The Deep State Rides Again

How the Washington Establishment Continues
to Try to Overturn the Will of the Voters

By

Stephen Edward Browne

This book is dedicated to all those who tried to get the truth out to the public. Especially to those who, like Mary Pinchot Meyer and Dorothy Kilgallen, lost their lives in that attempt.

Paperback ISBN 978-1-7336436-0-3

"Once you eliminate the impossible, whatever remains, no matter how improbable, must be the truth."

Sir Arthur Conan Doyle

"History is the set of lies we agree on."

Napoleon

"Ye shall know the truth and it shall set you free"

From the Bible (John 8:32) and engraved in the lobby of CIA headquarters

"You will never find a more wretched hive of scum and villany."

Obi-Wan Kenobi

Table of Contents

Preface: The Deep State Rides Again

The Deep State is trying to get rid of President Trump, and this is not the first time they've tried to overturn the will of the voters. They tried this in the 1960's and the only difference is that this time they're not using bullets. The Deep State is a danger to our democracy. Our government, which we the citizens elect and pay for, has no business trying to overthrow the will of the voters, especially not by murdering our duly elected president. However, that's what happened on November 22, 1963. What was back then referred to as The Washington Establishment and what we now call the Deep State (or just the "Swamp") conspired to murder President John F. Kennedy. Having the government bureaucracy try to take over power from the existing leadership is not a new concept. This has been going on since the beginning of civilization. The Deep State in the U.S. consists of the crooked politicians, the FBI, the Justice Department, the intelligence community, the mainstream media and a few others. This hasn't changed since the early 1960's. With a few relatively minor differences, the current crop of bad actors from these same institutions are still at it. The Deep State that took out President Kennedy also included the mafia, the Pentagon and some anti-Castro Cuban exiles. Back then the intelligence community was primarily the CIA. Now the U.S. intelligence community has grown to also include over a dozen other major intelligence agencies in addition to just the CIA. Other than those relatively minor differences, the Deep State hasn't changed much in the last few generations. And the Deep State is still trying to overturn the will of the voters. They still, a few generations later, have no intention of allowing democracy to work. They don't believe in our representative republic or our Constitution. They are doing everything in their considerable and growing power to substitute their agenda and policies for those of the duly elected president. And what is worse, they're still succeeding and getting away with it. They're not using bullets this time, which gives us the illusion of progress, but the Deep State is still doing their best to either get rid of Donald Trump, our duly elected president, or stop him from implementing his agenda. While they're trying to have him thrown out of the White House, they're doing everything humanly possible, legal or otherwise, to make sure that he's unable to implement the agenda he was elected on. The objective of the Deep State hasn't changed in the last few generations. Whatever it takes, the Deep State has no intention of allowing our elected leaders to exercise power unless their agenda agrees with the Deep State.

The Deep State is doing this to President Trump because he had the nerve to challenge them. Like Kennedy, Trump persisted in believing that he was the elected president and not the Deep State. He believed that the Constitution and the voters gave him the authority. The Deep State isn't using bullets this time, but they threw everything else they could think of at him in an effort to keep him from wining the election and exercising power. The Deep State launched a multi-level attack on Trump starting when he was still just a candidate. They tapped his phones, made up fake documents, used those documents to start an investigation, and used the investigation to try to find something they could use to have him thrown out of office and put in prison. At the same time the mainstream media smeared Trump and his family at every opportunity. No matter what the question was, the media's answer was "Trump is bad." The Deep State was doing this for several reasons. First, they disagree with almost every part of Trump's agenda. For example, he wanted to stop illegal immigration and they wanted to continue it. They are also doing this because they wanted to make an example out of Trump. They want to make sure that no one ever tries the same thing again. The Deep State wants candidates from the Establishment who will do what they want. Trump was neither of those things and they wanted to both destroy him and make the process so ugly that no one else will dare to challenge them again. In a later chapter I describe the multi-level attack on New Orleans D.A. Jim Garrison. The Deep State launched a vicious multi-level attack on him for the same reasons. He challenged the Deep State, they disagreed with his agenda, and they wanted to make an example out of him so no one else would dare challenge them again. They went after him with (pun intended) trumped-up charges and smears in the mainstream media.

This book lays out for the reader what happened in Dallas on November 22, 1963 when President Kennedy was murdered, the events that led up to it, and what happened after. It also lays out the reasons behind what happened and what motivated the major players like Johnson and Hoover to participate in the conspiracy. Finally, it describes how our history is repeating and what we can do about it.

In this book I claim that many shocking things happened, then I spend a lot of time backing it up with facts. I claim, for example, that Lyndon Johnson shot his way into the White House. I also claim that Hoover joined Johnson in the conspiracy to assassinate President Kennedy. Then I spend a lot of time supporting those arguments. In the end I believe that the weight of the evidence supports my conclusions, but that will ultimately be for the reader to decide.

How I Came to Write This Book

Since 1963 many facts have surfaced that contradict the official conclusion of the Warren Commission. So many facts have surfaced that the government has been forced several times to change the "official" version of the Kennedy assassination. For example, in the late 1970's the United States House Select Committee on Assassinations (HSCA) came out with a report admitting that Oswald was not a lone gunman – that there was in fact a conspiracy to kill President Kennedy. Imagine that. Even the government now admits that the JFK conspiracy theory isn't just a theory.

I noticed that the CIA worked hard over the decades to cover up the conspiracy. This got me to wondering if they were part of it. Even the CIA has finally been forced to officially admit that they were part of the cover-up. According to a report by CIA Chief Historian David Robarge released to the public in 2014, CIA Director John McCone was "complicit" in a CIA "benign cover-up" by withholding information from the Warren Commission. According to this CIA report, CIA officers had been instructed to give only "passive, reactive, and selective" assistance to the commission, in order to keep the commission focused on "what the Agency believed at the time was the 'best truth' – that Lee Harvey Oswald, for as yet undetermined motives, had acted alone in killing John Kennedy." The CIA was also covering up evidence that the CIA may have been in communication with Oswald before 1963, according to the CIA's own official findings. And this is only what they "officially" admit.

This book didn't start out to be a book. It started as an interesting project for me in my spare time. History is a hobby for me. I read and listen to books for entertainment and the criteria I use to choose a book is based on what I think I might learn from it. One day I decided to start buying books on the Kennedy assassination. I thought it might be an interesting exercise to see if I could solve the question of who was behind it.

The JFK assassination was the crime of the century. I was three years old when Kennedy was murdered. I grew up in the sixties and seventies watching and listening to all the speculation about the unanswered questions surrounding his murder. It was impossible to miss. It affected the whole country and there was an enormous amount of media attention given to it. The questions the conspiracy theorists asked could not be answered and therefore the rumors persisted.

Even the government, which tried desperately to keep a lid on the cover up, eventually officially admitted that there was a conspiracy. The House Assassinations Committee in the late 1970's admitted that there was hard evidence of at least two shooters, one from the front and one from the back. Two shooters constitute a conspiracy, as the government was eventually forced to admit.

Once you conclude that there was a conspiracy to kill Kennedy the next obvious question is "Who was behind it?" Who else (besides Oswald) was involved? The importance of this question can't be overstated. Some people conspired to kill our president. I was interested to know who. I was also interested to see if I could figure it out. This is part of what pushed me to dig deeper.

As an amateur history buff, I gradually came to learn a few things about Kennedy in the early sixties. It was pretty obvious that the CIA had been involved somehow in the Kennedy assassination and the cover up, but I never expected to know specifically who at the CIA was involved. They do things in secret and didn't appear to be rushing to give me an update. From what little I knew (at that time) about the circumstances surrounding Kennedy in the early sixties I understood that the CIA had persuaded him to give a green light to the Bay of Pigs invasion and that, when it became a fiasco, he blamed the CIA and was threatening to come down on it. Some reports have Kennedy threatening to shatter the CIA and scatter it to the winds. Kennedy took responsibility in public but privately he felt that the CIA had deceived and manipulated him into the decision and he was truly angry about it.

As I learned how bureaucracies worked I started to suspect that there was someone high up in the CIA in the early sixties who said to themselves 'I'm not doing this (killing an American president) to save *my* skin, I'm doing this for my country....' In other words, the justification for killing Kennedy could be wrapped in patriotism rather than self-interest. If Kennedy really was planning on cutting back the CIA, or at least getting rid of the guys who persuaded him to go ahead with the Bay of Pigs invasion, then the guys who were about to lose their jobs could have justified their treason by telling themselves that they were doing it 'for the good of the country.' The logic goes something like this: 'The U.S.A. and the world need a strong CIA to contain Communism and if Kennedy is going to weaken the CIA then that's bad for the country – and for the world.' This would, of course, be a stretch but it seemed plausible to me that it might suffice as a justification for an evil bureaucrat whose job is threatened. It's all about the stories we tell ourselves. However, I still wasn't expecting to figure out which bureaucrat we were talking about.

I also didn't realize the level of animosity toward Kennedy from the Joint Chiefs of Staff at the Pentagon. They saw Kennedy as weak and indecisive and they saw the United States of America as needing someone with resolve to win the Cold War. After the Cuban Missile Crisis, the Joint Chiefs wanted to launch a strike and Kennedy did not. Kennedy wanted to work with Khrushchev to achieve peace and the Joint Chiefs viewed this 'collusion with the Russians' as tantamount to treason.

Then I happened to read *THE DEVIL'S CHESSBOARD: ALLEN DULLES, THE CIA, AND THE RISE OF AMERICA'S SECRET GOVERNMENT* by David Talbot and suddenly I had a name and a face to put on that faceless CIA bureaucrat – Allen Dulles. Allen Dulles was head of the CIA at the time of the Bay of Pigs and had deceptively pushed Kennedy into the Bay of Pigs fiasco and was later fired from the CIA by Kennedy for that reason. I was then shocked to see that Allen Dulles, of all people, was on the Warren Commission. Having the guy who was a prime suspect in Kennedy's killing sitting on the official committee set up to "investigate" the murder was just too much of a coincidence for me. It was then that I decided to look further into the Kennedy assassination to see if I could figure out who was behind it. I still had no intention of writing a book. I just wanted to see if I could figure it out, like solving a puzzle. I eventually bought and read dozens of books on the subject in addition to any documentary or video footage I could get my hands on. There's a mountain of Kennedy assassination material to choose from. I tried to stick to credible sources using known facts. I decided to stick to facts that could be proven because there has been so much myth, legend, disinformation, misinformation, rumors, obfuscation and spin, not to mention that much of the evidence was either buried or just plain destroyed, that I was concerned that I could get lost. There is a phrase – 'wilderness of mirrors' which has been used by one of the more colorful characters in the saga. His name is James Angleton and he was clearly one of the guys at the CIA working diligently at least on the cover up if not on the actual hit. I think the term is a good summation of the material available on the Kennedy assassination, and that's on purpose. The idea of creating a wilderness of mirrors is so that anyone wandering into it gets hopelessly lost and accomplishes nothing. I think that's exactly what the conspirators wanted. This exploration eventually led me to dig into the life of Lyndon Baines Johnson. As I dug into it and gradually pieced it together I realized with considerable dismay that

Johnson was part of the conspiracy. The hit on Kennedy was a coup d'état. Johnson had shot his way into the White House.

Johnson had enriched himself through corruption on an epic scale. He acquired political power and influence and sold it to the highest bidders. If you needed something fixed you paid the price and Johnson would fix it for you. This corruption caught up with him and he ended up having to order at least half a dozen murders before he had Kennedy killed. By 1963 Johnson had put himself in a position where he was going to end up disgraced and in prison unless he got to the White House where he could use the power of the presidency to quash the investigations into his background. All of this came as a surprise to me.

Johnson had Kennedy taken out so that he could assume the presidency. This struck me as something that my fellow citizens should know, and that's how this book came to be. Killing the president so you can take over isn't supposed to happen here in the U.S.A. Killing the leader so you can take over is only supposed to happen in third-world "banana republics," not in my country. The understanding that Johnson was behind the hit on Kennedy also answered many of the unanswered questions surrounding the Kennedy assassination. I finally felt like I knew what happened. Not only did the various pieces finally fit but it was the only scenario that answered the loose ends. Having Johnson behind the murder was the only way this could have happened the way it did.

Even if the background is black and the puppet strings are black and you can't see the puppet master in the darkened theatre that doesn't mean that there is no puppet master. Puppets don't dance and perform by themselves. They need someone pulling the strings. Just because Johnson was a master at hiding the strings doesn't mean that he wasn't behind the Kennedy assassination. Only Johnson could have appointed and controlled the Warren Commission. Only Johnson could have coordinated the hit because only he could guarantee the participants that, if they were successful in killing Kennedy, he and Hoover could keep a lid on the cover up. Otherwise the other conspirators would not have risked joining the conspiracy. They might have hated Kennedy but they weren't about to risk disgrace, prison and the electric chair unless there was a good chance they would get away with it.

That's how I came to write this book. I doubt very much that most people in America know that Lyndon Johnson was behind the Kennedy assassination. And we citizens need to know that it can and did happen right here in the United States of America.

The Warren Report was criticized from when it was first published and the criticism has only grown since then. As more and more evidence became public knowledge over time we the people have gradually acquired more and more of the pieces of the puzzle. We now have enough of the picture to see what really happened and therefore who had to be behind it. The time has come. Enough truth has seeped out around the edges. Even the government has admitted many of the facts that had previously been "officially" denied. People looking back on historical events have the advantage of having a 360-degree view not available to the people who were there at the time. We also now have the internet which helps in many ways, including the ability to search for historical evidence including videos of interviews of witnesses who were there at the time.

This book was made possible by a mountain of research, literature, books, magazine articles, DVD's, other videos, documentaries, home movies and other material produced by thousands of people devoting millions of hours to a search for the truth about Kennedy's assassination. For our representative republic to function the way it should we the people need to know the truth. This book is a summary of the information from all those others. My hope is that, having read this summary, the reader is then interested enough to not just take my word for it. I hope that, having read this summary, people decide to read some of the supporting material, including previous books, that I reference here. I hope people travel at least part of the way down the road I did and discover the truth for themselves.

This is not the first book to claim LBJ was behind the plot to kill JFK. Several books, like (for example):

- Phillip Nelson's book *LBJ: THE MASTERMIND OF THE JFK ASSASSINATION*
- Barr McClellan's book *BLOOD, MONEY AND POWER: HOW LBJ KILLED JFK*
- Stone & Colapietro's book *THE MAN WHO KILLED KENNEDY: THE CASE AGAINST LBJ*

have all claimed that Johnson was part of the conspiracy that killed Kennedy. I make reference to these and many other books as I attempt to build a case that, beyond a reasonable doubt, Johnson was part of the conspiracy that killed our president.

Jefferson believed that an educated populace was necessary to maintain our freedom. This book is my attempt to help with that. Once I realized that Kennedy was taken out by Johnson, it dawned on me that this was not the only time the Deep State was trying to overturn the will of the voters. It was happening again right before my eyes as I was writing this book. The Deep State was also trying to take out President Donald Trump, only this time not with bullets. The Deep State rides again.

Reasons Why Oswald Could Not Be a Lone Shooter

The Warren Commission said that Oswald was a nut who acted alone and killed Kennedy. This can't be true. The following are some of the reasons that their conclusion does not fit the known facts:

> Oswald was out of place. He was seen by multiple witnesses in the lunch room just before, during and after the shooting and could not have gotten to the sniper's nest and back in time. Oswald wasn't even one of the shooters, much less the lone shooter.

> If Oswald had scurried up to the sixth floor, shot JFK and scurried back down the stairs to the lunchroom in the brief minuets between when witnesses saw him in the lunchroom, he would have been spotted on the stairs by Victoria Adams and Sandra Styles. Victoria Adams was watching the motorcade with Sandra Styles from the fourth floor of the Texas School Book Depository. Adams said there was no one else on the stairs when she and Sandra ran down to see what was going on when the shooting started.[1] It took author Barry Earnest thirty-five years to find Victoria Adams. She said she was harassed, questioned multiple times and changes were made in her testimony, so she decided to disappear for her own safety.[2] The Warren Commission disregarded Victoria's testimony. Her testimony didn't fit the "Oswald as lone shooter" theory because the two women would have been on the stairs at the same time as Oswald if he had just shot JFK and then went down the stairs to the lunchroom where he was seen right after the shooting by Dallas police officer Marion L. Baker who had rushed into the building right after JFK was shot. She decided it was safer to leave town.[3]

> There were shots from the front. Kennedy was hit from the front as well as from the back. The presidential limousine had a front-to-back bullet hole in the windshield. Even assuming Oswald was a shooter there was more than one shooter so Oswald could not have been a "lone" shooter.

> The ammunition for the Mannlicher-Carcano rifle had been manufactured decades earlier. The fact that the bullets were no longer being made for it was one of the reasons the rifle was so cheap. A test of Mannlicher-Carcano ammunition

showed that, out of one batch of twenty rounds of this type of ammunition, seventeen of them failed to fire.[4] And we're asked by the Warren Commission to believe that Oswald got three in a row to work, the only three he fired. The odds against this are so high as to rule it out as a realistic possibility.[5]

According to multiple witnesses there were some shots very close together. This is not possible with a bolt action rifle being used by a lone gunman. Only an automatic weapon like a machine gun or multiple shooters could have produced shots that close together. Not even the government is claiming Oswald had an automatic weapon. Therefore, Oswald could not have been a lone shooter.

The rifle claimed by the Warren Commission as the murder weapon could not have made those shots. It was not sighted properly. Ronald Simmons of the Army Ballistic Test Center told the Warren Commission that the Mannlicher-Carcano rifle, Oswald's alleged murder weapon, could not even be tested until they added three metal shims to the scope make it accurate enough to test.[6] No one could have hit anything at that distance with a rifle that was not sighted.

The Warren Commission claimed Oswald carried the rifle into the Texas School Book Depository that morning. He is supposed to have claimed it was some curtain rods. Oswald could not have carried the murder weapon into the book depository the way the Warren Commission said he did. Even if it had been disassembled, it was too long to carry under his arm. He got in the car for his ride to work that day and had the package in the back seat. When they got to work he cupped his hand under the end and tucked the package up under his armpit. Whatever it was it could not have been the Mannlicher-Carcano rifle claimed by the Warren Commission, even if it was disassembled. The wooden stock, the longest single part, of the Mannlicher-Carcano was much too long to fit between Oswald's hand and his armpit so he could not have carried that weapon the way they said he did.[7]

A German Mauser rifle was found on the sixth floor, not the Italian Mannlicher-Carcano. This Mauser was likely one of the actual weapons used to shoot Kennedy. The cops weren't supposed to find it but they did. And they publicly identified it as a Mauser, not the Mannlicher-Carcano, which was found a day later and on a different floor.[8] The Warren Commission said Oswald used the Mannlicher-Carcano and made no mention of the Mauser. It disappeared into some taxpayer-funded black hole. If Oswald was a lone shooter, who was using the Mauser?

Oswald passed his paraffin test. Had he shot a rifle he would have had residue on his cheek. He had none.[9] Even the government wasn't trying to say Oswald shot President Kennedy and Governor Connally with a pistol. Therefore, Oswald wasn't even a lone shooter. He wasn't a shooter at all.

Rose Cherami predicted the assassination two days before it happened. She had heard about it from some anti-Castro Cubans who she was with while they were on their way to Dallas as one of the shooting teams. She told her story to multiple people and it was well documented. Then the assassination happened just like she predicted. The only way Rose could have predicted the assassination was if it was a conspiracy and she found out from some of the conspirators.

Oswald's voice stress test says he was telling the truth when he said he didn't shoot anyone.[10]

Clearly Oswald was not a lone shooter. Make no mistake, Oswald was involved in the Kennedy assassination. He was told he was being prepared to go on an undercover mission to go to Cuba to kill Castro while he was really being set up as the fall guy in the Kennedy assassination. The point I'm trying to make here is that Oswald wasn't a lone shooter. Based on the evidence, he couldn't have been. Once you accept that Oswald could not have been a lone shooter and there were at least two shooters you have just proven that Kennedy was killed by a conspiracy. Based on the findings of the House Select Committee on Assassinations (HSCA) in the 1970's, even the government now admits that Kennedy was killed by a conspiracy.

This is why the government has locked all the information away for generations. If it happened the way the government originally said it happened (as opposed to the way they later changed the story in the late 1970's to admit there actually was a conspiracy) then there would be no reason not to come clean. The government has locked all the information away for a few generations now to hide the truth from the public. That information is still locked away to this day.

Author Anthony Summers, in his book *NOT IN YOUR LIFETIME*, pointed out that:[11]

"The Central Intelligence Agency, for its part, over the years released assassination related documents only when under intense pressure at the insistence of Congressional committees or, in more recent years, when obliged to comply with the Records Act. Sometimes, released documents have turned out to be censored virtually out of existence."[12]

It Couldn't Have Happened Any Other Way
– a Summary

At some point you have to be a kook to continue to believe in the Warren Report. This is ironic because, for a few generations now, the mainstream media has painted anyone who questioned the official government version of the Kennedy assassination out to be a "conspiracy nut" or "conspiracy kook." This was intentional. Marginalizing those who sought the truth allowed the Deep State, the government and the mainstream media, to minimize their impact on public opinion. Anyone who looked into the killing of our president was labeled a kook and therefore there was no reason to listen to anything they had to say. God forbid we the people should actually search for or find out the truth.

Any objective analysis of the Kennedy assassination will come to the same conclusion. There's just no way that the Warren Commission's conclusion that Lee Harvey Oswald acted alone can be true because it doesn't fit the facts. Even the government now admits this. So, you have to ask the question; were they lying in the early 1960's when they said that Oswald was the lone shooter or were they lying in the late 1970's when they admitted there was more than one shooter? The answer is obvious. They were lying both times. After all, this is the government we're talking about.

A minimum of two shots came from the front. This was the finding of the doctors at Parkland Hospital before they were intimidated into changing their story. More on that later. They were well familiar with gunshot wounds and they found an obvious entry wound in the front of Kennedy's throat. They stood up and said so at the press conference that day. There was another shot, after the first shot to the throat, that hit Kennedy in the front of his head that took off part of the back of his head. There was blood splatter on the motorcycle cops riding to the left and rear of Kennedy. There was also a bullet hole in the windshield of the presidential limo. It was a front-to-rear hole. The glass shop folks at Ford who replaced the windshield were well familiar with the effects of gunshots on automobile glass. They clearly recognized the windshield bullet hole as the result of a front-to-rear shot. There were multiple witnesses in Dealey Plaza at the time who saw and smelled gun smoke and heard shots from the fence at the top of the now famous grassy knoll which was in front of the limousine. There were even a few people who witnessed the shooters. In the 1970's the House Select Committee on Assassinations reviewed acoustical and other evidence and concluded that shots had come from the direction of the knoll. That is, from the front.

Oswald was behind Kennedy at the Texas School Book Depository when Kennedy was shot. Oswald could therefore, not have taken the shots at Kennedy that came from the front. There is more evidence that Oswald was not a shooter and I will get into that in more detail later. However, the fact that there were shots from the front proves that the Warren Commission conclusion that Oswald was a lone shooter was wrong. Shots from the front mean at least two shooters, since there were also shots from behind, from the direction of the Texas School Book Depository. That means there was more than one shooter involved. The fact that there were multiple shooters means there was a conspiracy to kill Kennedy. This leads directly to several other questions like: Who else was involved, who set up the hit and who participated in the cover up? These are huge questions. Setting up a hit on the president is no small task. And covering up a conspiracy to kill the president is a considerably more difficult and complex task even than shooting the president. Several lone nuts have shot American presidents, but a cover-up is a huge and complex undertaking.

This book goes into detail on the answers to these questions. Once I accepted that there was a conspiracy to assassinate Kennedy, I started to understand the magnitude of the conspiracy necessary to plan and cover up something that big. I realized that whoever did it would need to have high-level cooperation from the FBI because they would obviously be called in to investigate.

The only person who could have kept the lid on a conspiracy that big was President Johnson. Corrupt leaders have been using their political power to squash opposition since before recorded time. It continues today. Lyndon Johnson didn't invent the concept, he just used it to deadlier effect than most other corrupt American politicians. Johnson planned to use the power he would have as president to quash the investigations into his past and avoid paying consequences for his crimes, including the killing of Kennedy.

Johnson was a brilliant, ruthless and driven politician who would stop at nothing to achieve the presidency. By 1963 he had put himself in a position where he would either go to the "big house" (prison) or the White House. Given those options he chose the White House, even if it meant killing JFK. The Kennedy assassination was not the first murder that Johnson had orchestrated, and his past had caught up with him. The Kennedys were going to dump him off the ticket for the 1964 election and he would be indicted for some of his many crimes and end up disgraced and behind bars.

Johnson decided to organize Kennedy's many enemies into a cabal that would not only kill the president but cover it up once it was done. Of the two tasks the cover up was the harder one. Johnson was uniquely qualified to do this. He had proven himself "master of the Senate" (to borrow the term from Robert Caro, one of Johnson's biographers) by getting enough United States Senators to do what he wanted. This was no easy task. Senators are notoriously egotistical and independent-minded individuals and Johnson had managed to control them as no one had before. He was able to bend them to his will. Also, Kennedy had made many enemies including at the highest levels of the mafia, the FBI, the CIA, the Pentagon, the wealthy oil barons of the time and among the anti-Castro Cubans who were unhappy that Kennedy had pulled the plug on invading Cuba. All Johnson had to do was get them to work together. He was good at this. He would provide the leadership and the cover and they would do the dirty work. And the rest, as they say, is history.

For those of you who, like me, are skeptical of "conspiracy theories" please read on. In the following chapters I lay out, in detail, that this is the only way that this could have happened. Only the new president would be able to cover up the assassination of a (now previous) president. As appalled as I was to come to this conclusion, there is no other way it could have happened. Sir Arthur Conan Doyle was right. Once you eliminate the impossible whatever is left, no matter how improbable, must be true. The Warren Commission's "conclusion" that Oswald was a lone nut with a rifle simply isn't true. It can't be. It doesn't fit the evidence. The only conclusion that does fit the evidence is that Johnson was behind it.

No one but Johnson could have appointed and controlled a presidential commission stocked with cronies willing to do a whitewash like the Warren Commission. Only a sitting president who was part of the conspiracy as vice president could have organized and run the assassination and cover-up that happened before, during and after the Kennedy assassination. The Kennedy assassination involved the CIA, the mafia, the FBI, the Pentagon and others and only President Johnson could have coordinated and run a conspiracy of that magnitude.

Here is a partial list of things only Johnson could have done:

- Only LBJ was in a position to control every aspect of the pre- and post-assassination conspiracies.
- Only LBJ took over the planning and coordination for the Dallas trip that day.[13]
- Only LBJ could have appointed and controlled the Warren Commission.

- Only LBJ could have convinced the other conspirators that he could cover up the assassination so they would not all end up in the electric chair.
- Only LBJ could have orchestrated the Kennedy trip to Dallas. JFK didn't want to go and only LBJ could have arranged the circumstances in Texas that convinced JFK to go play peacemaker.
- Only LBJ could have changed the motorcade route to go by the book depository. Only LBJ could have convinced everyone that the lunch venue had to be changed and thus the route.
- Only LBJ could have arranged to have the protection stripped from JFK in Dealey Plaza. LBJ was old friends with Secret Service Director James Rowley and only LBJ could have convinced him to go along with the plan.
- Only LBJ could have controlled the authorities in Dallas. He'd been doing it for years.
- Only LBJ could have held Air Force One on the ground while they played the shell game with the body to get the autopsy results faked. Only the president can hold Air Force One on the ground.
- Only LBJ had the skills necessary to get a bunch of conspirators to work together. This was no easy task and he'd been doing it for years in the Senate.

Johnson knew the major conspirators and had long and trusting relationships with them. And many of them also knew each other the same way. Johnson had to be involved. It was Johnson who appointed and controlled the Warren Commission. Johnson alone had the means, the motive and the opportunity. Without him it could not have happened the way it did. This is the only scenario that fits the known facts.

Johnson didn't do this alone. Just as he had in the Senate, he had to coordinate lots of egotistical, independent-minded folks and get them to work together. Fortunately for Johnson, Kennedy had made a long list of enemies who all wanted Kennedy removed from power. These included the mafia, the CIA, the anti-Castro Cuban exiles, Hoover at the FBI, the Joint Chiefs at the Pentagon and the oil barons, the same list just mentioned above.

The mafia were outraged at Kennedy for several reasons. First, Sam Giancana in Chicago had helped JFK to get elected and saw Kennedy as having double-crossed him by allowing Robert Kennedy to go after the mafia as Attorney General. Second, Carlos Marcello in New

Orleans had been rather rudely deported by Bobby Kennedy. He had been kidnapped and dropped off in the jungle in South America. He came close to losing his life during this episode, but he made it back to the United States. Once back, the Attorney General continued to try to have him convicted and deported. For Marcello, this was a life-or-death struggle. Giancana and Marcello were not the kind of guys to be taken lightly. They were willing and able to take out a hit on the president, and they did.

Allen Dulles and his crowd at the CIA were die-hard Cold Warriors who wanted to fight communist expansion. They saw Kennedy as a lightweight who was weak and indecisive. They wanted to make war and Kennedy wanted to make peace. Dulles was out of control when Kennedy took office and their relationship got progressively worse with each crisis. Dulles saw Kennedy as passing up chances to attack Cuba and the Soviet Union. Dulles wanted to invade Cuba. Kennedy was not so sure. Dulles and his Cold Warriors saw the Bay of Pigs as a missed opportunity. Then there came the Berlin Crisis and the Cuban Missile Crisis. With each crisis, the folks at the CIA grew more and more outraged that Kennedy would not give them the green light to attack. Meanwhile, Kennedy grew more and more interested in reaching out to Khrushchev and eventually even Castro to make peace. Kennedy's firing of Dulles and his efforts to bring the CIA under control only made things worse.

The CIA also wanted to ramp up the Vietnam war and Kennedy decided he wanted to pull out of Vietnam. This was the 'domino theory' in action. We had to fight back or the communists would gradually take over, one country at a time until the United States would end up isolated. The top echelon of the CIA had all been recruited and trained by Dulles and they all agreed with him that what Kennedy was doing was an outrage. The entire CIA did not participate in the Kennedy assassination and cover up. Clearly there were a few people at the top who went rogue and ran a covert operation that involved a few more CIA people and CIA contractors. And not everyone who was involved was told all the details of why they were doing what they were doing. Only those few with a "need to know" understood what was really going on.

The anti-Castro Cuban exiles were outraged at Kennedy because, between 1961 and 1963, he had done a 180-degree turn on them. He started out in 1961 by backing their efforts to retake their island from Castro, but the Bay of Pigs invasion failed. They were then told by their sponsors at the CIA that the Bay of Pigs invasion failed because Kennedy lost his nerve and pulled the rug out from under them. This outraged them. In 1962 Kennedy had promised Khrushchev, to resolve the Cuban Missile Crisis, that the U.S. would not invade Cuba and the Kennedy administration ended up having to actively try to keep the exiles from launching raids against Cuba. The anti-Castro Cuban exiles saw this about-face turn as a betrayal and many of them hated Kennedy for this reason. For some of them this turned their outrage to cold hatred for Kennedy. They saw getting rid of Kennedy as their only option to get back their homeland. And they were egged on by their CIA sponsors.

J. Edgar Hoover at the FBI was going to be fired by Kennedy. Hoover was outraged at this prospect. He had created the FBI as a dictatorship for himself and he was desperate to stay in power. He was not about to allow himself to be put out to pasture if there was any way to keep that from happening. The entire FBI did not willingly participate in the cover-up of the Kennedy assassination, but orders were orders at the FBI in those days and an order from Hoover was not to be ignored.

The Joint Chiefs at the Pentagon thought Kennedy was soft on communism and were outraged that Kennedy would not agree to let them launch World War Three. They were of the opinion that Kennedy had passed up several chances at a nuclear first strike, including the Bay of Pigs, the Berlin crisis and the Cuban Missile Crisis. They thought Kennedy was weak at a time when the country needed a leader who was more decisive. The Joint Chiefs also believed that the United States should strike now while the Russians were still relatively weaker in terms of numbers of nuclear weapons. In their view the window of opportunity for a successful first strike would not stay open much longer. Time was running out and in the meantime the military brass came to see Kennedy as a threat to the survival of the nation. And JFK's collusion with Khrushchev was seen by them as treason.[14] (Does this 'collusion with the Russians' charge sound familiar?) The Joint Chiefs also agreed with the CIA that the war in Vietnam should be ramped up. Johnson would do that and Kennedy would not. The entire Pentagon did not participate in the Kennedy assassination. A few of the top brass were all it would take.

The wealthy oil barons of the time hated Kennedy because he wanted to get rid of their oil depletion allowance. This was a huge tax break that would have cost them millions and they spent heavily on corrupt politicians like Johnson to keep their tax breaks in place. Their contribution to the conspiracy was most likely money to run the operation, but they could also supply some logistical support. D.H. Byrd is one example. He was one of the oil barons and he owned the Texas School Book Depository, and their connections to the corrupt authorities in Dallas would come in handy when Oswald needed to be arrested, framed and murdered.

And these different groups who all hated Kennedy all had ties to each other. The Joint Chiefs and the CIA were in agreement that communism was the big threat and that Kennedy was the problem. The CIA and the mafia were already working together to try to kill Castro. The CIA was sponsoring the anti-Castro Cuban exiles in their bid to take back Cuba. The mafia and J. Edgar Hoover all hung out together at a resort and race track owned by one of the oil barons. And Johnson was friends with all of them. He was the common thread that pulled them all together and made it work. One of these groups by themselves could not have pulled it all off. With Johnson's leadership they not only killed our president, they got away without being punished because Johnson and Hoover were able to keep a lid on the conspiracy with the cover up.

In addition to the things listed above that only Johnson could have done, there were a number of things that Johnson did that, while others could possibly have done them, are very suspicious:

- LBJ issued a gag order to keep the Bethesda medical staff from discussing the autopsy and the circumstances surrounding it.[15] Being honest about the autopsy would have given away the fact that there were shots from the front and therefore Oswald was not a lone shooter.

- LBJ pushed Texas Governor John Connally to insist on the Trade Mart as the site for the lunch that day even though it was harder to secure than the alternate site, the Women's Building. This change forced the parade route to go by the Texas School Book Depository in Dealey Plaza.[16]

- LBJ later placed the blame for making this decision on Kennedy aide Kenny O'Donnell which wasn't true.[17]

- LBJ kept trying to get Kennedy to agree to have Senator Yarborough switch places with Connally in the limo with Kennedy. John Connally was a friend of LBJ's and he didn't want John to get hurt. Johnson hated Yarborough and therefore would have preferred to have him in the line of fire.[18] As it happened Connally was seriously injured during the assassination.

- LBJ could have easily made peace with the Texas factions who were fighting. He kept the feud going in order to force Kennedy to have to make the trip to Texas when he really didn't want to.

- LBJ (and Hoover) were longtime friends with James Rowley, the head of the Secret Service, who had to be involved in order to help with the setup and the cover up.

Since we know Oswald wasn't a lone shooter and that some of the shots came from the front, we know that there was a conspiracy to assassinate Kennedy. The question then becomes who else was involved in that conspiracy. The only answer that fits the facts is that Johnson was involved. No one else could have done all the things listed above, and without them the conspiracy would have failed. They got away with it because Johnson was there as vice president to push Kennedy to visit Dallas and later in the White House to help keep the lid on the conspiracy. There's no other explanation that fits all the facts in this case.

In this book I will go into details on each of the points listed above, including showing where I got those details so the reader can, if they would like, go check it out for themselves. I'm not asking anyone to just take my word for all of this, I would encourage anyone who is interested to check out the facts for themselves.

The Real Lyndon Baines Johnson

The purpose of this chapter is to give readers an understanding of who Johnson was. I take the reader through Johnson's rising levels of corruption up to and including the murder of at least half a dozen people by the time he was vice president after the 1960 election. Only by understanding that Johnson was capable of murder, and the pressure LBJ was under by 1963, can anyone comprehend that Johnson was also capable of murdering President John F. Kennedy in order to attain the White House.

Most, if not all, of the people I talk to about this are shocked when I say that Johnson was behind the Kennedy assassination. I can understand this reaction. I too was shocked when I realized that Johnson was one of the conspirators. This comes not only as news to most people, it means that the murder of John F. Kennedy in Dealey Plaza was a coup d'état. That's not supposed to happen here in the United States of America. It's only supposed to happen in banana republic dictatorships. This is one of the reasons I decided to write this book. We as citizens need to understand that not only did it happen here, it's happening again. And if you count the murder of Robert Kennedy, this is the third time the Deep State has tried it.

Johnson was ambitious, very ambitious. And he was not in a position where his parents were going to help him get into an ivy league university like Harvard or Yale. He was going to have to make it on his own. Johnson's rise to power and wealth from humble beginnings had required regular legal and moral short cuts and he had decided to take those short cuts and continue the climb. Johnson wanted the White House. I would say he was obsessed with the idea of becoming president, but obsessed is not a strong enough word in this case. When something or someone got in his way he went around, over or through it or them. This pattern of corruption is well documented in Robert Caro's biographical series on Johnson, *THE YEARS OF LYNDON JOHNSON* and in Barr McClellan's book *BLOOD, MONEY AND POWER: HOW LBJ KILLED JFK*. I highly recommend these books as excellent background on the Real Lyndon Baines Johnson.

Johnson decided to go into politics and try to climb a corrupt and slippery pole. When he first ran for the Senate in 1941 he had the election stolen from him by crooked opponents who were more experienced in voter fraud than Johnson was at that time and who figured out how many votes they needed to manufacture in order to win. There was cheating on both sides, Johnson was just relatively new to the game and got beaten. Seeing this loss, Johnson decided not to let that happen again. In the 1948 Senate campaign he was willing to take the cheating to a higher level, all the way to the U.S. Supreme Court, in a way that his opponents couldn't match. This is discussed in more detail in the section on the Box 13 Scandal.

This chapter is organized into four sections:

1. Johnson's Personality – describes who Johnson was, which I believe is essential to understanding how he could possibly participate in the Kennedy assassination

2. Corruption on an Epic Scale – describes the various schemes Johnson used to enrich himself by selling his influence to the highest bidders and using corrupt deals to line his own pockets

3. The Murder of Doug Kinser – describes one of the murders that Johnson ordered Mac Wallace to commit and how Johnson arranged for Wallace to get off scott free after the killing

4. Other Murders by Johnson – describes how, by the time Johnson was one heartbeat away from the White House, he had commited at least half a dozen murders

Johnson's Personality

On the day Kennedy was murdered, Air Force One was flown back to Washington with Kennedy's casket on board. Upon landing in Washington, a grief-stricken Bobby Kennedy rushed past Johnson to get to the body of his slain brother. Johnson, now president, was offended that Bobby did not first stop and acknowledge him and show him due respect as president.[19]

Johnson gave Kennedy's shocked and grieving secretary, Evelyn Lincoln, until Noon the next day to vacate her office and clear out her things.[20]

Johnson's crude personality has been reported on in many books and articles and in at least one feature-length film. One of these traits he is best known for is holding meetings while on the toilet. This is just one of the more famous aspects of Johnson's personality. A more in-depth look at his personality shows him to be a narcissist and a sociopath. In their book *THE MAN WHO KILLED KENNEDY: THE CASE*

AGAINST LBJ authors Roger Stone and Mike Colapietro go into great detail on these aspects of Johnson's personality. I highly recommend their book. Other Johnson biographers like Robert Caro and Barr McClellan in their respective books also explore various aspects of Johnson's personality flaws in detail. Stone and Colapietro go deeper than Caro in exposing the worse aspects of Lyndon Baines Johnson.

Interestingly enough, Robert Caro is one of the more prolific of Johnson's biographers. In my opinion he had to have either known about, or strongly suspected, the murders Johnson ordered, including the Kennedy assassination. However, he seems to have chosen not to write about this side of Johnson's personality.[21] I suspect this is because he realized that he did not want to join the ranks of people who became bad life insurance risks.

Any understanding of what happened in Dealey Plaza has to start here with an understanding of who Johnson was. We Americans have a natural tendency to want to think that the people we put in the White House are good. We tend to give our President the benefit of the doubt. We would prefer not to think the worst of our elected leaders. After all, we chose them. In the case of Johnson, we have to face the fact that he was not a good man. He was in fact an evil genius. He was also an obsessed and driven politician who would stop at nothing to obtain his goal of becoming president.

Below I discuss some of the epic levels of corruption orchestrated by Johnson as well as some of the murders he ordered that have been documented. Johnson was responsible for at least half a dozen murders before he decided to have Kennedy bumped off so he could take his place in the White House. By the time he was one heartbeat away from the White House, which he had obsessively sought his whole adult life, he was no stranger to ordering the murder of people who got in his way.

Johnson created a political machine that had many tentacles. Two of those tentacles were Billie Sol Estes and Bobby Baker. Billie Sol Estes was a con man in Texas and Bobby Baker was a protégé of Johnson in Washington. They both became Johnson's partners in crime. They ran scams and gave Johnson a cut in return for LBJ using his power and influence to keep the scams from being busted. Baker and Estes were also 'cutouts' or 'circuit breakers' there to protect Johnson in case something went wrong and they got caught. They were used by LBJ as layers of insulation. They both ended up in the 'big house' (prison) while Johnson went on to the White House. This is partly because they both went too far, got too greedy, and they both ended up getting caught.[22] Once their problems hit the newspapers, they became problems for Johnson to contain. Johnson was able to get to the White House just in time to use the power of the presidency to quash the investigations into these scandals. Johnson himself was tarnished by the scandals but he managed to escape any serious consequences.

Corruption on an Epic Scale

By the time he was a Senator, Johnson controlled a river of corrupt money coming into the politicians and diverted much of it for himself.[23] The November 22, 1963 issue of *Life* magazine details another Senator complaining about only getting $3,000 out of a $25,000 payment, $12,000 of which was meant for the Senator. When he complained to Bobby Baker, one of Johnson's bag men, he was told "You're doing all right, you don't need it."[24] Like many politicians before and since who are ostensibly public servants living on a salary, Johnson went to Washington initially as a middle-class person earning a salary and ended up with tens of millions in net worth. As I detail below, he did this largely by creating corrupt partnerships which allowed him to sell his influence in Washington in return for large kickbacks.

Author Robert Caro is a Pulitzer-prize winning author who has done a lifetime of research into Lyndon Johnson. Because of his efforts we know much more about Johnson's early years and all the scams that started when he was young. Caro describes in his book series *THE YEARS OF LYNDON JOHNSON* a consistent pattern of increasing corruption and back-room dealing. Here are a couple of quotes from Caro's book(s):[25]

> Of Johnson's early years Caro describes Johnson as "Cultivating and manipulating older men possessed of power that could advance his ambitions, the young Lyndon Johnson employed obsequiousness and flattery so striking that contemporaries mocked him as a 'professional son'" and "Everyone knew that something wasn't straight. And everyone knew that if something wasn't straight it was Lyndon Johnson that had done it"[26]

This section is organized into nine sub-sections:

1. The sub-section on Ed Clark discusses how Johnson and Ed Clark had a partnership where Clark would run the operation in Texas while Johnson ran things in Washington. If you wanted to buy influence in Washington from Johnson you

went to see Ed Clark. Having Clark collect the money was another layer of protection. It was another way Johnson insulated himself from the possibility that illegal payoffs could be tied to him.

2. The Box 13 Scandal details how Johnson moved from the House to the Senate by stealing the 1948 Senate primary election.

3. The sub-section on station KTBC details how Johnson used his power in Washington to deny the request of a local Austin radio station for a better FCC license so he could buy it for peanuts. He then used his power to see that it was granted greatly expanded licenses by the FCC, which Johnson controlled. Johnson was able to make millions as the tiny, worthless radio station now turned into a greatly expanded radio and television operation.

4. The sub-section on the mafia details how Johnson would take payoffs from the mafia in order to keep anti-racketeering legislation bottled up in the Senate. This allowed the mafia to prosper before Kennedy was elected to the White House.

5. The sub-section on the crooked partnership between Johnson and Hoover introduces the mutually dependent relationship they developed where Hoover covered Johnson's tracks in return for Johnson helping Hoover stay in power

6. The section on Billie Sol Estes details one of the scandals that erupted into the open and almost took Johnson down. Billie Sol Estes had agricultural scams going on that involved cotton farming and fertilizer tanks. He would give Johnson a cut of his illegal profits in return for Johnson using his power in Washington to make sure that the USDA would look the other way while the Estes scams made millions. This was also one of the corrupt deals that led to Johnson ordering that someone, in this case a man named Henry Marshall, be murdered. Marshall was a USDA employee who could not be bribed into looking the other way. Marshall continued to investigate the Estes scam until ultimately Johnson ordered his murder, which is also covered in detail.

7. Brown & Root was part of Johnson's circle of corruption. This section goes into detail on how Johnson got a cut of the

profits from huge government contracts which were given to Brown & Root as a result of Johnson's power and influence. As Johnson's career grew, so did Brown & Root.

8. The Bobby Baker affair was another scandal that almost took LBJ down. Baker was a protégé and crony of Johnson's from the Senate and they ran many scams together. When the Bobby Baker scandals hit the newspapers, it was one more reason that Johnson had put himself in a position where he HAD to get to the White House or he was going to end up in prison. Johnson's past was catching up with him in late 1963 and scandals like this were going to get him dumped off the ticket for the 1964 election. If that happened, he would be out of power and unable to quash the investigations that would put him behind bars.

9. The TFX scandal was another problem for Johnson. Johnson got the TFX/F-111 contract taken from Boeing and given to General Dynamics in Fort Worth. It doesn't rank as high, in terms of danger to LBJ and damage to LBJ's reputation, as some of Johnson's more profitable scams, but it added to the weight of the problems pressing in on Johnson by November of 1963.

In his book *BLOOD, MONEY AND POWER: HOW LBJ KILLED JFK*, author Barr McClellan goes into detail on a number of things, including how the IRS had questions about the accumulation of wealth by Johnson. Frank Scofield of the IRS looked into Johnson's finances and got character assassination in return.[27] Johnson had the Deep State attack him personally. Scofield was indicted on the Hatch Act on trumped up charges.[28] Johnson's records were mysteriously burned in a suspicious series of fires, which made prosecuting LBJ more difficult.[29] Scofield was eventually found not guilty and after that Scofield got the hint and the IRS investigation and audit into Johnson came to an end.[30]

Author Phillip Nelson, in his book *LBJ: THE MASTERMIND OF THE JFK ASSASSINATION*, delves into Johnson's personality, making a good case that LBJ was a paranoid sociopath who was also a manic depressive. Nelson claims Johnson also had extreme narcissism, egomania and the compound effect of all of these personality traits in the same person is how you end up with people like Napoleon, Hitler and Stalin. Nelson also makes a good case that the rest of the JFK assassination documents need to be released and that LBJ's name should be removed from monuments, lakes and freeways.[31]

LBJ's Crooked Partnership with Ed Clark

Ed Clark was a crooked lawyer in Texas who teamed up with Johnson to sell political influence. He became more than just Johnson's lawyer. Thanks to author Barr McClellan we now know much more than we did before about Ed Clark and the law firm that he employed to keep Johnson's illegal activity from coming to light. Authors Robert Caro and Barr McClellan also describe how Johnson ran multiple scams with multiple partners. I have tried to summarize these below. I would highly recommend that the reader who is interested in more detail take advantage of the extensive research done by Caro and McClellan. I've seen hints that Caro is coming out with another volume on Johnson.

Johnson would take kickbacks from corrupt businessmen who wanted either protection from prosecution or help getting government contracts, or both. Johnson teamed up with attorney Ed Clark early in his career and the two formed a crooked partnership that lasted until after Johnson died. In 1937 Clark got the governor of Texas to endorse Johnson for the special election that year and send a letter to the state employees and the result was that Johnson went from the middle of the pack to winning and became a member of Congress.[32] The way McClellan describes their setup, Clark arranged things in the background and Johnson was the elected official of the partnership. Johnson was always careful to keep from getting his hands dirty. Johnson used other people to do the dirty work so that his name could not be directly tied to illegal activity. Ed Clark skillfully used the attorney-client privilege to keep investigators from being able to discover how the money moved around in Johnson's scams.[33] The two of them created a front company called Brazos-Tenth which was covered by attorney-client privilege.[34] Clark was one of the layers of protection that Johnson used to avoid going to prison. This allowed Johnson to provide the political cover for scam operators like Billie Sol Estes and Bobby Baker in return for a cut of their illegal profits.

This meant that, even if one of Johnson's scams led back to him, he still had the attorney-client privilege as a fallback position where he could avoid giving up financial records. Brazos-Tenth continued long after Johnson was no longer president. Payoffs made to keep people quiet were made out of Brazos-Tenth. Whoever was getting paid off had the payments stop if they started talking. For example, Madeline Brown (LBJ's mistress) had her income cut off when she started talking.[35]

Johnson's election to the U.S. House of Representatives in 1937 and then to the U.S. Senate in 1948 and eventually to Senate Majority Leader constituted a continual rise in power and influence. This allowed him to continue to get a bigger cut of bigger scams over that same period of time. Johnson was not the first crooked politician to use his office to enrich himself, he was just better at it than most. Along the way the Clark-Johnson partnership continued to prosper. If you were a scammer and needed a "favor" from the government you went to Clark at his office in Austin, Texas and arranged a payment and Clark got Johnson to put in the "fix" in Washington, D.C.

The Box 13 Scandal That Got LBJ to the Senate

In 1940 Johnson was a Congressional representative from Texas and was looking to move up to the Senate. Johnson tried in 1941 to run for the Senate but he lost. 1941 was Johnson's first Senate race. He actually got more votes than his opponent but was defeated by the more experienced team of then Texas Governor Wilbert Lee "Pappy" O'Daniel. When the O'Daniel team learned how many votes they were losing by, they manufactured the necessary votes to claim victory.

Having been outmaneuvered in the 1941 election, Johnson decided to try again in 1948. In the 1948 Senate race Johnson used the now infamous Box 13 to do the same thing to his opponents. Johnson's lawyer was Ed Clark. Clark was heavily involved with Johnson in raising cash for the campaign and dispensing it to where votes could be bought. Even with all the bribes Johnson did not have enough votes to win the Democratic primary election, so he had his cronies pay to revise ballot counts with enough votes to win in the days ahead with "amended" vote totals that went to Johnson.

This is where the now infamous "Box 13 Scandal" came to be in Alice Texas. Johnson and Ed Clark sent Don Thomas there and he paid to be allowed to add names to Johnson's total. Thomas was tired from the drive and running out of time and many names were added in alphabetical order, in the same handwriting and in the same color ink.[36] They would not stand up to scrutiny. Johnson tried to block Coke Stevenson's people from seeing the ballots.[37] Coke Stevenson got the legendary Texas lawman Frank Hamer involved and they got a brief look at the ballots.[38]

Author Barr McClellan in his book *BLOOD, MONEY AND POWER: HOW LBJ KILLED JFK* details how Johnson and his lawyers Ed Clark and Don Thomas had come to control the judges in Texas. When the results were contested by Johnson's opponent in the race, former Texas governor Coke Stevenson, the issue went before the Texas courts who then, of course, ruled in Johnson's favor. Stevenson then took the issue to the federal courts.[39] The Johnson camp then got lawyer Abe Fortas to call U.S. Supreme Court Justice Hugo Black and get him to rule in Johnson's favor.[40] Years later, President Johnson would nominate Fortas to the United States Supreme Court. Once he had been confirmed as the winner of the Democratic primary and was the Democratic nominee for the Senate race Johnson was able to win the Senate seat in the general election. In those days Texas was a heavily Democratic state and winning the Democratic primary meant winning the general election and the Senate seat.

Johnson had successfully stolen the 1948 Senate election, but the illegal things he had done would come back to haunt him in the years ahead. The "Box 13 Scandal" wouldn't just die. Johnson and Hoover were cronies, and the FBI wasn't going to investigate Johnson's voter fraud in the 1948 election.[41] Johnson was later investigated by other agencies and ended up having to get the White House to cancel the inquiry. Luis Salas was an election judge in Jim Wells County, Texas who acknowledged his role in the fraud in the 1948 Senate primary only after all the others involved in the scandal had died.[42]

KTBC – One Example of Johnson Lining His Pockets

Station KTBC is another example of Johnson using his power and influence in Washington to enrich himself. Authors Robert Caro, mentioned above, and Barr McClellan, author of *BLOOD, MONEY AND POWER: HOW LBJ KILLED JFK*, in their respective books on LBJ describe how Johnson, as a United States Congressional representative from Texas, used his connections with the FCC in 1943 to keep the radio station KTBC from being able to expand its broadcast rights or transfer its broadcast license. The owners of KTBC wanted to boost their weak signal and move to a better place on the dial. The station, unable to get the necessary approvals from the FCC, had very little value to anyone. The FCC also would not allow the station to transfer its license to a new syndicate of buyers for $50,000. With no other options, the owners of the station had to sell for peanuts. Johnson bought KTBC in 1943 for $17,500, and put it in his wife's name.

Once Johnson owned it (in his wife's name) suddenly the station got the necessary FCC approvals and Johnson made millions as the value of the station increased. KTBC grew from a tiny radio station to a TV and radio media conglomerate with a monopoly in the Austin market. In Austin the television fare at that time had been dubbed 'LBJ-TV' by the locals.[43] Johnson has used his influence with the FCC to gain a monopoly on broadcasting in the area when local competitors were still trying to find a way into the market.[44] On January 29, 1963 the Dallas News and Texas Observer published articles examining LBJ's television and cable interests. In conjunction with this Congressman Gross of Iowa had been raising persistent and pointed questions about the propriety, ethics and legality of Johnson's radio and television operations.[45] On December 9, 1963 Representative Gross said: "I submit . . . that every member of the Federal Communications Commission is going to be aware of the interests of the Johnson family in the field of radio and television. And I further submit that, in the case of the FCC, the chairman holds office at the pleasure of Lyndon Johnson."[46]

Having bought KTBC in 1943 for $17,500, Johnson sold the station in 1972 for nine million dollars. During the almost three decades that Johnson owned the station, buying advertising from KTBC became another way to buy influence with Johnson. This clearly indicates Johnson's willingness to use unethical means to line his own pockets once he was in power in Washington.

Thirty-eight former employees of Johnson's company sued the company over an incentive and profit-sharing plan, asserting that the profit-sharing plan owed them almost fifty thousand dollars. They were employees of the radio and television station, held in Mr. Johnson's name, when it was sold and they were left without jobs two years earlier.[47]

Johnson Charges the Mafia for Protection

In the 1950's Johnson's influence in the Senate was growing. Relatively quickly Johnson went from being a junior senator to being the Leader of the Senate. Johnson's biographer Robert Caro does an excellent job in his book series *THE YEARS OF LYNDON JOHNSON* in detailing how Johnson managed to accomplish this rapid climb. Johnson, with his growing influence, was able to eventually control what legislation did or did not get passed in the Senate. And his relationship with Sam Rayburn extended that reach to the House of Representatives, so Johnson effectively controlled what did or did not become law in the United States. In those days Sam Rayburn was the Speaker of the U.S. House of Representatives and a very powerful leader of the Democratic Party. Johnson had recruited Rayburn to be his mentor and ally and used that relationship to control the House as well as the Senate, giving Johnson effective control of the Congress.

At that time New Orleans mafia boss Carlos Marcello was running, among other things, an illegal gambling racket that included operations in Texas. Marcello wanted to make sure the government did not crack down on it. During this time Johnson was taking money from Marcello's organization to bottle up anti-racketeering legislation in the U.S. Senate. FBI Director J. Edgar Hoover was also part of this cozy relationship with the mafia, as will be shown below.

By the time Johnson was vice president, he had been doing business with mafia boss Marcello and his organization for a decade. During that time, he had been taking fifty thousand dollars a year in bribes to keep the federal government off the backs of the mafia. Illegal slot machines and illegal bookies using Marcello's betting wire had operations in Texas and paid off a percentage to Johnson so that Marcello could continue to operate.[48] Johnson and Marcello used a go-between named Jack Halfen. As insurance, Halfen kept eight hundred feet of home movie footage showing himself and his wife partying with the Johnsons on a Texas hunting trip, and there were plenty of people in Texas willing to talk with Justice Department officials like Robert Kennedy of the Halfen-Marcello-Johnson relationship.[49]

In fact, at the time of President Kennedy's assassination, there was a file of incriminating evidence on Attorney General Robert Kennedy's desk detailing the Marcello-Halfen-Johnson connection that the president's brother was debating whether to pursue.[50] Robert Kennedy was by then looking to expose Johnson's corruption in order to justify dumping him off the ticket for the 1964 election campaign.

Robert Kennedy and Lyndon Johnson hated each other. Bobby was horrified when the Kennedys were forced to accept Johnson on the ticket as Kennedy's V.P. running mate. Bobby was looking for ways to dump LBJ off the ticket for the 1964 election and Johnson's growing pile of scandals was just what he needed to get rid of Johnson. The first step in dumping Johnson off the ticket was for Bobby to leak dirt on Johnson to the press. They would then print it and the ensuing scandals would give the Kennedys the cover they needed to dump Johnson off the ticket. Johnson would be then left to fend for himself.

Hoover continued to run interference for Johnson. In spite of Bobby Kennedy's drive to wipe out the mafia, the FBI never tapped the phones of mafia bosses Meyer Lansky, Carlos Marcello or Santo Trafficante. These are the only three mob bosses not tapped.[51]

On November 22, 1963 President John F. Kennedy was assassinated.

Once he was president, LBJ stopped all bugging of the mafia. No more wiretaps.[52] And Halfen, the go-between for Johnson and mafia boss Marcello, was later given a full pardon by President Johnson in 1966.[53] By late 1964 the connections between Johnson and Marcello had become too obvious. The week of November 25, 1964 J. Edgar Hoover made direct attempts to prevent FBI personnel from examining the Marcello organization, with only limited success.[54]

The examples listed above demonstrate a cozy relationship between Johnson and the mafia. This is an example of influence peddling by Johnson. The mafia paid him off so they could continue operating. It also shows how Johnson was comfortable dealing with the mob, and with Marcello in particular. Later, when Marcello decided to take out a hit on Kennedy, this relationship will be of critical importance. Notice also that Hoover is right in there with Johnson, using his influence at the FBI to help LBJ keep his mafia ties from becoming public knowledge. In later generations the crooked politicians of the Deep State will use the FBI in the same way to shield them from prosecution for their influence peddling.

Johnson's Crooked Partnership with Hoover

During the period when Lyndon Johnson was vice president, he had given up much of his power in a bid to get closer to the White House. At the same time his scandals were catching up to him. He needed help from Hoover to keep a lid on the scandals. If he is implicated it will lead to his destruction. Hoover pitches in to lend a hand, using the FBI to cover for Johnson.[55]

Once Kennedy was dead, Johnson and Hoover shut Attorney General Robert Kennedy off from all investigations into the mafia and the scandals involving Bobby Baker and Billie Sol Estes.[56] The subsections below go into more detail on the scandals involving Johnson and Bobby Baker and Billie Sol Estes. Once he became president, Johnson also moved quickly to get rid of key members of Robert Kennedy's loyal staff.[57]

Author Mark North, in his book *ACT OF TREASON: THE ROLE OF J. EDGAR HOOVER IN THE ASSASSINATION OF PRESIDENT KENNEDY*, has a quote:[58]

> "Johnson did not hesitate to turn to Hoover for information about his administration's critics (which information, for ideological as well as strategic reasons, Hoover generously gave); for another, Johnson, like Hoover, harbored an inordinate interest in derogatory personal information. ... The two men were made for each other."[59]

The Billie Sol Estes Scandal

Billie Sol Estes was a Texas con man who teamed up with Johnson. The Estes scandal is important because it became one of the reasons Johnson had to participate in the Kennedy assassination. Estes ran the scams and Johnson used his influence to keep the government from investigating the scams. In return Estes paid Johnson a cut of the profits from the scams. This worked well for them both until Estes took it too far and, when his pyramid scheme collapsed, it became a public scandal. While Johnson was vice president he did not have enough power to keep a lid on the scandals. Once the Estes scandal hit the newspapers Johnson was forced to use his backup strategy of having Estes take the fall. In the end the Estes affair was one of the public scandals that, by 1963, had reached critical mass and was going to take Johnson down unless he got to the White House.

The Estes scandal is also notable for the fact that, in an attempt to try to keep a lid on the scandal, Johnson ultimately ordered the murder of a man named Henry Marshall. There is a subsection below on the murder of Henry Marshall. The pressure of keeping the Estes scandal from reaching all the way to LBJ was one of the reasons Johnson had to get to the White House. As president he would be able to quash the investigations and keep from going to prison. Henry Marshall wasn't the only person to lose his life due to the Billie Sol Estes scandal. Estes had an accountant named George Krutilek who also had to be murdered in order to silence him because he knew too much.

In the 1950's Billie Sol Estes began selling ammonia fertilizer. Estes slashed his prices to drive his competition out of business.[60] And then he sold nonexistent fertilizer storage tanks to farmers who then leased them back to him. This scam netted Billie Sol thirty million dollars.[61]

In his book *BLOOD, MONEY AND POWER: HOW LBJ KILLED JFK* author Barr McClellan documents how Billie Sol Estes came up with different illegal and fraudulent schemes to use fictional cotton allotments and fictional ammonia tanks to make millions. At that time cotton production exceeded demand so production was controlled to prop up the price of cotton. Each cotton farmer was "allotted" so much cotton acerage to farm.[62] These allotments therefore became valuable but could not legally be sold or traded unless the land was taken over by the government for eminent domain purposes.[63] For example, if a farmer was displaced by highway construction that would be a case of the government exercising eminent domain to force the sale of the land. Cases of eminent domain were rare but technically possible and Estes drove a truck through this tiny loophole. McClellan points out in his book *BLOOD, MONEY AND POWER* that, at one point, Estes had purchased 3,200 acres of allotments from 116 different farmers and this was illegal. Estes made a fortune doing this. Johnson was involved because Estes was kicking back money to Johnson to make sure the government would approve of the illegal cotton allotment transfers.[64]

During the 1950's, Johnson continued to help Estes get cotton allotments until the USDA tightened the rules.[65] This involved money for favors from Johnson via Cliff Carter, one of Johnson's aides, and all of this was transacted in cash so it was untraceable.[66] By 1960 the USDA was investigating Estes.[67]

Since Estes was being audited he got Johnson to call off the Department of Agriculture and even had the USDA put Estes on the Cotton Advisory Council, thus giving Estes the ability to go full steam ahead with the scams. [68] LBJ pressured the Secretary of Agriculture to allow Estes to continue to carry out his fraud. Johnson had the USDA rewrite their procedures to allow the massive fraud of Estes and the kickbacks to Johnson to continue.

The USDA official who was assigned to investigate Estes was named Henry Marshall.[69] Marshall refused Johnson's attempts at bribery and Johnson ultimately had him murdered. This is covered in more detail in the section below on the murder of Henry Marshall. Estes also made anhydrous ammonia fertilizer tanks available to farmers. However, Estes also created tanks out of thin air by claiming to have many more tanks than he actually had and used the nonexistent tanks as collateral on loans.[70] This appears to be where Estes got too greedy for his own good. The tank scam eventually developed into a pyramid scheme and Estes needed help from Johnson to cover it up when he went too far and it collapsed and was going to become a public scandal which would eventually lead back to Johnson.

Dunn Lights the Fuse

Author Phillip Nelson in his book *LBJ: THE MASTERMIND OF THE JFK ASSASSINATION* documents how one citizen tried to get the word out about what a hypocrite Billie Sol Estes was. Estes pretended to be an upstanding citizen and pillar of the community while in fact he was a dishonest scammer and con man. Dr. John Dunn was a dentist who appealed to local law enforcement authorities to investigate the Estes scandal. This did not work so he bought a newspaper in Pecos and started publishing the truth about Billie Sol Estes.[71] In 1961 the Pecos Texas School Board held an election. When Estes ran for the school board he lost to a write-in candidate. John Dunn's newspaper had opposed Estes in the school board election. He printed the first exposure of the Estes fertilizer tank mortgage fraud scheme. This took courage.[72] Then other newspapers took up the story which eventually made it to the national press. Estes eventually ended up in prison a few years later. The town of Pecos became divided into two camps, for or against Estes. The fight to expose Estes cost Dunn dearly. Just as the IRS Director who tried to look into Johnson's finances had come under personal attack by the media and the authorities, Dr. Dunn was destroyed personally and financially by the battle.[73] This reaction is typical of anyone who dares oppose the Deep State. They turn on you and destroy you, as will be seen multiple times in this book.

However, Dunn succeeded in finally getting a newspaper, his own, to publish accounts of what Estes was up to. The story was eventually picked up by the national media and, once the story had come to light, the Billie Sol Estes scandal became one more weapon Robert Kennedy could use against Lyndon Johnson. Bobby Kennedy wanted to dump Johnson off the ticket for the upcoming 1964 election and the first step in doing that was to have Johnson's scandals published nationally. In the summer of 1961 Attorney General Robert Kennedy initiated prosecution of Billie Sol Estes.[74] Once the disgraced Johnson was forced to step down he could and would be prosecuted and sent to prison. Johnson would not let this happen. The fuse lit by Dunn was a long one, but it eventually led to the assassination of President Kennedy. In 1962 stories were beginning to appear in Texas newspapers about Johnson's involvement with Estes.[75]

In 1962, after information came to light that Estes had paid off four Agriculture officials for grain storage contracts, President Kennedy ordered the Justice Department and FBI to open up investigations into Estes' activities and determine if the Secretary of Agriculture Orville Freeman had been "compromised" (he was cleared). Congress conducted hearings on Estes' business dealings, some which led back to Vice President Johnson.

George Krutilek, a Certified Public Accountant who worked for Billie Sol Estes, was questioned on April 2, 1962 by FBI agents. [76] He obviously knew too much and also had to be silenced. Two days later on April 4, 1962 the body of George Krutilek was found in his car with a hose stuck in the window. The El Paso County pathologist said Krutilek did not die from carbon monoxide poisoning.[77] This is covered in more detail below in the sub-section on George Krutilek. In April of 1962 Billie Sol Estes was indicted on 57 acts of fraud by a Federal grand jury.[78]

Congressman Cramer

The incident with Congressman Cramer is an excellent illustration of how Hoover and Johnson worked as a team. Hoover was willing to use the investigative power of the FBI to bury inconvenient evidence for Johnson to make sure LBJ's scandals do not destroy him. At the same time Hoover was also willing to use the intimidation power of the FBI to keep Johnson's potential enemies at bay.

By 1962 Johnson had ordered at least two murders in an attempt to keep the Estes scandal from destroying his career. The latest murder was an accountant who was working for Estes named George Krutilek. Congressman Cramer decided to take action, and Johnson reached out to Hoover for help.

Author Mark North, in his book *ACT OF TREASON: THE ROLE OF J. EDGAR HOOVER IN THE ASSASSINATION OF PRESIDENT KENNEDY*, said of vice presidential aide Walter Jenkins, that in April of 1962:[79]

> "Jenkins, upon learning that congressman Bill Cramer (R.-Fla.) was preparing impeachment proceedings based on the Vice President's and Mrs. Johnson's alleged association with Estes in two grain storage operations in Texas, asked DeLoach to have the FBI 'interview Cramer immediately'.

Emphasizing that Hoover 'would, of course, want of every possible assistance to the Vice President,' DeLoach recommended that, 'in [*sic*] this particular occasion it might be better if we received the information from a third party rather than from the Vice President's office.' The next morning *Thomas Corcoran, the lobbyist*, contacted DeLoach to report having learned that Cramer had plans to initiate impeachment proceedings against the Vice President. DeLoach thereupon briefed Hoover, recommending that Cramer be 'immediately' interviewed as a 'legitimate responsibility in the current Estes investigation.' Hoover had concluded ... 'We have already checked into the story told by Cramer and found it false; Cramer himself is a loud mouth; Corcoran is the devious "Tommy."'[80]

Hoover was using the FBI as an American Gestapo. President Truman had worried about this and he was right. Notice also how they do this – through aides. Jenkins is an aide to Johnson and Cartha DeLoach is an aide to Hoover. This gives Hoover and Johnson each another layer of insulation, of 'plausible deniability', should it ever become necessary.

Suppressing the Media

Farm and Ranch Magazine published an editorial which was critical of Johnson's involvement with Estes.[81] Jenkins reached out to DeLoach to have the FBI lean on the editor of the magazine.[82] FBI agents were dispatched to intimidate the editor.[83]

The Estes scandal was just one step away from being linked to Johnson. On June 23, 1962 there were newspaper reports of an assistant state's attorney general reading from telephone company records of calls from Billie Sol Estes to a member of LBJ's staff (three calls to Cliff Carter) one to an unlisted number in Washington.[84] Cliff Carter is on Johnson's staff in Washington. Cliff Carter said he got a few calls from Billie Sol Estes.[85] Carter said he told Billie Sol that he knew nothing about it (Billie Sol being arrested).[86] Adding to the pressure, Republicans were hot on the trail, trying to pin the Estes scandal on the Kennedy administration.[87]

In the middle of the scandal, Estes insisted on another face-to-face meeting with Johnson. Given how important containing the scandal was, Johnson agreed to fly to Pecos.[88] Unfortunately, the weather was bad that day and the pilots who flew Johnson's plane said they could not come and get him at his ranch due to the thick fog.[89] Johnson, callously disregarding the danger to the pilots, ordered them to fly anyway, and the plane crashed, killing both pilots.[90]

At this point Johnson is desperately using whatever it takes, including using the FBI as an American Gestapo, to keep a lid on the scandals.

The Murder of Henry Marshall

Henry Marshall was a Texas USDA official who was assigned to look into the activities of Billie Sol Estes. Once Henry Marshall had been assigned to investigate, it was only a matter of time before it blew up because Henry Marshall was an honest man. He uncovered the Estes fraud and refused to be bribed. Mac Wallace, LBJ's hitman, murdered Henry Marshall in 1961. Barr McClellan in his book *BLOOD, MONEY AND POWER: HOW LBJ KILLED JFK* and Phillip Nelson in his book *LBJ: THE MASTERMIND OF THE JFK ASSASSINATION* both do an excellent job of documenting this. Hitman Mac Wallace typically got his orders through Cliff Carter, one of Johnson's aides. Carter was another of LBJ's "layers" or "circuit breakers" to protect Johnson.[91]

Author Phillip Nelson, in his book *LBJ: THE MASTERMIND OF THE JFK ASSASSINATION*, documents that:[92]

> "Billie Sol Estes was released from prison in December, 1983. Three months later he appeared before the Robertson County grand jury. He confessed that Henry Marshall was murdered because it was feared he would "blow the whistle" on the cotton allotment scam. Billie Sol Estes claimed that Marshall was murdered on the orders of Lyndon B. Johnson, who was afraid that his own role in this scam would become public knowledge. According to Estes, Clifton C. Carter, Johnson's long-term aide, had ordered Marshall to approve 138 cotton allotment transfers. Billie Sol Estes told the grand jury that he had a meeting with Johnson and Carter about Henry Marshall. Johnson suggested that Marshall be promoted out of Texas. Estes agreed and replied: "Let's transfer him, let's get him out of here. Get him a better job. Make him an assistant secretary of agriculture." However, Marshall rejected the idea of being promoted in order to keep him quiet. Estes, Johnson and Carter had another meeting on 17th January, 1961, to discuss what to do about Henry Marshall. Also at the meeting was

Mac Wallace. After it was pointed out that Marshall had refused promotion to Washington, Johnson said: "It looks like we'll just have to get rid of him." Wallace, who Estes described as a hitman, was given the assignment."[93]

The hit went wrong. In June of 1961 Wallace went to see Marshall. Estes told a 1984 grand jury that he met Carter and Wallace at his home in Pecos after Marshall was killed.[94] Wallace described to Estes how he had waited for Marshall at his farm and Marshall refused to cooperate so Wallace attacked Marshall and rendered him unconscious.[95] Wallace had originally intended to kill Marshall and make it look like death by suicide, by carbon monoxide poisoning, but Marshall fought back and Wallace had to shoot him.[96] Wallace had panicked because he thought he heard a truck coming and used Marshall's own bolt action rifle to shoot Marshall five times.[97] This made the murder too obvious. It's just hard to commit suicide by shooting yourself five times in the back with a bolt action rifle.[98] Three of the shots which killed Henry Marshall were "rapidly incapacitating" and therefore it was impossible for this to have been a suicide.[99] Estes quoted Carter as saying that Wallace "sure did botch it up."[100]

Clint Peoples was an honest Texas Ranger who investigated and pursued the murder of Henry Marshall.[101] It was his opinion that three of the five shots would have killed Marshall and therefore five self-inflicted shots were impossible. And Marshall couldn't have fired the shots into his own side. Peoples thought Marshall was murdered and he reported this in June of 1962.[102] His efforts were rewarded when the Medical Examiner agreed and said that Henry Marshall had been shot in the back.[103] The Estes scandal grew and a grand jury investigation was ordered into the suspicious death of Henry Marshall.

Johnson was now forced to use his influence with the Texas authorities to cover-up the murder.[104] Johnson starts by having the grand jury hand-picked by Sheriff Howard Stegall so as to be able to control the outcome.[105] Three of the members of the grand jury were related to Sheriff Stegall.[106]

Then Johnson had the authorities trick Nolan Griffin into identifying the wrong suspect. Nolan Griffin was the gas station attendant who gave hitman Mac Wallace directions to the Marshall place on the day Marshall was murdered.[107] Griffin later said he was tricked into "identifying" the wrong guy.[108] Next, Johnson had to limit the amount of information the grand jury got from the official investigation. For this LBJ got Hoover to help out. Notice the repeating pattern of the Deep State, with the crooked politicians getting the FBI to help them out of a jam. This still goes on a few generations later.

The FBI Report of Evidence in the Estes Case

In May of 1962 Vice President Johnson was desperately trying, through FBI Director Hoover, to limit the amount of evidence the Texas grand jury got.[109] If he could keep a lid on the facts, he could keep the grand jury in Texas from handing down an indictment for the murder of Henry Marshall. If they got the full story on the Estes scandal, Johnson might not have been able to have the murder deemed a suicide. When the edited report was given to the grand jury, Johnson needed to personally be right there in Texas to use his influence to make sure that no indictment was handed down. Up until then Hoover had the report and had seventy-five agents working on it.[110] So, on May 25, 1962 Johnson flew to Texas, ostensibly to accept an honorary award from his alma mater.[111] Johnson did not even speak at his own, therefore somewhat awkward, ceremony.[112] LBJ was really there because the USDA was releasing the edited version of the Agriculture Department's report on Estes and it was due to arrive in Austin at the Attorney General's office the next day.[113]

On May 26, 1962 Attorney General Robert Kennedy announced that excerpts from the confidential report on the Estes scandal were flown to Texas that day.[114] On May 28, 1962 the Texas grand jury looking into the death of Henry Marshall asked for the full report on Estes. The federal government had only submitted 22 pages of the 175-page report. Will Wilson, Texas Attorney General, described getting the report as "like pulling teeth."[115]

On June 6, 1962 Senator John McClellan announced hearings into the Billie Sol Estes case.[116] We don't know how much evidence was withheld by Hoover in the Estes case.[117] We do know that the FBI and the Texas Rangers had very different opinions of what happened. On June 19, 1962 there were press reports that the Texas Rangers and the FBI were at odds in the investigation into the death of Henry Marshall because the Rangers said it was murder.[118] Here again we can see Hoover's hand helping Johnson. Clearly the FBI is being used to obstruct the investigation at the source so that it does not lead back to Johnson.

By using all his influence to hide evidence and stack the grand jury, Johnson was able to avoid an indictment for the murder of Henry Marshall. It was ruled a suicide. This will be overturned more than two decades later. At the same time Johnson was trying to distance himself from Estes, claiming he 'would not know him if he met him' or 'never heard of him' or 'only met him once.'[119]

Consequences for the murder of Henry Marshall had been sidestepped, but there still remained the investigation by the Department of Agriculture into the dealings of Billie Sol Estes. Author Mark North, in his book *ACT OF TREASON*, documents that, on October 18, 1961:[120]

> "...Estes and his attorney visited [Mr. Tucker at] the [Agriculture] department to protest the investigation ... [He] declared that if [it] were not cancelled, 'before night he would have a group consisting of about thirty-eight people including lawyers and accountants who would fly into Washington' and 'buy space in newspapers and magazines and go to New York and appear on television and embarrass the Administration....' He mentioned the death of Henry Marshall...."[121]

The *Chicago Tribune* reported on the Agriculture Department's report, raising the issue of Estes' threats to "go to the top".[122]

On October 27, 1961 the U.S. Department of Agriculture produced a 140-page internal report concerning the investigation into Estes and his scams and his threats to go to top officials if he didn't get his way.[123] On December 15, 1961 the USDA ruled that Estes cotton allotments were illegal and recommended that they be cancelled.[124] On December 22, 1961 Undersecretary of Agriculture Charles Murphy cancelled the Estes cotton allotments and overrode an adverse recommendation by the review division and adjudication board and appointed Estes to the Cotton Advisory Council.[125]

The USDA continued to investigate.[126] The new investigators who replaced Marshall went to work with the support of Bobby Kennedy.[127] Estes could not get any more cotton allotments so he turned to leasing non-existent fertilizer tanks.

In 1984 a grand jury reopened the case and ruled it a homicide. Back in 1962 it had been ruled a suicide.[128] Also in 1984 Estes claimed that Marshall was murdered on the orders of Johnson who was afraid that his own role in the scam would become public knowledge.[129]

In August of 1962 Estes was indicted on price fixing.[130] Also in August of 1962 Johnson's name was coming up in two congressional investigation subcommittees looking into Billie Sol Estes.[131] Johnson owned part of a company called Commercial Solvents which also did business with Billie Sol Estes.[132] In 1958 Estes took huge losses in order to drive his competition under and he got behind on his payments to Commercial Solvents and he owed it over $550,000.[133] Then he got them to loan him even more money.[134] On October 22, 1962 Estes was ordered to be tried immediately on charges of theft and swindling, overruling his lawyer's request for a delay.[135] On November 7, 1962 a jury found Estes guilty of swindling and sentenced Estes to eight years.[136] On November 9, 1962 a Senate subcommittee said it still planned to question Estes.[137] On November 13, 1962 the office of New York Governor Rockefeller announced that the governor had signed extradition papers for Maynard Wheeler, president of Commercial Solvents, to stand trial on antitrust charges stemming from the Estes case.[138] On December 11, 1962 Estes was ordered to stand trial on fourteen of twenty-nine counts of fraud and the trial is moved from Pecos to El Paso to find a jury.[139]

Hoover was forced to make a show of investigating Johnson. This he did not want to do so the investigation was half-hearted at best. The FBI agents stumbled across Johnson's money laundering corporation, Brazos-Tenth, set up and run by LBJ's crooked lawyer and partner, Ed Clark. Johnson, the man who should be untouchable, was becoming the focus of the investigation. The deeper the investigation got the closer and the more ties to Johnson were found. Senator John McLellan of Arkansas announced in 1962 that his permanent investigations committee would hold hearings and issued a subpoena of Estes who then demanded an immediate trial to avoid the subpoena.[140]

On March 10, 1963 Estes went on trial in Federal court and on March 28, 1963 Estes was convicted of mail fraud involving $24 Million.[141] On March 29, 1963 Senator McClellan announced that he would call Estes in front of his Senate committee soon.[142] On April 14, 1963 Estes was sentenced to 15 years in prison for mail fraud and conspiracy.[143]

On November 9, 1963 the press reported that Senate investigators planned to call Billie Sol Estes to finish up four months of hearings.[144] On November 12, 1963 Estes "took the fifth" twenty-six times in front of the senate subcommittee on investigations.[145] After forty-five minutes Senator McClellan indicated that the case was closed but, he said, there were some areas where law enforcement officers may want to examine the record carefully.[146]

All this time Bobby Kennedy was keeping up the pressure on Johnson.[147] He wanted to get enough dirt on Johnson and leak it to the press so Johnson could be dumped off the ticket for the next election. If the press got wind of the many Johnson scandals and found a way to tie one or more of them directly to Johnson, then the Kennedys would have the perfect excuse to get rid of Johnson as a liability. To that end Attorney General Robert Kennedy offered Estes his freedom if he would turn states evidence against Johnson. At that time Estes turned it down because, he said, he would be free for thirty minutes and then he would have been dead.[148]

On November 22, 1963 President Kennedy was assassinated in Dealey Plaza and everything changed.

On January 15, 1964 the press reported that the Texas Court of Criminal Appeals upheld that day the conviction of Estes on swindling charges and ruled that he must serve an eight-year prison sentence.[149] His attorney, John Cofer, also refused comment.[150] At that point Estes still has pending against him four more federal and state indictments containing more than thirty counts of theft, swindling, mail fraud, false statements and criminal antitrust violations.[151] On January 17, 1964 the press reported that The Internal Revenue Service found that Estes owes the government more than $18.2 million in back taxes and fraud penalties.[152]

Johnson was barely able to get to the White House in time to bury the Estes scandal before it got to him. The Estes scandal, combined with the Baker and other scandals (see below) all added to the pressure Johnson was under by 1963. He needed to get to the White House in order to keep all these scandals from taking him down. With Bobby Kennedy collecting dirt on Johnson and leaking it to the press, Johnson would not survive.

LBJ's Crooked Partnership with Brown & Root

Brown & Root was another of Johnson's crooked partnerships. Johnson used his influence to get Brown & Root increasingly massive federal contracts and they kicked back some of the equally massive profits to Johnson.[153] This is an example of the rise of the military-industrial complex that Eisenhower warned about in his farewell address. Brown & Root and Bell Helicopter both supported Johnson and both subsequently made fortunes during the Vietnam War.[154]

In their book *THE MAN WHO KILLED KENNEDY*, authors Roger Stone and Mike Colapietro document how Brown & Root was a small construction company primarily building roads when the depression hit and they turned to former Texas State Senator Alvin Wirtz to help get them the Marshall Ford dam project even though they had never built a dam before.[155] When the project hit a snag (the federal government didn't own the land it was being built on) they turned to Johnson to get President Franklin Delano Roosevelt to give the project the green light, which he did.[156] So, thanks to Johnson, Brown & Root got the Marshall Ford Dam contract, a project that Johnson salvaged and expanded. The IRS investigated Johnson and Brown & Root in regard to illegal contributions during the 1941 senate election. Brown & Root was not supposed to contribute to Johnson's campaign. This IRS inquiry grew until Johnson had it quashed by the White House.

Author Phillip Nelson, in his book *LBJ: THE MASTERMIND OF THE JFK ASSASSINATION*, documents that:[157]

> "In 1956 the columnist Drew Pearson managed to acquire copies of an investigation into Johnson's financial misconduct, including IRS records that showed that George and Herman Brown's company, Brown & Root, paid their employees bonuses with the understanding that they were to immediately deposit them and then send the same amount to one of Johnson's campaign funds. Pearson cited numerous examples of this scheme; for example, an employee named Randolph Mills at the Victoria Gravel Company, a subsidiary of Brown & Root, received a check for $2,500 that he deposited before immediately paying out the same amount to J. Frank Jungman, Lyndon's Houston campaign manager. In another case, Edgar Monteith, a Houston attorney, received several checks in 1941 that he and his partner, A. W. Baring, treated as revenue for their firm and then sent to the Johnson campaign as reimbursement for campaign expenses. Drew Pearson further wrote that "when asked specifically about the matter, Lyndon told the IRS that he 'had never heard of Monteith,' much less his financial support, though Monteith was the brother of a former Houston mayor.""[158]

> "Still another example of Johnson's illegitimate power can be traced to Brown & Root having been given a contract to build subchasers and destroyers, which was eventually worth $357 million, despite having no experience whatsoever in

shipbuilding. After landing the largest navy contract in history, paving the way to expand his construction business into shipbuilding, George Brown observed, "We didn't know the stern from the aft – I mean bow – of the boat." Before Johnson went to Washington to act as Brown & Root's personal emissary and "rainmaker," their company was practically bankrupt and Herman lived with his wife in a tent; shortly after Lyndon went to Washington, thanks to Herman and the Austin attorney, Alvin Wirtz, the contracts began to flow so quickly that the company became highly profitable and one of the largest independent government contractors; in 1962 it was acquired by Halliburton."[159]

Then Brown & Root bought the "Big Inch" and "Little Inch" pipelines in 1947 for $143 million.[160] These pipelines had been laid during WW II to bring oil to the Northeastern U.S. Brown & Root formed a company called Texas Eastern Transmission and Johnson and many of his cronies got stock, including Johnson's lawyer and partner Ed Clark.[161] Deregulation would make everyone involved rich if Johnson could get rid of Leland Olds, then the head of the Federal Power Commission and a strict enforcer of the rules. Johnson used a smear campaign to get rid of Leland Olds[162] He dug up old writings of Olds which he took out of context and used to accuse Olds of being a communist sympathizer. This worked and Johnnson was able to block an honest civil servant from re-nomination. Thus, Olds was unable to continue enforcing the 1938 Natural Gas Act. This ruined the career of Olds.[163] Then Johnson and his crony House Speaker Sam Rayburn did everything possible to protect the Oil Depletion Allowance. Johnson also got Brown & Root shipbuilding contracts even though they had never built boats before.[164]

Brown & Root grew over the years, making everyone involved a fortune off of government contracts arranged by Johnson, and the company was set to make hundreds of millions of dollars off the escalation of the war in Vietnam. Then President Kennedy issued National Security Action Memorandum (NSAM) #263 on October 11, 1963. This was JFK's order to start the *withdrawal* of troops from Vietnam.[165] He had decided that the Vietnam War was a bad idea and that the U.S. should pull out. This would have meant a severe limit on the profits Brown & Root could make from war-related contracts.

On November 22, 1963 President Kennedy was assassinated.

National Security Action Memorandum (NSAM) #273 on November 26, 1963 was LBJ's order to *increase* the U.S. involvement in Vietnam. Then in 1964 LBJ used the Gulf of Tonkin Incident to get congressional approval for the war in Vietnam. It later turned out that the Gulf of Tonkin incident was more of a pretext to go to war than a true provocation worthy of starting a land war in Asia.[166] Brown & Root made a fortune on construction contracts in Vietnam. They were given over a billion dollars in contracts. Bell Helicopter, which had helped Johnson in his 1948 Senate campaign with money and "transportation" was also given a huge contract to build the iconic Huey choppers for the Vietnam War.[167]

Author Phillip Nelson, in his book *LBJ: THE MASTERMIND OF THE JFK ASSASSINATION*, documents that:[168]

> "The Government Accounting Office found that his [Johnson's] friends at Brown & Root "were overcharging by hundreds of millions of dollars beyond what was legitimate for their construction work in Vietnam."[169]

Like his other schemes, Johnson used his influence to help Brown & Root make money and they kicked some of the huge profits back to Johnson. This is typical of the crooked politicians in the Deep State. They use their influence to help criminals make windfall profits and the criminal 'businessmen' then kick back a cut to the crooked politicians who helped them by using their power and influence to arrange lucrative business deals. The public interest is not high on the list of priorities of the denizes of the Deep State.

The Bobby Baker Scandal

As dangerous as the Billie Sol Estes scandal was to Johnson's career, the Bobby Baker scandal worried LBJ even more. These two scandals built to a head in 1963 to the point where Johnson, as vice president, could not contain them. Johnson *had* to get to the White House in order to gain enough power and influence to keep his scandals from taking him down with them. Of the two the Baker scandal was the one Vice President Johnson was almost unable to contain. Part of the problem was that the scandal had everything the press could ask for. There was sex, lies, corruption and even the mafia. If Johnson was implicated then he would be tied to all of it. At the same time Attorney General Robert Kennedy was feeding dirt on Johnson to the press as a prelude to dumping him from the 1964 ticket. Bobby Kennedy had been horrified from the first moment, during the 1960 Democratic convention, when he realized that Johnson had pushed his way onto the Kennedy ticket as the VP running mate. Bobby was still trying to get rid of Johnson and a necessary step on the way to dumping LBJ was to let his scandals erupt in the national media. Then LBJ could easily be cut from the ticket for the 1964 election.

The Bobby Baker scandal, added to the Estes scandal and the other scandals, put so much pressure on Lyndon Johnson that he felt he had no choice but to go ahead with the plot to murder President John F. Kennedy. If LBJ had not had Kennedy killed then he would end up disgraced in the press, dumped from the ticket, prosecuted for his crimes and very likely end up behind bars. Johnson had put himself in a position where his choices were stark – the Big House or the White House. He chose to murder Kennedy and take the White House.

Bobby Baker worked for Johnson in the Senate. This relationship eventually grew into another of Johnson's crooked partnerships where Baker ran scams and gave Johnson a cut of the profits while Johnson ran interference for Baker so he could keep the illegal operations running. Baker is another example of Johnson having a "layer of protection" so that, if they got caught, Johnson would not be the one behind bars. As it happened they got caught and Baker ended up behind bars. Once Baker was behind bars Johnson then offered to bribe him with a million dollars to keep quiet. And Baker never squealed on Johnson.

Edward Levinson was a Cincinnati mafia gambler who associated with Bobby Baker and Fred Black. Bobby Baker was Johnson's protege in the Senate. Johnson was a mentor to Baker, who eventually became a partner in crime to Johnson. Fred Black was a Washington lobbyist who also worked closely with Johnson on some of his scams. Levinson was a front man for Meyer Lansky's Sands Casino and was also associated with Jimmy Hoffa who fronted the money, from the Teamster Union funds, to invest in hotels with Levinson.[170] Levinson was also a friend of mafia boss Sam Giancana.[171] This was a dangerous mix because if the Baker scandal became public then Johnson's mafia ties might become public knowledge and ruin at least LBJ's political career and also perhaps his chances of remaining out of prison.

On December 29, 1961 Fred Black, Bobby Baker, Ed Levinson and Benny Sigelbaum formed Serv-U Corporation.[172] Fred Black was a lobbyist and friend and neighbor of Johnson, Baker and Hoover.[173] Black was a longtime friend of mobster Johnny Roselli.[174] Ed Levinson and Benjamin Sigelbaum arranged the financing for the Serv-U corporation for Fred Black and Bobby Baker, and Levinson and Sigelbaum were associated with the mafia.[175] Baker and Black formed Serv-U Corporation to provide vending machines to government contractors because the two of them are well-connected to the Washington power structure and, through Johnson, in a position to force government contractors to accept Serv-U vending machines in their offices and factories.[176] The Serv-U deal became the subject of allegations of conflict of interest and corruption after a disgruntled former government contractor sued and the lawsuit eventually generated a lot of press and that made it a public scandal. This lit another fuse that led to the Kennedy assassination.

The Baker scandal came to a head in 1963. Don Reynolds, who sold life insurance to Johnson, was testifying that he gave Johnson a stereo worth over $500 and bought $1,200 worth of advertising on Johnson's radio station. He also said that he saw Baker with a suitcase full of $100,000 as a payoff for steering the TFX contract to General Dynamics.[177] Reynolds also passed on a Baker comment that Johnson had said on inauguration day.[178] The comment was that Johnson had said that Kennedy would not live out his term and would die a violent death.[179] Baker didn't want to be a "rat," but Johnson dropped him when he became too hot.[180] Attorney General Robert Kennedy had sent *Life* magazine reporters to dig up dirt on Johnson and they wrote an article on the Baker angle which was ready to go.[181] Then Kennedy was killed and so was the story, to be replaced by an article based on the Zapruder film.[182] Baker went to jail and Johnson went to the White House.[183]

Don Reynolds was testifying against Johnson and Johnson wanted to smear him so he had a White House aide call a publisher with leaked dirt on Reynolds.[184] Senator Hugh Scott then demanded an investigation into the leaks.[185] Ted Lewis of the *New York Daily News* asks:[186]

> "Does the White House have the authority to order Hoover to turn over its secret files any time the administration wants to crack down on an embarrassing witness?"[187]

This use of the FBI to crack down on witnesses is typical of the Deep State and continues today. According to an article on November 29, 2018 from *The Daily Caller*, the FBI raided the home of Dennis Nathan Cain on November 19, 2018. Cain was a whistleblower who gave evidence on Hillary Clinton and her scheme to take money in return for using her influence as Secretary of State to allow the sale of Uranium One to the Russians. Notice that instead of investigating Hillary Clinton's crimes, the FBI is raiding the home of the whistleblower and thus protecting Clinton instead of investigating or prosecuting her.

The Baker Scandal Breaks Into the Open

On September 12, 1963 the *Washington Post* reported on a breach of contract suit against Baker and Black for Serv-U, and the Bobby Baker scandal was about to break out into the open.[188] In September of 1963 the Baker-Levinson scandal exploded, and this revealed close connections between Johnson and the mafia.[189] At this point the fact that the scandal had broken in the press beame a problem for Johnson. If Baker had decided to talk then Johnson's career would have come to a screeching halt.

In September of 1963 an investigation was begun by the Senate rules committee into Baker's business and political activities. Baker was investigated for allegations of bribery and using money allocated by Congress and arranging sexual favors in exchange for votes and government contracts. Under increasing pressure, Bobby Baker was forced to resign from his Senate job as the Secretary for the Majority on October 7, 1963.[190] When asked about this Vice President Johnson says "no comment."[191]

On October 23, 1963 the Senate rules committee planned to investigate Baker as the Baker scandal grew.[192] On October 31, 1963 the Senate rules committee was trying to decide whether to employ special outside counsel to direct the investigation into Bobby Baker.[193] The investigation was expected to touch "others in the executive branch," which was a likely reference to Johnson.[194]

On November 5, 1963 investigators for the Senate Rules Committee started looking into the Baker scandal.[195] The press reported that Baker had ties to Ed Levinson who had ties to the mafia.[196] A retired FBI agent named William Meehan was looking into Baker for the rules committee.[197] The mafia were likely funneling money to Johnson via Baker to buy influence and get protection from the federal government. The senate committee voted unanimously to hire outside counsel to direct the investigation into Baker.[198] This was all bad news for Johnson, who by now needed to have Kennedy murdered as soon as possible. If the hit was put off much longer, Johnson would be publicly disgraced and it would be too late for Johnson. If that happened, then Hoover would be forced to retire and Bobby Kennedy would continue to destroy the mafia. The conspirators were running out of time.

On November 19, 1963 the press reported on Baker and his mob connections.[199] Clifford Jones was the Lieutenant Governor of Nevada.[200] Later he ran a casino in Havana and was accused by the state gaming control board of being a front for Meyer Lansky's ownership of the Thunderbird Hotel.[201] After that Mr. Jones was connected to Bobby Baker.[202] Baker arranged a series of meetings between Jones and John Gates, the president of Intercontinental Hotels, Inc., a subsidiary of Pan Am.[203] Johnson was tied to Baker and, if Baker was tied to the mafia then Johnson would be tied to the mafia. Johnson was right on the edge of losing everything, and the fate of the others were now tied to Johnson's fate.

On November 20, 1963 the press reported that Senator Ralph Yarborough charged the night before that Baker had a hand in keeping him from a choice committee assignment in 1961.[204] Baker had told some people "We couldn't afford to have Yarborough have that seat, he would then be in a position to control Texas's judicial patronage or would be in a position" to prevent Lyndon from controlling it"[205] This bit of information shows how Johnson was able to control the corrupt political machine in Texas, which controlled the judges. Controlling the corrupt judges helped Johnson control the corrupt judicial system.

On November 22, 1963 President John F. Kennedy was assassinated and Johnson became president. The next day President Johnson gave Hoover complete control of the investigation into the death of President Kennedy.[206] From then on Attorney General Robert Kennedy was denied access to FBI files on the Baker investigation.[207] Once Kennedy was dead and Johnson was in the White House, Hoover could then go around the Attorney General and effectively report directly to the president. He could cut Bobby and the Justice Department out of the loop. On November 23, 1963 Hoover ordered FBI officials to stop talking and working with the Justice Department's organized crime section.[208]

Author Mark North, in his book *ACT OF TREASON: THE ROLE OF J. EDGAR HOOVER IN THE ASSASSINATION OF PRESIDENT KENNEDY*, documents that:[209]

> "...As a Justice Department lawyer later ... told ... the *New York Times*, John Kennedy was assassinated and 'the next day we stopped getting information from the FBI on the Bobby Baker investigation. Within a month the FBI ... wouldn't tell us anything.'"[210]

North also says in the same book that Hoover "cannot allow Johnson to be directly implicated (and very probably impeached) over the Baker/Levinson scandal."[211]

Just because Johnson is now president does not mean he is out of the woods. He is still in danger of having the various scandals ruin him. However, he now has the power of the White House to help him with damage control.

Author Mark North, in his book *ACT OF TREASON: THE ROLE OF J. EDGAR HOOVER IN THE ASSASSINATION OF PRESIDENT KENNEDY*, documents the escalation of tension in the Baker scandal:

On December 14, 1963:[212]

> "Press: "The National Broadcasting Company will televise live on Tuesday the opening day of the . . . investigation of . . . Baker . . . . .A protégé of Johnson when the latter was Senate Democratic Leader, Mr. Baker reportedly acquired a $2 million fortune while serving in his influential nineteen-thousand-dollar-a-year Senate post."[213]

On December 16, 1963:[214]

> "Press also reports on the testimony of a female associate of Baker, a Mrs. Novak: "A number of times, she said, he gave her large sums of cash to be deposited in the bank account of the motel. The sums varied from $1,000 to $13,000, usually in $100 bills. She would pick the money up in Mr. Baker's Senate office and take it to the bank, she said." This session is broadcast live by NBC."[215]

On December 17, 1963:[216]

> "Johnson cannot survive the growing scandals surrounding Baker without Hoover's help, nor can Hoover stave off retirement without Johnson's executive order. LBJ is soon to say of Hoover "I'd rather have him inside the tent pissing out than outside the tent pissing in.""[217]

On January 13, 1964:[218]

> "Baker press coverage continues. "In other testimony, a Nevada gambler, Edward Levinson, was identified as a major stockholder in the Serv-U corporation, the vending machine concern that is the nucleus of Mr. Baker's financial interests. Today's hearing also produced the first public corroboration of statements by the Capitol Vending Company that it's

president had made substantial payments to Mr. Baker in return for the latter's influence in arranging for a profitable contract at a Virginia defense plant. . . . Mr. Hill told the committee that he 'had heard' that Mr. Baker had negotiated a $100,000 loan from 'a union.' He did not elaborate. However, Mr. Hill [later] told a reporter that he had been told by an 'insurance man' about a loan and that the money had come from the Teamster's Union's Western Conference pension fund. . . . Testimony that . . . Levinson, a Las Vegas casino operator who long has been a figure in Newport, Kentucky gambling, was linked with Mr. Baker, was the first tentative substantiation of reports that gambling money might be involved in Mr. Baker's activities. Mr. Levinson has declined to discuss any relationship with Mr. Baker."[219]

On January 14, 1964:[220]

"Press: "An assertion that . . . Baker was linked to Las Vegas gambling interests was put into the public record today. . . . Mr. Baker was co-signer on a $175,000 bank loan in March, 1962 with Edward Levinson, Benny Siegelbaum and Fred A. Black. The four men used the money in a financial venture, it was stated. Mr. Levinson and Mr. Siegelbaum are operators of gambling casinos in Las Vegas, Nev."[221]

The pressure on Johnson is now so great that he finally loses it and on February 4, 1964 LBJ barged into House Speaker John McCormack's office saying that he would give Bobby Baker $1M to keep his mouth shut.[222] So focused is Johnson on his chances of losing everything that, at first, he does not even notice the other person in McCormack's office who is listening while he is offering a million-dollar bribe to Baker.

Mark North, in his book *ACT OF TREASON*, describes the February 4, 1964 encounter:[223]

"Johnson finally panics over the growing Baker scandal. On February 4, 1964 Washington lobbyist Winter-Berger is discussing public relations with Speaker of the House McCormack in McCormack's Washington office. Johnson then barged in and began ranting hysterically, oblivious to the lobbyist's presence. Johnson said "John that son-of-a-bitch Bobby Baker is going to ruin me. If that cocksucker talks I'm gonna land in jail. I practically raised that motherfucker and now he's gonna make me the first President of the United States to spend the last days of his life behind bars." When Johnson finally noticed Winter-Berger's presence,

McCormack explained that the visiting lobbyist was a close friend of Nat Voloshen. Johnson then became enthusiastic, exclaiming "Nat can get to Bobby. They're friends. Have Nat get to Bobby." When Winter-Berger volunteered that he had an appointment with Voloshen the next day, Johnson told Winter-Berger "Tell Nat that I want him to get in touch with Bobby Baker as soon as possible – tomorrow, if he can. Tell Nat to tell Bobby that I will give him a million dollars if he takes this rap. Bobby must not talk. I will see to it that he gets a million-dollar settlement.""[224]

And the subsequent results on February 19, 1964:[225]

"Baker at last appears before Senator Jordan's investigating Rules Committee, but refuses to talk, claiming fifth amendment privileges."[226]

"It is unknown whether Baker, in fact, ever receives one million dollars from Johnson.[227]

And on February 25, 1964:[228]

"Baker again appears before Committee. He again takes the fifth. Apparently, Johnson has now, with the aid of Hoover and Baker, weathered the worst of the scandal."[229]

"In April of 1964 the Baker hearings are permanently discontinued."[230]

The Baker scandal almost cost Johnson everything. Even with the power of the presidency he was barely able to contain it. Had he not had Kennedy murdered and made the leap from vice president to president, he would have ended up in prison. This was Johnson's motive for participating in the murder of Kennedy.

The TFX Scandal

The TFX scandal wasn't as dangerous to Johnson as the Baker and Estes scandals, but it added to the pressure LBJ was feeling by early 1963. All of these scandals taken together almost brought LBJ down. It had taken him a while to get everything to line up for the assassination, and the scandals had gotten out of hand in the meantime. He was barely able to have Kennedy murdered in time to save himself.

Johnson got the TFX/F-111 contract taken from Boeing and given to General Dynamics, located in Fort Worth, Texas. General Dynamics had an inferior design that was $400 million more expensive. The TFX became another scandal that threatened to erupt in 1963 and was another reason Johnson had to move up from vice president to president. Once Johnson was president the investigation was quashed.[231]

When John Connally resigned as Secretary of the Navy to run for governor of Texas, Johnson managed to get his guy Fred Korth installed as Connally's replacement.[232] There was a clear conflict of interest between Korth's duties and the awarding of the TFX contract because Korth had been the president of the bank that was backing General Dynamics in its bid for the TFX contract. Korth then ousted Boeing as the builder of the TFX fighter jet and gave the contract to General Dynamics.[233] On October 14, 1963 Fred Korth resigned as Secretary of the Navy.[234]

The TFX scandal caused another Senate investigation, this one under Senator McClellan. On November 19, 1963 the press reported that the Senate was looking into the Johnson's role in the awarding of the TFX contract to General Dynamics.[235] The TFX committee had closed its meeting on November 20, 1963 with a plan to resume hearings the next week and eventually get testimony from Fred Korth.

Two days later, on November 22, 1963 JFK was assassinated. As it happened, hearings were never resumed until 1969, after Johnson was no longer in office.[236] Don Reynolds told of seeing a suitcase full of money with $100,000 that Bobby Baker said was for Johnson to influence the TFX contract.[237] One by one all of the scandals and investigations were dropped once Johnson became president.[238]

The Murder of Doug Kinser

The shooting death of John Douglas "Doug" Kinser on October 22, 1951 is another example of Johnson having someone murdered because they were some kind of threat to him. It may even have been the first time Johnson ordered a hit on someone.

Johnson had a sister named Josefa. Josefa had a boyfriend named Doug Kinser. Johnson also had a hitman named Mac Wallace, who would go on to carry out many murders for Johnson. Wallace was jealous of Doug Kinser. This is where it gets complicated. Mac Wallace was sleeping with Josefa who was also sleeping with Doug Kinser who was also sleeping with Mac Wallace's wife Mary Andre. Kinser was an amateur actor who was not only sleeping with Mac Wallace's wife and girlfriend, but sometimes at the same time. Mac Wallace had several reasons to be unhappy with Doug Kinser.[239]

So, in 1951, when Kinser became a threat to Johnson, Wallace was sent in for the kill. Barr McClellan's book *BLOOD, MONEY AND POWER: HOW LBJ KILLED JFK* also sheds light on what happened to Doug Kinser. Josefa had an affair with Doug Kinser. Kinser had a small business, a miniature golf course. Kinser started asking for a Small Business Administration (SBA) government loan for his business.[240] This was interpreted by Johnson as a blackmail threat as Josefa had told Kinser about some of LBJ's shady dealings. This was another potential scandal for Johnson who couldn't afford any more scandals after the 1948 Box 13 election scandal and due to the upcoming election. Coke Stevenson was still looking to take Johnson's senate seat. Thus, Kinser was perceived as a danger to Johnson, so in 1951 Johnson and Ed Clark sent Mac Wallace to kill Kinser and promised him that after Wallace killed Kinser, Clark would make sure the judge would let him off.[241] Ed Clark was Johnson's "fixer" in Texas (see the section on LBJ's Crooked Partnership With Ed Clark). When Wallace killed Kinser he was let off by the judge even after he was caught and convicted for the killing.[242] Ed Clark had arranged for a lawyer, John Cofer, and a cooperative judge, and Wallace got a suspended sentence and walked free.[243] The punishment for the murder of John Douglas Kinser was unprecedented.[244] After the murder of Doug Kinser, Mac Wallace then went to work for D.H. Byrd. Byrd was one of the wealthy oil barons of the day, [245] and D.H. Byrd owned the Texas School Book Depository in Dealey Plaza.[246] The Texas School Book Depository is where Lee Harvey Oswald was working when Kennedy was assassinated. This is all covered in more detail later.

Other Murders Ordered by Johnson

In addition to Doug Kinser and Henry Marshall, Johnson also ordered the murders of Harold Orr, George Krutilek, Ike Rogers (and his secretary), Howard Pratt, Coleman Wade, Josefa Johnson and Johnson is very likely to have been involved in the murder of Dale Turner. And these are the ones we know of. Johnson was able to get away with these murders because he had control of the key judges and law enforcement authorities in Texas (see the section on Corruption in Dallas). Here I'm just trying to point out that Johnson was capable of ordering a hit on someone who got in his way. By 1963 Johnson has already ordered hits on at least half a dozen people, and Kennedy is standing between LBJ and the White House.

Here is a partial list of hits ordered by LBJ (note: Mac Wallace is reputed to have put the real total at seventeen, and as LBJ's hired gun he would know, but information on the others has yet to surface):

1. Doug Kinser – October 22, 1951 – Kinser was Josefa Johnson's boyfriend and appeared to be blackmailing LBJ – Kinser was murdered by Mac Wallace who was convicted but got a suspended sentence and walked away – Billie Sol Estes testified in 1984 that Johnson ordered the hit (see the section on the murder of Doug Kinser)

2. Henry Marshall – June 3, 1961 – Marshall was a USDA investigator who refused to be bribed – also murdered by Mac Wallace – the murder scene was arranged to try to look like carbon monoxide poisoning – Billie Sol Estes testified in 1984 that Johnson ordered the hit (see the section on the murder of Henry Marshall)

3. Dale Turner – 1961 – was a maid who suddenly "disappeared" because she had figured out that Johnson had an illegitimate son by Madeline Brown – she knew too much and therefore represented a danger to Lyndon Johnson

4. Josefa Johnson – December 25, 1961 – Josefa was Johnson's sister who had become an embarrassment and a danger to Johnson – she also knew too much, drank too much and talked too much when she drank – Billie Sol Estes testified in 1984 that Johnson ordered the hit

5. Ike Rogers and his secretary – these were two of the murders that Estes claimed in 1984 were committed by a group of four people (Estes, LBJ, Cliff Carter and Mac Wallace) – the other murders were Henry Marshall, George Krutilek, Harold Orr, Coleman Wade, Josefa Johnson, Doug Kinser and John F. Kennedy – Estes claimed that Johnson ordered the hits via Cliff Carter (a Johnson aide) and Mac Wallace carried out the actual murders – mostly to keep Estes and Johnson scams and scandals from coming to light and/or being connected to Johnson

6. Ike Rogers' secretary (see Ike Rogers murder, #5, above)

7. George Krutilek – April 4, 1962 – accountant for Estes who was starting to talk – found dead of carbon monoxide poisoning – Billie Sol Estes testified in 1984 that Johnson ordered the hit

8. Coleman Wade – 1963 – was a building contractor who built many of the storage facilities for Estes – Billie Sol Estes testified in 1984 that Johnson ordered the hit

9. President John F. Kennedy – November 22, 1963 – this was also one of the murders Estes claimed in 1984 that Lyndon Johnson had conspired to commit – Mac Wallace left his fingerprint on the sixth floor of the Texas School Book Depository[247]

10. Harold Orr – February, 1964 – Orr was involved with Estes and arrested with Estes and convicted for his role in the fraud – found dead of carbon monoxide poisoning – Billie Sol Estes testified in 1984 that Johnson ordered the hit

11. Howard Pratt – 1964 – Pratt was the Chicago office manager for Commercial Solvents, which was a vendor supplying fertilizer for Estes and of which Johnson was part owner – also found dead in his car of carbon monoxide poisoning

Dale Turner

Johnson had a mistress named Madeline Brown, who had a son by Johnson.[248] Dale Turner was a maid and nanny and mother figure to the boy.[249] One day she watched Lyndon and Madeline hug and had an epiphany.[250] She realized that Johnson was the father.[251] At that moment she became a liability because she knew too much and

Johnson wanted her gone.[252] Then she disappeared around the same time Josefa died.[253]

Josefa Johnson

Johnson's sister Josefa Johnson worked in Hattie Valdez's brothel.[254] She was into alcohol and drugs and was bisexual.[255] Josefa talked liberally about Johnson's illegal activities and the more drunk or high she got the more she talked about Johnson's activities.[256] This was in 1951 and sexual scandal was not acceptable in the early 1950's and Johnson was worried that Josefa might sink his career.[257] Doug Kinzer's murder served as a warning to Josefa to stop being an embarrassment and a threat to Lyndon Johnson's career.[258] For a while after the murder of Doug Kinzer, Josefa faded into the background and stopped embarrassing Johnson.[259] This gained her ten more years of life, because Josefa died in 1961.[260] She left a Christmas party with Johnson and Wallace and went home and died in the early morning hours.[261] There was no autopsy even though Josefa had died under suspicious circumstances.[262] Josefa's death may also have served as a warning to Billie Sol Estes, who would eventually include Josefa's name on a list of Johnson's murder victims.[263]

George Krutilek

Just as the Billie Sol Estes scandal was starting to break, George Krutilek was murdered right after he started to talk.[264] George Krutilek was the head accountant for Billie Sol Estes and was questioned by investigators on April 2, 1962.[265] Two days later George Krutilek was found dead with a hose attached to the exhaust pipe of his pickup.[266] An El Paso pathologist said that carbon monoxide poisoning was not the cause of death and called attention to a severe bruise on the side of George's head.[267] He was ignored and the coroner ruled the death a suicide.[268]

Coleman Wade

Coleman Wade was a building contractor who built many of the storage facilities for Estes. In 1963 Wade's plane crashed under suspicious circumstances. Later Estes would testify that Wade's death was done to protect Johnson.[269] Madeline Brown said that, but for these deaths, Johnson would have been forced out of office right then.[270] She was starting to realize what was going on with all these deaths.[271]

Harold Orr

Harold Orr was involved with Estes and arrested with Estes and convicted for his role in the fraud. He was sentenced to ten years in prison.[272] He died in 1964, also ruled an accident. The murder scene was staged to make it look like carbon monoxide (again), but the tools that were scattered around did not even fit the work he was supposedly doing.[273] He was planning to talk to get a lighter sentence.[274] This was also later listed by Estes as one of the murders done by Wallace to protect Johnson, who ordered the hit.[275]

Howard Pratt

Howard Pratt was the Chicago office manager for Commercial Solvents, which was a vendor supplying fertilizer for Estes. He was also found dead in his car of (what else?) carbon monoxide.[276]

John Kennedy

On the day Kennedy was assassinated, Johnson's hitman, Mac Wallace, left a fingerprint on the sixth floor of the Texas School Book Depository, where Oswald is alleged to have shot Kennedy from.[277] The Texas School Book Depository was owned by D.H. Byrd., who Wallace worked for. Only Lyndon Johnson had the means to bury the facts in all these cases. He controlled the Texas authorities. They were part of his corrupt political machine.

Suspicious Deaths

There are also some suspicious deaths not tied directly to Johnson, but which just happened to benefit Johnson at just the right time.

Johnson went to great lengths to make sure that no records could trace back to him from any of the illegal activity. So, for example, LBJ arranged for military aircraft to take Mac Wallace on trips instead of having him travel on commercial airlines.[278] Mac Wallace flew on military planes and the pilots did not know why they were flying this guy, they were just following orders.[279]

During the part of the 1948 election that became the Box 13 scandal, there were a bunch of names in the same handwriting, ink and in alphabetical order.[280] George Parr was the corrupt "Duke of Duval County" who was paid off to allow the voter fraud and Bill Mason was a radio announcer who tried to expose the corruption.[281] In 1952 Sam Smithwick was in prison for the murder of Bill Mason.[282] Sam Smithwick expected to be sprung from prison for murdering Bill Mason, but he suddenly ended up dead in prison of "suicide" because he was willing to talk.[283] He had written to Coke Stevenson, Johnson's opponent in the elections, looking for a shorter sentence.[284] Texas Governor Allan Shivers accused Johnson of having Smithwick murdered but nothing came of it.[285] Johnson's lawyer and partner Ed Clark, and not Johnson himself, may have been behind it, so this did not appear on "the list" above.[286] However Bill Mason, Sam Smithwick and Dale Turner should be added to the list of people Johnson may have had murdered.

As mentioned earlier, the purpose of this chapter is simply to point out that, by the time 1963 rolls around, Johnson had already ordered at least half a dozen murders, not counting the two pilots he killed when he ordered them into the air after they told him it was unsafe.

The 1960 Election

By 1960, Johnson was the second most powerful man in the United States. He was the Leader of the Senate at a time when President Eisenhower's health was failing and Eisenhower himself was slowing down. Johnson was also very close to Sam Rayburn, who was the Speaker of the House and an ally of Johnson's. By combining his control of the Senate with Rayburn's control of the House, Johnson had effective control of the Congress. Johnson was looking to move up to the White House.

Johnson had hoped to get the Democratic nomination for president at the 1960 convention. Prior to 1960, candidates were chosen at the convention. This is what Johnson wanted and what he planned on. However, the Kennedys made innovative use of the primaries to stack up enough delegates to win on the first ballot at the convention. This blew up LBJ's plan and Johnson had to scramble and pull strings just to get himself on the ticket as vice president because Kennedy had already chosen Senator Stuart Symington as his running mate. Johnson had not planned to have to be VP and certainly didn't plan on having to scramble to get there, but he managed to get on the ticket as VP and was then very close to being in the White House. He was one heartbeat away from his lifelong obsession.

The extremely narrow victory in 1960 over Nixon made Kennedy president and Johnson vice president. The Kennedys were skeptical of Johnson, at best. Bobby Kennedy hated Johnson and Johnson hated him right back. The Kennedys put LBJ on the ticket reluctantly under pressure from the party leaders and to 'balance the ticket.' The Kennedys knew the election was going to be very close and they needed Johnson to shore up their support in Texas and the south. Johnson was from Texas and knew how to talk to southerners so he was seen as being able to help get votes in the southern states where JFK was weak.

This chapter is organized into three sections:

1. Kennedy had to pull out all the stops to win. He was a dark horse candidate who came from behind to win. One example of this is how he used the Cuban angle against Nixon. This would come back to haunt him. Another example is how Joe Kennedy reached out to the mafia for help with the election. This would also come back to haunt the Kennedys.

2. Johnson was surprised by Kennedy's come-from-behind win and had to scramble to force Kennedy to put him on the ticket as the vice-presidential running mate.

3. Once the election was won Johnson tried for a power grab so that he wouldn't have to give up all the immense power and influence he had accumulated as the leader of the Senate. This bid failed and Johnson was left with vastly diminished power and influence. In this relatively weak state, Johnson would need Hoover's help to keep a lid on his scandals during his years as vice president.

Kennedy Pulls Out All the Stops

During the primary battle the Kennedy machine had decided to go all out and win enough primaries to win the nomination on the first ballot at the convention. This was a new innovation. In those days the candidate was picked at the convention. It was one of the main reason the parties held conventions in the first place. Traditionally, since the days before modern communications, they had to get together to pick a candidate. Now, the candidate is picked by the number of delegates they win during the primaries. The 1960 election was the turning point, and it was the Kennedy's innovative use of the primaries that caused the change. The Kennedy strategy worked and John F. Kennedy became the Democratic nominee for president that year, beating Lyndon Johnson.

Authors Roger Stone and Mike Colapietro, in their book *THE MAN WHO KILLED KENNEDY,* document how mafia boss Sam Giancana helped the Kennedys in the primaries, including Wisconsin and West Virginia and during the general election in Chicago.[287] This would also come back to haunt the Kennedys. Joe Kennedy understood the deals he made with the mafia for assistance during the 1960 campaigns and he understood the code that the mafia lived by. They expected things in return for their help.

In his book *LBJ: THE MASTERMIND OF THE JFK ASSASSINATION* author Phillip Nelson describes how Joe Kennedy spent over two million dollars in 1960 to secure victory in West Virginia.[288]

In the White House Richard Nixon was Eisenhower's vice president. During the waning days of the Eisenhower administration, Nixon was an especially active vice president. He took particular interest in Cuba because Castro had just taken power and was turning toward communism.[289] As an ardent Cold Warrior, Nixon took the lead in coordinating a plan to oust Castro.[290]

During the campaign, Kennedy decided to play a trick on Nixon.[291] Kennedy knew that Nixon was spearheading the White House effort to oust Castro, and he also knew that, as the plans were secret, Nixon could not talk about them.[292] Kennedy decided to push Nixon's button on the Cuba issue assuming that Nixon would automatically take the opposite side in one of the debates, and it worked.[293] Kennedy hinted, during his opening statement during the fourth debate, that the U.S. should take a more aggressive stance toward Cuba.[294] Nixon took the bait and went for the opposite position, and this boxed Nixon in.[295] Kennedy was the first to publicly advocate U.S. intervention in Cuba.[296] This would come back to haunt him, but it was an effective campaign tactic and just then Kennedy was trying to come from behind to win the White House.[297] Nixon was outraged at Kennedy for exploiting this issue while knowing that Nixon could not reply, even though he (Nixon) was the lead guy in the Eisenhower administration pushing for intervention in Cuba.[298] Even if he didn't realize it, part of Nixon's rage was likely due to his being angry because he had fallen for the bait and rather automatically taken the opposite side in the debate, just as Kennedy had thought he would.

Having won the White House by talking tough on Cuba, Kennedy would have a hard time backing out of the invasion that the CIA had planned. After the election, CIA Director Allen Dulles had Kennedy right where he wanted him, between a rock and a hard place.[299] Kennedy didn't want to invade Cuba because it would make the U.S. look like an aggressor nation, but he had campaigned on that issue. It was a close election and he had used that issue to gain an edge over Nixon. In the end Kennedy reluctantly agreed to the CIA plan for the Bay of Pigs invasion.

Even though he had to pull out all the stops to do it, Kennedy had made it to the White House.

Johnson Forces His Way Onto the Ticket

In 1960 Lyndon Johnson was the second most powerful man in the United States and he was looking to move up to the White House. He had been trying for this his entire adult life. He was obsessed with the idea of becoming president.

Author Phillip Nelson in his book *LBJ: THE MASTERMIND OF THE JFK ASSASSINATION* and Robert Caro, in his book series *THE YEARS OF LYNDON JOHNSON* describe how, in 1940, when LBJ was still a Congressional Representative from Texas, he turned down a valuable stake in an oil company worth $750,000 (in 1940 dollars) because, he said, it would kill him politically.[300] It wouldn't play well with the voters.[301] This was before he had real wealth and power. Given that Johnson was not shy about enriching himself, the only explanation for this was that he was, even back then, completely focused on the White House.

Both authors came to the same conclusion about this. If Johnson wanted to be a Texas Congressman, Senator or Governor, being in the oil business would not have come with a political cost. The only reason to turn down a gift of that magnitude was if you had your eye on the distant prize of the White House. Both authors use this as an example of how obsessed Johnson was with getting to the White House.

In 1958 Johnson got the Texas laws changed so he could run for vice president or president at the same time he ran for reelection for the Senate. In 1959 Robert Kennedy went to the LBJ ranch to see if Johnson was going to run. LBJ said "no" and then ran anyway.[302]

Johnson's plan to get to the White House was to take the conventional path. He saw himself as the most well-positioned candidate to get the nomination at the upcoming convention. His strength was in backroom dealing, and that was how it was done back in those days. He was planning on using his political influence to sew up the nomination at the convention. The Kennedys surprised Johnson. Their primary victories changed the game.

In his book *LBJ: THE MASTERMIND OF THE JFK ASSASSINATION,* author Phillip Nelson describes how Johnson had made a run for the White House in 1956 as a prelude for his more realistic attempt in 1960.[303] He also describes how Johnson was conflicted. He wanted the White House so badly that he was afraid of failure.[304] This caused his strategy to be somewhat dysfunctional. Johnson only declared his candidacy five days before the convention in 1960.[305]

So, there was Johnson in the days before the convention. He considered the presidency his destiny.[306] His lifelong dream of being president was being pulled out from under him by the Kennedys. He tried attacking Kennedy on JFK's not being healthy enough to be president.[307] Kennedy had Addison's disease, but this was not widely known. Johnson sent John Connally out to attack Kennedy on this.[308]

That didn't work, so his next move was to fight, as though his life depended on it, for the VP slot. He was out of position for the VP slot. He wasn't even on Kennedy's list of potential candidates for the job of vice president.[309]

According to author Phillip Nelson in his book *LBJ: THE MASTERMIND OF THE JFK ASSASSINATION*, Johnson enlisted the help of House Speaker Sam Rayburn, Senator Richard Russell, *Washington Post* publisher Phil Graham, lobbyist Tommy Corcoran and journalist Joseph Alsop in lobbying Kennedy for the job of vice president.[310] By this time Kennedy had decided on Senator Stuart Symington.[311] Johnson and Rayburn threatened to mount a fight on the floor of the convention unless Johnson was named vice president, and suddenly Johnson was the VP nominee.[312] Between the pressure and the blackmail and the fact that Johnson would help in the south, Kennedy caved in and switched to Johnson from Symington. John Kennedy saw no alternative even though Bobby Kennedy and others were against it.[313]

Johnson's Power Grab as Vice President

Kennedy won by such a razor-thin margin that Nixon could have asked for a recount. Nixon chose not to. Now that Johnson was vice president he was faced with the reality of giving up the immense power and influence he had as the Leader of the Senate. Johnson tried to have it both ways. He tried to both keep some of his power as Leader of the Senate and increase the power of the vice presidency.[314] Johnson wanted to remain as Chairman of the Senate Democratic caucus.[315] This was shot down when he tried it.[316] Johnson had an executive order drafted for Kennedy to sign. This included 'general supervision' of government activities, including NASA, the Defense Department, the CIA, the State Department and the Office of Civil and Defense Mobilization.[317] It also had reports, plans and proposals traditionally sent to the president go to the VP who would then approve and forward them on to the president.[318] Kennedy ignored it.[319] Johnson ended up with vastly diminished power and influence. He had risked the drop in power because he wanted the White House, and being vice president became his only potential path to get there. Otherwise he would have remained as Leader of the Senate.

Johnson took the job of vice president, a huge demotion, in order to get a step closer to his ultimate goal, the White House. While vice president, his power and influence went over a cliff. As Senate

Majority Leader he was the second most powerful man in the country. As vice president he lost almost all of his power and influence. Johnson did not want the job of vice president. He wanted the job of president. Part of this loss of power was to be expected and was a calculated gamble on Johnson's part. And part of this was Johnson convincing himself that he could hang on to some of his power while vice president, which turned out to be wishful thinking on his part.

LBJ's Choice in 1963: The Big House or the White House

Johnson's grandmother on his mother's side, Ruth Baines, said he would end up in prison (the Big House). Lyndon Johnson wanted to be in the White House. The situation in 1963 was that Johnson had to choose between the two. By 1963 Lyndon Baines Johnson had put himself in a position where he was either going to prison or the presidency. First the Estes scandals and then the Bobby Baker scandals were more coffin nails in Johnson's chances of being on the next ticket, the one in 1964. Once he was dumped from the ticket, he would be indicted and prosecuted. These scandals, on top of the Box 13 scandal, the TFX scandal, the self-serving KTBC deal and all the others, were eventually going to lead to Johnson and when they became public knowledge Johnson would lose everything, including his freedom. By Johnson's way of thinking, he had no choice. Kennedy had to go.

By 1963 mafia boss Carlos Marcello, FBI Director J. Edgar Hoover and Lyndon Johnson are all in the same boat, and it's sinking. Marcello will be deported, Hoover will be deposed and Johnson will be indicted. Their motivation is clear. In his book *OSWALD: ASSASSIN OR FALL GUY?,* author Joachim Joesten points out that there are men in the CIA and FBI who were capable of anything and one of the most powerful motives was operating: survival.[320]

President Kennedy was not Johnson's first murder. In the past his pattern had been to go ahead with whatever crime was necessary to get to the next step up in his career and gamble that he could use the power of the new office to avoid the consequences of whatever crime he had committed to get there. This had worked in the 1948 Senate race and it worked again in the case of the American coup d'état that put Johnson in the White House.

Along the way Johnson had corrupt dealings and to cover them up he and a few other men, including:

- Ed Clark – LBJ's attorney and lifetime partner in crime
- Billie Sol Estes – was involved with Johnson in various fraud schemes
- Mac Wallace – was an economist for the USDA and was Johnson's trigger man
- Cliff Carter – was Johnson's aide and one of his bag men – collecting cash

Had already conspired to murder a total of at least eight people:

- Henry Marshall – refused to be bribed to cover up Johnson's fraud with Estes
- George Krutilek – worked for Billie Sol Estes as an accountant
- Ike Rogers and his secretary
- Harold Orr – was involved with Estes
- Coleman Wade – a building contractor in Oklahoma associated with Estes
- Josefa Johnson – Johnson's sister who was a hooker and a potential embarrassment
- Doug Kinser – was having an affair with Josefa who was also having an affair with Mac Wallace

After the 1960 election Johnson tried to make the job of vice president into a much bigger role than it had ever been.[321] This fell flat with both the Senate and the White House, and they both rejected his attempted power grabs.[322] The net result of his demotion from Senate majority leader to vice president was that LBJ no longer had the power to quash the investigations into his scandals. This relative weakness, combined with his growing scandals, put Johnson in a very vulnerable position by 1963. Once the election was over Johnson's past came knocking and he was going to be indicted. With his diminished power he was unable to keep a lid on his past. This made his choices stark. He was going to prison unless he found a way to secure the presidency. If he became president he could use the power of the Oval Office to quash the investigations. He decided to gamble on killing Kennedy.

Author Phillip Nelson, in his book *LBJ: THE MASTERMIND OF THE JFK ASSASSINATION*, relates an incident between Robert Kennedy and Johnson. It happened at the LBJ ranch when Bobby was visiting to see if Johnson was going to run in the 1960 election.[323] Johnson reassured Bobby that he was not going to run, then he invited Bobby to go deer hunting with him and purposefully gave Bobby an overpowered shotgun that Bobby was unfamiliar with.[324] Bobby was knocked over by the recoil and Johnson then made fun of him.[325] This was how their relationship started. It went downhill from there.

Then, of course, Johnson did try for the White House in 1960, even after he had reassured Robert Kennedy he would not. When Bobby found out that his brother had put Johnson on the ticket he was horrified and tried everything to stop it, but to no avail. For his part, Johnson thought that Robert Kennedy had taken over his rightful place as the number two man.[326] This was at least partially true. President

John F. Kennedy increasingly looked to his brother for advice and gave Bobby increasing responsibility during his administration. Kennedy assigned Johnson to look after the Equal Employment Opportunity Commission (EEOC) and LBJ failed miserably.[327] The Kennedys thought LBJ was simply incompetent, but Johnson was actually stalling on Civil Rights because he wanted it to be part of *his* legacy as president.[328]

At first John Kennedy tried to stay on good terms with Johnson, but Johnson was uncooperative. Johnson was sent to Vietnam in 1961 by Kennedy and spent his time there undermining Kennedy's policies.[329] It took a while, but eventually John Kennedy came around to Bobby's view of Johnson. LBJ eventually lost almost all his influence with Kennedy, who thought Johnson was incapable of telling the truth. In the meantime, Johnson's scandals were undermining the credibility of the Kennedy administration.

In his book *ACT OF TREASON: THE ROLE OF J. EDGAR HOOVER IN THE ASSASSINATION OF PRESIDENT KENNEDY*, author Mark North points out that on March 26, 1963 there are press reports that:[330]

> " . . . Johnson refused to say tonight whether he would seek renomination with Kennedy next year. Reminded that Kennedy had publicly stated his support for Johnson saying that he would be happy to have Johnson with him, the Vice President replied that the decision 'will depend upon the delegates who have not yet been selected.'" Clearly LBJ sees the writing on the wall. Word has been circulating for months that he will be dumped, the Estes and Baker scandals threatening to consume him. It is common knowledge in Washington that he and the Kennedys have nothing but contempt for each other. Hoover, as well as Marcello, is mindful of this reality."[331]

First the Billie Sol Estes scandal was in the news. Estes made the cover of *Time* magazine on May 25, 1962 with an article about his fraud and corruption.[332] In March of 1962 Estes and three associates were charged with fraud, and his chief accountant, George Krutilek, was interviewed by investigators and then killed a few days later.[333] In May of 1962 Johnson flew to Austin to attend Mayor Tom Miller's funeral and made a side trip to Midland, Texas to meet with Estes and his lawyer.[334] The meeting took place in his plane on the tarmac, and Johnson never left the plane.[335] Later Estes claimed that LBJ promised him that if he kept his mouth shut he would not go to jail.[336] Estes also had to worry about getting killed. John Cofer, the same lawyer who got Mac Wallace off for the murder of Doug Kinzer, was assigned to Estes.[337]

Then the Bobby Baker scandal was on the front pages. Even though Johnson was not involved with Baker's business dealings after 1960, the Senate investigation looked into their questionable financial activities in the 1950's. This was another nail in the coffin of Johnson's future chances of staying on the ticket for the 1964 election. In October of 1963 Baker resigned as secretary of the Senate.[338] The Baker scandal continued through the death of John F. Kennedy. Even as president, LBJ was barely able to contain it.

On June 18, 1963 Robert Kennedy attended an EEOC meeting and began openly arguing with LBJ who slumped in his chair with his eyes half closed.[339] Bobby Kennedy and Lyndon Johnson were by then open enemies and President Kennedy's opinion of Johnson was dropping as well.[340] On June 28, 1963 there was open speculation as to the value of Johnson to the Kennedy ticket.[341] By the fall of 1963 Johnson was running on empty.[342] He had to do *something* or he was going to prison.

Author Phillip Nelson, in his book *LBJ: THE MASTERMIND OF THE JFK ASSASSINATION,* points out that Johnson lost all his influence and did nothing to help the Kennedys.[343] Johnson hated the VP job and only took it to get to be President. Nelson claims that Johnson was desperate to keep the VP job, yet he feared losing it. The only reason to keep going was to get to the Oval Office. Eventually Kennedy stopped inviting LBJ to meetings on important issues like Vietnam.[344] Johnson stalled on issues like civil rights so he could have it for his own legacy.[345] LBJ did nothing to help pass Kennedy's legislation.[346] The Kennedy's were going to dump Johnson and the only thing left to do was justify the decision.[347]

To justify dumping Johnson, the plan was for Bobby Kennedy to feed stories to the press on Johnson. Then, once he was demolished by the press, he could be easily dumped from the ticket. Bobby Kennedy had a two-pronged approach. He could have the Justice Department investigate Johnson at the same time he was feeding information to the press and showing them where to dig.

In his book *WHO REALLY KILLED KENNEDY*, author Jerome Corsi documents how *Life* magazine also wanted to look into how Johnson became rich on a civil servant's salary, just like Bobby Baker. Baker provided girls to lawmakers in return for control of their votes and support.[348] On November 8, 1963 *Life* magazine published a story about the Quorum Club and Bobby Baker.[349] On the cover was a picture of Bobby Baker in a mask at a party. The article talked about how Baker got rich while living on a civil servant's salary.[350] There was also a picture of Johnson with his arm around Baker and scantily clad waitresses at the Carousel Motel in Ocean City, Maryland.[351] The next *Life* magazine article was going to focus on Johnson's connection to Baker.[352] The editor, George Hunt, agreed to let the writer, William Lambert, use the nine-person investigative team to look into Johnson's financial picture.[353] The Bobby Baker scandal was going to become the Johnson scandal. The article was going to be published.[354] Johnson was not invited to a meeting of Kennedy's political advisors to discuss the 1964 election on Wednesday, November 13, 1963 (according to Robert Caro in *THE YEARS OF LYNDON JOHNSON – THE PASSAGE OF POWER*) and part of the discussion was whether or not Johnson would be on the ticket and how effective he would be in adding votes to the ticket in the upcoming election.[355] Kennedy told his secretary that he was going to dump Johnson. She wrote down his comments word for word and later repeated them to Johnson biographer Robert Caro.[356] Kennedy was going to start to withdraw from Vietnam (partly due to South Vietnamese President Ngo Dinh Diem being killed) and he was going to dump LBJ.[357] Johnson was a corrupt politician who had enriched himself at public expense.[358]

The next issue of *Life* magazine was going to bury Johnson.[359] It never came out. Once Kennedy was murdered and Johnson was president, the whole thing, all the research, everything, was shredded.[360] The article was replaced by the images from the Zapruder film of Kennedy being killed in Dealey Plaza.[361]

Articles in the news were not Johnson's only problem in late November of 1963. Don Reynolds was an insurance salesman who had come forward with information that Johnson had been getting kickbacks from a life insurance policy that Reynolds had sold to Johnson via Bobby Baker.[362] Reynolds also knew about other Baker misdeeds, including skimming like he did with Ralph Hill and Matthew McCloskey.[363] McCloskey was a major federal construction contractor.[364] Reynolds would testify that McCloskey had bribed to get the contract for a new federal building and then increased the cost from six million to twenty million, with some of the cost overrun kicked back to Johnson and Baker.[365] Reynolds had decided to testify in spite of the pressure to clam up. Now Johnson had no choice but to go ahead with the hit on Kennedy. Reynolds started to talk on November 22, 1963 about Johnson demanding kickbacks on two life insurance policies he had sold LBJ in 1957 and 1961.[366] This included buying an expensive stereo for Johnson and buying a bunch of advertising at LBJ's TV station.[367] Reynolds had documentation.[368] He also testified about the TFX hundred thousand dollars in a suitcase.[369] Reynolds was testifying while JFK was being killed.[370] When his testimony came to an end a secretary burst in and said JFK had been killed.[371] That ended his testimony.[372]   The hit on JFK happened on the last day possible to salvage LBJ's career.[373]

On October 11, 1963 President Kennedy issued National Security Action Memorandum (NSAM) # 263 which specified the withdrawal of American personnel from Vietnam, one thousand by the end of 1963 and the rest by the end of 1965.[374] *Vice* President Johnson then drafted a *presidential* order countermanding Kennedy's *presidential* order. This became NSAM # 273.   The date the draft was written was November 21, 1963, the day *before* the Kennedy assassination.[375]   This is a key point.   Only a vice president who knows he is going to be president the next day drafts a memo countermanding President Kennedy's order to withdraw from Vietnam the day before his president is murdered and he moves up to the White House.

E. Howard Hunt eventually confessed to being involved in the assassination.   He did not think Johnson was the mastermind but he believed that LBJ was in on it with CIA officers David Atlee Phillips and Cord Meyer.[376] (See the section on Rogue CIA Elements).

The conspirators appear to have gotten together the night before the assassination at Clint Murchison's estate for a final meeting to verify that they were going ahead.   This would have been their last chance to call it off, and they needed to make sure everything was in place and everyone was still prepared to go ahead.   Mae Newman confirmed the pre-assassination party the night before Kennedy was assassinated in Dallas.[377]   Mae was a maid and she said Mac Wallace was there too,[378] as was Hoover whose code name was "Bulldog."[379]   Hoover flew down for the party and then flew right back to Washington.   Johnson came in around 11:00 PM.[380]   This would have been after Richard Nixon had left.[381]

On November 22, 1963 JFK was assassinated in Dealey Plaza in Dallas.

In his book *LBJ: THE MASTERMIND OF THE JFK ASSASSINATION*, author Phillip Nelson describes how Johnson was able to use his power as President of the United States to quash the multiple investigations into his background.   One by one all of the scandals and investigations were dropped once Johnson became president.[382]

Insurance salesman Don Reynolds testified of witnessing a suitcase full of money with $100,000 that Bobby Baker said was for Johnson to influence the TFX contract.[383]   Reynolds continued to testify, even about the TFX contract, saying he was the bag man.[384]   Then Johnson launched an all-out attack on Reynolds, using the power of the government to dig up dirt and using his press contacts to print that dirt.[385]

This was illegal and created a sympathetic backlash which helped the people pursuing Johnson's scandals.[386] There were speeches in the House of Representatives charging the Johnson administration with destroying evidence and engaging in witness intimidation.[387]

At one point, Reynolds said:[388]

> "My God! There's a difference between testifying against a President of the United States and a Vice President. If I had known he was President, I might not have gone through with it."[389]

Author Phillip Nelson, in his book *LBJ: THE MASTERMIND OF THE JFK ASSASSINATION*, documents that:[390]

> "In a Senate speech on February 3, Senator Hugh Scott (R-PA) said he had received "veiled threats" for pushing the Bobby Baker probe. The Pennsylvanian declared that he would push for a full investigation and calling of "all witnesses, no matter how many veiled threats may be conveyed members of the Rules Committee." He spoke on the Senate floor of the "shocking" leak of confidential information about Reynolds. Since some of the information came from the Air Force files, he wrote to Secretary McNamara, "I am doubly concerned that leaks of internal memoranda can apparently be used to destroy witnesses whose testimony becomes embarrassing. The situation is particularly serious when it's realized that this information was denied to proper officials of the United States Senate . . . In a House speech, Representative Gross charged that the Johnson administration had engaged in an 'outrageous' attempt to 'intimidate' Reynolds and other witnesses who might give testimony that embarrassed the White House . . . The Army-Navy-Air Force Journal declared that the leaking of the Reynolds file seriously 'undermined' the confidential status of military files . . . A Washington Evening Star editorial spoke of the 'smear' and disclosed that persons connected with the White House had tried to peddle derogaroty information and allegations about Reynolds to the Star."[391]

Author Mark North, in his book *ACT OF TREASON: THE ROLE OF J. EDGAR HOOVER IN THE ASSASSINATION OF PRESIDENT KENNEDY*, describes how in January of 1964:[392]

"The publisher of another major publication received a phone call from a White House aide, who deprecated Reynolds. The caller read excerpts from what purported to be an FBI dossier. "Senator Hugh Scott demanded an investigation of the 'leak' of the 'raw FBI files,' (which) could only have occurred at the instance of some person . . . higher than the FBI in government.' . . . Hoover denied a leak to any unauthorized source. . . . Newsmen pinpointed it directly on the White House – . . . [Johnson] himself. This . . . use of power provoked Ted Lewis, of the *New York Daily News,* to put the question . . . 'Does the White House have the authority . . . to order . . . Hoover to turn over its secret files any time the administration wants to crack down on an embarrassing witness?'"[393]

On top of everything else that was happening at this time, the wife of the government accountant assigned to investigate Bobby Baker's files mysteriously turned up dead, found by her children in her bathroom.[394] There was no criminal investigation.[395] Don Reynolds left the country, afraid for his life.[396]

Senator John Williams of Delaware was investigating Bobby Baker and President Johnson pressured him to close down his investigation.[397] The senator's mail was being opened and read, and he was warned about this.[398] Johnson did everything possible to put pressure on Senator Williams.[399] LBJ continued to apply pressure to end the investigations using a combination of threats, blackmail, persuasion and promises to get the investigations stopped.[400] The Bobby Baker investigation eventually closed. At the same time Johnson did his best to bribe Bobby Baker into silence by offering him a million dollars to shut up, even ranting in Speaker John McCormack's office in front of a witness.[401] Then, when Attorney General Robert Kennedy was out of the office, Johnson grabbed RFK's Bobby Baker file from the Department of Justice and that killed the investigation.[402] The Democrats managed to close the investigations before the 1964 elections.[403]

President Johnson Avoids the Press

Author Mark North, in his book *ACT OF TREASON: THE ROLE OF J. EDGAR HOOVER IN THE ASSASSINATION OF PRESIDENT KENNEDY,* describes how Johnson avoids the press. Below are some examples of this:

"On November 28 he presents his first speech as president. He invokes God, simultaneously calling upon the American people to support him. The burgeoning Baker scandal is ever present on his mind and he does not miss the opportunity to distract the electorate. On December 1 he makes a formal visit to JFK's grave, in part for purposes of gaining further sympathy from the public. By December 5, however, the press begins to complain that he is avoiding them. This is nothing more than a continuation of vice-presidential policy. Johnson had always avoided noncontrolled press situations, in part for fear reporters would ask questions that might expose his dealings with men like Estes and Baker."[404]

On December 19, 1963 there were reports in the press claiming that:[405]

"Although . . . Johnson has not yet offered the networks an opportunity to televise his press conferences, he is not ignoring them completely. High officials of the three national networks are invited to lunch with the president at the White House on three successive days this week. . . . The networks . . . . do not yet know what policy Mr. Johnson will adopt. At another of his informal surprise meetings with the press on Wednesday he said that he wanted to maintain a flexibility – maybe 'a meeting of this kind today, maybe a televised meeting tomorrow with maybe a coffee session the next day.' Note that Johnson has not changed significantly in his attitude toward the press, still fearful, perhaps the more so, because of the Baker hearings."[406]

On January 6, 1964:[407]

"Johnson writes a letter to Edward F. Ryan, President of the Radio Television News Directors Association: "You may be sure that we will make full use of television in the months ahead, and television will be permitted to cover some of our press conferences. We would be most interested in any suggestions you have in making more effective use of television and radio.""[408]

On January 14, 1964 press:[409]

"A New York House member asked today why Johnson had held no televised news conferences. . . . Representative . . . Horton said he was concerned by what he called a 'news lockout at the White House.' This cannot be corrected, he said, by an occasional coffee klatch, barbeque or guided tour."[410]

On January 18, 1964 press:[411]

> ". . . Johnson . . . has invited newsmen to suggest ways for more effective use of the medium . . . Johnson has held no formal news conference in Washington since taking office last Nov. 22, but he has met informally with newsmen a number of times both here and at his Texas ranch – these sessions have not been broadcast."[412]

Crooked politicians make up a key component of the Deep State. From his many and varied scams, Johnson made himself very wealthy. He made tens of millions of dollars peddling influence. This kind of thing is still going on today. A few generations after Johnson, the Clintons made themselves very wealthy. They made hundreds of millions of dollars selling access and influence during the period while Hillary Clinton was Secretary of State and a political candidate with a good chance of becoming president. And the two-tier justice system is still in place in the United States. In fact, it has become even more obvious. Hillary Clinton has broken many laws and is not prosecuted while her political opponents are pursued relentlessly until they end up behind bars whether they have committed crimes or not. This is discussed in more detail in the last chapter – Why This Matters Today.

Kennedy's List of Enemies

In 1963 Kennedy wanted to make peace and the Deep State saw JFK as naïve and dangerous, a national security risk.[413]

Author Patrick Nolan, in his book *CIA ROGUES AND THE KILLING OF THE KENNEDYS*, said:[414]

> "These extremists had become convinced that America's future would not be secure until President Kennedy was removed from office."[415]

In August of 1963 the latest polls show President Kennedy running well ahead of any potential Republican presidential candidates.[416] He is therefore very likely to be reelected the next year.[417] The Deep State wanted Kennedy out, and they were going to have to take him out themselves because the voters liked him and wanted to keep him for a second term.

In addition to being the only obstacle between Johnson and the White House, Kennedy had made many enemies by the early sixties. These included, but weren't limited to, the CIA, the mafia, Hoover at the FBI, the Joint Chiefs of Staff at the Pentagon, the wealthy oil barons of the time and the anti-Castro Cuban exiles. This is an impressive and dangerous list of enemies, especially when you consider the fact that Johnson was willing and able to get them to act as a group. In the sections below, I go into each in turn and detail how and why the mafia, the CIA, the anti-Castro Cubans, Hoover, the Joint Chiefs and the oil barons had become JFK's enemies.

This chapter is organized into six sections:

1. The mafia, especially mob boss Sam Giancana in Chicago, helped the Kennedys get elected and after the election the Kennedys turned and attacked the mafia, especially mafia boss Carlos Marcello in New Orleans. The mob guys had been expecting the Kennedys to at least ease up on prosecutions. The last thing they expected was Bobby Kennedy's all-out attack on them. Giancana and Marcello were dangerous men to have as enemies.

2. The CIA under Allen Dulles was getting out of control before Kennedy took office and it got worse, culminating in the Bay of Pigs disaster where Dulles at the CIA tried to trap Kennedy into a position where he would have to agree to have the U.S.

military openly intervene in the invasion of Cuba. Kennedy was blatantly lied to by Dulles and others about the chances of success. This was done in order to get a reluctant Kennedy to give his approval for the operation. When Kennedy realized he had been purposely misled he fired Dulles and a few of his top guys. He also decided it was time to bring the CIA under control. He took their military function away, reduced their budget and put their foreign offices under the official control of the State Department. This infuriated Dulles and his Cold War crowd at the CIA, the vast majority of whom were still loyal to Dulles. They didn't want to be brought to heel. They wanted a stronger CIA while Kennedy was cutting their budget and reducing their responsibilities. They also wanted to escalate the Vietnam War and Kennedy wanted to pull out of Vietnam. They believed in the Cold War domino theory that the communists had to be fought everywhere. Kennedy wanted the opposite approach and solution to the same problems. He wanted to make peace with the Russians and Cubans. The CIA thought Kennedy had to go.

The guys at the CIA (and the Pentagon) who took Kennedy out didn't see themselves as bad men committing treason. They saw themselves as super-patriots doing the hard and dangerous things and making the tough decisions that their fellow citizens didn't really want to deal with or even know about. Our enemies were communists and were perfectly willing to use all manner of unethical and evil methods to gain an advantage on us. We needed to pull our heads out and fight back, even if that meant that meant doing some distasteful things. CIA officers Allen Dulles and James Jesus Angleton liked the movie *High Noon* where the sheriff fights crime alone because the civilian town people don't want to get their hands dirty.[418] That's how they saw themselves.

3. The anti-Castro Cuban exiles started out supporting Kennedy because he initially supported them in their attempts to retake their homeland from Castro. The Bay of Pigs disaster ruined their relationship with Kennedy. They were told by the CIA that Kennedy had canceled the necessary air strikes, and that that was why the Bay of Pigs invasion had failed. Then, to resolve the Cuban Missile Crisis, Kennedy promised not to invade Cuba and to call off the raids which had been taking place since the Bay of Pigs. He had to call out the Coast Guard to stop the Cuban raids still being sponsored by the

CIA. This infuriated the anti-Castro Cuban exiles. They saw getting rid of Kennedy as the only chance of taking back their homeland.

4.   J. Edgar Hoover had been the head of the FBI since before it was the FBI. He had created it as his own dictatorship. He had survived every change of administration since Warren G. Harding and had no intention of just stepping down to retirement. Only the president could give Hoover a retirement waiver and Kennedy had decided to force Hoover to retire. Hoover had no intention of letting this happen. Making an enemy of Hoover was dangerous. He was a very powerful and unscrupulous man and he had complete dictatorial control of the nation's crime investigation bureau. The Kennedys underestimated just how dangerous Hoover was to them.[419] They thought they could control Hoover and deal with him at the appropriate time.[420]

5.   By 1963, the Joint Chiefs of Staff at the Pentagon disagreed with Kennedy on almost every major issue the country faced. They saw the United States as much stronger than Russia and wanted each crisis to be used as an excuse to flex American military muscle. They wanted to have a nuclear showdown with the Russians while the U.S. had the advantage. As each crisis (the Bay of Pigs, the Berlin Crisis and the Cuban Missile Crisis) came up the Joint Chiefs became increasingly frustrated that Kennedy would not allow them to attack. Kennedy increasingly wanted to work with Khrushchev toward peace and the Joint Chiefs came to see this as treasonous collusion with our mortal enemy. They also wanted to ramp up the Vietnam War and believed, as did the CIA, in the Cold War domino theory. Kennedy himself became concerned that the military would try to take him out.

6.   The wealthy oil barons of the time hated Kennedy not only for his liberal politics but mainly because he wanted to get rid of their cherished oil depletion allowance. This would cost them each millions of dollars annually. They were powerful enemies who were used to buying influence in Washington. They were also dangerous enemies.

Now add Lyndon Johnson to the mix. By late 1963 Johnson was desperate. He was going to the Big House or the White House. And Johnson had decades-long, deeply mutually dependent and trusting relationships with the oil barons, Hoover and the mafia. Johnson wanted to ramp up the Vietnam War just like the Cold Warriors at the CIA and the Pentagon did. And he was as skilled and experienced as anyone at getting a crowd of powerful, egotistical men to work as a group to accomplish what he wanted. He was able to reassure them that, as long as Kennedy did not get out of Dealey Plaza alive, he (and Hoover) would be able to protect them with all the power and influence of the government.

And Kennedy's enemies had strong relationships with each other. The Cold Warriors at the Pentagon and the CIA were already working together in trying to force Kennedy to go along with their plans. The military brass and the oil barons knew each other. CIA Director Alen Dulles had worked for some of the Texas oil barons as a lawyer for his brother's law firm, Sullivan & Cromwell. The Cubans were sponsored by the CIA. The mafia and the CIA were already working together to try to kill Castro. James Angleton at the CIA had a direct line to Hoover. And Hoover was regularly invited to vacation for free at a race track and resort owned by the oil barons who also invited members of the mafia.

Oil baron D.H. Byrd owned the Texas School Book Depository in Dealey Plaza. Air Force General Curtis LeMay and D.H. Byrd were close.[421] LeMay gave Byrd a medal in 1963 for his role in founding the Civil Air Patrol, which at one point included a teenage Lee Harvey Oswald, and Johnson's hitman Mac Wallace worked for D.H. Byrd.

General Charles Cabell at the CIA was the one who asked President Kennedy for permission to send the aircraft to help the Bay of Pigs invasion and was not only turned down but later fired by Kennedy. His brother John Cabell was the Mayor of Dallas in November of 1963.[422] Dallas Police Chief Jesse Curry served at the pleasure of Mayor Earle Cabell.[423] The Cabell brothers hated Kennedy.

Author Phillip Nelson, in his book *LBJ: THE MASTERMIND OF THE JFK ASSASSINATION*, said that Johnson knew the major players and had long and trusting relationships with them and they all also knew each other the same way.[424] He also pointed out that Johnson had to be involved (he appointed the Warren Commission) and had the means, the motive and the opportunity to murder JFK. Oil baron H.L. Hunt and J. Edgar Hoover knew each other since the 1950's as poker playing buddies.[425] Nelson also claims that CIA officer Bill Harvey would be one of the guys who held the whole thing together, and that Johnson got his crooked lawyer Ed Clark to collect money for the operation from a bunch of people but the main contributors were oil barons H.L. Hunt and Clint Murchison.[426] Money was needed for things like paying the hitmen, moving men and equipment into place, paying off politicians and miscellaneous expenses. Nelson claims that they were able to talk in vague code because they had worked together and trusted each other for a long time.[427] Nelson also pointed out that not everyone knew the real agenda because information was compartmentalized.[428] The few at the top knew what was going on but the rest were told only what they needed to know to pull it off.[429]

As mentioned before, FBI Director Hoover, Vice President Johnson and mafia boss Marcello were all doomed if Kennedy stayed in office,[430] but there were lots of groups who would benefit if JFK were killed. According to author Jerome Corsi in his book *WHO REALLY KILLED KENNEDY*, the lucrative heroin trade would continue and the Kennedys would no longer be able to continue their prosecution of the mafia.[431] Johnson and the Pentagon lacked the covert operational capability, but the mafia and the CIA had that and the FBI could help with the cover up. And the oil men could fund the operation.[432] The prototype assassination plot was developed in Guatemala by the CIA. The Cuban exiles, who hated Kennedy, could be used as shooters. The military-industrial complex also benefitted from Kennedy's death because Johnson wanted to ramp up the Vietnam war. The CIA would also have a friend in the White House instead of Kennedy, who was threatening to shatter the CIA and scatter the pieces. Appointing Allen Dulles, who Kennedy fired from the CIA, to the Warren Commission completed the circle for the cover-up. Author Jerome Corsi also claimed Allen Dulles participated in the JFK assassination conspiracy not just for revenge but for ideology.[433]

Former U.S. Senator Richard Schweiker, whose Intelligence Committee investigation did the groundwork for what grew into the House Select Committee on Assassinations, pointed out:[434]

> "It means that for the first time in the whole Kennedy assassination investigation, we have evidence which places at 544 Camp Street intelligence agents, Lee Oswald, the Mob and anti-Castro Cuban exiles. It puts all these elements together."[435]

I would add to this list with what we now know about the address at 544 Camp Street in New Orleans. Ex-FBI agent Guy Banister was there and he was working for the CIA and the FBI. Oswald was controlled by the CIA, as was CIA contractor Clay Shaw. Pilot David Ferrie was working for the CIA, Banister and the mafia. So, in addition to the anti-Castro Cuban exiles we have the rest of the conspirators represented at the 544 Camp Street address they were operating out of in the summer of 1963.

Author Phillip Nelson pointed out that CIA officer Bill Harvey knew everyone, and he hated the Kennedys.[436] David Ferrie was in Dallas to fly people to Mexico if necessary.[437] Johnson assured the oil men they would get their oil depletion allowance.[438] The military and industrial folks got the Vietnam War they wanted. The hit men got paid money. And Johnson got the Oval Office and was able to shut down the investigations that had gotten too close to him.[439]

Evelyn Lincoln was Kennedy's personal secretary. In 1994 she stated in a letter that Johnson, Hoover, the mafia, the CIA and the Cubans in Florida were responsible.[440] She got it right.

The Mafia

The Kennedys got help from the mafia to get to the White House, then they turned on the mafia and attacked them with all the resources of the government. This turned the Kennedys and the mafia into enemies. The entire mafia didn't kill President Kennedy. A few of the mafia bosses like San Giancana in Chicago, Santo Trafficante in Florida and Carlos Marcello in New Orleans were involved and they got some of their underlings like Johnny Roselli and Jack Ruby involved. Giancana was the boss in Chicago and he had helped get Kennedy elected.[441] Trafficante was the boss in Florida and he was deeply involved with the CIA and the anti-Castro Cuban exiles. Trafficante was heavily invested in Cuban casino operations before Castro came to power and he was hoping to get back there once Castro was gone. Kennedy at first tried to get rid of Castro but eventually reversed course on Cuba and was blocking Trafficante from his dream of a return to Cuba. Marcello was being personally targeted by the Kennedys to the point where it became a fight to the death for him.

Making an enemy of the mafia is dangerous, particularly because the CIA had a history of using them to carry out assassinations. There are multiple accounts, for example, of the CIA contracting out to the mafia the assassination of Fidel Castro. Santo Trafficante was one of the mafia bosses who the CIA contacted for the hit on Castro. Since their Havana casinos and hotels had been appropriated by Castro when he took power and kicked the mob out of Cuba, the mafia was happy to take the assignment.

In his book *WHO REALLY KILLED KENNEDY?*, author Jerome Corsi goes into detail on the links between the mafia and the Kennedy clan. In the early 1950's the Eastern mafia was mostly Catholic and Jewish and the Western mob was mostly Protestant.[442] The mob takeover of the Teamster Union was also a move by the Eastern mob to take over the Western mob and not just the unions.[443] The Elkins crime family was part of the Western mob. They had started gambling operations in Reno and were moving to Las Vegas and the Eastern mafia wanted to take that over too, especially once Castro tossed the mob out of Havana in 1959.[444]

JFK's father Joe Kennedy had a long history with the mafia. He had controlled the import of scotch liquor into the U.S.[445] He had never really been accepted into the Eastern mafia because he was Irish, not Italian.[446] Old Joe encouraged his sons to use the McClellan Committee hearings to gain national attention.[447] The Kennedys established a partnership with the Elkins crime family and used their tapes and the McClellan Committee as a political springboard to national office.[448]

James Butler Elkins was a mafia boss in the Northwest.[449] His area of operations was mainly Portland and Seattle.[450] Once the mafia got control of the unions the Elkins family resisted being taken over by the Eastern mafia.[451] In 1956 Senator John F. Kennedy lost his bid to be the vice president on that year's Democratic ticket.[452] After this loss the Kennedys understood the importance of television in getting national expose and thus a shot at a national office like the White House.[453] The Kennedys decided to use the McClellan hearings to gain national exposure, and to use the tapes the Elkins family had made to make the case that the target of the McClellan committee hearings was the mafia and not the unions.[454] This was because the Democratic party wanted the unions as supporters and didn't want to offend them.[455]

Robert Kennedy had always seen the mafia as the enemy.[456] As a young attorney for the Subcommittee on Investigations in 1956, he found evidence that the mafia had gotten into the unions.[457] There were accounts of the mafia using violence to organize unions, including torture and murder.[458]

The bad blood between the Kennedys and the mafia traces back to the 1957 McClellan Committee, run by Senator John McClellan from Arkansas, who was looking into mafia ties to union labor and Jimmy Hoffa of the Teamsters. Then Senator John F. Kennedy was on the committee.[459] J.B. Elkins began his testimony in 1957. This helped JFK make the cover of *Life* magazine. Robert Kennedy wrote a book on the McClellan Committee in 1960. RFK said that J.B. was an interesting and controversial witness.[460] Robert Kennedy said that, once Elkins decided to cooperate, he went all the way. J.B. warned the Kennedys that going after the mob might cost them their lives.[461] Then Elkins turned his tapes over to the Kennedys.[462] And Jim Elkins was a good witness because he didn't lie or exaggerate. Robert Kennedy and the Elkins family became close. Elkins once stayed in the Robert Kennedy home in McLean, Virginia.[463] In 1957 Elkins sent RFK a Christmas card.[464] RFK was able to crack the Teamster case wide open.[465] The Elkins and the Kennedys stayed in touch as long as JFK and RFK were alive.[466]

Having gained the national exposure they needed, JFK's father, Joseph Kennedy, had made a deal with Sam Giancana, the head of the Chicago mob, to help get out the vote and to have the unions contribute to the 1960 Kennedy campaign.[467] Giancana and the mafia held up their end of the bargain. In 1960 the Eastern mob helped the Kennedys get to the White House and were outraged when the Kennedys turned on them.[468]

Kennedy won the 1960 election by a razor thin margin. The mafia help had made the difference and they thought they should, at the very least, be able to expect the Justice Department to let up on them. The way they saw it 'their guy' was now in the White House and since the Attorney General at the Justice Department reported to the president, and the FBI reported to the Attorney General, they should expect some relief from the pressure being applied by the Justice Department and the FBI under the Eisenhower administration. The exact opposite happened. JFK appointed Bobby Kennedy to be Attorney General and Bobby went after organized crime as well as the Teamsters and Jimmy Hoffa. This outraged the mob bosses who, to put it mildly, didn't take kindly to being "double-crossed" by the Kennedys. The coordinated attack run by Robert Kennedy, if it was allowed to continue, would have not only put them out of business it would have seen most of them end up in prison. This outraged Giancana in Chicago as well as Trafficante in Florida and Marcello in New Orleans, just to name a few. In addition, Attorney General Robert Kennedy had Carlos Marcello unceremoniously deported and dropped off in a South American jungle. This episode came close to costing Marcello his life as he and his attorney, in their expensive suits, had to bribe local thugs to help them find their way out. They realized that the local thugs were planning to kill them for their money and narrowly escaped with their lives. This experience was likely what pushed Marcello to take out a hit on JFK, especially when RFK continued to prosecute Marcello after he managed to get back to the U.S.

Author Mark Shaw, in his book *THE POISON PATRIARCH*, claims that Joe Kennedy was ultimately responsible for his son JFK's assassination. In his book he claims that old Joe insisted that RFK be named Attorney General.[469] Former White House Counsel Clark Clifford told Joe why it would be a mistake and Joe listened and then said that Robert Kennedy was going to be Attorney General.[470] Joe Kennedy had business dealings with mafia boss Frank Costello during prohibition.[471] Joe would import bootleg liquor from Canada under medicinal liquor licenses and sell the liquor on to the mafia, using them as his distribution arm.[472] And Joe Kennedy and the mafia all made tons of money.[473]

In Shaw's opinion, Joe's links to the mafia were a prelude to asking Giancana for help with the 1959 election. Joe supplied the money and the mafia supplied the union connections (and the Chicago political machine connections) to get JFK elected in both the primaries and the general election.[474]   The appointment of Robert Kennedy to be Attorney General was a shock to the mafia, because Joe had not told them of his plans to put Robert Kennedy in as Attorney General. The mafia felt betrayed.[475] In his book Shaw discusses how Joe Bonanno said he sent Smitty D'Angelo down to Florida to warn Joe Kennedy about trouble ahead if Bobby kept up the pressure on the mafia.[476] The mafia had given their help with the expectation that the Kennedys would repay the favors when the time came. Joe Kennedy told Smitty there would be no problem because Christmas was coming and the family would all be together and he would have a talk with "the boys" (JFK and RFK).[477]   This never happened because Joe had a massive stroke that left him incapacitated.[478] Joe Kennedy suffered his stroke in Palm Beach on December 19, 1961.[479]

The title of Mark Shaw's book *THE POISON PATRIARCH* refers to the deal made by old Joe Kennedy to get his son John Kennedy elected and how that led to the JFK assassination. His assertion is that, having accepted help from the mafia to get JFK elected, Joe the father was ultimately responsible for the series of events that led to the Kennedy assassination (or assassinations if you count Robert Kennedy). I agree with his thesis. If I have it right it goes like this:

1. Joe Kennedy got the mafia to help get JFK elected.
2. Joe Kennedy, once JFK was elected, insisted on Robert Kennedy as Attorney General.
3. Robert Kennedy as Attorney General attacked the mafia.
4. The outraged mafia retaliated and killed John and maybe Bobby Kennedy.

I believe that Shaw got this right. Joe Kennedy got Sam Giancana to help put JFK in the White House. And Joe's insistence on Bobby Kennedy as Attorney General did light a fuse that ended up with both brothers dead. Robert Kennedy increased his attacks on the mob. The mafia had thought that, if they helped put JFK in the White House, that they would be left alone by the government. In 2000 Tina Sinatra claimed that her father, Frank Sinatra, was the go-between for Joe Kennedy and Sam Giancana to arrange Giancana's assistance with getting JFK elected.[480] Tina Sinatra claims that Giancana told Frank "that's not right – you know he owes me" (he being Joe Kennedy).[481] Taped FBI conversations back up this assertion. Double-crossing the mafia was a fatal mistake that old Joe made. Shaw also claims that Joe likely made JFK appoint RFK to be Attorney General so that RFK could be president after JFK had his two terms. He was likely trying to create a dynasty.[482] Joe Kennedy had originally wanted to run for president himself in 1940 but WW II and Joe's isolationism derailed his plans to become president.[483] When Joe couldn't be president he turned to JFK and Joe was likely lining RFK up to take the White House after JFK's two terms.[484] Shaw also points out that historian and author Doris Kearns Goodwin said that, as Joe's hopes for the White House faded, he took more and more solace in the political fortunes of his sons, counting their successes as his own and, in a way, resurrecting his ambitions through his children.[485] The problem was RFK's attack on the mafia and the mafia subsequently turning on the Kennedys. Joe was unable to stop this due to the stroke that left him helpless and bound to a wheelchair. Author Mark Shaw blames Joe Kennedy for the chain reaction of events that ended in the death of JFK.[486] I agree with Shaw's logic here because it fits the facts as they happened.

Anthony Summers, in his book *NOT IN YOUR LIFETIME*, points out that in 1961 when his brother appointed him Attorney General, Robert Kennedy made clear that combatting organized crime was to be a priority. "It was" he said "a private government . . . resting on a base of human suffering and moral corrosion."[487] Until then, with FBI Director J. Edgar Hoover virtually denying the mob's existence, Kennedy had been merely a thorn in the side of that private government.[488] Now that RFK had power as the nation's top law enforcement officer he used it unrelentingly.[489] Summers also points out that in 1960, before the Kennedys came to power, there were only a few dozen convictions of organized crime.[490] In 1963 there were almost three hundred, and that number soon doubled.[491] Before the Kennedys were elected, government lawyers spent about sixty days in court and less than seven hundred days investigating the mafia.[492] In the last year of the Kennedy administration government lawyers spent over a thousand days in court prosecuting and over six thousand days investigating organized crime. [493] The mafia had a right to feel like they had been double-crossed and were under attack.

On September 13, 1961 President Kennedy signed into law three new bills to give federal, state and local police new authority to fight crime.[494]

On January 31, 1963 an FBI mafia summary is prepared and sent to Hoover stating that permission is being sought (from the Mafia National Commission) to retaliate against politicians who expose the mafia.[495]

In 1963 the Elkins family warned the Kennedys about a planned mafia hit on President Kennedy – from a high building with a high-powered rifle with a scope shooting at the motorcade.[496]

Sam Giancana

Sam Giancana participated in the Kennedy assassination because he felt he had been double-crossed.

At about the same time mafia boss Sam Giancana is being asked by Joe Kennedy to help get his son elected to the White House, the CIA under the Eisenhower administration is reaching out to Giancana to kill Castro. Giancana agrees to help the Kennedys get elected and also agrees to help the CIA murder Castro. Giancana clearly thinks that he is getting in bed with the government. This has worked well for him on a local level in Chicago and now he is trying to gain influence on a national level. His expectation is that he will have the whole game wired. With 'his guy' in the White House, he thinks he will have the Justice Department under control. GIancana has already met socially with J. Edgar Hoover at the Del Mar racetrack and the Del Charo hotel and resort as a guest of oil baron Clint Murchison. Hoover is doing his best to avoid investigating the mafia. By getting in bed with the CIA and the new Kennedy administration, Giancana sees a bright future for himself. No wonder he is usually photographed wearing sunglasses.

Then comes the shock of Robert Kennedy being named as Attorney General. This is a cold shower. Given Bobby's attitude toward organized crime, it is a disaster for the mafia. Then, as Attorney General, Robert Kennedy goes after the mafia with everything he's got, which is all the resources of the United States government. Giancana tries to reach out to Joe Kennedy to straighten things out, but just before Christmas of 1961 old Joe suffers a debilitating stroke that takes him almost entirely out of the game. At the very least, it prevents Joe from reining Bobby in. This put Giancana and the Kennedys on a collision course that would lead to Dealey Plaza.

Sam Giancana confessed to his brother Chuck that he was part of the Kennedy assassination.[497] Chuck Giancana wrote a book, *DOUBLE CROSS*, where he talked about Sam's involvement in the Kennedy assassination and also claimed that Sam said the money for the hit came from Texas oil men.[498]

On June 19, 1975, a week before his scheduled appearance before the Church Committee to be questioned about the CIA-mafia plots, Chicago mob boss Sam Giancana was murdered.[499]

According to Gaeton Fonzi in his book *THE LAST INVESTIGATION*, when the CIA wanted to kill Castro, CIA Director Allen Dulles gave the assignment to CIA Deputy Director Richard Bissell who then told Colonel Sheffield Edwards to find a way to kill Castro and he in turn asked his assistant James O'Connell.[500] CIA officer O'Connell reached out to Robert Maheu, who was former CIA and FBI and had worked for Howard Hughes in Nevada where he presumably gained mafia contacts.[501] Through Maheu they got in touch with mobster Johnny Roselli who was the link to mob bosses Giancana and Trafficante.[502] Author John Newman, in his book *OSWALD AND THE CIA*, has an account that agrees with this version of events.[503] When the CIA decided to hire the mafia to hit Castro, Robert Maheu and Johnny Roselli met with Joe Shimon and Sam Giancana at the Fontainebleau hotel in Miami.[504] Joe Shimon was a hitman for the government.[505]

James Douglass, in his book *JFK AND THE UNSPEAKABLE*, documents how: [506]

> "At the 1975 Senate hearings on U.S. intelligence operations chaired by Senator Frank Church, CIA officials testified reluctantly on their efforts to kill Castro. In late 1960, without the knowledge of President Dwight Eisenhower, the CIA had contacted underworld figures John Roselli, Sam Giancana and Santos Trafficante, offering them $150,000 for Castro's assassination. The gangsters were happy to be hired by the U.S. government to murder the man who had shut down their gambling casinos in Cuba. If they were successful they hoped a U.S.-sponsored successor to Castro would allow them to reopen the casinos."[507]

> "In the Spring of 1961, without the knowledge of the new President Kennedy, the CIA's Technical Services Division prepared a batch of poison pills for Castro. The pills were sent to Cuba through John Roselli. The murder plot failed because the CIA's Cuban assets were unable to get close enough to Castro to poison him. The CIA's purpose was to kill Castro just before the Bay of Pigs invasion. As Bay of Pigs planner Richard Bissell said later "Assassination was intended to reinforce the invasion plan. There was the thought that Castro would be dead before the landing." Very few, however, knew of this aspect of the plan."[508]

Anthony Summers, in his book *NOT IN YOUR LIFETIME*, points out that the CIA was claiming that the president needed a version of plausible deniability where the assassination of Castro was concerned. He put it this way:[509]

> "Senator George Smathers, himself a passionate opponent of Castro, also had a conversation with the president on the subject. Smathers would recall Kennedy expressed himself "horrified" at the idea of assassination "I remember him saying" Smathers said "that the CIA frequently did things he didn't know about, and he was unhappy about it." He complained that the CIA was almost autonomous."[510]

> "CIA officials, for their part, were to say that while it was not proper to discuss such things with the president, they assumed he was aware of and approved the assassination plots. As for the Attorney General Robert Kennedy, one reading of the record suggests he was furious when he learned of the mafia role in the plots. This occurred when in early 1962 he discovered the CIA was trying to protect Sam Giancana from prosecution, insisted on finding out why, and was then briefed on Giancana's part in the early murder plans by CIA attorney Lawrence Houston."[511]

In the meantime, Robert Kennedy was ramping up his attacks on the mafia, and they were having an effect. Mark North, in his book *ACT OF TREASON: THE ROLE OF J. EDGAR HOOVER IN THE ASSASSINATION OF PRESIDENT KENNEDY*, documents that by the end of 1961, 121 mafia members have been indicted.[512] The Justice Department went on to convict 96 in 1961 and 101 in 1962.[513]

On December 9, 1961 FBI recorded Sam Giancana telling Johnny Roselli that he had made contributions to JFK's campaign through his father, Joe Kennedy.[514] This information was sent to Hoover.[515] By early 1962 Giancana would be overheard on an FBI wiretap saying "The president will get what he wants out of you, but you won't get anything outta him."[516]

Giancana tried to get to JFK through his father and through Frank Sinatra to get JFK to get RFK to back off of prosecutions of the mafia.[517] On December 19, 1961 Joe Kennedy suffered a massive stroke in Palm Beach, Florida.[518] The stroke effectively takes Joe out of the picture. Without being able to use Joe Kennedy to get his sons to back off, Giancana was left trying to use Sinatra to get to Kennedy. This didn't work because Sinatra had lost what influence he had with Kennedy. A planned visit to Sinatra's home had been cancelled because it would look bad with Sinatra's ties to the mafia. This infuriated Sinatra, but there was little he could do to change it. Giancana feels he has been double-crossed. He helped the Kennedys get to the White House and then they turned on him.

On the morning of November 22, 1963, the day JFK is assassinated, Attorney General Robert Kennedy was conducting a meeting of his task force and prioritizing his top targets.[519] Sam Giancana of Chicago, Santo Trafficante of Florida, labor boss Jimmy Hoffa of the Teamsters and Carlos Marcello of New Orleans were his top four targets.[520] That day Johnny Roselli had flown to Dallas.[521] Roselli was supposedly there to say "stop the hit" but Chuck Nicoletti, Giancana's hitman, who was in Dallas that day, said that only Giancana, who had commissioned the hit, could call it off.[522]

Author Mark North, in his book ACT OF TREASON, points out that the mafia was happy JFK was gone:[523]

> "Ten days after the assassination, an FBI listening device picked Charles 'Chuckie' English . . . , one of . . . Giancana's underbosses, expressing the Mob's relief to his boss 'I will tell you something, in another two months from now, the FBI will be like it was five years ago. They won't be around no more. They say the FBI will get it [the investigation of Kennedy's murder]. They're gonna start running down Fair Play for Cuba, Fair Play for Matsu. They call that more detrimental to the country than us guys.'"[524]

On June 19, 1975, a week before Giancana is scheduled to appear before the Church Committee to be questioned about the CIA-mafia plots, he was murdered.[525] Giancana becomes one of dozens of murders of people who knew too much and were therefore a danger to the conspirators.

In 1975 Trafficante was recorded, during an FBI surveillance operation, saying to Marcello "Now only two people are alive who know who killed Kennedy."[526] Trafficante was suspected of ordering the hits on Giancana and Roselli.[527]

On August 7, 1976 the body of mobster John Roselli, a coordinator between the CIA and organized crime, was found mutilated and stuffed into a drum floating in Florida's Biscayne Bay.[528]

Carlos Marcello

At first glance it would seem that mafia boss Sam Giancana had the biggest ax to grind with the Kennedys. He had helped them get to the White House and, instead of laying off the mafia, they were attacking organized crime. However, I would argue that with Marcello it was a blood feud. Giancana's life was not threatened by the Kennedys. Marcello's was. Bobby Kennedy went so far as to have Marcello unceremoniously deported to a South American jungle. Marcello narrowly escaped with his life. This made it a blood feud. With Giancana, killing Kennedy was just business. With Marcello it was personal.

Author Mark Shaw, in his book *THE POISON PATRIARCH*, says that Robert Kennedy was going to continue to pursue Marcello so it became a blood feud, a fight to the death, for Marcello. Marcello was not going to just go to prison or be deported, he was going to fight back.[529]

Marcello had a heroin business going through French diplomats and Bobby Kennedy pursued him relentlessly.[530] Hoover had left the mafia alone, but Bobby Kennedy went after them with a vengeance. Oil baron Clint Murchison owned the Del Charo, a resort hotel and the nearby racetrack, the Del Mar, where J. Edgar Hoover went for a free month's vacation every year.[531] Richard Nixon, future Texas governor John Connally, and mafiosi like Meyer Lansky, Santo Trafficante, Johnny Roselli, Sam Giancana, Carlos Marcello and Frank Costello would also drop by for a fun time.[532] Hoover was rubbing shoulders with the mafia while not pursuing them. (For more on this, see the section on how Hoover ignored the mafia).

Authors Roger Stone and Mike Colapietro, in their book *THE MAN WHO KILLED KENNEDY*, have an excellent description of how Bobby Kennedy had Marcello and his lawyer dropped off in a Guatemalan jungle.[533] On April 4, 1961 Carlos Marcello and his lawyer, Mike Maroun, meet at the Immigration and Naturalization office in New Orleans for a hearing.[534] They are arrested and handcuffed and driven to the airport. From there they are flown to Guatemala.[535] They get kicked out of Guatemala and start toward San Salvador in a station wagon.[536] They soon have to abandon the car and end up on an old bus for six hours in the mountains between El Salvador and Honduras. As the authors put it:[537]

> "These two pudgy, aging men in Shantung silk suits were reduced to wandering. Starving and increasingly desperate to

come upon some vestige of civilization, they stuffed the $3,000 they had left between them into their crumbling alligator shoes. Fearful that the two Indian boys they have picked up to guide them were about to murder them with their machetes, Maroun and Marcello plunged down a thorn-ridden ravine, where Marcello tumbled through boulders and bayonet grass and broke three ribs."[538]

And, when Marcello made it back to the United States the next month, Bobby Kennedy was not going to let up. He continued to prosecute Marcello to the limit. Marcello was doing everything possible to stay in the U.S. and to stay in business. He was using legal tactics, appeals, delays, bribing juries and whatever else he could think of. It wasn't working. By 1963 his appeals are running out. In Marcello's world, this meant he had to go ahead with the hit on Kennedy in order to survive. Marcello's determination to assassinate Kennedy became one of the cornerstones that the conspiracy was built on. Hoover saw that Marcello had taken out a contract on Kennedy and did not pass that information on to Kennedy. Hoover did, however, have someone he gave this vital information to. He has been friends, neighbors and cronies with Lyndon Johnson for almost two decades.

On May 27, 1963 the U.S. Supreme Court declined to hear Marcello's appeal.[539] Now only a change in administration can save him. Once the administration finds a country to take him, Marcello is gone.[540] By the summer of 1963 it was all-out war between the Kennedys and Carlos Marcello, who Bobby Kennedy had deported to the jungles of Latin America two years earlier.[541] In the meantime Kennedy had stepped up his prosecution of Marcello and his organization, and Marcello was not taking it lying down.[542] Hoover, Johnson and Marcello are all doomed if Kennedy stays in office.[543] As noted earlier in this book, this is the same Marcello who, since the early 1950's, had been paying Johnson every year for protection against anti-mafia legislation. Hoover, Johnson and Marcello all know each other and they all hate Kennedy and see him as an obstacle.

Author Mark North, in his book *ACT OF TREASON*, points out that:[544]

> "Marcello astutely realized that the two officials who would be most able to prevent his prosecution after the fact, Hoover and Johnson, would personally benefit in very real ways from the assassination of President Kennedy – Hoover through perpetuation as Director, and Johnson, through the acquisition of power, as well as containment of the Estes scandal and Baker/Levinson connection. Marcello well knew of Hoover's

and Johnson's apathy toward the ongoing prosecution of the mafia. Accordingly, realization of the above factors triggered his decision to put out a contract on the life of JFK."[545]

Hoover got word of the Marcello JFK contract via the FBI field office in Miami who heard it from their informants in the Cuban exile community.[546] Only a few FBI agents in Miami knew of the warning.[547]

Author Anthony Summers, in his book *NOT IN YOUR LIFETIME*, documents that:[548]

"In autumn 1962, according to a former associate, the Mafia chief and three others convened on the mobsters three-thousand-acre estate outside New Orleans. For all his wealth Marcello preferred on this occasion to talk in a ramshackle building that did occasional service as a hunting lodge. One of the men present was Edward Becker, whose background involved work in the Casino business and undercover investigative work. Another was an oil geologist named Carl Roppolo, who hoped to bring the mobster in on a business deal. The third man there may have been a Marcello aide called Liverde. Becker is the source of the account that follows."[549]

"As the whiskey flowed, Becker said, the talk turned to Marcello's trials and tribulations under the Kennedy onslaught. As he talked of Robert Kennedy and the deportation episode, Marcello became enraged. Ranting on in his Sicilian-accented southern drawl he exclaimed that Robert Kennedy was "going to be taken care of."[550]

"Marcello referred to President Kennedy as a dog, Becker said, and his brother Robert was the tail. "The dog," he said, "will keep biting you if you only cut off its tail." If the dog's head were cut off the biting would end. The meaning was clear. Were John F. Kennedy to be killed, his brother would cease to be attorney general and harassment of the mafia would cease."[551]

"What he heard, Becker would tell the authorities repeatedly over the years, left him in no doubt. Marcello had "clearly stated that he was going to arrange to have President Kennedy murdered in some way." The impression Becker got was that this was something Marcello had been considering for some time."[552]

In August of 1962 Marcello puts out a contract on President Kennedy.[553] Marcello is under pressure from prosecutions of members of his organization and from his likely deportation and/or imprisonment.[554] In September of 1962 Hoover learned that the Marcello crime family had put out a contract on JFK in order to protect themselves from prosecution by Robert Kennedy and the Justice Department.[555]

In Mark North's book *ACT OF TREASON: THE ROLE OF J. EDGAR HOOVER IN THE ASSASSINATION OF PRESIDENT KENNEDY*, he documents that in September of 1962 Hoover learns of Marcello's plans to assassinate President Kennedy.[556] In North's opinion this is when Hoover shifts from trying to blackmail Kennedy into giving him a retirement waiver to trying to see that Marcello's hit succeeds.[557] North says that this is when Hoover senses the opportunity to stay in office.[558] Hoover and Johnson become even closer.[559] Hoover gets more information on the Marcello contract on JFK from the Philadelphia FBI office and also does not pass on the information to the authorities.[560]

For those unfamiliar with Silicon Valley startup investment funding, it's kind of like the game of who will be the first one in the pool or out on the dance floor. Everyone is standing around, thinking the same thing, but it takes one brave soul to actually jump in the pool or start dancing. Then everyone else who is interested joins in. Startup funding works the same way. Startup founders looking for investors make the rounds of the venture capital firms and, if they have a few interested investors, the investors stand around the pool looking at each other. Everyone is looking to see what everyone else is going to do. Then one investor says "Yes. I'm going to lead a round of funding." They then offer what's called a term sheet. This is the signal that they are "in." They have jumped in the pool. This then forces the other investors to make a decision – in or out, because the train is leaving. This is how things happen. This is how groups make difficult decisions. One person finally makes a decision and the others then have to decide if they are in or out. Marcello could act without the approval of the national mafia Commission. This is because Marcello's organization was older than the mafia Commission and he is not subject to the Commission.[561] In this case Marcello made a decision to act. He had his own reasons. And he told fellow mafia bosses Giancana and Trafficante. Then Hoover found out and you can bet he told Johnson. Johnson is a master at manipulation. He became the first effective leader of the Senate since the republic was founded by getting one hundred notoriously independent senators to bend to his will and act as a group. He could see how all of Kennedy's enemies could be manipulated to come together as a group and pull this off. The mafia, the CIA, the anti-Castro Cubans, Hoover, the Joint Chiefs and the oil barons could all get what they wanted. And Marcello's single act of taking out a hit on Kennedy is likely the spark that set it off. Hoover clearly decided he was in, otherwise he would have done his job and reported the wiretap threats to Kennedy. He did not. At that point the mafia and Hoover were in. Johnson clearly was in no position to refuse to join. He will go to prison unless he goes to the White House, so he decided he was in. At that point the mafia, Hoover and Johnson were in. At some point the CIA and the Pentagon become so frustrated with Kennedy that they decided to join the conspiracy, and the CIA was in control of the anti-Castro Cubans. Enough of the Cubans are outraged at Kennedy that a few can be found to join in. Johnson was already in bed with the wealthy oil barons. The rest of the hit and the cover-up was just working out the logistics.

On October 31, 1962 a Federal court ruled against mafia boss Carlos Marcello in his bid to have his narcotics charge overturned.[562] On December 5, 1962 a deportation order for Marcello was upheld by the courts.[563] On December 18, 1962 FBI agents Regis Kennedy of New Orleans and Paul Scranton and George Davis of Miami file reports on mafia bosses Carlos Marcello and Santo Trafficante.[564] FBI Director J. Edgar Hoover again sees the Marcello contract in more detail.[565] On November 16, 1963 David Ferrie is at Marcello's estate, supposedly to help with trial preparation.[566]

On the morning of November 22, 1963 Attorney General Robert Kennedy was conducting a meeting of his task force and prioritizing his top targets.[567] Sam Giancana of Chicago, Santo Trafficante of Florida, labor boss Jimmy Hoffa and Carlos Marcello of New Orleans were his top four targets.[568] David Ferrie was an associate of Carlos Marcello (who Bobby had deported in 1961) who was on trial.[569] Davie Ferrie was also working for the CIA.[570]

On November 22, 1963 President John F. Kennedy was assassinated in Dealey Plaza at 12:30 PM.

On November 22, 1963 at 1:45 PM Central Standard Time, while the Marcello jury goes into deliberation in New Orleans, Marcello was already aware that his hit on Kennedy had succeeded.[571]

In 1984 Jack Van Laningham was a fellow inmate who was willing to rat on Marcello.[572] Marcello confessed to Van Laningham that he hated Robert Kennedy from back when he was deported to the jungle in South America.[573] David Ferrie had introduced Oswald to Marcello in

New Orleans and Marcello claimed to have set Jack Ruby up in his club in Dallas.[574] He also said he had JFK ("the little son of a bitch") killed and he would do it again.[575] Van Laningham brought in a portable radio with an FBI bug in it.[576]

Author Roger Stone said in his book *THE MAN WHO KILLED KENNEDY* that he was with attorney Roy Cohn and "Fat Tony" Salerno, an underboss in the Genovese crime family, when Fat Tony said it was Carlos Marcello and Lyndon Johnson who were behind the Kennedy assassination and he also said that Kennedy got what was coming to him.[577] Fat Tony pointed out that the Kennedys took their money and their help and then turned on the mafia.[578]

The original plan was for Oswald to be shot while being arrested.[579] That plan failed and the conspirators had to improvise. Jack Ruby in Dallas worked for Marcello's organization which was based in New Orleans. It was Ruby's job to arrange with the Dallas cops to kill Oswald. The mafia paid Ruby to set this up because he had the relationships with the Dallas cops.[580] It was his responsibility. When the original plan failed and Oswald was taken alive it fell to Ruby to go to Dallas Police Headquarters and kill Oswald while he was in custody. This was a potential disaster for the conspirators. If Oswald talked or went to trial the entire conspiracy would easily be exposed. Since it was Ruby's job to have Oswald killed, it was still his job and he was then sent in to do the job himself. Johnny Roselli said Ruby was ordered by the mafia to kill Oswald to shut him up.[581] This is covered in the chapter on Jack Ruby. Here the focus is on Marcello.

The day after the Kennedy assassination David Ferrie arrived in Galveston, and Ruby made a phone call to Galveston.[582] From Ferrie's hotel there is then a call to the Town & Country Motel, Marcello's headquarters in New Orleans.[583] Later, Marcello will set Ferrie up in a lucrative service station franchise in an ideal location in New Orleans.[584] The next day, on November 24, 1963 Lee Harvey Oswald was murdered by Jack Ruby on national television.

Author Mark North, in his book *ACT OF TREASON*, points out that:[585]

> "With the death of Oswald, Hoover launches a disinformation campaign designed to prevent the media from gaining a clear picture of the assassination and thus Marcello's and his involvement. It begins in Dallas with directives to SAC J. Gordon Shanklin on November 24. The SAC publicly states that the Bureau had no contact with Oswald before the assassination and claims the Dallas P.D.-administered paraffin

test on Oswald, results of which strongly suggest his
innocence, in fact implicate him. Both assertions are complete
fabrications."[586]

544 Camp Street was the office some of the the conspirators worked
out of in New Orleans in the summer of 1963 before the Kennedy
assassination later that year. It was Guy Banister's office, and Lee
Harvey Oswald, David Ferrie, Sergio Arcacha Smith and the anti-
Castro Cuban exiles all used it as a base of operations. Guy Banister
was working for the FBI and CIA, as were Lee Harvey Oswald and
David Ferrie, who was also working for Marcello. Sergio Arcacha
Smith was operating a CIA-sponsored anti-Castro Cuban exile group.
A few days after the Kennedy assassination, FBI agents in New
Orleans claimed no connection between 544 Camp Street (the address
on Oswald's pro-Castro leaflets) and Sergio Arcacha Smith's office at
the same address.[587] They do this by referring to Smith's address as
531 Lafayette Street, which is the side entrance to the same building.[588]
During the week of November 25, 1963 Hoover gets reports that Ruby
is part of the Marcello criminal organization.[589] Joseph Civello was
Carlos Marcello's capo in Dallas and Ruby worked for Civello.
Hoover orders this covered up.[590]

On November 26, 1963 the FBI interviewed one of Ruby's piano
players, Robert Moore, who also worked in a store owned by Civello.[591]
Moore referred to Ruby as a frequent visitor at Civello's store and an
associate of Civello.[592] Joseph Civello had represented Marcello at the
Apalachin mafia national Commission conference in 1957.[593]

A week after Ruby murdered Oswald, Sam Campisi was sent by Carlos
Marcello to visit Ruby in jail.[594]

In early December Hoover again attacked the Dallas and New Orleans
FBI agents investigating the Marcello organization and the
investigation slowed to a crawl.[595] In mid-December of 1963 Hoover
shut down the FBI New Orleans investigation of the link between
David Ferrie and Carlos Marcello.[596] Hoover ordered his agents to
drop their investigation of Ferrie after December 18 and to make no
mention of him or of Carlos Marcello in the FBI supplemental report to
the Warren Commission on January 13, 1964.[597]

Santo Trafficante

Trafficante's father was an immigrant who established rackets in Florida.[598] Trafficante inherited the Florida rackets and the Sans Souci Casino in Havana.[599] Trafficante came to prominence in 1957 when Albert Anastasia, at the time regarded as one of the founders of the American mafia, of Murder Incorporated and the head of what became the Gambino crime family, died in a hail of gunfire while sitting in a barber's chair.[600] Anastasia had been attempting to move in on Trafficante's interests in Cuba.[601]

Trafficante was one of the guests who hung out with J. Edgar Hoover at the Del Charo resort hotel and the Del Mar racetrack owned by Texas oil baron Clint Murchison.[602] This was a tradition dating back to the 1950's and may help explain why Hoover did his best to avoid investigating the mafia. In addition to socializing with the head of the FBI, Trafficante sought to curry favor with politicians. Frank Ragano, a mafia lawyer, related a story. In 1957, when John Kennedy was a senator, he accepted an invitation from Santo Trafficante and his casino partner, Evaristo Garcia, to have sex with three Cuban hookers at the Commodoro Hotel in Havana while Trafficante and Garcia watched from a two-way mirror.[603]

There is no solid proof that Santo Trafficante ordered the hit on Kennedy. There is solid proof Trafficante knew about the hit and was obviously involved in it, but there is no hard evidence that he himself ordered the hit. The more likely scenario is that he agreed to lend his support and assistance because he hoped to get back into his casino business in Cuba. With Kennedy in the White House this was not going to happen. With Kennedy gone there was a chance the casino business might be restarted.

After Castro took over Cuba he booted the mafia out and shut down their casinos. Jack Ruby ran guns to Cuba before the revolution. Some of the mafia casino owners got out of Cuba before Castro took over. Others, like Trafficante, decided to stay and try to hang onto their casinos.[604] This was a mistake. Castro had Trafficante put in the Triscornia detention camp outside Havana.[605] Another inmate named John Wilson, a British journalist, who was there at the same time contacted authorities in the U.S. after Ruby killed Oswald on national television.[606] He said that Ruby visited 'Santos' (Trafficante) at the camp and brought food.[607] Two days after the Kennedy assassination the nation watched on live television while Jack Ruby killed Lee Harvey Oswald to keep him from talking. Then John Wilson's account surfaced, and Hoover quickly moved to label Wilson a psychopath.[608] The last thing the conspirators wanted was for Ruby's ties to the mafia to come to light. The conspirators were attempting to get the public to believe that Ruby and Oswald had no connection to each other or to the mafia. No hint of 'conspiracy' must be seen by the people or they would suspect what really happened.

During the Church Committee hearings in 1975 more details came to light on how the CIA reached out to the mafia through mobster Johnny Roselli to Sam Giancana and Santo Trafficante to kill Castro.[609] The CIA offered the mafia $150,000 for their help with Castro's assassination, and Trafficante and Giancana agreed because they hoped to overthrow Castro and get back into the casino business in Cuba.[610] In early 1961 the CIA started to supply the mafia with devices for murdering Castro, beginning with poison pills.[611]

The CIA operation to get rid of Castro was named Mongoose. Joe Shimon was at the original meeting between the government and the mafia at the Fontainebleau hotel in Miami. Shimon had started as a cop on the Washington, D.C. police force and he had worked his way up to the Justice Department and the White House.[612] He also worked for the Secret Service and the CIA.[613] Shimon later admitted that he was a hitman for the government.[614] He also later told the *Washington Post*'s Jack Anderson that Trafficante had told Shimon "I'll get you the assassins, I'll give you lots of names, but keep me out of it."[615] Apparently Trafficante did not want direct involvement in the plan to kill Castro. However, none of the six teams sent to Cuba to kill Castro was successful.[616] Shimon came to believe that six professional hit teams all failing to come back from Cuba could not have been a mere coincidence.[617] One or two, maybe, but six in a row meant that Trafficante was likely tipping them off.[618] Santo Trafficante had somehow managed to get out of jail in Cuba and come back to the United States with all his assets intact, and now all the Castro hit teams were disappearing without a trace.[619] When Shimon asked Giancana about Trafficante's reliability, Sam said Santo was a rat.[620]

In 1962 Florida mafia boss Santo Trafficante met at the Scott-Bryant hotel with a Cuban exile named Jose Aleman to discuss a loan Trafficante was arranging for Aleman from Jimmy Hoffa and the Teamsters.[621] Referring to the Kennedy prosecutions of the mafia, Trafficante said "Have you seen how his brother is hitting Hoffa, a man who is a worker, not a millionaire, a friend of the blue collars? He doesn't know that this kind of encounter is very delicate." Hoffa was in fact a millionaire "It is not right what they are doing to Hoffa." Trafficante went on "Hoffa is a hard-working man and does not deserve it."[622] In an apparent reference to the mob's help in getting Kennedy elected in 1960 and the Kennedy prosecutions of the mafia that had followed, Trafficante went on to say that these Kennedys were not honest "They took graft and they did not keep a bargain. Mark my word. This man Kennedy is in trouble, and he will get what's coming to him."[623] when Aleman disagreed, saying he thought the president was doing a good job and would be reelected to a second term, the mafia boss replied very quietly "You don't understand me." he said "Kennedy is not going to make it to the election. He is going to be hit."[624]

in September of 1963 Santo Trafficante again tells FBI informant Jose Aleman that Kennedy is going to be assassinated, and Aleman again reports the conversation to his Miami FBI contacts, agents George Davis and Paul Scranton.[625] Davis and Scranton said that Aleman was reliable, and Davis and Scranton forward the information to FBI Director Hoover who did not pass on the information.[626] Aleman continued to meet with Trafficante and continued to warn the FBI although he thought they were not taking him seriously.[627] The agents were passing the information to Hoover who was sitting on it and not passing on the warnings to the Kennedys.[628] On November 22 1963, hours after the assassination of the president, agents rushed to see Aleman.[629]

Bobby went after the mob and Jimmy Hoffa. On the morning of November 22, 1963, he was conducting a meeting of his task force and prioritizing his top targets.[630] Sam Giancana of Chicago, Santo Trafficante of Florida, labor boss Jimmy Hoffa and Carlos Marcello of New Orleans were his top four targets.[631]

John Martino was a friend of Florida mafia boss Santo Trafficante, and late in life he confessed to being part of the Kennedy assassination.[632] He had predicted the assassination to his wife the morning of November 22, 1963 and they watched it on television.[633]

On November 22, after Kennedy was assassinated, the two FBI agents came back to see Aleman about his prior conversations with Trafficante "They wanted to know more and more and I finally had to tell them he didn't say he was going to do it, he just said Kennedy was going to get hit."[634]

Frank Ragano was a mob lawyer for Jimmy Hoffa and Santo Trafficante and Carlos Marcello and Trafficante confessed to Ragano on his deathbed [635] 'we should have killed Bobby, not JFK'[636]

In 1975 Trafficante was recorded, during an FBI surveillance operation, saying "Now only two people are alive who know who killed Kennedy" in a conversation with Marcello.[637]   Trafficante was suspected of ordering the hits on Giancana and Roselli.[638]

The CIA

The entire CIA didn't get together at a big meeting where they all took a vote and decided to murder the president of the United States. That's not how the world works. The vast majority of people who work at the CIA are hardworking patriots who perform difficult and dangerous work for a civil servant's salary. Many of them are heroes who are not even allowed to wear medals and receive public credit and praise for their actions in the way that many military heroes are. In 1963 these quiet heroes went about their work having no idea that there were rogue elements high up in the CIA who had decided to participate in a conspiracy to murder their president. It wasn't the whole CIA who decided to murder Kennedy and cover it up. A few key people at the top of the CIA made a decision to go rogue and participate in the conspiracy to murder Kennedy and cover it up.

They did this for several reasons, most of them ideological. Director Allen Dulles and his inner circle at the CIA were hard core Cold Warriors. They believed that the United States needed to fight communism now or end up isolated, weakened and eventually destroyed. They believed in the domino theory, which is where one country after another falls to communism until an entire region or continent goes communist. CIA Director Allen Dulles was their leader. He had recruited and trained them. He had held them together. He had found money to pay them in the days after World War II when the OSS was out of business and the CIA had yet to be created. He had protected them from Senator Joseph McCarthy and his witch hunt for communists. Kennedy came along and had the inevitable clash with Dulles and fired him as Director of the CIA, but Dulles was still the leader of the Cold Warriors at the CIA. They still considered Allen Dulles to be their leader, even when he was tossed out.

This section is organized into seven sub-sections:

1. The Dulles Brothers – goes into how Allen Dulles and John Foster Dulles ran U.S. foreign policy during the Eisenhower administration long before Kennedy was even elected. They were used to running things and thought of themselves as being in charge. This did not sit well with Kennedy when he was elected. Kennedy persisted in thinking he had been elected president.

2. The Bay of Pigs – describes how the relationship went from bad to worse when Allen Dulles lied repeatedly to Kennedy

about the chances for success in the Bay of Pigs operation in order to trap Kennedy into agreeing to the invasion. Dulles knew it would fail without direct U.S. military support, the one thing Kennedy had refused. Dulles thought that, once the invasion was underway, Kennedy would be forced to give in and agree to the direct military support. Kennedy refused, the invasion failed, and Kennedy found out how he was lied to and manipulated. He fired Dulles and a few of his top guys.

3. Losing Control of the CIA – describes how the CIA was using its control of events on the ground to deliberately undermine Kennedy's official policies in favor of what the CIA wanted and how Kennedy attempted to gain control of the CIA and of American foreign policy.

4. Losing Control in Southeast Asia – describes how the CIA was running its own show in Vietnam and ignoring the orders of President Kennedy. They were using their control of events on the ground in Vietnam to force the implementation of their policies against the wishes of the president.

5. The CIA tries to implicate Cuba and the Soviet Union – describes how the CIA does its best to implicate Cuba and Russia in the JFK assassination as a pretext for an invasion of Cuba and/or an attack on the Soviet Union.

6. The Alarm is Turned Off – describes how the CIA infiltrated other U.S. government agencies and gives one specific example. A guy they planted at the FBI switched off the alarm bell that would have rung to alert the bureaucracy that Oswald was a potential threat to the president in Dallas.

7. Rogue CIA Elements – lists the prime suspects and the roles they played in the assassination and the cover up, at least until (some of them) were themselves murdered to keep them quiet.

Before Kennedy even took office, the CIA had, between the time of the election and the time of JFK's inauguration, run an operation that Kennedy did not approve of. In fact, that was probably why the operation had to take place when it did. Dulles wanted the democratically elected Prime Minister of the Democratic Republic of the Congo murdered. Once Kennedy was in office he would likely have specifically told the CIA not to have Lumumba murdered, so they did it before Kennedy was inaugurated.[639]

At some point Kennedy had lost control of the CIA, assuming he ever had it to begin with. During the height of the Cuban Missile Crisis Kennedy had ordered the CIA to halt all covert CIA raids on Cuba. Even after Kennedy issued this order, the CIA had continued launching attacks on Cuba. This was a huge provocation at a very tense time when the world was on the verge of World War Three. Had this been taken the wrong way by the Russians it might have tipped the delicately balanced situation into disaster. Again, this was not done by everyone at the CIA. In this case it appears to have been done by Bill Harvey with the support of his superiors, but it shows that Kennedy was no longer in control of the CIA.

More evidence that Kennedy was losing control of the CIA came after the Cuban Missile Crisis. On March 19, 1963 at a press conference in Washington, anti-Castro Cuban Antonio Veciana, leader of the CIA-sponsored Alpha 66 group, announced Cuban raids on Soviet shipping in Havana harbor. This was an example of the CIA intentionally defying and embarrassing the Kennedy administration.[640]

Since 1961, not long after he took office, Kennedy was furious with the CIA for the way they had lied to him about the Bay of Pigs operation and, after it turned into a fiasco, he was planning to do something about it. He was considering breaking up the CIA, reducing it in size and even putting his brother Robert Kennedy in charge of it.[641] This caused panic, fear and outrage at the CIA.[642] Kennedy was looking to end the U.S. involvement in the war in Vietnam and was looking to make peace with Cuba. In Vietnam and Cuba, the CIA was doing everything in their power to sabotage Kennedy's efforts to make peace.[643]

With the CIA in almost open rebellion against their Commander in Chief, the situation had come to a head by 1963. Author Mark Lane, in his book *LAST WORD: MY INDICTMENT OF THE CIA IN THE MURDER OF JFK*, documented that:[644]

> "On October 2, 1963, Richard Starnes, an editor of *The Washington Daily News* and a respected reporter, wrote from Saigon that the CIA had "arrogantly" rejected orders from President Kennedy about ending the war in Vietnam. He said that if an attempted military coup against Kennedy took place, it would be organized by the CIA. He stated that Kennedy was reluctant to confront the agency head on, perhaps because he was "simply afraid they'd kill him if he tried.""[645]

> "On that same day, Arthur Krock devoted his daily column, "In the Nation" in *The New York Times*, to "The Intra-Administration War in Vietnam." Krock, a three-time Pulitzer

Prize winner, was the nation's most famous conservative journalist as was referred to as the "Dean of Washington newsmen." He was very close to President Kennedy. Kennedy's Pulitzer Prize-winning book, *Profiles in Courage*, was drafted and written in Krock's Georgetown home. Krock wrote, quoting a "very high American official," that "the CIA's growth was 'likened to a malignancy' which the 'very high official was not sure even the White House could control … any longer.' 'If the United States ever experiences [an attempt at a coup to overthrow the government] it will come from the CIA . . .' The agency 'represents a tremendous power and total unaccountability to anyone' . . . The CIA may be guilty as charged." Starnes also reported President Kennedy had commissioned a major inquiry into the misconduct of the CIA. The Krock and Starnes predictions were published in October 1963. Kennedy was murdered the next month."[646]

And Allen Dulles, who was the root cause of the trouble between the CIA and Kennedy, was put in charge of the investigation into the Kennedy assassination.[647]

The Dulles Brothers

Long before John F. Kennedy won the 1960 election to become president, the Dulles brothers, for the two terms of the Eisenhower administration, had formulated and implemented the foreign policy of the United States. They decided what needed to be done, they persuaded Eisenhower to approve whatever operation it was, and they then implemented that policy. Sometimes Eisenhower gave his approval willingly and at other times they had to work on him for a while, but in the end, he almost always went along. John Foster Dulles was Secretary of State and Allen Dulles was the Director of the CIA. By the time Kennedy arrived in the White House Allen Dulles was used to formulating and implementing the foreign policy of the United States.

Here we can see the beginning of what we now refer to as the Deep State. These men were unelected bureaucrats with too much power who thought they knew better than the duly elected leaders and were arrogant enough to defy the will of those leaders. Here are the denizens of the Deep State attempting to implement their policy in defiance of trivial aspects of life like the Constitution and the will of the people or their elected representatives.

During World War II

President Franklin Delano Roosevelt was wary of Allen Dulles but let him operate in the open in Switzerland during World War II so he could more easily identify Dulles' Nazi connections.[648] Sullivan & Cromwell, the law firm where the Dulles brothers worked, allowed the Dulles brothers to play an intricate shell game to hide the assets of their German client firms like I.G. Farben and Merck to keep them from being confiscated by the United States as enemy property during wartime.[649] John Foster Dulles signed "Heil Hitler" on his correspondence with his client, chemical company I.G. Farben (makers of Zyklon B, the gas used in the death camps) before WW II.[650] By the end of the war many of their clients were under investigation by the Justice Department and John Foster Dulles was suspected of collaboration with the enemy.[651] However, Allen Dulles had his brother's back.[652] According to John Loftus, a Nazi hunter who eventually went to work in the Justice Department under President Jimmy Carter, shredding of Nazi documents was the favorite tactic of Allen Dulles and his associates who stayed behind to run the occupation of postwar Germany.[653] Allen Dulles was well placed to destroy any incriminating evidence so that no investigation could get traction against the Dulles brothers.[654] Supreme Court Justice Arthur Goldberg said that if President Franklin Delano Roosevelt had survived the war the Dulles brothers would have faced prosecution for war crimes.[655] He also said that both Dulles brothers were guilty of treason, but FDR died and no one else had the will to challenge them.[656] Allen Dulles was a cold man who had little or no empathy for others. Firms like Farben, Krupp and Siemens got labor from the concentration camps. Himmler cut himself and the SS in by charging the companies for the labor.[657] Dulles knew of the ongoing genocide in the death camps in Germany during WW II but did nothing to alert the U.S. government. He went along with the official U.S. State Department policy of looking the other way. Instead Dulles focused on the threat from communism. After the war, the WW II wartime alliance with Russia was dead and Russia and communism was the new enemy. Many of the Nuremburg defendants were released early due to quiet intervention by Allen Dulles, who worked with Nazis like spymaster Reinhard Gehlen to help in the Cold War against the Russians.[658] Once he became director, Allen Dulles turned the CIA from an intelligence gathering organization to an action machine that overthrew foreign governments.[659]

In his book *LEGACY OF ASHES: THE HISTORY OF THE CIA,* author Tim Weiner points out that Nazi Reinhard Gehlen was adopted by the Americans because the prevailing theory at the time was that, now that WW II was over, the Russians were the enemy and we needed whatever edge we could get in the Cold War.[660] We held our nose and adopted Gehlen and his organization for the same reason that we held our nose and adopted Wernher von Braun and his crew to build rockets. Yes, they had committed war crimes while they were working for Hitler, but (the thinking went) we needed their knowledge and talent because we were in a competition with communism. Whether it was the space race or the wider Cold War, we needed to keep up and, if possible, get ahead and win.[661] By 1947, many in the U.S. military leadership were starting to agree with this view. In his book on Dulles, *THE DEVIL'S CHESSBOARD: ALLEN DULLES, THE CIA, AND THE RISE OF AMERICA'S SECRET GOVERNMENT,* author David Talbot describes Allen Dulles as "emotionally numb" and viewing people as "useful."[662] This made him the perfect person to implement the strategy of using former Nazi war criminals for the benefit of the fight against communism. Morality didn't enter into the equation.

James Jesus Angleton also rescued former Nazi leaders like Eugen Dollmann after the war.[663] Angleton and Dulles both viewed the Russians as the enemy. The Cold War was on and Angleton and Dulles wanted to contain world communism. This was their priority, and if former Nazis could help then that was OK with Dulles and Angleton.[664] Angleton would eventually become part of the CIA when it was created.

After World War II, the Dulles brothers were set to become the Secretary of State and the head of the CIA in a Dewey administration. Thomas Dewey was the establishment's choice for President of the U.S. and the Dulles brothers would have been the choice for these two posts. Then the voters chose Harry Truman and that didn't happen.[665] The Dulles brothers had to wait for the Eisenhower administration.

Walter Bedel "Beetle" Smith, Eisenhower's aide from World War II, was chosen by Truman to run the CIA and Smith chose Allen Dulles as his second in command.[666] But later when it was time to choose his successor Smith had come to see Allen Dulles as amoral and therefore not suited to the job.[667] However, John Foster Dulles had gotten to Eisenhower first.[668] The Dulles brothers were wired into the establishment group that formed Eisenhower's support and he went along with the Dulles theory that having the two brothers running the

State Department and the CIA would make for a smooth working relationship.[669] So, Allen Dulles became the head of the CIA while his brother was Secretary of State.[670]

Eisenhower's view of national security was to use nuclear deterrent and covert action instead of a massive military buildup to achieve peace. He listened to John Foster Dulles and to Allen Dulles. The Dulles brothers agreed on an "us vs. them" worldview. The U.S. vs. Communism (Russia, China, etc.) and the "domino theory" so covert action was the way to go and the CIA was the way to do it.[671]

In 1953 the CIA overthrew Iranian Mohammad Mosaddegh, the democratically elected leader of Iran.[672] In 1954 the CIA overthrew Jacobo Arbenz, the democratically elected leader of Guatemala.[673]

Iran

The CIA was behind a coup in Iran in 1953. Dulles wanted to topple Mohammed Mossadegh but Eisenhower thought the U.S. should support Mossadegh instead of trying to overthrow him.[674] Mohammed Mossadegh was the democratically elected Prime Minister of Iran and he saw the British as exploiting his country's natural resources and interfering in his country's internal politics.[675] Iran just wanted to be independent. This was also Harry Truman's approach.[676] Since Eisenhower wasn't going along, the Dulles brothers changed tactics and used the Cold War angle, using the threat of Iranian oil fields falling into communist control.[677] Dulles simply wanted to put the Shah back on the Peacock Throne. The British government joined in trying to convince Eisenhower, and he eventually agreed.[678] In 1953, with Allen Dulles directing the operation by radio out of Geneva, Switzerland, the CIA launched a well-organized coup against the government of Iran.[679] As a result, Premier Mohammed Mossadegh was overthrown and a government friendly to the CIA was installed.[680]

The Iranians have never forgotten what the Dulles brothers did to them in the name of the United States, and we are still paying for their sins due to the effects of disastrous relations with Iran that are still with us today.

Guatemala

The 1954 Guatemalan coup d'état was another CIA operation pushed by Allen Dulles.[681] Allen Dulles owned stock in the United Fruit Company (UFC), as did his brother John Foster Dulles.[682] They also had ties to the company due to having done legal work for UFC while in private law practice.[683] The democratically elected Guatemalan government was undergoing land reforms which would prevent the UFC from continuing to exploit the Guatemalan people for the profit of the company.[684] In 1954 in Guatemala Jacobo Arbenz, though not a communist, was trying to reform his country and help his people with liberal policies.[685] The Dulles brothers had convinced Eisenhower to authorize a coup d'état in Guatemala to put a more compliant military dictatorship in place which would allow the UFC to get back to business as usual at the expense of democracy in Guatemala and the Guatemalan people.[686] When some military leaders began a plot against the democratically elected leader the CIA moved in to support them with armed fighter planes and Arbenz ended up fleeting the country.[687]

As a country which was created by throwing off colonial rule, the United States had no business becoming a colonial ruler, but the Dulles brothers didn't care.

MK-ULTRA

In 1953 CIA Director Allen Dulles inaugurated the MK-ULTRA program.[688] There were persistent rumors that American P.O.W.'s captured in Korea were subject to Chinese brainwashing techniques.[689] This made Dulles want to catch up and pass the communists in the area of brainwashing, just like Sputnik made the U.S. want to catch up and pass the Russians in the space race and the reports of Nazi Germany working on an atomic bomb pushed the U.S. to come up with the Manhattan Project.[690] If brainwashed people could be made to carry out tasks like murder or spying that they otherwise would be unwilling to do this could be used as an advantage by one side or the other. If the communists could do something that might be useful in the Cold War then Dulles was going to make sure that the U.S. had that capability and more and he created project MK-ULTRA.[691] MK-ULTRA involved mind-control experiments on human beings, and CIA officer Richard Helms oversaw the program.[692] They tried lots of things including electric shock therapy, LSD and whatever else they could think of to get people to act on command, even against their own conscience.[693] Dulles' amoral view of people as "useful" allowed him to have people tortured with electric shocks and used as human guinea pigs in the name of winning the cold war against communism. They started with Soviet prisoners and double agents and then moved on to drug addicts, mental hospital inmates, prisoners and others they saw as 'expendables.'[694] Frank Olson was a CIA officer who became a security risk when they gave him an overdose of LSD and they kidnapped and eventually killed him.[695] Dr. Donald Ewen Cameron experimented on Gail Kastner.[696] She was given so much electrical shock therapy that she broke teeth and fractured her spine while being shocked.[697]

When the Allies won World War II after invading Germany, the Nazis were put on trial in Nuremberg for doing what Allen Dulles and Richard Helms were doing in the name of the United States.

In 1956 Jesus Galindez disappeared because he was a threat to Rafael Trujillo, dictator of the Dominican Republic.[698] He had written a critical Ph.D. dissertation on Trujillo and Trujillo had him kidnapped off the streets in New York and flown to the Dominican Republic.[699] Robert Maheu and Associates was hired by the CIA to grab Galindez at his apartment, and he was drugged and transported by ambulance to a twin-engine Beechcraft and flown south to West Palm Beach, Florida and from there to the Dominican Republic where Trujillo had Galindez tortured and killed.[700]

Author David Talbot, in his book *THE DEVIL'S CHESSBOARD: ALLEN DULLES, THE CIA, AND THE RISE OF AMERICA'S SECRET GOVERNMENT*, documented that:[701]

> "The abduction of the Columbia University academic from the streets of Manhattan is the first flagrant example of what would come to be known during the War on Terror, with bureaucratic banality, as "extraordinary rendition" – the secret CIA practice of kidnapping enemies of Washington and turning them over to the merciless security machinery in undisclosed foreign locations."[702]

The U-2 Incident

The Dulles brothers were used to making their own policy and implementing it. They decided what they wanted and then figured out how to get it done. When they couldn't get a president to go along they had a habit of using their control of events on the ground to force the president into a position where he had no choice but to go along. In this book I will document multiple times when Allen Dulles or the people he put in charge used this tactic. The U-2 incident may be one of those times or it may not. There is no hard proof, but it fits the same pattern as the other examples.

In 1957, John Foster Dulles proposed to make the U-2 program public after the launch of Sputnik, but Eisenhower refused.[703] The Dulles brothers, at this point, wanted to let the secret of the U-2 spy planes out. Eisenhower did not. Eisenhower also wanted to cut the military budget and the Dulles brothers did not. Several people who would be in a position to know said that, at this point, the Dulles brothers cooked up a scheme to get both of the things they wanted. And it worked.

In 1960 Dulles asked Eisenhower for permission to fly a U-2 over Russia.[704] Eisenhower had reluctantly agreed to the flight and it was shot down.[705] The CIA claimed that a weather balloon had been lost and eventually the Russians put captured pilot Gary Powers on trial and convicted him.[706] He was kept for two years until he was eventually exchanged.[707]

Peter Janney, author of *MARY'S MOSAIC*, claims that the CIA engineered the May 1, 1960 downing of the U-2 flight over Russia as a way to torpedo the peace talks between the U.S. and the U.S.S.R.[708] Eisenhower was looking to cut the military budget and Dulles was opposed to the cuts. The way to avoid the cuts was to derail the peace process by having the Russians shoot down the U-2.[709]

Dulles was the CIA Director who assured Eisenhower that the Russians could not shoot down the U-2 spy plane, and then it was shot down over Russia and Francis Gary Powers was captured.[710] L. Fletcher Prouty thought that Dulles allowed the U-2 to be shot down so as to ruin the chances for a peace meeting between Eisenhower and Khrushchev in 1960.[711] Eisenhower was truly angry with Duller over the U-2 incident and told Dulles that the CIA was badly organized and badly run and as a result Eisenhower would leave his successor with a legacy of ashes.[712]

Gary Powers was the pilot of the U-2 that was shot down. He said he thought it was Oswald who gave the Russians the information they needed to shoot him down.[713]

Prouty and Janney may be right. I have yet to see proof, but given all the other times I've seen proof that Dulles and his crowd used this tactic I have to assume there's a good chance that Peter Janney is right. Dulles had a habit of maneuvering the president into a position where he had no choice but to do what Dulles wanted. Dulles may have somehow slipped the information to the Russians as a way to derail the peace talks he so desperately wanted to fail. In either case the Dulles brothers got what they wanted. The U-2 was exposed, the Cold War continued and the budgets weren't cut, they were increased.

The Church Committee found that the CIA had actively encouraged the assassinations of other foreign leaders, including Rafael Trujillo of the Dominican Republic in 1961 and President Ngo Dinh Diem of South Vietnam in 1963 (this last one was not while Dulles was Director).[714]

By 1960 Dulles was running a shadow government. Kennedy wanted to get rid of both Hoover and Dulles as soon as he was elected but didn't see himself as having a strong mandate to clean house given his slim margin of victory. Dulles and Hoover were viewed as pillars of the establishment, and JFK thought he would have to go with them for a year or so, then he could make changes.[715]

Author David Talbot, in his book *THE DEVIL'S CHESSBOARD: ALLEN DULLES, THE CIA, AND THE RISE OF AMERICA'S SECRET GOVERNMENT*, documented that:[716]

> "Dulles was confident enough that the Dulles era would continue under JFK that he boasted to that effect on the Washington dinner party circuit, within full earshot of Kennedy loyalists. Shortly after Kennedy took office, the painter William Walton, a close friend of JFK and Jackie, found himself at a gathering at Walter Lippmann's house where Dulles was a fellow guest. "After dinner the men sat around a while in an old-fashioned way and [Dulles] started boasting that he was still carrying out his brother Foster's foreign policy. He said, you know, that's a much better policy. I've chosen to follow that one." Walton, who loathed the CIA boss, couldn't believe Dulles' audacity. The spymaster knew that Walton was one of Kennedy's inner circle, but he felt no need to hold his tongue. He was clearly sending the new president a message – and Kennedy's close friend duly delivered it. Early the next morning Walton phoned Kennedy at the White House and reported what Dulles had told Lippmann and his guests. "God damn it" swore Kennedy, "Did he really say that?"[717]
>
> "The torch has been passed to a new generation of Americans," Kennedy declared in his inaugural address. But, in fact, the Dulles old guard was deeply reluctant to give up power to the New Frontier team. In fact, the power struggle

between the new president and his CIA director started before Kennedy was even sworn in, when Dulles took advantage of the transition period to carry out a brazen act of insubordination."[718]

The Congo

James DiEugenio, in his book *RECLAIMING PARKLAND*, says that:[719]

> "Dulles likely speeded up the murder of Patrice Lumumba because he knew that Kennedy would never approve it."[720]

Allen Dulles took advantage of the transition period between the 1960 election and Kennedy being sworn in. Having been elected only six months earlier, Patrice Lumumba was the Congo's first democratically elected leader following the end of Belgium's brutal colonial rule.[721] Lumumba was on the run from the CIA-backed Congolese military forces that opposed him.[722] Lumumba had broken free from house arrest and was trying to regroup and reform his government.[723] The Congo had been exploited first by the Belgians and then by western mining interests. Belgian King Leopold had used slavery to produce rubber and ivory and after Leopold the looting continued with gold, diamonds, copper and tin being the primary resources.[724] Global mining companies made huge fortunes there but Lumumba's election threatened to end the gravy train for the exploiters of the Congo.[725] He was a threat to western business interests.[726] Congo was the source of the uranium for the atomic bombs that were dropped on Hiroshima and Nagasaki.[727] Lumumba turned down millions of dollars in bribes and was trying to keep the Congo from being aligned with either Russia or the U.S. because he wanted to be independent.[728] Allen Dulles saw Lumumba as a threat to U.S. national interests.[729] The CIA engineered a military coup to put Mobutu Sese Seko in power and put Lumumba under house arrest. They wanted to kill him, but did not want to be seen getting their hands dirty, so Lumumba had been allowed to escape and was on the run. They were originally going to use poison toothpaste to kill him while in captivity but decided it would be better to let him escape and be killed by his opponents. This would let them do the dirty work and let the CIA escape the blame that would follow if Lumumba died while in captivity. As Lumumba made his way to his followers he was pursued, captured and beaten.[730] Kennedy had praised Lumumba and his movement and his followers hoped he could survive in captivity long enough for JFK to be sworn into office.[731] Once Kennedy was sworn in it would be more complicated. JFK was going to be sworn in on January 20. Three days before Kennedy's inauguration Lumumba was transferred to Katanga, beaten and killed.[732] After JFK was sworn in Allen Dulles briefed Kennedy on the Congo but did not tell him that Lumumba was dead.[733] The Kennedy White House remained unaware of Lumumba's fate for a month after JFK's inauguration.[734] There is a picture of Kennedy as he got the news of Lumumba's death.[735] He looks just devastated.

In 1960 the CIA was training 500 men in Guatemala to invade Cuba. The plan was unworkable, and Jake Esterline, the CIA project director for the invasion of Cuba, pointed out to Richard Bissell, the CIA Deputy Director who Dulles had assigned to oversee the project, that the plan would not work.[736] After the election Kennedy met with Dulles and Bissell at his father's place in Palm Beach, Florida.[737] Esterline had told Bissell that to overthrow Castro would require a full-scale invasion and not just the 500 Cuban exiles they had training in Guatemala.[738] Dulles and Bissell did not tell this to Kennedy. Eisenhower had not approved the invasion of Cuba but Kennedy didn't know that.[739] Eisenhower had been particularly disgusted by the U-2 fiasco and he had commissioned some reports on the CIA after the U-2 was shot down.[740] The reports said that there were serious shortcomings at the CIA because Dulles had spent most if not all of his time on covert operations and not on intelligence gathering.[741] Eisenhower's Board of Consultants on Foreign Intelligence activities issued recommendations on January 5, 1961.[742] They claimed the covert operations, psychological experiments and other activities were not worth the cost or the risk, and had distracted the CIA from its primary mission of gathering intelligence.[743] The board urged the president to separate the functions of the CIA.[744] Dulles reassured Eisenhower that he had things under control and that the CIA didn't need to be reorganized.[745] Eisenhower told Dulles that he, as president, should have reorganized the CIA long ago and that he had suffered an "eight-year defeat on this" and that nothing had changed since Pearl Harbor.[746] Earlier, Ike had asked the CIA to make sure that a surprise like Pearl Harbor didn't happen again. Eisenhower said that, because of the failures of the CIA to do its job, he (Eisenhower) would leave a "legacy of ashes" to his successor.[747]

The Bay of Pigs

Kennedy and the CIA got off to a bad start with the murder of Patrice Lumumba in the Congo. Dulles had substituted his judgement for that of the duly elected president. This was not what Kennedy wanted and he would likely have vetoed the idea once he was inaugurated, so the operation was given the green light in the time between the election and the inauguration. Kennedy was of the opinion that not only was the policy of murdering a democratically elected leader a bad idea but he also had a CIA which was willing to implement policy opposed to what the president wanted. Immediately upon taking office Kennedy was confronted with the Deep State fighting him for control. At issue was who was in charge.

The bad blood between Kennedy and the CIA then greatly accelerated with the Bay of Pigs. CIA Director Allen Dulles and his lieutenants wanted to invade Cuba and Kennedy was not agreeing to their plan. JFK wanted Castro ousted, but he did not want the United States to be seen as invading Cuba. He wanted plausible deniability. He therefore did not want direct U.S. military participation in the invasion. If the U.S. military invaded a nation that had not attacked the United States, that would make the United States look like an aggressor nation. The only way the CIA could get Kennedy to approve of the invasion was to promise that it would not require direct U.S. military participation. The problem was that the invasion would not succeed without direct involvement from the U.S. military, and the CIA knew it. This put Dulles and his guys in a quandary. They solved it by lying to Kennedy and saying that the Bay of Pigs invasion would succeed without help from the U.S. military. Dulles gambled that, once the invasion was in progress, Kennedy would cave in and agree to having the U.S. military pitch in and help out rather than allowing the operation to fail. Kennedy only reluctantly approved of the operation with the very specific understanding that the U.S. military would absolutely not be involved. Once the operation got underway the guys planning and running the operation asked Kennedy to approve U.S. military air strikes, and he refused. The operation failed and the Bay of Pigs was a total disaster. Dulles and his guys at the CIA blamed Kennedy. Kennedy blamed the CIA. Kennedy was furious with Dulles. Dulles and his crowd were furious with Kennedy. Each thought the other should be removed from office. Kennedy fired Dulles. Dulles retaliated. Things went downhill from there.

Eisenhower had approved the plan to train a force to invade Cuba. Richard Bissell was the CIA officer in charge of planning for the operation. The whole concept began with the assumption that, once the local Cuban people saw their liberators coming, they would join in the fight to help liberate their island homeland.[748] The idea was to take over the radio transmitter and broadcast for help and then for U.S. military forces waiting offshore to come ashore and lend 'assistance.'[749] This way the United States could be seen as helping to liberate the Cuban people, not as invading a peaceful neighbor. During the 1960 presidential campaign Kennedy, who was running against Nixon, decided to push on the Cuba issue assuming that Nixon would automatically take the opposite side in the debate and it worked.[750] Nixon could not disclose that plans were already underway and Kennedy could safely blast away at Nixon knowing that Nixon could not reply.[751] The headlines said "Kennedy advocates U.S. intervention in Cuba – calls for aid to rebel forces in Cuba."[752] Kennedy gave quotes to the press, and this came out before the fourth debate.[753] By now Kennedy was getting briefings from Dulles.[754] Nixon was outraged at Kennedy exploiting this issue while knowing that Nixon couldn't respond.[755] Thus, Kennedy was the first to publicly advocate intervention in Cuba when, in fact, it was Nixon's program.[756] Nixon had spearheaded the issue behind the scenes within the Eisenhower administration. This was one of the reasons he was so angry at losing votes over this issue. Nixon saw it as a dirty trick, and he could do nothing about it. And Kennedy knew it.[757] The strategy got Kennedy elected, but it backfired. Once he was president, the CIA blackmailed him over Cuba intervention. They would leak to the public if Kennedy backed out on the invasion plan. The CIA had Kennedy where they wanted him.[758] Kennedy reluctantly approved the Cuban invasion plan in spite of his reservations about the chances of success of the plan. At a January 21, 1961 meeting of Secretary of State Dean Rusk, Secretary of Defense Robert McNamara, Attorney General Robert Kennedy, Chairman of the Joint Chiefs of Staff Lyman Lemnitzer and others Dulles said that something had to be done. In only two months they had to move. Dulles had Kennedy over a barrel.[759] This would be a major political blowup if they didn't invade. And Dulles was also able to use the issue of the exiles. What would they do with all the Cuban exiles they had trained?[760] The unfortunate reality was that the invasion was unlikely to succeed. It had a very low likelihood of military success and almost no chance of it sparking an uprising.

CIA officer Jake Esterline created the original plan for the Bay of Pigs invasion while Eisenhower was still in office.[761] The idea was that there were anti-Castro rebels in the Escambray mountains and they just needed some help.[762] The Trinidad plan (as it was called at first) was to either invade Cuba all at once or, alternatively, a little at a time.[763] This alternative plan called for a series of secret landings of men and equipment to gradually build up the rebel forces in the mountains in preparation for the invasion.[764] They started training 500 anti-Castro Cuban exiles.[765] Esterline pointed out that the whole concept was based on the idea that there were Cubans in Cuba who would rise up.[766]

In late 1960 this concept changed because Castro had consolidated his hold on power and was cracking down on the dissidents that the original Cuba invasion plan was dependent on.[767] The idea of having a slow buildup of men and supplies was no longer viable, and CIA officer Richard Bissell had to change to a more conventional beach assault with planes providing air support.[768] The new concept was that the invasion would spark a popular uprising among Cubans who were against Castro, and the budget for the operation tripled.[769] Army General Lyman Kirkpatrick said "As the operation expanded, it reached a point where it simply was not plausibly deniable."[770]

This is the point where Dulles and his inner circle (like Richard Bissell) just started lying to President Kennedy. Instead of just telling only part of the truth, like they did with the murder of Lumumba, and leaving the president to find out later that he had been told half-truths, they just plain lied. Dulles assured Kennedy that the plan would succeed when he knew it would not, at least not as presented. Dulles knew that, now that it was a classic amphibious landing, it would be opposed by Castro's regular army and reserves. He also knew that, in order to succeed, they would need lots of close air support to keep the small invasion force from being overwhelmed. Kennedy was skeptical of the plan presented to him, and Dulles and his guys just lied when they said it would work. In Tim Weiner's book *LEGACY OF ASHES*, there's a quote from Dulles to Kennedy:[771]

> "Mr. President I stood right here at Ike's desk and told him I was certain that our Guatemalan operation would succeed, and the prospects for this plan are even better than they were for that one."[772]

This was also a lie. Weiner also points out that Dulles had in fact told Eisenhower that the chances for success in Guatemala were one in five, and zero without air cover.[773]

On June 16, 1954 at a meeting with President Eisenhower and a few others to go over the planned coup in Guatemala, Eisenhower told the Dulles brothers:[774]

> "Are you sure this is going to succeed?" and added "I want you all to be damn good and sure you succeed. I'm prepared to take any steps that are necessary to see that it succeeds. When you commit the flag, you commit to win."[775]

Later, when the coup was faltering and Dulles requested more airstrikes, Eisenhower approved them and the coup was a success.[776]

Allen Dulles may have considered this attitude when he tried to push President Kennedy into the Bay of Pigs. He appears to have either hoped or believed that, once Kennedy had 'committed the flag' he would take any steps necessary to win. In any case, that's the path Dulles took, and it backfired because Kennedy meant what he said when he refused to use the U.S. military to invade Cuba.

The whole Bay of Pigs invasion plan was a lie, and Dulles and Bissell knew it. There were a few air strikes in the plan that Kennedy approved, but not enough. Dulles was gambling that Kennedy would cave in and agree to the extra air strikes once the shooting started, because he wouldn't want to be seen as a failure. He wouldn't want to look like a weak and indecisive president who had sent in an inadequate force and failed. Dulles underestimated Kennedy. Kennedy, as it happened, was willing to publicly take the blame for the failure rather than compromise his principles. He had said he would not invade other nations, that the United States was not an aggressor nation. He had made a public pledge on April 12 that "There will not be, under any conditions, an intervention in Cuba by the United States armed forces."[777]

Peter Janney, in his book *MARY'S MOSAIC*, points out that Dulles assumed that Kennedy would have to agree to the extra air cover for the Bay of Pigs invasion once the shooting started. Kennedy held firm and did not.[778] The invasion failed and Kennedy blamed Dulles and fired Dulles and Richard Bissell.[779] He also fired Deputy Director General Charles Cabell, another CIA officer involved in the duplicity. Janney said:[780]

> "However, this did not change things at the CIA. Getting rid of Dulles didn't mean Dulles was gone. The entire upper echelon of the Agency, most of which had been recruited by Dulles, were loyal to him and would remain so."[781]

Janney also quotes Arthur Schlesinger, who said "We (Kennedy and his inner circle) were at war with the national security people." and quoted Kennedy as saying "How could I have been so stupid? I've got to do something about those CIA bastards"[782] Janney also quotes Kennedy as telling David Powers "They were sure I'd give in to them. They couldn't believe that a new president like me wouldn't give in and try to save his own face. Well, they had me figured all wrong."

In 2005, the CIA was compelled to release the minutes of a meeting held by its Cuba task force on November 16, 1960.[783] The group, which was trying to figure out what to tell the newly-elected president, realized that their invasion plan would not work without the help of U.S. military.[784] The CIA knew back then that the Bay of Pigs invasion was doomed to fail, but they did not tell Kennedy.[785] They also did not tell Kennedy about the ongoing plot to use the mafia to kill Castro.[786]

Anthony Summers, in his book *NOT IN YOUR LIFETIME*, recounts a conversation with E. Howard Hunt. As news of the debacle came in, he and the others there reacted with dismay and scorn:[787]

> "At CIA headquarters in our war room . . . we thought, as the indications came in, that the administration would feel more and more an obligation to unleash some United States power to equalize the situation. We kept receiving the administration's refusals with incredulity. I felt a sense of hollowness . . . somewhere along the way we lost a good part of our national will to prevail. I think it was a failure of nerve."[788]

On April 22, 1961 Kennedy convened the National Security Council.[789] He ordered General Maxwell Taylor to work with Allen Dulles, Robert Kennedy and Admiral Burke to perform an autopsy on the Bay of Pigs.[790] The Taylor Board of Inquiry met that afternoon.[791] Author Jerome Corsi, in his book *WHO REALLY KILLED KENNEDY*, points out that CIA historian Jack Pfeifer said that Allen Dulles was doomed after his "particularly abysmal performance" as a witness during the Taylor Committee investigation.[792] In the Taylor report it clearly states that the CIA knew before the invasion that there would be no additional air strikes approved unless they were launched from the beachhead secured by the invasion.[793]

The Taylor Committee report badly damaged Dulles and the report from CIA Inspector General Lyman Kirkpatrick sealed his fate.[794] Kirkpatrick was an honest man who wrote an honest report, which only surfaced in 1998.[795] Kirkpatrick had concluded that Dulles and Bissell had failed to be candid with two presidents and keep them accurately and realistically informed about the Cuban invasion operation.[796] Kirkpatrick made the point in his report that, even if Kennedy had agreed to double the number of air strikes, as the CIA had requested after the invasion had begun, the operation never stood a chance.[797] Even if the air strikes had knocked out the entire Cuban air force, the invaders would have still been outnumbered 100 to 1 by Castro's forces.[798] Castro had 32,000 regulars and 200,000 in his reserve militia, so the 1,500 landing on the beach didn't stand a chance against those numbers backed up by Soviet-supplied equipment.[799] Dulles made sure the report was buried.[800]

There were lots of rumors going around that Kennedy was going to implement layoffs at the CIA, and one of every five was eventually fired.[801]

David Talbot, in his book THE DEVIL'S CHESSBOARD, points out that:[802]

> "The Bay of Pigs debacle produced a "stuttering rage" among CIA officers aligned with Dulles, according to CIA veteran Joseph B. Smith – especially among those on the Cuba task force."[803]

The same was true of the Pentagon. Talbot quotes Lyman Lemnitzer, Chairman of the Joint Chiefs of Staff, saying that the Kennedy decision to hold back on the air cover for the invasion was "unbelievable, absolutely reprehensible, almost criminal."[804] The feeling was mutual. Kennedy dismissed Lemnitzer and his crowd as having an outdated outlook.[805]

By the time both the Taylor report and Kirkpatrick's inspector general's report were completed, Kennedy had a good understanding of how deeply he had been deceived.[806] This would be the last time he assumed that his military advisors, with their chests full of medals and ribbons, were more highly qualified than he was to judge military matters.[807] From now on he would not automatically assume they knew what they were doing.[808]

Dulles, for his part, reacted to the fiasco by attempting to control the spin. His first reaction was to publicly pin the disaster on President Kennedy. Dulles blamed the Bay of Pigs fiasco on JFK's "lack of determination." He had an article planted in the September 1961 issue of *Fortune* magazine. Charles Murphy was a Dulles ghost writer for Dulles' memoir and he wrote the article entitled "Cuba: The Record Set Straight."[809] Much of the article shifted blame from the CIA to the White House, and Kennedy was furious about the article.[810] He told his contacts that he was going to have to deal with the CIA. He said this to James "Scotty" Reston, the *New York Times* Washington correspondent.[811] Word quickly got back to the CIA that, while Kennedy was publicly taking the blame for the Bay of Pigs fiasco, he was privately blaming the CIA. It had become a duel between Dulles and Kennedy[812] Dulles knew that Kennedy wanted to fire him.[813]

The CIA had also gotten out of control at the operational level. President Kennedy had expressly forbidden any CIA officers from landing on the beach with the invasion force, and he had been disobeyed.[814] CIA agents had also told their Cuban counterparts to go ahead with the invasion even if Kennedy called off the invasion at the last minute.[815]   Robert Kennedy, when he found out later, considered this the same as treason.[816]   John Kennedy said privately that he would like to splinter the CIA into a thousand pieces and scatter it to the winds.[817]

Robert Kennedy was put in charge of Cuban policy, and he did not get along with William Harvey, the CIA officer in charge of Cuban operations.[818]

In James DiEugenio's book *DESTINY BETRAYED*, he says that in 1965 Dulles wrote a draft of an article about the Bay of Pigs that was never published.   In it Dulles points out that he did in fact lie to Kennedy, and he even says why. DiEugenio quotes Dulles:[819]

> "We did not want to raise these issues … which might only harden the decision against the type of action we required. We felt that when the chips were down – when the crisis arose in reality – any action required for success would be authorized rather than permit the enterprise to fail … We believed that in a time of crisis we would gain what we might have lost if we provoked an argument in advance."[820]

Here is Dulles himself admitting, in his own words, that he deceived Kennedy on the Bay of Pigs on the assumption that Kennedy would cave in and agree to the additional air strikes once the operation was underway instead of allowing it to become a public failure.[821]   Richard Bissell also later admitted that they lied to Kennedy.[822]

Losing Control of the CIA

The concept of plausible deniability, where the people who are responsible for making the decisions can claim not to know what is being done in their name, is very dangerous.   When the CIA was created, plausible deniability was built into the legislation that founded it.   The problem is that plausible deniability gives people like Allen Dulles the ability to run their own show with no accountability to anyone. In the United States of America, where government agencies are created by Congress, we're supposed to have civilian control of our agencies. Our elected representatives are supposed to be able to put limits on what they can do. This doesn't even work in theory, much less in practice. And increasingly the agencies created by Congress either lie to Congress or simply refuse to even answer their questions. Without accurate information on what is going on inside these agencies our elected representatives have no hope of controlling them. They wouldn't even know what questions to ask.

George Kennan was a diplomat for the United States at the beginning of the Cold War, and he had a hand in creating the CIA. He later called the concept of plausible deniability, in the context of the CIA, the greatest mistake he ever made.[823] President Truman, who reluctantly signed the legislation creating the CIA, came to have deep regrets. One month after Kennedy was assassinated, Truman published an article where he said he was "disturbed because the CIA had become an operational and at times a policy-making arm of the government. This has led to trouble ... There is something about the way the CIA has been functioning that is casting a shadow over our historic position and I feel that we need to correct it."[824]

Lyman Kirkpatrick, the inspector general of the CIA concluded that Allen Dulles and Richard Bissell had failed to be candid with either Eisenhower or Kennedy about the Cuban invasion operation. Dulles buried the report.[825] Kennedy fired Dulles while the new CIA headquarters at Langley was still being built. Bissell was canned six months later. Kennedy was diplomatic to both of them as they retired, even though he was furious with what they had done while at the CIA. At first, he was so angry he was tempted to destroy the CIA, then he wanted to put his brother Bobby in charge.[826] Bobby disagreed that he should be the Director of the CIA, then they agreed on John McCone, who got along well with Robert Kennedy.[827] JFK did end up giving Bobby responsibility for covert Cuban actions.[828] Dulles and Bissell never told McCone about some of the illegal CIA operations, like the program to open mail.[829]

On May 29, 1961, Kennedy sent a letter to each American Ambassador abroad.[830] The president wrote "You are in charge of the entire U.S. diplomatic mission and I expect you to supervise all its operations. The mission includes not only the personnel of the Department of State and the Foreign Service, but also representatives of all other United States agencies." That included, of course, the CIA.[831] The point of this letter was another attempt to try to get the CIA under control.[832] Part of the problem here was that the State Department, including Kennedy's choice for secretary of state, Henry Cabot Lodge, was also in almost open rebellion against Kennedy.[833] All the letter did was further alienate the CIA.[834]

James Douglass, in his book *JFK AND THE UNSPEAKABLE*, points out that National Security Action Memorandum (NSAM) #55 came out on June 28, 1961.[835] NSAM #55 informed the Joint Chiefs of Staff that it was they, not the CIA, who were going to be his military advisors from then on.[836]   Douglass quotes Air Force Colonel L. Fletcher Prouty, who back then was in charge of providing military support for the CIA's clandestine operations, described the impact of NSAM #55, addressed to General Lyman Lemnitzer, Chairman of the Joint Chiefs:[837]

> "I can't overemphasize the shock – not simply the words – that procedure caused in Washington: to the Secretary of State, to the Secretary of Defense and particularly to the Director of Central Intelligence. Because Allen Dulles, who was still the Director, had just lived through the shambles of the Bay of Pigs and now he finds out that what Kennedy does as a result of all this is to say that, 'you, General Lemnitzer, are to be my advisor.'   In other words, I'm not going to depend on Allen Dulles and the CIA. Historians have glossed over that or don't know about it."[838]

When Kennedy fired CIA Director Allen Dulles, Deputy Director Richard Bissell and Deputy Director Charles Cabell, it was a failed attempt to decapitate the CIA so that he could put his own guy in there and start to control it. Dulles had been there for years and had recruited and trained most of the top echelon of the CIA since long before there even was a CIA. With the exception of Bissell and Cabell, the whole Dulles Cold Warrior crowd were all still there. And they were still loyal to Dulles. Richard Helms and James Jesus Angleton were still there, and they stopped by regularly to see Dulles.[839] And Dulles still had the use of his office and the facilities of the CIA. Author David Talbot describes Dulles as being deposed but having his reign continue.[840] Talbot said that Dulles created a government in exile of anti-Kennedy folks.[841]   And Dulles continued to keep up with all his contacts.[842] Dulles was eventually replaced as Director of the CIA by John McCone, who seems not to have been fully aware of what was going on at the CIA.[843] His direct reports Helms and Angleton did not tell him everything. McCone was intentionally left out of the loop on major operations because Angleton and Helms remained staunchly loyal to Dulles and both were in key positions at the CIA.[844] Allen Dulles would always be their boss and they would consult him regularly even after his departure.[845] This was the Deep State in action, doing what they wanted to regardless of the agenda or policies of the duly elected or legally appointed leadership.

On October 21, 1962 during the Cuban Missile Crisis, after Robert Kennedy told CIA Director McCone to immediately halt all operations against Cuba, CIA Task Force W chief William Harvey sent two raiding parties into Cuba.[846] The world was on the brink of nuclear war and Bill Harvey defied his direct orders and launched raids at Cuba anyway.[847] He clearly did this with the support of his superiors because they protected him. They were told to fire him and did not.

In 1963 Kennedy was being eased out of control by the CIA and the Pentagon.[848] In 1963 the CIA continued to deliberately defy President Kennedy and attempted to escalate tensions with the Soviet Union.[849] One example of this was the continuing raids into Cuba against Kennedy's orders.[850] Another example was the CIA planting a bomb in the city of Hue, Vietnam, killing Buddhist demonstrators and blaming it on Diem's government.[851] The purpose in each case was to make a bad situation worse and force Kennedy into a war he was trying to avoid. Kennedy used the Peace Speech at American University to go over the heads of his administration and jump-start the stalled negotiations with Khrushchev, and it worked.[852]

On March 19, 1963 at a press conference in Washington, Antonio Veciana, the leader of the CIA-sponsored Alpha 66 anti-Castro Cuban exile group announced more Cuban raids in a deliberate attempt to embarrass the Kennedy administration.[853]

Kennedy would go on to make quiet cuts to the CIA budget in 1962 and 1963 and was aiming at a 20% reduction in the CIA budget by 1966 according to Kennedy historian Arthur Schlesinger.[854] Author Mark Lane, in his book *LAST WORD*, pointed out that Kennedy's intentions to scale back the CIA caused panic at the CIA and that the CIA probably looked at taking Kennedy out as an act of self-defense.[855]

In July of 1963 Kennedy went around his own national security apparatus and crafted a nuclear test ban treaty to propose to the Soviet Union.[856]

Truman's Warning

President Harry Truman did not want an American Gestapo. The Office of Strategic Services was the U.S. intelligence agency during WW II, before there was a CIA. Truman let the OSS lapse after World War II was over. Later, a retired Harry Truman wrote right around the time of the Kennedy assassination saying that the CIA should have been limited in its role. In his highly critical article he said the CIA had outgrown the charter he established for it. He never wanted it to become what it became. He wanted the president to have better information and that's why he reluctantly agreed to the legislation to establish the CIA. Truman wanted the CIA to be an intelligence coordinator for the White House.[857] He said that the CIA had become an operational and policy-making arm of the government, and that the CIA had become a liability. Truman pointed out that, with all the propaganda from the Soviet Union claiming imperialism and colonialism on the part of the United States, the last thing Truman thought we needed was to have the CIA doing exactly what the Soviets were accusing us of doing. Truman also said that now the CIA was not just threatening foreign governments but also threatening democracy at home.[858] He called for the CIA to be restricted to its original charter of gathering intelligence.[859]

In his book, *LAST WORD: MY INDICTMENT OF THE CIA IN THE MURDER OF JFK*, author Mark Lane points out that Truman was reluctantly persuaded in 1947 to create the CIA to act as an intelligence gathering arm of the president. Then, in late 1963 Truman called for the CIA to be restored and restricted to that role.[860]

Truman said:

> "I think it has become necessary to take another look at the purpose and operations of our Central Intelligence Agency – CIA...[861]

> "For some time, I have been disturbed by the way the CIA has been diverted from its original assignment. It has become an operational and, at times, a policy-making arm of the government. This has led to trouble and may have compounded our difficulties in several explosive areas.[862]

> "We have grown up as a nation respected for our free institutions and for our ability to maintain a free and open society. There is something about the way the CIA has been functioning that is casting a shadow over our historic position and I feel that we need to correct it."[863]

Dulles tried to get Truman to retract his harsh criticisms of the CIA. Truman would not recant but Dulles later claimed that Truman had second thoughts.[864] This was another lie by Dulles. Truman never changed his mind on the issue.[865]

Losing Control in Southeast Asia

Kennedy wanted to avoid a land war in Asia. He did not want to commit American combat troops. To that end he tried to encourage a neutral Laotian government. This would, in his opinion, solve the problem without direct American military intervention. However, this was not what the CIA wanted.

In 1960 the CIA forced out the freely elected leader of Laos and installed Prince Souvanna Phouma.[866] U.S. involvement in Vietnam had continued to ramp up and the U.S. wanted to organize Hmong tribesmen to assist in the effort to close what became known as the Ho Chi Minh Trail.[867]

In early 1962, as the *Times* of London reported "CIA agents had deliberately opposed the official American objective of trying to establish a neutral government and encouraged Phoumi and his reinforcement of Namtha and had negatived the heavy financial pressure brought by the Kennedy administration upon Phoumi by subvention from its own budget." Knowing he was backed by the CIA, Phoumi was openly defiant of Kennedy's intentions. The *Times* correspondent stated:[868]

> "The General apparently was quite outspoken and made it known that he could disregard the American embassy and the military advisory group because he was in communication with other American agencies."[869]

The CIA was trying to create a crisis that would push Kennedy to intervene. They did not want a coalition in Laos, they wanted American combat troops.[870] Kennedy wanted to guide Laos to a neutral position that would not require American combat troops to enforce America's will.[871] The CIA ploy failed to create a crisis sufficient to get Kennedy to intervene with troops.[872] Kennedy did have Jack Hazey, the CIA officer working with Phoumi, transferred.[873] Kennedy also got diplomat Averill Harriman to work out a compromise in Geneva with the Russians for a neutral Laos.[874] The CIA and the Pentagon were bitterly opposed to the agreement.[875] They tried to destroy it by supporting Phoumi's provocations and violations of the ceasefire.[876] In his book *JFK AND THE UNSPEAKABLE*, author James Douglass points out that in May of 1962 Averell Harriman told historian Arthur Schlesinger that Kennedy's policy in Laos was being systematically sabotaged by the Pentagon and the CIA "They want to prove that a neutral solution is impossible." Harriman said "And the only course is to turn Laos into an American bastion."[877]

In Southeast Asia the CIA systematically undermined Kennedy's policies. For example, Kennedy said that it was up to the South Vietnamese to win or lose the war. The United States could help but they have to do it themselves.[878] On the other hand, the State Department, the CIA and the Pentagon believed in the domino theory. Communists would take over entire continents by knocking over one country at a time. They believed that we needed to fight back against communism to keep from being eventually left isolated and weak in a mostly communist world. This is why the U.S. got pulled into a civil war in Vietnam.[879] Johnson, for his part, wanted to be a "wartime president" like Franklin Delano Roosevelt.[880] LBJ thought South Vietnam could become like South Korea – an ally.[881] Kennedy at first went along with funding and advisors but drew the line at sending combat troops.[882]

In 1963 Kennedy started keeping the CIA and Pentagon out of his high-level foreign policy discussions.[883] Kennedy also shut them out of the test ban treaty talks with the Soviet Union.[884] JFK went direct to the Russians.[885] At one point, Kennedy walked out of a strategy meeting with the Joint Chiefs, who had been advocating a first strike capability.[886] Kennedy was rapidly losing control of his own administration. The CIA would make major moves in Vietnam without Kennedy knowing.[887] When he made the Peace Speech to American University Kennedy called for a new attitude toward the Soviet Union.[888] The CIA and the Pentagon hated the sentiment of the speech.[889] Kennedy also stopped inviting Johnson to Vietnam strategy meetings.[890]

Author James Douglass, in his book *JFK AND THE UNSPEAKABLE*, also relates another incident where the CIA used plastic explosives in May of 1963 to bomb the city of Hue in Vietnam.[891] They blamed the subsequent deaths on the Diem government and used the resulting polarization between the Diem regime and the Buddhists to thwart Kennedy's plans for a negotiated withdrawal of American forces from Vietnam.[892] Douglass claims that both Diem and Kennedy had been outmaneuvered by the CIA.

In early September Kennedy found out that the CIA's Aid for Internatinal Development (AID) chief David Bell had cut off economic aid to South Vietnam, the commodity import program.[893] This was a designated signal for a coup, and it was taken this way by the generals in South Vietnam.[894] This was another example of how the CIA used control of events on the ground to force Kennedy to do what the CIA wanted – by leaving him with little or no choice.[895]

Author Joachim Joesten, in his book *OSWALD: ASSASSIN OR FALL GUY?*, pointed out that:[896]

> "Richard Starnes of the *New York World Telegram and Sun* who, in a courageous column December 11, 1963 dared to challenge former CIA chief Allen Dulles – under the title "Dulles is Shadow on Inquiry," Starnes writes about a conversation he recently had in the Far East with an American official of high rank and immense personal privilege who told Starnes:"[897]

> "I have a Q security clearance, which is the highest anyone can have, and I thought I pretty much knew what was going on. But I've been appalled at what I've seen here. I seriously question whether President Kennedy himself has any effective control over this monstrous bureaucracy."[898]

> "The reference is to the CIA, and if Americans dismiss Mr. Starnes with the thought that the CIA in the Far East is a different outfit than at home, I would remind them that the would-be assassins of President de Gaul also became disaffected in the Far East – in Vietnam, to be precise, where probably the high official (could it be Mr. Lodge?) was functioning when he talked to Starnes."[899]

The CIA was not the only part of the Deep State working against Kennedy. His own State Department and the ambassador he appointed to Saigon, Henry Cabot Lodge, was also doing his best to undermine Kennedy's policies.[900] This proved to be a lethal combination when Lodge showed up in Vietnam.[901] Lodge and the CIA were a long way away from Washington, and they worked together to implement their Vietnam policy regardless of what Kennedy wanted.[902]

Kennedy gave his peace speech on June 10, 1963. The CIA also learned of JFK's intention to end the war in Vietnam.[903] He was also considering putting Robert Kennedy in charge of the CIA and either scaling it back to its legal charter or dissolving it and replacing it with something more in line with what Truman had in mind when he created it.[904] Kennedy was also looking to make peace with Russia and Cuba.[905]

Mark Lane, in his book *LAST WORD*, points out that the CIA bypasses the checks and balances built into the government by the founders who wrote our Constitution.[906] The CIA makes and carries out its own policies often against the wishes of the executive branch and/or Congress, who are typically unaware of what is really going on.[907]

When Kennedy appointed Henry Cabot Lodge as ambassador to Vietnam, he didn't anticipate that Lodge would disobey his direct orders and work against him and with the CIA to undermine his policies in Vietnam.[908] Kennedy wanted Diem in Vietnam to be less repressive of the Buddhist population and to get rid of the Nhus (Diem's brother and sister-in-law Ngo Dinh Nhu and his wife, Madam Nhu) who were the cause of much of the trouble.[909] JFK wanted Lodge to go to Vietnam and meet with Diem and express Kennedy's wishes.[910] That's what he pictured his ambassador doing. Lodge took the job and went to Vietnam, but did almost none of what Kennedy wanted.[911] Lodge and the CIA thought the best policy was to replace Diem with the generals in a coup, and that was the strategy they pursued.[912] CIA Deputy Director Richard Helms at the CIA approved this strategy, and he felt no need to inform his new boss, CIA Director John McCone, before facilitating a coup in Vietnam.[913] Kennedy ended up having to send his friend Torbert Macdonald to bypass his own ambassador and meet with Diem, which Lodge was refusing to do after just having been appointed ambassador to Vietnam by President Kennedy.[914] Torbert Macdonald met with Diem and warned him that he would be killed and to take refuge at the U.S. embassy and get rid of his brother and sister-in-law. Diem would not budge. He refused.[915] Henry Cabot Lodge and the CIA wanted Diem deposed and replaced by the generals. This was not what Kennedy wanted, but the Deep State didn't care what Kennedy wanted. They were in Saigon and Kennedy was in Washington.[916] In September of 1963 Kennedy once again asked his ambassador in Vietnam to resume dialog with Diem, and once again Henry Cabot Lodge refused.[917]

On October 11, 1963 President Kennedy issued National Security Action Memorandum (NSAM) #262 which ordered the withdrawal of one thousand American personnel from Vietnam by the end of 1963 and the rest by the end of 1965.[918] Kennedy wanted to make a start on withdrawing from Vietnam even though they would have to win the 1964 election before he could publicly announce his intention of a complete withdrawal from Vietnam. This was a sensitive issue. Truman and Kennedy had both won by razor-thin margins. Had either of them publicly advocated withdrawal from Vietnam before the election their opponents would have had a field day blasting them as soft on communism. This would likely have swung enough votes to make the difference. President Kennedy knew he had to tread lightly until the next election. On October 13, 1963 President Kennedy had an approval rating of fifty-seven percent.[919] He was overwhelmingly likely to be reelected. However, he needed to have that happen before he could order the complete withdrawal. He knew that, even after the election, he would pay a heavy political price, but he believed it was the right thing to do. The CIA and the Pentagon also knew what JFK intended. The Deep State thought they know better than the duly elected president what needed to be done in Southeast Asia and around the world. Rogue elements in the CIA, accountable to no one, had decided that Kennedy needed to be taken out so they could be allowed to fight the Cold War.[920] Kennedy's moves toward peace with Khrushchev and Castro, his intent to pull out of Vietnam, his cuts in the CIA's budget and responsibilities, his firing of Dulles and refusal to take the advice of the Cold Warriors had all built up to the point where they had reached a decision. They didn't see themselves as bad men, committing murder and treason. They saw themselves as super-patriots, willing to make the hard decisions and do the difficult and dangerous work that their fellow citizens would rather not even know about.

On October 24, 1963 Ambassador Lodge and the CIA found out from the generals in Vietnam that the coup there would take place in November, and Lodge chose to let it happen because that's what he and the CIA wanted.[921] On Saturday, November 2, 1963 Diem was killed during the coup and Kennedy's option of negotiating a withdrawal with Diem was taken off the table.[922] Once again, the CIA had used control of events on the ground to override Kennedy's policy. Kennedy was disgusted upon hearing the news.[923]

Author Mark Lane, in his book LAST WORD, documented that:[924]

> "On October 3, 1963 [Arthur] Krock published an historic column in the *New York Times*. Entitled "The Intra-Administration War in Vietnam," – Krock revealed that the White House had declared war on the CIA and that the CIA was responding. Krock wrote, "the CIA had flatly refused to carry out instructions from ambassador Henry Cabot Lodge" and that in one instance the CIA had "frustrated a plan of action that Mr. Lodge had brought from Washington." The reason was that the CIA "disagreed with it." The issue that caused the CIA such concern was the efforts to end the war in Vietnam."[925]
>
> "Krock wrote that "the CIA's growth" was "likened to a malignancy" that his source, a "very high official," was "not even sure the White House could control … any longer.""[926]

"Krock wrote that by releasing this information the "executive branches have expanded their war against the CIA from the government councils to the American people via the press." Did we listen then? Are we listening now?"[927]

"Here are Arthur Krock's frightening and prophetic words. Relying upon the "high official," certainly with the president's approval, Krock wrote and the *New York Times* published these words:"[928]

"If the United States ever experiences an attempt at a coup to overthrow the government it will come from the CIA."[929]

"The next month Kennedy was assassinated."[930]

Kennedy was going to fire Ambassador Henry Cabot Lodge when he got back from the trip to Dallas.[931]

The CIA Tries to Implicate Cuba and the Soviet Union

The Cold Warriors at the CIA and the Pentagon wanted to fight communism. The Soviet Union was exporting communism and taking over one country after another and the United States, for the sake of national security, needed to fight back. The CIA and the Pentagon wanted a nuclear first strike against Russia to win the Cold War and Kennedy would not agree. JFK was trying to avoid starting World War Three. One of the reasons the CIA and the Pentagon participated in the Kennedy assassination was to get rid of Kennedy so that the CIA and the Pentagon would be unleashed to fight the good fight against communist aggression. If Kennedy's assassin could be seen as connected to Cuba and/or Russia, so much the better. This would give the Cold War crowd at the CIA and the Pentagon the excuse they wanted to invade Cuba and attack the Soviet Union. To this end the CIA tried several ways to implicate Cuba and/or Russia in the Kennedy assassination. Oswald was a creation of the CIA. Since it was their job to supply the patsy, they chose one who could be used to implicate Russia and Cuba. Oswald fit the bill perfectly. He was in the fake defector program so he already had a background of having lived for a while in Russia. He even had a Russian wife he brought back with him. Once back in the United States they had him go to New Orleans in the summer of 1963 to add pro-Castro activities to his resume. This way, once he was convicted posthumously in the court of public opinion of assassinating Kennedy, Russia and Cuba would also be included as scapegoats. This would provide the pretext for launching attacks on Cuba and/or Russia.

Obviously, Oswald was not recruited as a teenager to kill Kennedy. Oswald was recruited as a teenager into the Marines and the fake defector program. Only later was he chosen, partly because he had been in the fake defector program, as the patsy for the Kennedy assassination.

Below are nine sub-sections which go into different aspects of how the CIA set Oswald up to implicate Russia and/or Cuba in the Kennedy assassination.

1. Oswald on the CIA payroll – describes how Oswald was being paid as a CIA agent, starting while in the Marines and continuing until the Kennedy assassination and Oswald's death

2. Oswald's early years – describes how Oswald was recruited as a teenager into becoming a secret agent for the United States to be sent to Russia in the fake defector program

3. Oswald in the Marines – describes how Oswald was prepared for his mission to become a fake defector, including learning Russian and pretending to be a communist during the Cold War

4. Oswald Goes to Russia – describes his first mission as a fake defector in Russia and how he was able to easily go to Russia and how he was easily able to return with help from our government

5. The Bolton Ford Incident – describes how Oswald was being set up for his next mission three years before the Kennedy assassination

6. Oswald in New Orleans – describes the side trip Oswald was sent on in the summer of 1963 to polish his credentials as a pro-Castro communist in preparation for his next big mission

7. Oswald in Mexico City – describes how an Oswald imposter is sent to the Russian and Cuban embassies in Mexico City to apply for visas in Oswald's name – this is an attempt to also implicate the Cubans and the Russians in the assassination of President Kennedy

8. The Letter to the Soviet Embassy – describes how Oswald is alleged to have written a letter to the Soviet Embassy in Washington, D.C. that could later be used to implicate the Russians and the Cubans in the Kennedy assassination

9. Veciana is asked to reach out to his cousin – describes how, even after Johnson is president and had ditched the idea of starting World War Three over the Kennedy assassination, the CIA was still trying to use the JFK assassination as a pretext to invade Cuba and/or attack Russia

Oswald on the CIA Payroll

Oswald was a CIA operative. This is why he was on the CIA payroll. James Wilcott was the CIA finance officer who paid Oswald. When Kennedy was assassinated and Wilcott realized that it was Oswald that he had been paying with CIA money, and that the CIA was involved in the assassination, he quit the CIA in disgust. At the time of the Kennedy assassination, James Wilcott had been working for a few years as a CIA finance officer at the Tokyo CIA station.[932] When Kennedy was assassinated the station went on alert and Wilcott was assigned to security duty with CIA agents who knew Oswald.[933] As they passed the time they talked, and after a little drinking they told Wilcott that the CIA was involved in the Kennedy assassination.[934]

James Douglass, in his book *JFK AND THE UNSPEAKABLE*, quotes Wilcott:[935]

> "At first I thought 'these guys are nuts'" he said "but then a man I knew and had worked with before showed up to take a disbursement and told me Lee Harvey Oswald was a CIA employee. I didn't believe him until he told me the cryptonym under which Oswald had drawn funds when he returned from Russia to the U.S."[936]

Author Douglass points out that the man at the disbursing cage window who revealed the Oswald connection was, Wilcott said, a case officer who supervised agents.[937] The case officer said Wilcott himself had issued an advance on funds for the CIA's Oswald project under the cryptonym. "It was a cryptonym" Wilcott told the house committee "that I was familiar with. It must have been at least two or three times that I had remembered it and it did ring a bell."[938]

Wilcott and his wife both worked for the CIA at the same time. In a 1978 interview with the *San Francisco Chronicle* Jim Wilcott said "It was common knowledge in the Tokyo CIA station that Oswald worked for the Agency."[939] "That's true." Elsie Wilcott said "Right after the president was killed, people in the Tokyo station were talking openly about Oswald having gone to Russia for the CIA. Everyone was wondering how the Agency was going to be able to keep the lid on Oswald, but I guess they did."[940]

In an article based on what he learned at the Tokyo station, Jim Wilcott wrote "Oswald had been trained by the CIA at Atsugi Naval Air Station, a plush, super-secret cover base for Tokyo special operations. Oswald was recruited from the military for the express purpose of

becoming a double-agent assigned to the USSR. More than once I was
told something like 'so-and-so was working on the Oswald project back
in the late 50's.'"[941]

Author Douglass goes on to point out that things in the Kennedy
assassination conspiracy were compartmentalized so that only a few
people knew the big picture.[942] Most people, like Jim Wilcott, were on
a "need to know" basis.[943] Wilcott had no idea until after the
assassination that he had been handing out money to pay someone
involved in the Kennedy assassination.[944] Douglass also points out that
only people like CIA officers Richard Helms and James Jesus Angleton
knew the big picture.[945]

Authors Richard Belzer and David Wayne, in their book *DEAD
WRONG*, point out that William "Tosh" Plumlee said Oswald was U.S.
intelligence.[946] Tosh Plumlee worked for the CIA and he first met
Oswald during his intelligence training for the fake defector program at
Nags Head, North Carolina.[947] Then he saw him again in Hawaii when
Oswald was shipping out for Japan.[948] Then Plumlee saw Oswald yet
again in a safe house in Dallas at a gun running operation for the guys
in the Alpha 66 anti-Castro Cuban exile group.[949] Plumlee was told
Oswald was associated with Office of Naval Intelligence (ONI).[950]
Plumlee was on the mission, a flight into Dallas, to abort the
assassination.[951] Johnny Roselli was on that flight also.[952] Tracy
Barnes was part of the debrief session a few days later to discuss how
the abort mission went wrong.[953] Victor Marchetti was also in the CIA
and he also said Oswald was part of the fake defector program.[954]
Oswald tried to call his Nags Head contact from the Dallas jail just
before he was murdered.[955]

Otto Otepka worked in the State Department in 1960, and he asked CIA
officer Richard Bissell to report back on a list of defectors to see which
ones were fake defectors sent by the CIA.[956] Bissell handed the request
to CIA officer James Jesus Angleton because Angleton's department
was responsible for the fake defector program. Lee Harvey Oswald's
name was on the list.[957] Author James DiEugenio, in his book
DESTINY BETRAYED, describes how:[958]

> "Otepka, who had been an award-winning employee, now saw
> his career slide downhill. And then both his career and his life
> became a Kafkaesque nightmare. He was first taken off of
> sensitive cases. Stories began to appear in the press that his
> job could be eliminated. He was asked to take another
> position in State, but he declined. He was then called before a
> Senate committee to explain his methods for issuing security
> clearances. This happened four times in less than three years.

He still would not resign or suspend his defector investigation. Spies, phone taps and listening devices were then planted in his office. His office started to be searched after hours, and his trash was scoured for any of his notes. Even his house was being surveilled. Otepka could not understand what was happening to him. He could only conclude that the sensitive study of American defectors hidden in his safe was behind it all. That safe was later drilled into after he was thrown out of his original office and reassigned. Whoever drilled it then used a tiny mirror to determine the combination. The safecracker then removed its contents. On November 5, 1963 Otepka was formally removed from his job at state. Later on, author Jim Hougan asked him if he had been able to figure out if Oswald was a real or false defector. Otepka replied "We had not made up our minds when my safe was drilled and we were thrown out of the office." Just two and a half weeks after his forcible departure from State, Oswald, the man he had studied for months on end, was accused of killing President Kennedy."[959]

Oswald also left a lot of circumstantial evidence that he was a CIA agent. Oswald had his passport fast-tracked via teleprinter and granted within 24 hours, a process that normally takes about a week.[960] He also got considerable assistance from the government in returning from Russia, including a loan for the money to travel with.[961] And he faced no consequences for having defected to Russia and offered them top secret information he had gathered while in the U-2 program in Japan. A genuine defector would have faced prosecution.[962] Oswald also had a spy camera not available on the commercial market.[963]

In 1975 Senator Richard Schweiker got a look at some classified documents and said that Oswald had intelligence connections.[964] "Everywhere you look with him you see the fingerprints of intelligence." In 2007 Schweiker said that Oswald was a product of the CIA's fake defector program.[965] Schweiker said that the CIA had never come clean about Oswald.[966]

Oswald's Early Years

Lee Harvey Oswald had a difficult childhood.[967] His mother Marguerite Oswald was a single mom who struggled to keep a roof over their heads.[968] She worked retail jobs and had a hard time making ends meet.[969] Lee was put in an orphanage with his two brothers for a

year when he was three.[970]   His favorite TV show was I Led Three
Lives about an undercover agent.[971]   One of his teachers said "Oswald
was a child of average intelligence and low achievement who
responded to any interest or affection shown him at school."[972]

The Oswalds moved to New Orleans and at age 15 Lee joined the Civil
Air Patrol (CAP) and met pilot David Ferrie.[973]   Ferrie worried that
there was a photo of himself with Oswald in Civil Air Patrol when
Oswald was a cadet there.   The photo surfaced in 1993.[974]   Jerry
Parades was an instructor in the CAP in 1954-55, and Paradis is quoted
as saying "I sure could have told them that Oswald and Ferrie were in
the CAP." He stated that "I specifically remember Oswald.   I can
remember him clearly, and Ferrie was heading the unit then.   I'm not
saying they might have been there together.   I'm saying it is a
certainty."[975]

Ferrie recruited kids into the Marines.[976]   Two former CAP cadets said
that Ferrie had convinced four of them to join the Marines.[977]   Jack
Martin, who worked for the Banister Detective Agency, would tell the
FBI within three days of President Kennedy's assassination that Ferrie
had helped get Oswald into the Marine Corps.[978]

Oswald tried to sign up for the Marines while still underage.   When this
didn't work he studied his brother's Marine Corps manual until he
knew it backwards.   He joined the Marines six days after his
seventeenth birthday.[979]

Oswald in the Marines

Oswald spent his time in the Marines learning Russian and preparing
for the next phase of his mission as part of a fake defector program. He
pretended to be a Marxist and was allowed to immerse himself in
Russian culture while working at a secret CIA base at the height of the
Cold War.   Had he been a real Marxist or truly interested in
communism he would have been disciplined. Because he was training
to become a double agent his study of Russian language and culture
was not only tolerated, it was encouraged. He was sent to Russian
language school while in the Marines.

This section is organized into five sub-sections:

1.   Oswald's Odd Absences – as typical of intelligence agents in
     the military, Oswald had long absences that were thinly veiled
     by made-up medical excuses to be gone for other training

2. Oswald and the U-2 program – Oswald worked at a secret CIA U-2 base while in the Marines. At that time the U-2 was a secret spy plane in the era before there were spy satellites.

3. Oswald's Other Job – while in the Marines one of his "other" assignments was to pass disinformation to the Russians via the attractive Japanese hostesses at a club in Tokyo

4. The Military Teaches Oswald Russian – this was in preparation for his mission as a fake defector

5. Oswald's Marxism is tolerated – at the height of the Cold War, Marine Oswald is openly spouting Marxist ideology – this was tolerated because Oswald was preparing for his next mission

Oswald's Odd Absences

Oswald had some odd absences while in the military. This is typical of intelligence operatives.

While serving at Keesler Air Force Base, Oswald was thought to be using his weekend passes to go home to New Orleans.[980] However, his mother had since moved to Texas and Oswald did not visit his other relatives in New Orleans at that time.[981]

Oswald would also have long stretches on his service record where he was listed as being absent for medical reasons that didn't make sense. At one point he was flown from Taiwan to Atsugi for a minor ailment which could have easily been treated in Taiwan.[982] Author Anthony Summers, in his book *NOT IN YOUR LIFETIME*, points out that military intelligence operatives frequently use medical reasons as a cover for long absences which have to be officially explained.[983] What was really going on was either secret training or a mission of some sort.

Oswald and the U-2 Program

The U-2 was a (then) secret spy plane developed by the CIA to fly high in the atmosphere and take photographs of places where we had no access to before the advent of spy satellites. While in the Marines Oswald worked at a secret CIA U-2 base at Atsugi, Japan.[984] Oswald had a secret clearance to work on the U-2 program because he had access to classified information.[985]

John Donovan knew Oswald in the Marines and was Oswald's commanding officer for a while.[986] Donovan was ready to testify about Oswald and the U-2 program and the Warren Commission didn't want to talk about the U-2 program that Oswald worked on.[987] They went out of their way to avoid the subject.[988]

Oswald's Other Job in the Marines

One of Oswald's 'other' jobs while in the Marines was to pass disinformation to the Russians.[989] There was an expensive bar in Tokyo called the Queen Bee which featured very attractive Japanese women.[990] Some of them worked for the Russians and their job was to gather information from the American servicemen who frequented the place.[991] Oswald's 'other' job was to pass disinformation to them. Oswald spent many nights in the Queen Bee and other bars like it.[992] A night at the Queen Bee cost more than Marine Oswald made in a month, yet he never seemed to lack for money to go to the clubs.[993]

The Military Teaches Oswald Russian

Oswald began trying to learn Russian while still in Japan.[994] He was given leave to spend time with a very attractive female tutor to learn Russian.[995] Dan Powers was one of his fellow Marines and he saw Oswald in the company of the beautiful Eurasian woman while off the base and commented on it to Oswald.[996] Oswald told him the woman was half Russian and was teaching him the Russian language.[997] Oswald didn't do well on a Russian language test in February of 1959, but by that summer he could converse in Russian.[998] His quick jump in Russian language skills was because Oswald learned Russian at the Monterey Army Language School, later known as the DLI (Defense Language Institute).[999]

Oswald's Marxism is Tolerated

Any other Marine who, at the height of the Cold War, had been spouting Marxism would have been a discipline problem. However, Oswald's Marxism was tolerated because he was preparing for his next mission as a fake defector to the Soviet Union.

Oswald had his name written in Russian on one of his jackets and his Marine buddies sometimes called him Comrade Oswaldskovich, which Oswald thought was very funny.[1000] Oswald himself often joked about his obsession with Russian culture and language.[1001]

Nelson Delgado was Oswald's roommate at El Toro Marine air base in California.[1002] He asked Oswald about his obsession with Marxism and things Russian "They let you get away with this in the Marine Corps, in a site like this?"[1003] Captain Block, a Marine officer, asked Oswald about his reading Russian books and playing Russian records and Oswald replied that he was in conformance with Marine Corps policy.[1004] The matter was dropped.[1005]

Researcher and author Mark Lane interviewed James Botelho, who was Oswald's roommate at Santa Ana, California while they were in the Marines together.[1006] Botelho said "I'm very conservative now" (in 1978) "and I was at least as conservative at that time. Oswald was not a communist or a Marxist. If he was I would have taken violent action against him, and so would many of the other Marines in the unit."[1007]

Botelho eventually became a judge, and Judge Botelho said Oswald's 'defection' was nothing but a U.S. intelligence ploy:[1008]

> "I knew Oswald was not a communist, and was in fact anti-Soviet. Then when no real investigation occurred at the base, after Oswald's presence in the Soviet Union was made public, I was sure that Oswald was on an intelligence assignment in Russia. Two civilians dropped in at Santa Ana, asked a few questions, took no written statements and recorded no interviews with witnesses. It was the most casual of investigations. It was a cover investigation so that it could be said there was an investigation. Oswald, it was said, was the only Marine to defect from his country to another country, a communist country, during peacetime. That was a major event. When the Marine Corps and American intelligence decided not to probe the reasons for the defection, I knew then what I know now. Oswald was on an assignment in Russia for American intelligence."[1009]

While in the Marines at El Toro Oswald bragged to a friend named David Bucknell that, after he was discharged, he was going undercover to Russia and would come home a hero.[1010] In a letter home to his brother, Oswald wrote "Pretty soon I'll be getting out of the Corps, and I know what I want to be and how I'm going to be it."[1011]

Oswald Goes to Russia

Oswald went to Russia as a fake defector, but he failed to convince the Russians that he was a real defector. His hosts did assign a woman to keep an eye on him and Oswald decided to marry Marina and bring her back to America with him. Oswald was by then a spy. He was able to quickly get a hardship discharge, supposedly to be with his ailing mother, but this was just for show.[1012] Oswald was going on his next mission, in this case to Russia as a fake defector. Oswald filed his petition for a hardship discharge on August 17, claiming he needed to go home to support his mother because she needed medical attention.[1013] This was approved in only ten days, when the normal time was three to six months.[1014] And in fact, his mother was not in dire need of medical attention.[1015] She had earlier claimed to be hurt by a candy jar falling on her nose while working one of her retail jobs.[1016] His mother was supposedly in such dire need of medical attention that the Marines let him out early, but then Oswald only spent one day with his 'ailing' mother before departing for Russia.[1017] For a Marine supposedly traveling on a budget, Oswald traveled first class, staying (for example) in the finest hotels in Finland.[1018] There were a lot of fake defectors around the same time as Oswald, and they also followed the same route.[1019]

Since the Marines are technically part of the U.S. Navy, The Office of Naval Intelligence (ONI) is the group that keeps track of Marines who become spies. The ONI is in turn controlled by the CIA, and at that time the department of the CIA that was responsible for managing the ONI was run by CIA officer James Jesus Angleton.[1020] (See the subsection on James Jesus Angleton). Oswald had his fake defector training in Nags Head, North Carolina and his handler was located there.[1021] As a spy known to the ONI, Oswald was able to keep his security clearance, even though he publicly stated that he was a defector to the Soviet Union at the height of the Cold War.[1022]

On October 1, 1959 Oswald went to the U.S. embassy in Moscow and announced that he wanted to defect.[1023] Normally an ex-marine with sensitive knowledge would have been locked up immediately.[1024] As usual Oswald glided through this and other incidents which would have been roadblocks for anyone doing this without the CIA behind them.

For an enlisted man to defect should have caused a damage assessment. For two enlisted men who defected (for real) before Oswald and for two who defected after Oswald, there were damage assessments.[1025] In Oswald's case, there was no damage assessment.[1026] This is because he was a known spy and not a real defector.

Oswald almost had his fake defector mission cut short because the Russians didn't believe him to be a real defector and didn't want him to stay.[1027] Oswald promptly slit his wrist in such a way that he would be found and have to go to a hospital.[1028] The Russians relented and allowed him to stay, but they sent him to Minsk, 450 miles away from Moscow.[1029]

At the beginning of 1961 Oswald was trying to return to the United States. He was asking the U.S. State Department to give him back his passport.[1030] About this time Oswald met Marina and they started dating and then got engaged and married.[1031] In June of 1961 Oswald told Marina he was trying to return home.[1032] Then he told the U.S. and Soviet authorities about his marriage to Marina.[1033] The State Department gave him back his passport and even loaned him the money for the return trip.[1034]

On June 13, 1962 Oswald, with Marina and their baby, arrived in the U.S. at Hoboken, New Jersey.[1035] When the Oswalds arrived in the U.S. they were greeted by Spas T. Raikin, a representative of the Traveler's Aid Society.[1036] Raikin was, at that same time, Secretary General of the American Friends of the Anti-Bolshevik Nations, an anti-communist organization with extensive intelligence connections, including the U.S. Army Intelligence, the FBI and anti-communist activists headquartered in New Orleans in the same building where Oswald will soon be working out of.[1037] With Raikin's help the Oswalds passed smoothly through U.S. customs and immigration.[1038] From there they went to Fort Worth where Oswald got a job and eventually met one of his CIA babysitters, George de Mohrenschildt.[1039] On October 11, 1962 Oswald got a job at the Jaggars Chiles Stovall Company who were doing work for the U.S. Army map service which involved information obtained from U-2 spy flights.[1040]

Oswald could easily have been prosecuted under espionage laws upon his return to the U.S. from Russia due to his statements about passing secrets to the Russians[1041] Had Oswald been a genuine defector he would have been prosecuted.[1042]

On November 10, 1960 the Office of Naval Intelligence (ONI) office got involved again, transferring and forwarding Oswald's intelligence file from Glenview, Illinois to Algiers, Louisiana (near New Orleans).[1043]

On April 16, 1963 Oswald was in touch with the head of the Fair Play for Cuba Committee (F.P.C.C.) on his activities in Dallas and requested more literature to pass out.[1044] This was because he had been told to polish up his pro-Castro credentials in preparation for his next mission.

The Bolton Ford Incident

The Bolton Ford incident is important because it shows that Oswald was being set up almost three years before the assassination. The Bolton Ford dealership was in New Orleans and the incident happened while Oswald was still in Russia.

In Jim Garrison's book *ON THE TRAIL OF THE ASSASSINS*, he describes how Oswald's name was used at the Bolton Ford dealership on North Claiborne Avenue in New Orleans.[1045] Salesmen Fred Sewell and Oscar Deslatte said that two men claiming to represent Friends of Democratic Cuba arrived at the Bolton dealership on January 20, 1961, three months before the Bay of Pigs fiasco.[1046] One of the men was Latin and the other was a thin young Anglo-Saxon who obviously was in charge.[1047] They said they wanted to buy ten Ford pickup trucks, and they wanted a bid from Bolton Ford.[1048] The Latin identified himself as Joseph Moore but said the bid had to be in the name of Oswald.[1049] The young Anglo-Saxon confirmed that and said that he was the one with the money.[1050] Instead of asking the buyers to sign, Deslatte himself printed the name Oswald on the form.[1051] The real Lee Oswald was in the Soviet Union that day, and would be for more than another year.[1052] Following Kennedy's assassination, Sewell and Deslatte called the FBI, and the FBI agents picked up the bid form carefully with tongs.[1053] One of the incorporators of the Friends of Democratic Cuba was Guy Bannister.[1054] Guy Banister was the ex-FBI agent who was using his private detective agency in New Orleans as a front for the CIA. See the section on Guy Banister.

Oswald in New Orleans

Oswald was told that his next mission was to go to Cuba as a fake defector to kill Castro. His job was to get close enough to Castro to either kill him or have him killed with a fast-acting cancer bioweapon the CIA developed in secret labs in New Orleans in the summer of 1963. Oswald was told that, in order to get a Cuban visa to be able to travel to Cuba, he needed to pretend to be pro-Castro. Since he had been spouting Marxism since he was a teenager and had lived in Russia, the next phase of his preparation for the mission to kill Castro was to polish up his pro-Castro credentials. So, Oswald was told to go to New Orleans in the spring and summer of 1963 to start a chapter of the Fair Play for Cuba Committee, pass out leaflets, and cause some incidents where he would be officially recorded by the press while doing these things. He was told that his would help on the next phase of his mission, which was to be sent once again as a fake defector, this time to Cuba. His real mission was to be the patsy in the Kennedy assassination, but that's not what Oswald was told. He was told to be seen as a pro-Castro activist and then he was told to go back to Dallas. This was ultimately done to implicate Castro and perhaps Russia in the assassination of Kennedy. Since the CIA was supplying the patsy, they were going to supply one with Cuban and Soviet Russian communist connections. This would allow the Cold Warriors who were controlling Oswald to justify an attack on Cuba and/or the Soviet Union.

Author Phillip Nelson, in his book *LBJ: THE MASTERMIND OF THE JFK ASSASSINATION*, claims that CIA officer Bill Harvey met with CIA contractor Guy Banister in 1962.[1055] He points out that Harvey and CIA officer James Jesus Angleton were setting Oswald up to be the patsy in the Kennedy assassination.[1056]

On April 24, 1963 Oswald was laid off from Jaggars Chiles Stovall and tells his wife he is going to New Orleans to look for work and that she should follow in a few weeks.[1057] He temporarily moves in with his aunt and uncle Charles "Dutz" Murret, who is a shipyard worker and a bookie in the mafia organization of Carlos Marcello.[1058]

Jim Garrison also points out in his book *ON THE TRAIL OF THE ASSASSINS*, that in the spring of 1963 an Oswald impersonator applied in person to dozens of potential employers in New Orleans.[1059] His height was listed at 5' 9" when the real Oswald was 5' 11".[1060] The impersonator had Oswald's 'chicken-scrawl' handwriting down, but had to put his own height on the forms because he was there in person.[1061] This was done to pretend that Oswald looked for work in New Orleans.

On May 9, 1963 Oswald's handlers got him a fake job at the Reily Coffee Company, which is little more than a front for the CIA. Oswald's job there was a cover for his real activities. The owner, William B. Reily, was a wealthy supporter of the CIA-sponsored Cuban Revolutionary Council.[1062] Author James Douglass points out in his book *JFK AND THE UNSPEAKABLE*, that researcher William Davey found a declassified government document which showed that Reily's Coffee company had been part of the CIA's New Orleans network since 1949.[1063] According to a CIA memorandum dated January 1, 1964, this firm (Reily's) was of interest as of 1949.[1064] In a 1968 interview with the New Orleans District Attorney's office, CIA contract employee Jerry Patrick Hemming confirmed that William Reily had worked for the CIA for years.[1065] The Reily Coffee Company was located at the center of the U.S. intelligence community in New Orleans, close by the offices of the CIA, FBI, Secret Service and Office of Naval Intelligence (ONI).[1066] Directly across the street from Naval Intelligence and the Secret Service was another office that Oswald worked in, the private detective agency of former FBI agent Guy Banister.[1067] Jim Garrison documents in his book *ON THE TRAIL OF THE ASSASSINS*, that, once Oswald was gone, all the folks who worked with Oswald at the Reily Coffee Company left and went to work at NASA in New Orleans.[1068] This is because NASA was providing temporary employment for CIA folks who were in between assignments.

Oswald's girlfriend in New Orleans was Judyth Vary Baker, and she was working on a fast-acting cancer for use on Castro which they later used on Jack Ruby.[1069]

This section is organized into four sub-sections:

1. Setting Up Shop at 544 Camp Street – describes how Guy Banister's office was the center of activity for everything the "intelligence community" (CIA, FBI, etc.) were doing in New Orleans in 1963 and how Oswald used that as his "headquarters" for his pro-Castro activities

2. Handing out F.P.C.C. Leaflets – describes how Oswald was adding pro-Castro activities to his resume to allow him show the Cuban embassy that he should be given a Cuban visa

3. Oswald Creates an Incident – describes how Oswald got arrested to get his name in the news to add to his pro-Castro activist credentials

4. Judyth Vary Baker – was Oswald's girlfriend while he was in New Orleans – through her account we were able to learn more about why Oswald was doing what he was in New Orleans in the summer of 1963

Setting Up Shop at 544 Camp Street

Guy Banister had his office at 544 Camp Street. Banister was a former FBI Agent who, in the early 1960's, worked both for the FBI and the CIA. Guy Banister Associates appeared to be a private detective agency. Jack Martin worked for Guy Banister. Martin's job was to handle any actual private detective work for people who just happened to see that there was a private detective agency there and needed a private detective. This was done to keep up appearances.

Guy Banister Associates was a hub for covert U.S. Intelligence operations. There were anti-Castro Cuban exiles who needed to be organized and supplied with weapons. There were guns and ammunition all over the offices. There were nearby training camps for the anti-Castro Cubans and they stopped by Guy Banister Associates on their way to and from the camps. Daniel Campbell was an ex-Marine hired by Banister to help with the volume of traffic in small arms for the Cubans.[1070] David Ferrie was a pilot who worked at Guy Banister Associates. He was listed as an 'investigator.' In fact, Ferrie worked for the CIA and the mafia (Carlos Marcello).

Guy Banister had Oswald set up shop in a room upstairs at Banister's 544 Camp Street office. Oswald even stamped the 544 Camp Street address on some of the Fair Play for Cuba Committee (F.P.C.C.) flyers he handed out. Later, both Banister's secretary and her daughter will be among the many people who identified Oswald as working upstairs at Guy Banister's office at 544 Camp Street. Banister was virulently anti-communist, anti-Kennedy, and anti-Castro. When his secretary asked him why Oswald, working out of Banister's office, is handing out pro-Castro leaflets, he told her not to worry about it.[1071]

Handing out F.P.C.C. Leaflets

In the meantime, Oswald gets on with what he has been told was his real job. Oswald had been told his job was to make himself look like a pro-Castro communist. On May 26, 1963 Oswald got in touch with the Fair Play for Cuba Committee (F.P.C.C.) about opening a New Orleans chapter.[1072] On May 29, 1963 at the Jones Printing Company, next to Reily Coffee, Oswald ordered a thousand handbills for the F.P.C.C.[1073] Some of the handbills were hand-stamped with the address 544 Camp Street, which is the office of ex-FBI agent Guy Banister and his 'investigator' David Ferrie.[1074] On June 16, 1963 Oswald was seen on the dock passing out leaflets to sailors from the aircraft carrier U.S.S. Wasp.[1075] On August 16, 1963 Oswald went to the International Trade Mart in New Orleans with two hired hands and handed out pro-Castro leaflets and got recorded doing it.[1076] This was Oswald doing his 'job.'

Oswald Creates an Incident

Oswald needed to create an incident so that he had some published record of his pro-Castro activities to point to. To do this he worked with another CIA-sponsored operative, Carlos Bringuier. Bringuier was an anti-Castro Cuban exile and a member of the CIA-supported Student Revolutionary Directorate. Oswald wrote to the Fair Play for Cuba Committee and described the confrontation he got into with Carlos.[1077] The letter was sent five days before the actual confrontation occurred, on August 4, 1963, so Oswald knew ahead of time that he was going to stage the confrontation.[1078]

Oswald made a trip to a men's clothing store to see Carlos Bringuier on August 5, 1963. This was a setup so Oswald and Bringuier could get into an altercation a few days later so Oswald could get noticed by getting arrested as a pro-Castro activist.[1079]

On August 9, 1963 Oswald gets 'attacked' by anti-Castro Cubans led by Carlos Bringuier while handing out literature with the 544 Camp Street address printed on it. Oswald and Carlos Bringuier knew each other and worked out the 'attack' in advance, then Oswald spent the night in jail.[1080]

A week after Oswald was released from jail, he was back passing out more leaflets. He was interviewed by local radio commentator William Stuckey, who invited him to debate Bringuier on the radio.[1081] On August 21, 1963 Oswald and Bringuier appear on the radio in New Orleans.[1082]

Oswald had succeeded in his task of getting noticed as a pro-Castro communist activist. This was exactly what he has been told to do.

Judyth Vary Baker

Judyth Vary Baker had an affair with Oswald while he was in New Orleans. Because they fell in love and he confided in her, we have a window into what Oswald was doing in New Orleans, some of what he was thinking and his motives for his actions.

Judyth Vary Baker was a brilliant high school student who was doing groundbreaking cancer research while still in high school.[1083] She was invited to do advanced work at the best laboratories in the country and guided to work on secret projects having to do with the Cold War and the effort to keep ahead of the Russians.[1084] Dr. Alton Ochsner was a famous doctor based in New Orleans who was the first to find a link between smoking and cancer. He was also a sponsor of Judyth Baker and virulently anti-communist. He invited Judyth to come to New Orleans in the spring of 1963 when she was 19 years old.[1085] She was promised a scholarship and entrance to medical school.[1086] She agreed to come to work for Ochsner for the summer of 1963.[1087]

Ochsner was in charge of a secret CIA project to create a bioweapon, in this case a fast-acting cancer intended to be used on Castro as a means of killing him with plausible deniability.[1088] If Castro died of cancer, the United States could pretend not to be involved. Castro would appear to have died of natural causes. Oswald was assigned to work on the project along with researcher Dr. Mary Sherman, pilot David Ferrie, CIA contractor Clay Shaw, Judyth Vary Baker and others, all under the direction of Dr. Ochsner.[1089] They had a secret laboratory that consisted of several locations around New Orleans where they worked on developing the fast-acting cancer bioweapon, first in mice and then in monkeys and, eventually, in humans.

Judyth Baker and Lee Oswald both had cover jobs at the Reily Coffee Company while they worked to develop the fast-acting cancer.[1090] Oswald's cover job was as a maintenance man and Judy's was as a secretary.[1091] Oswald also needed to learn how to safely handle the cancer so he could transport it to Cuba for use on Castro.[1092] Baker was spending most of her time working on the cancer project with Dr. Mary Sherman while Oswald and Ferrie were working on the cancer project and also working out of Banister's office running guns and supplies to the Cubans. At the same time Oswald was establishing his pro-Castro credentials in preparation for the mission to Cuba to deliver the cancer bioweapon to kill Castro. Clay Shaw was also involved. Shaw was a CIA contractor who was involved in the cancer project and also the gun smuggling operation, among other things.

When Judy first arrived and she had only met Oswald and Ferrie but had yet to meet Dr. Ochsner, and she wanted reassurance that they were indeed working for the government. So, Oswald took Baker to meet Guy Banister at his office at 544 Camp Street and Banister confirmed that Oswald was working on an official government project.[1093]

Oswald also showed Baker where they stored all the guns and other military supplies for the anti-Castro Cuban exiles they were training and equipping.[1094] Later Judy did meet with Dr. Ochsner.[1095] Lee and Judyth were in love, but Baker had a fiancé and Oswald was married. Oswald admitted he beat his wife, so Judyth went ahead and married Robert Baker.[1096] Robert Baker was only there for a day or so when they got married and then he was gone and she was left in New Orleans.[1097] Then Oswald took her to meet Dr. Ochsner, and Oswald went with her and talked to Ochsner first.[1098]

Jack Ruby was a mafia functionary in Dallas who worked for mafia boss Carlos Marcello in New Orleans. Ruby, whose nickname was "Sparky," came to New Orleans for a visit with Oswald and met Judyth and pointed out that he had known Oswald since he a young boy.[1099]

Marina Oswald showed up in New Orleans for a while. When Marina and Lee would fight Lee would come to Judyth Baker's rooming house.[1100] CIA contractor Clay Shaw, who was working on the bioweapon project, was sympathetic to the young lovers and arranged hotel rooms for Lee and Judy to use.[1101] Judyth understood that the mafia and the CIA were working together to use the fast-acting cancer as a means of killing Castro. Oswald told Judy his next mission was to kill Castro.[1102] Oswald told Judyth Baker that the plan was to give the fast-acting cancer to friendly doctors in Cuba to give to Castro.[1103] At one point the cancer bioweapon wasn't working fast enough and Baker came up with the idea of using X-rays to reduce Castro's immune system to allow the cancer to work faster.[1104]

Oswald and Baker realized that some of the people they were working with also wanted to kill President Kennedy. The Kennedy policy of having promised not to invade Cuba was seen as one of the main reasons to want to kill JFK. Most of the group were virulently anti-communist and anti-Castro and hated Kennedy's policy of not invading Cuba. Oswald and Baker thought that if they were able to finish the cancer project to kill Castro soon enough, perhaps the anti-Kennedy crowd would be satisfied and would decide that there was no need to kill Kennedy.[1105] The idea was that the mafia, the CIA and the military wanted Castro out of power and perhaps if Castro died they would not feel the need to kill Kennedy.[1106]

Oswald worked with Guy Banister in uncovering student radicals.[1107] At the same time Oswald was working on his pro-Castro credentials. He did this by getting arrested while supporting Castro so that the publicity created by that would help him to be better able to get a Cuban visa so he could enter Cuba as a double-agent.[1108] Oswald was told he was going to be bringing the cancer bioweapon to either Mexico

City or Cuba.[1109] Oswald was fired from Reily because Reily was a right-wing outfit and he was pretending to be a left-wing, pro-Castro activist.[1110]

Once the fast-acting cancer was working on mice and then monkeys, the next assignment was to experiment on prisoners from Angola, the big Louisiana state prison. The idea was to use the prisoners as human guinea pigs. This caused the Clinton incident and also caused Baker to be disowned by Dr. Ochsner. The group working on the cancer project were on their way to Jackson and stopped in Clinton.

August 28, 1963 was the freedom march in Washington, D.C. by Martin Luther King, Jr. and others, and this encouraged black people to demand their right to vote. This led to voter registration drives in many places around the country, including the town of Clinton, Louisiana. Clay Shaw, Lee Oswald and David Ferrie were spotted in the town of Clinton, Louisiana. Later, when Kennedy was assassinated, people remembered the incident. Their visit to Clinton was actually a visit to the state mental hospital in Jackson. They just planned to wait in Clinton by a phone booth for a call to join with the convoy with the prisoners on its way from Angola to Jackson and arrive with the convoy at the hospital because this would be easier to explain than arriving at separate times.[1111] The Clinton 'incident' happened because Shaw, Ferrie and Oswald were on their way to Jackson, but stopped to wait in Clinton because they thought they would be less conspicuous waiting in Clinton for the convoy.[1112] This tactic backfired because there was a black voter registration drive in Clinton that day, the convoy was hours delayed and while they sat there they were spotted and people remembered them later.[1113]

Baker had been told that there was only one human guinea pig and he was a volunteer.[1114] Then she found out that there were in fact multiple human subjects and none of them were volunteers.[1115] Baker wasn't OK with that so she wrote to Dr. Ochsner, who was in charge of the project, protesting the use of human beings on the grounds that they were unaware that they were being used in an experiment that involved live cancer cells that would kill them.[1116] Dr. Ochsner called Baker and was furious, screaming at her that she never should have written anything down, that she should have objected verbally, and he told her that both she and Lee Oswald were expendable.[1117]

The experiments on the prisoners from Angola Prison took place at the state mental hospital in Jackson, not far from Clinton.[1118] The prisoners were delivered to the state hospital in Jackson and experimented on, and the combination of high doses of X-rays and the fast-acting cancer caused the prisoners to have a fatal dose of cancer after 72 hours. Within a month the first prisoner died. This was considered a success.

Lee Oswald told Judyth Baker that the Kennedy assassination was happening because of Billie Sol Estes and Bobby Baker and to remember those names.[1119] And on November 20, 1963 he also told her to remember Bishop (a fake name) was really CIA officer David Atlee Phillips, and that he was involved in the JFK assassination.[1120] Maurice Bishop was an alias that David Atlee Phillips used.

President John F. Kennedy was assassinated on November 22, 1963 in Dallas.

After the Kennedy assassination pilot David Ferrie called Judyth Baker and told her it had all gone wrong and also for her to keep quiet, that they were going to try to get Oswald and fly him out of there. Then she watched the whole thing on TV, and she saw Jack Ruby shoot Oswald on national television.[1121]

Ferrie then called Judyth again and said for her to keep quiet or she would be killed. He told her to become a nobody or be killed. This meant do not become a famous doctor or a famous anything. Just keep a low profile or be murdered, so she kept her secrets for forty years.[1122]

Oswald in Mexico City

Less than two months before Kennedy was murdered, the CIA again attempted to implicate Cuba and the Soviet Union in the assassination. This was done by having an Oswald imposter show up at the Cuban and Soviet Russian embassies in Mexico City and apply for visas to go to the Soviet Union via Cuba. That way, when they blame Oswald for the assassination of Kennedy, they will have a pretext to invade Cuba.

Oswald was in Mexico City, supposedly applying to both the Soviet embassy and the Cuban consulate for visas to get to Cuba. The idea was that he was applying to the Soviet embassy for a visa and to the Cuban embassy for a transit visa on the theory was that he was going to stop by Cuba on the way to the Soviet Union. The plan fell apart on several levels. The Cubans would not issue a transit visa without first seeing the visa from the Soviet Union and the Soviet embassy had a process that would take weeks if not months to issue a visa. So, no transit visa could be issued by the Cuban consulate in the few days he was there. This worked fine for the conspirators because they never intended for Oswald to go to Cuba. He was going to die right after

Kennedy was murdered. They just wanted him to be seen applying for the visas. But there was another problem. The person there claiming to be Oswald was not Oswald. This was also not a problem for the conspirators.

The visit of an Oswald impersonator to the Soviet and Cuban missions in Mexico City was an attempt by the conspirators to implicate the Cubans and Soviets in the Kennedy assassination. This would give the CIA and the Pentagon a handy excuse to, at a minimum, invade Cuba. It might even lead to war with Russia. The original plan was for Oswald to be shot while resisting arrest for the murder of Kennedy. With Oswald dead there would be no live Oswald to compare to the recording of the fake Oswald coming and going from the Soviet embassy in Mexico City. But then Oswald messed up the plan by not being killed on schedule. Then the recording of the Oswald in Mexico City came to light and it became obvious that the imposter didn't match the real Oswald. Then the CIA had to change its "official" story.

The Oswald Imposter

The pictures and recordings of "Oswald" were not of Oswald – it was an imposter chosen by the CIA.[1123]

On November 23, 1963 at 10:01 AM Johnson received a phone briefing on Oswald from FBI Director J. Edgar Hoover. It included the following exchange:[1124]

> LBJ: "Have you established any more about the visit to the Soviet embassy in September?"[1125]
>
> Hoover: "No. That's one angle that's very confusing for this reason – we have up here the tape and the photograph of the man who was at the Soviet embassy using Oswald's name. That picture and the tape do not correspond to this man's voice nor to his appearance. In other words, it appears that there is a second person who was at the Soviet embassy down there."[1126]

This phone exchange proves several things. First, it proves that there was an Oswald impersonator in Mexico City. Second, it proves that, since there was more than one person involved with Oswald in the Kennedy assassination, there was a conspiracy. Third, it proves that Hoover and Johnson both knew that there was a conspiracy.

Oswald took Continental Trailways bus number 5133 in the early morning hours of September 26, 1963 to Mexico, and on the way, he made a point of talking to people about his background.[1127]

Other people who interacted with the Oswald impersonator in Mexico said that he did not match the real Lee Harvey Oswald. Anthony Summers, in his book *NOT IN YOUR LIFETIME*, describes how, when he was a law student in Mexico City's National University in 1963, Oscar Contreras was talking with some friends when a man came by and introduced himself.[1128] The man was careful to spell out his name.[1129] He did this so they would remember it later and be able to implicate Oswald. Contreras, who was himself 5' 9" clearly recalled looking down at the man, so he could not have been the real Lee Harvey Oswald who was taller.[1130]

Summers also describes how Eusebio Azcue was at the Cuban consulate when a man came in claiming to be Oswald. Azcue assumed when Kennedy was assassinated that the Lee Harvey Oswald arrested in Dallas was the same guy who showed up at the consulate. Then, a few weeks later, Azcue watched a cinema news reel that included scenes of Oswald under arrest for murder and being shot and killed by Jack Ruby.[1131] Those pictures of the alleged assassin, the former consul told the House Assassinations Committee in 1978, in no way resembled the man who had shown up in his office.[1132] Azcue remembered the visitor as about 35 years old, of medium height with features quite different from the authentic Oswald.[1133] The film, as Azcue said, shows a young man with a youthful, unlined face which was, according to the consul, dramatically different from the deeply lined face of the man who, he said, came asking for a visa.[1134] The Lee Oswald arrested in Dallas was just twenty-four, five foot, nine and a half inches tall and very slim. Shown still photographs of the authentic Oswald, Azcue continued to say he believed "this gentleman was not, is not the person or the individual who went to the consulate."[1135]

On October 1, 1963 Oswald decided to leave Mexico City.[1136]

Sylvia Duran worked at the Cuban Consulate in Mexico City when the Oswald impersonator showed up looking for a visa.[1137] When she was shown film of the real Lee Harvey Oswald she said it was not the man who she met in Mexico City because the man she met with was shorter than the real Oswald and had blonde hair.[1138] The CIA wanted someone to identify the impersonator as Oswald, so they told the Mexican authorities to arrest Sylvia Duran.[1139] She was arrested and brutally interrogated and told to keep quiet about it. When she was released she started talking so the CIA had her arrested again.[1140] The CIA wanted to make sure that the Mexican authorities took responsibility for her arrest and interrogation.[1141] The CIA did not want anyone to know that all this was being done at the request of the United States.[1142] Duran was still not positive in her identification of Oswald.[1143]

The CIA Story Changes

In 1963 David Atlee Phillips was in charge of CIA operations against the Cuban embassy in Mexico City.[1144] Mark Lane, in his book *LAST WORD: MY INDICTMENT OF THE CIA IN THE MURDER OF JFK*, points out that Phillips was assured that the patsy would not be alive to dispute the facts.[1145] This was important because Phillips was arranging for an Oswald imposter to be in Mexico City to apply for visas to Cuba and Russia.[1146]

The plan was for Oswald to be killed while being arrested shortly after Kennedy was assassinated. Since Oswald didn't die on schedule this presented multiple problems for the conspirators. One of these problems was that, now that Oswald was alive and talking to the media who crowded into the Dallas Police Headquarters, everyone knew what he looked and sounded like. This made it difficult, if not impossible, to claim that the imposter who showed up at the Russian embassy in Mexico City was Oswald. There was a recording of everyone who called and pictures of everyone who came and went. Had Oswald died on schedule they would likely have been able to bury the discrepancies.[1147] He lived, and this created a problem. Now the CIA had to change their story, and this became somewhat of an embarrassment.

The CIA had arranged alternatives in case the "lone gunman" theory failed to convince people – they were going to blame Cuba or Russia or the mafia as fallbacks.[1148] The whole idea was to have multiple layers of protection so the blame didn't fall on the CIA.[1149] David Atlee Phillips established the legend that Oswald had been to Mexico City during September of 1963, from September 26 through October 3, 1963.[1150]

The CIA first said that, on October 1, 1963, Lee Oswald contacted the Soviet Embassy in Mexico City.[1151] It later sends the Warren Commission a photograph of someone, who is not Oswald, entering the embassy.[1152] After that the CIA said it was all just a mistake.[1153]

Once the CIA saw that no one was buying the Oswald trip to Mexico City angle (and by implication the "let's start a war with Cuba" angle), the CIA started backpedaling on the "Oswald in Mexico City" scenario because it was more likely to implicate the CIA than Cuba or Russia.[1154]

The CIA Mexico City station started the backpedaling by saying that its audio tapes of the Oswald phone calls to the Soviet embassy had been routinely destroyed and therefore no voice comparisons were possible to determine if the speaker really was Oswald.[1155] This was another lie because the FBI was already listening to the tapes of the Oswald phone calls, so they still existed at that time.[1156]

Later, CIA officer David Atlee Phillips testified to the House Select Committee on Assassinations (HSCA) that on October 8, 1963 he signed off on a cable to CIA headquarters reporting Oswald's visit to the Soviet Embassy in Mexico City.[1157] This was yet another lie because records surfaced showing he was on leave at the JM/WAVE CIA station in Miami and didn't return until October 9, 1963 so he could not have signed off on the cable from Mexico City.[1158]

On November 27, 1976 David Atlee Phillips was questioned by the HSCA about his role in the CIA supplying the Warren Commission a photo of a man misidentified as Lee Harvey Oswald, about the tape recordings and transcripts of "Oswald's" visit to the Russian embassy. Phillips testified that surveillance cameras were not working when "Oswald" approached the embassy and that the tape recordings had been routinely destroyed.[1159] The claim that the camera wasn't working was still another lie.[1160] They had multiple cameras and there were hundreds of other photographs from the time when the CIA claimed the camera wasn't working.[1161] The CIA later claimed this was a mistake and the materials were just mislabeled, but they changed their story about having recordings or photographs. They claimed the camera was broken, but that was a lie because there was more than one camera.[1162] Freedom of Information Act (FOIA) requests eventually unearthed twelve pictures of the Oswald imposter's visit to the Soviet Embassy in Mexico City.[1163]

The CIA flew the tapes up from Mexico City and claimed that they were routinely recycled.[1164] This was another lie.[1165] Copies of the tapes were kept at home by Winn Scott, the CIA Station Chief in Mexico City.[1166] And when Scott died CIA officer James Jesus Angleton showed up to make sure he got the evidence by threatening to cut off his widow's benefits if she did not cooperate.[1167] The day after the funeral he turned up at the widow's door accompanied by John Horton, the then current CIA Mexico City station chief.[1168] Angleton wanted access to the dead man's study.[1169] The next day, after Angleton had left, a truck removed three large boxes and four suitcases containing the tapes.[1170]

The next problem with this whole scenario, as Lyndon Johnson eventually came to realize, was that it was risking the start of World War Three. Once he was president, Johnson decided that, since the Russians had nuclear weapons pointed our way and he might therefore be in danger from a nuclear exchange, the whole idea of using the Kennedy hit as a pretext to start World War Three didn't seem like such a great idea after all. He already had what he wanted. He was now in the White House rather than the Big House. And he knew very well that the Russians were not behind the Kennedy assassination. He also realized that if he started firing nuclear missiles at the Russians, they would likely fire back. However, before he completely tossed out the whole concept of the threat of World War Three, he decided to use it to his advantage. The back story that the plotters had created for Oswald could still be useful to Johnson. Oswald was a defector to Russia who had been recorded by the press in New Orleans passing out pro-Castro leaflets. This plus just the rumor of a visit to Mexico City by Oswald to obtain Soviet and Cuban visas created enough of a scare that the Russians and the Cubans might be behind the assassination of Kennedy. Johnson was able to use the rumors and speculation of a Soviet or Cuban plot to assassinate Kennedy to scare some reluctant folks into agreeing to join what became the Warren Commission and doing a whitewash. He used the threat of nuclear war as a way to convince reluctant folks like Supreme Court Chief Justice Earl Warren and Senator Richard Russell into signing on to a commission charged with issuing a whitewash report that Oswald was a lone nut gunman and therefore there was no conspiracy and no reason to start World War Three. This was an example of Johnson's genius. He was able to find a way to manipulate the situation to get the result he wanted and needed.

In his book *JFK AND THE UNSPEAKABLE*, James Douglass points out that Johnson did not want to begin and end his presidency with a global war.[1171]

In December Hoover then shut down the investigations in Mexico City and New Orleans into conspiracy angles.[1172] The crime was already solved. Oswald was a lone nut.[1173]

The Letter to the Soviet embassy

In addition to having Oswald supposedly visit Mexico City to apply for visas to incriminate Cuba and Russia in the Kennedy assassination, Oswald is also alleged to have written an incriminating letter to the Soviet Embassy in Washington. This is very likely just another attempt by the CIA to implicate Russia. There is no proof that Oswald typed the letter.

Ruth Paine, one of Oswald's CIA babysitters, claimed that Oswald used her Russian alphabet typewriter to type the letter on October 9, 1963 and left it where she could see it on October 10.[1174]

On November 18, 1963 the letter showed up at the Soviet Embassy in Washington. It appeared to implicate the Soviet Union in the assassination of Kennedy, which will happen in a few days.[1175]

On November 22, 1963 Kennedy was assassinated.

On November 23, 1963, the day after the Kennedy assassination, the FBI conducted a search of the Paine's residence. When the agents arrived, Ruth Paine informed them about "Oswald's" letter to the Soviet embassy, and gave them the original.[1176]

Veciana is Asked to Reach Out to His Cousin

On February 1, 1964 CIA officer David Atlee Phillips was using his alias, Maurice Bishop. As Maurice Bishop, he reached out to Antonio Veciana. Veciana was the leader of Alpha 66, one of the larger and more effective anti-Castro Cuban exile groups. Phillips asked Antonio Veciana to contact his cousin, a Cuban intelligence officer stationed in Mexico City, and offer him lots of money if he will agree to claim that he had met with Lee Harvey Oswald.[1177] Veciana attempted to do this but could not make the contact before his cousin was recalled to Cuba.[1178]

This is extraordinary. Johnson had already decided not to use the Kennedy assassination to start World War Three. He made that call right after the Kennedy assassination, two months earlier, and the CIA was *still* trying to find a way to implicate Cuba in the assassination as a pretext to invade Cuba.

The Alarm is Turned Off

CIA Director Allen Dulles planted people in other government agencies so the CIA could control as much as possible. This was not restricted to federal government agencies. He even went so far as to place people in the local police departments in major cities. One of the agencies they placed people in was the FBI. This is one of the deeper parts of the Deep State, and this was how the CIA turned off the FBI alarm that was supposed to catch people with profiles like Lee Harvey Oswald.

In his book *JFK AND THE UNSPEAKABLE*, James Douglass describes how this process worked.[1179]   Colonel L. Fletcher Prouty was tasked in 1955 with setting up a Pentagon office to provide support to the CIA.[1180] Allen Dulles wanted people planted in other agencies, and he tasked Prouty with doing this.[1181]   They were to ostensibly work for their respective agencies, but they would take orders directly from the CIA.[1182] Douglass lists examples like the State Department, the Federal Aviation Administration (FAA), the Customs Service, the Treasury, the FBI and all around and through the government, up in the White House and other agencies where they planted CIA operatives.[1183] By the time of the Kennedy presidency, the CIA had a secret team of its own employees throughout the entire U.S. government. When Allen Dulles was fired from the CIA, his deputy Richard Helms took over the network.[1184]   Author James Douglass describes this as a government within a government, accountable to no one except the CIA.[1185] Kennedy had no idea, when he got to the White House, what he was up against.[1186]

Douglass claims that FBI Director Hoover understood that the CIA had infiltrated the FBI, and he wasn't happy about it.[1187]   Douglass also claims that on October 9, 1963, an FBI official in Washington D.C. turned off an alarm system that was about to identify Lee Harvey Oswald as a threat to national security.[1188]   Douglass quotes author John Newman on how Marvin Gheesling, a supervisor in the Soviet espionage section at FBI headquarters, had remarkable timing "Gheesling turned off the alarm switch on Oswald literally an instant before it would've gone off."[1189]   Four years earlier, when Oswald threatened to give U.S. military secrets to the Russians, the FBI issued a 'flash' on Oswald.[1190] Anyone who got information or anything to do with Oswald was to respond to a security watch that covered all the FBI offices.[1191]   Gheesling cancelled this just in time for Oswald to be the patsy for the Kennedy assassination.[1192]   After the assassination, when the FBI was taking heat for not having flagged Oswald, Hoover ordered "send this guy to Siberia" and Gheesling was transferred to the FBI Detroit office.[1193]

Rogue CIA Elements

The entire CIA didn't kill Kennedy. A few of the people near the top went rogue and decided to eliminate Kennedy. They used the facilities, budget and apparatus of the CIA and got some of their underlings to participate. The vast majority of the people who work at the CIA are patriots who work hard and take serious risks without even the potential for public recognition when they accomplish something for their country.

Making an enemy of the CIA is dangerous. They have an entire murder department and they even hire the mafia to assassinate leaders like Fidel Castro. Kennedy and the leaders of the CIA became enemies, starting with Allen Dulles, the Director of the CIA when Kennedy was elected president.

Kennedy eventually wanted to make peace with Cuba and the Soviet Union. Dulles and his crowd at the CIA wanted to cancel the peace initiatives and invade Cuba. Kennedy wanted to withdraw our advisors from Vietnam. Dulles and his guys at the CIA wanted to ramp up the Vietnam War, including sending combat troops. And not just a few. He wanted to send in half a million combat troops. Kennedy did not want to continue murdering the democratically elected leaders of sovereign foreign countries. Dulles and the top echelon of the CIA wanted to continue knocking off foreign leaders who would not go along with their policies. Dulles and his Cold Warriors believed in the domino theory. Kennedy saw it differently. He wanted to make peace.

We don't know all the names of those CIA folks who were involved in the Kennedy assassination conspiracy, or even how many of them there were in total. The prime suspects include:

- Allen Dulles – CIA Director (appointed by Eisenhower)
- Richard Helms – CIA Director (appointed by Johnson)
- James Jesus Angleton – CIA Chief of Counterintelligence (responsible for Oswald)
- David Atlee Phillips – CIA Chief of Operations, Western Hemisphere (in charge of Cubans)
- Bill Harvey – CIA Officer in Miami (also former FBI)
- Frank Sturgis – CIA Officer (also later involved in Watergate)
- E. Howard Hunt – CIA Officer (also later involved in Watergate)
- Clay Shaw – CIA Contractor in New Orleans (also worked on cancer bioweapon)

- David Ferrie – CIA Contractor in New Orleans (also worked for mafia boss Carlos Marcello)
- Guy Banister – CIA Contractor in New Orleans (also worked for the FBI at the same time)
- Cord Meyer – CIA Assistant Deputy Director of Plans (ex-wife was having an affair with JFK)
- David Sanchez Morales – CIA hitman (was likely one of the shooters in Dealey Plaza)

The people on this list of CIA employees and contractors likely knew most, if not all, of what was going on. They understood that they were working on either the murder of the president or the cover-up or both. The group above enlisted the help of other CIA contractors like George de Mohrenschildt and Ruth Paine. And I could even include Lee Harvey Oswald in this second group. This second group of contractors was used by the folks at the top to accomplish specific tasks. As near as I can tell, information for these lower-level folks was on a "need to know" basis. This second group of CIA-connected folks were not actual CIA employees. They were more like contractors, and they were only told what they needed to know to play their part in the overall plan. George de Mohrenschildt, for example, appears not to have been told everything that was going on. We may never know how much Ruth Paine knew about the overall plan, but she likely was not privy to everything. Some of them, like de Mohrenschildt, became victims themselves when they were killed because they knew too much and murdering them would ensure their silence. Oswald obviously became a victim and was murdered to ensure his silence. He figured out too late that he was the patsy.

These rogue elements murdered Kennedy because they were opposed to his policies and refused to acknowledge that the duly elected leaders of the United States were in charge and not the Deep State. Johnson would implement their policies and Kennedy would not, so they participated in the conspiracy to kill President Kennedy and cover it up so JFK could be replaced by LBJ. The net result was that they got a president who would go along with the policies that the CIA wanted. America's sending half a million combat troops to the Vietnam War was one direct result of the assassination of President Kennedy.

Like Johnson, Hoover, and the others who conspired to murder Kennedy, these CIA folks seem unlikely to rise from their graves and confess. However, we know that the CIA had a hand in the conspiracy and the cover-up and we also know what actions the folks listed above took. It doesn't take a rocket scientist to connect the dots from there.

Author Phillip Nelson, in his book, *LBJ: THE MASTERMIND OF THE JFK ASSASSINATION*, asserts that:[1194]

> "The nucleus of CIA men at the top knew precisely who could be trusted implicitly to devise the operational planning that would ensure success. Their recruitment of men like Bill Harvey, David Morales, David Atlee Phillips and over a dozen others lower in the hierarchy would proceed over a period of many months."[1195]

Allen Dulles

The Dulles brothers worked at the law firm Sullivan & Cromwell. They did work for Brown Brothers Harriman, which was investing in German rearmament in the 1930's.[1196] This helps to explain why John Foster Dulles signed "Heil Hitler" on his correspondence with clients like I.G. Farben (makers of Zyklon B, the gas used in the gas chambers) before WW II.[1197]

Allen Dulles was the originator of the Deep State in America. Dulles had been running his own show since before World War II. In the years before the war, Allen Dulles and his brother John Foster Dulles helped their Nazi German clients hide assets from the U.S. government.[1198] Supreme Court Justice Arthur Goldberg said that if FDR had survived the war the Dulles brothers would have faced prosecution for war crimes.[1199] He also said that both Dulles brothers were guilty of treason, but FDR died and no one else had the will to challenge them.[1200] Multiple times Dulles continued to pursue his own policies even when this was in direct opposition to the orders of the president of the United States. An example of this was Operation Sunrise.[1201] The official policy of President Franklin Delano Roosevelt was unconditional surrender, but Dulles went off on his own and negotiated separate terms with a Nazi German friend of his who was in Northern Italy near the end of the war.[1202] Dulles was off on his own, pursuing his own policy, regardless of what the elected leaders of the country wanted. This is the definition of the Deep State.

Allen Dulles rescued Nazi spy chief Reinhard Gehlen from an allied prison to use him to set up an anti-communist spy ring in what became West Germany.[1203] In 1959 Gehlen signed a contract to work for the CIA for five million dollars per year.[1204] The CIA was forming out of the OSS and wanted help and advice and absorbed and funded the Gehlen network. The CIA was on the side of U.S. corporate interests like the United Fruit company. The CIA created coups in Iran, Guatemala, Congo, Laos and Vietnam under Eisenhower and Kennedy and in Indonesia under Johnson. In spite of Kennedy's desire to work with the democratically elected leader of Indonesia, the CIA continued to attempt to overthrow the government until it finally succeeded in 1965.[1205] Dulles created this culture at the CIA and, even though Kennedy fired him in 1961 after the Bay of Pigs fiasco, his reign continued.

In his book on Dulles, *THE DEVIL'S CHESSBOARD: ALLEN DULLES, THE CIA, AND THE RISE OF AMERICA'S SECRET GOVERNMENT,* author David Talbot describes Allen Dulles as "emotionally numb" and viewing people as "useful."[1206] This made him the perfect person to implement the strategy of using former Nazi war criminals for the benefit of the fight against communism. For Dulles, morality didn't enter into the equation.

Instead of the Dulles brothers being prosecuted for war crimes they were able to help the Nazi spies continue to operate after the war, only now for the Americans. The Dulles brothers saw the enemy as the Russians and communism. And the former Nazis could help, just like we used German scientists to help our rocket programs in the space race.

When the Office of Strategic Services (OSS) was dissolved after World War II, Dulles created the Office of Policy Coordination (OPC).[1207] President Truman was skeptical of creating an American central intelligence agency because he didn't want America to have a Gestapo.[1208] He let the OSS lapse after the war and was only later persuaded to create the CIA. In the meantime, Dulles created the OPC and even found funding for it from hidden Nazi treasure looted from Jewish families which Dulles had tracked down after the war.[1209] The OPC ran much of its operations without either White House or Congressional oversight. Buried in the State Department bureaucracy the OPC engaged in sabotage, subversion and assassination.[1210] Truman thought the purpose of any American spy service should be simply to gather information and report to the White House and the National Security Council.[1211] Dulles disagreed with Truman on this and went off on his own.[1212] This was not the first time Dulles had disagreed with the president and implemented his own policy. Many of the OPC recruits were ex-Nazis. The OPC had 47 overseas stations with 3,000 employees and another 3,000 contractors.[1213] Dulles had created his own private spy agency and was engaged in direct combat with communism. In Wikipedia, under Deep State, there should be a picture of Allen Dulles. In World War II Dulles had gone against the wishes of his superiors to run Operation Sunrise.[1214] Now he was going against the wishes of Truman to run his own fight against the Soviet Union and communism.[1215] In 1948, the Dulles brothers were set to become the Secretary of State and the head of the CIA in a Dewey administration. Dewey was the establishment's choice for President of the U.S. and the Dulles brothers would have been the choice for these two posts. Then Truman won and that didn't happen.[1216] But that didn't stop Allen Dulles from going ahead with his plans anyway. He viewed the cause of fighting against world communism to be more important than the opinion of whoever happened to be occupying the White House. This is a key point. In the United States of America, we have this concept of civilian control of the military and the agencies created by Congress. The elected representatives of the people of the U.S. are supposed to be in charge, but Allen Dulles thought he knew better. In 1938 Allen Dulles, while running for Congress, said that democracy works only if intelligent people make it work.[1217] He was willing to either disobey orders or simply run his own show right under the nose of the Truman administration which had other ideas. Truman's opinion was that, even if we had an American spy agency, it should just be passively gathering information and not actively running operations. Truman would have been amazed to discover what was actually going on in the OPC.[1218] Later Dulles would use money skimmed from the Marshall Plan to fund operations.[1219]

J. Edgar Hoover at first saw Dulles as a rival, and he had amassed a file on Dulles.[1220] Dulles had many affairs. So, Allen Dulles and his deputy James Jesus Angleton in turn also kept files on Hoover.[1221] Angleton claimed he had pictures on Hoover, including one of Hoover giving his companion Tolson a blow job.[1222] Hoover was feeding names to Senator Joseph McCarthy for his crusade, and when McCarthy attacked the CIA, Dulles refused to comply with the subpoena of himself or any of his employees.[1223] Dulles saw the CIA as a "superagency" operating above the normal checks and balances, including supervision by the White House, the Senate and the House of Representatives.[1224] This the essence of the Deep State.

The overthrow of the governments of Iran, Guatemala and the Congo while Dulles was still the Director of the CIA during the Eisenhower administration set the tone for the rest. Western business interests like British oil companies or American fruit or mining companies were exploiting the people and the natural resources of these countries. America, the country born of throwing off exploitative British colonial rule, had no business implementing exploitative colonial rule in other countries. About the best thing I can say in defense of these abhorrent policies is that at least the Dulles brothers got Eisenhower to agree before they did this in Iran and Guatemala. However, I believe these were mistakes. We're still paying for the trouble they caused in Iran, but I digress.

In 1953 Allen Dulles ran the CIA's MK-ULTRA program. There were persistent rumors that American P.O.W.'s captured in Korea were subject to Chinese brainwashing techniques. This made Dulles want to catch up and pass the communists in the area of brainwashing, just like Sputnik made the U.S. want to catch up and pass the Russians in the space race and the reports of Nazi Germany working an atomic bomb pushed the U.S. to come up with the Manhattan Project.[1225] If brainwashed people could be made to carry out tasks like murder or spying that they otherwise would be unwilling to do this could be used as an advantage. If the communists could do something that might be useful in the cold war then Dulles was going to make sure that the U.S. had that capability and more and he created project MK-ULTRA, which involved mind-control experiments on human beings. So, Dulles started to do experiments on human beings. CIA Deputy Director Richard Helms oversaw the program. They tried lots of things including electric shock therapy, LSD and whatever else they could think of to get people to act on command, even against their own conscience.[1226] Dulles' amoral view of people as "useful" allowed him to have people tortured with electric shocks and used as human guinea pigs in the name of winning the Cold War against communism.[1227] They started with Soviet prisoners and double agents and then moved on to drug addicts, mental hospital inmates, prisoners and other people they viewed as 'expendables.'[1228] These were American citizens. CIA officer Frank Olson became a security risk when they overdosed him on LSD, so they kidnapped and eventually killed him.[1229] Gail Kastner was experimented on.[1230] Dr. Donald Ewen Cameron experimented on her.[1231] She was given so much electrical shock therapy that she broke teeth and fractured her spine while being shocked.[1232] Had Kennedy known of this program he would have had it stopped. Dulles put Helms in charge of the program, and they simply didn't tell the political leaders what they were doing, so no one knew to order them to stop. And this was done with taxpayer money. Here again we can see the Deep State mentality at work. They simply don't tell the elected officials and those legally in charge what they're really up to.

Mary Meyer was married to Cord Meyer. Cord was a high-level CIA officer and she knew Dulles well. Mary detested Allen Dulles and "compared him to Machiavelli, only worse."[1233] Dulles was consistently willing to overthrow democratically elected governments in foreign countries in favor of colonial rule by the United States. He did this in Iran, Guatemala and the Congo and the CIA continued this policy in Laos, Vietnam and Indonesia after he was no longer the official Director of the CIA. Dulles was the CIA Director who assured Eisenhower that the Russians could not shoot down the U-2 spy plane – then it was shot down over Russia and Francis Gary Powers was captured.[1234]

The Deep State mentality that Dulles personified continued through the days between the 1960 election and when Kennedy was inaugurated. Kennedy would not have sanctioned the murder of the duly elected leader of the Congo, so Dulles had him murdered just before Kennedy was sworn in. Then Dulles briefed Kennedy on the situation in the Congo, but did not tell him for a month that Lumumba was already dead. (See the section on the Congo). Dulles was always willing to implement his policy regardless of what the elected leaders wanted.

Kennedy knew he had to deal with Dulles, but did not think he had enough of a mandate at first to make big changes. He had won with a razor-thin margin. He thought he needed to build up his political capital before he could make bold changes.

The Bay of Pigs fiasco occurred on April 17, 1961. Less than a week later a group of retired French generals tried to seize power from de Gaulle in France. This was one month before Kennedy was scheduled to visit France. de Gaulle quickly concluded that U.S. intelligence was backing the coup.[1235] de Gaulle was viewed as an obstacle to NATO because he refused to have French troops under NATO command and insisted on having his own nuclear arsenal not under the control of the U.S.[1236] Dulles was forced to issue a denial of CIA involvement in the French coup attempt.[1237] Kennedy didn't believe Dulles and later it turned out that the CIA was in fact in touch with the French coup plotters and that Dulles had organized a secret army in France after the war with buried arms caches.[1238] The point was to have a quick-reaction force ready to rise up and resist the Russians if they attacked west and tried to take over Western Europe.[1239] Then the 'stay-behind army' became unnecessary because Stalin decided not to attack and eventually the remains of the secret army were used by the French coup plotters.[1240] Kennedy was furious all over again with Dulles for running his own foreign policy. Dulles kept Kennedy in the dark on all of this and when it erupted it further destroyed what little remained of the relationship between Kennedy and Dulles.[1241] This all happened one month before Kennedy was to visit Paris and threatened to trash the U.S. relationship with France. When Kennedy assured de Gaulle that he had nothing to do with the coup he, unfortunately and embarrassingly, could not vouch for his own CIA.[1242] The French people rose up and resisted the coup and it failed.[1243] de Gaulle purged his disloyal security forces and Kennedy needed to do the same.[1244]

If Kennedy had any second thoughts about firing Dulles, the embarrassment of having to admit to de Gaulle that he could not vouch for his own CIA not having a hand in the attempt to oust the legendary French leader must have sealed the fate of Allen Dulles and his tenure as the Director of the CIA. However well justified, firing Dulles was considered an outrage to Dulles and his crew at the CIA.

Just before the Paris coup attempt and the Kennedy trip to Paris, The Bay of Pigs fiasco came up and Kennedy realized how Dulles and his guys had deceived him and tried to trap him. He decided to fire Dulles, but that didn't change anything. Dulles was still in charge. He still used his offices and the facilities of the CIA. His subordinates still came to him on all the important issues. Author David Talbot, in his book *THE DEVIL'S CHESSBOARD: ALLEN DULLES, THE CIA, AND THE RISE OF AMERICA'S SECRET GOVERNMENT*, points out that Dulles had been deposed, but his reign continued.[1245] Loyalists like CIA officers James Jesus Angleton and Richard Helms remained on the job, and they still looked to Dulles for leadership, not John McCone, his replacement and officially the new Director of the CIA. Dulles created a "government in exile" at his house on Q street.[1246] A steady stream of anti-Kennedy folks came by. Angleton stopped by a few times a week.[1247]

So, as time went by and Kennedy continued to turn away from the Cold War mentality and toward peace, Dulles and his crowd at the CIA became increasingly frustrated with Kennedy. Firing Dulles only made them angrier and gave them more reason to hate and despise Kennedy. At the height of the Cuban Missile Crisis, with the world on the brink of nuclear war, the CIA sent two raiding parties into Cuba.[1248] Dulles had taught them well. They were continuing to use their control of events on the ground to force the president into actions against his will.

Kennedy decided to fire Allen Dulles as CIA Director. He also decided to fire CIA Deputy Directors Charles Cabell and Richard Bissell. In addition to having completely opposite views on almost every important issue facing the United States, these firings outraged the top CIA officers. And this was only the beginning. Kennedy put the CIA offices around the world under the authority of the State Department, took military operational responsibility away from the CIA and put it under the Pentagon and cut the CIA budget. From the perspective of the Cold Warriors at the CIA, each fresh outrage was followed by more. During the Cuban Missile Crisis Kennedy promised Khrushchev that the United States would not invade Cuba. This not only outraged the CIA, it outraged the anti-Castro Cuban exiles who the CIA was sponsoring. At some point the rogue elements at the CIA had more than they would stand for and they decided to join the conspiracy to replace Kennedy with Johnson, even if it meant murdering the president of the United States.

Kennedy was moving away from the CIA and the Pentagon and wanted to work directly with Russia to end the cold war.[1249] The CIA and the Pentagon thought Kennedy was naïve and dangerous.[1250] Eisenhower and Dulles were comfortable building the CIA around ex-Nazis like Gehlen, but Kennedy was not so sure.[1251] He wanted to pursue peace as exemplified by his Peace Speech at American University.[1252]

Vice President Johnson became the wild card in this mix. By 1963 Johnson was either going to be president or go to prison. He had killed people before and had no moral qualms about doing it again. His desperation gave the other conspirators the opportunity for collective action. If he became president, he could provide the necessary air cover to make sure none of the conspirators ended up in prison. Johnson and the Cold Warriors in the Pentagon and the CIA saw things the same way. Johnson and Dulles got along well.[1253] Dulles also had good relationships with the Texas oil barons. He had done work for them as a lawyer with Sullivan & Cromwell.[1254] Dulles went down to Texas to visit LBJ on his ranch in the summer of 1963.[1255] Dulles also visited Dallas three weeks before the Kennedy assassination.[1256] Dulles also had another direct connection to the power structure in Dallas. Dallas Mayor Earle Cabell was the younger brother of former CIA Deputy Director Charles Cabell, who Kennedy had fired after the Bay of Pigs fiasco along with Allen Dulles.

As David Talbot points out in his book *THE DEVIL'S CHESSBOARD: ALLEN DULLES, THE CIA, AND THE RISE OF AMERICA'S SECRET GOVERNMENT*:[1257]

> "In the weeks leading up to the assassination of President Kennedy on November 22, 1963, the flurry of meetings at Dulles' house intensified. Among the CIA men coming in and out of Q Street were several who later came under investigation by the House Select Committee on Assassinations and other probes for their possible connection to the president's murder. And on the weekend of the assassination, Dulles hunkered down for unexplained reasons at a secret CIA facility in northern Virginia known as "The Farm" despite the fact that he had been removed from the Agency two years earlier."[1258]

I point this out because I don't believe it was a coincidence that Allen Dulles just happened to be at his office at the CIA where he could monitor and direct the Kennedy assassination that fateful weekend.

President John F. Kennedy was assassinated on November 22, 1963.

Author Peter Janney, in his book *MARY'S MOSAIC*, points out that Bobby Kennedy directly confronted CIA Director McCone on the CIA being involved. He asked in a way that McCone couldn't lie, but McCone was not in control of the CIA.[1259] Dick Helms, James Angleton, Bill Harvey, Cord Meyer, Tracy Barnes and Bob Crowley still carried the flag for Dulles behind the scenes.[1260] Bobby Kennedy asked the wrong man.[1261]

Then Lyndon Johnson, suddenly now President Johnson, appointed Dulles to the Warren Commission. Allen Dulles was Johnson's first choice to be the chairman of what became the Warren Commission, but then went for Earl Warren as a better choice.[1262] Clearly, Johnson wanted Dulles to control the commission, which Dulles did. He was the only one of the commissioners who did not have a full-time job, and he was able to devote the time necessary to physically be there to control the meetings. Most of the work was done by staffers, and being a commissioner allowed him to pull rank, especially with the other commissioners having a full work load and therefore not being at most of the meetings. Johnson realized this in advance, and also realized that having Warren as the figurehead had several advantages. First, it would become known as the Warren Commission and not the Dulles Commission, putting the spotlight on Warren and his position of credibility as chief justice of the United States Supreme Court. This gives the Warren Report the added credibility, in the mind of the public, of having the Supreme Court behind it. Second, Warren had managed to get a consensus in the landmark Brown vs. Board of Education ruling, no easy feat. This demonstrated a skill that Johnson wanted to make use of in getting an effective whitewash job done for the assassination. He wanted the Commission to unanimously endorse the 'Oswald as lone nut' theory, and Warren's skill in gaining a consensus would be needed.

Author Jerome Corsi, in his book *WHO REALLY KILLED KENNEDY?*, said that:[1263]

> "The day JFK removed Allen Dulles from directing the CIA was the day JFK signed his death warrant. Even removed from the CIA, Dulles was more than capable of organizing the coup d'état from behind the scenes, the place where Dulles was truly most comfortable. It should come as no surprise that

LBJ appointed Allen Dulles to the Warren Commission. This completed the circle, positioning Dulles so he could make sure Warren Commission assigned all the blame for JFK's assassination to Lee Harvey Oswald, the operative chosen by the CIA to play the role of patsy."[1264]

"Allen Dulles had a deep motive to see JFK killed that stemmed not simply from revenge, but more importantly from ideology. Truly, Allen Dulles came to hate everything JFK represented..."[1265]

Mark North, in his book *ACT OF TREASON: THE ROLE OF J. EDGAR HOOVER IN THE ASSASSINATION OF PRESIDENT KENNEDY*, points out that at the commission's first executive session, Dulles gave each of his colleagues a book supporting the theory that American assassinations were always perpetrated by lone nuts.[1266] North also quotes the *New York Times* that:[1267]

> "members conceived of the commission's purpose in terms of the national interest. Allen Dulles said that an atmosphere of rumor and suspicion interferes with the functioning of the government, especially abroad, and one of the main tasks of the commission was to dispel rumors ... McCloy said that it was of paramount importance to 'show the world that America is not a banana republic, where a government can be changed by conspiracy' ... Cooper said that one of the commission's most important purposes was to 'lift the cloud of doubt that had been cast over American institutions' ... Ford said that dispelling damaging rumors was a major concern of the commission, and most members of the commission agreed."[1268]

Willy Morris was an assistant editor at Harper's. He was working with Dulles one day on an article where Dulles was going to put his spin on the Bay of Pigs. Dulles said "That little Kennedy. He thought he was a god."[1269]

Richard Helms was a career CIA man who eventually became Director of the CIA in 1966. During his time at the CIA he was responsible for things like the MK-ULTRA program and the cover up of the Kennedy assassination. The Garrison investigation and prosecution of CIA asset Clay Shaw for the murder of President Kennedy happened in the late 1960's while Helms was CIA Director. Helms used the CIA to make sure the prosecution failed. (see the chapter on the Garrison prosecution of Shaw).

After Allen Dulles was fired, Kennedy appointed John McCone to head up the CIA in 1961. McCone served until 1965 when he resigned and Johnson appointed Richard Helms. This meant that, for a while, there was someone in charge of the CIA, John McCone, who was not from the Deep State. While McCone was in charge, Helms and James Angleton and others from the Deep State wing of the CIA kept McCone in the dark about some of the worse things they were doing at the CIA until Johnson promoted Helms. Once Helms was CIA Director, the Deep State was officially back in charge of the CIA and they didn't have to keep the CIA director in the dark as to what was going on.

During his long career at the CIA, Helms was, among other things, in charge of the MK-ULTRA program. When he was forced to resign as the Director of the CIA in 1973, Helms systematically destroyed all the records on MK-ULTRA that he could get his hands on. Fortunately, seven boxes of financial records were in an offsite storage facility and they survived.[1270] Otherwise we would have very little evidence of what had happened.

In 1953 Allen Dulles put Richard Helms in charge of MK-ULTRA.[1271] By then it was a mind control program to see if they could brainwash someone into committing murder and not having any memory of it after.[1272] They were hoping to be able to commit murder without it being traced back to the CIA.[1273] This would come in handy if they wanted to bump off a foreign head of state, for example Fidel Castro, without blame falling on the CIA. This project evolved into a widespread program of using a combination of drugs, torture and hypnosis in experiments carried out on college campuses in the U.S. as well as on military installations.[1274] The closest they came to their goal was to be able to create a patsy who would appear to shoot while the true assassin was nearby to make the kill shot.[1275] As a sociopath, Richard Helms saw the results of the MK-ULTRA program as more important than the lives of the subjects of these experiments.[1276]

Operation PAPERCLIP was a program to bring one thousand Nazi 'scientists' to the U.S. after WWII.[1277] The definition of 'scientists' in this case included those who had experimented on Nazi concentration camp victims. Helms wanted to build and expand on what the Nazis had done.[1278] In 1948 a project called ARTICHOKE started using captured prisoners of war and double agents.[1279] An attempt was made to find a way to make people tell the truth that involved drugs and torture.[1280] On May 15, 1952 Allen Dulles and Frank Wisner got a report on the four-year effort of Project ARTICHOKE.[1281] By 1950 the project was renamed BLUEBIRD.[1282] Operation BLUEBIRD used North Korean prisoners and involved giving them amphetamines and barbiturates to see if they could be hypnotized into doing things against their will.[1283] Richard Helms wrote the original proposal for Allen Dulles for MK-ULTRA.[1284] A few months later Dulles approved MK-ULTRA in the summer of 1952.[1285] MK-ULTRA was a program to look into ways to control behavior using human guinea pigs.[1286] Allen Dulles, Frank Wisner and Richard Helms were personally responsible for setting up and running MK-ULTRA, the search for mind control drugs and techniques using secret prisons in which to run experiments on human subjects.[1287] To start with, seven prisoners in Kentucky were kept high on LSD for seventy-seven days.[1288]

When Allen Dulles was promoted from second in command to Director of the CIA in 1953, he was concerned that communist countries had an edge in the field of brainwashing or mind control.[1289] If America's enemies the communists had the ability to brainwash (for example) American pilots who had been shot down in the Korean War, then the United States need to put serious effort into mind control and brainwashing.[1290] Helms was using LSD, heroin, sleeping pills, other drugs, torture, hypnosis, electric shock therapy, sensory deprivation and other methods, most often on unwitting human beings who were not volunteers. They were trying to produce effects like brainwashing, amnesia, hypnosis and mind control among other things. Their idea of mind control started with getting someone to tell the truth. They also were looking to develop what eventually became "date rape" drugs, something that could be slipped to someone in a bar that would render them pliable. The ultimate goal was to make people programmable, so they could be given instructions which they would then carry out later. They were hoping to get to a point where they could get a subject to kill someone and have no memory of who sent them. The closest they appeared to get was to get a subject to shoot at someone, but it was unreliable enough that they needed to have a real assassin nearby to take the kill shot and have the hypnotized subject set up to take the blame for the murder.[1291]

In 1953 Frank Olson, a CIA employee who worked on the program at Camp Detrick in Maryland, started to have concerns and doubts about both the ethics and the effectiveness of what the CIA was doing.[1292] He made the mistake of discussing these doubts with his co-workers and superiors, and they slipped him a dose of LSD.[1293] He reacted badly to it and became psychotic, so the CIA then kidnapped and murdered him.[1294] His family sued and won in court was eventually paid off.[1295]

Richard Helms saw the results of the MK-ULTRA program as more important than the lives of the subjects of the experiments.[1296] When he was ordered by CIA Director McCone, a Kennedy appointee, to shut the program down he just changed the name from MK-ULTRA to MK-SEARCH and kept going.[1297] Here again we can see the Deep State mentality in action. Helms didn't care what the duly elected and appointed leaders ordered him to do. He had his own amoral agenda and he carried it out, with taxpayer money.

They tested on inmates, for example, at the prison in Vacaville, California.[1298] Author Mark Lane, in his book *LAST WORD: MY INDICTMENT OF THE CIA IN THE MURDER OF JFK*, points out the immense scope of the project.[1299] The Church Committee hearings eventually uncovered the fact that 12 hospitals or clinics, 44 colleges or universities, 3 prisons and 15 research foundations were involved.[1300] Ted Kaczynski was one of the subjects, and he was emotionally stable before the experiments.[1301] He later became famous as the Unabomber.[1302]

In 1963 CIA Director John McCone was trying to rein in the Agency.[1303] Then CIA Inspector General John Earman wrote that experimenting on human guinea pigs without their knowledge or consent was "distasteful and unethical."[1304] Here we have the duly elected representative, Kennedy, appointing the head of the CIA, McCone, to do his job. When McCone found out about the MK-ULTRA program he tried to shut it down.[1305] And here we have the Deep State, Richard Helms, ignoring the wishes of the people duly elected and appointed to keep track over the agency. Since Helms didn't want the MK-ULTRA program shut down, he didn't.[1306] In 1964 he changed the name from MK-ULTRA to MK-SEARCH, shut down a few of the safe houses they were using, and kept the program going.[1307] In fact, the program expanded and a few years later hundreds of inmates at Vacaville, California were being experimented on.[1308] By this time McCone had resigned and Johnson had promoted Richard Helms to be the Director of the CIA. During 1968 the program was used in an attempt to get Vietnamese prisoners to cooperate using massive doses of LSD.[1309] When that didn't work they were operated on and portions of their skulls were cut away and electrodes were attached.[1310] They tried to get the prisoners to attack each other, but this failed.[1311] The prisoners were then executed and their bodies were burned to get rid of the evidence of the experiments.[1312] This getting rid of the evidence is very similar to the attempts by the Nazis at the end of World War II to destroy the evidence of what they had done.

One of the scientists who Helms had working on MK-ULTRA was named Sidney Gottlieb. Sidney Gottlieb was in charge of MK-ULTRA and the CIA's Technical Services Division (TSD).[1313] Gottlieb experimented on Americans at a federal prison facility in Lexington, Kentucky.[1314] One person was given LSD for 174 straight days.[1315] Gottlieb also paid drug addicted prostitutes in New York and San Francisco to slip drugs to unsuspecting victims and bring them back to CIA safe houses were they would be given LSD and observed and recorded via two-way mirrors.[1316] Barbara Smithe was a young wife of one of the friends of George Hunter White, who worked with Gottlieb at the CIA.[1317] She attended a party without her husband and White slipped her LSD.[1318] She spent the next twenty years in and out of mental institutions.[1319] Gottlieb had thousands of subjects in the U.S. and he even managed to expand into Canada, using a Canadian Doctor named Donald Ewen Cameron.[1320] They used drugs and electric shock therapy to try to destroy the minds of human beings, to try to wipe their minds clean so they could start over.[1321] Gail Kastner was a nineteen-year-old honors student when she went to Cameron for mild depression.[1322] After his treatment, she sucked her thumb and used the floor instead of the toilet.[1323] He destroyed her life.[1324] In poverty in her seventies she was eventually awarded $100,000 by the courts.[1325] Sidney Gottlieb was responsible for destroying countless lives.[1326] In 1972 Gottlieb himself described his work as useless.[1327]

In 1964 CIA Director John McCone and (then) Deputy Director of Plans Richard Helms testified before the Warren Commission. Not being part of the Deep State, McCone was an outsider and was able to have plausible deniability, but Helms just flat lied.[1328] He knew that Oswald was a CIA creation and lied about it.[1329] He also made sure that the files that were handed over were scrubbed prior to being delivered.[1330]

Author James Douglass, in his book *JFK AND THE UNSPEAKABLE*, said that:[1331]

> "After President Kennedy fired Bissell from the CIA for his role in the Bay of Pigs, Richard Helms, his successor as Deputy Director of Plans, took up where Bissell had left off in conspiring to kill Castro. Helms testified to the Church Committee that he never informed either the president or his

newly appointed CIA Director John McCone of the assassination plots. Nor did he inform any other officials in the Kennedy administration. Helms said he sought no approval for the murder attempts because assassination was not a subject that should be aired with higher authority. When he was asked if President Kennedy had been informed, Helms said that "nobody wants to embarrass a president of the United States by discussing the assassination of foreign leaders in his presence." He also didn't seek the approval of the Special Group Augmented that oversaw the anti-Castro program because, he said "I didn't see how one would have expected that a thing like killing or murdering or assassination would become a part of a large group of people sitting around a table in the United States government.""[1332]

Richard Helms is a good example of the Deep State mentality. Quite certain that he does not want the elected representatives of the people of the United States to know what he's been up to, he destroys records before leaving office at the end of his tenure as CIA Director, just like the Nazis tried to hide the evidence of their crimes as World War II was winding down.[1333] Without information on what the denizens of the Deep State are up to, our elected representatives don't even know what questions to ask. And the Deep State certainly isn't going to volunteer any information.

In his book *NOT IN YOUR LIFETIME*, author Anthony Summers gives this example of an exchange between the Senate Intelligence Committee charged with oversight of the CIA and Richard Helms:[1334]

> Senator Morgan: "You were charged with furnishing the Warren Commission with information from the CIA, information that you thought relevant?"
>
> Helms: "No sir. I was instructed to reply to inquiries from the Warren Commission for information from the Agency. I was not asked to initiate any particular thing."
>
> Senator Morgan: "In other words, if you weren't asked for it, you didn't give it."
>
> Helms: "That's right sir."

I bring this up because Richard Helms was one of the people running the CIA who was still loyal to Allen Dulles at the time of the Kennedy assassination. I point these things out to show who was running the CIA at the time of Kennedy's assassination. It wasn't John McCone, the Director that Kennedy appointed. It was guys like Richard Helms and James Angleton, who were still taking their directions from their leader, Allen Dulles. Helms got a promotion to become Deputy Director for Plans when Dulles and Bissell were fired after the Bay of Pigs fiasco.

By 1963 Kennedy was making steps toward peace and the Deep State establishment saw JFK as naïve and dangerous.[1335] The Deep State saw Kennedy as a national security risk.[1336] Richard Helms had a top aide called Sam Halpern who was candid about what the CIA thought about the Kennedys. The view from Helms and the CIA was that the Kennedy's had botched the Bay of Pigs and had no idea how to run clandestine operations.[1337]

The Church Committee, following the CIA's top-secret inspector general's report, discovered that the Deputy Director of Plans, Richard Helms, had agreed that CIA officer Desmond Fitzgerald should claim to be a personal representative of Attorney General Robert Kennedy.[1338] As the CIA's own internal report admitted, Helms had also decided it was OK not to get approval from Robert Kennedy for Fitzgerald to claim to speak in RFK's name.[1339]

Richard Helms, with his Deep State mentality, thought he knew better than the elected leader and was willing to implement his policy in direct opposition to Kennedy's. Helms had CIA officer David Atlee Phillips direct his CIA-sponsored anti-Castro Cuban exile groups to continue to attack Cuba. Kennedy was trying to reach out to Castro to make peace while Helms led the effort to sabotage Kennedy's efforts at rapprochement with Cuba.[1340] Since Angleton and Helms were keeping CIA Director McCone in the dark, Kennedy was unable to get answers on this from the CIA Director he had appointed.

President Kennedy was assassinated on November 22, 1963. The CIA was involved in both the assassination and the cover up. In his book *LBJ: THE MASTERMIND OF THE JFK ASSASSINATION*, author Phillip Nelson documents that Helms was aware of at least one of the French shooters who was in Dallas on the day Kennedy was assassinated.[1341]

In his book *CIA ROGUES AND THE KILLING OF THE KENNEDYS*, author Patrick Nolan makes a strong case that Richard Helms was a sociopath.[1342] He points out that Helms was pathological liar and lacked empathy and conscience.[1343] In addition to not telling the whole truth, Helms was just a plain liar. For example, on October 31, 1977 Richard Helms plead guilty to lying to the Church Senate Intelligence Committee about the CIA's involvement in overthrowing President Salvador Allende in Chile.[1344] This was one lie that he was caught in and prosecuted for. Helms was fined and handed a two-year suspended sentence. In his only public speech as CIA Director he said the nation "must to a degree take it on faith that we too are honorable men."[1345] And that was exactly the problem. We needed honorable men in positions like Director of the CIA, and we unfortunately had Deep State men like Richard Helms.

On March 12, 1964 Richard Helms, then Deputy Director of Plans of the CIA, the man in charge of all the Agency's covert operations, met with Lee Rankin and told the Warren Commission General Counsel they would have to take his word that Oswald was not connected with the CIA.[1346]

While CIA officers James Jesus Angleton and Richard Helms technically reported to the new CIA Director, John McCone, they were still doing what Allen Dulles wanted done. And they were not telling McCone. Dulles was their leader. McCone was an outsider, not even "one of them," much less their leader. He was kept in the dark. In November of 1975 the Church Committee issued a report that said that Helms had kept McCone in the dark on certain covert operations.[1347] McCone tried several times to resign as CIA Director, but Johnson kept persuading him to stay. He eventually resigned in 1965, and on June 1, 1966 President Johnson promoted Richard Helms to be the Director of the CIA.

As CIA Director, Helms used the CIA, at Johnson's direction, to spy on the American people. Johnson was unhappy that the peace movement was making him unpopular. He told Helms to find proof that foreigners, particularly communists, were behind the peace movement in America.[1348] The CIA was forbidden by law from domestic spying. In a blatant violation of the legal mandate of the CIA, Helms ordered operation CHAOS which went on for seven years.[1349] He used James Jesus Angleton's counterintelligence department to hide this project.[1350] Agents grew long hair and infiltrated the peace movement.[1351] The CIA compiled an index of three hundred thousand Americans and compiled extensive files on over seventy-two hundred of them.[1352] The CIA was illegally spying on Americans.[1353]

On January 3, 1967 mafia functionary Jack Ruby died of cancer as a prisoner in Dallas.[1354] He had been injected with the fast-acting cancer developed by the CIA in New Orleans in the summer of 1963. In February of 1967 it became public knowledge that Jim Garrison, the District Attorney of New Orleans, was investigating CIA asset Clay Shaw for the murder of President Kennedy.[1355] The Shaw trial would take place in 1969. On June 4, 1968 Robert Kennedy was assassinated in Los Angeles. During all this time Helms, as Director of the CIA, was doing his best to keep a lid on the cover up. According to Victor Marchetti, who was a special assistant to the deputy director of the CIA in 1967, CIA Director Richard Helms started his daily morning meetings by asking if "they needed anything in New Orleans."[1356] This was in reference to the Garrison prosecution. Here is the Director of the CIA using the resources of the CIA to make sure that the Garrison prosecution of Clay Shaw fails.[1357] While Helms was Director of the CIA, the CIA tried to shut down the Garrison investigation. (See the chapter on the Garrison investigation.)[1358]

Author Phillip Nelson, in his book *LBJ: THE MASTERMIND OF THE JFK ASSASSINATION*, states:[1359]

> "The post assassination cover-up appears to have been handled primarily by Allen Dulles and Richard Helms."[1360]

James Jesus Angleton

James Jesus Angleton appears to have been the CIA officer ultimately responsible for supplying the patsy, Oswald, for the Kennedy assassination. Angleton was heavily involved in the cover-up and was likely also involved in the murder of Mary Meyer as part of that cover-up.

James Angleton was loyal to Allen Dulles. Dulles had given Angleton almost unlimited power within the CIA.[1361] Also like Dulles, Angleton rescued former Nazi leaders like Eugen Dollmann after World War II.[1362] At the end of World War II, Angleton and Dulles both viewed the Russians and communism as the enemy. The Cold War was on and Angleton and Dulles wanted to contain world communism. This was their priority, and if former Nazis could help then that was OK with Dulles and Angleton.[1363]

James Jesus Angleton led the charge at the CIA on the policy of using American money to make sure that Italy did not turn toward communism. President Kennedy had voiced support for an "opening to the left" while he visited Italy on his last trip to Europe.[1364] This was opposed by the CIA who saw it as a slippery slope toward communism for Italy. This is another example of Kennedy having one policy and the CIA having another.[1365] The CIA wing of the Deep State regularly implemented the policy they wanted, regardless of the policies or agenda of the elected political leadership.

Like his mentor and sponsor Allen Dulles, Angleton had a Deep State mentality when it came to Congressional oversight. Author Jefferson Morley quotes James Jesus Angleton in his book *THE GHOST: THE SECRET LIFE OF CIA SPYMASTER JAMES JESUS ANGLETON.* When asked during the Church Committee hearings why the CIA had ignored a direct order, Angleton said "It is inconceivable that a secret intelligence arm of government has to comply with all the overt orders of government."[1366]

Author Anthony Summers pointed out in his book *NOT IN YOUR LIFETIME*, that:[1367]

> "Analysis of available information shows that Angleton's department monitored Oswald's progress from the time of his defection until the assassination."[1368]

Author Phillip Nelson, in his book *LBJ: THE MASTERMIND OF THE JFK ASSASSINATION*, points out that James Jesus Angleton was the only person who could have set up Oswald as the patsy in the Kennedy assassination.[1369] Nelson further points out that CIA officer Bill Harvey reported to Cord Meyer and James Angleton at the CIA, and that CIA assets Guy Banister, David Ferrie and Clay Shaw in New Orleans reported to Bill Harvey.[1370]

According to author Phillip Nelson, in his book *LBJ: THE MASTERMIND OF THE JFK ASSASSINATION*:[1371]

> "Both Shaw and de Mohrenschildt had taken their orders directly from the man controlling the details of the operation from his CIA position in Mexico, under the code name of Maurice Bishop, David Atlee Phillips. Phillips, as did his peer David Morales, in charge of the operational and logistical end of the plan, took his orders from Bill Harvey who reported only to two men at the highest levels of the CIA, James Jesus Angleton and Cord Meyer. According to information furnished by E. Howard Hunt … Harvey and the others were being guided by Cord Meyer, operating out of his London CIA offices."[1372]

Angleton was still loyal to Dulles after Dulles was fired by Kennedy from the CIA. Angleton and Helms kept their new boss, CIA Director John McCone, in the dark on what was going on at the CIA.[1373] Angleton also refused to tell Otto Otepka at the State Department that Oswald was a fake defector, preferring to ruin Otto's career instead.[1374] Angleton was in charge of the work the Office of Naval Intelligence (ONI) did for the CIA. He was therefore in charge of Oswald, because, as a Marine, Oswald was overseen by the ONI.

Author Phillip Nelson, in his book *LBJ: THE MASTERMIND OF THE JFK ASSASSINATION*, said:[1375]

> "The preponderance of the evidence at this point in time indicates that James Angleton was deeply involved in the preassassination conspiracy in many ways as previously described but clearly with respect to moving Lee Harvey Oswald into position. The post assassination cover-up appears to have been handled primarily by Allen Dulles and Richard Helms."[1376]

Dulles called Angleton and they discussed how to steer President Johnson's new assassination commission away from the CIA.[1377] CIA officer John Whitten was put in charge of the CIA's investigation into Oswald's background.[1378] Angleton tried to thwart Whitten and succeeded.[1379] Once Whitten realized Angleton had information he had not shared he complained to Helms and Helms responded by taking Whitten off the case and giving it to Angleton.[1380]

Angleton appears to have been involved in the death of Mary Meyer to keep her quiet. Her ex-husband, CIA officer Cord Meyer, was in agreement with Angleton about the need to kill Mary.[1381] (see the chapter on the murder of Mary Meyer.)

One of the more obvious examples of illegal domestic spying on Americans by James Angleton was a program to open and read the mail of American citizens. For two decades, Angleton had fourteen thousand letters a year steamed open and photographed and then resealed.[1382] This operation was called HT-LINGUAL.[1383] The results were shared with J. Edgar Hoover, with whom Angleton had a direct line.[1384]

Angleton was also involved in MK-ULTRA, which got to the point where a subject could pull out a weapon and fire and later not remember what had happened.[1385] It was unreliable so you would have to have two shooters, one hypnotized and programmed patsy with a gun and one real assassin to take the kill shot.[1386] According to author Patrick Nolan in his book *CIA ROGUES AND THE KILLING OF THE KENNEDYS*, this technique would later be used in the assassination of Robert Kennedy. The book makes for interesting reading. (See the chapter on the murder of Robert Kennedy).

CIA Director Allen Dulles and Deputy Director Richard Bissell never told the new CIA Director, John McCone, about Angleton's illegal program of opening mail from 1952 onward.[1387] They also didn't tell McCone about the assassination plots against Fidel Castro.[1388] These were temporarily suspended after the Bay of Pigs. McCone only found out about the Castro assassination plots two years later. He found out about the mail opening program when the public did.[1389]

CIA officer Winn Scott kept a copy of the Oswald Mexico City tapes at his home. (See the section on Oswald in Mexico City.) When Scott died in 1971, Angleton immediately showed up to threaten the grieving widow with the loss of her benefits if she did not allow him to ransack Scott's private study and haul away the material he found.[1390]

On December 17, 1974 Angleton was fired by then CIA Director William Colby when Colby got a tip from journalist Seymour Hersch that *The New York Times* was about to publish a story about operations CHAOS and HT-LINGUAL.[1391] CHAOS was Angleton's program of infiltrating and spying on the peace movement in the United States and HT-LINGUAL was his program of opening the mail of Americans.[1392]

After he was fired, James Angleton was then willing to talk to Bernie Yeoh, who ran Accuracy in Media (AIM) to put his spin on the recent bad news about his departure from the CIA.[1393] Author Leo Damore had interviewed Yeoh.[1394] Angleton admitted to Bernie Yeoh that he had Mary's diary.[1395] He gave Yeoh a copy and this is presumably how Damore came into possession of it.[1396] (See the chapter on the murder of Mary Meyer.)

James Jesus Angleton had stonewalled the Warren Commission.[1397] David Slawson, who had been a staff attorney for the Warren Commission, called Angleton on it in the *New York Times* and Angleton called Slawson at home to threaten him into silence.[1398] Even after he was fired, Angleton was still obstructing justice.[1399] Angleton called Slawson at home and, at first, he was friendly, then he pointed out that he knew Slawson's boss, the head of USC.[1400] He then asked if what Slawson said in the *New York Times* was accurate and then Angleton said he hoped that Slawson would remain a friend.[1401] Author Philip Shenon, in his book *A CRUEL AND SHOCKING ACT*, summed up the effect of the call that Angleton made to Slawson:[1402]

> "As he put the phone down, Slawson thought the message was obvious: "The message was: We know everything you're doing. We'll find it out. Just remember that. The CIA is watching you." He and his wife, Karen, were both alarmed by the call. What did it mean that the apparently powerful figure at the CIA would contact them out of the blue to suggest that Slawson was asking too many questions about the Kennedy assassination? Slawson was convinced that Angleton was giving him a warning: "Keep your mouth shut.""[1403]

This even though Angleton was supposedly fired from the CIA.[1404] Angleton had been "officially" fired but was still showing up for work and occupying his office at the CIA months after he was supposedly no longer there.[1405]

Angleton began to talk when he was near death – he said he expected to join his CIA cronies in hell.[1406] This may have been one of the few times Angleton was telling the truth.

David Atlee Phillips

Beyond meeting with Oswald in Dallas and lying to the House Select Committee on Assassinations, it's hard to tell what part CIA officer David Atlee Phillips played in the assassination. In the fall of 1963 Phillips was reporting to Richard Helms who was then the CIA Deputy Director of Plans.[1407] Oswald said Phillips was a key part of the plot, but he did not elaborate.[1408] (See the subsection on Judyth Vary Baker). E. Howard Hunt and David Atlee Phillips came up with the plan for the coup in Guatemala.[1409] (See the section on E. Howard Hunt.) They were later asked to come up with a coup plan for Cuba.[1410] This eventually morphed into the plan to kill President Kennedy.

In early September of 1963 Lee Harvey Oswald went from New Orleans to Dallas to meet with Phillips.[1411] This meeting was witnessed by Antonino Veciana.[1412] At that time Phillips was in charge of anti-Castro Cuban exile groups like Alpha 66, and Veciana was the head of Alpha 66.[1413] E. Howard Hunt later said that Phillips was part of the JFK conspiracy.[1414] This corroborates what Oswald said.[1415] Author Phillip Nelson, in his book *LBJ: THE MASTERMIND OF THE JFK ASSASSINATION*, claims that Phillips was recruited into the conspiracy along with Bill Harvey, David Sanchez Morales and Frank Sturgis.[1416] On November 20, 1963 Lee Harvey Oswald told Judyth Vary Baker that Phillips was the traitor.[1417] Oswald said Phillips was behind this (the Kennedy assassination) and to remember his name, David Atlee Phillips.[1418]

According to author Phillip Nelson, in his book *LBJ: THE MASTERMIND OF THE JFK ASSASSINATION*:[1419]

> "Both Shaw and de Mohrenschildt had taken their orders directly from the man controlling the details of the operation from his CIA position in Mexico, under the code name of Maurice Bishop, David Atlee Phillips. Phillips, as did his peer David Morales, in charge of the operational and logistical end

of the plan, took his orders from Bill Harvey who reported only to two men at the highest levels of the CIA, James Jesus Angleton and Cord Meyer. According to information furnished by E. Howard Hunt ... Harvey and the others were being guided by Cord Meyer, operating out of his London CIA offices."[1420]

Shaw here refers to New Orleans CIA asset Clay Shaw (see the section on Clay Shaw).

There was an FBI memo dated November 23, 1963 from Hoover to all FBI supervisory personnel that stated that the FBI agents who had questioned Oswald had listened to a tape recording of a conversation between "Lee Oswald" and someone in the Cuban embassy who "Oswald" had telephoned.[1421] This call was made from the Russian Embassy in Mexico City to the Cuban Consulate in Mexico City on October 1, 1963, and the Hoover memo noted that the voice on the tape was not Lee Harvey Oswald.[1422] Based on the evidence that David Atlee Phillips (a.k.a. Maurice Bishop) was in charge of Western Hemispheric operations for the CIA (as Maurice Bishop he was involved in the anti-Castro Cuban movement and Lee Harvey Oswald), Phillips had been subpoenaed to appear before an executive session of the House Select Committee on Assassinations.[1423] He was asked under oath where they could locate a tape of the conversation between 'Oswald' and the Cuban embassy while he was in the Russian embassy.[1424] Phillips lied under oath and said that the tape had been recycled within a week of when the call was made and was therefore unavailable because it no longer existed.[1425] Then he was handed the Hoover memo (mentioned above) which proved that the tape was available in late November of 1963.[1426] This proved that the committee had trapped Phillips and the CIA in a lie. He had just been shown proof that he had committed perjury and was liable for prosecution.[1427] Phillips then took the memo and folded it and put it in his pocket and left the meeting without saying anything.[1428]

Mark Lane was the first to publicly raise questions about the Warren Commission. In his book *LAST WORD: MY INDICTMENT OF THE CIA IN THE MURDER OF JFK*, he claims that David Atlee Phillips was the leading CIA official in charge of defamation of those who did not accept the Warren Commission's view of the events and who helped prevent the publication of *RUSH TO JUDGEMENT*.[1429]

David Phillips tried to use the CIA-sponsored Cuban raiders to force Kennedy into an all-out war with Cuba.[1430] Kennedy was trying to make peace while the Deep State was trying to start a war. In 1962 Phillips directed Antonio Veciana to have Alpha 66 attack merchant cargo ships in Havana harbor on September 10 and October 8.[1431] This is in direct opposition to Kennedy's orders. Here we have the Deep State in open defiance of the direct orders of the elected leader. On March 19, 1963 Alpha 66 announces at a press conference in Washington, D.C. that it had raided shipping in Havana and caused a dozen casualties.[1432] Phillips is doing all this under his alias Maurice Bishop, and the CIA will deny that anyone named Maurice Bishop works for the CIA. Later, Veciana will admit to House Select Committee on Assassinations (HSCA) investigator Gaeton Fonzi that the purpose of the attack on the Soviet vessel in Cuban waters was "to publicly embarrass Kennedy and force him to move against Castro."[1433] Veciana revealed that "Maurice Bishop" (David Atlee Phillips) kept saying that Kennedy would have to be forced to make a decision and the only way was to put him up against a wall."[1434] David Atlee Phillips, pretending to be Maurice Bishop, targeted Soviet ships in an attempt to create another Soviet-American crisis.[1435]

Bill Harvey

After the Bay of Pigs fiasco, Kennedy still wanted Castro out, but without any overt action by the United States. President Kennedy put his brother Bobby in charge of the Special Operations Group. Operation Mongoose to overthrow or kill Castro was created in November of 1961 by the White House.[1436] The idea was to help Cuba overthrow Castro. Bill Harvey was a rising star at the CIA and was put in charge of Operation Mongoose. Harvey was loyal to the CIA and perhaps to the FBI. He went from the FBI to the CIA but there is some speculation that Harvey remained in close touch with Hoover.[1437] In May of 1962 poison pills were given to Bill Harvey who then gave them to mobster Johnny Roselli who then passed them on to the Cuban contact used in the first poison pill attempt on Castro.[1438]

In November of 1961 CIA Deputy Director Richard Bissell told Bill Harvey to apply the ZR/RIFLE assassination plan to Castro.[1439] Harvey reestablished the CIA connection to mobster Johnny Roselli.[1440] At the end of November 1961 Kennedy fired Allen Dulles and Richard Bissell for the Bay of Pigs debacle. Kennedy then appointed John McCone as Director of the CIA.[1441] Bill Harvey continued to use the mafia and McCone would have disapproved so he was kept in the dark.[1442] Kennedy wrote a memo to Dean Rusk to establish Operation Mongoose which was then headed up by Bill Harvey and Operation Mongoose was run out of the CIA station in Miami, code named JM/WAVE.[1443] The chief of operations at JM/WAVE was David Sanchez Morales.[1444]

(See the subsection below on David Sanchez Morales). JM/WAVE had an official staff of over 300 and 54 front corporations and became one of the largest employers in the state of Florida.[1445] JM/WAVE even had its own navy with hundreds of boats.[1446]

When CIA officer Bill Harvey was reporting to Robert Kennedy they didn't get along. Harvey thought of RFK as an amateur and questioned his judgement.[1447] Al Haig, who later became Secretary of State, said that Bobby Kennedy was in charge and they were running two raids per week into Cuba via the CIA.[1448] Bobby micro-managed the operations and Bill Harvey was not happy being micro-managed, especially by Bobby.[1449] E. Howard Hunt (See the section on E. Howard Hunt) remembered the friction between the younger Kennedy and William Harvey.[1450] Harvey had played a leading role after the Bay of Pigs and blamed the Kennedys for the failure. In a reference to the Bay of Pigs disaster, Harvey liked to display behind his desk a poster that read "The Tree of Liberty is Watered With the Blood of Patriots" and Robert Kennedy wasn't happy with either the poster or Harvey.[1451] Bill Harvey was becoming increasingly angry at RFK's interference. They were barely on speaking terms. Then the Cuban Missile Crisis happened.

In his book *THE GHOST: THE SECRET LIFE OF CIA SPYMASTER JAMES JESUS ANGLETON*, author Jefferson Morley describes how the tension between the White House and the national security agencies came to a boil at a meeting at the Pentagon at the height of the Cuban Missile Crisis:[1452]

> "Bill Harvey announced he had ordered six scouting teams to infiltrate Cuba in advance of the expected invasion. Robert Kennedy told him to call it off. Harvey said the mission was urgent. Kennedy told him to recall the teams. Harvey objected. The Attorney General insisted. The younger man was staring down the older man when Harvey exploded "If you fuckers hadn't fucked up the Bay of Pigs we wouldn't be in this fucking mess." Robert Kennedy just walked out of the meeting. "Of course I was furious." He said later "You were dealing with people's lives, the best of the Cubans, the ones who volunteer, and you're going to go off with a half-assed operation such as this?" Most of the CIA men in the meeting agreed with Harvey but they held their tongues "Harvey has destroyed himself today." Said John McCone "His usefulness has ended.""[1453]

Ramon was an anti-Castro Cuban exile who liked President Kennedy and passed on details he had heard about the planned Kennedy assassination plot, including that Bill Harvey was involved.[1454] He also knew about CIA asset Guy Banister in New Orleans.[1455] Wesley Swearingen was an FBI agent who Ramon passed the information to, and he also knew Banister.[1456] Swearingen said he could see the assassination coming a year in advance but his superiors would not believe that the CIA would kill President Kennedy.[1457] The FBI closed ranks and Swearingen was transferred to Kentucky for trying to warn everyone.[1458]

Several elements of the Deep State mentality are on display here. Note that only Bill Harvey is willing to openly defy Kennedy to his face. The rest of the Deep State folks who agreed with him kept their mouths shut in public but made it their full-time job to work in opposition to Kennedy policies. The world is on the brink of nuclear war and Bill Harvey defies his direct orders from Robert Kennedy and launches raids at Cuba anyway. This cost Harvey his current assignment, but not his job.[1459] He was still at the CIA, but they had to move him to Italy where he would be out of sight of the Kennedys.[1460]

According to author Phillip Nelson, in his book *LBJ: THE MASTERMIND OF THE JFK ASSASSINATION*:[1461]

> "Both Shaw and de Mohrenschildt had taken their orders directly from the man controlling the details of the operation from his CIA position in Mexico, under the code name of Maurice Bishop, David Atlee Phillips. Phillips, as did his peer David Morales, in charge of the operational and logistical end of the plan, took his orders from Bill Harvey who reported only to two men at the highest levels of the CIA, James Jesus Angleton and Cord Meyer. According to information furnished by E. Howard Hunt … Harvey and the others were being guided by Cord Meyer, operating out of his London CIA offices."[1462]

On January 1, 1963 Bill Harvey was replaced but the Cuban raids continued, on a smaller scale, but they continued, despite a directive from President Kennedy that they be stopped.[1463] This shows that it was not just Bill Harvey who was behind the continued raiding in direct opposition to Kennedy's policies and orders.

Bill Harvey later admitted to the Church Committee that he and Richard Helms kept the anti-Castro mafia alliance secret from then CIA Director John McCone.[1464] Richard Helms, Bill Harvey and James Jesus Angleton all believed that extraordinary efforts were justified to defeat communism.

In addition to being the chief of operations for JM/WAVE, David Sanchez Morales was a hitman for the CIA. He said that Bill Harvey had recruited him to kill President Kennedy.[1465]

Bill Harvey was in on the planning of the Kennedy assassination. He met with mobster Johnny Roselli several times.[1466] Bill Harvey worked so closely with Johnny Roselli, that Harvey's daughter took to calling Roselli "Uncle Johnny."[1467] Harvey was the one who came up with the idea of using Corsicans from France since Sicilians from Italy could lead back to the mafia. This led to Michele Mertz, who often used the name of Jean Suetre[1468] Years later it came to light that one of the shooting teams was French. Author Phillip Nelson, in his book *LBJ: THE MASTERMIND OF THE JFK ASSASSINATION*, said that Jean Suetre was in Dallas on the day JFK was killed and was then deported, and that Michele Mertz and Michele Roux were also there.[1469] Exactly which French shooters were there in Dallas that day is still not clear. Authors Belzer and Wayne, in their book *DEAD WRONG*, said that Mertz was in Dallas that day, using the name of Suetre. Marcello and Trafficante were both familiar with the Corsican mafia.[1470]

> Note: Author Richard Belzer thought Michele Mertz was using the name of Jean Suetre. Author Phillip Nelson wrote that he thought it was Jean Suetre using the name of Michele Roux and that Lucien Sarti used the name of Michel Mertz.[1471] There still appears to be some confusion on this point.

Author Phillip Nelson, in his book *LBJ: THE MASTERMIND OF THE JFK ASSASSINATION*, pointed out that Richard Helms was aware of the French shooters.[1472] (See the section on Richard Helms). In 1975 the Church Committee looked into the CIA's ZR/RIFLE program to recruit foreigners for dirty work like black bag jobs and assassinations.[1473] CIA Director Richard Helms testified about two people, code-named WI/ROGUE and QJ/WIN, who appeared on the CIA payroll from just before to just after the Dallas assassination.[1474] Nelson also points out that CIA officer Bill Harvey reported directly to Helms on this, and that several researchers concluded that these two were actually Lucien Sarti and Jean Souetre (a.k.a. Michel Mertz and Michel Roux) the French assassins were one of the shooting teams in Dealey Plaza during the Kennedy assassination.[1475] Nelson also believed that Bill Harvey reported to Cord Meyer and James Angleton at the CIA.[1476] He also said that CIA assets George de Mohrenschildt and Clay Shaw reported to David Atlee Phillips, and that CIA assets Guy Banister and David Ferrie reported to Bill Harvey, as did Phillips and David Sanchez Morales.[1477]

Author Phillip Nelson, in his book *LBJ: THE MASTERMIND OF THE JFK ASSASSINATION*, said that Lyndon Johnson knew the major players and had long and trusting relationships with them and they all also knew each other the same way.[1478] Nelson also claims that CIA officer Bill Harvey would be one of the guys who held the whole thing together.[1479] Bill Harvey had meetings with Guy Banister in 1962 and early 1963.[1480] Harvey and Angleton were setting Lee Harvey Oswald up to be the patsy in the Kennedy assassination.[1481] Oswald was sent to New Orleans to make him look like a Castro supporter. He was given a fake cover job with the Reily Coffee Company in the same neighborhood with all the intelligence offices.[1482] The Reily Coffee Company was owned by William B. Reily who was linked to the CIA front Cuban Revolutionary Council.[1483] Within sight of each other were the offices of the CIA, FBI, ONI (Office of Naval Intelligence), the Secret Service and CIA asset Guy Banister's office.[1484]

Senator Richard Russell, the head of the congressional committee to oversee the CIA, asked about the ability to keep former CIA agents quiet.[1485] Bill Harvey would show up drunk to meetings, and they tried to quietly retire him.[1486] Harvey was bitter and was willing to blackmail the CIA.[1487]

Bill Harvey died after talking to the Church Committee where he said "they didn't ask the right questions."[1488] This quote highlights the fact that the CIA folks did not volunteer information to the Congressional oversight committees. Harvey's death also shows how the death toll among those who knew too much continued to climb.

Frank Sturgis

Frank Sturgis was born Frank Fiorini. In 1952 he adopted the last name Sturgis, which was his stepfather's last name. Sturgis went to Cuba in the 1950's to help Castro and in 1958 made his first contact with the CIA.[1489] Frank Sturgis had been in Cuba helping Castro and after the revolution had been appointed by Castro to deal with the casinos owned by the mafia.[1490] Then he defected and joined the anti-Castro Cubans.[1491]

Marita Lorenz was a former 'mistress' of Castro, who Sturgis rescued from Cuba in 1960.[1492] He also convinced her to go back to Havana twice, once to steal documents from Castro and once to try to kill Castro.[1493] According to Lorenz, E. Howard Hunt was with the CIA and Sturgis and Hunt knew each other in the late 1950's and early

1960's in Cuba and Miami. Hunt initially used the name "Eduardo" when meeting with Sturgis.[1494]

On October 28, 1962 the Cuban Missile Crisis was resolved and Khrushchev announced he will dismantle the missile sites in Cuba. In return, Kennedy agreed to halt Operation Mongoose raids and promised not to invade Cuba. On December 4, 1962 a group of twelve anti-Castro Cuban exile guerillas were arrested in No Name Key as they were about to embark on a raid to Cuba.[1495] Among those arrested was Jerry Patrick Hemming, one of the founders (along with Sturgis) of an anti-Castro group, the International Anti-Communist Brigade.[1496]

In 1963 Frank Sturgis invited E. Howard Hunt to a safe house in Miami for a meeting with David Sanchez Morales. Nicknamed 'El Indio,' Morales was a hitman for the CIA. Morales said that Bill Harvey had recruited him to kill President Kennedy.[1497] Morales and Sturgis wanted Hunt to join the conspiracy.[1498] Hunt also hated President Kennedy.[1499] Sturgis, to get Hunt to join, said "You're somebody we look up to. We know how you feel about the man [Kennedy]. Are you with us?"[1500] Hunt later claimed to play only a peripheral role in the Kennedy assassination.[1501]

Author Phillip Nelson, in his book *LBJ: THE MASTERMIND OF THE JFK ASSASSINATION*, says that the CIA conspirators at the top recruited Bill Harvey, David Sanchez Morales, Frank Sturgis and David Atlee Phillips to join the conspiracy.[1502]

In 1963 the FBI seized a large amount of explosives at an anti-Castro Cuban exile training camp near New Orleans.[1503] Within a month of this, the Coast Guard assisted the British Navy in capturing a group of CIA-armed Cuban exiles in the Bahamas.[1504] Then the Federal Aviation Administration issued strong warnings to six American civilian pilots, including E. Howard Hunt's associate Frank Sturgis, who had been flying CIA-backed raids over Cuba.[1505]

Jerome Corsi, in his book *WHO REALLY KILLED KENNEDY*, claims that Frank Sturgis, Roscoe White and Sergio Arcacha Smith are prime suspects as shooters as is Michele Mertz.[1506] He also says that mobster Johnny Roselli was likely in charge of the shooters.[1507] Roscoe White was a Dalla Police officer.

During a trial in which E. Howard Hunt was suing a publication which claimed Hunt was involved in the assassination, a trial in which he lost, Marita Lorenz had a chance to testify under oath. She had a lot to say. Lorenz had known Frank Sturgis and others like E. Howard Hunt since 1960. She had been trapped as a 'mistress' of Castro and Sturgis not only rescued her but sent her back to try to kill Castro. She was also involved in the training of the Cubans in the CIA-sponsored camps in Florida.[1508] Hunt's role was to deliver lots of cash to keep the operation going.[1509]

According to Marita Lorenz, Frank Sturgis led a meeting in September of 1963 where they studied street maps of Dallas.[1510] In addition to Lorenz, the group included Lee Harvey Oswald, Pedro Diaz Lanz (the former head of the Cuban Air Force), Orlando Bosch (a Cuban exile leader and CIA operative), Jerry Patrick Hemming (a CIA operative and former Marine) and the Novo brothers.[1511] The Novo brothers were Guillermo and Ignacio Novo, two of the Cuban exile leaders.[1512] The Novo brothers were also assassins.[1513] Then, a week before the assassination, this same group took a road trip to Dallas in two cars, drove nonstop for two days and checked into a hotel in Dallas.[1514] They brought high-powered rifles with them, including scopes, and while in Dallas, E. Howard Hunt showed up with more money.[1515] Hunt later confirmed that his job was paymaster in Dallas, stopping by a few times with more money.[1516] Marita Lorenz also testified that mafia functionary Jack Ruby stopped by the hotel rooms.[1517] Lorenz further testified that she got homesick for her daughter and had Sturgis taker her to the airport where she flew home on November 19 or 20, 1963.[1518] She was on an airplane from Miami to New York with her daughter when Kennedy was assassinated.[1519]

Later, Lorenz testified about a subsequent meeting she had with Frank Sturgis where he said:[1520]

> "We killed the president that day. You could have been part of it – part of history. You should have stayed. It was safe. Everything was covered in advance. No arrests. No real newspaper investigation. It was all covered. Very professional."[1521]

In their book *COUP D'ETAT IN AMERICA*, authors Alan Weberman and Michael Canfield use forensic photography to make a strong case that Frank Sturgis and E. Howard Hunt were arrested in Dealey Plaza shortly after Kennedy was assassinated. Three men were photographed being led away by police after being found on a train. The train was in Dealey Plaza and was pulling out, but was stopped by Lee Bowers when he spotted three men in the train from his observation platform in the train yard. The three have become known as the "three tramps" because of their appearance. However, upon closer inspection, they're not really tramps. Their clothes look like they went shopping at the Salvation Army, but they are clean, the men are clean shaven, they have good shoes and they appear to be well fed. Authors Weberman and Canfield use forensic photography to make a compelling case that two of the "tramps" were actually Sturgis and Hunt. Their book, among many other things, includes acetate overlays of photographs of Sturgis and Hunt so as to make direct photographic comparisons. I urge anyone who is interested to look for themselves.

On June 17, 1972 E. Howard Hunt and Frank Sturgis, along with others, were arrested burglarizing the Watergate offices of the Democratic National Committee.[1522]

E. Howard Hunt

E. Howard Hunt was a CIA officer. In the early 1950's the Dulles brothers worked with the United Fruit Company to take control of Guatemalan railroads. In 1954 the Guatemalan coup, masterminded by E. Howard Hunt, was in the interest of United Fruit.[1523] Also involved in the Guatemala coup in 1954 with Hunt were CIA officers David Atlee Phillips and David Sanchez Morales.[1524] In March of 1959 the decision was made to create a group of Cuban exiles to invade Cuba. The CIA's Allen Dulles and Richard Bissell were pushing it and President Eisenhower approved. Tracy Barnes reported to Bissell on the project to assist Cuban exiles in ousting Castro, and E. Howard Hunt was then put on the project.[1525] Phillips and Hunt were chosen in 1960 by Richard Bissell who had been appointed by Allen Dulles to overthrow Castro in Cuba.[1526] The idea was to use their successful Guatemalan coup as the model for the Cuban coup.[1527]

E. Howard Hunt and Frank Sturgis knew each other in the late 1950's and early 1960's in Cuba and Miami. Sturgis had been working with Castro since before the Cuban revolution and was put in charge of the casinos by Castro before Castro threw the casinos out of Cuba.[1528] Then Sturgis defected and joined the anti-Castro Cubans.[1529] It was at this point, if not sooner, that Hunt and Sturgis started working together.

Hunt also got David Atlee Phillips involved in what became the Bay of Pigs project. One of Phillips' jobs was to make the invasion look like the U.S. was not involved.[1530] The idea was that the invasion was not supposed to look like an attack by the United States.[1531] It was supposed to look like the Cuban exiles did this on their own.[1532] Then, once they had established a beachhead on Cuba and "requested help," the U.S. would "step in" and provide assistance.[1533] This was supposed to give the U.S. plausible deniability.[1534] The idea was for the U.S. to be able to say 'Hey, we weren't involved until the Cubans rose up to overthrow Castro and then asked for our help.'

The Bay of Pigs was a failure. Allen Dulles and E. Howard Hunt then worked with *Fortune* magazine journalist Charles Murphy on an article called "Cuba: The Record Set Straight" to pin the blame for the failure on President Kennedy.[1535]   Author James DiEugenio, in his book *DESTINY BETRAYED*, claimed that this was the beginning of the "Kennedy cancelled the air strikes and therefore caused the Bay of Pigs to fail" myth.[1536] This myth was also used by the CIA to tell the anti-Castro Cuban exiles that it was Kennedy who had pulled the rug out from under them.[1537]   DiEugenio also says that Allen Dulles, E. Howard Hunt, David Atlee Phillips, David Morales, Sergio Arcacha Smith, David Ferrie, Clay Shaw, Guy Bannister and others were involved in the Bay of Pigs as well as being prime suspects in the Kennedy assassination.[1538] His point is that they all knew each other and all worked together on both projects.

Anthony Summers, in his book *NOT IN YOUR LIFETIME*, recounts a conversation with E. Howard Hunt. As news of the debacle came in, he and the others there reacted with dismay and scorn.[1539]

> "At CIA headquarters in our war room we thought, as the indications came, that the administration would feel more and more an obligation to unleash some United States power to equalize the situation. We kept receiving the administration's refusals with incredulity.   I felt a sense of hollowness. Somewhere along the way we lost a good part of our national will to prevail. I think it was a failure of nerve."[1540]

When the Bay of Pigs invasion was a complete failure, E. Howard Hunt was quoted in regard to the effect this had on the Cuban exiles. "The failure of the Bay of Pigs had a disastrous effect." Hunt said "They were outraged that a country so powerful as the United States only ninety miles away from their homeland could have permitted a disaster such as the Bay of Pigs to have taken place."[1541]

The Taylor Committee was formed to study the Bay of Pigs fiasco under General Maxwell Taylor.[1542] CIA historian Jack Pfeifer said that Allen Dulles was doomed after his terrible performance as a witness during the Taylor Committee investigation.[1543]   General Taylor was then recalled to active duty and became an advisor to the president and Chairman of the Joint Chiefs of Staff.[1544]

After the Bay of Pigs fiasco, Hunt started setting up safe houses and handing out money to the Cuban exile community, sometimes carrying over one hundred thousand dollars with him in a briefcase.[1545] They called him Uncle Sam.[1546] The CIA was financing the establishment of a small army and navy of Cuban exiles to launch raids into Cuba.

Hunt made use of the anti-Castro Cuban exiles who had made it to the United States.[1547] The Cuban Revolutionary Council became an umbrella group to encompass and represent many of the other anti-Castro Cuban exile groups. Training camps were set up in Florida, Panama, Guatemala and Nicaragua. Hunt's recommendation was to eliminate Castro before or during the invasion.[1548] He also suggested that the United States not count on a popular uprising until after the invasion had been a success.[1549]

During the House Select Committee on Assassinations (HSCA) investigation, Gaeton Fonzi was a staff investigator looking into the Kennedy assassination. Robert McKeown put Fonzi on to Ron Cross so Fonzi and an associate on the HSCA stopped by to see Cross who had been a CIA case officer at the JM/WAVE station when it was in full swing.[1550] Cross was retired by this point but remembered seeing Sturgis in Castro's camp in the mountains before Castro came to power.[1551] Cross was candid, and said that Hunt would occasionally stop by the JM/Wave station.[1552] Cross confirmed to Fonzi that David Phillips used Maurice Bishop as his alias.[1553] He also said he thought that Knight was Hunt's alias.[1554]

On February 2, 1963 CIA officer Tracy Barnes was put in charge of operations with Hunt reporting to him.[1555]

In 1963 Frank Sturgis invited E. Howard Hunt to a safe house in Miami for a meeting with David Sanchez Morales. Nicknamed 'El Indio,' Morales was a hit man for the CIA. Morales said that Bill Harvey had recruited him to kill President Kennedy.[1556] Morales and Sturgis wanted Hunt to join the conspiracy.[1557] Hunt also hated President Kennedy.[1558] Sturgis, to get Hunt to join, said "You're somebody we look up to. We know how you feel about the man [Kennedy]. Are you with us?"[1559] Hunt later claimed to play only a peripheral role in the assassination.[1560]

According to author Phillip Nelson, in his book *LBJ: THE MASTERMIND OF THE JFK ASSASSINATION*:[1561]

> "Both Shaw and de Mohrenschildt had taken their orders directly from the man controlling the details of the operation from his CIA position in Mexico, under the code name of Maurice Bishop, David Atlee Phillips. Phillips, as did his peer David Morales, in charge of the operational and logistical end of the plan, took his orders from Bill Harvey who reported only to two men at the highest levels of the CIA, James Jesus Angleton and Cord Meyer. According to information furnished by E. Howard Hunt ... Harvey and the others were

being guided by Cord Meyer, operating out of his London CIA offices."[1562]

Kerry Thornley went to the print shop and picked up the flyers Oswald had printed.[1563] Thornley had been recruited into the conspiracy by E. Howard Hunt.[1564]

In their book *COUP D'ETAT IN AMERICA*, authors Alan Weberman and Michael Canfield use forensic photography to make a strong case that Frank Sturgis and E. Howard Hunt were arrested in Dealey Plaza shortly after Kennedy was assassinated. Three men were photographed being led away by police after being found on a train. The train was in Dealey Plaza and was pulling out, but was stopped by Lee Bowers when he spotted three men in the train from his observation platform in the train yard. The three have become known as the "three tramps" because of their appearance. However, upon closer inspection, they're not really tramps. Their clothes look like they went shopping at the Salvation Army, but they are clean, the men are clean shaven, they have good shoes and they appear to be well fed. Authors Weberman and Canfield use forensic photography to make a compelling case that two of the "tramps" were actually Sturgis and Hunt. Their book, among many other things, includes acetate overlays of photographs of Sturgis and Hunt so as to make direct photographic comparisons. I urge anyone who is interested to look for themselves.

On June 17, 1972 a group of Nixon White House operatives known as The Plumbers, including E. Howard Hunt and Frank Sturgis, were arrested burglarizing the offices of the Democratic National Committee in Washington's Watergate complex.[1565]

Mark Lane, in his book *LAST WORD: MY INDICTMENT OF THE CIA IN THE MURDER OF JFK*, has an excellent first-hand account of a lawsuit in which he participated as a lawyer. Lane recounts how Liberty Lobby published an account in *The Spotlight* by a former CIA officer who accused E. Howard Hunt of being involved in the Kennedy assassination.[1566] Hunt filed a defamation suit and won a large judgement, mainly because the lawyer for Liberty Lobby didn't put up a fight.[1567] Hunt denied being in Dallas that day, and claimed that he was facing family issues due to the publication.[1568] He claimed his family had read the article and questioned him, thus he wanted more money.[1569] Hunt won the lawsuit and was awarded $650,000.[1570] Liberty Lobby was facing bankruptcy and the case was overturned on appeal in 1983 and in 1985 Mark Lane was hired to retry the case. Lane insisted that they retry the case on the merits.[1571] Hunt had been in Dallas that day and did conspire to assassinate Kennedy.[1572] Lane took depositions from David Atlee Phillips, Richard Helms, G. Gordon

Liddy, Stansfield Turner and Marita Lorenz as well as cross examination of Hunt. Lane took the jury through Hunt's many and varied explanations of where he was on that day.[1573] Lane and Liberty Lobby won and Hunt lost. Hunt had lied under oath and was caught in those lies. He said that he was home watching TV with his family when Kennedy was killed and he had also said in the previous trial that having his children read the article in the *The Spotlight* had caused him much family pain as they then wondered if he was in Dallas that day and involved in the murder of Kennedy. Lane asked him in court and under oath why his children would think he was in Dallas if he was home watching TV with them when JFK was killed.[1574] The jury did not find Hunt to be credible.[1575] The testimony of Marita Lorenz placed E. Howard Hunt in Dallas on November 21, 1963, along with Frank Sturgis and Jack Ruby, all in the same motel room.[1576] She also described how Sturgis later admitted that they had killed Kennedy.[1577] The foreman of the jury, Leslie Armstrong, said on the courthouse steps that Lane had clearly demonstrated that Hunt and the CIA had assassinated Kennedy.[1578] Later, Mark Lane tracked down Jerry Patrick Hemming who said that there were three cars in the caravan, but other than that everything Marita Lorenz said was true.[1579] The Novo brothers (Guillermo and Ignacio) who went there with Lorenz and Hemming were assassins.[1580] The Novo brothers would later be charged in the 1976 car bomb murder of Orlando Letelier. Letelier was a vocal opponent of Augusto Pinochet who assumed power in Chile in a CIA-backed coup in 1973.[1581]

Marita Lorenz also testified that she saw Hunt pay off the Kennedy assassination team in Dallas.[1582]

In 1985 the *Washington Post* and the rest of the mainstream media avoided coverage of the verdict in the trial where Hunt lost in court and it was obvious that the CIA was involved in the Kennedy assassination.[1583]

E. Howard Hunt said on his deathbed that Lyndon Johnson was at the top of the chain of command on the JFK assassination, and directly below him was CIA officer Cord Meyer.[1584] Hunt did not think Johnson was the mastermind but he believed that LBJ was in on it with David Atlee Phillips and Cord Meyer.[1585]

CIA officer E Howard Hunt made a death bed confession. His son, St John Hunt, wrote a book about his father's deathbed confession, which was taped. Hunt claimed he was a bench warmer on the day of the Kennedy assassination. This confirms the CIA's role from the beginning.[1586]

Clay Shaw

Clay Shaw was a wealthy businessman in New Orleans who worked with the CIA.[1587] Shaw founded the International Trade Mart in New Orleans. Allen Dulles and the CIA had a fifty-million-dollar fund deposited in the J. Henry Schroeder bank.[1588] Dulles was a director of the bank and eventually became their chief counsel.[1589] In 1956 the J. Henry Schroeder bank financed the opening of a Swiss company called Permindex which worked with the World Trade Center Corporation.[1590] In 1961 the Italian press charged that Permindex was used by the CIA to supply money to Corsican assassins like Michele Mertz to kill French President Charles de Gaulle.[1591] In the late 1960's New Orleans District Attorney Jim Garrison established that Clay Shaw was a member of the board of both Permindex and the World Trade Center Corporation.[1592]

During the Garrison investigation, Maurice Gatlin was sought for questioning. Maurice Gatlin had served as a bag man for the CIA, Clay Shaw and CIA asset Guy Banister.[1593] Gatlin had brought cash to France to pay for the assassins to kill Charles de Gaulle, and he suddenly became unavailable for questioning by Garrison because he died from a fall from a sixth-floor balcony.[1594]

Clay Shaw was involved with the projects that Oswald, Ferrie, Banister and the others were working on in New Orleans in the summer of 1963. In the late 1960's, Shaw became the focus of the Garrison investigation which was the only official prosecution in connection with the Kennedy assassination. Clay Shaw narrowly escaped being convicted of conspiracy to commit murder by having the CIA interfere in Garrison's investigation and Shaw's trial. The Garrison investigation and prosecution of Clay Shaw is covered in more detail in a later chapter. After Shaw was dead and therefore could no longer be prosecuted, the CIA admitted that Shaw was in fact connected to the CIA. Richard Helms had a long career with the CIA, topped off by being Director of the CIA from 1966 to 1973. In 1979 Helms testified under oath that Clay Shaw was connected to the CIA.

In his book *LAST WORD: MY INDICTMENT OF THE CIA IN THE MURDER OF JFK*, author Mark Lane said:[1595]

> "Had Shaw survived until after June 5, 1984, when Garrison discovered that Shaw had been associated with the CIA, he might have faced legal difficulties. There is no statute of limitations for murder in Louisiana; even if there were a time-limiting statute it would have been tolled in the event of

deliberate concealment of material facts. Shaw had died almost ten years before Garrison learned that the CIA admitted that the connection had existed. His death prevented him from facing the possibility of a motion to reopen the murder case against him."[1596]

According to author Phillip Nelson, in his book *LBJ: THE MASTERMIND OF THE JFK ASSASSINATION*:[1597]

> "Both Shaw and de Mohrenschildt had taken their orders directly from the man controlling the details of the operation from his CIA position in Mexico, under the code name of Maurice Bishop, David Atlee Phillips. Phillips, as did his peer David Morales, in charge of the operational and logistical end of the plan, took his orders from Bill Harvey who reported only to two men at the highest levels of the CIA, James Jesus Angleton and Cord Meyer. According to information furnished by E. Howard Hunt … Harvey and the others were being guided by Cord Meyer, operating out of his London CIA offices."[1598]

Author James DiEugenio, in his book *DESTINY BETRAYED*, says that Allen Dulles, E. Howard Hunt, David Atlee Phillips, David Morales, Sergio Arcacha Smith, David Ferrie, Clay Shaw, Guy Bannister and others were involved in the Bay of Pigs as well as being prime suspects in the Kennedy assassination.[1599] Author Phillip Nelson, in his book *LBJ: THE MASTERMIND OF THE JFK ASSASSINATION*, says that Bill Harvey reported to Cord Meyer and James Angleton at the CIA, and that Guy Banister, David Ferrie and Clay Shaw reported to Bill Harvey.[1600]

Clay Shaw was working with Oswald and Ferrie on, among other things, the cancer bioweapon project.[1601] Once it was ready to be tested on human subjects, they had several human guinea pigs from the state prison in Angola, Louisiana sent to the state mental hospital in Jackson, Louisiana.[1602] Shaw drove his black Cadillac with Ferrie and Oswald to Clinton, Louisiana to wait for the phone call that the convoy was on its way from Angola to Jackson.[1603] The idea was that they would join the convoy and all arrive at the hospital as part of the convoy.[1604]

Then two things happened that would cause the trip to enter the historical record. First, there was a voter drive in Clinton, Louisiana that day. Martin Luther King, Jr. had given his famous "I have a dream" speech in Washington, D.C. and inspired a voter drive among African Americans.[1605] The pay phone where they had chosen to wait for the call about the convoy just happened to be near where the voter drive was going on. Second, the convoy was delayed.[1606] This meant that the big black Cadillac was sitting in little Clinton, Louisiana for hours and the white people in it got noticed and were remembered later.[1607]

When Clay Shaw died, on August 15, 1974, he was embalmed before there could be an autopsy.[1608] This was illegal and the cause of death could not be determined.[1609]

David Ferrie

David Ferrie was a pilot who worked for the CIA and for mafia boss Carlos Marcello.[1610] Oswald joined the Civil Air Patrol at the age of 15 and met David Ferrie.[1611] Ferrie then recruited Lee Harvey Oswald into the Marines and the CIA when Oswald was still a teenager.[1612] Ferrie also worked with Oswald in the summer of 1963 in New Orleans on several CIA projects. One of those projects was to create a fast-acting cancer to use to kill Fidel Castro while making it look like the U.S. was not involved. Another project was to make Oswald appear to be a supporter of Fidel Castro so he would be able to travel to Cuba to deliver the cancer bioweapon. Oswald was not told that the real project they were working on was a plot to kill President Kennedy. He was told he was being groomed to help kill Castro. In fact, Oswald was being set up to be the patsy in the Kennedy assassination. He only gradually figured this out, and only realized he was the patsy when it was too late. David Ferrie was part of that setup. Ferrie was also virulently anti-communist, anti-Kennedy and made no secret of his views.[1613] While all this was going on, they were also smuggling weapons and supplies to the anti-Castro Cuban exiles that they were training in the camps near New Orleans. Ferrie flew dozens of CIA missions to Cuba before the Bay of Pigs invasion.[1614]

In the summer of 1963 the CIA was trying to implicate Cuba and/or Russia in the upcoming assassination of President Kennedy. Since the CIA was, among other things, supplying the patsy for the assassination, they wanted to make sure that the patsy would also implicate at least Cuba. If some lone nut kills the president, that's a tragedy. If the lone nut could also appear to have been sent by Castro (and, by implication, the Soviet Union), then the assassination of President Kennedy could be blamed on Cuba and maybe even the Russians. This would give the CIA and the Pentagon an excuse to invade Cuba and maybe even launch an attack on Russia.

So, Oswald was ordered to go to New Orleans and help with the gun smuggling, the training of Cubans and the cancer project. While he was there he was also told to appear to be a Castro supporter. His cover job was at the Reily Coffee Company, but he spent his time on the various CIA projects while also handing out pro-Castro leaflets and creating incidents to get media coverage as a Castro supporter.

While in New Orleans, Oswald worked with David Ferrie. Oswald had known Ferrie since he joined the Civil Air Patrol as a teenager before he joined the Marines. Ferrie was who guided Oswald into the Marines and into the CIA. Now they work together on the various CIA projects together. They both used Guy Banister's office as a base of operations. Ferrie was listed on the books as an investigator for the Banister Detective Agency. Jack Martin, who worked for the Banister Detective Agency, would tell the FBI within a few days of the Kennedy assassination that Ferrie had helped get Oswald into the Marine Corps.[1615]

Ferrie's apartment was used for some of the mice and the lab experiments necessary to develop the cancer bioweapon. Once the weapon was developed, it was tested on human subjects. This is why Ferrie, Clay Shaw and Oswald made a trip to the state mental hospital in the summer of 1963.

According to author Phillip Nelson, in his book *LBJ: THE MASTERMIND OF THE JFK ASSASSINATION*, Bill Harvey reported to Cord Meyer and James Angleton at the CIA and Guy Banister, David Ferrie and Clay Shaw reported to Bill Harvey.[1616] Author James DiEugenio, in his book *DESTINY BETRAYED*, said that Allen Dulles, E. Howard Hunt, David Atlee Phillips, David Morales, Sergio Arcacha Smith, David Ferrie, Clay Shaw, Guy Bannister and others were involved in the Bay of Pigs as well as in the Kennedy assassination.[1617]

Guy Banister's secretary Delphine Roberts remembered Ferrie as 'one of the agents' at 544 Camp Street. "Many times, when he came into the office, he used the private office behind Banister's and I was told he was doing private work. I believed his work was somehow connected with the CIA rather than the FBI."[1618] Some of the pro-Castro leaflets Oswald handed out were hand-stamped with the address 544 Camp Street, which was the office of ex-FBI agent Guy Banister and his investigator David Ferrie.[1619] Both Banister and Ferrie were ardent anti-Castro activists.[1620] Ferrie and Oswald worked with the ant-Castro Cubans, organizing training and running guns and supplies to the training camps near New Orleans.[1621]

Sergio Arcacha Smith was one of the leaders of the anti-Castro Cuban exiles.[1622] He was the New Orleans delegate of the FRD (Fronte

Democratico Revolucionario) which a CIA document on Arcacha Smith states was created and sponsored by the CIA.[1623] The CIA used the FRD as a front for recruitment of a brigade for the Bay of Pigs invasion.[1624] Arcacha admitted in 1967 that he and David Ferrie, while working for the CIA, helped train the Bay of Pigs invasion force.[1625] When the FRD was phased out Arcacha established a New Orleans chapter of the Cuban Revolutionary Council, the Cuban 'government in exile' organized by the CIA.[1626] In addition to working with David Ferrie, Arcacha Smith was on his way to Dallas to kill Kennedy and the Louisiana State Police appear to have found diagrams of the Dallas sewer system in Dealey Plaza at Smith's apartment.[1627] Arcacha Smith had a woman named Rose Cherami with him on his way to Dallas to kill JFK, which is how we know about his involvement. (See the section on Rose Cherami predicting the Kennedy assassination). In July of 1963 a group of anti-Castro Cubans arrive in New Orleans from Miami and were directed to a training camp by Lake Pontchartrain. During the Garrison investigation it came out that Oswald and Ferrie were seen at this camp.[1628]

By the summer of 1963 New Orleans mafia boss Carlos Marcello was locked in mortal combat with the Kennedys.[1629] By this time Marcello had already said he plans to have President Kennedy killed. Marcello was also openly getting help from Guy Banister and David Ferrie in his fight to keep from being deported.[1630] Ferrie made at least one flight to Guatemala to gather evidence for Marcello's defense.[1631] On November 9 and 16, 1963, not long before the Kennedy assassination on November 22, there were meetings between Ferrie and Marcello. Ferrie claimed they were mapping strategy for Marcello's trial.[1632] On the day Kennedy was killed, Ferrie was in court with mafia boss Carlos Marcello.[1633] He then drove to Houston, Texas.[1634] While in Texas he made a collect call from a motel back to Marcello's New Orleans headquarters. He then went to a skating rink and made a bunch of calls on a pay phone.[1635] He was there to fly some of the shooters to Mexico if necessary.[1636] Marcello would subsequently finance a lucrative service station franchise in an ideal location in New Orleans for Ferrie.[1637]

Lee Harvey Oswald had David Ferrie's library card in his possession when he was arrested. This led to the arrest of Ferrie which caused a problem for J. Edgar Hoover. The connection to Marcello was becoming too obvious. Hoover intervened to keep the FBI agents from looking into Marcello's organization.[1638] The FBI made a show of investigating and the matter was soon dropped.[1639]

In his book *ACT OF TREASON: THE ROLE OF J. EDGAR HOOVER IN THE ASSASSINATION OF PRESIDENT KENNEDY*, author Mark North has the following quote:[1640]

> "CBS producer Peter Noyes recalls a conversation he once had with ... a former member of the NBC television camera team that had covered the murders of the president and Oswald. Sometime toward the middle of the week of November 25, as interest in Ferrie was reaching a crescendo in New Orleans and Dallas, the NBC men had a discussion about Ferrie's links to Oswald and Marcello with a group of FBI agents and newsmen that he remembered everyone found most provocative. However, the FBI soon put a damper on his interest in the subject. For, immediately after the discussion broke up, one of the agents took him aside and told him that he should never discuss what they had just been talking about with anyone, 'for the good of the country.'"[1641]

Ferrie worried that there was a photo of himself with Oswald in Civil Air Patrol when Oswald was a cadet there.[1642] A photo surfaced in 1993 and was shown on the PBS Frontline Special about Oswald.[1643] When Mike Ewing of the House Select Committee on Assassinations (HSCA) interviewed Parades he told him that he was surprised that the FBI never interviewed him about the matter since:[1644]

> "I sure could have told them that Oswald and Ferrie were in the CAP." He stated that "I specifically remember Oswald. I can remember him clearly, and Ferrie was heading the unit then. I'm not saying they might have been there together. I'm saying it is a certainty."[1645]

Parades said Oswald first attended meetings at Lakefront, but when Ferrie left Lakefront to start up a new troop at Moisant Oswald followed him there.[1646]

In 1984 Jack Van Laningham was a fellow inmate who was willing to rat on Marcello. Marcello confessed to Van Laningham.[1647] He hated Robert Kennedy from back when he was deported to the jungle in South America.[1648] David Ferrie had introduced Lee Harvey Oswald to Carlos Marcello in New Orleans.[1649] Marcello claimed to have set Jack Ruby up in his club in Dallas.[1650] He also said he had President Kennedy ("the little son of a bitch") killed and he would do it again.[1651] Van Laningham brought in a portable radio with an FBI bug in it.[1652]

Hoover had his agents drop the investigation of Ferrie and make no mention of it in the FBI supplemental report of January 13, 1964.[1653]

In the late 1960's, a few years after the Kennedy assassination, Jim Garrison, the District Attorney for New Orleans, eventually decided that rogue elements within the CIA, including Clay Shaw, Guy Bannister, David Ferrie and a bunch of Cuban exiles had turned on President Kennedy.[1654]   David Ferrie was initially Garrison's prime suspect.[1655]   In February of 1967 Ferrie was named as a defendant in the Garrison investigation.[1656]   Ferrie said that Garrison had just made him a dead man.[1657]   People (like Maurice Gatlin mentioned above) started getting killed when Garrison started looking into the Kennedy assassination.[1658]   Garrison was apparently getting too close to the truth. Ferrie turned out to be right about the danger to himself.[1659]   On February 22, 1967 David Ferrie was found dead in his apartment.[1660]

Jack Martin, the investigator hired by Guy Banister to do any actual private investigations that happened to walk into the office, was reluctant to talk to Garrison because he didn't want to die like all the others.[1661]

Guy Banister

Guy Banister was an FBI agent who rose to become the Special Agent in Charge (SAIC) of the Chicago office in the early 1950's.   Then his extramarital affairs and drinking caused him to have to leave the FBI. However, he remained on good terms with Hoover.   Hoover made a point of finding jobs for former FBI agents and using them as contractors.   Former FBI agents could be very useful to Hoover as cutouts.   Hoover could have them do illegal things that the FBI was not supposed to do like break-ins and wiretaps.[1662]   Banister went from the FBI to become the Assistant Superintendent of the New Orleans Police Department in 1955, but his drinking and erratic behavior caused him to have to leave that job also.   At one point he pulled out a gun and shouted "There comes a time when the world's problems can be better solved with a bullet than the ballot!"[1663]   Banister was also virulently anti-communist, anti-Kennedy and, like Ferrie, made no secret of his views.[1664]   This made him a good fit for the needs of the intelligence community, who were also strongly anti-communist and anti-Kennedy, so Banister then opened his own office to work undercover for the FBI and the CIA.   He hired an associate name Jack Martin to handle any walk-in clients looking for detective work due to having an office as a front for the clandestine work.

Author Anthony Summers, in his book *NOT IN YOUR LIFETIME*, quotes Banister's secretary, Delphene Roberts, who said:[1665]

"Mr. Banister had been a special agent for the FBI and was still working for them. There were quite a number of connections which he kept with the CIA and the FBI too. I know he and the FBI traded information due to his former association."[1666] She also says "I think he received funds from the CIA. I know he had access to large funds at various times in 1963." Summers points out that she added that known intelligence agents and law enforcement officers often visited Banister's office and that she accepted the comings and goings as normal because, so far as she was concerned "The visitors and her boss were doing something to try to stop what was taking place, the danger that was facing this country because of Cuba."[1667]

David Ferrie also worked out of Guy Banister's office on 544 Camp Street. He was officially listed as an investigator for Banister.[1668]

Banister's office became the hub of activity for covert intelligence projects in New Orleans. These projects included supplying training, guns and munitions to anti-Castro Cuban exiles at nearby camps and spying on radical college students in New Orleans.[1669] This is how, in the summer of 1963 when Oswald needed to brush up his pro-Castro credentials, he was sent to New Orleans to Guy Bansiter. The Banister office also became Oswald's base of operations.[1670] Oswald wrote to the New York headquarters of the Fair Play for Cuba Committee (F.P.C.C.) that he wanted to start a New Orleans F.P.C.C. chapter.[1671] Guy Banister had Oswald set up shop in a room upstairs at Banister's 544 Camp Street office. Later, both Banister's secretary and her daughter will be among the many people who identified Oswald as working upstairs at Guy Banister's office.[1672] Banister hated Castro, so his secretary asked him why Oswald, who was working out of Banister's office, was handing out pro-Castro leaflets, and told her not to worry about it.[1673]

FBI Director Hoover still kept a line on Bill Harvey and used him as a mole in the CIA. Guy Banister was also doing the same thing for Hoover even though he was officially retired from the FBI.[1674]

In the meantime, Oswald got on with what he had been told was his real job, which was to make himself look like a pro-Castro communist. On May 26, 1963 Oswald got in touch with the Fair Play for Cuba Committee (F.P.C.C.) about opening a New Orleans chapter.[1675] On May 29, 1963 at Jones Printing Company, next to Reily Coffee, Oswald ordered a thousand handbills for the F.P.C.C.[1676] Some of the handbills were hand-stamped with the address 544 Camp Street.[1677]

In 1960 Sergio Arcacha Smith came to the U.S. He was sponsored by the CIA as an anti-Castro Cuban exile.[1678] Banister helped him get set up to raise funds for his cause and they both moved their offices in 1962 to the Newman building at 544 Camp Street.[1679] Arcacha Smith worked with Guy Banister, David Ferrie and Lee Oswald on anti-Castro activities.[1680]

CIA officer Bill Harvey met with Guy Banister in 1962.[1681] Harvey and James Jesus Angleton were setting Oswald up to be the Patsy.[1682]

According to author Phillip Nelson, in his book *LBJ: THE MASTERMIND OF THE JFK ASSASSINATION*, Bill Harvey reported to Cord Meyer and James Angleton at the CIA and Guy Banister, David Ferrie and Clay Shaw reported to Bill Harvey.[1683] Author James DiEugenio, in his book *DESTINY BETRAYED*, said that Allen Dulles, E. Howard Hunt, David Atlee Phillips, David Morales, Sergio Arcacha Smith, David Ferrie, Clay Shaw, Guy Bannister and others were involved in the Bay of Pigs as well as in the Kennedy assassination.[1684]

Guy Banister even pitched in to help the effort to keep mafia boss Carlos Marcello from being deported.[1685] David Ferrie was working on this project as well.[1686] Another secretary, Mary Brengel, was taking dictation on a letter for this project when she said she was surprised about the contents.[1687] Banister had always been against organized crime, but Banister said "There are principles being violated and if this goes on it could affect every citizen in the United States." So, Banister had decided to switch sides in this case and help Marcello.[1688]

On November 22, 1963, the day President Kennedy was assassinated, Jack Martin (the only actual private investigator at Banister's detective agency) and Guy Banister got in an argument that turned into a beating where Banister tried to kill Martin with the butt of a revolver.[1689] Only the intervention of Banister's secretary saved Martin's life.[1690] Martin later said that what had provoked the reaction was his question "What are you going to do, kill me like you all did to Kennedy?"[1691] Banister told his secretary not to talk to the FBI about Oswald and gave her some time off so she wouldn't be in the office for a while.[1692]

The FBI made no real attempt to investigate their friend Guy Banister. They even claimed not to make the connection between the 544 Camp Street stamped on Oswald's leaflets and Guy Banister's office.[1693] They referred to Banister's office as being at 532 Lafayette Street. This was a ruse. The office was on the corner of Camp and Lafayette and 532 Lafayette was just a side door to the same place.[1694] The FBI, as usual, went out of its way to not see the obvious connection. The FBI report of the interview with Banister showed that he was asked questions about anti-Castro exiles but none at all about Oswald or use of the 544 Camp Street address on Oswald's handouts.[1695]

On July 1, 1964 Guy Banister died of a heart attack.[1696]

Jack Martin, the investigator hired by Guy Banister to do any actual private investigations that happened to walk into the office, was reluctant to talk to Garrison because he didn't want to die like all the others.[1697] The 'others' were the other people around Banister, including Lee Oswald, David Ferrie, Maurice Gatlin and Guy Banister himself.

Cord Meyer

Cord Meyer had a vision of a one-world government that would put an end to war.[1698] In 1945 he married Mary Pinchot. They shared the same vision of a world at peace. She was an intelligent and talented writer and editor and their marriage was a partnership of equals where they both worked together on the same goal.[1699] Together they went to the United Nations conference on International Organization in San Francisco.[1700] John F. Kennedy also attended the conference. The three already knew each other, but there was some kind of confrontation between Cord and John at the conference that clouded their relationship from then on.[1701] At one point, Kennedy, as a journalist, asked to interview Cord and was turned down.[1702] Cord was still idealistic and advocated world government as a writer and scholar.[1703] Unfortunately for Cord, the world federalist movement was eclipsed by the Cold War. He became frustrated by his inability to impact events.[1704] This frustration spilled over into his personal life and marriage, which suffered and deteriorated. By 1951, with their marriage cooling off and the Cold War heating up, Allen Dulles recruited Cord Meyer into the CIA.[1705] This move appeared to Mary to be Cord abandoning his idealism and selling out.[1706] Cord did well at the CIA and eventually was put in charge of projects like Operation Mockingbird and Radio Free Europe. He was awarded the Distinguished Intelligence Medal three times.[1707] The young couple moved to the Washington, D.C. area for Cord's job, but they could no longer be partners like they had been when they were first married. Cord was not allowed to talk about his work and, even if he could, he and Mary would have been on opposite sides. Mary still believed in working for world peace while Cord was putting all his effort into being a Cold Warrior. Mary was now shut out and increasingly vocal in her opposition to the CIA, its mission, strategy and tactics.[1708] Mary particularly detested Allen Dulles and compared him to Machiavelli, only worse.[1709] By the mid-1950's Mary had gone from being Cord's partner and biggest supporter to being shut out and opposed to what he was doing. Mary was uncomfortable as a "CIA wife" and was increasingly alienated from Cord.[1710] Mary was free and uninhibited and Cord was cold and dismissive.[1711] In 1956 Mary told Cord she wanted a divorce.[1712] Mary cited "extreme mental cruelty" as her reason for the divorce.[1713] Cord Meyer was devastated by the divorce. He was furious. In his book *MARY'S MOSAIC*, author Peter Janney quotes CIA officer Robert Crowley "Cord was so angry being dumped he hated her from then on."[1714] Janney also quotes journalist Charlie Bartlett, a close friend and Yale classmate of Cord Meyer "Cord was shaken after his divorce. He played on the wild side. He was drinking too much and making an ass out of himself."[1715]

Cord Meyer had always despised John F. Kennedy and other newly rich folks he considered inferior, because he came from old money.[1716] After the divorce Mary Meyer eventually started an affair with Kennedy which continued in the White House. Cord had still held a grudge against Kennedy since the conference in 1945. The incident at the conference may have been an attempt by Kennedy to seduce Mary. Regardless of what the incident was, Cord hated Kennedy from 1945 on.[1717] The affair Mary was having with Kennedy deepened Cord's hatred of Kennedy.[1718] At the same time, Cord was loyal to Allen Dulles, who had protected him from Senator Joseph McCarthy's attempt to add Cord's scalp to his belt.

Author Peter Janney, in his book MARY'S MOSAIC, pointed out that:[1719]

> "Under Cord Meyer's tutelage, Mockingbird became a stunning success. Whenever the CIA wanted a news story slanted in a particular way, it got it. This amounted to a subversion of democracy's most precious cornerstone, the free press."[1720]

> "During the 1950's, the CIA initiated Operation Mockingbird, a project designed, the reader will recall, to influence the American media to slant news stories favoring the CIA's agenda or point of view, particularly those having to do with international events and foreign policy. The program had been started by Allen Dulles's top lieutenant Frank Wisner, a friend of Phil Graham's and at one time Cord Meyer's boss. Wisner successfully "recruited" a number of prominent journalists to the CIA, including his friend Phil Graham, who soon helped run Mockingbird within mainstream media outlets. Using newspapers, magazines, radio and television,

even Hollywood, the CIA's disinformation spin machine went to work shaping public opinion and perceptions, undermining the integrity and independence of an indispensable pillar of the democratic process."[1721]

By 1963 Kennedy had become the champion of world peace, even against the opposition of his own administration. During his Peace Speech Kennedy articulated the vision that Cord Meyer had once championed. Kennedy went around his own national security apparatus and crafted a nuclear test ban treaty to propose to the Soviet Union.[1722] He was also reaching out through informal channels to make peace with Castro.[1723] He had rejected the Cold Warrior mindset of the CIA and the Pentagon and he was pursuing peace. He was also sleeping with Mary Pinchot Meyer, Cord Meyer's ex-wife.

It appears that Cord Meyer's hatred of Kennedy got the best of him. Below are several examples of authors who assert that Cord Meyer was part of the conspiracy to assassinate Kennedy. Most, if not all, of these appear to trace back to the deathbed confessions of CIA officer E. Howard Hunt.

According to author Phillip Nelson, in his book *LBJ: THE MASTERMIND OF THE JFK ASSASSINATION*, Bill Harvey reported to Cord Meyer and James Angleton at the CIA and Guy Banister, David Ferrie and Clay Shaw reported to Bill Harvey.[1724] E. Howard Hunt said on his deathbed that LBJ was at the top of the chain of command on the hit and directly below him was Cord Meyer.[1725] Hunt did not think LBJ was the mastermind but he believed that LBJ was in on it with David Atlee Phillips and Cord Meyer.[1726]

According to author Phillip Nelson, in his book *LBJ: THE MASTERMIND OF THE JFK ASSASSINATION*:[1727]

> "Both Shaw and de Mohrenschildt had taken their orders directly from the man controlling the details of the operation from his CIA position in Mexico, under the code name of Maurice Bishop, David Atlee Phillips. Phillips, as did his peer David Morales, in charge of the operational and logistical end of the plan, took his orders from Bill Harvey who reported only to two men at the highest levels of the CIA, James Jesus Angleton and Cord Meyer. According to information furnished by E. Howard Hunt ... Harvey and the others were being guided by Cord Meyer, operating out of his London CIA offices."[1728]

President John F. Kennedy was assassinated on November 22, 1963 in Dallas, Texas.

Author Peter Janney, in his book *MARY'S MOSAIC*, points out that Bobby Kennedy directly confronted CIA Director John McCone to see if the CIA was involved. He asked in a way that McCone couldn't lie, but McCone was not in control of the CIA.[1729] Dick Helms, James Angleton, Bill Harvey, Cord Meyer, Tracy Barnes and Bob Crowley still carried the flag for Dulles behind the scenes.[1730] Bobby Kennedy asked the wrong man.[1731]

Mary Meyer had read the Warren report and confronted Cord Meyer who told his boss at the CIA, James Jesus Angleton.[1732] Mary had connected the dots and furiously confronted Cord with what she had dug up.[1733] She was planning to go public with what she had found, and she was not someone who could be ignored.[1734] If she made good on her threats, as she intended, the public would believe that she had inside information.[1735] Mary had the potential to ignite more of a firestorm than the conspirators could afford, so they had to silence her.[1736] Mary's murder by the CIA is covered in more detail in a later chapter. There was an attempt made to make the murder appear to have been by a local man named Ray Crump in a failed sexual assault gone wrong.

Author Peter Janney in his book *MARY'S MOSAIC*, pointed out that James Jesus Angleton could not afford to be seen as being involved in any way in the murder of Mary Meyer, so he had CIA officer Wistar Janney (author Peter Janney's father) call *Washington Post* editor Ben Bradlee and Cord Meyer with the 'news' that Mary Meyer had been murdered.[1737] He also pointed out that Cord Meyer knew in advance his ex-wife was going to be murdered.[1738] In addition, he said that two years after Cord's death, his former research assistant and Meyer family friend Carol Delaney was quoted in C. David Heymann's book *THE GEORGETOWN LADIES' SOCIAL CLUB* as saying the following: "Mr. Meyer didn't for a minute think that Ray Crump murdered his wife or that it'd been an attempted rape, but, being an Agency man, he couldn't very well accuse the CIA of the crime, although the murder had all the markings of an in-house rubout."[1739]

David Sanchez Morales

David Morales was a hitman for the CIA whose nickname was 'El Indio,' which loosely translates to the 'big indian.' In their book *THE MAN WHO KILLED KENNEDY*, authors Roger Stone and Mike Colapietro documented that:[1740]

"Morales's lawyer Robert Walton had said multiple times that El Indio confessed his guilt in the JFK assassination. Morales told Walton, "I was in Dallas when we got that mother fucker, and I was in Los Angeles [where Robert Kennedy was murdered] when we got the little bastard."[1741]

Author David Talbot, in his book *THE DEVIL'S CHESSBOARD: ALLEN DULLES, THE CIA, AND THE RISE OF AMERICA'S SECRET GOVERNMENT*, said that:[1742]

"According to Morales's daughter, he was the CIA's "peon." Her father was utterly devoted to the Agency. "He did whatever he was told. They gave him a lifestyle that he would never have had under any other circumstances ... He did everything for the Company. His family wasn't his life – the Company was his life.""[1743]

Allen Dulles decided to interfere in Guatemala and overthrew the government. The CIA folks involved in that operation included E. Howard Hunt, Edward Lansdale, Tracy Barnes, Grayston Lynch, Rip Robertson, David Sanchez Morales and David Atlee Phillips.[1744]

Author James DiEugenio, in his book *DESTINY BETRAYED*, said that Allen Dulles, E. Howard Hunt, David Atlee Phillips, David Morales, Sergio Arcacha Smith, David Ferrie, Clay Shaw, Guy Bannister and others were involved in the Bay of Pigs as well as in the Kennedy assassination.[1745]

E. Howard Hunt, Edward Lansdale, Grayston Lynch, Rip Robertson, David Sanchez Morales and David Atlee Phillips were all in Dealey Plaza on the day Kennedy was assassinated.[1746]

David Morales was a hitman for the CIA who died suddenly in 1978 before he could testify before the HSCA could hear his testimony.[1747] He was in all three of the groups listed above. E. Howard Hunt also named Morales as being involved in the Kennedy assassination.[1748]

A man fitting Morales' description was involved in the Kennedy assassination. Morales was likely in Dallas that day, in the Texas Book Depository. Morales died in 1978 under suspicious circumstances just days before he was to testify before the House Select Committee on Assassinations.[1749]

According to author Phillip Nelson, in his book *LBJ: THE MASTERMIND OF THE JFK ASSASSINATION*:[1750]

"Both Shaw and de Mohrenschildt had taken their orders directly from the man controlling the details of the operation from his CIA position in Mexico, under the code name of Maurice Bishop, David Atlee Phillips. Phillips, as did his peer David Morales, in charge of the operational and logistical end of the plan, took his orders from Bill Harvey who reported only to two men at the highest levels of the CIA, James Jesus Angleton and Cord Meyer. According to information furnished by E. Howard Hunt ... Harvey and the others were being guided by Cord Meyer, operating out of his London CIA offices."[1751]

E. Howard Hunt eventually confessed to being involved in the assassination. He did not think Johnson was the mastermind but he believed that LBJ was in on it with CIA officers David Atlee Phillips and Cord Meyer.[1752]

In 1963 Frank Sturgis invited E. Howard Hunt to a safe house in Miami for a meeting with David Sanchez Morales. Nicknamed 'El Indio,' Morales was a hitman for the CIA. Morales said that Bill Harvey had recruited him to kill President Kennedy.[1753] Morales and Sturgis wanted Hunt to join the conspiracy.[1754] Hunt also hated President Kennedy.[1755] Sturgis, to get Hunt to join, said "You're somebody we look up to. We know how you feel about the man [Kennedy]. Are you with us?"[1756] Hunt later claimed to play only a peripheral role in the assassination.[1757]

Author Phillip Nelson, in his book *LBJ: THE MASTERMIND OF THE JFK ASSASSINATION*, says that the CIA conspirators at the top recruited Bill Harvey, David Sanchez Morales, Frank Sturgis and David Atlee Phillips to join the conspiracy.[1758]

Author Gaeton Fonzi, in his book *THE LAST INVESTIGATION*, says:[1759]

> "On June 1, 1965 David Sanchez Morales is assigned as a deep cover operative working as a public safety officer for the Agency for International Development in Lima, Peru."[1760]

> "On March 1, 1967 David Sanchez Morales joins former JM/Wave station chief Ted Shackley to implement the Phoenix Program in Vietnam. It is a plan devised by future CIA director William Colby to eliminate the Viet Cong infrastructure. It results in the assassination of forty thousand individuals. Morales works under cover of the Agency for International Development's Vien Tien Community Development Administration."[1761]

Mobster Johnny Roselli was set to testify in 1976 while the HSCA was getting established and then he turned up dead, floating in the water near Miami.[1762]   In the early 1960's Roselli had worked with and for David Morales, who was in charge of JM/WAVE at that time.[1763]   They had a very close relationship according to Brad Ayers, author of *THE WAR THAT NEVER WAS*.[1764]   Morales had been part of Operation Phoenix in Vietnam, a program to hunt down and murder the Viet Cong leaders.[1765]   Morales was an assassin for the CIA and was the main "action man" for David Atlee Phillips.   Morales was also supposedly involved in the capture of Che Guevara.[1766]   Morales said he was worried about the CIA killing him because he "knew too much," and he put a very sophisticated alarm system in a house he built about thirty miles from the Mexican border.[1767]

Author Gaeton Fonzi, in his book *THE LAST INVESTIGATION*, says:[1768]

> "On May 7, 1978 David Sanchez Morales, although officially retired from the CIA, returns from a regular trip to Washington to his home near Phoenix, Arizona.   He tells friends he began feeling ill shortly before leaving Washington and that night has a sudden heart attack.   The ambulance is late in arriving and reportedly has equipment problems. Morales dies the next morning at a Tucson medical center.   He had told a friend he feared for his life from his own people because he knows too much."[1769]

The Intelligence Community Today

The intelligence community is still involved in attempting to undermine the will of the voters. Author Theodore Malloch, in his book, *THE PLOT TO DESTROY TRUMP*, refers to Professor Stephen F. Cohen of Princeton and points out that John Brennan, CIA Director from 2013 to 2017, shared the dossier with James Clapper, Director of National Intelligence from from 2010 to 2017, and FBI Director James Comey to get the anti-Trump ball rolling:[1770] This is discussed in more detail in the last chapter – Why This Matters Today.

The U.S. intelligence community makes up a key component of the Deep State.   Back in 1960 this was primarily the CIA.   Now the intelligence community makes up over a dozen major agencies in addition to the CIA.   These include the Defense Intelligence Agency (DIA), the Office of Naval Intelligence (ONI), the National Reconnissance Office (NRO), the National Security Agency (NSA), the National Geospatial-Intelligence Agency (NGA) and others.   These are overseen by the Director of National Intelligence, a Cabinet-level appointee. Back in 1960 Allen Dulles was the member of the Deep State who was in charge of the intelligence community. By 2010 James Clapper had become the member of the Deep State who was appointed by Obama as the Director of National Intelligence. He would become part of the Deep State plot to get rid of Trump. This is also covered in the chapter on Why This Matters Today.

The anti-Castro Cuban Exiles

The anti-Castro Cuban exiles started out as supporters of President Kennedy. In 1961 he had given the green light to the Bay of Pigs invasion and they saw this as a chance to take back their homeland with the help of the United States. By 1963 Kennedy had reversed course and was trying to keep the anti-Castro Cuban exiles from attacking Cuba. Also, by 1963 he was reaching out to make peace with Castro. This 180-degree turn caused some of the anti-Castro Cuban exiles to join the conspiracy to kill Kennedy.

This section is divided into six sub-sections:

1. The Bay of Pigs – when the Bay of Pigs invasion failed, their CIA sponsors told the Cuban exiles that it had failed because Kennedy had pulled the rug out from under them at the last minute. This enraged the Cuban exiles.

2. Operation Mongoose – after the Bay of Pigs fiasco, the Kennedy administration agreed to sponsor raids on Cuba from bases in Florida. This meant that the CIA was funneling guns and money to the growing army of Cuban exiles. It was called Operation Mongoose.

3. The Cuban Missile Crisis caused Kennedy to promise Khrushchev that the U.S. would not invade Cuba and, in addition, would cease the Operation Mongoose raids. The Cuban exiles were already enraged by having been told that Kennedy had lost his nerve and caused the Bay of Pigs invasion to fail. The promise not to invade Cuba enraged them further. The situation got worse when the Kennedy administration cracked down on the raids.

4. The Crackdown – the CIA was telling the anti-Castro Cuban exiles to continue the raids. The CIA had sponsored the exiles with money and support and was still sponsoring them, even after Kennedy ordered the raids stopped. This caused the Kennedy administration to have to use the other Federal agencies like the Coast Guard to crack down on the raiders. The crackdown further enraged the exiles, pouring gasoline on the fire of their hatred for Kennedy.

5. Reaching out to Castro – Kennedy decided to make peace with Castro. This meant that they would never be able to take back

their homeland. When the exiles, who already saw Kennedy as a traitor, heard this it was the last straw. Some of them decided to participate in the CIA plot to kill Kennedy.

6. Rose Cherami predicts the assassination – two of the anti-Castro Cuban exiles were on their way to Dallas to kill Kennedy when they dropped off a woman in Louisiana. On the way they had talked about their intention to kill Kennedy. She ended up in the hospital and told the doctors and nurses that Kennedy was going to be killed in Dallas. Two days later Kennedy was murdered in Dallas, just like Rose had predicted.

In his book *ACT OF TREASON: THE ROLE OF J. EDGAR HOOVER IN THE ASSASSINATION OF PRESIDENT KENNEDY*, author Mark North recounts a conversation on November 9, 1963 between William Somerset and Joseph Milteer. Somerset was an informant for the Miami police and Milteer was active in the Cuban exile community:[1771]

Somerset: "I think Kennedy is coming here on the eighteenth or something like that to make some kind of speech…"

Milteer: "You can bet your bottom dollar he is going to have a lot to say about the Cubans."

Somerset: "Yeah. Well he will have a thousand bodyguards, don't worry about that."

Milteer: "The more bodyguards he has the easier it is to get him."

Somerset: "Well, how in hell do you figure is the best way to get him?"

Milteer: "from an office building with a high-powered rifle… He knows he's a marked man…"

Somerset: "They are really going to try to kill him?"

Milteer: "Oh yeah, it is in the working… They will pick somebody up within hours afterwards, just to throw the public off"

North also points out that Somerset then informs[1772]

"his police contact who informs captain Charles Sapp who reports to his chief of police, the Secret Service and the FBI. The Secret Service checked on Milteer's whereabouts but he was not questioned. Milteer thinks the Cuban exiles are behind the hit as Milteer is active in the Cuban exile community."[1773]

On November 22, 1963 Milteer phones Somerset to say he is in Dallas to see Kennedy, who is due in shortly. He also comments that Kennedy will never be seen in Miami again. He then joins the crowd to watch the Kennedy motorcade in Dealey Plaza.[1774] He is close enough that he witnesses Kennedy being assassinated.[1775]

Five days before the Kennedy assassination, Harold Reynolds of Abilene, Texas picked up a note left for one of his neighbors, Pedro Gonzalez, who was the president of a local anti-Castro group called the Cuban Liberation Committee.[1776] The note was from Lee Oswald, who Reynolds had seen attending meetings with Gonzalez.[1777] (See the section on the Abilene Incident).

A Cuban exile pilot who was working with Wayne January at Redbird airport near Dallas getting a plane ready to take several passengers the next day confided in Wayne that President Kennedy was going to be killed the next day, and it happened just like he said it would.[1778] (See the section on the Wayne January incident in the chapter on the murder of Robert Kennedy).

The Bay of Pigs

When the Bay of Pigs invasion was a complete failure, E. Howard Hunt was quoted in regard to the effect this had on the Cuban exiles. "The failure of the Bay of Pigs had a disastrous effect." E. Howard Hunt said "They were outraged that a country so powerful as the United States only ninety miles away from their homeland could have permitted a disaster such as the Bay of Pigs to have taken place."[1779]

Pepe San Roman, the commander of Brigade 2506 of the exiles who invaded the Bay of Pigs later said:[1780]

> "Every day it became worse, and then I was getting madder and madder. And I wanted to get a rifle and come and fight against the U.S. For me the government of the United States had been the utmost of everything, bigger than my father, than my mother, than God. It was so low, so low a blow to us with so many plans and so many hopes. They knew before they sent us, in my mind, that they were not going to go ahead with it."[1781]

Mario Kohly was a Cuban politician who formed part of the Cuban government in exile. Anthony Summers, in his book *NOT IN YOUR LIFETIME*, said that Mario Kohly, Jr. quoted his late father as saying "John Kennedy sold out the American people. John Kennedy was a traitor... He was a communist."[1782]

Anthony Summers, in his book *NOT IN YOUR LIFETIME*, recounts a conversation with E. Howard Hunt. As news of the debacle came in, he and the others there reacted with dismay and scorn:[1783]

> "At CIA headquarters in our war room . . . we thought, as the indications came in, that the administration would feel more and more an obligation to unleash some United States power to equalize the situation. We kept receiving the administration's refusals with incredulity. I felt a sense of hollowness . . . somewhere along the way we lost a good part of our national will to prevail. I think it was a failure of nerve."[1784]

CIA Director Allen Dulles, for his part, reacted to the fiasco by attempting to control the spin.[1785] His first reaction was to publicly pin the disaster on President Kennedy.[1786] Dulles blamed the Bay of Pigs fiasco on JFK's "lack of determination."[1787] He had an article planted in the September 1961 issue of *Fortune* magazine. Charles Murphy was a ghost writer for Dulles' memoir and he wrote the article entitled "Cuba: The Record Set Straight."[1788] Much of the article shifted blame from the CIA to the White House.[1789] Authors E. Howard Hunt and Charles Murphy claimd that it was British Prime Minister Harold Macmillan who convinced Kennedy out of committing troops to Laos.[1790] The idea was to make Kennedy look like a weak-minded fool who is easily influenced and incapable of fighting the Cold War because he had no vision or backbone.[1791] The article goes on to claim that Kennedy cancelled the necessary air strikes.[1792] This was a lie, but it was necessary to pin the blame on Kennedy.[1793] It also states that the original plan was approved by the Pentagon, which was also a lie and for the same reason.[1794] The article ends up by saying that Kennedy thought there were lessons to be learned from the Bay of Pigs.[1795] While this is true, the context in which it is used in the article makes it appear that Kennedy agrees that the Bay of Pigs fiasco was his fault.[1796] Kennedy blamed himself for believing the CIA's lies and deceptions to him about the Bay of Pigs, and he took the public blame for the mess, but when he said there were 'lessons to be learned,' he meant that now he knew not to trust Allen Dulles and his guys at the CIA.[1797] The use of this phrase in the article was a clever way to use Kennedy's own words to appear to pin the blame on himself. This was not the case.[1798]

This article was used by the CIA to start the myth that it was all Kennedy's fault.[1799] This myth was also used by the CIA to encourage the already outraged Cuban exiles to focus their anger on Kennedy.[1800]

Author James DiEugenio, in his book *DESTINY BETRAYED*, said that Allen Dulles, E. Howard Hunt, David Atlee Phillips, David Morales, Sergio Arcacha Smith, David Ferrie, Clay Shaw, Guy Bannister and others were involved in the Bay of Pigs as well as in the Kennedy assassination.[1801]

Operation Mongoose

After the fiasco of the Bay of Pigs, Kennedy agreed to sponsor a force of Cuban exiles that would be based primarily in south Florida and launch raids into Cuba to destabilize the Castro regime. The goal was to get rid of Castro. This becomes known as Operation Mongoose. The CIA called its Mongoose unit "Task Force W."[1802]

CIA Operation Mongoose to kill Castro was created in November of 1961 by the White House. In November of 1961 Richard Bissell told Bill Harvey to apply the ZR/RIFLE plan (the CIA program to recruit foreigners for dirty jobs like assassinations) to Cuba. Harvey reestablished the connection to mobster Johnny Roselli. At the end of November 1961 Kennedy fired Allen Dulles and Richard Bissell for the Bay of Pigs debacle. Kennedy then appointed John McCone as Director of the CIA.[1803] Bill Harvey continued to use the mafia and McCone would have disapproved so he was kept in the dark.[1804] Kennedy wrote a memo to Dean Rusk to establish Operation Mongoose which was then headed up by Bill Harvey and Mongoose was run out of the CIA's JM/WAVE station in Miami.[1805] The chief of operations at JM/WAVE was David Sanchez Morales.[1806] JM/WAVE had an official staff of 300 and 54 front corporations and was one of the largest employers in the state of Florida.[1807] JM/Wave even had its own navy with hundreds of boats.[1808]

After the Bay of Pigs fiasco, E. Howard Hunt started setting up safe houses and handing out money to the Cuban exile community, sometimes carrying over one hundred thousand dollars with him in a briefcase.[1809] The CIA was financing the establishment of a small army and navy of Cuban exiles to launch raids into Cuba.

In November of 1961 the CIA's David Atlee Phillips had Cuban exile Antonio Veciana create the anti-Castro Cuban exile group which eventually becomes known as Alpha 66.[1810] Alpha 66 becomes one of the larger and more effective of the many anti-Castro Cuban exile groups.[1811]   On September 10, 1962 David Atlee Phillips directed Antonio Veciana to attack cargo ships in Cuban waters, and on October 8, 1962 Phillips told Veciana to attack Soviet merchant ships in Havana harbor.[1812]

The Cuban Missile Crisis

In 1962 CIA Director John McCone was worried that Khrushchev would put missiles in Cuba. He insisted on resuming the U-2 flights to monitor the situation.[1813]   When the pictures were analyzed he was proved right.[1814]   Kennedy announced the situation to the country on October 22.[1815]

On October 21, 1962 during the Cuban Missile Crisis, after Robert Kennedy tells CIA Director McCone to immediately halt all operations against Cuba, CIA Task Force W chief William Harvey sends two raiding parties into Cuba.[1816]   The world is in a tense standoff, on the brink of nuclear war, and Bill Harvey defies his direct orders and launches raids at Cuba anyway.[1817]   He clearly did this with the support of his superiors because they protected him. They were told to fire him and did not.

Part of the resolution to the crisis was by Kennedy promising Khrushchev not to invade Cuba and to stop the Operation Mongoose raids.[1818]   The anti-Castro Cubans were already furious at Kennedy for not approving the extra air strikes once the Bay of Pigs invasion was underway. The promise not to invade Cuba came as an additional shock.[1819]   Exile attorney Mario Lazo called it a "soul-shattering blow."[1820]

Author Anthony Summers, in his book *NOT IN YOUR LIFETIME*, points out that the view among the anti-Castro Cuban exiles was that Kennedy had not only blown a chance to get rid of Castro but had now ended up giving Castro a guarantee to stay in power.[1821]

For the anti-Castro Cuban exiles, the Cuban Missile Crisis changed everything. During the crisis, in order to bring the world back from the brink of nuclear disaster, Kennedy had promised Khrushchev that the United States would not invade Cuba. This meant that Kennedy had done a 180-degree turn from the 1961 invasion of Cuba to, by 1963, actively trying to keep the Cuban exiles from launching raids on Cuba. The anti-Castro Cuban exiles saw this as a betrayal and many of them hated Kennedy for this reason. They saw getting rid of Kennedy as their only option to get back their homeland. Their outrage from the

Bay of Pigs disaster had, for some of them, turned to cold determination to participate in the attempt to assassinate Kennedy so that Johnson would be in charge. These men were heavily armed and saw Kennedy as an obstacle to getting their homeland back. By 1963 Kennedy was trying to make peace with Cuba. The CIA knew this and was telling the Cuban exiles about it. Having Kennedy make peace with Castro was the last thing the Cuban exiles wanted. And they were being egged on by their CIA sponsors, who showed them how they could participate in the Kennedy assassination.

The Crackdown

Adding fuel to the firestorm of anger among the Cuban exiles over the settlement of the missile crisis that left Castro in power was what came next. The U.S. government, through the CIA, had set up the training camps and recruited the Cuban exiles. It had supplied them with everything they needed to launch raids into Cuba. Now the same government was cracking down on them.[1822] On December 4, 1962 a group of twelve anti-Castro Cuban exile guerillas were arrested in No Name Key as they are about to embark on a raid to Cuba.[1823] Kennedy also cut the funding for the Cuban Revolutionary Council.[1824] The CRC was an umbrella organization meant to coordinate the efforts of many of the anti-Castro Cuban exile groups. The head of the CRC resigned in protest.[1825] E. Howard Hunt said that U.S. assistance to the exiles was "A fraud. A fraud perpetrated on the Cuban people and on the American people."[1826]

In October of 1963, just weeks before the Kennedy assassination, Allen Dulles openly criticized the Kennedy administration in a speech titled "The Art of Persuasion: America's Role in the Ideological Struggle" where he said that America should try to be respected instead of trying to be loved.[1827] He basically said that Kennedy was an appeaser who wanted the world to love him and America when the American president (and America itself) should be feared and respected.[1828] This new policy of not attacking Cuba is also criticized by Kennedy's political opponents like Richard Nixon.[1829]

At the same time the Kennedy administration was trying to stop the raids, the CIA was still going ahead with them.[1830] In 1963 it funded the DRE (an anti-Castro Cuban exile group) in the amount of $51,000 a month (in 1963 dollars).[1831] The CIA was still trying to start a war by forcing Kennedy's hand with continued raids.[1832] Author James Douglass, in his book *JFK AND THE UNSPEAKABLE*, says that on

March 19, 1963 at a press conference in Washington Antonio Veciana, the head of the Alpha 66 anti-Castro Cuban exile group, announced more Cuban raids. This was an intentional embarrassment to the Kennedy administration.[1833] He also points out that, many years later, Antonio Veciana admitted to an investigator for the House Select Committee on Assassinations (HSCA) that the purpose of the attack on the Soviet vessel in Cuban waters was "to publicly embarrass Kennedy and force him to move against Castro." Veciana revealed that "Maurice Bishop" (David Atlee Phillips) kept saying that Kennedy would have to be forced to make a decision and the only way was to put him up against a wall.[1834]

The government at this point literally had two opposing policies. The Kennedy administration was trying to stop the raids and the CIA was trying to keep them going. This was bound to further infuriate the anti-Castro Cuban exiles. The CIA was still giving them funding and orders for more raids. At the same time the Coast Guard was arresting and handcuffing them.[1835] The Customs Service and the FBI were also cracking down on the training camps and weapons dumps.[1836]

Alpha 66 and other anti-Castro Cuban exile groups sponsored by the CIA continued to launch raids into Cuba. This went on before, during and after the Cuban Missile Crisis. In April of 1963 they bombed an oil refinery near Havana.[1837] In May a military camp was attacked.[1838] The CIA denied it was behind the raids.[1839] On April 5, 1963 the Kennedy administration announced it was assigning more Navy and Customs planes and boats to crack down on the continuing raids.[1840] In June 1963 Federal agents enforcing the Kennedy crackdown seized an aircraft and explosives intended for use in a bombing raid against the Shell Oil refinery in Cuba.[1841]

Author David Talbot, in his book *THE DEVIL'S CHESSBOARD: ALLEN DULLES, THE CIA, AND THE RISE OF AMERICA'S SECRET GOVERNMENT*, pointed out that once Kennedy promised not to invade Cuba the anti-Castro Cuban exiles went from being pointed at Castro to being pointed at Kennedy.[1842]

Author Anthony Summers, in his book *NOT IN YOUR LIFETIME*, points out that Charles Sapp, the head of the intelligence unit of the Miami Police, began getting alarming warning signs from the Cuban community.[1843] Sapp said:

> "Since President Kennedy made the news release that the U.S. government would stop all raiding parties going against the Castro government" he wrote "the Cuban people feel that the U.S. government has turned against them. Violence hitherto

directed towards Castro's Cuba will now be directed towards various governmental agencies in the United States."[1844]

Summers points out that he was referring specifically to President Kennedy as the target.[1845]

Reaching Out to Castro

Kennedy followed up the test ban treaty by reaching out to Castro in Cuba to make peace.[1846] In the fall of 1963 Castro made it known that he was ready to talk.[1847] Lisa Howard was a journalist who had interviewed Castro in April of 1963 and she also told Kennedy that Castro was ready to talk.[1848] Howard briefed the CIA on her way back from her interview with Castro.[1849] The CIA did not want the U.S. to make peace with Cuba. They wanted to attack Cuba, and they tried to stop this peace process.[1850] CIA Director McCone argued against it and was joined by National Security Advisor McGeorge Bundy.[1851] They both said word of the process might leak out and cause problems.[1852] The State Department was also opposed to normalizing relations with Cuba.[1853] Lisa Howard wrote an article urging JFK to quietly approach Castro.[1854] Kennedy agreed with her approach, but he wanted to make sure that word did not leak out.

In his book *LAST WORD: MY INDICTMENT OF THE CIA IN THE MURDER OF JFK*, author Mark Lane expresses the opinion that Richard Helms led the effort at the CIA to sabotage Kennedy's efforts at rapprochement with Cuba.[1855] At the same time that Kennedy was reaching out to Castro, the CIA was still trying to kill Castro. When Kennedy fired CIA Deputy Director Richard Bissell, Richard Helms was promoted to take his place. Helms continued the policy of attempting to kill Castro. Helms did not tell either the president or the new CIA Director, John McCone, about the attempts on Castro's life.

CIA Director John McCone testified that assassination was not part of the CIA's anti-Castro program.[1856]

CIA officer Nestor Sanchez met with Rolando Cubela, one of Castro's aides, in the hope that they could get him to help kill Castro. On October 11, 1963 Sanchez reported that Cubela wanted reassurance from Robert Kennedy that the United States would support his attempt to overthrow Castro.[1857] In 1975 the Church Committee uncovered the fact that Richard Helms had approved a plan for CIA officer Desmond Fitzgerald to pretend to be a personal representative of Robert Kennedy for the purpose of asking Rolando Cubela to assassinate Castro using a poison pen to be delivered later.[1858] This was done on October 29, 1963 without Robert Kennedy's knowledge.[1859] Later, the pen was being delivered on the day Kennedy was assassinated.[1860]

On November 5, U.S. diplomat William Atwood briefed National Security Advisor McGeorge Bundy on Castro's willingness to talk.[1861] Atwood was using Lisa Howard to arrange a dialog with his Cuban counterpart Carlos Lechuga.[1862] Bundy gave President Kennedy an update, and Kennedy wanted to take every precaution to make sure word did not leak out.[1863] Atwood and Lechuga met and Atwood proposed going to Cuba but Kennedy thought it would be too risky.[1864] He was worried that Atwood might be spotted, so French journalist Jean Daniel was then used as the conduit between Kennedy and Castro.[1865]

Kennedy also decided to send a message to Castro in one of his public speeches, so in his November 18, 1963 speech he said "Every nation is free to shape its own economic institutions in accordance with its own national needs and will."[1866] He also said that "A small band of conspirators had made Cuba a victim of foreign imperialism, an instrument of the policy of others, a weapon in an effort dictated by external powers to subvert the other American republics. This, and this alone, divides us. As long as this is true, nothing is possible. Without it, everything is possible. Once this barrier is removed, we will be ready and anxious to work with the Cuban people in pursuit of those progressive goals which a few short years ago stirred their hopes and the sympathy of many people throughout the hemisphere."[1867] The speech was intended to convey an open door and that was the way Castro interpreted it.[1868]

In his book *LAST WORD: MY INDICTMENT OF THE CIA IN THE MURDER OF JFK*, author Mark Lane reports on a conversation he had with journalist Lisa Howard in September of 1963. Mark Lane asked Lisa Howard, in light of the CIA's opposition to her efforts to make peace, if she felt safe.[1869] Her reply was "JFK is with me on this. I feel safe as long as he is around."[1870] Mark Lane goes on to point out that Castro and Daniel were meeting to discuss normalizing relations between the U.S. and Cuba when they got word of Kennedy's assassination.[1871] Lisa Howard decided to continue to try to make peace between Cuba and the United States, even after Kennedy was killed.[1872] She became an inconvenient loose end who wouldn't take a hint.[1873] She became ill and died suddenly at the age of thirty-five while driving to a pharmacy trying to save herself.[1874] Lane describes her death as very suspicious.[1875]

The CIA had known for months about Lisa Howard and her efforts, and if the CIA told the anti-Castro exiles about the back-channel efforts to make peace with Castro this would have given them a motive to kill Kennedy.[1876]

Jean Daniel was a French journalist on his way to Cuba to interview Fidel Castro.[1877] He was asked to stop by to see President Kennedy on October 24, 1963.[1878] Kennedy asked him to bring up the subject of normalizing relations between the U.S. and Cuba and report back what Castro had to say.[1879]

Jean Daniel was meeting with Castro when they got word that Kennedy had been killed. Castro understood and said that everything was changed now, that everything would be different.

Rose Cherami Predicts the Assassination

Rose Cherami was born Melba Christine Marcades. At some point she took the stage name Rose Cherami. Rose Cherami proved several things. The first thing she proved was that Oswald was not a lone shooter. Rose predicted the assassination. She was able to do this because she knew some of the conspirators. This proves that Oswald was not alone. In addition, she proved that the FBI and the Dallas police were involved in the conspiracy. This is because neither of them wanted to investigate the fact that she predicted the assassination. If they were running a real investigation and not a sham cover-up they would have shown some interest in someone who predicted the assassination. Rose also shows the involvement of the anti-Castro Cubans because that's who she learned of the assassination from.

On November 20, 1963, two days before the Kennedy assassination, Rose was driving from Miami to Dallas with two anti-Castro Cuban exiles, Sergio Arcacha Smith and Emilio Santana.[1880] Both are associated with the CIA.[1881] Sergio Arcacha Smith had his office in the same building with CIA asset Guy Banister and worked with Banister and Lee Harvey Oswald, David Ferrie and the others in New Orleans.[1882] The purpose of the trip from Miami to Dallas was to kill Kennedy.[1883] Rose was along as a drug courier for mafia functionary Jack Ruby.[1884] Rose had worked as a stripper for Ruby, who she knew as Jack Rubenstein.[1885] Rubenstein was Ruby's original name. Now Rose was a former stripper and current heroin addict who had been forced to go on the trip by the fact that her child was being held hostage until she completed the drug deal.[1886] On the way from Miami to Dallas they stoped at the Silver Slipper brothel.[1887] While there, Rose got drunk and rowdy and got slapped around and thrown out of the place.[1888]

Outside, Rose decided to hitchhike and almost got run over by a car.[1889] She was hit and brought to the nearest hospital, Moosa Memorial, by a motorist named Frank Odom.[1890] From there she was taken to jail and interviewed by police Lieutenant Francis Fruge and subsequently taken to the East Louisiana State Hospital at the request of Dr. Derouin, who Fruge had contacted.[1891] The ambulance ride to get treatment for Rose's withdrawal symptoms took two hours, and during the ride Fruge questioned Rose.[1892] She said she was on the way to kill the president with two 'Italians' (she mistakenly thought the Cubans were Italians), but that she first had to get some money and get her baby.[1893] It all sounded pretty far-fetched, and Rose was a heroin addict in bad shape, so Fruge did not take her Kennedy assassination story seriously.[1894] In the hospital she spoke again of the Kennedy assassination to happen two days later. Then the assassination happened just like she said it would, and word spread around the hospital.[1895] Fruge, seeing the assassination happen just as she had predicted, called the hospital and told them to keep Rose there until he could get there.[1896] She said she was supposed to get $8,000 from the person holding her baby, then meet a seaman bringing the heroin into Galveston on a ship.[1897] Fruge looked into her drug connection story and it checked out. Dr. William Weiss and an intern named Wayne Owen from the hospital confirmed that she had predicted the assassination.[1898] Fruge called the Dallas police and talked to Will Fritz, chief of homicide. Fritz told Fruge that Rose was of no interest to the Dallas police.[1899] Fruge also contacted the Louisiana State Police to help him check out various parts of Rose's story. They also confirmed that her story about the hotel reservations and that the ship in Galveston checked out.[1900] Colonel Morgan of the Louisiana State Police talked to Captain Will Fritz of the Dallas Police and also found out that Fritz and the Dallas police did not want to question Rose.[1901] By this time Nathan Durham, the chief customs agent, was holding Rose for further questioning, and he found out that the FBI did not want to question Rose.[1902] Since no one wanted to question Rose, she was released.[1903]

On September 4, 1965 Rose was found at 3:00 AM on Highway 155 east of Big Sandy, Texas, where a motorist said he had been driving and suddenly saw a woman and some suitcases in the road and braked hard to avoid running her over.[1904] She had a gunshot wound.[1905] And her body had been moved to the road from where she was shot on the side of the road.[1906] Her blood was on the property where she had been shot, and that property belonged to the head of security for H.L. Hunt, one of the oil barons.[1907]

Many years later it was uncovered by the House Select Committee on Assassinations (HSCA) that diagrams of the sewer system in Dealey

Plaza were found in Sergio Arcacha Smith's apartment.[1908] This is significant because there is an above-ground sewer drain built into the curb on the north side of Elm Street which could have been used as a sniper's location. The huge drain conduits under there empty into the Trinity River which is dry most of the time.[1909] This would offer both concealment and an escape route. A shot from this location would have hit Kennedy from the front. The drain is still there in Dealey Plaza.

J. Edgar Hoover and the FBI

The entire FBI didn't assist in the cover up. A few people at the top and a few of their underlings did. The vast majority of the people at the FBI work hard and take serious risks to help keep the rest of us safe. The real problem was J. Edgar Hoover himself, and he had dictatorial control of the FBI back then.

This chapter is organized into ten sections:

1. How Hoover got started – describes how Hoover was head of the FBI from the beginning and how he built it up from scratch to become his personal fiefdom with Hoover as its dictator

2. Hoover's history of evidence tampering – describes how Hoover, from the beginning, was willing to manufacture evidence to railroad people, especially communists and union organizers, into jail or deportation

3. Hoover the publicity hound – describes how Hoover was relentless in using the accomplishments of the FBI to promote himself to the public as America's top law enforcement professional

4. Hoover the freeloader – describes how Hoover continually accepted "accommodations" from free lunch every day to free gifts and lavish vacations at the expense of people who wanted to have influence with Hoover and the FBI

5. Hoover ignored the mafia – describes how Hoover denied the existence of the mafia until he was forced by the publicity generated by the Apalachin mafia Commission meeting to take some limited steps to investigate organized crime

6. Hoover the dirt collector – describes how Hoover kept his blackmail files on everyone who could be useful to him in his quest to remain in power through the administrations of Harding, Coolidge, Hoover, Roosevelt, Truman, Eisenhower, Kennedy, Johnson and Nixon.

7. Hoover the racist – describes how Hoover ignored the Klan as long as he could, segregated the FBI and only allowed a few black people to work there, and then only as his personal

servants – it also describes how Hoover tried to keep the civil rights movement from being effective

8. Truman's opinion of Hoover – describes how Truman had Hoover's number – Truman thought Hoover was trying to create an American Gestapo or secret police and was unimpressed

9. Hoover before the JFK assassination – describes how Hoover helped in the JFK assassination, primarily by keeping a lid on the warnings of the hit that were recorded by FBI agents

10. Hoover after the JFK assassination – describes how Hoover got involved in the cover up of the assassination by using Gestapo tactics to intimidate witnesses and manufacture or bury evidence as necessary to make sure the conspirators were not brought to justice

Hoover did most of his work on the assassination in the cover up after the killing. He started helping the conspiracy before the assassination by not informing Kennedy about the threats to his life from the mafia, but most of the heavy lifting Hoover and the FBI did was after the assassination during the cover up. He ordered his minions to destroy or manufacture evidence and intimidate witnesses. This allowed the cabal to keep a lid on the conspiracy.

As mentioned earlier, Hoover was facing a crisis by 1963. He was going to be retired against his will by President Kennedy unless something happened. Hoover was desperate to remain in power. He couldn't imagine not being in charge of *his* Bureau. Hoover had become the Deep State. In his mind the FBI was *his*. He had created it and it belonged to him. He was not just its curator for the sake of the American people, who the FBI really belonged to. He was not just a public servant. He *was* the FBI. He also hated the Kennedys. He couldn't believe that he had to actually report to Robert Kennedy, the Attorney General, who he despised. He had always bypassed whoever was currently the Attorney General, ignored the official chain of command, and gone directly to the president. Having John F. Kennedy appoint his brother Robert F. Kennedy as Attorney General changed all that. Now he had a buzzer on his desk which Robert Kennedy could push to summon him. Hoover also despised President Kennedy for his views on communism and civil rights, and for his womanizing. Hoover was anti-communist and Kennedy wanted to talk peace with Khrushchev. Hoover was a racist and Kennedy had decided to support Martin Luther King, Jr. in his fight for civil rights. Hoover also saw

President Kennedy and his many affairs as morally indefensible and a threat to national security. Hoover despised the Kennedys and, in order to survive, Hoover needed Kennedy out of the way so Johnson could become president.

The Kennedys underestimated just how dangerous Hoover was to them. They were wary of him, but they thought they could control Hoover and deal with him at the appropriate time.[1910]

Hoover was also very close to Lyndon Johnson. Johnson would be happy to give Hoover a waiver which would allow him to remain in office past the mandatory retirement age. The president has the authority to waive this requirement, and several key people had already had this done for them.

Before anyone can understand how J. Edgar Hoover could allow himself to be mixed up in the assassination and especially the cover-up of the Kennedy assassination, it would be useful to first cover some background on who Hoover really was and how he got to a point where he was willing to join the conspiracy. Some background on the relationship between Hoover and Johnson will also help in this regard.

J. Edgar Hoover had been in on the beginning of the formation of the Federal Bureau of Investigation. He had been named to head it up before it was the FBI, when it was still called the Bureau of Investigation during the Warren G. Harding administration. The FBI had been born and grew up under his leadership. It was his baby. He was an autocrat and had created a dictatorship for himself. He ran the Bureau with an iron fist, getting rid of anyone who dared to defy or even outshine him. He had also managed to stay in office for two generations, from 1924 to 1972. This meant he had survived many changes of administrations; Harding, Coolidge, Hoover, Roosevelt, Truman, Eisenhower, Kennedy, Johnson and Nixon. One of the ways he did this was by collecting dirt on everyone and anyone who could be blackmailed into helping him stay in power.

By the early 1960's Hoover was facing a career-ending crisis. He was rapidly approaching the mandatory government retirement age. When he turned seventy years old he would be forced to step down. Born on January 1, 1895, he would turn seventy while Kennedy was in the White House. The FBI had become his life and he absolutely refused to give it up. In order to stay in power, he would need the president to sign an executive order granting him a waiver. This had been done for other high ranking federal officials and could be done for him, but this would have to come from the president and President Kennedy wasn't going to go along. Hoover had tried persuasion and blackmail, but nothing worked. Kennedy thought there needed to be a change and was determined to retire Hoover and put someone else in charge.

In the meantime, Hoover had become very close with Lyndon Johnson. They had been neighbors and friends for almost twenty years and, more importantly, they were cronies. They shared information on who was doing what. Johnson had become a very powerful leader in the Senate during the Eisenhower administration and Hoover had become an institution as head of the FBI for decades. They both knew how to use information as a weapon to gain power. Johnson was able to get the senators to do what he wanted partly because he knew all their weaknesses. Hoover was able to get what he wanted from members of Congress or from the administration because he knew where the bodies were buried. Hoover had a file on everyone who was anyone and the information in those files allowed him to put pressure on them. Most of the politicians had secrets they didn't want made public. When necessary, Hoover was not above making up facts to ruin someone with. Those files gave Hoover leverage over the members of the Washington establishment. This had worked for decades, but it wasn't going to work anymore. Not with Kennedy in the White House. Kennedy wasn't afraid of Hoover. Maybe he should have been.

By the early 1960's Hoover was in a bind. He was fighting for survival. He needed a way out. At that same time Hoover and Johnson had become so close that Hoover regularly helped Johnson cover his tracks. Johnson's scandals were coming to a head in the early 1960's and Hoover was using his power as the dictatorial head of the FBI to help keep Johnson from being brought down by his scandals. Johnson had gone from being the second most powerful man in the United States as Leader of the Senate to being a vice president with very limited power. Vice President Johnson needed more power and influence to keep a lid on his scandals and Hoover pitched in to lend a hand.

A few examples will help the reader understand who J. Edgar Hoover really was. In his book *ENEMIES: A HISTORY OF THE FBI,* author Tim Weiner goes into detail on how Hoover built the FBI from scratch. He also describes how Hoover was an American Machiavelli. Wiener's section on the Palmer raids and Hoover's willingness to trample civil liberties and manufacture evidence to railroad people to jail or deportation makes for interesting reading. In his book *PUPPETMASTER: THE SECRET LIFE OF J. EDGAR HOOVER,* author Richard Hack details Hoover's personal and professional life. I would recommend both of these books to anyone who wants to know more about Hoover and who he really was.

On April 25, 1963 Hoover stated on the Paul Harvey show that he is not going to retire.[1911]

How Hoover Got Started

Hoover was the mastermind of the infamous Palmer Raids of 1919 to 1920. He was the driving force behind the planning and execution of them. They should have been called the Hoover raids. This was one of the largest violations of the Constitution and civil rights in our history.[1912] Hoover tried to deny bail and even lawyers to the people he rounded up.[1913] Hoover created lists of thousands of leftists and union sympathizers and had them arrested and beaten.[1914] Then they were detained, tried and deported.[1915] The Palmer Raids, under President Wilson and U.S. Attorney General A. Mitchell Palmer, were run by Hoover who rounded up and deported those he considered 'subversives.'[1916] The raids went over well with the public – at first.[1917] Then there was a backlash against the wholesale nature of the raids when the public found out that individual civil liberties were trampled and the Bureau had overstepped its authority.[1918] Harvard liberal Felix Frankfurter took the Bureau to court in defense of the rights of the people who had been rounded up for deportation.[1919] Judge Anderson ruled against the Bureau and the Justice Department did not challenge the ruling.[1920] Louis Post, the Assistant Secretary of Labor, then threw out three quarters of the fourteen hundred cases he reviewed, and Hoover opened a file on Post to start collecting dirt on him and tried to get him removed from office.[1921] Palmer went to a cabinet meeting and demanded that President Wilson get rid of Post.[1922] Wilson was skeptical of Palmer's point of view but Palmer said otherwise after the meeting.[1923] Wilson was slipping away both physically and mentally at this point.[1924] Congress cut the Justice Department's budget by one third – Post was called before Congress and defended himself and his actions so well that Palmer was then called before Congress to defend his actions and the Palmer Raids[1925] Post published a Report to the American People in 1920 in which he and Frankfurter accused Palmer and Hoover of violating civil rights of people who were arrested and subjected to illegal search and seizure.[1926] Hoover opened a file on Supreme Court Justice Frankfurter to start collecting dirt on him.[1927] Based on the 'success' of the raids, Palmer had been hoping to ride his crest of popularity all the way to the White House and become president. Then the real story came out and he was hauled before Congress. Hoover pulled together all his facts and figures and Palmer read the whole thing for a day and a half before Congress.[1928] Palmer's chances of getting the nomination sank.[1929] It became clear that the Palmer Raids were unpopular and then suddenly Hoover claimed to know nothing about the raids when asked before Congress about them.[1930]

In the 1920's William J. Burns was America's most famous private detective, and he became the Director of the Bureau of Investigation (BOI) during the Harding administration.[1931] Hoover was the second in command under Burns, who was happy to allow Hoover to effectively run the BOI.[1932]

In the 1930's Hoover was busy creating an American Gestapo. He asked for and got stronger subversion laws.[1933] He kept lists of 'subversives,' people who were to be rounded up in the name of national security in the event the country went to war.[1934] This included people who subscribed to socialist publications.[1935] He also continued illegal wiretaps even after the Supreme Court ruled against them.[1936]

Hoover's History of Evidence Tampering

Manufacturing evidence for the cover-up of the Kennedy assassination was nothing new for Hoover. By the early 1960's Hoover had decades of experience fabricating 'evidence' against whoever he was trying to have convicted or deported. Hoover had been doing this since before the Palmer raids of 1919-1920.[1937] Hoover particularly targeted political activist Emma Goldman for deportation.[1938] He edited the trial testimony of Leon Czolgosz, the assassin of President McKinley, to make it look like she had encouraged him to shoot the president.[1939] The backlash created by the disastrous Palmer raids made Hoover furious, so he started keeping files on the lawyers who were attempting to offer a defense for those he targeted.[1940] Later it was discovered that Hoover had planted spies in the unions to help manufacture evidence for the subsequent trials.[1941]

Congressman Cornelius Gallagher was one example of how Hoover had no problem creating 'evidence' where none existed. Gallagher questioned Hoover's methods, and Hoover decided to make an example of him. Gallagher was an honest man and had no skeletons in his closet that could be used for blackmail, so Hoover created all the 'evidence,' including phone transcripts, and used it to destroy Gallagher's career.[1942] In the Lindbergh kidnapping case Hoover made up evidence.[1943] He had his assistant Charles Apple say that Bruno Hauptman's handwriting matched the samples on the ransom notes, even though they did not.[1944] Hauptmann was convicted and executed. Hoover was responsible for either planting or building the typewriter that was used to convict Alger Hiss.[1945] In the 1990's Chemist Fred Whitehurst went public with the fact that his reports had been changed to create evidence and strengthen cases.[1946] This proved that the policies and the culture Hoover had created at the Bureau had outlived him.[1947] Since Oswald never had a lawyer, Hoover's long history of manipulating and creating evidence would have made rigging the Kennedy case a walk in the park for Hoover.

Hoover could also choose to selectively enforce laws. In 1934 General Smedley Butler was approached by powerful corporate interests in America who wanted to use veteran's groups as part of a military strategy to take over the White House.[1948] They wanted to stage a coup d'état, and once the plot had gotten far enough to have enough evidence to prosecute the plotters for treason, Butler went to Hoover.[1949] Hoover said he didn't have the authority to open an investigation.[1950] Hoover would later choose to look the other way on issues from civil rights to organized crime.

Hoover the Publicity Hound

J. Edgar Hoover was a publicity hound who cultivated the media, including Hollywood, to project the image of himself and *his* Bureau as valiant crimefighters and his point of view in general.[1951] Hoover only highlighted the successes of the Bureau, never the stumbles or failures. He saw them as *his* successes and *his* stumbles and made sure that the public only saw the wins and not the losses.

Hoover started collecting information in files, including statistics on national crime and on the accomplishments of the Bureau of Investigation, statistics which Hoover shared with his superiors and Congress to highlight his accomplishments. The St. Valentine's Day Massacre in 1929 forced the issue of violent crime into the spotlight of publicity.[1952] In 1932 the Lindbergh kidnapping caused President Hoover to authorize J. Edgar Hoover and the Bureau of Investigation to assist in the case.[1953] That same year Congress passed the Lindbergh Law which made kidnapping a Federal crime.[1954] The Bureau of Investigation (BOI) became the Federal Bureau of Investigation (FBI) in 1935, with Hoover in charge as the first Director of the FBI. Hoover constantly sought the spotlight for his (the Bureau's) accomplishments, even if he had to stretch or invent what was presented to the media and the public. Hoover was very conscious of his public image and the image of his Bureau.[1955] Hoover even tried to influence the movies to get them to stop glamorizing the gangsters and start glamorizing the "G-men," especially Hoover. Hoover even resented when Bureau agents became famous. He wanted the spotlight on him, not on his agents. An example of this was FBI Agent Melvin Purvis. Hoover forced him out of the Bureau when he became famous for getting Baby Face Nelson, John Dillinger and Pretty Boy Floyd.[1956] How dare he take the spotlight away from Hoover. Senator McKellar grilled Hoover and asked if he (Hoover) had ever made any actual arrests. Hoover was forced to admit he had not, and this stung Hoover's ego.[1957] Soon afterwards, on Hoover's orders the arrest of Alvin Karpis was staged so Hoover could take credit for the arrest.[1958]

Hoover tried to take advantage of every opportunity to highlight the effectiveness of the Bureau with himself taking center stage as the head of the Bureau. Every high-profile arrest was exploited, even when the actions of Hoover and the FBI hurt rather than helped the public good, or were less than competent or honorable, as in the case of the four German spies who landed on our shores.[1959] Hoover made sure to spin the publicity in his direction.[1960] Alerted as a courtesy by the New York City police that they were going to arrest Harry Brunette, Hoover barged in and took over, making a mess of the arrest and taking all the credit.[1961] The New York City Fire Department had to be called due to the ensuing firefight which lit the building on fire.[1962]

Hoover had a book published about the FBI and himself, *THE FBI STORY* by Don Whitehead became a best seller.[1963] It was pushed by one of Hoover's pet media outlets.[1964] Hoover either encouraged the positive books and articles or did his best to squash the negative books and articles. Dorothy Schiff of the *New York Post* wrote a series on Hoover and this panicked Hoover, who had not known of the series in advance and therefore had no control over it.[1965] For the most part, his efforts worked and the public had a mostly positive impression of Hoover as the nation's chief law enforcement officer.

Hoover the Freeloader

Hoover had a companion for almost his entire adult life named Clyde Tolson. Tolson worked at the FBI and became Hoover's alter ego and number-two man. Their relationship was more than just professional. They spent almost all their time together. They lived near each other. They ate most of their meals together. They rode to work together.

When Hoover died, the folded flag was handed to Tolson at the burial service. And Hoover left his estate to Tolson.

Hoover and Tolson ate lunch almost every day at a restaurant called Harvey's at the Mayflower hotel and never paid the tab.[1966] Hoover also arranged for stays at luxury hotels (like the St. Moritz in New York) and meals at expensive restaurants (like the Stork Club in New York) to be provided to he and Tolson for free.[1967] Hoover was friends with Del Webb who owned hotels in Las Vegas and Hoover often stayed for free while in Las Vegas.[1968] Hoover also arranged extravagant vacations to luxurious hotels, like a week in Miami, Puerto Rico, Cuba and the Bahamas which he and Tolson took in 1936 at the expense of the Bureau without claiming any vacation time.[1969] Hoover referred to this celebrity freeloading as accepting "accommodations" from various hotels, resorts, restaurants, clubs, etc. on multiple "business" trips to New York or wherever. And inevitably Tolson went along on these junkets. Hoover also accepted many expensive gifts, including an early television set from David Sarnoff of RCA.[1970] Hoover was in his complimentary suite at the Waldorf Astoria in NYC when the Japanese attacked Pearl Harbor.[1971] Every August Hoover and Tolson would go to Del Mar, California for a free vacation for days at the horse races and evenings with movie stars, mafia and celebrities.[1972] During these paid vacations he would occasionally take a side trip to a local FBI office near his vacation spot, but this was a fig leaf to claim he was on a business trip when in fact he was on vacation.[1973]

The freeloading also meant that others gained influence over Hoover. Oilmen Sid Richardson and Clint Murchison owned the Del Charo, a resort hotel and the nearby racetrack, the Del Mar, where Hoover went for a free month's vacation every year.[1974] Other guests who were there at the same time included future U.S. president Richard Nixon, future Texas governor John Connally and mafiosi Meyer Lansky, Santo Trafficante, Johnny Roselli, Sam Giancana, Carlos Marcello and Frank Costello.[1975] Hoover and the oil barons hated the Kennedys as much as the mafia and Johnson, and they all socialized together.[1976] Socializing with the mafia may have had some influence on the fact that Hoover tried his best to look the other way and claim the mafia did not exist.

Hoover Ignored the Mafia

Hoover had to be pushed into investigating the mafia. Until the Apalachin meeting brought the mafia to the attention of the public, Hoover had even denied the existence of the mafia. This position conveniently allowed him to sidestep the question of why the FBI wasn't investigating organized crime. Why Hoover chose not to go after the mafia is an interesting question. In those days the mafia was part of the power structure. The mob paid off crooked politicians like Hoover's friend Johnson and they were all friends. Hoover was friends with Johnson and the oil barons and they were all friends with the mafia. And Johnson was friends with the oil barons. One big happy family.

In the early 1950's oil baron Clint Murchison had purchased the Del Mar racetrack and built a new luxury hotel, the Del Charro, in La Jolla, California.[1977] He reserved a private cottage for Hoover's free use.[1978] While using the facilities, Hoover was mixing socially with organized crime bosses.[1979] Hoover was quoted by Secretary of State J. Howard McGrath as saying that there was no such thing as a national crime syndicate.[1980] By the time he said that Hoover had been introduced by Lewis Rosenstiel, Clint Murchison and Myer Schine to Frank Costello, Meyer Lansky, Sam Giancana and Santo Trafficante representing the heads of the New York, Las Vegas, Chicago and Miami mafia crime families.[1981]

In 1957 there was a big organized crime meeting in Apalachin, New York. Alert law enforcement noticed all the fancy cars and ran their plates to see what was going on. They raided the meeting and the resulting national publicity forced Hoover to at least pretend to have the FBI investigate organized crime.[1982]

There were rumors that Hoover (and his lifetime companion Clyde Tolson) were closet homosexuals and that Hoover's self-imposed ignorance of the mafia was more than just gratitude to Clint Murchison and Sid Richardson for all the free time spent at the racetrack and resort. The rumors said that Meyer Lansky had a picture of Hoover and Tolson in a "compromising situation."[1983] This picture, if it ever existed, has never surfaced. If the rumors were true it would help explain Hoover's reluctance to investigate the mafia. A similar rumor involved CIA officer James Jesus Angleton, who is supposed to have had a copy of the same or a similar picture.[1984] There were other rumors swirling around Hoover.[1985] These may or may not be true. Again, proof has never surfaced. The rumors may have simply grown out of speculation caused by the fact that Hoover and Tolson were constant companions who never married in an era when homosexuality was viewed as a crime. For whatever reason, Hoover did his best to ignore the mafia. And his benign neglect allowed it to grow into an important part of the power structure of the era.

In Mark North's book *ACT OF TREASON: THE ROLE OF J. EDGAR HOOVER IN THE ASSASSINATION OF PRESIDENT KENNEDY*, he expresses the opinion that Hoover refuses to appear in person before the House Judiciary Subcommittee in May of 1961 out of fear his self-imposed ignorance of the mafia will be revealed.[1986]

Hoover the Dirt Collector

The FBI files were in three sections.[1987] The first was the central records for the official stuff, the second section was for off-limits records (illegal stuff like COINTELPRO) and the third was Hoover's personal blackmail files.[1988] Much of this was illegal, in violation of the Federal Records Act of 1950, which specified the legal use and proper handling procedures for such records.[1989] Hoover used *his* files for his own purposes. Hoover collected information from criminal informants and also farmed out "retired" FBI agents to locate their offices near FBI field offices and work with the local FBI office doing things that the FBI was not legally allowed to do.[1990] This was a way for Hoover and the FBI to have plausible deniability if they got caught.[1991] FBI agents performed illegal break-ins, but having contractors do it was an additional layer of protection for Hoover and the FBI and their reputation.[1992] This system of outside contractors was used for placing illegal bugs and wiretaps, for example.[1993] The recordings that resulted from illegal wiretaps were outside the normal controls because they were unknown to the courts or Congress or other oversight authorities which would normally order and control the output.[1994] Hoover ran many phone tapping operations without the knowledge of Attorney General Robert Kennedy. An example of this was a massive operation to tap phones in Las Vegas.[1995] The last chapter of this book contains accounts of how the FBI wing of the Deep State is still up to dirty tricks involving surveillance.

Typical of the attempts Hoover made to use blackmail as leverage over Kennedy to get a presidential waiver to stay in office was Judith Campbell. In the early 1960's Judith Campbell was a beautiful young woman who had affairs with several famous men, including mobster Johnny Roselli, mafia boss Sam Giancana and eventually John Kennedy. She appears to have been introduced to Kennedy by Frank

Sinatra. The FBI was taping phone conversations of mafia figures and Campbell was recorded having conversations with Giancana. Attorney General Robert Kennedy came across the mob tapes of Campbell as did Hoover. RFK and Hoover both knew that JFK was having an affair with Campbell, and when they heard the tapes they also knew that she was sleeping with Giancana during that same period. This was a problem for several reasons. In 1961 a sex scandal brought down the government of British Prime Minister Harold Macmillan. Hoover saw the potential for leverage in this information and brought it up to President Kennedy.

Author Phillip Nelson, in his book *LBJ: THE MASTERMIND OF THE JFK ASSASSINATION*, said Hoover was:[1996]

> "...a 'master blackmailer'... according to one of his closest colleagues, William Sullivan. He used his huge cache of official and confidential files to blackmail anyone whom he deemed necessary, including congressmen, senators, high-level officials in every department or agency up to and including a succession of presidents, from Roosevelt to Nixon (but no doubt excluding his namesake, Herbert Hoover, who appointed him to his position). In most cases, his blackmailing of presidents was related to forcing them to allow him to continue in his position, and it was done through innuendo and hints that he would drop about having knowledge of certain indiscretions."[1997]

In 1934 a federal law was passed to prohibit wiretaps.[1998] Hoover ignored the law and continued illegal wiretaps on whoever he chose.[1999]

Hoover continued to collect information in his secret personal files to use as potential blackmail on anyone who could be of use to him.[2000] The information he and his FBI collected for various purposes included information gathered via illegal break-ins and illegal wiretaps.

Hoover had all his files full of dirt on powerful people in Washington. Hoover was paranoid about communism.[2001] Truman was not.[2002] Hoover was continuing illegal wiretaps and Truman ordered them stopped.[2003] Hoover had a Deep State mentality and did not cut them off. Even without presidential authorization he continued the wiretaps.[2004] He believed that, in order to safeguard the civil liberties of the majority he (Hoover) would have to violate the civil liberties of a few communists and radicals.[2005] Hoover quietly supplied Senator Joseph McCarthy with files on suspected communists for his crusade.[2006]

Hoover kept a file on President Kennedy and his many affairs.[2007] Kennedy's sex life got him in trouble. He had sex with spies like Ellen

Rometsch, Maria Novotny and Suzy Chang. He also had sex with Judith Exner Campbell and Marilyn Monroe. A few days before she died Marilyn threatened to expose her affairs with JFK and RFK.[2008] Hoover had all this information in his files. Hoover knew all about the Kennedys and Marilyn.[2009]

This was typical of Hoover's attempts to use blackmail as pressure on Kennedy to give Hoover a waiver to avoid being retired against his will. It was also typical in that it failed to work on Kennedy, who was determined to see Hoover replaced as head of the FBI.

Hoover the Racist

Hoover was a racist.[2010] Born in 1895, Hoover's racial attitudes were very likely a product of the era he grew up in.

Hoover showed the same basic attitude toward the Ku Klux Klan (KKK) as he originally had toward the mafia. Hoover didn't try to deny the existence of the KKK (as he had the mafia), but he also didn't do anything to oppose it until he was forced. The KKK, like the mafia, was part of the existing power structure. Senator Harry Byrd from West Virginia was a member of the KKK. Lyndon Johnson was friends with Harry Byrd. One big happy family. Hoover had no incentive to go after the Klan. Hoover was perfectly happy avoiding the whole question of the KKK by claiming that Klan activity was a matter for the states to handle. Hoover claimed that, since he headed up the *Federal* Bureau of Investigation, Klan activity wasn't his jurisdiction. Just like the mafia was ignored until it made national headlines, not until the Civil Rights movement made national headlines was Hoover reluctantly forced to take some action against the Klan.

Hoover sent memos to Robert Kennedy claiming links between Martin Luther King, Jr. and the Communist Party of the United States of America.[2011] He claimed that Stanley D. Levison, an advisor to Martin Luther King, Jr., was a communist.[2012] Levison had previously given the communist party some advice.[2013] RFK and JFK did not take Hoover's communist warnings seriously.[2014] On June 22, 1963 President Kennedy warned Martin Luther King, Jr. about Hoover bugging his phones.[2015] King thought that, because Kennedy walked him to the rose garden to talk, Kennedy was also worried about his own phones being tapped as well.[2016] On July 17, 1963 President Kennedy held a press conference to say that civil rights leaders were not communists.[2017] This was specifically to counter Hoover, who had been saying that the civil rights leaders were communists.[2018]

Hoover kept African-Americans out of the FBI except for a few personal servants who performed personal tasks for Hoover as part of their official duties.[2019] Hoover looked the other way when African-Americans were murdered in the South, including Emmett Till, who was murdered in Mississippi in 1955.[2020] Hoover said that no civil rights were violated and no Federal laws were broken so there was no reason for the FBI to get involved.[2021] Hoover had a counterintelligence program known as COINTELPRO.[2022] Under this program Hoover ordered his agents to plant evidence (and stories in the press) against communists, the New Left, the Ku Klux Klan and the civil rights movement.[2023] The program was expanded to include on-the-job harassment, IRS audits and police interrogations.[2024] This was first placed under Alan Belmont, Assistant Director of the Domestic Intelligence Division of the FBI and was eventually expanded to include black bag jobs and illegal wiretaps.[2025] Hoover believed the ends justified the means.[2026]

Hoover did his best to keep the Black Panthers and other African-American from becoming a cohesive force in America. He used COINTELPRO to undermine them and teamed up with local law enforcement to raid, arrest and imprison them. One example of this would be the treatment of Black Panther leaders Fred Hampton and Mark Clark. In the pre-dawn hours on December 4, 1969 Chicago Police Sergeant Daniel Groth commanded the team that broke into the Chicago apartment of Black Panther leaders Fred Hampton and Mark Clark.[2027] Officers shot both men to death.[2028] In 1983, the Black Panther survivors of the raid and the families of Hampton and Clark were awarded $1.85 Million in a lawsuit against federal, state and Chicago officials and officers.[2029] Groth acknowledged under oath that his team of officers had carried out the assault on Fred Hampton and Mark Clark at the specific request of the FBI.[2030] Hoover and the FBI drove actress Jean Seberg to suicide when they leaked false information that she was pregnant by a member of the Black Panthers in an attempt to discredit the Panthers.[2031]

On November 16, 1963 Hoover, speaking before the Catholic Youth Organization, and accepting an award, denounced the civil rights movement.[2032]

Truman's Opinion of Hoover

In his book *PUPPETMASTER: THE SECRET LIFE OF J. EDGAR HOOVER*, author Richard Hack points out that Hoover crashed FDR's funeral as a way to meet President Truman.[2033] Hack also points out that:[2034]

> "Since his early days as a Senator, Truman found Hoover to be far too unregulated and pompous and was outspoken about his concerns over the extent of the FBI's authority. On May 12, 1945 the new president wrote himself an internal memo crystalizing his thoughts:"[2035]

> "We want no Gestapo or secret police. FBI is trending in that direction. They're dabbling in sex life scandals and plain blackmail when they should be catching criminals. They also have a habit of sneering at local law enforcement officers. This must stop. Cooperation is what we must have."[2036]

Hoover and Truman were never going to get along because Hoover wanted to be in charge and Truman saw things the other way around.[2037] Here was the Deep State mentality again. Hoover believed he knew better than the president and didn't care what Truman wanted. Truman believed that he was the duly elected president and that the Constitution gave him the authority to be in charge, not Hoover.

Author Richard Hack, in his excellent book *PUPPETMASTER: THE SECRET LIFE OF J. EDGAR HOOVER*, relates the following story:[2038]

> "Hoover arranged for a little-known agent named Marion Childs III to pay a visit to the new president and convey his message of welcome. Childs, as it happened, had grown up in Missouri. His father, Marion Childs, Jr. was a longtime friend of Truman's. As a surprised Truman welcomed Childs into the Oval Office, he was highly curious as to why the agent had come. "With a message from Mr. Hoover," Childs replied. "Mr. Hoover wants you to know that he and the FBI are at your personal disposal and will help you in any way you ask." Truman was not playing the game and sent Childs packing with a message for the Director "Any time I need the services of the FBI I will ask for it through my Attorney General." Truman announced, dismissing Childs and Hoover in the same sentence."[2039]

Truman was not impressed with Hoover. Writing to his wife Bess in 1947 Truman said:[2040]

"I'm sure glad the Secret Service is doing a better job. I was worried about that situation. Edgar Hoover would give his right eye to take over and all congressmen and senators are afraid of him. I'm not and he knows it. If I can prevent it, there'll be no NKVD or Gestapo in this country. Edgar Hoover's organization would make a good start toward a citizen spy system. Not for me."[2041]

Hoover did his best to boost his popularity while Truman did his best to look after the public interest. This left Truman at a disadvantage. An author named Max Lowenthal had written a book called *FEDERAL BUREAU OF INVESTIGATION,* which was about to be published by William Sloane Associates.[2042] Hoover wrote to President Truman suggesting that Lowenthal was a communist sympathizer.[2043] In fact, Lowenthal was a primary supporter of Truman who helped Truman get the vice president job, and Truman had helped edit the manuscript and had even seen a copy of the finished book.[2044] Hoover got Congressman George Dondero of Michigan to denounce Lowenthal for his still-unpublished book.[2045]

Hoover Before the JFK Assassination

As mentioned previously, most of the heavy lifting Hoover did for the conspiracy was after the assassination, during the cover up phase. However, some assistance was needed from Hoover prior the assassination. Hoover first had to make sure to sit on the warnings that were gathered by FBI agents where mafia bosses like Santo Trafficante or Carlos Marcello were overheard saying that Kennedy was going to be killed. For Hoover, in his position, to not pass these warnings on was a felony. Also, once it became clear that Dallas was likely to be the site of the assassination, Hoover moved to replace the FBI agent in charge of the Dallas FBI office with someone who could be relied upon to order other local Dallas FBI agents to use Gestapo tactics on witnesses who knew too much as well as to tamper with evidence. Having done those things beforehand Hoover was ready to play his major part in the cover-up once Kennedy was murdered.

The Kennedys wanted to retire Hoover and replace him. Hoover did not want to be deposed and put out to pasture. And Hoover had his famous files where he kept embarrassing evidence on political leaders to give him the leverage to stay in power. Hoover discovered that Kennedy was having an affair with Judith Campbell, who was also having an affair with Sam Giancana at the same time. Hoover tried several times to use this kind information as leverage with the Kennedys to keep from losing his job. Kennedy was not intimidated by Hoover's attempts at blackmail.

After the 1960 election, Joe Kennedy insisted that JFK make Bobby Attorney General. Hoover was not happy reporting to Bobby Kennedy.[2046] In his book *LBJ: THE MASTERMIND OF THE JFK ASSASSINATION*, author Phillip Nelson quotes Hoover upon finding out that "that skinny squealing little liberal shit" was going to be his boss.[2047] Both Kennedy brothers thought Hoover needed to be reined in. Hoover was approaching retirement and they decided to let that happen because it was time for a change. They underestimated the lengths to which Hoover would go to stay in power. Bobby wanted Hoover to clear all speeches and press releases through him.[2048] Hoover had regularly bypassed whoever was the Attorney General and dealt directly with the president, and President Kennedy put a stop to this.[2049]

Hoover and Robert Kennedy disliked each other immediately after the election. Hoover refused to cooperate in Bobby's war on the mafia.[2050] Hoover was a dictator who was outraged at having to report to Robert Kennedy. RFK had a buzzer and a direct phone installed on Hoover's desk.[2051] Hoover was outraged. Robert Kennedy showed up in Hoover's office without an appointment.[2052] Hoover was outraged. Robert Kennedy questioned why the FBI did not have minority agents.[2053] Hoover was outraged. Hoover moved the buzzer and hotline to his secretary's desk and Robert Kennedy had the phone and buzzer moved back to Hoover's desk.[2054] Robert Kennedy appeared at the office on the weekend and requested files while Hoover was out. Hoover wanted to filter what Robert Kennedy saw from his files and therefore had to show up at the office on Saturdays to make sure Robert Kennedy could not get at *his* files without Hoover being there to filter what Robert Kennedy saw.[2055]

On February 14, 1961 the press announced that Admiral Rickover was, at President Kennedy's request, being kept beyond his normal retirement date.[2056] This was exactly what Hoover wanted from President Kennedy, a presidential waiver.

J. Edgar Hoover thought someone was impersonating Oswald.[2057] On June 3, 1960 he sent a letter to the State Department asking them to look into it:[2058]

> "Since there is the possibility that an imposter is using Oswald's birth certificate," Hoover said "any current information the Department of State has concerning subject (Oswald) would be appreciated"[2059]

At some point Hoover realized that he was not going to get what he wanted from Kennedy. The buzzards were circling. In 1961 former agents start to speak out on Hoover's autocratic style and the effectiveness of the FBI[2060] On February 17, 1962 Philadelphia mafia boss Angelo Bruno was recorded by the FBI speculating that RFK wanted to get rid of Hoover.[2061] In June of 1962 the FBI recorded Marilyn Monroe telling a friend that she talked with Robert Kennedy about his desire to get rid of Hoover.[2062]

In June of 1962 Kennedy issued NSAM 161 to strip Hoover of his duties on the Interdepartmental Intelligence Conference and gave control of the position to RFK, thus signaling the beginning of the end of Hoover and his reign over the FBI.[2063]

Hoover continued to rub Kennedy's nose in the fact that he knew about the affair with Judith Campbell who was also having an affair with mafia boss Sam Giancana.[2064] This was an attempt to blackmail President Kennedy into keeping Hoover in office past his mandatory retirement date.[2065] In June of 1962 the Federal retirement age was seventy. Only the president could give a waiver and Kennedy had said that under no circumstances would he agree to Hoover staying in office.[2066] Hoover would turn seventy on January 1, 1965. Without a presidential waiver he was going to have to retire.

Hoover had dirt on the Kennedys but they also had dirt on him and if he lost his job he would lose his ability to use his leverage. He also wanted to build the new FBI building (which became the J. Edgar Hoover building) and it was yet to be built.[2067]

In September of 1962 Hoover learned that the Marcello crime family had put out a contract on Kennedy in order to protect themselves from prosecution by the Kennedys and the Justice Department.[2068] Hoover had a legal duty to report that to the Kennedys and he did not.[2069] He was now in clear violation of the law.[2070] Hoover got word of the Marcello JFK contract via the FBI field office in Miami who heard it from their informants in the Cuban exile community.[2071] Only a few FBI agents in Miami knew of the warning.[2072]

In his book *ACT OF TREASON: THE ROLE OF J. EDGAR HOOVER IN THE ASSASSINATION OF PRESIDENT KENNEDY*, author Mark North expresses the opinion that this is the point at which Hoover shifted from trying to blackmail Kennedy into giving him a retirement waiver to trying to see that the assassination of Kennedy was a success.[2073] This was the point at which Hoover decided to join the conspiracy to assassinate President Kennedy.

On December 18, 1962 FBI agents Regis Kennedy of New Orleans and Paul Scranton and George Davis of Miami file reports on mafia bosses Marcello and Trafficante, and Hoover again sees the Marcello contract, this time in more detail.[2074] Hoover at that point had confirmed and credible evidence of an assassination plot against the president of the United States and did not pass on that information. Clearly Hoover, by his actions, showed that he had joined the conspiracy. Otherwise he would have passed on the information on the threat to President Kennedy's life.

In April of 1963, as things were heating up in Dallas, Hoover replaced the Special Agent in Charge (SAIC) in Dallas with the more loyal Gordon Shanklin.[2075] Gestapo tactics are going to be needed to intimidate witnesses. Hoover will also need someone he can depend on to destroy or fabricate 'evidence' as necessary, and Shanklin was his choice. Shanklin will prove more than up to the task.

On June 6, 1963 the Senate Judiciary Committee approved a bill that would provide that future directors of the FBI would be appointed by the president and subject to senate approval and would limit the term of the FBI director to fifteen years.[2076] The feeling in Congress was that having an FBI director in office for so long was a bad idea.[2077] On June 13, 1963 Bill 603 was passed by the Senate, which had clearly sided with Kennedy on the issue of Hoover's retirement.[2078]

In July of 1962 Robert Kennedy leaked to the press that Hoover would have to retire on January 1, 1965. This meant that President Kennedy was telling the press (via RFK) that Hoover will not be given a waiver.[2079] Johnson was becoming increasingly dependent on Hoover and Hoover was facing being forced out by his retirement age and JFK's unwillingness to give him a pass.[2080] Hoover's attempts to blackmail President Kennedy into giving him a retirement waiver by threatening to reveal his affairs had failed.

In August of 1962 mafia boss Carlos Marcello put out a contract on President Kennedy.[2081] Marcello was under pressure from prosecutions of members of his organization and from his likely deportation and/or imprisonment.[2082] Marcello could act without the approval of the mafia Commission because Marcello's organization was older than the mafia Commission and he was not subject to the Commission.[2083]

On February 1, 1963 Hoover perjured himself many times while testifying before congress.[2084]

On March 15, 1963 Hoover stated publicly that he had no intention of resigning from his job.[2085] He emphasized that he intended to stay and get the job done.[2086] Given that he was facing retirement and Kennedy would't give him a waiver, one can only assume he had some other plan to avoid retirement.[2087]

Hoover collected dirt on JFK and revealed it to RFK on the assumption he will pass it on to JFK and President Kennedy and J. Edgar Hoover openly take shots at each other in speeches and in the press.[2088]

Richard Case Nagell Tries to Warn Hoover

Richard Case Nagell was a spy for the CIA and his assignment was to go become a double agent for the Russians in Mexico City.[2089] When he pretended to go to work for the Russians they told him there was a plot to kill Kennedy and they wanted to try to stop it.[2090] The Russians wanted no part of Kennedy getting killed. Khrushchev and Kennedy were getting along, and the Russians were justifiably worried they would be blamed if Kennedy was shot, so the Russians sent Nagell to make sure Kennedy was not killed. They told Nagell to warn Oswald, and if Oswald wouldn't listen he was to kill Oswald.[2091] Nagell tried to warn Oswald but Oswald didn't listen. By September of 1963 Nagell had met with Oswald in New Orleans and warned him, but failed to get the answer he wanted out of him.[2092] Then Nagell lost contact with his CIA case worker.[2093] This put Nagell in a difficult situation. He did not want to kill Oswald, as he had been told to do by the Russians. And he didn't want to be killed by the Russians for not following their orders. He also didn't want to be framed for Kennedy's assassination and then get killed as the patsy. He decided to send a registered letter to Hoover at the FBI warning him of the plot to kill Kennedy, and he does this on September 17, 1963.[2094] The FBI later claimed to be unable to find the letter.

Other Warnings

In Mark North's book *ACT OF TREASON: THE ROLE OF J. EDGAR HOOVER IN THE ASSASSINATION OF PRESIDENT KENNEDY*, the author documents the following warning:[2095]

> "… Still another allegation mentioning an associate of the Marcellos arrived at headquarters. It was Eugene De

Laparra's allegation that in March or April he had overheard Vincent Marcello's friend Ben Treagle say that there was 'a price on the president's head' and that somebody would kill Kennedy when he came south." North goes on to say "Hoover had reportedly heard this story in September, 1963. He ignores this second report also."[2096]

In mid-November, 1963 the FBI records a Cuban exile talking to others in his group saying that "we are waiting for Kennedy the 22 November" and "we're going to see him one way or the other – we're going to give him the works when he gets to Dallas" because of Hoover JFK learns nothing of these threats.[2097]

In his book *ACT OF TREASON: THE ROLE OF J. EDGAR HOOVER IN THE ASSASSINATION OF PRESIDENT KENNEDY*, author Mark North recounts a conversation on November 9, 1963 between William Somerset and Joseph Milteer. Somerset is an informant for the Miami police and Milteer is active in the Cuban exile community:[2098]

> Somerset: "I think Kennedy is coming here on the eighteenth or something like that to make some kind of speech..."
>
> Milteer: "You can bet your bottom dollar he is going to have a lot to say about the Cubans."
>
> Somerset: "Yeah. Well he will have a thousand bodyguards, don't worry about that."
>
> Milteer: "The more bodyguards he has the easier it is to get him."
>
> Somerset: "Well, how in hell do you figure is the best way to get him?"
>
> Milteer: "from an office building with a high-powered rifle... He knows he's a marked man..."
>
> Somerset: "They are really going to try to kill him?"
>
> Milteer: "Oh yeah, it is in the working... They will pick somebody up within hours afterwards, just to throw the public off"

North also points out that Somerset then informs "his police contact who informs captain Charles Sapp who reports to his chief of police, the Secret Service and FBI. [2099] The Secret Service checked on Milteer's whereabouts but he was not questioned. Milteer thinks the

Cuban exiles are behind the hit as he is active in the Cuban exile community."[2100] Once again, Hoover does not pass on the warning.

On November 16, 1963 Lee Harvey Oswald tried to send a warning about the assassination. He met with an FBI contact who he trusted and a warning was sent via Telex which was seen the following morning.[2101] Hoover tried to hide it, but William Walter was a clerk in the FBI office in New Orleans and he saw it.[2102] Author Mark Lane was in New Orleans and he gave a talk at Tulane University.[2103] He was approached by William Walter.[2104] On November 17 William Walter was in the FBI and he got a Telex on a threat to assassinate JFK in Dallas on November 22.[2105] Later it was removed from the file.[2106] The FBI did nothing, did not even notify the Secret Service, even though the warning had gone out under J. Edgar Hoover's name.[2107] After the Freedom of Information Act (FOIA) was passed in 1976, Mark Lane was able to obtain a copy of the warning Telex, which specifically warns of an attempt to assassinate President Kennedy during his trip to Dallas on November 22 or 23.[2108] The Telex is in Garrison's book ON THE TRAIL OF THE ASSASSINS, on page 221.

Hoover After the JFK Assassination

Author Mark North, in his book, ACT OF TREASON: THE ROLE OF J. EDGAR HOOVER IN THE ASSASSINATION OF PRESIDENT KENNEDY, points out that:[2109]

> "Though the effort to aid the Marcello contract had been successful, he has now to turn the opportunity to his advantage by containing the matter and obtaining a retirement waiver from Johnson. The growing Baker-mafia scandal complicates his task by threatening to dethrone LBJ at the outset. Hoover, quite simply, has to save Lyndon once again in order to save himself. No fool, LBJ soon perceives the reality of the situation. In this regard his not inconsiderable political skills are quickly brought to bear in aide of the two's mutual goals."[2110]

The morning after the Kennedy assassination Hoover submitted a five-page report to Johnson claiming Oswald is a lone nut shooter and a communist.[2111] Later that day Hoover called Johnson and said that there was someone, not Oswald, claiming to be Oswald in Mexico City, and that there was a recording of the conversation.[2112] This is important because it is proof that Hoover knew there was a conspiracy,

248

even though he later claimed in his report that Oswald was a 'lone gunman.'[2113] This taped conversation is hard evidence of duplicity on Hoover's part.[2114]

Hoover also pitched in on the disinformation campaign with the media.[2115] He leaked stories to the national press to counter the statements of witnesses who saw gun smoke and heard shots coming from the fence behind the grassy knoll.[2116] He played up the 'Oswald is a communist nut' angle.[2117]

Before the assassination Hoover had replaced the head of the FBI office in Dallas with the loyal Gordon Shanklin who can be counted on to use Gestapo tactics during the cover-up.[2118] This started right away with Shanklin lying to the national media. Hoover had Shanklin lie to the press about Oswald not having any contact with the FBI prior to the assassination and about Oswald's paraffin test. Oswald did have contact with the FBI and Shanklin said he did not.[2119] Oswald passed his paraffin test (he could not have shot a rifle) and Shanklin said he flunked it, the exact opposite of the truth.[2120]

Right after the assassination there was a call on the public for evidence and eyewitness reports.[2121] Hoover needed to have an inventory of every scrap of evidence and make sure that all of it was sanitized in some way. With Shanklin in place in Dallas, Gestapo tactics could be used on witnesses to make them either shut up or change their stories. Any photographic evidence that had not already been confiscated by government agents in place in Dealey Plaza could now be collected. Much effort will put into making sure that the number and direction of shots agree with the official myth that Oswald was the lone shooter. Any witnesses to shots from the front would be intimidated and any evidence of shots from the front would be buried. At first, people were willing to help. Their president had just been brutally murdered in front of them. They trusted their government. They wanted to help solve the crime. They came forward and told their stories and handed over their evidence.

Pilot David Ferrie was arrested in New Orleans because his library card was found in Oswald's possessions.[2122] The various connections to mafia boss Carlos Marcello were starting to become too obvious, so during the week of November 25 Hoover tried to shut down the FBI investigation into Marcello's organization.[2123] Later, he would shut it down completely.

Ruby Murders Oswald

At 11:15 AM on November 24, 1963 Oswald blurted out to reporters as he was being transferred "I'm just a patsy!" and at 11:20 AM Ruby entered the basement and moments later executed Oswald.[2124]

On November 30 Hoover obtained the Hughes film, strongly suggesting the presence of two gunmen on the sixth floor, just as numerous eyewitnesses' testimony had predicted.[2125]

In early December Hoover again attacked the Dallas and New Orleans FBI agents investigating the Marcello organization and the investigation slowed to a crawl.[2126]

Hoover also took steps to make sure no one heard of the multiple warnings the FBI had that Marcello was going to have Kennedy killed.[2127] The FBI agents who first heard of the warnings were ordered to go back and tell their contacts to keep their mouths shut 'in the national interest.'[2128]

Hoover claimed that the Dallas police had violated Oswald's civil rights and therefore the FBI was taking over the investigation.[2129] On November 25 Hoover sent reinforcements to Dallas to help Shanklin control events on the ground.[2130] The Dallas authorities cooperated and claimed publicly that the FBI was now in charge.[2131]

On Sunday Hoover told Shanklin to sanitize Oswald's file to get rid of any evidence of FBI contact with Oswald.[2132] This was destruction of evidence and obstruction of justice.[2133] Shanklin immediately followed orders.[2134]

On December 18, 1963 Hoover ordered a halt to the FBI New Orleans office investigation of the link between CIA asset David Ferrie and mafia boss Carlos Marcello.[2135] He does this because the last thing he wanted was for the truth to see the light of day.

Three weeks after Kennedy was murdered, Hoover put a stop to all investigations of the Kennedy assassination so that he and Johnson would not be exposed.[2136]

Reassure the Public

At first, Johnson and Hoover had no interest or intention to create a presidential commission to investigate the Kennedy assassination.

Johnson had things wired in Texas and Oswald was set up to take the blame. Johnson decided not to use the "Russians were behind it" angle or the "Castro was behind it" angle or some combination of both to start World War Three. He decided to just go with "Oswald did it alone."

Then Oswald was captured alive and, to keep him quiet, they had to send Ruby in to murder Oswald on national television. This was too much for the public, who could see for themselves that it looked like Ruby was sent in to silence Oswald. This made the calls for a congressional investigation loud enough that Johnson could not ignore them. Once Congress decided to investigate, Johnson had no choice but to create a presidential commission. Had he not done so, there might have been an actual investigation that he was not controlling. Creating what became known as the Warren Commission allowed Johnson to create something he could control and head off all the other investigations.

Hoover reluctantly gets into the act when he sees the writing on the wall. He has his 'investigative' report written on the evening of the assassination, and he sends it to President Johnson the next morning. He expresses his opinion that the crime is solved. The last thing either of them wanted was an actual investigation, then Oswald was captured alive and Ruby had to be sent in to kill Oswald and the situation had changed due to public opinion.

On November 24, 1963 Hoover created a memo. He also called Johnson aide Walter Jenkins to relay the sentiment in the memo, which included the following passage:[2137]

> "The thing I am most concerned about, and so is Mr. Katzenbach, is having something issued so we can convince the public that Oswald is the real assassin. Mr. Katzenbach thinks that the president might appoint a presidential commission of three outstanding citizens, to make a determination. I countered with a suggestion that we make an investigative report to the Attorney General with pictures, laboratory work, etc., then the Attorney General can make the report to the president and the president can decide whether to make it public. We have no information on Ruby that is firm, although there are some rumors of underworld activity in Chicago."[2138]

Hoover realized that the Warren Commission was a necessary whitewash. After the spectacle of Ruby murdering Oswald, the public needed a group of distinguished officials to tell them that Kennedy's assassination wasn't a political murder. Because this was a coup d'état against the U.S. government, the conspirators needed someone to reassure public that it wasn't a coup d'état against the U.S. government. So, what Hoover wanted was for the Warren Commission to read his scanty report and turn to the American people and say 'Hoover is right, Oswald did it and he acted alone.' He just wanted their seal of approval. The last thing Hoover wanted was a bunch of people snooping around his precious files. They might actually find something. Hoover wants to filter what everyone else saw, that way he can only let them see what he wanted them to see. So, while Hoover urged Johnson to create the Warren Commission, he then wanted it to wrap up as quickly as possible with as little actual investigation as possible. He wanted the commission to just take his word for everything.[2139]

Hoover quickly completed his summary report on the assassination. Instead of then turning it over to Johnson or the Warren Commission, he first leaked it to the press. This was an attempt by Hoover to force the commission to come to his conclusions.[2140]

On March 10, 1964 President Johnson stated publicly that he intended to waive Hoover's retirement.[2141] On May 8, 1964 he did just that, and Hoover was saved from having to be put out to pasture.[2142]

After the Kennedy assassination, Hoover immediately ordered RFK's hotline returned to Miss Gandy's desk, reportedly stating at the time "put that damned thing back on Miss Gandy's desk where it belongs."[2143]

In early January of 1964 Attorney General Robert Kennedy returns to work, and the FBI ceased sending an official car to pick up Robert Kennedy during his travels.[2144]

Author Anthony Summers, in his book *NOT IN YOUR LIFETIME*, points out that:[2145]

> "In 1977, when the FBI went through the motions of releasing 100,000 pages from its Kennedy assassination files, the U.S. media uttered an uncritical cheer. At the press conference to mark the event, reporters seemed uninterested or ill-equipped to ask probing questions. The author found himself virtually alone in pressing the FBI spokesman into an admission that up to 10% of the Kennedy file will not be released. One reason for retaining the records, the spokesman said, was to protect individual's privacy. The other was the familiar one –

national security – even after the passage of the JFK Records Act in 1992, which mandated the release of all Kennedy assassination material unless a real case could be made for retention, the FBI continued to resist full disclosure."[2146]

The last chapter, Why This Matters Today, goes into detail on how FBI Director James Comey carried on the Deep State tradition of using the power of the FBI to protect the Deep State while undermining the will of the voters.

That last chapter also goes into detail on how the rest of the Justice Department is used by the Deep State to do the same thing, even if they have to convict innocent people who just happen to get in the way.

The Joint Chiefs of Staff and the Pentagon

The Joint Chiefs of Staff at the Pentagon disagreed with Kennedy on almost every major issue they faced. They saw the United States as much stronger than Russia and wanted each crisis to be used as an excuse to flex American military muscle. They wanted to have a nuclear showdown with the Russians while the U.S. still had the advantage. As each crisis (the Bay of Pigs, the Berlin Crisis and the Cuban Missile Crisis) came up the Joint Chiefs became increasingly frustrated that Kennedy would not allow them to attack. The Pentagon saw each crisis as an opportunity to start World War Three and, as Kennedy passed up each opportunity, the Joint Chiefs became more and more frustrated that Kennedy would not act. Kennedy increasingly wanted to work with Khrushchev toward peace and the Joint Chiefs came to see this as treasonous collusion our mortal enemy. They also wanted to ramp up the Vietnam War and believed, as did the CIA, in the Cold War domino theory. By late 1963 the gap between Kennedy and the Joint Chiefs had widened into a canyon. They saw Kennedy as a traitor and a threat to the national security of the country. Kennedy himself became concerned that the military would try to overthrow the government.

The same dynamic that destroyed the relationship between Kennedy and the CIA played out in Kennedy's relationship with the Pentagon. Their relationship started out badly and went rapidly downhill from there.

This chapter is organized into seven sections:

1. Air Force General Curtis LeMay – describes how Curtis LeMay used his guts, brains and drive to go from being the son of a handyman to the Chief of Staff of the United States Air Force

2. The Joint Chiefs of Staff – describes how the Joint Chiefs and President Kennedy had opposite views on just about every important issue – especially a first nuclear strike

3. Let's start World War Three – describes how the Joint Chiefs advocated for a first nuclear strike against the Soviet Union and how Kennedy refused to go along

4. Losing control of the military – describes how the military tried to use the Cuban Missile Crisis as an excuse to start World War Three

5. The question of Vietnam – describes how Kennedy decided to pull America out of Vietnam over the objections of the military who wanted to ramp up the war in Vietnam

6. Eugene Dinkin goes AWOL – describes how an American cryptographic code operator stationed in Metz, France decoded secret military messages describing the Kennedy assassination a month before it happend and tried to warn the president

7. The Shell Game and the Autopsy – describes how the military doctors working on the Kennedy autopsy were ordered by their superiors not to do a proper autopsy so as to cover up the existence of a conspiracy to assassinate Kennedy

Most of the military back then were Republicans and the Joint Chiefs very likely voted for Nixon, who was a Republican and was seen by them as a fellow Cold Warrior. L. Fletcher Prouty said that the people at the Pentagon were not happy about Kennedy being elected. He mentioned their "shock and dismay."[2147]

In the early 1960's the Pentagon was not at all happy with Kennedy's election or administration or policies. They viewed Kennedy as a lightweight and a rich kid who had his wealthy father buy him the White House. This was only partially true. Kennedy's father had pushed Kennedy to run for office and had paid for the campaign. And Kennedy may have been young and inexperienced compared to Eisenhower, but he was not a lightweight. He was smart enough to realize that starting a land war in Asia was a bad idea. He also understood that no one would win a nuclear war between Soviet Russia and the United States. And he was brave enough to stand up to the Pentagon and the CIA when they tried to intimidate him. He also understood that he had been elected, not them.

The CIA, the State Department, the Pentagon and many of the politicians like Nixon were Cold Warriors who believed in the domino theory. They thought that communists in Russia and/or China would continue to push to take over one country after another until an entire region, like southeast Asia, went communist. Kennedy started out in

1961 with only one foot in their camp. Kennedy's views evolved while those of the hard-core Cold Warriors didn't. Kennedy gradually grew farther and farther apart from his CIA and the Joint Chiefs and they eventually ended up in 1963 with opposite views on the most important issues facing the country.

The few areas of agreement they had started with in 1961 soon evaporated as Kennedy's views evolved. The Joint Chiefs in general and Curtis LeMay in particular wanted a nuclear first strike while Kennedy was opposed to a nuclear first strike. The Joint Chiefs wanted a nuclear buildup while Kennedy wanted nuclear disarmament. Kennedy wanted to make peace with Khrushchev and the Russians. The Joint Chiefs wanted to take out the Russians while the U.S. was relatively stronger and had the advantage in nuclear weapons. The Pentagon believed that the Russians were building up their capabilities and that the window of opportunity for a successful first strike would not stay open much longer. Therefore, they wanted to strike as soon as possible. They were therefore horrified that Kennedy was balking at this.

The joint Chiefs wanted to invade Cuba. At first this was one of the few issues on which Kennedy and the Pentagon could come to agreement. In 1961 Kennedy was willing to go along with invading Cuba, but only if the United States was not seen as invading Cuba. Kennedy did not want the U.S. to be seen as an aggressor nation and using the U.S. military to invade Cuba would look bad. By 1963 Kennedy had done an about-face on Cuban policy and had promised Khrushchev that the U.S. would not invade Cuba. By 1963 Kennedy was even looking to normalize relations with Castro. Kennedy wanted to make peace with Cuba while the Joint Chiefs still wanted to invade Cuba. On the issue of Cuba Kennedy and the Pentagon had gone from agreement in 1961 to disagreement by 1963.

At first Kennedy and the Pentagon were able to agree on the U.S. policy toward Vietnam. This also changed. In 1961 Kennedy was willing to send more money and advisors to Vietnam. This was also what the Pentagon wanted. By 1963 Kennedy had decided that U.S. involvement in Vietnam was a bad idea. He had given orders to start the withdrawal and was planning to have the U.S. completely out of Vietnam within a few years. On this issue Kennedy and the Pentagon had again gone from agreement in 1961 to disagreement by 1963. Meanwhile the Pentagon wanted to dramatically ramp up U.S. involvement in Vietnam, including sending combat troops.

The issue of what to do in Vietnam was a difficult one for every American president who faced it. Any president from Truman to

Eisenhower to Kennedy who had pulled out of Vietnam would have been a one-term president. His opponent would have said 'my opponent is soft on communism.' Truman was elected by a razor thin margin, as was Kennedy. Had either of them pulled out of Vietnam, or even talked about pulling out, they would have lost the next election. And they knew it. Kennedy had decided to wait until after the 1964 election to pull out of Vietnam during his second term because he knew he would pay a political price. This would allow him to get elected and still do what he saw as the right thing.

By 1963 Kennedy and the Joint Chiefs of Staff were on opposite sides of most, if not all, of the important foreign policy issues. The Joint Chiefs were Cold Warriors who believed that communists were aggressive expansionists who were going to try to take over the world one country at a time in an attempt to gradually isolate the United States of America. They believed that the U.S. had to aggressively fight communism at every opportunity. They saw the Bay of Pigs, the Berlin Crisis and the Cuban Missile Crisis as opportunities to fight back, and they saw Kennedy as having missed those opportunities. And they viewed Vietnam as the place to hold the line on communist expansion. They viewed Kennedy as weak and indecisive and a danger to our national security. Kennedy was appalled by how close the world came to nuclear disaster during the Cuban Missile Crisis and wanted to work with Khrushchev to make peace. Kennedy negotiated a nuclear test ban treaty with the Soviet Union, and he had to go around his own national security apparatus to get it done.

The Joint Chiefs also believed at that time that the United States should strike now while the Russians were weaker. In their view the window of opportunity for a successful first strike would not stay open much longer. Time was running out and, in the meantime, the military brass were coming to see Kennedy as a threat to the survival of the nation. And Kennedy's collusion with Khrushchev was seen by them as treason.[2148] (Does this 'collusion with the Russians' charge sound familiar?) The Joint Chiefs also agreed with the CIA that the war in Vietnam should be ramped up. Johnson would do that and Kennedy would not. The entire military-industrial complex run out of the Pentagon did not participate in the Kennedy assassination. Just like the CIA and FBI, a few of the top brass were all it would take.

Kennedy himself was concerned that the military would try to take him out and take over. A military coup was a drastic step that would likely not have been accepted by the American people. However, there was another, less obvious, option open to a few of the members of the Joint Chiefs of Staff. A conspiracy was forming among other elements of the Deep State. Vice President Johnson was participating in a group that included the mafia, the CIA, the anti-Castro Cuban exiles, the FBI and the wealthy oil barons of the day. A few key people at the top of the military chain of command would be needed to cooperate in a conspiracy and the Pentagon could have a new Commander in Chief who would agree with them on their policies. And they could do all this without an obvious, and therefore unpopular, military takeover.

Kennedy was also rapidly losing control of the military. During the Cuban Missile Crisis, for example, the Pentagon had executed several provocative maneuvers at the height of the crisis. Had these been taken the wrong way by the Russians they would have started World War Three, which was what the Joint Chiefs wanted and were trying to accomplish.

The military took control of Kennedy's body and played a shell game with the corpse and corrupted the autopsy. This could only have been done by the military, and only with the highest authority.

Air Force General Curtis LeMay

Curtis LeMay was a brilliant and accomplished general in the United State Air Force. He rose on his own merit from humble beginnings to become a war hero and eventually the Chief of Staff of the United States Air Force. He led from the front and demanded that others not shirk their duty. Due to dangerous missions and high casualty rates in the bombing raids over Germany in World War II, there were a lot of bombers turning back. When LeMay was put in charge he led the raids himself and said that anyone who turned back would face a court martial. LeMay's leadership turned things around.

His success in the European theatre caused him to be put in charge of the bombing raids over Japan. LeMay's bombing campaign against Japan in World War II was devastatingly effective. The conventional bombing killed between a quarter and half a million Japanese and left millions homeless. This was more than were killed in Hiroshima and Nagasaki combined. LeMay's conventional bombing campaign was so effective that the bombers were running out of targets and a few major cities like Hiroshima and Nagasaki had to be spared on purpose. This was done so that, if nuclear bombs were later used, their effectiveness would be more obvious. Had they not been spared the effect of the nuclear bombs might not have been as obvious and therefore might not have caused the Japanese to surrender.

In 1948 Curtis LeMay was returned to the United States to head the Strategic Air Command where he proceeded to transform it from an ineffectual force with a few leftover World War II bombers with untrained crews to an effective deterrent force.

Curtis LeMay was also opinionated and outspoken. He was a colorful standout in a long line of successful and outspoken American Generals and Admirals, much like Douglas MacArthur. He is quoted as having said "That was the era when we might have destroyed Russia completely and not even skinned our elbows doing it." The difference between LeMay and the other Joint Chiefs is that he was willing to say in public what the others were thinking and saying privately.

In his book *LBJ: THE MASTERMIND OF THE JFK ASSASSINATION*, author Phillip Nelson has a quote from a *Washington Post* column by Marquis Childs:[2149]

> "At a Georgetown dinner party recently, the wife of a leading senator sat next to General Curtis LeMay, chief of staff of the Air Force. He told her a nuclear war was inevitable. It would begin in December and be all over by the first of the year. In that interval, every major American city – Washington, New York, Philadelphia, Detroit, Chicago, Los Angeles – would be reduced to rubble. Similarly, the principal cities of the Soviet Union would be destroyed. The lady, as she tells it, asked if there were any place where she could take her children and grandchildren to safety; the general would, of course, at the first alert be inside the top-secret underground hideout near Washington from which the retaliatory strike would be directed. He told her that certain unpopulated areas in the far west would be safest."[2150]

In that same book, author Nelson also says:[2151]

> "General LeMay talked openly about a preemptive attack in which one hundred million people would be killed. He persistently recommended taking aggressive action regarding an attack on Cuba in order to over throw Castro, beginning with the Bay of Pigs invasion and continuing through the Cuban Missile Crisis, as Kennedy continually resisted his recommendations. LeMay was a proponent of the concept of "nuclear first strike," saying that we should give the Russians the "Sunday punch" before they did it to us. Under Eisenhower, LeMay had the authority to order a nuclear strike without presidential authorization if the president could not be

contacted. Kennedy made it clear that that authority was no longer applicable."[2152]

General LeMay wasn't alone among the Joint Chiefs or the Pentagon in his views about a nuclear first strike. He was just willing to be more outspoken.

The Joint Chiefs of Staff

There were 28 civilians, federal agents and military generals and admirals at the Kennedy autopsy and Air Force General Curtis LeMay was in overall charge.[2153] One of the top military brass, very likely General LeMay, ordered the doctors to avoid doing a proper autopsy so as to avoid documenting the fact that several shots came from the front. This was necessary to cover up the conspiracy. This could only have been done by the U.S. military. A civilian could not have given orders to the military doctors at Bethesda.

In 1963 the Deep State had completely opposite views from President Kennedy on what policies the United States should pursue. Author Brian VanDeMark, in his book *ROAD TO DISASTER*, does an excellent job of describing how the Deep State came to believe it could win the Vietnam War. I highly recommend his book. The point here is that, by 1963, the Deep State believed that the United States could and should send combat troops to Vietnam and Kennedy, in the meantime, had decided we should pull out of Vietnam. The Deep State had also decided that Kennedy was unfit for office, and that he should be replaced. And some of them were willing to act on that belief by joining the conspiracy that Johnson was coordinating.

The building of the Berlin Wall and the crisis of the tanks at Checkpoint Charlie in October of 1961 had convinced General Lucius Clay that Kennedy was unfit for the presidency.[2154] He thought Kennedy had lost his "nerve."[2155]

During the Cuban Missile Crisis Air Force Chief of Staff General LeMay wanted to bomb the missile sites in Cuba.[2156] The Pentagon recommended a full-scale invasion as a follow-up to LeMay's bombing strikes.[2157] Their assumption was that the CIA was correct in their assessment that the medium-range nuclear-tipped missiles were not yet operational.[2158] What the Pentagon and the CIA did not know was that the Russians had over forty thousand troops to resist just such an invasion.[2159] And they had ninety-eight tactical nuclear weapons and the means to deliver them to repel an invasion, in addition to the medium-range missiles that had been spotted by the U-2 reconnaissance flights.[2160] Secretary of Defense Robert McNamara said, when he learned of the additional troops and missiles some 30 years later that, had we invaded Cuba at that time, we would have been involved in a nuclear war.[2161]

Author Jefferson Morley, in his book *THE GHOST: THE SCERET LIFE OF CIA SPYMASTER JAMES JESUS ANGLETON*, said that, in regard to Kennedy's handling of the Cuban Missile Crisis:[2162]

> "With the benefit of hindsight many scholars regard the peaceful resolution of the crisis as JFK's finest moment as president of the United States. What the liberal account of the October crisis tends to overlook is the impact on President Kennedy's government. JFK's refusal to go to war in October 1962 despite the advice of the Joint Chiefs stoked the *Seven Days in May* mood of rebellion that already pervaded the councils of U.S. national security agencies. The generals felt the president was abandoning the U.S. policy of containment of the Soviet Union in favor of accommodation."[2163]

The mention above of *Seven Days in May* is in reference to a book and movie about a U.S. military plot to overthrow the government due to the military disagreeing with the president's desire to sign a nuclear disarmament treaty with the Soviet Union. Kennedy thought it conceivable that the U.S. military would depose him.[2164] When he learned that the book *Seven Days in May* was going to be made into a move, he offered the use of the White House as a set for the filming of the movie.[2165]

Kennedy at one point asked General LeMay how the Soviet Union would react to an invasion of Cuba by the United States. LeMay said they would not respond because the U.S. had overwhelming military superiority.[2166] Kennedy didn't believe that the Soviets would just do nothing if we attacked.[2167] "They, no more than we, can let these things go by without doing something." He told LeMay "They can't after all their statements permit us to take out their missiles, kill a lot of Russians and then do nothing."[2168]

Robert Kennedy had a message for Khrushchev at the height of the Cuban Missile Crisis:[2169]

> "President Kennedy implores Chairman Khrushchev to accept his offer and to take into consideration the peculiarities of the American system. Even though the president himself is very much against starting a war over Cuba, an irreversible chain of events could occur against his will. That is why the president

is appealing directly to Chairman Khrushchev for his help in liquidating this conflict. If the situation continues much longer the president is not sure the military will not overthrow him and seize power. The American Army could get out of control."[2170]

Author Jefferson Morley, in his book *THE GHOST: THE SCERET LIFE OF CIA SPYMASTER JAMES JESUS ANGLETON*, said that:[2171]

> "Another point not emphasized in the liberal narrative of the October crisis: The president feared that 186 years of constitutional government in the United States of America was in jeopardy. A military coup was a real possibility. *The American Army could get out of control.* That wasn't paperback fiction, it was the reality of power in John Kennedy's Washington. War never came. At noon on Sunday, October 28, the White House received a communication from Chairman Khrushchev that began: "Dear Mr. President." The missiles would be removed, he told Kennedy. The Soviet leader said he had installed the missiles only to help Cuba deter the threat of an American invasion. With the president's assurances that there would be no invasion, Khrushchev said the missiles were unnecessary. The crisis was over. "Most of us felt limitless relief." Wrote Arthur Schlesinger. Not the men at the pentagon. They felt limitless dismay."[2172]

In order to end the crisis, Kennedy ended up promising Khrushchev that the U.S. would not invade Cuba. The Joint Chiefs were furious at this.[2173] Kennedy's opinion of his military advisors was not much higher than theirs was of him.[2174] He told Arthur Schlesinger "The military are mad. They wanted to do this."[2175] The Bay of Pigs was a humiliation for the Joint Chiefs, and the Cuban Missile Crisis enraged them.[2176]

When Kennedy invited the Chiefs to the White House so he could thank them for their support during the crisis, LeMay exploded: "We lost! We outta just go in there today and knock 'em off."[2177]

General Curtis LeMay wanted to repudiate the deal. "Why don't we go in and make a strike on Monday anyway?" He asked.[2178] He wanted Kennedy to hold out for more concessions. "We could have not only gotten the missiles out of Cuba, "LeMay said, "we could have gotten the Communists out of Cuba."[2179]

Author Jefferson Morley, in his book *THE GHOST: THE SCERET LIFE OF CIA SPYMASTER JAMES JESUS ANGLETON*, said that:[2180]

"What has been all but forgotten over time is the conservative critique of Kennedy's diplomacy which prevailed in the Pentagon, the CIA, the Cuban colony in Miami and much of the Republican Party."[2181]

"By the time the Cuban Missile Crisis ended relations between the Kennedy administration and the Joint Chiefs of Staff (Taylor excepted) were at an all-time low." wrote Pentagon historian Steven L. Rearden.[2182]

Vice President Lyndon Johnson sided with LeMay and the Joint Chiefs on military issues like invading Cuba to take out the missiles and expanding the war in Vietnam.[2183]

Author David Talbot, in his book *THE DEVIL'S CHESSBOARD: ALLEN DULLES, THE CIA, AND THE RISE OF AMERICA'S SECRET GOVERNMENT*, quotes a young Daniel Ellsberg (who would later become famous for the Pentagon Papers) who "observed the seething fury" among the uniformed at the Pentagon:[2184]

"There was virtually a coup atmosphere in Pentagon circles. Not that I had the fear there was about to be a coup – I just thought it was a mood of hatred and rage. The atmosphere was poisonous, poisonous."[2185]

Author Richard Kohn, in his book *STRATEGIC AIR WARFARE: AN INTERVIEW WITH THE GENERALS*, quotes Generals LeMay and his deputy Burchinal on the "lost opportunity" of the Cuban Missile Crisis:[2186]

"We could have gotten the communists out of Cuba," LeMay declared.[2187]

"We walked Khrushchev up to the brink of nuclear war, he looked over the edge, and had no stomach for it," said General David Burchinal, who served as LeMay's deputy during the crisis. "We could have written our own book at that time, but our politicians did not understand what happens when you have such a degree of superiority as we had, or they simply didn't know how to make use of it. They were busily engaged in saving face for the Soviets and making concessions, giving up the ... Jupiters deployed overseas – when all we had to do was write our own ticket."[2188]

The CIA agreed with the Pentagon on the subject of the Kennedys. The Deep State saw Kennedy as a national security risk.[2189] Richard Helms at the CIA had a top aide called Sam Halpern who was candid about what the CIA thought about the Kennedys.[2190] The view from

Helms and the CIA was that the Kennedy's had botched the Bay of Pigs and had no idea how to run clandestine operations.[2191]

The Cuban Missile Crisis also had an effect on Kennedy. He wanted to work toward peace so that the world would not find itself on the brink of nuclear war again. In 1963 Kennedy started keeping the CIA and the Pentagon out of his high-level foreign policy discussions. Kennedy also shut them out of the test ban treaty talks with the Soviet Union. He went around his own national security apparatus to craft a nuclear test ban treaty.[2192] Kennedy went direct to the Russians.[2193] In his Peace Speech at American University on June 10, 1963, Kennedy called for a new attitude toward the Soviet Union.[2194] The CIA and the Pentagon hated the sentiment of that speech.[2195] The Joint Chiefs were also against the nuclear test ban treaty. Strategic Air Command (SAC) General Thomas Power, Admiral Lewis Strauss and Admiral Arthur Radford all openly denounced the treaty.[2196]

On November 22, 1963 Kennedy was assassinated in Dallas.

The military tipped off the Dallas police as to who Oswald was.[2197] This can be traced to an error in the address attributed to Oswald.[2198] Lieutenant Jack Revell was the intelligence officer for the Dallas police.[2199] He left the depository and rode back to the Dallas police station with a man from the Office of Naval Intelligence (ONI) and upon arriving at the police station he met with FBI agent James Hosty and immediately made out a report which is a list of the employees of the Texas School Book Depository.[2200] At the top of the list is a Harvey Lee Oswald of 605 Elsbeth.[2201] Lee Harvey Oswald lived at 602 Elsbeth and this address could not be found anywhere on his employment records at the Texas School Book Depository.[2202] The House Select Committee on Assassinations (HSCA) interviewed Colonel Robert Jones of the Fourth Army Command out of San Antonio, Texas and he said that on the day of the assassination he got word from Dallas that they had arrested a suspect and his name was Alex James Hidell.[2203] He went to the Army military intelligence files and cross-referenced this name to Harvey Lee Oswald of 605 Elsbeth.[2204] This mistake in military intelligence files tells us that it was the U.S. Military who tipped off the Dallas police as to the identity of their suspect.[2205]

After the assassination, the military destroyed its file on Oswald. The Warren Commission requested the military file on Oswald but never got it, and when the House Select Committee on Assassinations (HSCA) asked for the same information years later the military said it had been 'routinely destroyed.'[2206]

Let's Start World War Three

The Joint Chiefs at the Pentagon repeatedly pushed Kennedy for a nuclear first strike. They considered the Bay of Pigs, the Berlin Crisis and the Cuban Missile Crisis all as missed opportunities for a nuclear first strike. Having missed these opportunities, they even tried to convince Kennedy to create an excuse for a nuclear first strike. Their idea was called Operation Northwoods, which was a plan for a false flag operation where the CIA had people pretending to be Cubans attacking the United States. This would then be used as a pretext for the U.S. launching a nuclear attack. Kennedy would not agree to any of these, preferring not to start World War Three with a nuclear first strike. He was of the opinion that the Russians would retaliate in kind. The Joint Chiefs grew increasingly frustrated with Kennedy for not wanting to go along with their plans. On July 20, 1961 General Hickey, Chairman of the Net Evaluation Subcommittee of the Joint Chiefs of Staff, General Lyman Lemnitzer, Chairman of the Joint Chiefs of Staff and CIA Director Allen Dulles presented a plan for a period of heightened tensions followed by a surprise nuclear attack on the Soviet Union.[2207] The plan, called Operation Northwoods, had the approval of all the Joint Chiefs and the Pentagon.[2208] It included a series of fake attacks on the U.S. military base at Guantanamo Bay, Cuba that could be then blamed on Castro.[2209] It also included attacks in Miami, Florida and Washington, D.C., followed by ships being sunk, including boatloads of Cuban refugees, also being blamed on Castro.[2210] Then planes would be hijacked and blamed on Castro.[2211] President Kennedy eventually got up and left the room in disgust in the middle of the meeting.[2212]

Author James Douglass, in his book *JFK AND THE UNSPEAKABLE*, documents that, after the Berlin Crisis was over General Lucius Clay sent a telegram to Secretary of State Dean Rusk:[2213]

> "Today we have the nuclear strength to assure victory at awful cost. It no longer suffices to consider our strength as a deterrent only and to plan to use it only in retaliation. No ground probes on the highway, which would use force, should or could be undertaken unless we are prepared instantly to follow them with a nuclear strike. It is certain that within two or more years retaliatory power will be useless as whoever strikes first will strike last."[2214]

Douglas goes on to say:[2215]

"To Lucius Clay's regret, the president had not been prepared to instantly follow Clay's assault on the Berlin Wall with a nuclear first strike. Like his cohorts in the Pentagon at the height of the Cuban missile crisis, Clay had wanted to seize the moment, so the United States could "win" the Cold War by striking first. His analysis, like theirs, was that time was running out. In the meantime, the military conscience was coming to see the president's conscience as a threat to the nation's survival. Moreover, his deepening collusion with Khrushchev seemed treasonous."[2216]

On March 13, 1962 the Chairman of the Joint Chiefs of Staff, General Lyman Lemnitzer proposed Operation Northwoods again to Secretary of Defense Robert McNamara.[2217] In September of 1962 Kennedy had Lemnitzer replaced as Chairman of the Joint Chiefs of Staff. However, Lemnitzer was not alone in his desire for an attack on Cuba.[2218] He claimed that Operation Northwoods was backed by all the Joint Chiefs.[2219] Kennedy was fighting the Cold War mentality, not just Lemnitzer. Replacing Lemnitzer didn't fix the problem.[2220] The problem was the Deep State.

Losing Control of the Military

In 1963 Kennedy was being eased out of control by the CIA and the Pentagon.[2221] There were attempts to provoke the Soviet Union into actions that would justify a preemptive nuclear first strike by the U.S.[2222] This was not what Kennedy wanted, but it was what the Deep State wanted.

During the height of the Cuban Missile Crisis, on October 28, 1963, the Air Force launched an unarmed ICBM from Vandenberg AFB in California destined for the Marshall Islands in the Pacific.[2223] The world was on the brink of nuclear war. This launch could easily have been interpreted by the Russians as a preemptive nuclear launch. The Russians had no way of knowing whether or not the missile was armed.

The U.S. had, at that time, a program where Strategic Air Command (SAC) bombers flew in shifts so they were always in the air and ready to strike, as a deterrent to the Soviets. They had established "turn around points" where they normally turned back. During the Cuban Missile Crisis, they provocatively went well past their previously established "turn around points." Given the heightened tensions of the crisis, this also could have easily been interpreted by the Russians as a preemptive strike.[2224]

Air Force Generals Thomas Power and Curtis LeMay came up with the concept of Mutually Assured Destruction (M.A.D.).[2225] During the Cuban Missile Crisis General Power made the decision on his own to raise the security level of the Strategic Air Command to DEFCON 2, only one step away from active nuclear war, without telling President Kennedy before he did so.[2226]

The Deep State was trying to provoke a nuclear war because they thought the United States would "win" a nuclear showdown with the Russians.

The Question of Vietnam

The Joint Chiefs of Staff were not happy that Kennedy won the election, but at first Kennedy and the Pentagon were able to agree on the U.S. policy toward Vietnam. This also changed. In 1961 Kennedy was willing to send more money and advisors to Vietnam. This was also what the Pentagon wanted. However, by 1963 Kennedy had decided that U.S. involvement in Vietnam was a bad idea. He had given orders to start the withdrawal and was planning to have the U.S. completely out of Vietnam within a few years. On this issue Kennedy and the Pentagon had gone from agreement in 1961 to disagreement by 1963. Meanwhile the Pentagon wanted to dramatically ramp up U.S. involvement in Vietnam, including sending combat troops.

The issue of what to do in Vietnam was a difficult one for every American president who had faced it. Any president from Truman to Eisenhower to Kennedy who had pulled out of Vietnam would be a one-term president. His opponent would have said 'my opponent is soft on communism.' Truman was elected by a razor thin margin as was Kennedy. The "soft on communism" angle had been used by multiple politicians to come from behind to beat their opponents and win political races in the United States for years. In Florida, George Smathers used the issue to unseat Senator Claude Pepper.[2227] Richard Nixon used the communism issue to beat Congressional Representative Helen Gahagan Douglas, and Everett Dirksen defeated Senator Scott Lucas the same way.[2228] Had either Kennedy or Truman even talked of pulling out of Vietnam they would have lost their elections, and they knew it. Kennedy had decided to wait until after the 1964 election to pull out of Vietnam because he knew he would pay a political price. This would allow him to get elected and still do what he saw as the right thing.

When Kennedy met with Eisenhower after the election but before the inauguration, he had asked what Eisenhower thought should be done in Laos.[2229] Eisenhower said he should send in the troops to prevent a communist takeover, but Kennedy was skeptical of this advice.[2230] Eisenhower had been in office for eight years and had avoided starting a land war in Asia. Kennedy had been advised by Douglas MacArthur not to start a land war in Asia.[2231] Yet here was Eisenhower, on the way out, telling Kennedy to start a land war in Asia. Kennedy thought that starting a land war in Asia was the easy part. He also understood that the hard part would be ending that war. Eisenhower could give Kennedy the easy answer, which he did, knowing that Kennedy, not Eisenhower, would then have to be responsible for what happened after that. The Joint Chiefs also wanted to send in the troops, and Kennedy might have gone along except for a series of events that made him take a closer look at the advice he was being given by the Pentagon.[2232] The Bay of Pigs fiasco opened Kennedy's eyes. After that he would never again trust the advice he was getting. This caused him to look more critically on the opinions he was getting from the same people to send the troops in to Laos. In addition, they kept increasing the number of troops they claimed they needed. Kennedy saw this as another warning sign. Kennedy asked more pointed questions and his advisors did not have good answers.[2233] They kept saying they needed more and more troops and material, and ultimately advocated the use of nuclear weapons, and Kennedy wasn't buying it.[2234] He looked for another solution to the problems in Laos.

By mid-1961 the military had tried to get Kennedy to use nuclear weapons in both Berlin and Southeast Asia.[2235] Kennedy started simply walking out of meetings.[2236] At one point he said "These people are crazy."[2237] The Joint Chiefs thought the same of Kennedy. They thought the use of overwhelming force was necessary to achieve victory.[2238]

On July 23, 1962 Secretary of Defense Robert McNamara convened a conference on the Vietnam War at Camp Smith in Hawaii.[2239] He had ordered General Harkins on May 8 to create a plan to begin a withdrawal from Vietnam.[2240] The general had not done so, and McNamara again ordered General Harkins to create a withdrawal plan.[2241]

In 1963 President Kennedy appointed Henry Cabot Lodge as the U.S. ambassador to Vietnam, and the appointment backfired on Kennedy.[2242] Lodge had a Deep State mentality. He thought he knew better than

Kennedy and was willing to pursue his own policy on the ground in Vietnam.[2243] On October 24, 1963 Lodge and the CIA found out from the generals in Vietnam that the coup would take place in November, and Lodge chose to let it happen because that's what he and the CIA wanted.[2244] On Saturday, November 2, 1963 President Diem was killed during the coup and Kennedy's option of negotiating a withdrawal with Diem was taken off the table.[2245] Once again, the CIA had used control of events on the ground to override Kennedy's policy. Kennedy was disgusted upon hearing the news.[2246]

On October 11 President Kennedy issued National Security Action Memorandum (NSAM) # 263 which specified the withdrawal of American personnel from Vietnam – one thousand by the end of 1963 and the rest by the end of 1965.[2247] *Vice President* Johnson drafted a *presidential* order countermanding Kennedy's order.[2248] This became NSAM # 273. The date the draft was written was November 21, 1963, the day *before* the Kennedy assassination.[2249] This is a key point. Only a vice president who knows in advance he is going to be president the next day drafts a memo countermanding Kennedy's order to withdraw from Vietnam the day before his president is murdered and he moves up to the White House.

Kennedy said that it was up to the South Vietnamese to win or lose the war, that the United States could help but the Vietnamese would have to do it themselves.[2250] On the other hand, the State Department, the CIA and the Pentagon believed in the domino theory. Communists would take over entire continents by knocking over one country at a time. They believed that we needed to fight back against communism to keep from being eventually isolated and weak in a mostly communist world. This is why the U.S. got pulled into a civil war in Vietnam.[2251] Lyndon Johnson, for his part, wanted to be a "wartime president" like Franklin Delano Roosevelt.[2252] South Vietnam could become like South Korea – an ally. Kennedy at first went along with funding and advisors but drew the line at combat troops.[2253]

The Joint Chiefs wanted Johnson to be president. He agreed with them on all the issues they disagreed with Kennedy on. Johnson wanted to escalate the Vietnam War. He would give them what they wanted, and once he was president he did exactly that. Johnson also refused to sign the test ban treaty with the Russians.[2254] He also later signed National Security Action Memorandum # 288 which was to result in full escalation of the Vietnam war.[2255] The Joint Chiefs got what they wanted.

Eugene Dinkin Goes AWOL

In 1963 Eugene Dinkin was a U.S. military cryptographic code operator stationed in Metz, France. He decoded messages going back and forth between the plotters of a military conspiracy against President Kennedy for an assassination attempt in November in Dallas.[2256] One month before the Kennedy assassination he alerted his superiors to the message traffic he was seeing, and they did nothing to warn the president.[2257] He then decided to try to get the word out to warn the president of the danger, and when he heard he was going to be locked up as a psychotic he went AWOL and managed to locate some journalists.[2258] He found some in Geneva, Switzerland in the United Nations office and told them his story.[2259] Then he went to Luxembourg where he reported it to several embassies and from there to Germany where he reported it to *Overseas Weekly*.[2260] Then he was talked into turning himself in and they locked him up as a psychotic.[2261] They then took him to Washington, to Walter Reed Hospital, where he was given strong drugs and tortured with electric shock 'therapy' until he changed his story.[2262] Dinkin filed a civil action lawsuit in 1975 where he described his efforts to warn the Kennedys.[2263]

Eugene Dinkin's experience proves several things. First, he proves that there was a conspiracy to assassinate President Kennedy. A lone nut gunman has no need for secure communications to coordinate with someone in France. Second, and more important, he proves that the U.S. military was involved in that conspiracy. This secure system was not open to just anybody. And the reaction of Dinkin's chain of command is telling. If they had nothing to hide they would have alerted the president to the danger. The fact that they hunted him down and put him in a mental institution so they could torture him into changing his story clearly implicates the military in the conspiracy. The only odd thing is that they didn't just kill him as they did so many others. If he hadn't changed his story they probably would have.

The Shell Game and the Autopsy

The point of the autopsy was to create some 'evidence' to support the fairy tale that Oswald, shooting alone from the Texas School Book Depository, had killed Kennedy. To do this several things had to happen. First, Kennedy's body had to be taken illegally from Parkland Hospital and brought back to Washington. Next, the body had to be worked on somewhere between Parkland Hospital in Dallas and the official autopsy in the Washington, D.C. area so as to make, among other things, the entry wound in the throat look like an exit wound. Doing this allows the conspirators to reverse the direction of the shot. If the throat wound is an exit wound the shot could be presented to the public as having come from behind.

Once he was pronounced dead at Parkland Memorial Hospital in Dallas, President Kennedy's body was put in an ornate bronze casket. When the body arrived in Bethesda it was in a gray shipping casket while Jackie Kennedy was still accompanying the ornate bronze casket. When the body left Parkland, the wounds were intact except for the small throat wound which had been used for a tracheotomy. When the body showed up in Bethesda the wounds had been altered somewhere in between.

During the autopsy in Bethesda, the U.S. military doctors were ordered by their U.S. military superiors not to complete the autopsy. This was because a complete autopsy would become hard evidence of shots from the front and thus a conspiracy. Hard evidence of a conspiracy had to be avoided at all costs.

Only the military could have played a shell game with the body. Only the military could have ordered the military doctors not to complete the autopsy. These actions also implicate the military in the Kennedy assassination and cover up.

The autopsy in Bethesda shows the complicity of both the military and the Secret Service. The Secret Service had to make sure to grab the body in Dallas and bring it back to Washington because the Parkland doctors were not under the thumb of the conspirators. The military doctors back in Bethesda could be ordered around by the military brass. The doctors at Parkland Hospital in Dallas were not so easily controlled. The conspirators had to be certain that the Secret Service would grab the body in Dallas. Left on their own the doctors in Dallas might perform a real autopsy. James Rowley, the head of the Secret Service, ordered Secret Service Agent Roy Kellerman to make sure he got the body to Air Force One to take back to Washington.[2264]

The Wounds at Parkland

For many years the best information available on Kennedy's wounds was what was announced at the press conference at Parkland Memorial Hospital the day of the assassination. The doctors there were well familiar with gunshot wounds because they saw them every day. They were also very familiar with Kennedy's wounds because they had just treated him right after the shooting. And the Deep State hadn't yet had time to get to them and intimidate them into either silence or changing their story.

What they said that afternoon was that Kennedy had been shot at least twice from the front, once in the throat and once in the right temple or forehead. The bullet in the throat had not emerged. The bullet in the head was the kill shot and it blew a hole in the back of his head. They also said he could have been shot from behind, but they had not done an autopsy and could not be sure. They had just tried to save his life, they weren't there to do an autopsy.

Their announcements to the assembled press and their answers to questions were plain and simple. They didn't hesitate. They knew what they were talking about. They were doctors with ample experience in gunshot wounds and familiarity with Kennedy's wounds.

Dr. Robert R. Shaw, Chairman of the Department of Thoracic Surgery at the hospital, said "The first bullet entered President Kennedy's trachea in the front of his neck, coursing downward into his right lung." *New York Herald Tribune*, November 28, 1963[2265]

Dr. William Kemp Clark said "Mr. Kennedy was hit by a bullet in the throat just below the Adam's apple." *New York Times*, November 23 – he also said that Kennedy was struck by a bullet at the necktie knot and added "It ranged downward in his throat and did not exit." *New York Times*, November 27, 1963[2266]

Dr. Robert McClelland, who worked on Kennedy's throat wound, told Richard Dudman of the *St. Louis Post Dispatch* that the wound was an entry wound.[2267]

Dr. Charles Crenshaw said "It was small, about the size of the tip of my little finger. It was a bullet entry wound. There was no doubt in my mind." He said about that wound "I had seen dozens of them in the emergency room."[2268]

Dr. Malcom Perry decided to perform a tracheotomy on the president's throat where the bullet had entered his neck.[2269] This procedure made the bullet wound a little bigger, because it involved inserting a tube to help with breathing.[2270]

Then Dr. Crenshaw noticed that the right rear of Kennedy's brain was gone. It looked, he said "like a crater, an empty cavity. All I could see there was mangled bloody tissue. From the damage I saw there was no doubt in my mind that the bullet had entered his head through the front."[2271]

Author Anthony Summers, in his book *NOT IN YOUR LIFETIME*, documents that:[2272]

> "Mortician Thomas Robinson did tell Assassinations Committee staff that he recalled seeing "a small wound, about a quarter of an inch at the temples in the hairline to the right side of the head.""[2273]

> "Another member of the Dallas medical team, Dr. Charles Crenshaw, claimed in a 1992 book that the wounds he saw indicated gunfire from the front."[2274]

James Douglass, in his book *JFK AND THE UNSPEAKABLE*, said that:[2275]

> "Twenty-one out of twenty-two witnesses at Parkland Hospital, most of them doctors and nurses, trained medical observers, agreed in their earliest statements that JFK's massive head wound was located in the right rear of his skull, demonstrating a fatal head shot from the front. The exit wound in the back of his skull was unforgettable."[2276]

Douglass goes on to say "Doctors Malcom Perry and Kemp Clark drew that same conclusion.[2277] At a press conference in a classroom at Parkland Hospital at 3:15 that afternoon, cited in the *New York Times* the following day, Dr. Perry said repeatedly at the press conference that the throat wound he had seen was an entrance wound.":[2278]

> Question: "Where was the entrance wound?"

> Perry: "There was an entrance wound in the neck."

> Question: "Which way was the bullet coming on the neck wound, at him?"

> Perry: "It appeared to be coming at him."

> Question: "Doctor, describe the entrance wound. You think from the front, in the throat?"

> Perry: "The wound appeared to be an entrance wound in the front of the throat. Yes, that is correct."

At about 1:00 PM Malcom Kilduff, the White House assistant press secretary, while announcing the death of President Kennedy, points to his own right temple to demonstrate the direction and location of the shot that killed the president – he said "He died of a gunshot wound in the brain ... of a bullet right through the head."[2279]

Dr. Robert McClelland compared the exit wound in the back of the head to the size of a baseball.[2280]

The first press reports are accurate and depict the small entry wound in Kennedy's right temple.[2281]

The doctors at Parkland assumed Kennedy had been hit twice and that both shots were from the front. One hit him in the throat and the other hit him in the temple and exited the back of his skull. They did not turn Kennedy over to see the wound in the back.[2282]

Dr. Charles Carrico, Dr. Charles Crenshaw, Dr. Richard Dulaney, Dr. Ronald Jones, Dr. Robert McClelland, Dr. Paul Peters, Dr. Kenneth Salyer and ER Nurse Audrey Bell all saw the large exit wound at the right rear of Kennedy's head while he was at Parkland Memorial Hospital.[2283]

The Shell Game and the Alterations

The government played a shell game with the body and the two caskets to give them time to alter the wounds between Parkland Memorial Hospital in Dallas and the official autopsy at Bethesda Naval Hospital. The body left Parkland in an ornate bronze casket and showed up in Bethesda in a cheap shipping casket. In the meantime, Jackie Kennedy was still traveling with the ornate bronze casket.

James Rowley, the head of the Secret Service, ordered Secret Service Agent Roy Kellerman to make sure he got the body to Air Force One to take back to Washington.[2284] Once the body is loaded into the ornate bronze casket, the Secret Service grab the casket and illegally take it from Parkland Hospital to Love Field airport. The body was legally supposed to stay at Parkland hospital where they would have performed a proper autopsy. The conspirators couldn't have that. An autopsy would prove that shots came from the front, so they had the Secret Service take the body by force from the authorities in Parkland Memorial Hospital by gunpoint and transported it to Love Field.

When the Secret Service team were trying to leave with the body, Dr. Earl Rose, the Dallas County Medical Examiner blocked their way. Justice of the Peace Theron Ward was also there. They tried to stop the Secret Service from taking the body. Dallas Police Sergeant Robert

Dugger was there also.[2285]   The Secret Service forced their way through.[2286]   Kennedy's body left Parkland in an ornate bronze casket, but it showed up in Bethesda in a plain gray shipping casket. And it showed up 90 minutes earlier than the official ornate bronze casket.

In the meantime, Air Force One was still sitting on the ground at Love Field. The pilot wanted to take off and Johnson ordered him not to. Air Force One is actually two identical planes. To this day they travel in pairs. Whichever one the president is on is designated Air Force One. The other one is a backup. Typically, the backup plane carries the vice president, and they "leapfrog" while in the air. The president's plane takes off first, but slows down so the vice president's plane can land first. This is done so the vice president can be there to greet the president when he arrives.[2287]   Johnson knows this. After insisting that they stay on the ground in Dallas to wait for Kennedy's body, and insisting that he be sworn in before they take off, he then arranges to have Judge Sarah Hughes summoned to swear him in.   This takes enough time for Jackie to show up with the ornate bronze casket. Johnson then insisted that everybody, including Jackie, attend his swearing-in. People were sent to round up everyone. This left the ornate bronze casket unattended for fifteen minutes while Johnson was being sworn in.[2288]

Author Phillip Nelson, in his book *LBJ: THE MASTERMIND OF THE JFK ASSASSINATION*, points out that, during that fifteen-minute period when the ornate bronze casket was unattended, Kennedy's body could easily have been switched to the plain, gray metal shipping casket that it showed up in when it first arrived in Bethesda.[2289]   We don't know that this is when the switch occurred, we only know that the body showed up in Bethesda in a plain gray shipping casket, not the ornate bronze casket.   However, this period when the casket was unattended would have been an ideal time for the switch, and one of very few such opportunities for a switch.

Nelson also points out that, while the ornate bronze casket was driven from Andrews Air Force Base, where Air Force One landed, to Bethesda Naval Hospital in a gray Pontiac hearse, the shipping casket which contained Kennedy's body could have been flown by helicopter to Bethesda. The drive was about 45 minutes. This would have saved considerable time as the flight would take less than ten minutes.[2290]

Whenever the switch took place, Kennedy's body showed up in a cheap shipping casket in Bethesda 90 minutes before the official ornate bronze casket. And, by the time the official autopsy started, Kennedy's body had been mutilated to make the shots from the front appear to be shots from the rear. The shell game with the body and the caskets and the transportation was orchestrated for that reason. They needed some time to manipulate the evidence to cover up the fact that Kennedy was shot from the front. The throat wound, for example, was greatly enlarged so as to appear to be an exit wound.

Dennis David was one of the Naval sailors who helped carry in Kennedy's casket. He said it was a plain gray shipping casket.[2291] They offloaded the gray casket from the black hearse at 6:35 PM, almost 90 minutes before the ornate casket was offloaded from the gray ambulance by the official Joint Casket Bearer Team at around 8:00 PM.[2292]

The motorcade with the gray Navy ambulance, the ornate bronze casket and Mrs. Kennedy didn't arrive until 6:55 PM and wasn't carried into the morgue until 8:00 PM.[2293] Dennis David saw that motorcade approaching and knew that the president's body was not in the ornate casket because he had just carried it in twenty minutes earlier.[2294] Just to make sure, Dennis David later talked to Dr. J. Thornton Boswell, who said that Kennedy's body arrived in the cheap shipping casket.[2295] Donald Rebentisch was one of the sailors who offloaded the casket and he later confirmed David's account.[2296] Joe Hagan worked for Joseph Gawler's Sons, a local funeral home that was summoned to embalm Kennedy's body.[2297] On his "first call sheet" the handwritten notation read "Body removed from metal shipping casket at NSNH at Bethesda."[2298] Paul O'Connor was an autopsy technician for the Kennedy autopsy. He told the HSCA in 1977 that Kennedy's body had arrived in a "cheap, metal, aluminum casket" in a "rubberized body bag."[2299] Jerrol Custer was an X-ray technician for the Kennedy autopsy. He saw two caskets, one of which was bronze.[2300] Ed Reed also served as an X-ray technician. He testified that the casket was a "typical aluminum military casket."[2301] James Jenkins, another Navy corpsman who served as an autopsy technician, said that the casket was "awful clean and simple" and "not something you'd expect a president to be in."[2302]

Mrs. Kennedy and Robert Kennedy showed up at 6:55 P.M. with the ornate bronze casket in the gray hearse, 20 minutes after the cheap shipping casket had arrived. They were let off at the front door and Mrs. Kennedy went inside to proceed up to the seventeenth floor. In the meantime, Jerrol Custer was taking X-rays of Kennedy upstairs to be processed when he saw Jackie entering the main lobby as she arrived.[2303] Notice that Mrs. Kennedy, who had accompanied the ornate bronze casket from Dallas, had just arrived in Bethesda Naval Hospital and is passed on the way by Jerrol Custer carrying X-rays of her husband's body. The gray ambulance was taken around back with the ornate bronze casket to be offloaded by FBI agents James Sibert and Francis O'Neill and Secret Service agents Bill Greer and Roy Kellerman before 7:30 PM.[2304] For an hour there was a break in the chain of custody of the body. The gray Pontiac ambulance with the (empty) ornate casket sped away from the front door.[2305] The guys on the official unloading team chasing it got lost and eventually found it at the back.[2306] In the meantime the body was taken to somewhere else on the grounds of the hospital to be transferred back to the ornate casket for the official 'autopsy' after they had time to work on it in private.[2307] The ornate bronze casket was officially carried into the Bethesda morgue at 8:00 PM by the Joint Casket Bearer Team in full Marine dress uniform with white gloves.[2308] No FBI or Secret Service agents were part of the Joint Casket Bearer Team that unloaded the casket.[2309]

The entry wound in the throat had been enlarged and obliterated by the time the official autopsy began.[2310] The rear head wound had been enlarged to five times its original size and now extended so that it was not just in the rear of the skull, as it had when it was first seen in Dallas, but the top and right side as well.[2311] What had been a small entry wound in the temple or forehead now appeared to be a large exit wound.[2312] Much more of Kennedy's brain was missing.[2313] In Dallas one third of it was gone, now two thirds of it was missing.[2314] All evidence of front entry wounds had been destroyed.[2315]

Everyone involved, of course, had to sign a gag order from the White House under verbal and written threat of court martial.[2316]

What has not yet come to light is where and when the alterations were done. We know the body was put in the ornate bronze casket in Dallas. We know it showed up in Bethesda in a plain shipping casket. We don't know when and where the first switch was made or when or where the body was switched back to the ornate bronze casket. Maybe the first switch was made during Johnson's swearing-in at Love Field. Maybe the switch back was made between when Jackie was dropped off at the front door of Bethesda Naval Hospital and when the official offloading team lost track of the gray Pontiac ambulance for almost an hour. We may never know exactly how that was done. What we do know is that, by the time the official autopsy started, the obvious outward signs of shots from the front had been destroyed. At that point what the conspirators needed was to make sure that the inward signs were not documented. They needed to make sure that the wounds were not sectioned or tracked so that there would be no hard evidence of which direction the shots that made those wounds came from. For example, they needed to make sure that the throat wound, which was a shot from the front, was not tracked by cutting into the throat and sectioning the organs of the throat so as to definitively determine the direction that shot came from. Fortunately for the conspirators, they had planned ahead. They had forcibly grabbed the body from Dallas, mutilated it on the way to the autopsy, and now they had control of the doctors and other staff in Bethesda. They could order the doctors performing the autopsy to avoid completing the normal medical procedures that they would usually follow to finish a proper autopsy. And they could swear everyone to secrecy and enforce that order with the threat of a court martial. And they did.

The Autopsy and the Evidence

There were 28 civilians, federal agents and military generals and admirals at the autopsy and Air Force General Curtis LeMay was in overall charge.[2317]

Years later, during the Garrison investigation and trial of Clay Shaw, it came out that the military doctors at Bethesda Naval Hospital were ordered by their military superiors not to complete the autopsy. They were specifically ordered not to track the wounds, which is a standard part of an autopsy. This is because determining the track of the bullets would have provided hard evidence of the direction of the shots.[2318]

Author James Douglass, in his book *JFK AND THE UNSPEAKABLE*, quoted Paul O'Connor who was there helping the doctors:[2319]

> "It got very tense, Admiral [Calvin] Galloway, the chief of the hospital command, started getting very agitated again, because there was a wound in his neck … and I remember the doctors were going to check that out when Admiral Galloway told them 'Leave it alone. Don't touch it. It's just a tracheotomy.' He stopped anybody from going further. Doctors Humes and Boswell, Dr. Finck were told to leave it alone. 'Let's go to other things.'"[2320]

When Dr. Finck was asked, under oath, who ordered him not to track the wounds he claimed not to remember.[2321]

The Shoulder Shot

The Warren Commission based its findings on the FBI summary report while ignoring the report of the two FBI agents were at the autopsy,

Francis X. O'Neill and James W. Sibert.[2322] They said the back wound was in the shoulder, not in the neck.[2323] They also said:[2324]

> "This opening was probed by Dr. Humes with a finger at which time it was determined that the trajectory of the missile entering at this point had entered at a downward position of 45-60 degrees. Further probing determined that the distance traveled by this missile was a short distance inasmuch as the end of the opening could be felt with the finger."[2325]

This report was ignored because it was accurate and did not fit the official theory, which had *moved* the back wound to the neck to support the Magic Bullet fiction.

The bullet holes in the shirt and coat of JFK are hard proof that the single 'magic' bullet theory is invalid.[2326] President Kennedy's shirt and jacket are still available in the national archives.[2327] They match up and show where the shoulder shot entered in the back below the shoulder blade to the right of the thoracic vertebrae.[2328] This matches the diagram signed and verified by Dr. George Berkely, Kennedy's personal physician.[2329] Dr. Humes, the autopsy doctor, said "six inches below the neckline to the right of the spinal column."[2330] Clint Hill of the Secret Service said "six inches below the neckline to the right of the spinal column."[2331] Glen Bennet of the Secret Service said "about four inches down from the right shoulder."[2332]

The sixth floor of the Texas School Book Depository is sixty feet above street level, so the bullet would have had a downward trajectory when striking Kennedy. The Warren Commission would have us believe that this bullet magically, upon entering Kennedy's shoulder, turned upward and came out the front of his throat without hurting anything in between and then went on to almost kill Governor Connally.

The placement of the shoulder shot, which can clearly be seen from the bullet holes in the jacket and shirt, are hard proof that the Magic Bullet theory is invalid.[2333]

Jerrol Custer, the X-Ray technician, and Floyd Reeby, the autopsy photographer, both today say that the X-rays and the photographs being shown to the public and being kept in the National Archives are not the ones they took – they are fake.[2334]

On December 18, 1963 the *Washington Post* printed an article regarding the autopsy findings "A bullet was found deep in his shoulder. It hit the president in the back shoulder five to seven inches below the collar line."[2335] That same day *The New York Times* said:

"The first bullet made what was described as a small, neat wound in the back and penetrated two or three inches."[2336]

The autopsy doctors assumed the wound in the back to be a superficial entry wound because it could be probed less than an inch or so, and upon hearing of the bullet found at Parkland they assumed it was the bullet they had not found.[2337] Only later did it become important to the cover-up for there to be a Magic Bullet.[2338]

Mark North, in his book ACT OF TREASON, documents that the press reported that:[2339]

> "Dr. Malcom O. Perry, a surgeon at Parkland Hospital who attended President Kennedy shortly after he was shot said today that physicians seeking to save the president's life noted that he had been wounded in the throat and head but did not seek to trace the course of the bullets. *Washington Post* prints an article regarding the autopsy findings "A bullet was found deep in his shoulder. It hit the president in the back shoulder five to seven inches below the collar line." *New York Times*: "The first bullet made what was described as a small, neat wound in the back and penetrated two or three inches.""[2340]

James Jenkins was at the autopsy and he said:[2341]

> "What sticks out in my mind" he recalled years later "is the fact that Commander Humes, the presiding surgeon, put his little finger in the back wound and, you know, said that he could probe the bottom of it with his finger, which would mean to me that it was very shallow."[2342]

> "I remember looking inside the chest cavity and I could see the probe through the pleura, the lining of the chest cavity. You could actually see where it was making an indentation, where it was pushing the skin up. There was no entry into the chest cavity. No way that could have exited in the front, because it was then low in the chest cavity, somewhere around the junction of the descending aorta, the main artery carrying blood from the heart or the bronchus in the lungs."[2343]

Robert Groden was the photographic consultant to the House Select Committee on Assassinations (HSCA).[2344]   When the HSCA hired Groden, as he put it:[2345]

> "One of the first things I did was ask to see the autopsy photographs in the National Archives. I wanted to find out how it was the Warren Commission concluded the shots came from the rear when all the doctors at Parkland Hospital, every one of them, wrote in their reports that Kennedy's head was blasted out. When I saw the autopsy photographs I was shocked. After years in photo optic work I knew what I saw, and that was a matte line in the photograph of the president's head. That's when two photographic elements come together visually and there's an overlap. I saw a soft edged matte insertion forgery of very high quality which made it appear as if there was a small wound of entry in the rear of the president's head."[2346]

Groden did some photo optical tests on copies of the photographs to confirm what he saw. Then he said:[2347]

> "I wrote a report about it to Blakey saying that, based on my professional opinion, the autopsy photographs of the president's head had been retouched."[2348]

Author Joachim Joesten, in his book *OSWALD: ASSASSIN OR FALL GUY?*, documents that:[2349]

> "Inexplicably, in the one and same *Report*, two different locations of the entry wound are given by the FBI, on one hand, and the autopsy report on the other. The autopsy report says (p. 90) the hole is about 5 ½ inches from the tip of the right mastoid process, the bony point immediately behind the ear. This puts the hole near the spine at a high shoulder level. The FBI says (p. 95) that the hole in the coat is 5 3/8 inches below the top of the coat collar, and 5 ¾ inches below the top of the shirt collar, both a little over one inch to the right of the center seam. This puts the FBI hole at least three inches below the autopsy hole."[2350]

> "In the photographs the president is clearly sitting straight, coat smooth on his shoulders. The coat collar would have had to be around his ears for the holes to coincide, and the shirt would have had to crumple upward in precisely the same

manner. Corroborative evidence that the hole in the coat is lower than the location given by the autopsy comes from the *Report* itself. This incident is interesting because it makes clear how it is that the Commission, trying to bolster one part of its case – on the missing bullet – unwittingly provides evidence which undermines another part."[2351]

Jerrol Custer, the X-Ray technician, and Floyd Reeby, the autopsy photographer, both say that the X-rays and the photographs being shown to the public and being kept in the National Archives are not the ones they took – they are fakes.[2352] The photograph of the back of JFK's head was faked to hide the huge hole in the back of his head – the X-rays are forgeries.[2353] Dr. Mantik, the Eisenhower Medical Center radiation expert who examined the X-rays, thought they had been tampered with, and thought the fakery was designed to divert attention from evidence indicating a shot from the front.[2354]

Autopsy photographer John Stringer was asked about the photos he took and he said there were identification tags in the shots he took of the brain yet these are absent from the photos in the archives.[2355] When shown actual photos of the brain from the National Archives, Stringer was genuinely puzzled since the edge numbers on the film, which showed both the film used and the technique employed, were not used by him.[2356]

Jim Garrison, in his book *ON THE TRAIL OF THE ASSASSINS*, documents that:[2357]

> "15 to 20 photographs and x-rays of President Kennedy's body were taken during the autopsy and handed over to Agent Roy H. Kellerman of the Secret Service, yet none of these was examined by the Warren Commission. Instead, the chief pathologist, Commander James Humes, arranged for artists to draw pictures of various parts of the autopsy for the Commission. Not even the artists were allowed to see the photos and x-rays. They drew their pictures from the pathologists' verbal recollections. Finally, on Sunday November 24, 1963 Commander Humes, by his own admission, burned his autopsy notes."[2358]

A frangible bullet leaves a cone of fragments and particles embedded in the victim, with the smaller particles at the tip of the cone where the bullet enters and the larger fragments lodging closer to the base of the cone.[2359] The cone thus points in the direction the shot came from.[2360] Kennedy had a cone of fragments consistent with an entry wound from the front, in the temple.[2361]

The Harper Fragment

X-rays taken that night show an intact rear skull where a large occipital fragment of the president's skull, which will be found the next day in Dealey Plaza, was blown out, proving the X-rays are fraudulent, created to disguise a massive exit wound in the rear.[2362]

Secret Service Agents Clint Hill and Winston Lawson both said a portion of the right rear of Kennedy's skull was missing, which they saw when they got to Parkland.[2363] Then at 5:30 PM on Saturday, November 23 William Harper found a skull fragment about twenty-five feet behind and to the left of the point on Elm Street where a shot had blown out the back of the president's skull.[2364] He took the fragment to his uncle, Dr. Jack C. Harper at Methodist Hospital, who turned it over to Dr. A.B. Cairns, the hospital's chief pathologist.[2365] They said it came from the lower back part of the human skull, and that it had lead fragments on it.[2366] This has since become known as the Harper Fragment.[2367]

In his book *JFK AND THE UNSPEAKABLE*, author James Douglass documents that:[2368]

> "Dr. David W. Mantik, a radiation oncologist with a PhD. in physics tested the autopsy X-rays at the National Archives in 1993 to 1995 to determine their authenticity. He used an optical densitometer to measure the levels of light on different areas of the official X-rays, in which the denser parts of the skull would ordinarily produce whiter images on the X-rays and the more vacant parts would produce darker images. Mantik was puzzled by the X-rays remarkable contrast between the front and back of Kennedy's skull, apparent even to the naked eye. By taking optical density measurements of the X-rays, what he discovered was, as he put it "quite astonishing. The posterior white area transmits almost one thousand times more light than the dark area!" There was far too much bone density being shown in the rear of JFK's skull relative to the front. The X-ray had to have been a composite. The optical density data indicated a forgery in which a patch had been placed on an original X-ray to cover the rear part of the skull – corresponding to the gap left in the part by the Harper Fragment, evidence of an exit wound. The obvious purpose was to cover up evidence of a shot from the front that,

judging from the original Parkland observations, had created an exit hole the size of one's fist in the back of the head."[2369]

The Intimidation of the Doctors

The intimidation of the doctors falls into two categories, the civilian doctors in Dallas and the military doctors in Bethesda. By far the easiest to control were the military doctors in Bethesda. This is why the conspirators went to such lengths to illegally take Kennedy's body from Dallas, where they couldn't control the doctors, to Bethesda where they could. That still left the doctors in Dallas to deal with. They had seen the wounds. They were very familiar with gunshot wounds, which they saw every day. They had to be gagged somehow. The doctors and staff in Bethesda could be ordered to be quiet. They could even be ordered to botch the autopsy. The doctors in Dallas had to be intimidated into silence.

The Doctors and Staff in Bethesda

Author James Douglass, in his book *JFK AND THE UNSPEAKABLE*, described how it started:[2370]

> "Late Friday afternoon November 22, 1963, Dr. Robert B. Livingston made a phone call from his home in Bethesda, Maryland to the Bethesda Naval Hospital. Dr. Livingston was Scientific Director for two of the National Institutes of Health. Because his scientific responsibilities related to the president's wounds and autopsy, Dr. Livingston paid careful attention to the news reports from Dallas. He learned that "there was a small frontal wound in the president's throat." Dr. Livingston's call was put through at Bethesda Hospital to Commander James Humes, the naval doctor chosen to head the autopsy team – Livingston has described their conversation.:"[2371]

> "Dr. Humes said he had not heard much reporting from Dallas and Parkland Hospital because he had been occupied preparing to conduct the autopsy. I told him about reports describing the small wound in the president's neck. I stressed that, in my experience, that would have to be a wound of entrance. I emphasized the importance of carefully tracing the

path of this projectile, and of establishing the location of the bullet or any fragments. I said carefully that, if that wound were confirmed as a wound of entrance, that would prove beyond per a venture of doubt that a bullet had been fired from in front of the president. Hence, that if there were shots from behind, there had to have been more than one gunman. At just that moment there was an interruption in our conversation. Dr. Humes returned after a pause to say 'Dr. Livingston I'm sorry but I can't talk with you any longer. The FBI won't let me.'"[2372]

"Dr. Livingston then wondered aloud to his wife, who had overheard his end of the conversation, why the FBI would want to interfere with a discussion between physicians relating to the important problem of how best to investigate and interpret the president's wounds."[2373]

After the autopsy, everyone involved was called into the commander's office and forced to sign orders requiring them to never discuss what they had seen with anyone, under penalty of court martial.[2374]

On Sunday, November 24, 1963 Dr. Humes, one of the JFK autopsy surgeons, claims to have burned his autopsy notes after preparing a fresh draft.[2375]

The Warren Commission did not allow the doctors to use photos during their testimony.[2376] They were forced to used sketches.[2377] Doctors Humes and Boswell had multiple meetings with Specter to get their story straight before they testified before the Warren Commission.[2378] No photographs were allowed. This was because photographs were too precise. They would show the actual locations of the wounds. They found an inexperienced young illustrator named Harold Rydberg to make the drawings because he would go along with the exercise where a more experienced medical illustrator would have been considerably more critical of what they were doing.[2379] This is because they showed up to the meeting with no pictures, no X-rays, no official measurements.[2380] All they had was their memories, because that way there was no paper trail.[2381] Later, if they were busted, they could just claim faulty memory.[2382] In the discussions that the doctors had previously with Arlen Specter they had already decided to go along with his Magic Bullet theory.[2383] The purpose of the meeting was to come up with diagrams that would fit this theory.[2384]

The Doctors in Dallas

Author Peter Janney, in his book *MARY'S MOSAIC*, quotes Audrey Bell, the supervising nurse at Parkland Memorial Hospital in Dallas. She said that people were continually calling Dr. Perry all night:[2385]

> "from people at Bethesda Naval Hospital who were trying to get him to change his mind about the opinion he'd expressed at the Parkland Memorial Hospital press conference the day before; namely, that President Kennedy had an entrance wound in the front of his neck."[2386]

By the time Dr. Perry testified before the Warren Commission he had caved to the pressure and changed his story.[2387] In the weeks after the assassination, there were lots of 'government men' hanging around Parkland Memorial Hospital, and one of them was Elmer Moore, a Secret Service agent.[2388] His job was to put pressure on Perry and the other doctors to get them to either change their stories or shut up, and by mid-December he had succeeded.[2389] Secret Service chief Rowley had assigned Moore to work full time with Warren and the commission on issues like this.[2390] Elmer Moore later said he was 'just following orders.'[2391] This was the same defense the Nazis used during their war crimes trials at Nuremberg.

Author James Douglass, in his book *JFK AND THE UNSPEAKABLE*, pointed out that:[2392]

> "When the government took charge with its official story of the lone assassin firing from the rear, the doctors were pressured by the Warren Commission to change their initial observations of Kennedy's body. The Warren Commission Staff Counsel Arlen Specter, a future U.S. Senator, confronted the Dallas doctors with a question that contained the answer the Commission was seeking:[2393]

> "Assuming that the bullet passed through the president's body, going in between the strap muscles of the shoulder without violating the pleura space and exited at a point in the midline of the neck, would the hole which you saw on the president's throat be consistent with an exit point, assuming the factors which I've just given to you?"[2394]

> "As Charles Crenshaw, who was not asked to testify, pointed out later "Specter had asked the doctors 'if the bullet exited from the front of Kennedy's throat, could the wound in the front of Kennedy's throat have been an exit wound?'"[2395]

Douglass adds: "The doctors went along with Specter's show of logic "Yes, assuming the bullet exited from the front of Kennedy's throat, that wound indeed could have been an exit wound.""[2396]

Dr. Crenshaw said later that he had kept quiet out of fear for his life.[2397] He said that these folks had killed the president of the United States and would not hesitate to kill a doctor.[2398]

Dr. Charles Crenshaw and the other Parkland doctors kept quiet for 30 years, but they agreed on a few things.[2399] The wound in Kennedy's throat was an entry wound, as was the entry wound at the right front by the hairline that blew out the back of his head.[2400] Crenshaw broke his silence 30 years later.[2401] He and the other doctors had kept quiet out of fear.[2402] After thirty years of keeping his mouth shut, Dr. Crenshaw wrote a book where he said that the shots had come from the front.[2403]

The Murder of William Pitzer

Lieutenant Commander William Bruce Pitzer was the head of the audio-visual department of the Naval Medical School in 1963, and he was called on the day of the Kennedy assassination to assist with documenting the autopsy at Bethesda Naval Hospital.[2404] A few days later he showed the results to a friend and co-worker, First Class Hospital Corpsman Dennis David, who would later say that it was abundantly obvious to both of them from the film and photographs that shots had come from the front.[2405] Pitzer was in possession of evidence that the Kennedy assassination was a conspiracy, and Pitzer himself would be a witness.[2406] This made him a danger to the conspirators. Bill Pitzer was shot to death on October 29, 1966 in the television production studio where he worked.[2407] He had been about to retire from the military and start a new career and he also intended to broadcast the photographic and film (35mm slides and 16mm film) evidence he had kept from the Kennedy autopsy.[2408] The evidence he had was missing and his widow was threatened into silence.[2409]

In August of 1965 the CIA had asked Army Special Forces Lieutenant Colonel Daniel Marvin to murder Pitzer, and he had turned the job down.[2410] Almost thirty years later Marvin was watching a television documentary on the Kennedy assassination when he saw that Pitzer was murdered as one of many murders associated with the Kennedy assassination and cover-up.[2411]

The Wealthy Oil Barons of the Day

In the early 1960's Texas was a very conservative place and Kennedy was a liberal by the standards of that time. The wealthy oil barons were very conservative and despised Kennedy and his policies. At some point Kennedy decided to get rid of their oil depletion allowance and this outraged the oil barons of the time who already disliked Kennedy. The oil depletion allowance was personally worth millions of dollars per year to the oil barons. Getting rid of it would have cost them each a fortune – personally. Sid Richardson, H.L. Hunt, Clint Murchison, D.H. Byrd and others were major supporters of Lyndon Johnson in order to maintain their oil depletion allowance. They had been contributing generously to Johnson in order to make sure that this kind of legislation was bottled up in the Senate. Now Johnson was temporarily out of power as vice president and Kennedy was planning to get rid of their cherished tax breaks. This was a crisis and they weren't going down without a fight.

Kennedy was planning on reducing or eliminating the 27% oil depletion allowance.[2412] One of his specific targets was H.L. Hunt, who paid few taxes on his huge income. Hunt was making over one million dollars (in 1963 dollars) a week while paying almost no taxes.[2413] At this same time, he was supporting and contributing to right-wing causes and to Senator Joseph McCarthy and his "Facts Forum," a news service featuring taped radio programs and subsidized reports.[2414]

Oilmen Sid Richardson and Clint Murchison owned the Del Charo, a resort hotel and the nearby racetrack, the Del Mar, where Hoover went for a free month's vacation every year.[2415] Other guests who were there at the same time included future president Richard Nixon, future Texas governor John Connally and mafiosi Meyer Lansky, Santo Trafficante, Johnny Roselli, Sam Giancana, Carlos Marcello and Frank Costello.[2416] Hoover and the oil barons hated the Kennedys as much as the mafia and Johnson, and they all socialized together.[2417]

Chicago mafia boss Sam Giancana confessed to his brother Chuck that he was part of the Kennedy assassination.[2418] Chuck Giancana wrote a book, *DOUBLE CROSS*, where he talked about Sam's involvement in the Kennedy assassination and also claimed that Sam said the money for the hit came from Texas oil men.[2419]

Author Phillip Nelson, in his book *LBJ: THE MASTERMIND OF THE JFK ASSASSINATION*, said that Johnson knew the major players and had long and trusting relationships with them and they all also knew each other the same way.[2420] He also pointed out that Johnson had to be involved (he appointed the Warren Commission) and had the means, the motive and the opportunity to murder JFK. Oil baron H.L. Hunt and J. Edgar Hoover knew each other since the 1950's as poker playing buddies.[2421] Nelson also claims that CIA officer Bill Harvey would be one of the guys who held the whole thing together, and that Johnson got his crooked lawyer Ed Clark to collect money for the operation from a bunch of people but the main contributors were oil barons H.L. Hunt and Clint Murchison.[2422] Money was needed for things like paying the hitmen, moving men and equipment into place, paying off politicians and miscellaneous expenses. Nelson claims that they were able to talk in vague code because they had worked together and trusted each other for a long time.[2423] Nelson also pointed out that not everyone knew the real agenda because information was compartmentalized.[2424] The few at the top knew what was going on but the rest were told only what they needed to know to pull it off.[2425]

D.H. Byrd had recently purchased the Texas School Book Depository building [2426] As noted earlier in this book, Mac Wallace was Lyndon Johnson's hitman. After the murder of Doug Kinser, Mac Wallace then went to work directly for D.H. Byrd.[2427] Byrd is one of the wealthy oil barons of the day, [2428] and D.H. Byrd now owned the Texas School Book Depository in Dealey Plaza.[2429] The Texas School Book Depository is where Lee Harvey Oswald was working when Kennedy was assassinated right below the window of the depository. Mac Wallace left a fingerprint on the sixth floor of the depository by the "sniper's nest."[2430] After the Kennedy assassination, Byrd had the sniper's window taken out and proudly displayed in his home like a trophy.[2431] Byrd was also a close friend of General Curtis LeMay. LeMay gave Byrd an Air Force commendation for founding the Civil Air Patrol, where Oswald was a member as a teenager.[2432]

The conspirators appear to have gotten together the night before the assassination at Clint Murchison's estate for a final meeting to verify that they were going ahead. This would have been their last chance to call it off, and they needed to get together to make sure everyone was still prepared to go ahead with the operation. Mae Newman confirmed the pre-assassination party the night before Kennedy was assassinated in Dallas.[2433] Mae was a maid and she said Mac Wallace was there too,[2434] as was Hoover whose code name was "Bulldog."[2435] Hoover flew down for the meeting and then flew right back to Washington.[2436] Johnson came in around 11:00 PM.[2437] This would have been after Richard Nixon had left.[2438]

Jerome Corsi, in his book *WHO REALLY KILLED KENNEDY*, quotes Johnson's mistress, Madeline Brown:[2439]

When Johnson showed up, according to Madeline Brown, Johnson's mistress "Tension filled the room upon his arrival," Brown wrote. "The group immediately went behind closed doors. A short time later Lyndon, anxious and red-faced, re-appeared. Squeezing my hand so hard it felt crushed from the pressure, he spoke with a grating whisper – a growl into my ear not a love message, but one I will always remember: '*After tomorrow those goddamn Kennedys will never embarrass me again – that's no threat – that's a promise.*'"[2440]

A video of her description of the meeting can be viewed on YouTube.

At that meeting were:

- Clint Murchison – Oil Baron
- H L Hunt – Oil Baron
- Lyndon Johnson – Vice President of the U.S.
- Mac Wallace – LBJ's hitman
- J. Edgar Hoover – FBI Director
- Clyde Tolson – Hoover's companion
- Robert Thornton – former mayor of Dallas
- John McCloy – ended up on the Warren Commission
- George Brown – founder of Brown & Root
- John Kerrington (I'm not sure of the spelling of his last name.)
- Bruce Alger – former Texas congressman

John McCloy was a hard-line Cold Warrior who left the Kennedy administration over differences between his and Kennedy's approach to the Soviet Union. After he left the administration, McCloy went to work for a law firm where he represented anti-Kennedy oilmen Clint Murchison and Sid Richardson, who he had known since his days at Chase Manhattan.[2441] He was also a longtime associate of H.L. Hunt.[2442] After the assassination, Johnson appointed McCloy to the Warren Commission.

On September 4, 1965 Rose Cherami was found at 3:00 AM on Highway 155 east of Big Sandy, Texas. She had predicted the Kennedy assassination. She knew too much and had to be killed. A motorist said he had been driving and suddenly saw a woman and some suitcases in the road and braked hard to avoid running her over.[2443] She had a gunshot wound.[2444] And her body had been moved to the road from where she was shot on the side of the road. Her blood was on the property where she had been shot, and that property belonged to the head of security for H.L. Hunt.[2445]

Eugene Hale Brading was at Hunt's office building in Dallas the day before the assassination.[2446] The next day he was arrested in Dealey Plaza after the shooting.[2447] He gave an alias and was released. Brading had been in the Dal-Tex building. While in Dallas, Brading stayed at the Cabana Hotel.[2448]

The son of H.L. Hunt was one of the sponsors of an ad in the *Dallas Morning News* that criticized Kennedy on November 22, 1963.[2449] The FBI advised H.L. Hunt to get out of town, according to *The Realist* March 1964 the FBI, "within an hour of the shooting, went to H.L. Hunt and advised him to get out of Dallas fast. Under an assumed name he took American Airlines flight 42 to New York."[2450]

CIA Director Allen Dulles also had connections to the Texas oil barons. He had worked for them through his law firm, Sullivan & Cromwell.[2451] And when Kennedy fired Dulles, he also fired Richard Bissell and General Charles Cabell. Charles was the brother of Earle Cabell, the Mayor of Dallas in 1963.[2452]

291

The Setup of Oswald and the Trip to Dallas

This chapter is organized into four sections:

1. Corruption in Dallas – describes how, by 1963, Johnson had control of the authorities in Dallas and how this made Dallas the ideal city in which to assassinate Kennedy so he could be president

2. The setup of Thomas Arthur Vallee in Chicago – describes how the conspirators had at least two other contingency plans set up in Chicago and Miami, including patsies set up to take the fall

3. Richard Case Nagell tries to warn Oswald – describes how an American double agent was sent by the Russians to warn Oswald that he was being set up and to try to stop the assassination

4. The setup of Lee Harvey Oswald in Dallas – describes the elaborate preparations in Dallas, including an Oswald double, to set Oswald up to take the fall for the assassination

There were actually three plots to kill President Kennedy; Tampa, Chicago and Dallas. This was to ensure that he was in fact dead in 1963 before he could dump Johnson off the ticket. The conspirators weren't going to give the whole plan a single point of failure that depended on one trip that might be cancelled. Below is a description of how the corruption in Dallas made that city the ideal place for the conspirators to murder Kennedy. While Dallas was the ideal place to kill Kennedy, it was only one of several options. There is also some detail on the plots in Tampa and especially Chicago. The reason to take the time to bring these up is to point out that there was a huge conspiracy to assassinate Kennedy. The conspirators went to the trouble to set up separate 'lone nut' patsies in Tampa, Chicago and Dallas, complete with motorcade routes that made sharp turns just underneath the windows of the places where the patsies worked. This may help the reader to understand the magnitude of the effort that went into planning the Kennedy assassination.

M. Wesley Swearingen was an FBI agent who found out from Ramon, a Cuban exile, in 1962 that plans were being put together in different cities that Kennedy might travel to; Chicago, Miami and Dallas.[2453]

Author Phillip Nelson, in his book *LBJ: THE MASTERMIND OF THE JFK ASSASSINATION*, quotes Ramon:[2454]

> "The different teams will make sure that Kennedy is killed, without it looking like a Mafia hit, that's where the CIA comes in, and then the patsy, who takes the first shot, will be killed. It is a very simple plan. The idea is to make it look like there was just one assassin. We practiced this in Florida when Castro was the target. The problem was that we couldn't get close to Castro because his security knows who we are. Shooting Kennedy will be much easier than shooting Castro."[2455]

Ramon liked Kennedy and passed on details, including that CIA officer Bill Harvey was involved. He also knew about CIA asset Guy Banister.[2456] Swearingen also knew Banister and said he could see the assassination coming a year in advance but his superiors would not believe that the CIA would kill Kennedy.[2457] The FBI closed ranks and he was transferred to Kentucky for trying to warn everyone.[2458]

Corruption in Dallas

Johnson had for years put government influence up for sale and the local Dallas mafia were customers, getting help with matters as diverse as gambling and deportation.[2459] However, by 1963, Vice President Lyndon Johnson and the mafia in Texas were all going to prison if the Kennedys remained in power. Johnson and the mafia, as has been discussed, had a mutually profitable working relationship where the mafia had been paying Johnson to keep the government off their backs. The same was true of the Dallas authorities, who were also in bed with the local Dallas mafia. Many of these same authorities were cronies of Johnson, including the judges, the Dallas Police Chief Jesse Curry and District Attorney Henry Wade. With Johnson able to control the corrupt authorities in Dallas and with LBJ and the mafia wanting Kennedy dead, Dallas was a very dangerous place for President Kennedy. As will be discussed shortly, there were contingency plans to murder Kennedy in Tampa and Chicago. These were put in place to make sure that Kennedy did not live long enough to dump Johnson. However, the ideal spot for the conspirators was Dallas. This was the city where Johnson had the most direct control over the authorities. In Chicago, Johnson would have had to rely on mafia boss Sam Giancana to control things, as he would have had to rely on mafia boss Santo Trafficante in Tampa. But Dallas was in Johnson's home turf of Texas and Johnson had been building his power base there for decades. Having the Kennedy assassination and the subsequent cover-up in Dallas made things easier for Johnson to control.

The authorities in Dallas and the local mafia had created a mutually profitable working relationship, all orchestrated by Lyndon Johnson. Carlos Marcello in New Orleans was the mafia boss in charge of Dallas, and Marcello's local guy in Dallas was Joseph Civello. Civello was arrested at the Apalachin mafia meeting in upstate New York where he was there representing Carlos Marcello.[2460] Marcello and Civello had a lucrative gambling empire, aided by the local Dallas officials who were in their pockets.[2461] The Anonymous Zuroma Club was an illegal gambling house run by the local mafia in Dallas.[2462] Lyndon Johnson was there as a frequent guest, and LBJ met Joe Civello there.[2463] Dallas Mayor Earle Cabell was also a frequent guest at the Anonymous Zuroma Club and he was close to Joe Civello and Sam Campisi.[2464] Sheriff Bill Decker was also a regular at the Zuroma Club.[2465]

With House Speaker Sam Rayburn's death in 1961 the mafia lost its last protection against national antiracketeering legislation.[2466] Once Johnson was gone from the Senate the anti-mafia bills passed the House and Senate and became tools that Bobby Kennedy used in the war on the mafia.[2467] When John Kennedy was elected in 1960 he put his brother Robert Kennedy in as Attorney General, and Bobby went after the mafia, including Carlos Marcello and Joe Civello.[2468] This disrupted the natural order of things in Dallas. Normally the local corrupt judges like Sarah Hughes and Harold "Barefoot" Sanders, who were in league with the corrupt District Attorney, Henry Wade, and Lyndon Johnson, would have stopped the prosecution of the mafia, but now they had their hands tied by the federal prosecution coming from Washington.[2469] The current case at that time was the United States vs. John Ely Stone, and was presided over by Judge Sarah Hughes.[2470] For years the local authorities had turned a blind eye to the local mafia, but Attorney General Robert Kennedy had forced the prosecution.[2471] With the assassination of President Kennedy, the prosecution of the local mafia, and the Stone case, were effectively stopped, and they could all get back to business as usual.[2472]

The Dallas police and prosecutors had a long history of either burying or creating evidence to put innocent people behind bars. They had been doing it for years. One minor difference in this case was that Lee Harvey Oswald was white while most of the previous victims had not been, but the mechanisms necessary to railroad someone through this process functioned like a well-oiled machine. They already knew how, they just had to apply their skills to Oswald. No matter what the facts were, Oswald was guilty.

Author James DiEugenio, in his book *RECLAIMING PARKLAND*, documents that:[2473]

> "In 2006 Dallas elected Craig Watkins, its first black DA. He was the first DA in over a half century who was not from, to put it kindly – the good ol' boys network. To put it unkindly, well, let's use Watkins' own words to describe what preceded him: "There was a kind of cowboy kind of mentality and the reality is that kind of approach is archaic, racist, elitist and arrogant." Watkins never worked for Wade or met him. Therefore, once in office he was free to go ahead and review many of his cases with an independent eye. What was the result? No other county in America, and almost no state for that matter – has freed more innocent people from prison in recent years than Dallas County where Wade was DA from 1951 through 1986."[2474]

> "In the review Watkins instituted, nearly thirty convictions, three for murder, have been overturned so far. And there are over 200 more to go. This review has caused both the DA's office and the DPD to be exposed for what they really were."[2475]

> "Watkins has said that many of the cases won under Wade "were riddled with shoddy investigations, evidence was ignored, and defense lawyers were kept in the dark." Take for instance the case of James Lee Woodard. Woodard spent 27 years in prison for a murder that DNA testing later showed he did not commit. But what makes it worse is that "Wade's office withheld from defense attorneys photographs of tire tracks at the crime scene that didn't match Woodard's car." A lawyer overseeing the review said that many corners were cut to get the case finished. And it was hard for her to be precise about who was more involved in that, the DA's office or the detectives running the case. Another person involved in the review, a professor of criminology at UT, has commented that it was a "win at all costs" mentality. "When someone was arrested, it was assumed they were guilty. I think prosecutors and investigators basically ignored all evidence to the contrary and decided they were going to convict these guys."[2476]

> "There was another case reversal in which the man accused of rape had a solid alibi. As the *Dallas Morning News* reported, Johnny Earl Lindsey was at work when the crime was

committed, and his supervisor vouched for his alibi. Plus, he had timecards to prove it. The case made against him was made upon eyewitness testimony and faulty police lineups. Sounds familiar."[2477]

In 1963 Earle Cabell, the mayor of Dallas, and his brother Charles Cabell hated Kennedy because Kennedy had fired Charles Cabell from the CIA after the Bay of Pigs fiasco.[2478] Dallas Police Chief Jesse Curry was an FBI Academy graduate who served at the pleasure of Mayor Earle Cabell.[2479] Since Curry worked for Earle Cabell, this allowed Johnson to control Curry, who stuck by Johnson during and after the Kennedy assassination.[2480]

So, Oswald was going to be guilty no matter what the 'evidence' showed. In fact, the authorities came up with three different explanations as to how Kennedy could have wounds from the front while Oswald was shooting from behind. The only consistent part of the three explanations is they all concluded that Oswald was guilty. The first explanation was that Oswald shot at Kennedy before the limousine made the left onto Elm from Houston. On November 26, 1963 the *New York Times* journalist John Herbers quoted Assistant District Attorney Bill Alexander:[2481]

> "The known facts about the bullets and the position of the assassin suggested that he started shooting as the president's car was coming toward him, swung his rifle in an arc of almost 180 degrees, and fired at least twice more."[2482]

This didn't fit the facts and had to be dropped for the second theory, which was that Kennedy was turned around and was looking back and waiving to someone when he was hit. This second theory also had to be abandoned as evidence came out to contradict it.[2483] The third theory they came up with was that the wound in the front was not an entrance wound, but an exit wound. This 'Magic Bullet' fiction was the explanation they stuck with. During this entire exercise the whole focus of the Dallas, and now also the Federal, authorities was on how to fit the facts to the 'lone gunman' theory. At no time did they consider the possibility of shots from anywhere but the Texas School Book Depository, or that anyone but Oswald could possibly have been shooting. This wasn't an investigation, it was a frame-up.

The Dallas homicide department concealed and manipulated evidence.[2484] They had discovered the Mauser and made it disappear.[2485] (See the subsection on the Mauser Rifle). They had questioned Lee Oswald all day without recording anything.[2486] They had let several suspects arrested in Dealey Plaza go without even their mugshots.[2487] They had failed to check out the Nash Rambler station wagon and then had lied about the incident, denying that Deputy Roger Craig had even been at police headquarters.[2488] (See the section on Roger Craig). And they had allowed Oswald to be killed while in police custody, in the basement of its own headquarters surrounded by police officers and then immediately closed its books on the investigation, claiming it was solved.[2489] Dallas police captain Fritz stated to the press: "Oswald said absolutely nothing before or after he was shot. The case is closed."[2490]

Witnesses heard shooting from the Dal-Tex building, and the guy who came out of that building had no explanation for being there.[2491] The clamor of the onlookers forced local authorities to arrest him and he was taken to the sheriff's office where he was held for questioning, but they did nothing and then released him without even keeping a record of his name.[2492] This may have been Chuck Nicoletti. Another man was arrested at the Dal-Tex building, and he gave his name as Jim Braidon and was released after being checked out.[2493] But his real name was Eugene Hale Brading and he was an ex-convict with a history of several dozen arrests.[2494] A few days earlier he had an appointment with one of the sons of H.L. Hunt, the oil billionaire.[2495] He claimed he was in the Dal-Tex building at the time of the assassination because he was looking for a pay phone.[2496] An off-duty officer named Tilson chased a suspect and lost him but got his license plate number which he reported but never heard anything about it again.[2497] Three men dressed as tramps were seen and photographed being arrested but there is no other record of them at all.[2498] The supposed 'tramps' were clean, clean-shaven and had good shoes.[2499] More on them later. Will Fritz, the Dallas Police Chief of Homicide, was contacted twice by the Louisiana State Police about the Rose Cherami incident where she predicted the assassination. First, he was contacted by Lieutenant Francis Fruge.[2500] Then he was contacted by Colonel Morgan.[2501] Both times Fritz said he had no interest in questioning Rose Cherami, so she was eventually released. And then there's the Dallas police department's abysmal performance in the Tippit case.[2502] They concealed three bullets, they made automatic cartridges found at the scene disappear, they tried to hide the revolver cartridges, and they failed to pursue any leads on the two men seen by witnesses.[2503]

Johnson's crooked attorney Ed Clark was running the Texas side of the Johnson partnership (see the section on Johnson's crooked partnership with Ed Clark). District Attorney Henry Wade was former FBI and hung out with Hoover and Johnson in Washington and at parties in the Johnson home.[2504] Wade was on the Johnson team.[2505] During the 1950's Wade was also a regular at the Anonymous Zuroma Club.[2506]

Wade refused to push hard to prosecute gambling.[2507] Henry Wade did not prosecute the Dallas mob after the successful raid by the Dallas police on the bookmaking operation of John Eli Stone in the early 1950's.[2508] He also allowed a Civello mafia member named Joe Ianni to go free after beating a man to death with a wooden club in front of witnesses.[2509] This was because Wade was in bed with the local mafia.[2510]

When Robert Kennedy decided to go after the Dallas mafia, he correctly saw Johnson as part of that corrupt gang.[2511] Johnson was a lot of things, but he wasn't stupid. He knew that Attorney General Robert Kennedy was out to get him.[2512] Meanwhile there were more rumors of Johnson being booted from the ticket.[2513]

Robert Kennedy continued to close down Civello and Marcello gambling operations in Dallas.[2514] Robert Kennedy's organized crime task force approach to attacking the mafia was having a dramatic effect and he was directly threatening Giancana, Civello and Marcello.[2515] He was also going after the Stone brothers, part of the Civello-Marcello organization in Dallas.[2516] In September of 1962 there were IRS raids on multiple Marcello gambling operations in Louisiana and Texas, and Marcello was outraged.[2517]

Mark North, in his book *BETRAYAL IN DALLAS*, said that, by 1962:

> "Marcello, Civello, Johnson and Hoover all perceived a common and mortal enemy in JFK."[2518]

And Robert Kennedy also continued to prosecute Carlos Marcello personally and to try to get him deported, this time for good.[2519] The combination of the corrupt District Attorney in league with the vice president and the mafia made Dallas the ideal place to murder the president and get away with it.[2520] Hoover and Wade would protect Marcello while he did to the government what the government was trying to do to him.[2521]

Congressional Representative Albert Thomas of Texas was key to the space program.[2522] Johnson seized on the opportunity created by the news of Representative Thomas and his decision to retire due to illness.[2523] Kennedy was desperate to keep the space program on track and was attempting to change Thomas' mind about retiring, and this gave Thomas the ability to summon Kennedy to Texas.[2524] This was perfect because Thomas was a longtime crony of Johnson, and Johnson got Thomas to get Kennedy to agree to visit Texas in the fall of 1963.[2525] On September 26, 1963 Kennedy confirmed the trip to Texas, including stops at Houston and Dallas and also including motorcades.[2526] Kennedy has no idea what he has just agreed to. He thinks he is simply 'unpopular' as a liberal in that conservative part of the country.

Robert Kennedy continued to close down Civello and Marcello gambling operations in Dallas.[2527] Robert Kennedy's organized crime task force approach to attacking the mafia was having a dramatic effect and he was directly threatening Giancana, Civello and Marcello.[2528] He was also going after the Stone brothers, part of the Civello-Marcello organization in Dallas.[2529] In September of 1962 there were IRS raids on multiple Marcello gambling operations in Louisiana and Texas, and Marcello was outraged.[2530]

In the meantime, as mentioned above, Robert Kennedy was still pursuing the Stone brothers, who were part of the Dallas operations of Carlos Marcello. On October 21, 1963 the grand jury returned indictments and the four defendants were scheduled for trial.[2531] Robert Kennedy was also still trying to get Marcello deported and was getting closer to his goal.[2532] Robert Kennedy also had a spectacular success in October when $56 Million in heroin was seized (almost $400 Million in today's dollars).[2533] That month Marcello twice talked about Kennedy being assassinated, once in Miami and once in New Orleans, and these conversations were both monitored by FBI informants, so Hoover was in on it.[2534]

When Kennedy was assassinated and Johnson was sworn in, Judge Sarah Hughes stopped the Stone prosecution.[2535] FBI Special Agent in Charge (SAIC) of the Dallas office, Gordon Shanklin, employed Gestapo tactics to keep the local witnesses quiet.[2536] Johnson got critical support from the corrupt mayor of Dallas, Earle Cabell.[2537] When three members of the Dallas City Council attempted to launch an investigation into Oswald's murder, Cabell quashed it.[2538] Johnson later supported Cabell for the Democratic Party nomination for U.S. Representative from Texas.[2539]

Sarah Hughes ruled the wiretap evidence in the Stone case inadmissible, destroying the case.[2540] The result was inevitable. The Stone trial came to a close on September 21, 1964 and they got a slap on the wrist.[2541] The mafia gambling operations were soon back in business.[2542] Johnson had evidence destroyed – he ordered Connally's clothes cleaned, the interior of the limousine stripped and replaced and the JFK coffin flown out to sea on the East Coast and dumped in deep water.[2543]

In 1970 the Racketeer Influenced and Corrupt Organizations (RICO) Act gave federal prosecutors the power they needed to break up the Dallas mafia.[2544] Under pressure from the federal prosecution of the mafia, the Dallas police force was reorganized to conform to the new RICO model.[2545] Dallas officials had realized that RICO meant they too would go down with the mafia if they continued to stonewall.[2546]

The federal strike force found embarrassing relationships between the Dallas Mafia and local officials. It was reported that "at least a dozen and perhaps more voices on taped telephone conversations ... have been identified as Dallas policemen."[2547]

The Setup of Thomas Arthur Vallee in Chicago

Lee Harvey Oswald in Dallas wasn't the only patsy. The conspirators couldn't afford to risk having the assassination plan fail if, by chance, they were unable to get Kennedy to go to Dallas or he happened to cancel the trip. To give themselves the best possible chance of success they also had plans for Chicago and Tampa. The Tampa plot was foiled when local law enforcement did their jobs and Kennedy's protection was properly deployed. I've also seen evidence of attempts to set up plots in Los Angeles, at a screening of the film PT-109, and in Washington, D.C. but these don't seem to be as well developed as the Tampa and especially the Chicago plots. The point is that the conspirators were hedging their bets by setting up plots in multiple cities to make sure they got Kennedy by late 1963. The assassins were ready to be deployed and would be sent to whatever city they were needed.

On October 29, 1963 President Kennedy's trip to Chicago to see the Army-Navy football game at Soldier Field was announced.[2548] The trip was set for November 2, and the planned route had a difficult left-hand turn onto Jackson and past tall warehouses.[2549] Secret Service Agent Abraham Bolden said that on October 30 there was a tip about a four-man shooting team with high-powered rifles.[2550] Then they got a tip from a local landlady who said that four men were renting a room from her boardinghouse. She had seen rifles with scopes and a map of the president's route and phoned the authorities.[2551] Secret Service Agent J. Lloyd Stocks spotted two of the suspects and started tailing them but he himself was spotted. The two were arrested.[2552] They were later released. They had nothing incriminating on them.[2553]

The patsy in Chicago was Thomas Arthur Vallee. He was a former Marine with outspoken views against Kennedy and worked at a printing company along the motorcade route.[2554] He was placed under surveillance prior to November 2 and arrested on November 2. When arrested he had an M1 rifle, a hand gun and three thousand rounds of ammunition. He had a history of mental illness.[2555] Vallee had also worked at the same U-2 base in Japan as Oswald.[2556] He also participated (like Oswald) in the training of anti-Castro Cubans.[2557] The plate on Vallee's car was registered to Lee Harvey Oswald.[2558]

Abraham Bolden

Abraham Bolden of the Secret Service was the first black Secret Service agent. Kennedy was who got him the job promotion. Bolden was working in the Chicago office when he heard of the threat to Kennedy. He tried to get the warning out and was set up, framed and sent to prison.[2559]

On October 30, 1963 Maurice Martineau, in charge of the Chicago Secret Service office, told other agents, including Abraham Bolden, of the Chicago plot to kill Kennedy during his upcoming visit. Bolden had been promoted and assigned to the White House at Kennedy's request, but had requested a transfer because he was unhappy about the lax security around Kennedy.[2560]

After the Chicago attempt on Kennedy's life failed, Maurice Martineau collected all the evidence. He had everyone give oral reports, not written reports, to the head secretary, Charlotte Klapkowski and turn in their notebooks.[2561] Secret Service Chief James J. Rowley had ordered Martineau to keep everything strictly secret. Bolden had already objected to the lack of security around Kennedy, then he watched as the report on the Chicago plot was buried.[2562] Bolden knew too much and his superiors knew he was willing to tell what he knew. On November 17 Bolden was suddenly told to report to Washington D.C. to the IRS which offered him an "undercover" assignment. If he took the new assignment he was to be given a new identity and to turn in all his identification and birth records.[2563] Bolden smelled a trap and turned the assignment down. He thought he was being set up to disappear for good. He also told his wife and the secretary at the office that he thought the president was going to be killed.[2564] Then Kennedy was assassinated. Maurice Martineau was following the party line and was telling everyone else to do the same.[2565] Then the Secret Service had everyone turn in their identification and issued completely new and different identification. This was because there were fake Secret Service agents with real Secret Service identification in Dealey Plaza the day Kennedy was assassinated.[2566] Bolden had become one of those guys who "knew too much," and his Deep State superiors knew he knew too much. What ensued was a game of cat and mouse where Bolden tried to find ways to get the word out and they tried to find ways to gag him. On a training trip to Washington, D.C. in May of

1964 he tried to contact J. Lee Rankin of the Warren Commission. He was ordered to quit his training class and go back to Chicago immediately.[2567] Upon his return he was arrested, framed and went to trial. When the jury could not reach a decision, a mistrial was declared.[2568] They tried again and this time he was convicted and sentenced.[2569] While in prison they tried to put him in a psychiatric unit where they tried to drug him into being unable to remember anything.[2570] Fortunately his wife and his lawyer got him transferred. They had set up a prearranged signal where he could call for help when, as he suspected, something dangerous happened. He was eventually released.[2571] While in prison his family was harassed and attacked.[2572] While in prison he got a visit from someone representing Jim Garrison, the New Orleans Attorney General attempting to prosecute Clay Shaw for conspiracy to murder John F. Kennedy. For talking to him Bolden was put in solitary confinement.[2573] Bolden somehow survived and was eventually released.

The Setup of Gilberto Lopez in Tampa

Kennedy had gone to Miami a few weeks before Dallas. There had been warnings of an attempt on Kennedy's life in Miami "from an office window with a high-powered rifle." The plan for a motorcade was scrapped and a helicopter was used instead, and Kennedy survived.[2574] This may have been due to the conversation Joseph Milteer had with William Somerset. Somerset was an informant for the Miami police and Milteer was active in the Cuban exile community. Somerset told his police contact who informed captain Charles Sapp who told the Chief of Police. Part of that conversation was that Kennedy would be shot "from an office window with a high-powered rifle"[2575] which leads me to think that was the source.

A few weeks after the Miami scare, Kennedy was in Tampa on November 18.[2576] This was early in the same week he later visited Dallas. Tampa Police Chief J.P. Mullens confirmed the existence of the plot in Tampa. The motorcade had to make a hard left turn in front of the Floridian Hotel, a tall building.[2577] Tampa law enforcement made an extra effort that day and Secret Service protection was properly deployed.[2578] The Tampa patsy was Gilberto Lopez. Lopez was under surveillance as a possible assassination threat. He was a young Cuban exile.[2579] He had a lot in common with Lee Harvey Oswald. In mid-1963 Lopez moved to another city and became involved in the Fair Play for Cuba Committee. Lopez also got in a fight over pro-Castro statements, and Lopez was no longer living with his wife.[2580] Lopez also traveled to Mexico City, and he had a job near the motorcade route.[2581]

Richard Case Nagell Tries to Warn Oswald

Richard Case Nagell was a spy for the CIA. His assignment was to go and pretend to become a double agent for the Russians in Mexico City. When he pretended to go to work for the Russians they told him there was a plot to kill Kennedy and they wanted to try to stop it. The Russians wanted no part of Kennedy getting killed. Khrushchev and Kennedy were getting along, and the Russians were worried they would be blamed if Kennedy was shot. The Russians sent Nagell back to make sure Kennedy was not killed. They told Nagell to warn Oswald, and if Oswald wouldn't listen he was to kill Oswald. Nagell tried to warn Oswald but Oswald didn't listen. This put Nagell in a difficult situation. He did not want to kill Oswald, and he didn't want to be killed himself (by the Russians for not following 'orders'). He also didn't want to be framed for murder himself. He sent a registered letter to Hoover at the FBI warning him of the plot to kill JFK. The FBI got rid of the letter and later claimed to be unable to find it. When he got no reply, he decided to shoot up a bank and get arrested so he would be in custody when Kennedy was assassinated. He thought he would only be charged with a misdemeanor. He planned to expose the plot in court. The evidence in his car disappeared and he was not allowed to discuss the plot in court. He was sent to prison and eventually murdered.

Richard Case Nagell had been told by his handlers that they would deny any knowledge of him if he were caught.[2582] He knew Lee Harvey Oswald in Tokyo when they were both stationed in Japan.[2583] As a double agent, he got orders from both the U.S. and Russia. The Russians told him to keep an eye on Oswald.[2584] In September of 1963 Nagell was ordered by the Russians to disrupt the plot to kill Kennedy by taking Oswald out, one way or another. If he could persuade Oswald that he was the patsy and to get out on his own, fine. If not, he was to kill Oswald.[2585] Nagell met with Oswald in New Orleans and tried to warn him, but Oswald would not quit.[2586] At this point Nagell was stuck between a rock and a hard place. His Russian orders were to kill Oswald, which he did not want to do. He then sent a registered letter to J. Edgar Hoover.[2587] As Nagell put it:

"I informed the Director of the Federal Bureau of Investigation and others in his communications with the CIA as early as September 17, 1963 that Lee Harvey Oswald and two of his Cuban associates were planning to assassinate the president of the United States."[2588]

After sending the registered letter, Nagell then walked into a bank in El Paseo on September 20, 1963 and fired a few shots into the ceiling of the bank and then went outside to wait for the police.[2589] This way he would be in custody when Kennedy was killed and couldn't be blamed or made a patsy. He was eventually released from prison, but after three attempts on his life he agreed, in 1990, to stay quiet in return for his life.[2590] Then on October 31, 1995 the Assassination Records Review Board (ARRB) mailed Nagell a letter. They wanted to talk.[2591] On November 1, 1995, the day after the ARRB's letter was mailed from Washington, D.C., Richard Case Nagell was found dead in the bathroom of his Los Angeles house under suspicious circumstances.[2592]

The Setup of Lee Harvey Oswald in Dallas

In addition to the efforts to set up Thomas Arthur Vallee in Chicago and Gilberto Lopez in Miami, there was an even larger effort to set up Lee Harvey Oswald in Dallas. There was at least one Oswald double running around creating incriminating incidents that would be remembered later. The incidents all had several things in common. The Oswald double would do something outrageous so that the people would remember the incident and then become witnesses. The Mercury dealership is a good example. The Oswald double drove the car like a maniac so the salesman would remember the incident. The Oswald double also talked about having been in Russia and said he would soon be coming into some money. The rifle range incidents were the same. The Oswald double at one point shot at other people's targets. This ensured that they would remember the incident. These incidents could later be used to convict Oswald in the court of public opinion. The sections below go into Oswald's background and list the various incidents.

This Section is organized into fifteen sub-sections:

1. George de Mohrenschildt – describes how one of Oswald's CIA babysitters helped to guide him through the next phase of his setup in Dallas and New Orleans

2. Ruth Paine – describes how de Mohrenschildt passed Oswald off to Ruth Paine, his next CIA babysitter, who helped to guide Oswald into place at the Texas School Book Depository

3. The Silvia Odio Incident – describes how an incident was created by the conspirators to incriminate Oswald and make him look like a nut who wanted to murder the president

4. The ammunition incident – describes how an incident was created by the conspirators to incriminate Oswald – an Oswald double goes into an ammunition store and is rude and obnoxious so the people at the store will remember the incident later

5. The Agent Hosty Incident – an FBI agent visits Oswald's residence and scares his wife and Oswald went to the local FBI office to raise hell – this is to distance himself from the FBI as Oswald is also an FBI informant in addition to being a CIA operative

6. The Redbird incident – describes how three people, one of them either Oswald or an Oswald double, show up to try to rent a plane for the afternoon of the assassination to fly to Cuba – this is so they will be remembered later and is another attempt to incriminate Oswald

7. The Ralph Yates incident – describes another attempt to incriminate Oswald by having an Oswald double hitchhike to the Texas School Book Depository with a rifle-size package under his arm and talk the whole time about shooting the president when he is in town – this is so the incident will be remembered later after the assassination

8. The rifle range incidents – describes multiple incidents where an Oswald double showed up for target practice at rifle ranges around Dallas and did something obnoxious or otherwise memorable so that the incidents will be remembered later

9. The Mercury dealership incident – describes how an Oswald double showed up at a car dealership in Dallas and drove a car in a memorable way and talked about his background in Russia and how he was planning on coming into some money soon – this is also done to incriminate Oswald

10. The gunsmith incident – describes how an Oswald double went to a gunsmith to have a scope mounted on a rifle – this was also done to incriminate Oswald

11. The Abilene incident – unlike the incidents manufactured to incriminate Oswald, this incident is real and is therefore studiously ignored by the authorities after the assassination

12. Marina Oswald – describes the relatively minor role of Marina Oswald in the whole affair

13. Oswald before the shooting – describes Oswald's activities leading up to the assassination

14. Oswald after the shooting – describes Oswald's activities in the brief time between the assassination and when he himself is murdered by Jack Ruby while in police custody

15. Oswald tries to contact his handler – describes how Oswald, in desperation just before his death, tried to reach his CIA handler – he was unsuccessful because he was by then long past the point of being expendable

Oswald was also sent to New Orleans for the summer of 1963 to polish his credentials as a Castro supporter. While in New Orleans he was to pretend to be pro-Castro and to create a few incidents of his own to get his name in the news as being pro-Castro. He was told this was part of his preparation for his undercover mission to Cuba. This was a lie. In reality he was being prepared for his role as the patsy in the Kennedy assassination. The objective of the CIA here was to not only take Kennedy out, but to implicate Cuba and the Soviet Union in the process. Painting Oswald out to be a lone nut who takes out the president accomplishes one thing. It gets rid of Kennedy. Having Oswald, the pro-Cuban communist, take out the president accomplishes two things. It gets rid of Kennedy and makes Cuba, and by extension Russia, the additional scapegoats.

By 1963 the CIA and the Pentagon have been pushing for years for a first nuclear strike. They have tried repeatedly to get Kennedy to agree. They've tried using the Bay of Pigs invasion, the Berlin Crisis and the Cuban Missile Crisis as excuses for a nuclear first strike. When Kennedy refused to use these opportunities to start World War Three, they came up with Operation Northwoods as a plan to create a fake crisis to use as an opportunity to attack Cuba and/or Russia. Now that they're going to have a patsy as the fall guy for the Kennedy assassination, they want that patsy to be a pro-Castro communist patsy. They want to use this opportunity to create a pretext for a first strike. This is why Oswald was sent to New Orleans to polish his pro-Castro credentials. He had already been to Russia and spouted Marxism, so he could already be easily painted out to be a communist. The side trip to New Orleans was to add the 'pro-Castro' angle.

By having Oswald get arrested in a fracas while he is handing out pro-Castro literature in New Orleans and having an Oswald imposter show up in Mexico City looking for visas to Russia and Cuba, they create a pretext for an attack on Cuba and/or Russia. The Russians understood this and tried to cancel the Kennedy assassination. They sent Richard Case Nagell to either warn Oswald or, failing that, to murder him in an attempt to derail the assassination. The Russians did not want to be blamed for the murder of Kennedy and did not want to give the CIA and the Pentagon an excuse for a first strike. Khrushchev had been working with Kennedy toward a peaceful resolution to the Cold War.

The last thing the Russians wanted was for the Cold Warriors at the CIA and Pentagon to have an excuse for a nuclear first strike on Russia.

After the assassination Robert Kennedy will send artist Bill Walton as an emissary to Russia to tell Khrushchev that he does not blame the Soviet Union for the murder of his brother. Also after the assassination the CIA, having been busted on the fact that the Oswald in Mexico City was an imposter, will continue to try to find another way to implicate Cuba and/or Russia in the assassination. David Atlee Phillips will tell Antonio Veciana to try to bribe his cousin in the Cuban consulate in Mexico City to claim that he met with Oswald. Even once Johnson was president and had decided not to use the Cuba/Russia angle to start World War Three the CIA was still trying to manufacture evidence to implicate Cuba in the Kennedy assassination.

CIA asset David Ferrie recruited Oswald while he was still a teenager in New Orleans in the 1950's. Oswald showed up at Ferrie's Civil Air Patrol meetings and Ferrie convinced Oswald to join the Marines. At some point, probably right from the start, Oswald was convinced that this was the way to become a secret agent man for the government. His assignment was to join the Marines and, eventually, be sent to Russia as a fake defector. We still don't know exactly what Oswald was told along the way, but the basic outlines are pretty obvious. Once Oswald came back from Russia he was the perfect patsy for the Kennedy assassination. At some point he was obviously told that his next mission was to be sent undercover to Cuba. This was a lie, but he apparently believed it, at least for a while. In their book *DEAD WRONG* authors Belzer and Wayne claim that Oswald was told he was being sent to Cuba to kill Castro. This is the scenario which makes the most sense and fits the facts. Oswald's girlfriend, Judyth Vary Baker, said the same thing in her book *Me & Lee*. To prepare himself for that mission Oswald was told to pretend to be a pro-Castro Marxist and make sure to get his name in the paper so he would have some 'proof' to show the Cubans when he went to apply for a visa to travel to Cuba. He would then be able to show the Cuban consulate in Mexico City evidence that he was a pro-Castro activist in the United States. He would again be a fake defector. This is what he was told to do by his handlers in the U.S. intelligence community. Lee Harvey Oswald had volunteered to become a secret agent for his country and was planning to go to Cuba to carry out his mission.

This also conveniently made Oswald the perfect patsy for the Kennedy assassination. He could be painted as a communist sympathizer and a lone nut. Some of this was true. Oswald kept to himself and was kind of quirky, so the lone nut part was plausible. This was handy for the conspirators and was obviously part of the reason Oswald was picked to play the role of the patsy. Looking at the profile of the other 'lone nut' patsies who were chosen for the same role in Miami and Chicago it's obvious the same criteria was used to choose all three.

The conspirators had many incriminating things that they wanted Oswald to do so that later on they could point to these events and say "See, he's obviously guilty." This would convict Oswald in the court of public opinion. Since the plan called for Oswald to die, he wouldn't be around to defend himself in a court of law. Some of the incriminating things they had Oswald running around doing were so Cuba and/or the Soviet Union would also be implicated in the assassination of President Kennedy. This was because the conspirators were still hoping to use the assassination of Kennedy as an excuse to invade Cuba and/or start a war with the Soviet Union. Johnson dropped this part of the plan later. He did not want to risk World War Three, but the fact remains that some of the incriminating things they had Oswald doing were done so they could also implicate Cuba and Russia.

Since Oswald obviously wasn't told he was going to be set up as the fall guy in the Kennedy assassination, he couldn't be asked to do everything on the list of incriminating activities. Contrary to popular belief, Oswald wasn't stupid. He could be plausibly told to pass out Fair Play for Cuba leaflets in New Orleans without him catching on to the real plan, but for some of the other things they needed an Oswald double. I have no idea where they got the Oswald double or what ever happened to him, but there is plenty of credible evidence that there was someone imitating Oswald in 1963.

The real Oswald claimed to be a Marxist, handed out leaflets in New Orleans and worked at the Texas School Book Depository. Like the trip to Russia and the Russian wife, these were obviously things that involved the real Lee Harvey Oswald. These things made sense to ask the real Oswald to do. However, there were a number of incriminating activities that the conspirators wanted to be able to point to after the assassination to implicate not only Oswald, but also Cuba and the Soviet Union. To this end they had a lot of 'Oswald' activities. Below are some examples of the Oswald double's activities:

- Part of the plan called for 'Oswald' to go to a rifle range near Dallas and draw attention to himself. So, the Oswald double was tasked with going to the rifle range. In this case 'Oswald' drew attention to himself by shooting at the target next to his. This made sure he would be remembered. The real Oswald was clocked in at work at the Texas School Book Depository when this happened.

- on November 1, 1963 a young man drew attention to himself while buying rifle ammunition at Morgan's Gun Shop in Fort Worth. He was rude and impertinent and boasted about having been in the Marines. Three witnesses thought he looked like Oswald. The real Oswald was busily occupied in Dallas at that time

- The double was also tasked with going to a car dealership and talking about Russia and claiming he was going to come into some money soon. In this case he asked to test drive a car and drove like a maniac so they would remember him later. He was also sure to tell them his name was Oswald.

- Someone claiming to be Oswald showed up at the Cuban and Soviet embassies in Mexico City and applied for a visa. The Cuban consulate said he would need a Soviet visa to obtain a transit visa to go to Cuba ostensibly on his way to Russia. He was turned down by both. In this case the FBI looked into the camera and audio surveillance of the Soviet embassy and said that whoever it was claiming to be Oswald did not look or sound like the real Oswald. Someone was impersonating Oswald who didn't even look or sound like Oswald, so this wasn't the double. It was just someone in Mexico City the CIA told to to pretend to be Oswald.

- Silvia Odio was a Cuban exile living in Dallas when three strangers showed up at her apartment. Two of them were Cuban and one was either the real Oswald or the double. I think this was the real Oswald, but it's hard to be sure. Even if this was the real Oswald, the fact that he was there with two others shows that there was a conspiracy to kill Kennedy.

- Oswald showed up at Redbird airport with a couple who tried to rent a plane which they obviously wanted to hijack to Cuba on the day of the assassination. The owner of the plane rental outfit chose not to rent them a plane but later identified Oswald as being with them. It's unclear which Oswald accompanied the couple to the airport. This might have been the real Lee Harvey Oswald. Even if this was the real Oswald, the fact that he showed up with two other people proves that Oswald was not acting alone.

- Oswald hitched a ride to the Texas School Book Depository with a long package wrapped in brown paper. He did this twice – once on the day of the assassination and once two days earlier - Ralph Leon Yates was a refrigeration mechanic with a Texas Butcher's Supply Company in Dallas, making his rounds to meat outlets on Wednesday, November 20, 1963 – at 10:30 AM Ralph Yates was driving on the R.L. Thornton Expressway – he noticed a man hitchhiking in Oak Cliff at the Begley Avenue entrance to the expressway – Yates stopped to pick up the man.[2593] I suspect because this happened twice that the first one, the one two days before the Kennedy assassination, was the Oswald double. This is because the real Lee Harvey Oswald brought a brown paper package with him on the morning of the assassination. Therefore, the first one was likely the double.

Several of these Oswald sightings had to be covered up later. The conspirators got too ambitious and had too many Oswalds running around. The Silvia Odio incident, the Redbird incident, the two hitchhikers both bringing rifles to the depository and the imposter in Mexico City all had to be buried or explained away if the Warren Commission was to be able to claim there was no conspiracy. After all, if there was no conspiracy, who were all these people with Oswald? How could Oswald be in two places at once? He couldn't be a lone nut if he had accomplices, so they had to cover some of their tracks.

In 1975 Senator Richard Schweiker got a look at some classified documents and said that Oswald had intelligence connections.[2594] He said: "Everywhere you look with him, there are the fingerprints of intelligence." In 2007 Schweiker said that Oswald "was a product of a fake defector program run by the CIA." Schweiker also said "I certainly don't believe the CIA gave us the whole story."[2595]

George de Mohrenschildt

George de Mohrenschildt was a CIA "asset." By that I mean he was sort of a contractor. He was given jobs to do by the CIA like collect information while traveling behind the Iron Curtain. In return he was paid in several ways. As a petroleum geologist he would be given government contracts for work done in foreign countries where the CIA had influence. He was based for a while in Dallas where he was tasked with being one of Oswald's babysitters.

In the early 1960's George de Mohrenschildt was an oil exploration consultant. He said to JFK assassination researcher and author Edward J. Epstein that he had been "dealing with" the CIA since the 1950's.[2596] He would sometimes, for example, travel behind the Iron Curtain in Eastern Europe. He would allow the CIA to quiz him on what was going on. This would allow the CIA a subtle way to keep an eye on things.[2597] As his relationship with the CIA grew, he was given other kinds of tasks. In the summer of 1962 de Mohrenschildt was told by the CIA to babysit Lee Harvey Oswald. He confirmed the assignment with the CIA's J. Walter Moore.[2598] In return de Mohrenschildt asked for help getting an oil exploration contract in Haiti.[2599] This was typical of how de Mohrenschildt's arrangement worked with the CIA. He got lucrative foreign government contracts in return for carrying out assigned tasks.

George de Mohrenschildt went to Guatemala in January of 1961 and stayed for four months while the CIA was training anti-Castro guerillas in Guatemala in preparation for the Bay of Pigs invasion. Oswald requested to return home from Russia in February of 1961.[2600]

On October 12, 1962 Oswald got a job in Dallas at Jaggars Chiles Stovall.[2601] The firm did secret work for the government, processing pictures taken by U-2 spy planes.[2602]

Oswald had just come back from his first big mission where he was a fake defector to the Soviet Union. At this point, he was back in the United States with his Russian wife, Marina and their daughter. He was told to get in touch with George de Mohrenschildt and get to know the Russian community in the Dallas area. Lee Harvey Oswald was pretending to be a blue-collar guy who could barely feed his family. George de Mohrenschildt was well-connected and part of the upper-crust of society. Suddenly this rich guy who knows Jackie Kennedy starts inviting Oswald and his wife to dinner parties, spending time with him, finding jobs for him and introducing him around to his friends. This didn't just happen, this was part of the setup of Oswald. George de Mohrenschildt's job was to help Oswald and keep an eye on him for the CIA.

According to author Phillip Nelson, in his book *LBJ: THE MASTERMIND OF THE JFK ASSASSINATION*:[2603]

> "Both Shaw and de Mohrenschildt had taken their orders directly from the man controlling the details of the operation from his CIA position in Mexico, under the code name of Maurice Bishop, David Atlee Phillips. Phillips, as did his peer David Morales, in charge of the operational and logistical end

of the plan, took his orders from Bill Harvey who reported only to two men at the highest levels of the CIA, James Jesus Angleton and Cord Meyer. According to information furnished by E. Howard Hunt ... Harvey and the others were being guided by Cord Meyer, operating out of his London CIA offices."[2604]

On February 2, 1962 de Mohrenschildt introduced Oswald to Ruth Paine.[2605] She was to be Oswald's next babysitter.

In March of 1963 de Mohrenschildt got a Haitian government contract for $285,000. This was a payoff from the CIA for his Oswald babysitting duties. In April he left Dallas.[2606] None of de Mohrenschildt's CIA contacts were mentioned in the Warren Report.[2607] For his Warren Commission testimony George de Mohrenschildt ran Oswald down as not very bright and mean to his wife.[2608]

New Orleans District Attorney Jim Garrison, in his investigation of the Kennedy assassination, determined that de Mohrenschildt was unaware of what lay in store for Oswald.[2609] Later de Mohrenschildt wrote an unpublished book "I am a Patsy" where he took back the bad things he had said about Oswald to the Warren Commission.[2610] Then he noticed that his phone was bugged and he was being followed.[2611] In 1976 he reached out to George H.W. Bush to get the CIA off his back when he started writing about Oswald. Bush wrote back and told de Mohrenschildt he was not the target of federal authorities.[2612] In addition to writing, de Mohrenschildt was also starting to talk. This was dangerous. JFK assassination researcher and author Edward J. Epstein was interviewing de Mohrenschildt in 1977 and de Mohrenschildt was about to be called by the House Select Committee on Assassinations (HSCA) when he was murdered in a way to make it look like a suicide.[2613] An investigator for the HSCA was on his way to meet with de Mohrenschildt when he was killed.[2614]

The murder scene was staged to look like a suicide, but there was a tape recording of his death. A maid had been instructed to make an audio tape of a soap opera. Unknown to the murderer, she had left a tape recorder running.[2615] On the recording can be clearly heard the beeping sound the alarm system makes when someone opens the door.[2616] Then there's the shotgun blast, then the beeping noise again. So, someone came in and murdered de Mohrenschildt. A woman on the local Coroner's Jury pointed it out. She had the same alarm system and knew what that meant.[2617] They shut her down and ruled it a suicide.[2618]

Ruth Paine

Ruth Paine was Oswald's next CIA babysitter after George de Mohrenschildt. Ruth's relationship with the CIA was similar to de Mohrenschildt's in that she was not a CIA employee but more of a contractor. Her ties to the CIA were many. Her father and sister were both CIA employees, and her husband worked for a government contractor and had a security clearance, but this assignment may have come to Ruth from Allen Dulles by way of Mary Bancroft, who was both mistress and assistant to Dulles. Ruth Paine's mother-in-law, Ruth Forbes Paine Young, was a lifelong friend of Mary Bancroft. By whichever route Ruth got the assignment to shepherd Oswald through the process, she did an excellent job. She guided the sheep right to the slaughter.

Ruth Paine was the one who got Oswald the job at the Texas School Book Depository. The importance of this point can't be overstated. If Oswald was a lone nut who just wanted to shoot the president, how did he know to get a job at the Texas School Book Depository? How would he know, six weeks before the Kennedy visit to Dallas, that the motorcade would take that route? That route was way out of the ordinary. Normal rules for presidential motorcades prohibit sharp turns, especially under tall buildings with lots of places for snipers. There is no way this could have been planned by a lone nut who just wanted to shoot the president. Oswald had to be guided to the point where he could be presented to the public as the patsy. The whole conspiracy depended on Oswald being in that building. It couldn't be left to chance. This is why Ruth Paine's background is important. Upon closer examination it turns out that she was CIA. In her defense she may not have known what was in store for Oswald. She was, similar to de Mohrenschildt, likely not told everything in advance.

Ruth Paine was there during Oswald's time in the Dallas area. She was there to help Oswald while he was in New Orleans, and she was there when Oswald returned to Dallas just before the assassination. Oswald's wife Marina and his children lived with Ruth Paine during much of this time while Oswald was off doing his real job as a CIA operative. Oswald privately referred to Ruth as "The Pain" and did not trust her.[2619]

Ruth Paine worked for the CIA.[2620] For Ruth, working for the CIA was a family tradition. William Avery Hyde, Ruth's father, worked undercover for the CIA.[2621] His cover job was to work for the Agency for International Development (AID) in Latin America. He posed as an insurance executive giving advice to the U.S. State Department.[2622]

The CIA planted operatives like this all over AID and the State Department. CIA operatives can't exactly hang a sign out saying "I work for the CIA," so they have cover jobs. William Avery Hyde's reports went to the CIA.[2623]

Sylvia Hyde Hoke, Ruth's older sister, followed dad into the family business. Sylvia worked for the CIA. And Ruth went to stay at her sister's home in September of 1963 in Falls Church, Virginia, near CIA headquarters not long before the Kennedy assassination.[2624] Sylvia's husband John also worked for the CIA and also used the same cover, the Agency for International Development, as his father-in-law.[2625]

Ruth's mother-in-law, Ruth Forbes Paine Young, was a lifelong friend of Mary Bancroft. Mary Bancroft was the long-time mistress of, and secretary to, Allen Dulles since Switzerland during World War II.[2626]

Ruth's husband Michael Paine worked at Bell Helicopter in Fort Worth, Texas. He had a security clearance. His step-father, Arthur Young, had invented the Bell Helicopter. He was part of the military-industrial complex.[2627]

When de Mohrenschildt left for Haiti, it was time for Ruth to step in as Oswald's babysitter. In February of 1963 George de Mohrenschildt gave a dinner party where he introduced Lee Harvey Oswald and his wife Marina to Ruth Paine.[2628] George de Mohrenschildt had held up his end of the deal with the CIA and they paid him off with a government contract for work in Haiti for over two hundred thousand dollars.[2629] Oswald had been handed over and now Ruth Paine was his new babysitter.

In April Ruth invited Marina Oswald to move in with her while Lee went to New Orleans.[2630] In May Ruth even drove Marina to New Orleans and helped them move in.[2631] She did the same when the Oswalds later returned to Dallas. In June of 1963 Marina wrote to Ruth to say that Lee Oswald did not want to live with her anymore.[2632] In July 11, 1963 Ruth Paine sent a letter to Marina to invite Marina and her children to stay with her again.[2633] She also let's Oswald use her garage to store his possessions.[2634]

Oswald spent the summer of 1963 in New Orleans. On his way back to Dallas, he had the side trip to Mexico City. He had filled out a change of address form at the post office in New Orleans. On October 11, 1963, someone in New Orleans filled out a duplicate change of address for Oswald. The second one was not in Oswald's handwriting.[2635] When Oswald returned from New Orleans, Ruth Paine arranged the job for Oswald at the Texas School Book Depository.[2636]

After the Kennedy assassination, Ruth Paine volunteered "evidence" damming Oswald to the Police, the FBI and the Warren Commission. She allowed them to search her home while she was not there. This resulted in the authorities 'finding' the pictures of 'Oswald with the rifle' that ended up on the cover of *Life* magazine. She showed them a copy of a letter she claims Oswald wrote to the Soviet embassy on her Russian typewriter. Her testimony to the Warren Commission painted Oswald out to be a lone nut communist. She claimed to have seen the sniper rifle in her garage. Ruth Paine was very helpful to those trying to posthumously convict Oswald in the court of public opinion.

During the Garrison investigation, Ruth Paine was evasive when questioned about her and her sister's backgrounds. Knowing that her sister also works for the CIA, Ruth was evasive when Garrison asks her about this, claiming she did not know. When Garrison asked Ruth Paine if her sister worked for the government, the exchange went like this:[2637]

> Paine: "She has worked – she did something with G9 – what is this? Well, it would be a government job."
>
> Garrison: "What did she do with the government?"
>
> Paine: "She majored in psychology. One of the things I recall is making testing angles. How to test a Bedouin to know whether he can be a good oil drill operator, this kind of thing."
>
> Garrison: "Do you know what government agency she has worked for?"
>
> Paine: "No, just worked for the government."
>
> Without access to government documents identifying Ruth Paine's sister as a CIA employee, Garrison asked Paine "Do you know why the investigative file on Sylvia Hyde Hoke is still classified in the archives as Secret?"
>
> Paine: "No. Is it?"
>
> Garrison: "Yes. Most of the file is still classified. Do you have any idea why they would do that? It seems there is no reason."
>
> Paine: "No."

Later, during the Contra War in Nicaragua, Ruth Paine was there collecting information for the CIA.[2638]

The Silvia Odio Incident

In 1963 Silvia Odio was part of the anti-Castro Cuban exile community in Dallas. Her father was in one of Castro's prisons. In late September of 1963, Oswald and two anti-Castro Cuban exiles showed up at her door. Her sister answered the door and they asked for Silvia.[2639] When Silvia came to the door the three of them introduced Oswald as "Leon Oswald," but the conversation was in Spanish and he did not say much.[2640] The two Cuban exiles said they were looking for her support for their anti-Castro group. They wanted her to write a letter soliciting funds for their group. They talked for a while and then left. A few days later, one of the Cubans called her and said that "Leon" was crazy and was talking about killing JFK.[2641]

This was another attempt to incriminate Oswald. The idea was to have Oswald stop by the apartment of an anti-Castro Cuban exile witness who would later be able to testify that Oswald was in the company of two other anti-Castro Cuban exiles. In this contrived incident, Silvia Odio was the witness. This was the conspirators planting evidence that could later be used to incriminate Oswald.

The conspirators created this incident when they were still hoping to use the Kennedy assassination as an excuse to invade Cuba. They created an incident where Oswald was connected to Cubans. Later, when Johnson bailed out on this option and the conspirators went with the 'lone nut' theory instead of the 'Castro was behind it' theory, the incident became a liability and the Warren Commission tried to cover it up. If Oswald was a lone nut, what was he doing with two Cubans? In fact, the Silvia Odio incident was proof of a conspiracy, and therefore the Warren Commission wanted to bury it. The Warren Commission was created was to tell the public that there was no conspiracy, so they had to bury the incident.

The FBI interviewed Silvia Odio in December of 1963.[2642] Their first attempt to bury the incident was to investigate Silvia instead of investigating the three visitors.[2643] They were hoping they could find some dirt to discredit her somehow. Silvia turned out to be a solid, credible witness with her sister to back her up, so they were stuck and had to come up with something else.[2644] By the time they got around to addressing the issue it was July of 1964 and it was late in the process. Referring to the incident, Lee Rankin said "At this stage we are supposed to be closing doors, not opening them."[2645]

So, the next thing the FBI did was come up with three guys who they claim were the three who showed up at Silvia's door. They came up with Loren Eugene Hall, William Seymour and Lawrence Howard.[2646] This was a hastily arranged and temporary patch and it did not hold for long, but it held long enough for the Warren Commission to declare success and disband, at which point there is no one to answer challenges. Later, Hall recanted the whole story about he and the other two guys.[2647] Silvia Odio never changed her story.

The Ammunition Incident

On Friday, November 1, a man bought ammunition for his rifle in a conspicuous way at Morgan's gun shop in Fort Worth, Texas.[2648] He was described as being rude and impertinent and made a point of saying he had been in the Marines.[2649] He appeared to be trying to call attention to himself. A man named Dewey Bradford was in the shop with his wife and brother-in-law. They later remembered the incident.[2650] When Kennedy was assassinated and they saw Oswald's picture in *Life* magazine they identified Oswald as the rude young man buying ammunition.[2651] The real Oswald was in Dallas at that time.[2652] This was another attempt to create an incident that would incriminate Oswald later.

The Agent Hosty Incident

In early November of 1963 FBI Agent James Hosty stopped by Ruth Paine's house looking for Oswald, and he talked to Ruth Paine.[2653] On November 7, 1963 Oswald stopped by the local Dallas FBI office and left a threatening note for Hosty telling him to stay away from his wife.[2654]

After Oswald was murdered, Hoover wanted to be able to claim that the FBI had no contact with Oswald, so he called Gordon Shanklin and told him to make sure Oswald's file had nothing in it to embarrass the FBI. Shanklin gave the note Oswald left for Hosty back to Hosty and told him to get rid of it. Hosty tore it up but that wasn't good enough for Shanklin so Hosty flushed the pieces down the toilet.[2655]

This was, of course, destruction of evidence, but it was nothing compared to the lengths the conspirators would go to in order to cover up the assassination.

The Redbird Incident

The Redbird incident was another attempt to implicate Oswald and Cuba. On November 20, two days before the Kennedy assassination, three people showed up at Redbird airport where Wayne January owned a plane rental business.[2656] Oswald was one of the three visitors, but he stayed in the car. The other two were a man and a woman who attempted to rent a plane in such a way that Wayne January refused to rent them a plane.[2657] They claimed they wanted a plane for two days later (the day Kennedy was to be assassinated), but they ask such suspicious questions as to make it obvious they planned to hijack the plane to Cuba.[2658] They weren't trying to rent a plane. They kept asking such leading questions that no sane person would rent them a plane. The idea was to leave a witness who would later come forward after the Kennedy assassination and say that Oswald tried to rent a plane to hijack to Cuba. After the assassination, Wayne January recognized Oswald.[2659] He contacted the FBI and reported the incident.

This creates a problem for the FBI. Once again, since they had abandoned the 'Cuba put Oswald up to it' angle in favor of the 'lone nut' angle, they now had a problem.[2660] Just like the Silvia Odio incident, how could Oswald be a lone nut if there were other people there with him trying to rent a plane to hijack to Cuba? So, the FBI decided to simply change the date on which Wayne January claimed to have met with the three to July.[2661] This allowed the FBI to claim that Wayne January must have been mistaken since the incident took place four months earlier, instead of just two days before Kennedy was assassinated. This evidence tampering did not come to light until 1991 under the Freedom of Information Act (FOIA).[2662]

The Ralph Yates Incident

On November 20, two days before the Kennedy assassination, Ralph Leon Yates picked up a hitchhiker. The hitchhiker was going to the Texas School Book Depository with a long package he claimed was curtain rods.[2663] The hitchhiker wanted to talk about the upcoming visit to Dallas by President Kennedy and he asked Ralph about the possibility of shooting the president while he was in town. Then they talked about the motorcade route.[2664] When he got to work, Ralph told a coworker, Dempsey Jones, about the rather odd conversation he had with the hitchhiker.[2665] After the Kennedy assassination Yates gave his statement to the FBI. Unfortunately, they already had Buell Wesley

Frazier on the record as giving Oswald a lift the morning of the assassination with a package of 'curtain rods.'[2666] Two Oswalds with 'curtain rods' was one too many. Somebody in the conspiracy had screwed up. Now they had a problem.[2667] They tried to get Buell Wesley Frazier to change his story, but he stuck to it. He had given the real Oswald a lift. Frazier worked with Oswald, so there was no mistaking who he had given a ride to. The FBI did everything they could to get Ralph Yates to change his story, but he wouldn't budge. Both men were given polygraph examinations. Yates was given three of them.[2668] On January 2, 1964 Hoover told FBI Agent Gordon Shanklin that Yates had not yet been completely discredited and to deal with the problem. Ever the loyal Gestapo, Shanklin obeyed orders. The next time Ralph Yates was brought in for questioning, on January 4, 1964, he brought his wife with him.[2669] When he passed his polygraph test for the third time, they told him to go immediately to Woodlawn Hospital, a mental institution, so the two of them drove to Woodlawn, where Ralph was admitted.[2670] Yates was 28 years old when he picked up the hitchhiker. He died eleven years later in a mental hospital at age 39. The last eleven years of his life were a hell of mental hospitals, drugs, torture by electric shock treatments and repeated attempts to get him to change his story.[2671] He never changed his story and died for telling the truth.

The Rifle Range Incidents

The rifle range incidents were additional attempts to implicate Oswald. The conspirators wanted to leave witnesses who would come forward later to say that Oswald was seen at rifle ranges around the Dallas area practicing in the weeks before the Kennedy assassination. Each time the Oswald double doing the shooting would do something annoying or otherwise memorable so the witnesses would be sure to remember him.

On September 28, 1963 Oswald asked Malcom Price for help sighting his rifle at the Sports Drome rifle range.[2672] The conspirators once again painted themselves into a corner with too many Oswalds being in two places at the same time. Oswald was supposed to be in Mexico City trying to get Russian and Cuban visas at their respective embassies at the same time he was getting his rifle sight adjusted at a Dallas rifle range.[2673] Howard Price claimed to have seen Oswald on November 10 at the Sports Drome rifle range. He said that Oswald asked him for help sighting the scope on his rifle.[2674] Price said he saw Oswald practice his shooting two other times as well.[2675] Garland Slack saw Oswald at the Sports Drome rifle range on November 10 and 17. He remembered 'Oswald' because the man shot at Slack's targets, clearly in an effort to be remembered.[2676] On November 10, 1963 Oswald was with his wife and daughters at the Paine residence. This is the same time the Oswald double was at the Sports Drome rifle range being seen by witness Garland Slack.[2677] The second time he was there he showed up without a gun and had someone pass a rifle over a fence to him. The rifle was wrapped in rags or something.[2678]

On November 20, 1963 two witnesses saw 'Oswald' at another rifle range while the real Oswald was working at the Texas School Book Depository.[2679] The FBI dealt with the problem of too many Oswalds by telling the owner of the rifle range to keep his mouth shut.[2680]

On November 16, 1963 the Oswald double is seen by Dr. Wood and his son at another local rifle range. Wood's 13-year-old son remembered very specifically that the rifle had a different scope than the one the Warren Commission said he was using.[2681] The FBI tried persistently to get the boy to change his story.[2682]

The Mercury Dealership Incident

On November 9, 1963 another Oswald impersonator test drove a new car at a Dallas Lincoln-Mercury dealership. He also drew attention to himself in a way that would help the people he saw to remember him later. He drove the car recklessly, so the car salesman would remember him.[2683] He said he didn't have the money now but would soon be coming into some money. He was refused credit and complained that he might have to go back to Russia to buy a car.[2684] The 'Oswald' who came to the Mercury dealership was only five feet tall.[2685] Oswald was five feet, eleven inches tall.[2686] The man said his name was Lee Oswald.[2687] The Warren Report dismissed the Mercury dealership incident as unimportant.[2688]

Al "Guy" Bogard was the salesman who had talked to "Oswald." He positively identified Lee Harvey Oswald as the man who had come to test drive the car.[2689] Unfortunately for Bogard, Oswald was positively identified as being somewhere else at that date and time, so Bogard became another problem for the authorities to deal with.[2690] They repeatedly 'interviewed' Bogard, including once in a Dallas jail cell on December 17, 1964, and gave him a lie detector test.[2691] He was harassed and beaten and eventually driven to suicide.[2692] He was found dead of an apparent suicide on February 15, 1966.[2693]

The Gunsmith Incident

Another attempt by the conspirators to create an incident which would cause a witness to come forward later with incriminating evidence against Oswald was the gunsmith incident. Someone named Oswald brought a rifle into a gunsmith to have a telescopic sight fitted. The problem for the conspirators that this created was that, on the other hand, they were telling the public that Oswald bought a rifle which already had a scope attached. Unless the authorities found another Oswald in the Irving or Dallas area who had a scope mounted, then this was evidence of a conspiracy.[2694]

The evidence, having been planted a month earlier, was brought to light by having 'someone' make an anonymous call, on the same day that Oswald was murdered by Jack Ruby, to the FBI and a television station to say that Oswald had his rifle scope worked on at a gun shop in Irving, Texas.[2695] The gunsmith in Irving, Texas, Dial Ryder, found a repair ticket with the number 1A374 that was for mounting a scope on a rifle. This all worked as the conspirators expected, creating more incriminating evidence against Lee Harvey Oswald, until they "found" the Mannlicher-Carcano rifle Oswald was alleged to have used to kill Kennedy. The customer paid $4.50 for drilling and $1.50 for bore sighting the weapon.[2696] The gunsmith drilled three holes for the scope. The Mannlicher-Carcano only required two holes to mount a scope.[2697]

Once they traced the rifle back to the mail-order firm in Chicago who sold it, they confirmed that the rifle came with a scope already attached.[2698] Once the Dallas police realized this problem, they first tried to say Oswald had two rifles. Then they just said it was a misunderstanding and tried to sweep the issue under the rug.[2699] They never mentioned it again.[2700]

The Abilene Incident

Abilene Texas is about 200 miles west of Dallas. Less than a week before the assassination, Harold Reynolds of Abilene picked up a note left for his neighbor, Pedro Gonzalez.[2701] The note was an urgent request to call Lee Oswald, and had a couple of Dallas phone numbers to use. When handed the note, Gonzalez became nervous and immediately used a public telephone.[2702] After the Kennedy assassination, Reynolds would recall seeing Lee Harvey Oswald with Gonzalez and other anti-Castro Cuban exiles. Gonzalez was president of an anti-Castro group known as the Cuban Liberation Committee.[2703] Clearly, Gonzalez understands that his involvement in the Kennedy assassination has left him in danger. Gonzalez left town and was last heard of in Venezuela.[2704]

Marina Oswald

Marina Oswald was Lee Harvey Oswald's Russian wife. How they met is interesting. Marina had an uncle, Ilya Prusakova, who was a colonel in the Soviet MVD, which would be similar to the U.S. FBI. She was assigned by the MVD to get to know the fake defectors from the U.S. who were in Russia and report back. Oswald was the second one she met.[2705] They were married a few weeks later, about the same time Oswald started the process of returning to the U.S.[2706] Oswald brought Marina and their new baby back to the U.S. with him. He does this easily, even though he was a defector at the height of the Cold War.[2707]

Once back in the U.S., as mentioned earlier, they are 'befriended' by first George de Mohrenschildt and then by Ruth Paine (see the respective sections on George de Mohrenschildt and Ruth Paine). Oswald and Marina have another daughter, but they don't get along. Their marriage was rocky. Immediately after the Kennedy assassination, Marina was taken into custody by the authorities and denied access to a lawyer.[2708] She was threatened with deportation if she did not cooperate.[2709] This included threatening to keep her children here in the U.S. to be raised as orphans.[2710] Marina agreed to say whatever they wanted her to say. She was kept in seclusion, away from the press.[2711] In the short run, she testified against Oswald for the Warren Commission. In the long run, her story changed multiple times and the value of her testimony diminished accordingly.

Oswald Before the Shooting

On November 9, 1963 Lee was happy and watched college football that afternoon. Meanwhile, at the same time, an Oswald look-alike applied for a job at the Southland Hotel.[2712] He asked how tall the building was and if you could see downtown.[2713]

Another Oswald look-alike visited Hubert Morrow, the manager of Allright Parking Systems.[2714] Morrow recalled that a man identifying himself as Oswald applied for a job as a parking attendant.[2715] Morrow first wrote the man's name as Lee Harvey "Osborne" and the man corrected him that it was "Oswald."[2716] The real Oswald did not usually spell out his middle name of Harvey and typically referred to himself as Lee Oswald.[2717]

The Mannlicher-Carcano

There is no proof that Oswald owned a rifle. Common sense will tell anyone who is paying attention that, if Oswald had wanted to buy a rifle to shoot the president with, he could have just purchased a rifle for cash at any number of places in the Dallas area, and it would have been completely untraceable.[2718] In 1963 that was how it worked. The Warren Report expects us to believe that Oswald was stupid enough to mail order a rifle under the alias of Alec Hidell and then have an Alec Hidell identification on him when he was arrested shortly after Kennedy was killed. Oswald was a lot of things, but he wasn't stupid. There is a good chance that Oswald did not own the rifle that the Warren Report said he owned.

The rifle the authorities claimed was his was not the rifle that was ordered from the mail-order company in Chicago.[2719] The Warren Report claims Oswald ordered an Italian Mannlicher-Carcano rifle on March 12, 1963 from Klein's Sporting Goods in Chicago.[2720] The Warren Report also tells us that Oswald used a coupon from an ad in *American Rifleman* and had it sent to his post office box, which was in the name of A. Hidell.[2721] The ad and coupon which was in the Warren Report did not appear until November of 1963, and it was in *Field and Stream*.[2722] If the ad did not appear until November of 1963, it was clearly not used by Oswald to order a rifle to shoot Kennedy. Also, the ad which did appear in *American Rifleman* was for a different model than the one we're told Oswald used.[2723]

The ammunition for the Mannlicher-Carcano had been manufactured decades earlier. The fact that the bullets were no longer being made for it was one of the reasons the rifle was so cheap. A test of Mannlicher-Carcano ammunition showed that, out of one batch of twenty rounds of this type of ammunition, seventeen of them failed to fire.[2724] And we're asked by the Warren Commission to believe that Oswald got three in a row to work, the only three he fired. The odds against this are so high as to rule it out as a realistic possibility.[2725]

The Warren Report tells us the Mannlicher-Carcano was well-oiled. There was no rifle cleaning equipment found among Oswald's possessions.[2726]   Ammunition isn't sold by the bullet.   No other ammunition for it was ever found, except for the three empty cartridges planted at the scene and the one live round in the chamber.   We are asked to believe that, somehow, Oswald only had four bullets with him that day.

The Motorcade Route

In November of 1963, President Kennedy was unhappy with Vice President Johnson for several reasons. One of them was the fact that Johnson would not patch up the differences he was having with feuding factions of the Democratic Party in Texas.[2727] This was on purpose – Johnson did not want to patch it up. He wanted Kennedy to have to come to Dallas to patch it up. And Johnson insisted on the Trade Mart instead of the Women's Building because that would force the motorcade to make the slow left turn in front of the Texas School Book Depository which would allow Dealey Plaza to become a shooting gallery.[2728] The intersection of Elm and Houston had high buildings on three of the four corners, and the grassy knoll just to the west of the Texas School Book Depository had a few good sniper positions. As usual, Johnson had someone else do the dirty work for him. In this case he had Texas Governor John Connally be the one to insist to Kennedy aide Kenny O'Donnell that it had to be the Trade Mart.[2729] Later, the choice would be blamed on O'Donnell, but that was just a smoke screen.[2730]

Once the decision on the Trade Mart instead of the Women's Building was made, Secret Service Agent Forrest Sorrels made the final adjustment, likely on orders from above, to add the abrupt dogleg turn in Dealey Plaza to the motorcade route.[2731] Kennedy was now set to make a hard left turn in front of the Texas School Book Depository. The big, long presidential limousine would have to slow almost to a stop to make the turn. This would make Kennedy a sitting duck in the shooting gallery which has been prepared with multiple sniper teams.

The Warren Report said that Oswald acted alone. Had this been true, he would have had to know in advance that the motorcade would be going right by the Texas School Book Depository so he could try to get a job there. This is, of course, impossible. This doesn't work even if we assume that Oswald did not plan that far in advance and just saw that Kennedy was in town and decided, on short notice, to murder the president. The route that was published in the Dallas newspapers did not show the motorcade route going past the Texas School Book Depository. The closest the route came to the depository was an impossible shot from the depository while the limousine was speeding by a block away on Main Street.[2732] Even this route was not published in the newspaper until the morning of the assassination and there was no way Oswald could have seen it before he got to work at 8:00 AM.[2733]

As author Joachim Joesten put it in his book, *OSWALD, ASSASSIN OR FALL GUY?*:

> "Yet we are asked to believe, we are told by the Dallas police, that he arose that morning firmly resolved to kill President Kennedy and that he took along his rifle for that purpose, on the bare chance that the motorcade might happen to pass nearby."[2734]

The Curtain Rods

We are also asked to believe that Oswald brought a sniper rifle with him the morning of the assassination. Buell Wesley Frazier gave Oswald a ride to work that day. He said Oswald had a long package with him, wrapped in brown wrapping paper.[2735] It was raining that morning. When he got out of the car, Oswald held the package under his armpit, keeping it dry by cupping one end in his hand and tucking the other end under his armpit. That made it two feet long, at most.[2736] This means that the package that Oswald brought into the Texas School Book Depository that day could not possibly have contained the Mannlicher-Carcano rifle that the Warren Commission claims Oswald had in the package.[2737] The Mannlicher-Carcano's longest piece is much too long for Oswald to have been able to carry this way. The longest of the pieces of the Mannlicher-Carcano is almost 34.8 inches, or almost three feet long.[2738] Even if it had been disassembled, it could not have fit in the package Oswald had with him that morning. Because his story didn't fit their 'Oswald did it' theory, they tried to get Frazier to change his story, but he stuck to it.[2739] Frazier was grilled multiple times and given polygraph examinations, but he would not change his story.[2740]

Oswald After the Shooting

The police performed a paraffin test on Oswald. He tested positive only on his hands, which is natural since he has been handling boxes all morning.[2741] He tested negative on his cheeks, which meant he has not shot a rifle, particularly not one like the Mannlicher-Carcano.[2742] Since not even the government was attempting to claim Oswald shot Kennedy with pistols in both hands, Oswald did not kill President Kennedy. Based on the evidence, he couldn't have done it.

The Photographs

Ruth Paine allowed her house to be searched when she was not even there. During this search the incriminating photographs of Oswald were allegedly found. They show Oswald holding the sniper rifle in one hand and some communist literature in the other, with a pistol on his hip. I believe the photos were fake and were planted (see the subsection on the mainstream media for a more detailed analysis of the photographs). The photographs show most of Oswald's face (except his chin) on the body of someone else. There are a number of obvious problems with the photographs. The face is the exact same on more than one photograph, which makes it look like whoever created the images only had the one shot of Oswald's face to work with. Oswald had a pointed chin. The man in the images has a square jaw. There is an obvious line between the chin and the rest of the face. The angles of sunlight are different between the face and the rest of the photographs. The photographs were taken on a bright, sunny day. The day we are told they were taken was actually cloudy. There are many more problems with the photographs. The bottom line, in my opinion, is that the photographs were created for a single purpose. They were made to convict Oswald in the court of public opinion. In that regard the pictures were a stunning success. Printed on the cover of *Life* magazine, they made Oswald look guilty. He looked like a communist kook who was proud to pose with weapons. This is what the conspirators needed. They needed the average person to view Oswald as guilty, so they could get away without anyone looking too closely at what really happened.

Oswald Tries to Contact His Handler

Oswald decided on November 23, 1963 to contact his handler. This was a drastic step only to be taken in extreme circumstances, and for Oswald, the situation he found himself in qualified. Oswald was trying to contact his handler through a 'cutout' named John Hurt in Raleigh, North Carolina.[2743] They never put the call through.[2744]

The Stripping of the Protection from JFK in Dealey Plaza

The normal protections provided to President Kennedy were systematically stripped away so the snipers in Dealey Plaza would have clear shots. The protective top on the limousine was removed. The Secret Service agents on the back bumper of the limousine were called off. The number of motorcycles was cut down from twenty-four to four. The four remaining motorcycles were told to stay to the rear of the limousine. The Dallas Police and 1,000 Dallas County Sheriff's deputies were all told to stand down. The Dallas police officers were told that the Secret Service would take over at Main and Houston so that Kennedy would be covered while going through Dealey Plaza. However, there was not one real Secret Service agent stationed in Dealey Plaza. There were several fake Secret Service agents in Dealey Plaza, but the only real agents were in the motorcade itself and they all continued on to Parkland with the motorcade.

Authors Roger Stone and Mike Colapietro, in their book *THE MAN WHO KILLED KENNEDY: THE CASE AGAINST LBJ*, point out that:[2745]

> "Likewise, LBJ's relationship with Secret Service Director Rowley is also underestimated by many of those examining the JFK murder. They both served in the National Youth Administration under Roosevelt and were friends beginning in the forties. There is no other way to explain the serious lapses in Secret Service protocol during the Kennedy trip to Dallas on November 22, 1963."[2746]

According to author Phillip Nelson in his book *LBJ: MASTERMIND OF THE JFK ASSASSINATION*:[2747]

> "Rowley knew the men in his agency whom he could trust to carry out his orders, even the most bizarre of them, which would all but abandon the president in Dealey Plaza."[2748]

James Rowley was former FBI. He had worked for Hoover before he transferred to the Secret Service.[2749] So, Rowley was close to both Hoover and Johnson. This fact helps to explain how he could have been persuaded to be part of the conspiracy.

The normal number of motorcycles surrounding the presidential limousine was twenty-four. The day before the assassination the president had been in Houston and this was how many motorcycles surrounded the limousine.[2750] They rode on all sides to screen the president from potential harm. In Dallas the number of motorcycles was cut down to four.[2751] And of the four who were left, Rowley had them stay to the rear of the presidential limousine.[2752]

Dealey Plaza was an ideal place for an ambush.[2753] This is why Johnson arranged to have Kennedy drive through it. The intersection at Houston and Elm has tall buildings on three corners. The sharp left turn from Houston to Elm would force the long presidential limousine to slow to a crawl for the shooters.[2754] U.E. Baughman was the former head of the Secret Service. He told journalists that it was a basic rule that people be kept out of upper floors of tall buildings, yet the authorities gave no such orders.[2755]

Dallas County Sheriff Bill Decker also told his men to stand out in front of the building at 505 Main Street instead of providing security for the motorcade.[2756] Decker specifically told his over 1,000 deputies:[2757]

> "You are in Dealey Plaza as observers. No matter what you see or hear, take no law enforcement action. You are there in respect for the presidency of the United States as observers and not law enforcement officers."[2758]

The Dallas police were also told to end their protection at the entrance to Dealey Plaza, the intersection of Main and Houston. They were told that the Secret Service would take over from there.[2759]

One of the Secret Service agents, Donald Lawton, can be seen in a YouTube video.[2760] He is ordered off the rear bumper of the limousine as it is pulling out of Love Field the day of the assassination. His job was to ride the rear bumper as added protection for the president and he can't believe he is being ordered off.[2761]

In another of the too many 'strange coincidences' of the Kennedy assassination, a dozen of the most experienced members of the White House Secret Service detail were either on vacation at the last minute or had transferred out in the sixty days before Kennedy was murdered.[2762]

President Kennedy was a sitting duck. He never had a chance. This is because the conspirators could not take the chance that Kennedy would emerge from Dealey Plaza alive. If he was just wounded, they would all be rounded up and executed for treason. In those days the electric chair was still in use. Treason rated a ride on 'old sparky.' As long as Kennedy died, Johnson could be counted on to run the cover-up and they would all get away with it. As it turned out, that is what happened.

Johnson Ducks Well Before the Shooting Starts

Johnson knew what was coming and he ducked well before the shooting started. Johnson normally rode sitting up like Miss America in a parade, waving and smiling at everyone. He wanted to be seen. Not this time. Johnson not only ducked, he got lower and lower as the car got nearer and nearer to Dealey Plaza. By the time the motorcade entered Dealey Plaza he was invisible to the crowd from the car he was riding in because he was crouching down practically on the floor of the convertible.

This chapter is organized into five sections:

1. The positioning of the sniper teams – here is my best estimate of where the different sniper teams were positioned to shoot from in front of and in back of the presidential limousine

2. The number and direction of shots – there is still, to this day, an ongoing debate about how many shots were fired and from which direction – here I give my best estimate

3. Fake Secret Service agents in Dealey Plaza – describes how, even though there were no Secret Service agents in Dealey Plaza, there were Secret Service agents in Dealey Plaza that day

4. Where was Oswald? – describes Oswald's movements inside the Texas School Book Depository during the shooting – proving that he was not on the sixth floor when Kennedy was shot

5. Roger Craig and the station wagon – describes how Dallas County Sheriff's Deputy Roger Craig saw either Oswald or his double get into a Nash Rambler station wagon in Dealey Plaza

Johnson knew what was coming because he had set it up. By the time the motorcade got to Dealey Plaza, Johnson was so low in the convertible he was not visible from the sidewalk. Mary Mitchell was a citizen who had come out to see the parade and she described Johnson's car as "Senator Yarborough's car" because he was the only politician visible from the sidewalk as the car went by.[2763] The cops riding alongside Johnson's car also noticed Johnson duck well before the shooting started. Officer J.B. Martin said:[2764]

> "According to the guys who were escorting his car in the motorcade, our new president is either one jumpy son of a bitch or he knows something he's not telling about the Kennedy thing ... he started ducking down in the car a good thirty or forty seconds before the first shots were fired."[2765]

Officer J.B. Martin had his statements suppressed for 30 years.[2766]

An Associated Press photographer, James "Ike" Altgens, took a photograph of Johnson's car just before the shooting started. Everyone else in the car is visible except Johnson, who has ducked down so far as to be out of sight.[2767] Because of this photograph, Johnson later had to come up with a story line to explain his actions. The yarn he came up with was that Secret Service Agent Jack Youngblood had leaped into the car and sat on him to protect him.[2768] This was a lie. Youngblood said he did not remember doing this, but if the new president wanted to give him a medal for his actions he was not going to get in a fight with President Johnson over it. Youngblood would have been visible in the photograph if he was sitting on Johnson. This was something Johnson made up later. I urge anyone who is interested to look for themselves at the photograph taken by Altgens. It is easily found with a Google search using a few key words like 'altgens photo Johnson convertible.' You can see for yourself that Johnson is so low as to be invisible below the top of the door of the convertible. In addition, Senator Yarborough said that Johnson made up the story about Youngblood leaping into the car and sitting on him. Yarborough said:

> "It just didn't happen. ... It was a small car. Johnson was a big man, tall. His knees were up against his chin as it was. There was no room for that to happen."[2769]

Had this happened, Agent Youngblood would be visible in the photograph. He is not, as anyone who looks at the photograph can see. Johnson also had his car moved farther back in the order of motorcade. Normally he rode right behind the president's limousine. In this case he had his car moved back one and had a carload of Secret Service agents in between his car and Kennedy's.[2770] Before the assassination, White House aide Joseph Shimon told his daughter that Johnson had asked for extra security. He then quizzed her on what that meant and praised her when she said that meant that something was going to happen and that Johnson knew about it in advance.[2771]

The Positioning of the Sniper Teams

Snipers work in a team of two consisting of a spotter and a shooter. No one seems to know how many sniper teams were in Dealey Plaza that day, or where they were positioned. Here is my best estimate. We know for sure there was at least one shooter behind the fence at the top of the grassy knoll. There may have been two, one dressed as a Secret Service agent and one dressed as a cop. Ed Hoffman saw the fake Secret Service agent shoot Kennedy and Jean Hill ran to the grassy knoll and saw a cop putting away a rifle just after Mary Moorman had just taken a polaroid photograph of what appears to be a cop shooting at Kennedy.[2772] We also know there was a shooter in the Texas School Book Depository. I think there were also shooters at the base of the grassy knoll and in the Dal-Tex building. There are also reports of a shooter on the County Records building on the southeast corner of the intersection of Elm and Houston in Dealey Plaza. Let's start with the shooter in the Texas School Book Depository.

The Texas School Book Depository

Multiple witnesses saw gunmen on the sixth floor of the Texas School Book Depository. The presidential limousine was allowed to make the agonizingly slow left turn from Houston onto Elm. Had Oswald been a lone nut gunman, the time to take the shot would have been right before the limousine made that left turn. Had whoever was firing from the southeast corner window of the book depository building been a lone gunman, that would have been the ideal time to take the shot. When the limousine slowed down to make the left turn, it was going the slowest it was going to go. The limousine was right below the window and the shooter had a clear frontal shot. It would have been the easiest shot and, for a lone shooter with only a few shots, it would have been the time to take that crucial first shot, the one that could be aimed carefully. For a lone shooter, there was no reason to wait until the limousine was accelerating away down Elm Street before opening fire.

As author Mark Lane put it in his book *LAST WORD: MY INDICTMENT OF THE CIA IN THE MURDER OF JFK:*[2773]

> "He was so close that he could have thrown the rifle at the president."[2774]

Clearly Mark Lane was using humor to make his point, but I've stood at the sixth-floor window and looked down and I agree with his point. Had Oswald been a lone shooter at that window, that would have been the time to take the shot. The reason that shot was not taken was because there was more than one shooter. Had he taken that shot, the limousine might have sped off and, if the shot had missed, they would all end up getting the electric chair for treason. They waited until the limousine had rounded the corner and was in the kill zone where they didn't have to depend on one shooter. They had multiple shooting teams lined up from front and back and the grassy knoll sniper position provided an even easier shot than the shot from the book depository. The shot from the grassy knoll didn't even require a scope because it was almost at ground level with the street where the depository shot was from the sixth floor.

Witnesses Arnold Rowland and Ruby Henderson saw two men in the now famous window in the southeast corner of the sixth floor of the Texas School Book Depository.[2775] One of them had a rifle with a scope and a dark complexion. The witnesses thought he was either Black or Mexican.[2776]

Witness Richard Randolph Carr saw a man on the top floor looking out of the second window from the southeast corner of the book depository building.[2777] Then, when he got down to the street, he saw the same man was running toward him and watched him getting into a Nash Rambler station wagon before the wagon went on to pick up 'Oswald' by the book depository.[2778]

Another witness, Carolyn Walther, saw two men with a gun on the sixth-floor window.[2779] Caroline Walther looked up at the book depository from across the street and saw a man with a rifle looking for the motorcade, and another man behind him was wearing a brown suit coat.[2780] Across the street from Caroline Walther was James Worrell, who stood under the book depository window and looked up to see a rifle barrel sticking out.[2781] And after the shooting he saw a guy in a suit coat run out the back of the book depository building.[2782]

The shooter with the dark complexion could have been David Sanchez Morales or one of the Cubans like Sergio Arcacha Smith or one of the Novo brothers. The other one may have been Mac Wallace. We know Mac Wallace was there because he left his fingerprint there.[2783] Author Barr McClellan found a fingerprint examiner to do a blind examination (with no idea of either the crime or the owner of the fingerprints) and the print matched so Mac Wallace left a fingerprint on the sixth floor of the Texas School Book Depository.[2784] We know Morales was involved because he recruited E. Howard Hunt to join the conspiracy.[2785]

We know about Arcacha Smith from Rose Cherami and we know about the Novo brothers because they drove there with E. Howard Hunt and Marita Lorenz.[2786]

Author Barr McClellan said in his book *BLOOD, MONEY & POWER: HOW L.B.J. KILLED J.F.K,* that Mac Wallace was there with a dark suit and a Secret Service badge.[2787] McClellan also said Wallace had a shooter there with him.[2788]

Witness James Tague said that no one did anything for six or seven minutes after the shooting.[2789] He said that, if Oswald was in the Texas School Book Depository, he had all the time in the world to just walk away.[2790] The building was open for fifteen or twenty minutes before it was sealed.[2791] Bystanders and police picked up evidence and handed it over to 'Secret Service agents.'[2792] They rapidly lost control of the crime scene.[2793]

The Fence at the Top of the Grassy Knoll

Witnesses Bill Newman and his wife were interviewed by ABC affiliate WFAA and they claimed the shots came from the grassy knoll.[2794]

Several police officers thought the shots came from the knoll area. The reaction of Dallas County Sheriff Bill Decker, riding in front of the president, was to call on the radio "Notify Station Five to move all available men out of my department back into the railroad yards." The railroad yards were just behind the fence at the top of the grassy knoll where the House Select Committee on Assassinations (HSCA) acoustics experts placed a gunman.[2795]

In all 277 of the more than 700 witnesses to the shooting have been identified, and 107 of these 277 have given their statements as to the origin of the shots that killed the president.[2796] 75% or 77 of the 107 reported that at least one shot came from the president's right front, the area of the grassy knoll with the wooden fence on top.[2797]

Fifty-five witnesses saw and heard shots from the grassy knoll.[2798] This is a slope of grass just to the west of the Texas School Book Depository with a fence at the top of the hill and a parking lot behind the fence. At the time of the shooting the now famous grassy knoll was in front and to the right of the presidential limousine. The government did its best to convince everyone that there were only three shots and that they had all come from the sixth floor of the Texas School Book Depository, which was behind and well above the presidential limousine at the time of the shooting.

This is what happens when you kill the president of the United States in broad daylight in front of a crowd in a major city. There are witnesses.

Witness Frankie Riley, an electrician at Union Terminal, "Heard three shots which seemed to come from the trees on the north side of Elm Street at the corner up there."[2799]

Another witness, Thomas J. Murphy, heard two shots and said they came from a spot just west of the depository, that is the grassy knoll.[2800]

Mary Woodward, Maggie Brown, Aurelio Lorenzo and Ann Donaldson all worked at the Dallas Morning News. They were all on the grassy knoll in front of the fence. They spoke of "a horrible, ear-shattering noise coming from behind us and a little to the right." They were ignored by the Warren Commission even though their story was printed in the next day's paper.[2801]

Witness John Chisolm said "I looked behind me to see if it was a fireworks display." His wife Mary said "It came from what I felt was behind us." They were also on the grassy knoll in front of the fence and also not called by the Warren Commission.[2802]

Witness A.J. Milliken, who had been on the grassy knoll, said of the final gunfire "I hear two more shots come from the arcade between the bookstore and the underpass. And then three more shots came from the same direction, only farther back. Then everybody started running up the hill." Mr. Milliken was also not called by the Warren Commission.[2803]

Witness Jean Newman was also on the grassy knoll and said that "The shots came from my right." Mrs. Newman was also not called by the Warren Commission.[2804]

Abraham Zapruder was standing on the concrete colonnade on the grassy knoll making his now famous film. He said that one of the shots came from the grassy knoll.[2805]

Six witnesses said they smelled gunpowder from the grassy knoll. Three of them were in the motorcade; the mayor's wife, Mrs. Cabell, Senator Ralph Yarborough and Congressman Ray Roberts. Police Officer Earl Brown, on duty at the railway bridge, and Mrs. Donald Baker, at the other end of the knoll also said they smelled gunpowder.[2806] Smelling gunpowder from the motorcade as it was going by on the street level would not have been possible if the only firing had come from the sixth floor of the Texas School Book Depository, sixty feet above and well behind the limousine. Patrolman Joe Smith ran to the grassy knoll when the firing started. He also smelled gunpowder at the top of the grassy knoll.[2807]

From a high vantage point on a nearby building, witness Jesse Price saw a man in his twenties, wearing a white shirt and khaki pants, run toward the railroad siding while carrying something.[2808]

Tom Tilson was an off-duty Dallas policeman. He was driving by Dealey Plaza with his daughter when he heard the news on the radio. Then he said:[2809]

> "The man came down that grassy slope on the west side of the triple underpass - had a car parked there. A black car. He threw something in the backseat and went around the front hurriedly and got in the car and took off. I saw all of this and I said 'That doesn't make sense. Everybody running to the scene and one person running from it.'"[2810]

He chased after the car and lost it in traffic, but not before he managed to get the license plate number.[2811]

The Dallas Morning News reported on November 23, 1963 that O.V. Campbell, a vice president of the book depository, was standing with Superintendent Truly in front of the building when the shots were fired.[2812] He ran toward the grassy knoll west of the building where he thought the shots had come from.[2813]

Beverly Oliver was on the south side of Elm, across the street from the knoll, and she filmed the entire assassination with an 8mm camera.[2814] She also saw the puff of smoke.[2815] Then her film was confiscated by men claiming to be government agents.[2816]

Witness Ed Hoffman was watching from the side of the Stemmons Freeway.[2817] He saw a stocky man in a dark blue suit and a black hat shoot President Kennedy.[2818] He then tossed the rifle to another guy and waited for the reaction from the crowd.[2819] The shooter was confronted by a policeman and he showed the cop some identification, then mingled with the crowd, then got in a station wagon and left.[2820] As for one of the shooters at the top of the knoll, witness Ed Hoffman saw a guy in a suit take a shot at Kennedy and then toss his rifle to someone who quickly left. Then he pretended to be a Secret Service agent when a policeman confronted him.[2821] This would preclude the shooter who took up a position behind the fence at the top of the grassy knoll from being one of the French shooters. A guy with a French accent would have a hard time passing himself off as a Secret Service agent.

The shot from the front was with a hunting round. It came from the grassy knoll. Whether it came from the fence at the top of the grassy knoll or the sewer opening at the base of the grassy knoll is not yet known for sure.

Emmet Hudson was a groundskeeper who said the shots came from the grassy knoll.[2822]

Reporter Cheryl McKinnon and others saw puffs of smoke.[2823]

Lee Bowers

Lee Bowers was a railroad man in a tower in the railroad yard behind the fence at the top of the grassy knoll. He had an excellent view of the parking area behind the fence. He saw three cars come into that area twenty minutes before the Kennedy assassination.[2824] First was a station wagon, second was a 1957 Ford driven by a guy with a microphone and third was an Impala.[2825] Ed Hoffman would later say that one of the shooters left in the station wagon.[2826] James Files claims to have driven Chuck Nicoletti's Impala to Dealey Plaza.[2827] And he smoked Pall Mall cigarettes, which is the same brand of cigarette butts found in abundance at the scene of the shooting from behind the fence.[2828] James Files also claims to have taken the head shot from behind the fence on the grassy knoll.[2829] This is hard to verify and it may or may not be true. However, a home movie taken at the time shows Chuck Nicoletti's Impala was parked where Files says he parked it.[2830] The 2003 interview with James Files can be seen on YouTube.

Bowers describes the same two men that Ed Hoffman does. One is stocky and wearing a suit and the other is slim and casually dressed. He notices them because he knows everyone else.[2831] These two were unknown to Bowers. Then, over by where the two were, something happens. He also said that the two men were using walkie-talkies.[2832]

Bowers also said that something like a flash of light or smoke drew his attention to the fence at the top of the grassy knoll when Kennedy was shot.[2833]

Gordon Arnold

Gordon Arnold had recently joined the U.S. Army. He was on leave after having completed basic training.[2834] He had a home movie camera with him and was looking for the best place to watch the motorcade. He decided the triple underpass was the best location, but was stopped by a guy who said he was Secret Service.[2835]   From there he went to the grassy knoll and began filming when the motorcade came by. He ended up in the line of fire from the fence behind him and, on instinct from his training, dropped to the ground when the shooting started.[2836]   When he hit the ground he was seen by Senator Yarborough.[2837]   Then two guys in police uniforms confiscated his film.[2838] He went to Fort Wainwright, Alaska, where he was stationed, and kept his mouth shut until 1978 out of fear for his life.[2839]

Sam Holland

Sam Holland was on the railway bridge over Elm Street when the motorcade approached. He said he saw a puff of smoke coming from the fence at the top of the grassy knoll when he heard four gunshots.[2840] He also said he saw "a plainclothes detective or FBI agent or something like that" before the shooting.[2841]

Holland said:

> "I looked over to where the shots came from and I saw a puff of smoke still lingering underneath the trees in front of the wooden fence."[2842]

Asked where the shots came from, he said:

> "Behind that picket fence, close to the little plaza. There's no doubt whatsoever in my mind."[2843]

Holland saw a puff of white smoke from the grassy knoll, and Holland also saw a station wagon backed up to the fence.[2844]   This was the third car down, right where he saw the smoke.[2845]   And it looked like someone had been standing there for a long time and there was mud on the back bumper of the wagon like someone had stood on it, or cleaned their foot on it.[2846]

Mary Moorman and Jean Hill

Jean Hill and Mary Moorman were watching the motorcade from the south side of Elm, across the street from the Texas School Book Depository. Mary was taking Polaroid pictures and handing them to

Jean Hill. Once the shooting happened, Jean Hill ran across the street to chase after the shooter, she was stopped by men who identified themselves as Secret Service agents who then confiscated the pictures.[2847] The last picture Mary Moorman took was at the instant of the shooting.[2848]

Mary Moorman took four or five Polaroid pictures.[2849] The last one captured the shooter dressed as a cop.[2850] Fortunately, she had not given that picture to Jean Hill, and she was able to keep it.[2851] It can be found online now as the Moorman picture. The Warren Commission avoided Mary and her picture.[2852] Jean Hill was close to the limo, and she had the first few Polaroids that Mary took.[2853] After the shooting she saw a man in a brown coat running, later she would realize it was Jack Ruby when she saw him shoot Oswald on television.[2854] Then she saw a cop behind the fence putting a rifle away and then two men who claimed to be Secret Service grabbed her and confiscated her pictures.[2855] Then she was taken away to be interrogated for hours about what she saw and heard.[2856] She was warned to change her story and was threatened if she did not.[2857] Jean Hill finally snuck out after eight hours of this abuse.[2858] Her boyfriend was B.J. Martin, one of the motorcycle cops in the motorcade.[2859] She gave him her notes and someone broke into his locker and stole the notes.[2860] She was harassed for months by the FBI to change her story, which she never did, and there were threats and attempts on her life.[2861] Then Arlen Specter "interviewed" her while he tried to get her to change her story, and threatened to have her put in a mental institution. [2862] Officer B.J. Martin was Jean Hill's boyfriend (and he was married at the time) and his statements were suppressed for 30 years.[2863] He saw Johnson duck 30-40 seconds before the shots were fired.[2864]

The Sewer Opening at the Base of the Grassy Knoll

There is a drain on Elm Street, built right into the curb, right in front of where Kennedy was shot. The maze of huge drain conduits under Dallas empty into the Trinity River, which is either a trickle or dry most of the time.[2865]

Authors Richard Belzer and David Wayne, in their book *DEAD WRONG*, said that it appears that CIA officer Bill Harvey came up with the idea of using French assassins because they would be harder to trace back to the conspirators.[2866] This led to Michele Mertz, who often used the name of Jean Suetre. Mertz was in Dallas that day, using the name of Suetre.[2867]

Years after the assassination it came to light that one of the shooting teams was French. Author Phillip Nelson, in his book *LBJ: THE MASTERMIND OF THE JFK ASSASSINATION*, said that Jean Suetre was in Dallas and was then deported, and that Michele Mertz and Michele Roux were also there.[2868] Exactly which French shooters were there is still not clear. Authors Belzer and Wayne, in their book *DEAD WRONG*, said that Mertz was in Dallas that day, using the name of Suetre. Marcello and Trafficante were both familiar with the Corsican mafia.[2869]

> Note: Author Richard Belzer thought Michele Mertz was using the name of Jean Suetre. Author Phillip Nelson wrote that he thought it was Jean Suetre using the name of Michele Roux and that Lucien Sarti used the name of Michel Mertz.[2870] There still appears to be some confusion on this point. It reminds me of the term 'wilderness of mirrors' which Angleton was fond of.

Author Jerome Corsi, in his book *WHO REALLY KILLED KENNEDY?*, said that in 1976 an FOIA request unearthed a CIA document from the spring of 1964 regarding a Corsican assassin who was in Dallas the day of the assassination and was detained and deported.[2871] Souetre said he wasn't ever in the U.S. and he was in France on the day of the assassination, so it was Mertz who was using his name.[2872]

What we know for sure is that Eugene Dinkin picked up secure United States military traffic between the conspirators while he was stationed in France.[2873] This would seem to corroborate the assertions that there were French shooters. It would also make sense that the conspirators, many of whom had French connections, would look for shooters who would be harder to trace back to them.

The French shooters could have come through the mafia or the CIA. Marcello had a heroin business going through French diplomats.[2874] Allen Dulles had French connections, as did others on the CIA side of the conspiracy. Dulles had an entire army stashed in France since the end of World War II. Maurice Gatlin had served as a bag man for the CIA, Clay Shaw and Guy Banister.[2875] He had brought cash to France to pay for the assassins to kill Charles de Gaulle. Author Noel Twyman said that Bill Harvey and David Morales also had connections to the French mafia.[2876]

Author Phillip Nelson said, in his book *LBJ: THE MASTERMIND OF THE JFK ASSASSINATION*, that Christian David was offered the contract to kill Kennedy but he turned it down and Lucien Sarti accepted the contract. Lucien Sarti had two accomplices and used the name John Marty.[2877] He also said that Johnny Roselli helped to recruit the French shooters and the mafia shooters that took up positions in the Dal-Tex building and/or the County Records building.[2878] In addition, Nelson said that the French shooters who took up positions in front of the president used hunting rounds.[2879] Clearly this fits with the evidence. The kill shot that came from the front, the one that entered Kennedy's temple or forehead at the hairline, came out the back of his skull and made a hole the size of a baseball or an orange. This is consistent with an unjacketed hunting round. Military bullets have copper jackets so that they don't splinter and cause as much internal damage. Hunting rounds are made to splinter and cause more internal damage.

At some point in the planning, U.S. military code operator Eugene Dinkin picked up the message traffic going back and forth between the conspirators and their contacts in France who were arranging for one of the shooting teams.[2880]

The French shooter may have been the one in the sewer opening built into the sidewalk at the base of the grassy knoll. This is because that sniper position offered both concealment and a means of escape. The huge drain conduits under there empty into the Trinity River which is dry most of the time.[2881] A French guy is not going to be able to pass himself off as Secret Service or as a Dallas cop, so he could not have been one of the snipers shooting from behind the fence at the top of the knoll. However, a French shooter could have taken a shot from the drain opening and then gotten away using the sewer system. A French accent would not have been a problem that way.

The Dal-Tex Building

The Dal-Tex building is at the same intersection of Houston and Elm in Dealey Plaza as the Texas School Book Depository. It sits across Houston Street from the Depository. The depository is on the west side of Houston and the Dal-Tex building is on the east side. To make room for an entrance to the parking lot behind the depository, the depository is set back a bit from Elm Street. This setback gives the Dal-Tex building a clear view of Elm and makes it an ideal place for a sniper to shoot at a stretch limousine which has just made a slow left turn from Houston onto Elm. Any shots from the Dal-Tex building would have to go right past the Texas School Book Depository to reach Kennedy on Elm Street. This appealed to the conspirators, who were planning on claiming that Oswald shot Kennedy from the Texas School Book Depository. A shot from the Dal-Tex building would seem to have come from the Texas School Book Depository.

Eugene Brading (a.k.a. Jim Braidon) arrived in Dallas on November 21, the day before the assassination, and checked into suite 301 of the Cabana hotel with Morgan Brown.[2882] Brading was also at H.L. Hunt's office building in Dallas the day before the assassination. H.L. Hunt was one of the oil barons.[2883]

Author Jerome Corsi, in his book *WHO REALLY KILLED KENNEDY?*, says:[2884]

> "Roselli claimed he knew a gunman shooting from the grassy knoll fired the first shot that hit JFK. This first shot supposedly went through the windshield of JFK's limousine and hit him in the throat. Roselli claimed that the second and third shots came from gunman Charles Nicoletti, a Giancana hit man, who was shooting from the third floor of the Dal-Tex building behind JFK. Roselli claimed the second shot hit JFK in the back and the third shot hit Connally. Finally, according to Roselli, the fourth shot fired and the second shot from the grassy knoll was the fatal headshot that killed JFK."[2885]

Witnesses heard shooting from the Dal-Tex building, and the guy who came out of that building had no explanation for being there.[2886] The clamor of the onlookers forced local authorities to arrest him and he was taken to the sheriff's office where he was held for questioning, but they did nothing and then released him without even keeping a record of his name.[2887] This may have been Chuck Nicoletti, Sam Giancana's hitman who is reported to have been shooting from the Dal-Tex building that day. I'm not sure. Then a second man, Eugene Hale Braiding, was arrested coming out of the Dal-Tex building.

Just after the assassination of President Kennedy, Eugene Hale Brading was noticed by the elevator man in the Dal-Tex building as not someone he recognized and he ran to find a policeman who detained Brading for questioning.[2888] Brading gave them his alias name 'Jim Braidon' and claims he was visiting his parole officer. These were both lies, but they worked and he was released.[2889]

The Number and Direction of Shots

The number of shots is of critical importance. The Warren Commission said there were only three shots. They said this because, with a bolt-action rifle, Oswald could only have gotten off three shots in the six seconds of actual shooting. The Warren Commission had to bend over backwards to fit all the bullet damage into three shots. Any more than three shots meant more than one shooter, and the Warren Commission would do anything to avoid admitting that there was more than one shooter and therefore a conspiracy. The whole point of the Warren Commission was not to find the truth, it was to claim that there was no conspiracy, so they were forced to do whatever was necessary to fit all the damage into three shots.

The direction of the shots is of equally critical importance. The Warren Commission said there was only one shooter and he was behind the limousine. The Warren Commission also did whatever they had to do to bury any evidence of shots from the front. Shots from the front meant more than one shooter and therefore a conspiracy. The whole point of the Warren Commission was to convince the public that there was no conspiracy, so shots from in front of the limousine had to be avoided at any cost.

Author Anthony Summers, in his book *NOT IN YOUR LIFETIME*, documents that:[2890]

> "In spite of being shot himself in the hail of gunfire, Governor Connally, an experienced hunter, remembered that, because of the rapidity of the shots, "The thought immediately passed through my mind that there were two or three people involved or more in this, or that someone was shooting with an automatic rifle."[2891]

The Magic Bullet Theory was made up by the Warren Commission when they had evidence of many more than three shots. They weren't trying to find the truth, they were trying to cover it up. They were trying to claim that Oswald was a lone shooter with a bolt-action rifle. This limited them to three shots in the time shown on the Zapruder film. So, they had to do several things. They had to ignore or bury evidence of more than three shots. They also had to ignore or bury evidence of shots from the front because Oswald was behind Kennedy when he was shot. And when evidence came up that they couldn't ignore or bury, they had to combine multiple shots into one. This was how the fairy tale of the Magic Bullet was born. Arlen Specter took the front entry in Kennedy's throat and combined it with the rear entry wound in his right shoulder and all of Governor Connally's multiple wounds and claimed that they all came from a single, Magic Bullet. Never mind that Kennedy's throat wound was from the front, it could be changed to an exit wound, and they did. Never mind that Kennedy's shoulder wound didn't line up with the throat wound, it could be moved, and they did. Never mind that Kennedy's shoulder wound was shallow. Facts didn't matter. What mattered was that they had a story to tell the public that didn't involve a conspiracy.

Governor Connally never agreed with the Magic Bullet theory. His story never changed. He said all along that he and Kennedy were hit by two different shots. He said that a shot hit Kennedy, then a shot hit him (Connally) and then a third shot hit Kennedy again. He also said:[2892]

> "We heard a shot. I turned to my left and the president had slumped. He said nothing. As I turned I was hit and I knew I was hit badly. I knew the president had been hit and I said "My God, they're going to kill us all." Then there was a third shot, and the president was hit again. It was then that Mrs. Kennedy cried out."[2893]

Governor Connally's testimony is important because he was a very credible witness and he was positive that he and Kennedy were hit with separate bullets. His wife, who was there also, corroborated his testimony.[2894]

There is other evidence that the Magic Bullet theory is nonsense. The wound in Kennedy's back was in his right shoulder, as can be seen from the shirt and coat he was wearing. Congressman Gerald Ford, who was on the Warren Commission, later *moved* the shoulder wound so that it would be easier for the Warren Commission to lie and say that a single Magic Bullet hit both Kennedy and Connally, but the truth is they were hit with at least three separate shots. The placement of the shoulder shot, which can clearly be seen from the bullet holes in the jacket and shirt, are hard proof that the Magic Bullet theory is invalid.[2895]

Witness Eugene Aldredge and a reporter named Carl Freund noticed a bullet mark on the sidewalk a few days after the assassination and contacted the FBI. A week later he noticed that someone had tried to fill in the mark. Based on the direction of the mark, it could not have been made by a shot from the book depository window.[2896] The authorities were desperate to keep the shot count down to three and they could not afford any more shots.

A bullet hit the grass about 100 yards from the sixth-floor southeast window of the Texas School Book Depository.[2897] It landed near a manhole cover on the south side of Elm.[2898] The authorities digging up the bullet were photographed multiple times and one of the photographs shows one of the government agents slipping it in his pocket.[2899] In addition to the photographs, there were numerous witnesses and journalists there to record the event and it was reported in the newspapers.[2900] Author Donald Byron Thomas has a detailed account of this in his book *HEAR NO EVIL*. Any additional shots were bad news for the authorities, so they used the simple expedient of ignoring the evidence.

During the shooting, bystander James Tague was struck by a fragment of a bullet that first hit the curb. He reported the incident to Dallas Deputy Sheriff E.R. ("Buddy") Walthers and Dallas Police Officer Clyde Haygood.[2901] Two journalists, Tom Dillard and James Underwood, also took photographs of the mark on the curb.[2902] Tague was interviewed by FBI Agent Kreutzer.[2903] The authorities did their best to bury the incident. They did this because the last thing they needed was to have to account for more shots. Not until July of 1964 when Martha Jo Stroud, Assistant U.S. Attorney for Dallas, sent an official letter to the Warren Commission with a photograph, did the Commission ask the FBI to look into it, which they reluctantly did.[2904] The authorities eventually had to admit it existed. There was too much evidence to bury it.

The Tague fragment appears to have been one of the factors putting pressure on the Warren commission when Arlen Specter came up with the Magic Bullet theory. There were obviously more than three shots, and with the missed shot that struck the curb and then Tague, they had to come up with *something* to explain them all. This was when Specter came up with the idea of combining multiple shots into one, and why we now we have the Magic Bullet fiction.

Nurse Audrey Bell said that four to six fragments came out of Governor Connally.[2905] This is important because later the Warren Commission will show a whole bullet and claim it as the Magic Bullet. They will claim that it went into and out of Kennedy and Connally multiple times and still ended up whole. This is absurd. Kennedy's wounds don't line up neatly like the Warren Commission would like them to. This is why Gerald Ford had to 'move' the entrance wound in Kennedy's back. Anyone can Google an image of the Magic Bullet, otherwise known as CE 399 (Commission Exhibit #399), and see for themselves that there are no fragments missing from it.

Several accounts also have Kennedy hit in the head from behind just before he is hit from the front by the kill shot. This may or may not be true. It's hard to tell at this point.

The kill shot clearly comes from the right front, enters at the hairline in Kennedy's forehead or temple and takes off part of the back of his head. The two motorcycle cops riding to the left and rear of the limousine are both splattered with blood and brains. Bobby Hargis was one of the cops who got splattered. He was the closest of the two to the left and rear. To his left and rear was B.J. Martin. He was also splattered. Hargis said he was struck so hard by splatter that he thought he himself had been hit.[2906] Hargis then dropped his bike and charged up the grassy knoll.[2907]

The kill shot knocked a piece of Kennedy's skull onto the trunk of the limousine. This was recovered almost immediately by Jackie and given by her to Dr. Marion Jenkins at Parkland Hospital.[2908] There was another piece of skull, now referred to as the Harper Fragment. It was found by Billy Harper in the street about twenty feet or so behind and to the left of where Kennedy was hit.[2909]

As near as I can tell there were nine or ten total shots, five from the back and four or five from the front. There may have been two or more shooters from the right front. At the top of the grassy knoll there are accounts of one dressed as a cop and one dressed as a Secret Service agent. There may also have been a shooter in the above-ground sewer opening built into the curb at the base of the grassy knoll. There were also shooters in the Texas School Book Depository and the Dal-Tex Building. A total of four or five shooting teams each taking up to a few shots, depending on whether or not they had a good shot to take. The conspirators couldn't take the chance that Kennedy would emerge from Dealey Plaza alive. If Kennedy dies there then Johnson will be in charge and they can cover up any evidence that doesn't fit the fairy tale that Oswald was a lone shooter, which is in fact what happened. If Kennedy emerges only wounded then they all go to prison or the electric chair. Knowing this, they had enough sniper teams to make sure Kennedy was dead. They understood that killing the president of the United States is not something you do halfway.

Here is my best estimate of the number and direction of shots:

Shots from the back:

- Hit JFK in the back – hole in back of coat and shirt (#1)
- Hit the curb and a bystander, James Tague (#2)
- Hit John Connally from behind (#4)
- Hit JFK in the head from behind (#5)
- Hit the chrome strip on the top of the windshield (#7)

Shots from the front:

- Hit JFK in the throat – may be the windshield shot (#3)
- Hit JFK in the forehead – right front by hairline (#6) – this was the kill shot
- Recovered from the grass (#8)
- Scar on the sidewalk (#9)

Estimates differ on which shots happened in which order. Here is my estimate:

Shots in order:

1. The first shot hit JFK in the back – may have come from the top of the County Records building
2. The second shot hit the curb and then James Tague
3. Then JFK got hit in the throat with the third shot – this may have been from the sewer and come through the windshield – this would have been a shot from the front
4. Connally was hit in the back (#4) from the side as he turned to see what was going on with JFK
5. Kennedy was hit four times – once in the back from behind (#1 overall) – once in the throat from in front (#3 overall shot) and two closely-spaced shots to the head once the limo stopped (#5 and #6 overall) – one from behind and one from in front
6. See #5 above – the two closely-spaced shots to the head once the limo stopped are #5 and #6 overall – one from behind and one from in front - #6 would be the second of those two shots
7. another (#7) from behind hit the chrome molding strip above the windshield[2910]
8. another from the knoll was recovered from the grass (#8)
9. Scar on the sidewalk (#9) from the front (not from the depository or the rear)

Note – there were also some fragments (a separated jacket and core) found in the limousine which may have come from a tenth shot, but it's hard to be sure at this point. CE 567 is the separated jacket and core.[2911]

There also might have been a first shot that missed the limousine entirely. Virginia Baker and Royce Skelton both testified to seeing a first shot bounce off the pavement just behind the car, as did Secret Service Agent Warren Taylor and witness Harry Holmes.[2912]

CE 567 (Commission Exhibit # 567) consists of fragments found in the limousine which are likely to be from Connally's wounds, and CE 580 is a bullet recovered from the limousine itself.[2913]

In my opinion there were multiple sniper teams each taking multiple shots from both the front and rear.

Fake Secret Service Agents in Dealey Plaza

The CIA provided fake Secret Service with credentials created using the same equipment used by the CIA to make credentials for real Secret Service agents. The only real Secret Service agents in Dealey Plaza at the time of the shooting were with the motorcade and they stayed with the motorcade as it went on to Parkland Hospital. The fake Secret Service agents were able to control events long enough for the shooters to get away. At least one of the fake Secret Service agents was one of the shooters. Then they quietly left before the real Secret Service agents showed up about twenty minutes after the shooting. During that critical time, they were able to confiscate film from many witnesses and stall the police and sheriff's deputies who rushed to apprehend the shooters.

There was a fake Secret Service agent behind the fence at the top of the grassy knoll. He shot Kennedy, handed off his rifle, and then presented his credentials to a police officer. Two other men exited the Texas School Book Depository Building just after the shooting. They also had authentic Secret Service credentials.[2914] In 1963 the CIA printed the credentials for the Secret Service. How handy. The CIA appears to have provided the authentic credentials for the fake Secret Service agents.[2915] This did not become known until a FOIA request was finally complied with in 2007.[2916]

Author Barr McClellan, in his book *BLOOD, MONEY & POWER*, says that Johnson's fixer in Austin, Ed Clark, called Johnson aide Cliff Carter to arrange for the real credentials for the fake Secret Service agents in Dealey Plaza that day.[2917] Authors Richard Belzer and David Wayne, in their book *DEAD WRONG*, say that it was Chauncy Holt who drove Chuck Nicoletti to Dallas and dropped off the Secret Service badges that day.[2918]

Dallas Police Officer Joe Smith and a deputy sheriff saw a man behind the fence at the top of the grassy knoll, so Smith drew his pistol and confronted the man.[2919] The man showed Smith his Secret Service credentials. Smith said:

> "This character produced credentials from his hip pocket which showed him to be Secret Service. I've seen those

credentials before and they satisfied me and the deputy sheriff, so I immediately accepted that and let him go and continued our search around the cars."[2920]

Seymour Weitzman was a Dallas County Deputy Constable who rushed behind the fence at the grassy knoll where he encountered "Secret Service agents."[2921] Dallas Police Department Sergeant D.V. Harkness went around to the back of the Texas School Book Depository to make sure it was sealed off six minutes after the shooting. He also found some "Secret Service agents" there.[2922]

Witness Gordon Arnold had his film confiscated by a fake Secret Service agent.[2923] Jean Hill had all of the pictures Mary Moorman had taken and given to her confiscated by fake Secret Service agents.[2924]

The Warren Commission showed no interest at all in the fact that there were fake Secret Servicemen with real credentials in Dealey Plaza that day. When you're not running a real investigation, there is no need to do any real investigating. That would just open a can of worms.

Other than the Secret Service agents who were in the motorcade, all of whom stayed with the motorcade as it went on to Parkland Memorial Hospital, there were no real Secret Service agents in Dealey Plaza.[2925] The first one to arrive was Forrest Sorrels at least twenty minutes after the shooting.[2926]

Secret Service Agent Abraham Bolden said that, after the assassination, the Secret Service went to the trouble and expense of replacing all agent credentials with a new type of credentials.[2927] They knew they had been compromised and they had no idea who had real Secret Service credentials, so they had to replace them all.

Where was Oswald?

Lee Harvey Oswald was in the lunch room on a lower floor of the Texas School Book Depository when Kennedy was shot. He was seen there by multiple people.

A coworker of Oswald's named Williams saw him on the sixth floor in the late morning well before the shooting (which happened later at 12:30 PM) as the work crew was knocking off early to go watch the parade.[2928] At 11:50 another coworker named Gibbons saw Oswald on the first floor in the 'Domino room' where the employees ate lunch.[2929] A foreman named Bill Shelly saw Oswald on the first floor at 11:45 or

11:50, and Eddie Piper spoke to Oswald right at Noon, again on the first floor.[2930] At this same time, between Noon and 12:15, another employee, Bonnie Ray Williams, ate his lunch on the sixth floor near what will later be known as the 'sniper's nest' and sees no one else.[2931] Just after Noon Oswald tells Piper he is going to the second floor lunch room to get a Coke, and he is seen there at between 12:15 and 12:20 by Carolyn Arnold.[2932] By this time two of the actual assassins are spotted by multiple witnesses at the sixth floor southeast window, one of them with a rifle.[2933] Most of the witnesses who see them assume the snipers are with the Secret Service protection detail for the president.

Oswald ate lunch in the 'Domino room' on the first floor of the Texas School Book Depository. He was there with James Jarman, Jr. and Harold Norman.[2934] After eating lunch Oswald went to the second-floor lunchroom where there was a Coke machine to get a Coke. He was drinking it when Kennedy was shot at 12:30 PM. Ninety seconds after Kennedy was shot, a police officer confronted Oswald in the lunchroom with a Coke in his hands.[2935] Police Officer Marion Baker had been on a motorcycle when President Kennedy was shot. He thought the shots had come from an upper floor of the Texas School Book Depository, and he ran into the depository and almost immediately confronted Oswald.[2936] This confrontation between Oswald and Officer Baker took place sometime between 12:31 and 12:32. Oswald's supervisor, Roy Truly, had rushed in with the officer. Baker turned to Truly and said "Do you know this man? Does he work here?" Truly said "Yes." Baker immediately turned around, went out of the lunch room and continued climbing the stairs.[2937]

Oswald was spotted at various times at various places around the Texas School Book Depository by the people he worked with. Author James DiEugenio, in his book *RECLAIMING PARKLAND*, goes through each of the times when Oswald was spotted in the Texas School Book Depository, tracking his movements around the time of the Kennedy assassination. Then he compares those to the Warren Commission's analysis of those same times and places, and they are different. Not by a lot, but they were different. He concludes:[2938]

> "Those are not random mistakes in the recording of important testimony. In each dispute, the original testimony has been altered in one direction: it allows the Commission the leeway to put Oswald on the sixth floor. Without the alterations, you can't. Between Williams on the sixth floor at 12:20, Arnold on the first floor at 12:25, and Adams on the stairs right after the shooting, Oswald's placement on the lower floors at the time of the murder is all but puncture proof. Another witness,

Jack Dougherty, was on the fifth floor at the time of the shooting. Once he heard a shot, he took an elevator to the sixth floor. As revealed in the Adams testimony, that elevator is within feet of the stairs. He did not see Oswald either."[2939]

Oswald was charged with firing a bolt-action rifle at Kennedy from the Texas School Book Depository, but no one saw him shoot Kennedy, and he was seen in the lunchroom minutes before and after the shooting.[2940]

Carolyn Arnold was a secretary for a vice president of the book depository. As such, she knew Oswald.[2941] She saw him in the lunchroom between 12:15 and 12:20.[2942] Had Oswald been intending to shoot the president, he would have been upstairs, as the motorcade was scheduled to pass by the Texas School Book Depository at 12:25.[2943] In fact, witness Arnold Rowland and his wife did see snipers at that time, apparently waiting for the president, in the now famous sixth-floor window on the southeast corner facing Elm Street.[2944] They assumed the men with a rifle were there to protect the president. Later, Hoover had the FBI interview Mrs. Arnold again and get a second statement that said "I did not see Lee Harvey Oswald at the time President Kennedy was shot."[2945] The Warren Commission then did not call her to clarify her testimony, and only used her revised second statement.[2946]

Victoria Adams and her friend Sandra Styles, having watched the president get killed, immediately used the only flight of stairs to go see what else was happening.[2947] Had Oswald, as the Warren Commission later claimed, rushed down those same stairs to be calm and collected when confronted by the police, Victoria and Sandra would have noticed.[2948] They did not see anyone else on the stairs.

Roger Craig and the Other Oswald

Roger Craig was a Dallas County Deputy Sheriff who saw Oswald (or the Oswald double) get into a Nash Rambler station wagon that stopped at the grassy knoll right after the assassination. This created evidence of a second Oswald. He was also one of a group of officers searching the Texas School Book Depository when they found a Mauser and not a Mannlicher-Carcano rifle. His testimony did not fit the party line and he was harassed and fired from his job in an attempt to get him to change his testimony. When that failed they murdered him to shut him up.

Deputy Sheriff Roger Craig had been told to stand in front of the courthouse on Main Street with the other deputies.[2949] When the shots were fired he ran toward the gunfire in Dealey Plaza.[2950] While looking for evidence on the south side of Elm he heard a whistle and, as he said:[2951]

> "I turned and saw a white male in his twenties running down the grassy knoll from the direction of the Texas School Book Depository building. A light green Rambler station wagon was coming slowly west on Elm Street. The driver of the station wagon was a husky looking Latin with dark wavy hair wearing a tan windbreaker type jacket. He was looking up at the man looking toward him. He pulled over to the north curb and picked up the man coming down the hill. I tried to cross Elm Street to stop them and find out who they were. The traffic was too heavy and I was unable to reach them. They drove away going west on Elm Street."[2952]

The man he saw getting into the station wagon was either Oswald or the Oswald double. Later, Craig would positively identify the man as Oswald, not knowing there was an Oswald double. Craig had been attracted by their rush to leave the scene while everyone else was rushing to get to the scene.[2953] In an effort to do his job he reported the incident to a 'Secret Service agent,' also not knowing at that time that the Secret Service agents in Dealey Plaza were imposters.[2954]

Other witnesses saw the same incident as Roger Craig. Helen Forrest saw Oswald get into the Rambler station wagon, as did James Pennington, who were both standing in Dealey Plaza at the time.[2955] Oswald was also seen by two passing motorists, Marvin Robinson and Roy Cooper. Robinson had to jam on his brakes when the station wagon stopped in front of him to pick Oswald up.[2956]

Deputy Roger Craig then went on to search the Texas School Book Depository, and was with Deputy Eugene Boone and Deputy Constable Seymour Weitzman when they found a 7.65mm German Mauser rifle with a 4 by 18 scope.[2957]

Later that afternoon Craig found out they were holding a man suspected of killing the president, so he called homicide chief Captain Will Fritz who invited him to come to his office to look at the suspect.[2958]

James Douglass, in his book *JFK AND THE UNSPEAKABLE*, recounts the conversation:[2959]

> "Shortly after 4:30 PM Craig looked into Captain Fritz's office and identified the man being held there as the same man

he had seen running down the grassy knoll to the station wagon – Lee Harvey Oswald.

As Fritz and Craig entered the office together, Fritz said to Oswald "This man saw you leave."

Oswald became a little excited – he said "I told you people I did."

Fritz said, in a soothing tone of voice, "Take it easy son. We're just trying to find out what happened."

Then Fritz asked Oswald "What about the car?"

Oswald leaned forward and put both hands on Fritz's desk. He said "That station wagon belongs to Mrs. Paine. Don't try to drag her into this."

Then he leaned back in his chair. He said, in a low voice "Everybody will know who I am now."

Craig has emphasized that Oswald made this statement in a dejected tone of voice – he said "Everybody will know who I am now." As if his cover had just been blown."

Douglass further points out that, at this point Fritz ushered Craig from his office and Fritz got an urgent phone call from Sheriff Decker to come see him immediately, which he did.[2960] We don't know what was so urgent that Decker had to discuss with Fritz. However, after that Fritz would deny that Craig had even been in his office, much less identified Oswald.[2961]

It turns out that, in the meantime, they had decided that Oswald had gotten away on a bus at the same time as the incident happened on Elm Street with Oswald getting into the station wagon. There were even more witnesses on the bus, so they decided to go with the 'bus Oswald' story instead of the 'station wagon Oswald' story. The 7.65mm German Mauser rifle had also, in the meantime, magically changed into a 6.5mm Italian Mannlicher-Carcano rifle. Roger Craig now knew too much, all from just doing his job. So now they had to cover things up, and Roger Craig had to be made to change his story. He had become a 'loose end' to be dealt with.

Craig was never called by the Warren Commission, and he was fired from his job in 1967 because he continued to tell the truth.[2962] That same year he was asked to testify in Jim Garrison's prosecution of Clay Shaw for the Kennedy assassination and there were two attempts to shoot him, one of which grazed his head.[2963] After that he was almost killed by a bomb that went off when he started his car.[2964] Having survived that attempt he was forced off the road by two men who had waited for him and ended up in the hospital for a year.[2965] On May 15, 1975 Roger Craig was shot to death before he could testify in front of the House Select Committee on Assassination.[2966]

The Aftermath and the Cover-up Including the Intimidation of Witnesses

The conspirators had plenty of time to plan out what would happen once the shots rang out in Dealey Plaza, and they were well prepared. They immediately pounced on anyone with a camera and confiscated their film.[2967] They had men posing as Secret Service agents to do this and stall anyone, police officers or bystanders, who might try to chase or arrest one of the shooters.[2968] These guys obviously knew what was coming and they made note of who had a camera so they could be right there to confiscate the film immediately after the shooting.[2969] There is credible evidence that one of the shooters behind the fence at the top of the grassy knoll handed off his rifle to an accomplice and then posed as one of the fake Secret Service agents. After making sure their accomplices got away these fake Secret Service agents then quietly left the scene before any real Secret Service agents could show up about twenty minutes after the shooting.[2970]

This chapter is organized into six sections:

1. The government lie machine – describes how the government set up a giant washing machine to put evidence in one end and have it come out the other end supporting the party line

2. The aftermath and the cover-up gives specific examples of evidence that was either manufactured or buried and witnesses who were intimidated to change their stories

3. The shooting of Tippit – describes how Oswald was framed for the murder of Dallas Police Officer J.D. Tippit and goes into detail on evidence tampering and witness intimidation

4. The Texas Theatre – describes how two Oswald's were arrested at the Texas theatre – one was taken out the front and booked and the other was taken out the back and released

5. The Oswald double flies away – describes how the Oswald double was spirited out of Dallas that evening by the CIA – based on several witnesses including one who was on the flight with him

6. The Zapruder Film – describes how the Zapruder film was modified and then buried out of sight for as long as possible

because it contained evidence of shots from the front and therefore of a conspiracy to assassinate Kennedy

The Government Lie Machine

The government set up a machine, like a giant funnel. At one end they fed in the witnesses and the evidence of what happened and at the other end came out the fairy tale that Oswald was a lone assassin. At each level of the funnel the evidence of the truth was evaluated to see if it could be ignored, changed or eliminated. This was true of witnesses and physical evidence. It started before the assassination even happened. There was an Oswald double running around doing incriminating things that could later be used to convict Oswald in the court of public opinion.

On the day of the assassination evidence was destroyed and witnesses were intimidated. Witness intimidation worked on a lot of people, and this technique was used a lot. Anyone who had seen what actually happened and wouldn't change their story fell into one of several categories. If they could be safely ignored, like Acquilla Clemons, they were. In several cases the FBI simply changed their written statements to say what they wanted them to say, like with Julia Ann Mercer and Wayne January. If they wouldn't shut up and couldn't be safely ignored there were increasing attempts at intimidation, including physical threats and attempts at murder. If these failed to intimidate the witness into either silence or changing their story, they were murdered for real. The body count eventually got to be at least fifty people.

Many people were intimidated into going along. This is understandable. Time and time again I ran across accounts of people like, Dr. Crenshaw, whose attitude was basically 'These guys just killed the president of the United States. They will not hesitate to kill little old me.' Getting a visit from government agents with official badges and being told to 'change your story or else' can be very intimidating. It's not like you can call the authorities because that's who is threatening you and telling you to shut up and go along.

And of course, Oswald himself had to be killed. Imagine how inconvenient it would have been for the conspirators to have Lee Harvey Oswald getting a real lawyer and putting up a defense that showed the case against him to be a total sham.

Physical evidence was treated the same way. Any evidence that did not fit the story line was destroyed or buried. Evidence that needed to be manufactured was created either before, during or after the assassination. As the echoes of the shots were fading in Dealey Plaza the fake cops and fake Secret Service agents were collecting film from witnesses who had cameras. Someone planted three Mannlicher-Carcano rifle cartridges on the sixth floor for the cops to find, along with the rifle itself. The Secret Service agents at Parkland Hospital started destroying crime scene evidence by scrubbing out the limousine. At some point Kennedy's body was switched into a shipping casket so it could be sent ahead to Bethesda and have some work done on it to obscure the evidence of shots from the front. The doctors working on the autopsy in Bethesda were ordered not to trace the track of the bullets through the body. These orders were given by military brass. This is because those tracks would show that there had been shots from the front. Many of the official photographs and X-rays were modified, the originals destroyed or buried and replaced with fakes that fit the story line. Even these "official" photos and X-rays were never given to the Warren Commission, which had to make due with sketches made by artists who themselves were not allowed to see even the faked autopsy pictures.

Near the end of this funnel, making any last-minute changes, was the Warren Commission. The government lie machine served up "witnesses" and "evidence" to the Warren Commission that had passed through the various filters in the funnel so that what came out the other end of the Government Lie Machine was "evidence" that could be massaged into the Warren Report and the transformation was almost complete. The final step was for the Big Lie to be sold to the public via the mainstream media. A lot of evidence of other shooters was filtered out before it got to the Warren Commission, but the Warren Commission was able to either willfully ignore evidence or try to bully witnesses into changing their stories to fit the frame-up of Oswald. The conspiracy with multiple shooters was transformed by the Government Lie Machine into the fairy tale of Oswald the lone nut shooter. The witnesses and evidence still didn't quite fit, but it was close enough that the commission was able to package the lie in such a way that it could be sold to the public by the mainstream media. And our mainstream media was willing to pitch in and help out by proclaiming the Warren Report to be something the public could have faith in. After all, our government had produced it. The mainstream media then proceeded to tell us what a great and thorough job the Warren Commission did and to label anyone who questioned this as a "conspiracy nut" so they could be marginalized.

In April of 1963, as things were heating up in Dallas, Hoover replaced the Special Agent in Charge (SAIC) in Dallas with the more loyal Gordon Shanklin.[2971] Gestapo tactics are going to be needed to intimidate witnesses. Hoover will also need someone he can depend on to destroy or fabricate 'evidence' as necessary. Once the murder of Kennedy took place, Shanklin went to work.

Author Mark North, in his book *BETRAYAL IN DALLAS*, said:

> "Shanklin employed Gestapo tactics in the hope that locals would, in Hoover's words "shut up."[2972]

Here are a few examples of how the system worked:

- Rose Cherami was simply ignored at first because she accurately predicted the assassination. Neither the FBI or the Dallas police wanted to talk to her. She was killed later.

- Victoria Adams (the girl on the stairs) was intimidated into silence and had her testimony changed because she could testify that Oswald could not have made it from the lunch room to the sixth floor and back. She kept getting visits from the authorities. She left town.

- Julia Ann Mercer had seen Jack Ruby unloading one of the shooters at Dealey Plaza an hour before the shooting so she had her testimony changed by the FBI without her knowledge.

- Domingo Benavides witnessed the Murder of Tippit by someone other than Oswald. He was threatened and intimidated but would not change his story. Then his brother (who looked very much like him) was murdered in a case of mistaken identity and he decided to change his story.

- Marina Oswald and her children were taken into custody. Marina was threatened with deportation and the loss of her children if she does not cooperate. She then starts saying anything they want and her testimony therefore becomes meaningless. Marina becomes a propaganda tool.

- Ralph Yates gave a lift to a hitchhiking Oswald who needed a ride to the Texas School Book Depository. The Oswald had a package of 'curtain rods' with him. This turned out to be one too many Oswalds with curtain rods, so Yates had to be made to change his story. He refused to change his story, so they stuck him in an insane asylum while they tortured him into an early grave.

- Acquilla Clemons saw two people, neither of them Oswald, murder Officer Tippit. There was an attempt made at intimidation, but Acquilla wouldn't change her story. Luckily for her, she could be simply ignored, so she wasn't killed.

- Lee Bowers in the rail yard tower was kidnapped and intimidated into changing his story. He was also later murdered. He had seen too much.

- Ed Hoffman witnessed one of the shooters behind the fence in the rail yard. Fortunately for him he had an uncle on the Dallas police force and his father and uncle convinced him not to go to the authorities with his story or he would be in danger.

- George Whitaker at the Ford plant was afraid to tell his story (about the hole in the windshield being a shot from the front) at the time of the assassination. He kept his mouth shut for years.

- The doctors at Parkland were intimidated into changing their story and then remaining silent. Only thirty years later did Dr. Crenshaw feel safe enough to break his silence.

- Eugene Dinkin saw the coded military message traffic going back and forth between the shooters in France and the conspirators in the United States. He was hunted down and put in an insane asylum where they tortured him with shock treatments until he got his mind right and changed his story. He later filed a lawsuit.

- Judyth Vary Baker (Oswald's girlfriend who was the lab technician in New Orleans) was warned to keep her mouth shut and keep a low profile or she would be killed, so she kept quiet for forty years.

- Richard Case Nagell tried to warn Oswald and the FBI. After several failed attempts on his life he agreed to keep quiet in return for a longer life. He was also eventually murdered.

- Wayne January refused to agree to rent a getaway plane to the conspirators. Later, when the conspirators changed the cover story to omit the Cuba angle, his testimony was not only not needed, it would point to a conspiracy. He had his written statement changed by the FBI without his knowledge.

- Robert Vinson was on the plane with the Oswald double when they flew out of Dallas the evening of the assassination. Vinson was drafted into the CIA and forced to keep quiet for decades.

- Mary Pinchot Meyer had insider knowledge and couldn't be intimidated so she was murdered.

- Dorothy Kilgallen found out too much, was going public with what she knew, and couldn't be intimidated so she was murdered.

- William Pitzer took videos and photographs of the autopsy and was planning on going public with the real story so he was murdered.

- Jack Ruby started to talk so he was murdered.

- Even George de Mohrenschildt, one of Oswald's babysitters in Dallas, was killed once he started talking.

Buell Wesley Frazier worked with Oswald at the book depository. He had given Oswald a ride to work on the morning of the assassination. He said that the package Oswald had with him could not have contained the rifle.[2973] It was simply not long enough. He was given a polygraph.[2974] He was interrogated for hours, including threats to charge him as an accomplice.[2975] Frazier would not change his story, so they then concentrated on getting Ralph Yates to change his story.

The FBI would start with subtle threats to see if that worked first. W.W. Litchfield said he saw Oswald at Ruby's club. This did not fit with the official story that Oswald and Ruby did not know each other, so his story had to be changed. He described what happened when he talked to the FBI. They told him he had to be "absolutely sure" because, if he was wrong, he could face Federal charges. On the other hand, if he was willing to say he wasn't sure, he was safe. Of course, he decided to tell them what they wanted to hear. He said he wasn't sure. Here is the conversation in his own words:[2976]

> "...when the federal agents talked to me, they said, "You know, if you say you are positive and it wasn't him, it's a

361

federal charge," and I said "Well, I'm not that positive." ...
They said, "If you give false information as to an exact
statement – "not an opinion, but if I say I'm positive, that's a
statement."[2977]

In this way the FBI got what they wanted out of Litchfield without
having to more overtly threaten him.

Mrs. Arnold had her statement changed.[2978] She had seen Oswald
eating lunch a few minutes before the assassination. She did not find
out until many years later that her statement had been changed.[2979]

Wayne January reported the Redbird plane rental incident. He had his
written statement changed by the FBI and did not find out until many
years later. By changing the date on which Wayne said the incident
happened to be July instead of two days before the assassination, the
FBI was able to dismiss his memory as mistaken.[2980] This took care of
the problem. This evidence tampering did not come to light until 1991
under the Freedom of Information Act.[2981]

The FBI also told witnesses to shut up. The *New York Times* on
December 6, 1963 reports:

> "Most private citizens who had cooperated with newsmen
> reporting the crime have refused to give further help after
> being interviewed by agents of the Federal Bureau of
> Investigation. Dallas city and county police withdrew their
> help the same way. One high officer said he wished he could
> answer questions because 'it would save us a lot of work.'"[2982]

A witness named Price who had met Oswald at a rifle range and looked
through his telescope for him was told by the FBI not to talk.[2983] He
was quoted as saying:

> "I cannot tell you a thing. If the FBI says it is OK for me to
> talk, why then I'll be glad to tell you what I know, but up to
> then it is strictly classified."[2984]

Milton Klein of Klein's Sporting Goods in Chicago, who supposedly
sold the Mannlicher-Carcano rifle to Oswald, said:

> "I've had more than enough publicity, and the FBI has warned
> me to keep my trap shut."[2985]

The FBI, of course, has no authority to tell citizens not to talk, but this
worked on a lot of people.[2986]

The last thing J. Edgar Hoover wanted was for evidence that the mafia was involved to come to light. Then David Ferrie was arrested. His library card was found in Oswald's possessions. The connection to Marcello was starting to become too obvious, so during the week of November 25 Hoover tried to shut down the FBI investigation into Marcello's organization.[2987] Later, he would shut it down completely.

Author Mark North, in his book *ACT OF TREASON: THE ROLE OF J. EDGAR HOOVER IN THE ASSASSINATION OF PRESIDENT KENNEDY*, recounts the following incident:[2988]

> "CBS producer Peter Noyes recalls a conversation he once had with ... a former member of the NBC television camera team that had covered the murders of the president and Oswald. Sometime toward the middle of the week of November 25, as interest in Ferrie was reaching a crescendo in New Orleans and Dallas, the NBC men had a discussion about Ferrie's links to Oswald and Marcello with a group of FBI agents and newsmen that he remembered everyone found most provocative. However, the FBI soon put a damper on his interest in the subject. For, immediately after the discussion broke up, one of the agents took him aside and told him that he should never discuss what they had just been talking about with anyone, 'for the good of the country.'"[2989]

The FBI's evidence tampering was not limited to witness intimidation, but extended to physical evidence. Oswald had a German Minox spy camera which was about three inches long and looked like a cigarette lighter.[2990] Dallas police found it while searching among Oswald's possessions.[2991] The FBI did not want to say 'Oswald was a spy' because he was supposed to just be a lone nut gunman, so they called it a light meter.[2992] Earl Golz was a reporter for the *Dallas Morning News* and he noticed the discrepancy in 1978 when he talked to Detective Gus Rose.[2993] Rose did the original inventory and said "I know a camera when I see it."[2994] He told Golz:[2995]

> "The thing we got at Irving, out of Oswald's sea bag, was a Minox camera. No question about it. The FBI tried to get me to change the records because it wasn't a light meter. I don't know why they wanted it changed."[2996]

In 1979 the FBI released photographs that it claimed were taken with Oswald's Minox camera.[2997]

The Aftermath and the Cover Up

The first reaction of the government agents to the shooting appears to have been to collect everyone's film. This was made easier by knowing what was coming. Knowledge that the shooting was going to take place in Dealey Plaza allowed these men to make note of who had cameras and be standing near them when the shooting started. That way they could immediately confiscate the film. This happened to Gordon Arnold, Jean Hill, Mary Moorman, Beverly Oliver and many others. Not surprisingly, this also happened when Robert Kennedy was assassinated, but more on that later.

Their second reaction was to get control of other physical evidence, like Kennedy's body and the limousine itself, and ship them off where evidence of shots from the front could be destroyed. As mentioned earlier, Kennedy's body was illegally grabbed and sent to Bethesda Naval Hospital where military doctors could be ordered around by the conspirators.

The limousine was a crime scene. It was partially cleaned while parked at Parkland Memorial Hospital while Kennedy was in the operating room and then shipped back to Washington. From there it was sent to Cleveland and Detroit to have any remaining evidence destroyed. However, several people noticed a bullet hole in the windshield and it was later confirmed to be a shot from the front.

Journalist Richard Dudman of the *St. Louis Post-Dispatch* and Frank Cormier of the Associated Press saw a hole in the windshield of the presidential limousine. Dudman published this in the *St. Louis Post-Dispatch* on December 1, 1963:[2998]

> "Another unexplained circumstance is a small hole in the windshield of the presidential limousine. This correspondent and one other man saw the hole which resembled a bullet hole as the automobile stood at the hospital emergency entrance while the president was being treated inside the building."[2999]

Authors Richard Belzer and David Wayne claim in their book *DEAD WRONG* that shot number seven hits the windshield of the limo. They also point out that:[3000]

> "The bullet hole in the windshield was observed by two Dallas police officers, Sergeant Stavis "Steve" Ellis and officer H.R. Freeman as well as journalist Richard Dudman while the limo sat parked near the emergency room at Parkland Memorial

Hospital. The bullet hole was just left of center in the front windshield. Sergeant Ellis testified that he observed a bullet hole, not chipped glass "you could put a pencil through it.""[3001]

Secret Service Agent Roy Kellerman was in the limousine and went down to the White House garage to look at the limo the day after the assassination.[3002] He saw the bullet strike on the chrome molding strip over the windshield.[3003] He tried to point out to Arlen Specter, during his Warren Commission testimony, that there were more than three shots but he was ignored because this would have blown up the 'lone nut gunman' theory. If they admitted to more than three shots, they would have to have admitted that there was a conspiracy and that was exactly what they were trying to avoid.[3004]

The History Channel ran a series called *THE MEN WHO KILLED KENNEDY.* In Episode 7 of the series called "The Smoking Guns" there is a video, now available on YouTube, of Doug Weldon, a professor at Western Michigan University, explaining how George Whitaker came to see the bullet hole in the windshield of Kennedy's limousine. Whitaker worked at the Ford plant where the car was sent to have the windshield replaced.[3005] He later said it was a bullet hole from the front. This information did not come out for years. Evidently Mr. Whitaker was concerned for his safety if he spoke up at the time it happened. I urge anyone who is interested to see the Doug Weldon video on YouTube.

The last thing the conspirators wanted was for news of a bullet coming through the windshield of the limousine from the front to get out. They sent the limousine to the Rouge plant at Ford in Detroit to have the windshield destroyed and replaced. Mr. Whitaker was smart to be concerned for his safety had he spoken up.

There was also a bullet which hit the chrome strip at the top of the windshield. The conspirators were doing their best to keep the number of shots from going past the three they claimed Oswald had shot. Any more than three shots would have meant more than one shooter and thus a conspiracy.

Authors Roger Stone and Mike Colapietro, in their book *THE MAN WHO KILLED KENNEDY: THE CASE AGAINST LBJ*, point out that:[3006]

> "A few days following the assassination, the limousine was driven by Carl Renas, the head of security for the Dearborn Division of the Ford Motor Company, to Hess and Eisenhart in Cincinnati, Ohio to replace a chrome molding strip damaged in the shooting. Hess and Eisenhart was the specialty-car company that had a hand in the car's original

design and engineering. During the transfer of the vehicle, Renas noticed that the molding had been hit "with a primary strike" and "not a fragment." He was told by the Secret Service to "keep his mouth shut.""[3007]

This was a consistent pattern. The authorities did their best to keep news of more shots from leaking out to the public. They also wanted to bury or destroy any evidence of shots from the front.

Right after the assassination there was a call on the public for evidence and eyewitness reports.[3008] Hoover needed to have an inventory of every scrap of evidence and make sure that all of it was under his control. With Shanklin in place in Dallas, Gestapo tactics can be used on witnesses to make them either shut up or change their stories. Any photographic evidence that has not already been confiscated by government agents in place in Dealey Plaza could now be collected. Much effort would be put into making sure that the number and direction of shots agreed with the official myth that Oswald was the lone shooter. Any witnesses or evidence of shots from the front would be buried. At first, people were willing to help. Their president had been brutally murdered in front of them. This was in the era before Watergate and they trusted their government. They wanted to help solve the crime. They came forward and told their stories and handed over their evidence.

Homicide captain Will Fritz got a call from Johnson, who ordered him to stop his investigation "You have your man." Fritz had been attempting to investigate the homicide of Kennedy. He halted his inquiry.[3009]

On November 22, 1963 Julius Hardie was in Dealey Plaza when he noticed two men with rifles on top of the underpass.[3010] He called the authorities and got a visit from the FBI.[3011] They buried his testimony.[3012]

Building engineer J.C. Price was on the roof of the terminal annex building on the south side of Dealey Plaza.[3013] He saw a man run from the area behind the wooden fence.[3014] Price stated that the man had something in his right hand and "was running very fast which gave me the suspicion that he was doing the shooting."[3015]

Witness Richard Carr, on the seventh floor of the new courthouse, watched as two men ran from behind the Texas School Book Depository.[3016] The men entered a waiting station wagon and speed off north on Houston Street.[3017]

Twenty-year-old James Worrell, Jr. witnessed the assassination from the corner of Elm and Houston and panicked as the shooting began.[3018]

He quickly raced northward up Houston Street where he saw a man exit from the back door of the depository and walk quickly south on Houston.[3019]

Jean Hill saw a man running or trying to get away from the top of the slope west of the book depository and she told Mark Lane that she had already given her story in an affidavit.[3020] Lane asked if she was ever at any time told not to say something or this, that and the other and she said "The only thing that I was told not to say was not to mention the man running."[3021] Lane asked why and Mrs. Hill said:[3022]

> "Well, it was an FBI or Secret Service that told me not to, but they came in to me just right after I was taken – I was there in the press room – and told me in fact – I told him it was Featherstone [a reporter on the *Dallas Times-Herald*] that told me. He [Featherstone] said, "You were wrong about seeing a man running." He said, "You didn't . . ." I told Mr. Lane that Mr. Featherstone had told me that and I said, "But I did," and he said, "No; don't say that anymore on the air." . . . And I made it clear to Mark Lane, because I mentioned his name several times. . . " Specter: "You mean Featherstone?" Mrs. Hill: "Yes; that the shots had come from a window up in the Depository and for me not to say that any more, that I was wrong about it, and I said, "Very well," So, I just didn't say anymore that I ran across the street to see the man. . ."[3023]

Featherstone was not questioned, and many others who saw someone running away were not questioned.[3024]

While the wholesale confiscation of film was going on, other government agents were posing as fake Secret Service agents to give the shooters time to get away.

Oswald was spotted at various times at various places around the Texas School Book Depository by the people he worked with. Author James DiEugenio, in his book *RECLAIMING PARKLAND*, goes through each of the times when Oswald was spotted in the Texas School Book Depository, tracking his movements around the time of the Kennedy assassination. Then he compares those to the Warren Commission's analysis of those same times and places, and they were different. Not by a lot, but they were different. He concludes:[3025]

> "Those are not random mistakes in the recording of important testimony. In each dispute, the original testimony has been altered in one direction: it allows the Commission the leeway to put Oswald on the sixth floor. Without the alterations, you can't. Between Williams on the sixth floor at 12:20, Arnold

on the first floor at 12:25, and Adams on the stairs right after the shooting, Oswald's placement on the lower floors at the time of the murder is all but puncture proof. Another witness, Jack Dougherty, was on the fifth floor at the time of the shooting. Once he heard a shot, he took an elevator to the sixth floor. As revealed in the Adams testimony, that elevator is within feet of the stairs. He did not see Oswald either."[3026]

James Rowley, the head of the Secret Service ordered Secret Service Agent Roy Kellerman to make sure he got the body to Air Force One to take back to Washington.[3027]

Three weeks after Kennedy was murdered, FBI Director J. Edgar Hoover put a stop to all investigations of the Kennedy assassination so that he and Johnson would not be exposed.[3028]

District Attorney Henry Wade was told to just charge Oswald with plain murder and go for the death penalty because it would hurt foreign relations if he alleged conspiracy.[3029] Johnson had his aide Cliff Carter call multiple times that weekend to make sure Wade got the point.[3030]

J. Edgar Hoover wanted "something issued" to convince the public that Oswald was the real assassin.[3031]

The motorcade stopped when the first shots were fired.[3032] The Warren Commission didn't want to hear about the motorcade stopping.[3033] Senator Yarborough said in his written statement that the motorcade stopped.[3034] He said later he was disappointed to find out that many other people waited to see what he had to say before they filed their statements.[3035] This is understandable. People wanted to know whether or not to lie on their statements. There were risks in telling the truth in the new country that emerged from Dealey Plaza.

Kennedy aides Kenny O'Donnell and Dave Powers were in the motorcade. They thought the shots had come from the grassy knoll, but they were told by the FBI that it couldn't have happened that way. Kenny O'Donnell said:[3036]

> "I told the FBI what I had heard, but they said it couldn't have happened that way and that I must have been imagining things. So, I testified the way they wanted me to. I just didn't want to stir up any more pain and trouble for the family."[3037]

Richard Dodd and James Simmons were railroad workers who witnessed the assassination and both said that the information they provided to the FBI was changed by the FBI.[3038] Dodd said the shots came from the grassy knoll and the FBI said he did not know where the shots came from.[3039] Simmons said there was a puff of smoke from under the tree at the top of the grassy knoll and the FBI said that he claimed the shots had come from the Texas School Book Depository.[3040]

Witness J.C. Price found out that the FBI reversed the meaning of his statements before passing them on to the Warren Commission.[3041] A number of other witnesses had all their statements converted into lies.[3042] The FBI omitted all evidence of shots from the grassy knoll.[3043] Dallas Police Chief Jesse Curry at first sent officers over to the underpass but the next day said the shots came from the book depository.[3044] Sheriff Bill Decker sent all his men to the railroad yard (Decker and Curry were in the lead car) but when he testified to the commission he was not asked and did not say where the shots had come from.[3045]

The authorities seized on a man who claimed he saw Oswald in the sixth-floor window.[3046] H.L. Brennan was a steamfitter who wasn't even looking up at the window during the shooting, but he became their star witness.[3047] Warren Commissioner Gerald Ford, in an article for *Life* magazine, featured Brennan.[3048] Brennan's foreman, Sandy Speaker, told author Jim Maars:[3049]

> "They took [Brennan] off for about three weeks. I don't know if they were Secret Service or FBI, but they were federal people. He came back a nervous wreck and within a year his hair had turned snow white. He wouldn't talk about [the assassination] after that. He was scared to death. They made him say what they wanted him to say."[3050]

Lee Bowers

Lee Bowers was a railroad man in a tower in the railroad yard behind the fence at the top of the grassy knoll. He had an excellent view of the parking area behind the fence. He saw several cars that were not supposed to be there. He saw the shooters and he saw what appeared to be a flash and a puff of gun smoke. He was a good witness. Too good. He had to be intimidated and eventually murdered to keep him quiet. It wouldn't do to have a solid witness to someone shooting at Kennedy from behind the fence at the top of the grassy knoll. Someone might think there had been a conspiracy to assassinate President Kennedy.

Lee Bowers started getting death threats after talking to the Warren Commission and to author Mark Lane.[3051] Bowers told his minister that he not had publicly told everything he knew.[3052] Bowers' friend, Walter Rischel, told reporters that Bowers had been afraid to tell what he knew.[3053] Then Bowers disappeared for a few days, and when he came back he was missing a finger.[3054] His brother Monty did not believe the excuse Lee gave for his missing finger and the lost time.[3055] Later, Bowers was murdered by being drugged when he stopped for coffee and then run off the road by another car.[3056]

Ed Hoffman Is Told to Be Quiet

Ed Hoffman was a deaf mute who had an excellent view of the fake Secret Service agent who shot at JFK from behind the fence at the top of the grassy knoll.[3057] Hoffman was watching from the side of the Stemmons Freeway.[3058] He saw a stocky man in a dark blue suit and a black hat shoot President Kennedy.[3059] The man then tossed the rifle to another guy and waited for the reaction from the crowd.[3060] The shooter was confronted by a policeman and he showed the cop some identification, then mingled with the crowd, then got in a station wagon and left.[3061]

Hoffman tried to tell the authorities what he saw.[3062] Fortunately for him, they could not understand sign language. His father Frederick understood sign language and so Ed told him.[3063] Frederick told Ed to keep it to himself, that he was in danger.[3064] When Ed still wanted to contact the authorities, Frederick got his brother, Ed's uncle Bob, to give him the facts of life.[3065] Robert Hoffman was a Lieutenant Detective on the Dallas police force, and he also told his nephew Ed to keep quiet for his own safety.[3066] Ed Hoffman survived to tell his story because of the efforts of his father and uncle.

The Mauser Rifle

The authorities found a Mauser sniper rifle in the Texas School Book Depository. They examined it and reported to the press that they found a Mauser. This was one of the rifles actually used to shoot Kennedy. Later when they realized that the official story was supposed to be that a Mannlicher-Carcano rifle was used, they sent the Mauser down the official taxpayer-sponsored black hole reserved for evidence that did not fit the party line and from then on only talked about the Mannlicher-Carcano.

A German 7.65mm Mauser rifle with a 4 by 18 scope was found on the sixth floor of the Texas School Book Depository by Deputy Constable

Seymour Weitzman, Deputy Eugene Boone and Deputy Roger Craig.[3067] Weitzman made a sworn statement which described the weapon in detail.[3068] They announced it at a press conference.[3069] There is a UPI photograph of Dallas County District Attorney Henry Wade holding up the Mauser.[3070]

The next day they said they had an Italian Mannlicher-Carcano which was 6.5mm.[3071] Dallas County Sheriff Bill Decker told all three officers to change their stories.[3072] Deputy Sheriff Boone was the first to comply, then later Weitzman agreed to recant his sworn statement.[3073] However, Roger Craig refused to lie.

Roger Craig was never called by the Warren Commission, and he was fired from his job in 1967 because he continued to tell the truth.[3074] That same year he was asked to testify in Jim Garrison's prosecution of Clay Shaw for the Kennedy assassination and there were two attempts to shoot him, one of which grazed his head.[3075] After that he was almost killed by a bomb that went off when he started his car.[3076] Having survived that attempt he was forced off the road by two men who had waited for him and he ended up in the hospital for a year.[3077] On May 15, 1975 Roger Craig was shot to death before he could testify in front of the House Select Committee on Assassination.[3078]

The conspiracy rolled on and the Mauser was consigned to history. The new star of the show was the Mannlicher-Carcano.

Julia Ann Mercer

Julia Ann Mercer saw mafia functionary Jack Ruby unloading a guy with a rifle on the grassy knoll not long before Kennedy was shot. She was stuck in traffic and got a good look at him. After the assassination she went to the authorities and, like a good citizen, reported what she saw. She picked Ruby out of a set of mugshots. She gave them her statement. Since this evidence didn't fit the 'lone nut gunman' fairy tale being peddled by the government, her testimony was altered and she was never called as a witness.

Julia Ann Mercer was stalled in traffic at 11:00 AM on the day of the assassination next to a green pickup truck parked on the north side of Elm just west of Dealey Plaza.[3079] She watched as a man pulled out a rifle case wrapped in paper and carried it up the slope.[3080] She then pulled up next to the driver, who she did not know, and they made eye contact.[3081] The driver was Jack Ruby, which she would later realize when she saw his picture in the news media after he shot Oswald.[3082]

371

When Kennedy was assassinated she gave the FBI her statement.[3083]
She later recognized Jack Ruby from his pictures in the media.[3084] The
last thing J. Edgar Hoover wanted was a statement from a credible
witness saying that Ruby was involved in the Kennedy assassination.
The authorities, controlled by the conspirators, were doing their best to
keep that connection out of public view.   Years later, when Jim
Garrison showed Julia her statements, which had been printed in the
Warren Commission exhibits, she said they had been altered.[3085]

> "They have me saying just the opposite of what I really told
> them."[3086]

> "I have no doubts about what the driver's face looked like. I
> do not know whether the other three pictures shown me were
> other men who looked like Ruby, or whether they were three
> other pictures of Jack Ruby, but they definitely showed me
> Jack Ruby and I definitely picked him out as looking like the
> driver."[3087]

> "I again recognized Jack Ruby when I saw him shoot Oswald.
> And I said to my family, who were watching TV with me
> "That was the man I saw in the truck.""[3088]

> "He was only a few feet away from me in Dealey Plaza. How
> could I not recognize Jack Ruby when I saw him shoot
> Oswald on television?"[3089]

The FBI had also said there was a sign on the side of the truck which
said Air Conditioning.[3090] Julia said:

> "Every time I was questioned, which included at least two
> times by the FBI, I clearly stated that there was no printing on
> the truck."[3091]

The statement from the official records was signed and notarized, but it
wasn't Julia's signature. She demonstrated this to Garrison by signing
her name. Julia said:[3092]

> "Neither of the signatures on the two pages of this affidavit is
> mine, although they're fairly close imitations, except for the
> way the capital A is written in my second name, Ann. I've
> always used a pointed capital A and whoever signed my name
> on these two pages used a round capital A each time. Also, I
> note that a woman has signed her name as a notary public, and
> it's indicated that this alleged statement was sworn to and
> subscribed before her. This also is untrue."[3093]

Julia said she had been the only woman in the room when she gave her statement.[3094] The authorities had gone to great lengths to make her story appear to be irrelevant.

The Warren Commission ignored anyone who said they saw more than one person on the sixth floor. Carolyn Walters said she saw two men in an upper floor of the book depository, one with blonde hair and a white shirt and a rifle and the other with a brown suit jacket, so she was not called to testify.[3095] Instead the Warren Commission asked to hear from 16-year-old African American Amos Lee Euins who said he saw a man with a rifle shooting out of the sixth floor window of the book depository.[3096] Forrest Sorrels of the Secret Service discounted Amos Lee's testimony because he did not see the shooter well enough to tell if he was white or black, but because he said he saw a lone shooter he was good enough for the Warren Commission.[3097]

Oswald passed his paraffin test and this was reported in the press.[3098] FBI Agent Shanklin announced that he flunked it, the exact opposite of the truth.[3099]

The Shooting of Tippit

Forty-five minutes after the Kennedy assassination, a citizen used the radio in Tippit's police car to call in the death of Officer Tippit.[3100] He described the suspect as a white male approximately thirty years old, five feet eight inches, slender build, has black hair, a white jacket, a white shirt, and dark trousers.[3101]

The original plan was for Oswald to be shot while being arrested.[3102] Author Jerome Corsi, in his book *WHO REALLY KILLED KENNEDY?*, said:[3103]

> "Sam Giancana claimed that the original plan to eliminate Oswald involved having Officer Tippit and Roscoe White kill Oswald in what would have been portrayed as an attempt to apprehend the escaping assassin."[3104]

> "According to Giancana the plan went awry when Tippit lost his nerve."[3105]

> Giancana also said "When the plan to kill Oswald failed, the assignment went to Jack Ruby."[3106]

That plan failed when Tippit changed his mind and the conspirators had to improvise. It was Jack Ruby's job to arrange with the Dallas cops to kill Oswald. The mafia paid Ruby to set this up because he had the relationships with the Dallas cops.[3107] This was Ruby's responsibility – it was his key part in the overall plot to kill Kennedy. When that didn't happen, the plotters had to come up with a few things on the fly. They still had to kill Oswald, so they sent him to the Texas theatre to 'meet with his contact.' They also had to now get rid of Tippit. He had not followed the plan, and he knew too much. He had not killed Oswald while arresting him, and now he was a liability. This is why Tippit ended up being murdered, and why the authorities went to such lengths to pin it on Oswald, even when Oswald, again, couldn't have done it.

First the original plan failed and Oswald was not killed by Tippit while being arrested. Then the improvised backup plan to have Oswald killed in a shootout at the theatre while being arrested failed and Oswald was in custody. Since it was Jack Ruby's responsibility to have Oswald killed while being arrested, and he failed at this key job, it fell to Ruby to go to Dallas Police Headquarters and kill Oswald while he was in custody. Mobster Johnny Roselli said Ruby was ordered by the mafia to kill Oswald to shut him up.[3108] This is covered in the chapter on Jack Ruby. Here the focus is on the shooting of officer Tippit.

Oswald did not murder Tippit. The same authorities who claimed he was the lone nut gunman who murdered Kennedy in cold blood also claimed Oswald murdered Tippit. The facts don't point to Oswald as killing Tippit. There were witnesses who saw the shooting, and none of them identified Oswald. A few of them were forced to identify Oswald under threat of death, but that's not the same as Oswald actually being guilty.

Authors Richard Belzer and David Wayne, in their book *HIT LIST*, say that James Files, who was Chuck Nicoletti's driver and bodyguard, knew who killed Tippit and it was Gary Marlow.[3109] They also point out that, unlike Oswald, Marlow fits the description of the killer based on the testimony of the witnesses who were at the Tippit shooting.[3110] Recall that James Files also claims to have taken the head shot from behind the fence on the grassy knoll.[3111] Files may or may not have taken the shot that killed Kennedy, but much of his story checks out, so he has some credibility. Clearly, he was there that day. I could find no hard proof of the rest of his story. The 2003 interview with James Files can be seen on YouTube.

What we know for sure is that Oswald did not kill officer Tippit. He appears to have been nowhere near the scene of the shooting, and he did not fit the description of the killers (there were two) from the witnesses. Acquilla Clemons saw the shooting. Mr. and Mrs. Wright saw the shooting. Domingo Benavides saw the shooting. A rather flaky woman named Helen Markham saw the shooting. None of them identified Oswald as the shooter in spite of repeated attempts by the authorities to get their help in framing Oswald.

Domingo Benavides was a witness to the murder of Tippit. He even collected two of the spent cartridges and gave them to Officer James M. Poe of the Dallas police.[3112] Benavides was interviewed as a witness but would not go along with naming Oswald as the shooter, so he was repeatedly threatened by police and told to keep his mouth shut. While he was still refusing to finger Oswald his brother Eddie, who resembled Domingo, was fatally shot in the head. Domingo was convinced it was a case of mistaken identity.[3113] He thought they meant to kill him. When the police wouldn't investigate Eddie's murder, Domingo's father in law, J.W. Jackson, started to investigate. Then Jackson was shot at, and instead of trying to solve that crime, the police warned Jackson to mind his own business.[3114] Eventually Domingo gave in to the intimidation and decided to change his mind and identify Oswald as the killer of Officer Tippit.[3115] An interview of Domingo Benavides can be seen on YouTube.

Earlene Roberts was harassed to death because she would not change her story.[3116] Roberts was Oswald's landlady and had seen him just minutes before the Tippit shooting, a mile away.[3117] Her timeline made it obvious that Oswald could not have killed Tippit.[3118] She was harassed continually at all hours of the day and night by the authorities.[3119] Being in poor health to begin with, she died not long after the harassment began.[3120]

Warren Reynolds saw a man carrying a pistol fleeing from the scene of the Tippit murder, and it wasn't Oswald.[3121] He wouldn't change his story, so he and his family were harassed, threatened, and Reynolds was finally shot in the head.[3122] The prime suspect in the shooting was Darrell Wayne Garner, who was released when his girlfriend, Betty McDonald, gave him an alibi.[3123] Betty, also known as Nancy Jane Mooney, was one of Jack Ruby's strippers.[3124] Once she had provided the alibi, she was a liability to the conspirators because now she knew too much. She was arrested and died in jail.[3125]

Acquilla Clemons

The official version of the shooting of officer Tippit has Oswald, as usual, acting alone. Acquilla Clemons said there were two people who murdered Tippit, and neither of them was Oswald. This was not what the authorities wanted to hear. She said one was shorter and stocky and the other was taller and thinner and she said they left in different directions.[3126] The taller and thinner one was described by Clemons as wearing a white shirt and khaki pants, which was not what Oswald was wearing at that time.[3127] When Clemons' account did not match what the authorities wanted, they attempted to threaten her into silence. Jim Garrison, in his book *ON THE TRAIL OF THE ASSASSINS*, said that:[3128]

> "Clemons said Dallas police officers told her not to tell anyone what she had seen lest she be killed, a familiar piece of law enforcement advice in Dallas that day."[3129]

Author Mark Lane interviewed Acquilla Clemons. In his book *LAST WORD: MY INDICTMENT OF THE CIA IN THE MURDER OF JFK*, he said:[3130]

> "She said that Dallas police officers wearing guns had visited her and said that if she talked to anyone about what she had seen she "might get hurt." She also said that one of the police officers said that if she talked to the Warren Commission, she "might get killed.""[3131]

Mark Lane also said:[3132]

> "Her more specific testimony would have destroyed the case that was being fabricated." And that "Physical evidence also supported the facts revealed by Clemons and even confounded and confused some of the Warren Commission members."[3133]

The FBI interviewed Acquilla Clemons, but when she did not tell them what they wanted to hear they did not take her statement.[3134] They later claimed it was due to her poor health. Clemons was a diabetic, hardly a reason to keep her from being a witness.[3135] This appears to be the only excuse the FBI could come up with on short notice.

Author Anthony Summers, in his book *NOT IN YOUR LIFETIME*, says that Acquilla Clemons reported that one of the murderers told the other one to go:[3136]

> Interviewer: "Was there another man there?"

> Mrs. Clemons: "Yes, there was one. Other side of the street. All I know is, he tells him to go on."

> Interviewer: "Mrs. Clemons, the man who had the gun, did he make any motion to the man across the street?"

> Mrs. Clemons: "No more than tell him to go."

Interviewer: "He waived his hand and said 'Go on.'?"

Mrs. Clemons: "Yes, said 'Go on.'"

Mr. and Mrs. Wright

By the time Frank Wright got up and went to look at the murder scene only one of the suspects was still there. He said:[3137]

> "I saw a man standing in front of the car." He said "He was looking toward the man on the ground." This man, Wright said "ran as fast as he could go and he got into his car. His car was a little gray old coupe. It was about a 1950 – 1951 Plymouth. He got in the car and he drove away as quick as you could see."[3138]

Mrs. Wright called the police and then went to join her husband at the crime scene. She said the ambulance was there right away: "It wasn't but a minute 'til the ambulance got there."[3139]

Mr. and Mrs. Wright lived at 501 East Tenth Street, about half a block from the Tippit murder scene.[3140] They were watching television when they heard the shots and Mr. Wright went to see what happened while Mrs. Wright called the police.[3141] The ambulance was just two blocks from the scene and got there in a few minutes.[3142] Neither the Wrights nor the ambulance attendants were called by the Warren Commission.[3143] Mr. Wright said:[3144]

> "It seems to me that I saw him [Tippit] just as he hit the ground. I saw him turn over and he didn't move anymore. I saw a man standing in front of the car. He was looking toward the man on the ground. He had on a long coat. It ended just above his hands. I didn't see a gun. He ran around on the passenger side of the police car. He ran as fast as he could go and he got into his car. His car was a gray little old coupe. It was about a 1950-1951, maybe a Plymouth. I've seen what came out on television and the papers but I know that's not what happened. I knew a man drove off in a gray car. Nothing in the world is going to change my opinion. I saw that man drive off in a gray coupe just as clear as I was born."[3145]

Helen Markham claimed to witness the Tippit shooting, but she changed her story several times.[3146] Other witnesses saw two shooters and there were two different kinds of bullets recovered from Tippit's body during the autopsy.[3147] There were also two kinds of shells picked up at the crime scene.[3148] Cops typically mark their initials on evidence like shells to establish a chain of evidence. Officer Joseph Poe marked the shells he was handed by Domingo Benavides, but the shells in the National Archives from the Tippit shooting do not have initials on them.[3149]

The FBI is unable to match the slugs taken from Tippit's body to Oswald's pistol.[3150]

The jacket the cops found was light and Oswald's was dark. The jacket they found had a laundry tag but Marina said she washed Oswald's clothes and he did not use a laundry.[3151]

When Oswald left his rooming house he was wearing a brown plaid coat.[3152] Whoever killed Tippit was wearing a white coat.[3153]

Oswald could not have made it to the Tippit crime scene in time because the timeline does not work, so the Warren Commission adjusted the timeline.[3154] This is the same thing that happened to the timeline of Oswald's movements within the Texas School Book Depository. They 'adjusted' the times so that they could claim it was possible for Oswald to be on the sixth floor during the shooting when he was not.

Oswald had two wallets, one in his residence and one on him. There was a third wallet planted at the crime scene which very conveniently linked him to the alias of A. Hidell and thus to the Kennedy murder weapon. The third wallet was mysteriously "found" at the crime scene.[3155] There is no evidence that Oswald owned that wallet or created those fake identification cards.[3156]

Helen Markham

Helen Markham was a flake, but she was the star witness for the Warren Commission's prosecution of Oswald for the murder of Tippit. She was the best they could come up with. Markham said it took twenty minutes for the ambulance to get there, and in the meantime, she had a conversation with Tippit.[3157] The other witnesses said the murderer shot Tippit three times in the chest and calmly finished him off with a bullet in the head. The other witnesses also said that the ambulance arrived almost immediately, including the ambulance drivers who were stationed nearby.[3158] Joseph Ball was a lawyer for the Warren Commission. He said Markham's testimony had been "full of mistakes – she had been an utter screwball, utterly unreliable"[3159]

Jim Garrison, in his book *ON THE TRAIL OF THE ASSASSINS*, has a sample of the testimony of the only 'witness' to the Tippit murder who the authorities could get to 'identify' Oswald:[3160]

> Mr. Ball "Now, when you went into the room, you looked these people over, these four men?"
>
> Mrs. Markham "Yes sir."
>
> Mr. Ball "Did you recognize anyone in the lineup?"
>
> Mrs. Markham "No sir."
>
> Mr. Ball "You did not? Did you see anybody? I've asked you that question before. Did you recognize anybody from their face?"
>
> Mrs. Markham "From their face, no."
>
> Mr. Ball "Did you identify anybody in these four people?"
>
> Mrs. Markham "I didn't know nobody."
>
> Mr. Ball "I know you didn't know anybody, but did anybody in that lineup look like anybody you had seen before?"
>
> Mrs. Markham "No. I had never seen none of them before."
>
> Mr. Ball "No one of the four?"
>
> Mrs. Markham "No one of them."
>
> Mr. Ball "No one of all four?"
>
> Mrs. Markham "No sir."
>
> > Note – here Garrison interjects an author's note: "Ultimately, out of desperation, the commission's attorney had to resort to putting a leading question to his own witness, which is absolutely inadmissible in any real court, in order to telegraph to the witness what he wanted to hear:[3161]
>
> Mr. Ball "You recognized him from his appearance?"
>
> Mrs. Markham "I asked. I looked at him. When I saw this man I wasn't sure, but I had cold chills just run over me."

That was the identification on which the authorities depended to convict Oswald of the murder of Tippit. This was the best they could do in terms of getting someone to "identify" Oswald. No wonder they tried so hard to threaten someone else into fingering Oswald for the Tippit murder.

At 7:10 on November 22, 1963 Oswald was charged with the murder of police officer Tippit.[3162]

The Texas Theatre

Oswald was told to go to the Texas theatre and meet his 'contact,' so he showed up at the Texas theatre and started looking around for his 'contact.' He had not yet realized that there was no one there to contact. At this point the conspirators were still hoping he will be shot while being arrested, and that they could salvage most of the original plan. They made sure he had a gun and sent a bunch of cops over to the theatre to arrest him. They even sent the Oswald double there so he would be seen going into the theatre without paying as a pretext to send the cops. Oswald tried in vain to make contact at the theatre because his contact was not at the theatre. At this point Oswald had been cut loose by his handlers and his last job was just to die, preferably while being arrested. Since he had a gun on him there was a good chance the conspirators hoped he would be killed while being arrested at the theatre. This almost happened because Oswald pulled out a gun and tried to fire at the cops arresting him in the theatre. Most people who open fire on a bunch of cops trying to arrest them don't live very long. However, Oswald somehow survived his arrest at the theatre and ended up being taken alive. His luck is about to run out.

Oswald and his double were both arrested at the Texas Theatre. The real Oswald was held and the double was released. The double was seen by multiple witnesses during his arrest and his flight out of Dallas. Ruby was there in the theatre to watch the arrest. The real Oswald was arrested on the main floor and brought out the front of the theatre. His double was arrested in the balcony and brought out the back of the theatre. The double was later flown out of Dallas on a CIA plane.

Johnny Calvin Brewer was the manager of Hardy's shoe store, just a few doors east of the Texas Theatre. He spotted a man who appeared to be hiding from the police in the doorway of his store and then watched as the man ducked into the Texas Theatre without buying a ticket.[3163] He checked with Julia Postal, the ticket taker, confirmed that the man had not bought a ticket, and they called the police.[3164] Warren H. "Butch" Burroughs operated the concession stand at the Texas Theatre. He had not seen Oswald come in, but had sold him popcorn at 1:15 PM, almost the exact time of Tippit's murder.[3165] Oswald sat next to someone, waited a minute, then moved next to someone else. Clearly, he was expecting to make contact with someone he did not know and was looking for a signal.[3166] Equally clearly, whoever he was supposed to make contact with was not there. He was a spy who had been left out in the cold. He had been cut off. He did this for a while and then got up to get the popcorn from the concession stand at 1:15 PM, then he continued trying to make contact.[3167] Not long after that the police came in and arrested Oswald, causing a scuffle during which Oswald pulled a pistol and tried to shoot Officer McDonald.[3168]

George Applin was attending the movie when the first Oswald was arrested, and he got up and moved to the back when the lights came on and the police moved in on Oswald.[3169] While in the back, he warned Jack Ruby, who he did not know, that he would be safer if he moved.[3170] Ruby ignored him as Oswald tried to use his gun on the police at the last minute.[3171] Two days later Applin recognized Ruby from the television news.[3172]

George Applin did not identify Ruby until 1979 out of fear for his life.[3173] He said:

> "I'm a pretty nervous guy anyway because, I'll tell you what, after I saw that magazine where all those people they said were kind of connected to some of this had come up dead, it just kind of made me keep a low profile."[3174]

Lee Harvey Oswald was hustled out the front door and taken down to Dallas Police Headquarters to be booked.[3175] A few minutes later Butch Burroughs saw a *second* Oswald arrested, handcuffed and brought out the *back* door of the theatre.[3176] Bernard Haire owned Bernie's Hobby House just two doors east of the Texas Theatre. He went outside to see what was happening but the crowd had grown so large that he could not see anything, so he went out the back door of his shop to get a better view.[3177] He watched the police bring "Oswald" out the back door of the theatre and put him in a police car and drive off.[3178] Haire was shocked to find out in 1987 that the real Oswald had been brought out the *front* door.[3179]

Butch Burroughs and Johnny Calvin Brewer both have interviews on YouTube.

The Oswald Double Flies Away

Once Lee Harvey Oswald was in custody the Oswald double had to be spirited out of Dallas as quickly and quietly as possible. It wouldn't do to have any more Oswald sightings. Someone might start to suspect a conspiracy. The Oswald double was spotted waiting in a car by a restaurant when Lee Harvey Oswald was already in custody. The Oswald double was also seen by Robert Vinson who flew out of Dallas the night of the Kennedy assassination on a CIA plane with the Oswald double.

FBI Director J. Edgar Hoover thought someone was impersonating Oswald.[3180] On June 3, 1960 he sent a letter to the State Department asking them to look into it:[3181]

> "Since there is the possibility that an imposter is using Oswald's birth certificate," Hoover said "any current information the Department of State has concerning subject (Oswald) would be appreciated"[3182]

Lee Harvey Oswald was in custody at Dallas Police Headquarters by 2:00 PM.[3183] Also at about 2:00 P.M. on the day of the Kennedy assassination, auto mechanic T.F. White was listening to the events on the radio while working at Mack Pate's garage across from the El Chico restaurant in the Oak Cliff section of Dallas.[3184] He saw a man in a red 1961 Falcon drive into the parking lot of the restaurant and remain in the car.[3185] As White said later "The man appeared to be hiding."[3186] White told Mack Pate about the man when Pate returned from lunch and then walked up close enough to the car to recognize the driver and get the license plate number – Texas PP4537.[3187] The driver stared him full in the face when he was ten yards from the car.[3188] A few weeks after the assassination, on December 4, 1963 journalist Wes Wise was giving a talk at the El Chico restaurant when Mac Pate introduced him to T.F. White and they convinced White to tell what he had seen.[3189] Wise said "I just wish you had gotten the license number."[3190] White then gave Wise the license number, and it was tracked to Carl Amos Mather of Garland, Texas.[3191] Mather worked for a company that was a CIA contractor doing high-security communications work.[3192] He also happened to be a good friend of Officer J.D. Tippit.[3193]

So, the Oswald double was seen at 2:00 PM in the parking lot of the El Chico restaurant in the Oak Cliff section of Dallas, not far from where Tippit was shot and the Oswalds were arrested at the Texas theatre.

Clearly, this was not Lee Harvey Oswald, who was in police custody. This was the Oswald double.

At 3:30 PM an Oswald double is flown out of Dallas a CIA C-54 cargo plane.[3194]

Robert G. Vinson was in the Air Force and he had visited Washington on unofficial business. He had gone there to complain about being passed over for his promotion one too many times.[3195] While in Washington he talked to Colonel Chapman, who was talking on the phone while reviewing Vinson's paperwork.[3196] Vinson overheard Colonel Chapman, a liaison officer between Congress and the Pentagon, say that the president should cancel his trip to Dallas because "something" had been reported.[3197] When Colonel Chapman got off the phone he told Vinson he would look into the issue of Vinson's promotion, and Vinson took a bus the next day to Andrews Air Force Base for the trip home on November 22, 1963.[3198] He registered to take the next flight home to Colorado Springs and ended up being put on a CIA flight to Lowry Air Force Base in Denver.[3199] There were two other men on the C-54, but no one spoke to him at all.[3200] The other two stayed in the pilot and copilot seats, and there was no paperwork whatsoever.[3201] Somewhere over Nebraska the pilot announced that the president had been shot and the plane turned south.[3202] At about 3:30 PM Vinson saw they were coming into Dallas, and they landed alongside the Trinity river on a road under construction.[3203] The engines never shut down, and a tall Cuban and Oswald got on the plane.[3204] Vinson did not know Oswald at that time, but he recognized him later from the media coverage. Again, no one spoke as the plane took off and flew to Roswell Air Force Base in New Mexico.[3205] The four others all dashed off the plane and Vinson was left sitting there in an empty plane, so he got off and walked to the only building with lights on and asked where they were.[3206] He was told he was at Roswell and eventually was able to take a bus home.[3207] He and his wife realized that they should keep quiet and see what happened.[3208] He was eventually recruited by the CIA but turned them down, so they drafted him into the CIA.[3209] The CIA had the Air Force order Vinson to be put to work on the SR-71 Blackbird program at Nellis Air Base near Las Vegas.[3210] Vinson kept his secret until 1992 when Congress passed the JFK Records Act which allowed him to legally break the secrecy agreements he had been forced to sign.[3211] Thirty years after the Kennedy assassination Vinson was able to go public with his story, starting with news anchor Larry Hatteburg on Wichita's KAKE TV Channel 10 News.[3212] In 2003 the book *FLIGHT FROM DALLAS* was published with his story.[3213] The parking lot of the El Chico restaurant was a five-minute drive from where the CIA plane landed and took off again with the Oswald double.[3214]

One of the many unanswered questions in the Kennedy assassination is what ever became of the Oswald double. I strongly suspect he ended up in an unmarked grave. Once he was done playing his part, the conspirators had no reason to allow him to live. And they had every reason to kill him. In addition, since the real Lee Harvey Oswald was already dead, no one would miss the double. I would be very surprised if he lived into old age.

Robert Vinson's interview can be viewed on YouTube.

The Zapruder Film is Altered and Hidden

The Zapruder film is a shocking record of what happened. Even in the edited version, Kennedy can clearly be seen to have been shot from the front.[3215] For this reason, several things had to happen. First, the film had to be modified to make it less shocking. The original Zapruder film had evidence of up to eight shots from three different directions.[3216] Even once it was edited, it was still too shocking. So, it had to be hidden from the public for many years. Once it was released it had to be on as limited a basis as possible. Only after many years had gone by would the public be allowed to view the film, and then only the edited version.

The presidential limousine stopped when the first shots rang out. Multiple witnesses said the limousine stopped when the first shots were fired.[3217] The limousine either stopped or slowed down to such a crawl that it might as well have been stopped for a few moments. Dallas motorcycle Police Officer James Chaney said the limousine came to a complete stop.[3218] The wife of Mayor Earle Cabell testified that the motorcade came to a complete stop.[3219] Mary Woodward also said the limousine came to a stop.[3220] Senator Yarborough said the limousine stopped.[3221] However, this stop is not shown on the publicly available version of the Zapruder film because the original has been altered and we can only see the edited version.[3222]

Author Peter Janney's book, *MARY'S MOSAIC*, has the most detailed description of how exactly the Zapruder film was altered. He points out that the Zapruder film showed up at the CIA's National Photographic Interpretation Center (NPIC) twice the weekend of the assassination.[3223] The first time was at the request of John McCone, then the Director of the CIA.[3224] He called Arthur Lundahl, the distinguished Director of the NPIC, who alerted the NPIC's expert, Dino Brugioni, to have a team ready when the Secret Service showed up at 10:00 PM on Saturday night.[3225] Dino called in Ralph Pearce and Bill Banfield, their best guys.[3226] The NPIC team working on the original version also included Homer McMahon, and another technician named Morgan Bennet Hunter.[3227] He was interviewed in 1997 by Jeremy Gunn of the Assassination Records Review Board (ARRB).[3228] He said that, in his opinion, eight shots had been fired at the president's limousine from three different locations.[3229]

The first visit, on the evening of the assassination, was to make briefing boards for the CIA Director for official purposes.[3230] During the first visit it became obvious that there was more than one shooter.[3231] CIA

Director McCone told Attorney General Robert Kennedy that there was obviously more than one shooter.[3232] Dino Brugioni later described to author Peter Janney how graphic the first (unedited) Zapruder film was, and how the spray from Kennedy's head was three or four feet high in the air, and how this extended to many more frames than the Zapruder film we're all allowed now to see.[3233] The film they brought to the NPIC the second time had made a stop at the CIA's Hawkeye facility at Kodak's headquarters in Rochester, New York. They edited out the part where the limousine stopped, and added some finishing touches like alterations to the head wound in the frames after the kill shot.[3234] The purpose of all these alterations was to get rid of as much evidence as possible of shots from the front. The final edited version (that anyone can now see on YouTube) was still too graphic. Even the altered Zapruder film still made a shot from the front too obvious, so they hid it away from public view. The public finally got a look at the edited version in 1975, twelve years after the Kennedy assassination.[3235]

The first visit was on Saturday night, and on the next night, Sunday night, 'Secret Service Agent Bill Smith' showed up with another version of the Zapruder film.[3236] The briefing boards in the National Archives are from the second visit to the NPIC.[3237] The purpose of the second visit was to make briefing boards to show that there were only three shots.[3238]

Life magazine continued to help the conspiracy by denying access to the Zapruder film as a moving picture or video. This was because anyone who views the film can see that Kennedy is shot from the front. *Life* only published still shots. In its regular weekly issue on November 29, 1963 *Life* published only 31 out of over 400 frames of the Zapruder film.[3239] They were careful not to include any sequence of frames which would depict Kennedy's head moving backward as a result of a shot from the front.[3240]

Eleven Hollywood film experts have said that frame 257 shows what the back of JFK's head should look like but on frame 317 the Zapruder film was edited to include a black splotch added to cover up the massive exit wound in the back of Kennedy's head.[3241]

The Murder of Anyone Who Would Talk

Anyone who couldn't or wouldn't be intimidated had to be either silenced or ignored. If they couldn't be ignored, they were killed. As I outlined above in the section labeled The Government Lie Machine, the government had to change the real story (Kennedy was killed by a conspiracy) to the fairy tale that Oswald was a lone gunman. To do this they first confiscated and destroyed as much evidence as possible. This started immediately after the shooting by confiscating film. They also intimidated witnesses who had seen something that didn't fit their story about Oswald being a lone shooter. Most people could be intimidated into either silence or changing their story, but some could not. Of those who would not or could not be intimidated, they fell into two categories; those who could be ignored and those who couldn't. Those who could be ignored were allowed to live. Those who couldn't were murdered. At this point the conspirators were committed. They saw themselves as having no choice but to do whatever else was necessary to keep a lid on the conspiracy. Failure was not an option. If they had to kill more people, so be it. The list of additional murders continued to grow and grow. Over fifty people eventually lost their lives to keep the lid on the conspiracy. This list of murders grew for several reasons. One reason was that, once you had done something for the conspirators, you were of no use to them. Once your part was over, you were a liability. A good example is Oswald. Another good example is Jack Ruby. Once Ruby had killed Oswald, he quickly became a liability and had to be silenced. Another reason the list of murders grew was that there were several investigations of the assassination and of the CIA. First there was the Warren Commission, then there was the Garrison investigation. David Ferrie had to be murdered before he could be arrested and tried during the Garrison investigation. Mafia boss Sam Giancana was murdered just as he was about to testify before the Church Committee. CIA asset George de Mohrenschildt was murdered just before he could be interviewed for the House Select Committee on Assassinations.

There are also odd spikes on the chart of the murders during the Warren Commission, the Garrison Investigation, the House Select Committee on Assassinations and the Church Committee.

The death rate from unnatural causes among the witnesses of the Kennedy assassination is so astronomically high as to be impossible. In addition to that, the chart of occurrences of these odd deaths spiked during the four investigations mentioned above. There is also an odd spike of six deaths among FBI officials, all of whom just happened to have been part of the cover-up, in the six months after Hoover died. There's no possible way all these murders happened this way just by coincidence. The reason these people were murdered was to keep a lid on the conspiracy to kill Kennedy. This is one of those points where you have to be a kook to believe that all these deaths were just a coincidence.

Authors Richard Belzer and David Wayne wrote a book called *HIT LIST: AN IN-DEPTH INVESTIGATION INTO THE MYSTERIOUS DEATHS OF WITNESSES TO THE JFK ASSASSINATION*. I recommend this book to anyone who is interested in knowing more about the details of the background of each of these people and how they are connected to the Kennedy assassination. The list of fifty deaths I have below is not an exact match to the deaths listed in *HIT LIST*, but they are very close and *HIT LIST* goes into over three hundred pages of details on why each death is related to the Kennedy assassination and why the deaths are suspicious. Anyone who doubts that fifty people died to keep the lid on the cover-up should read *HIT LIST*.

The List

1. J.D. Tippit – was a Dallas police officer who was supposed to kill Oswald while arresting him.[3242] Tippit was killed because he decided he did not want to kill Oswald.[3243] Then he knew too much and had to be killed to keep him from talking and the authorities went to great lengths to try to blame Tippit's murder on Oswald, the all-purpose patsy. (See the section on the shooting of Tippit.)

2. Lee Harvey Oswald – was killed because he knew too much. He had been used as the patsy and would have talked if he had lived. (See the chapter on the setup of Oswald). In the original plan he was supposed to die while being arrested.[3244] Jack Ruby had responsibility for this part of the plan because he had the relationships with the Dallas police, and when it went wrong he was sent in to fix the problem by shooting Oswald.[3245] (See the section entitled Ruby is Sent to Silence Oswald.)

3. Jack Ruby – had done his part for the conspiracy by killing Oswald.[3246] Then when he started talking he had to be killed to keep him quiet. (See the chapter on Jack Ruby.)

4. Jack Zangetty – knew too much and made the mistake of talking.[3247] He predicted that Ruby would kill Oswald.[3248] He was killed for talking.[3249]

5. Rose Cherami – knew too much and was willing to talk so she had to be killed.[3250] She had predicted the Kennedy assassination and talked to the local and Louisiana state police, so she was killed to keep her from talking.[3251] (See the section on Rose Cherami.)

6. Karyn Kupcinet – was killed as a warning to her father, Irv Kupcinet, to quit looking into Jack Ruby's connection to the Kennedy assassination.[3252] Irv Kupcinet was a fearless investigative reporter who was getting too close for comfort.[3253] After his daughter's death he backed off of his investigation.[3254]

7. Jim Koethe – was a reporter who had found out too much and had to be killed to silence him.[3255]

8. Bill Hunter – was a reporter who had found out too much and had to be killed to silence him.[3256]

9. Dorothy Kilgallen – was killed because she found out too much and was going to print with what she knew.[3257] She was a prominent reporter and therefore couldn't be ignored so she had to be killed and her manuscript stolen and buried. Kilgallen was a television personality and a nationally syndicated columnist with a star on the Hollywood Walk of Fame who was writing a book.[3258] The chapter on the Kennedy assassination was what she was killed for.[3259] Kilgallen had talked to Ruby while he was in jail and, whatever he told her, it got her killed.[3260] (See the section on Ruby Needs to be Silenced.) She claimed to friends that she was going to crack the Kennedy assassination case wide open.[3261] Her book, Murder One, was published after her death *without* the chapter on the Kennedy assassination.

10. Florence Pritchett Smith – was killed because she had a backup copy of Dorothy Kilgallen's manuscript, which she was given by Kilgallen.[3262] Kilgallen had given her the copy

in case her apartment was broken into and searched. [3263] Smith was killed the next day after Kilgallen was.[3264]

11. Betty McDonald – killed because she knew too much.[3265] McDonald had provided an alibi for Darrell Wayne Garner.[3266] Darrell Wayne Garner was the suspect in the shooting of Warren Reynolds.[3267] Warren Reynolds was a witness to the Tippit shooting who refused to lie and identify Oswald as Tippit's shooter.[3268] If Betty had decided to recant her alibi the plot would unravel, so she had to be killed to keep her quiet.[3269]

12. Eddie Benavides – brother of Domingo Benavides, was killed in a case of mistaken identity. Domingo Benavides was a witness to the murder of Tippit. He even collected two of the spent cartridges and gave them to Officer James M. Poe of the Dallas police.[3270] Benavides was interviewed as a witness but would not go along with naming Oswald as the shooter, so he was repeatedly threatened by police and told to keep his mouth shut. While he was still refusing to finger Oswald his brother Eddie, who resembled Domingo, was fatally shot in the head. Domingo was convinced it was a case of mistaken identity.[3271] He thought they meant to kill him. When the police wouldn't investigate Eddie's murder, Domingo's father in law, J.W. Jackson, started to investigate. Then Jackson was shot at, and instead of trying to solve that crime, the police warned Jackson to mind his own business.[3272] Eventually Domingo gave in to the intimidation and decided to change his mind and identify Oswald as the killer of Officer Tippit.[3273] An interview of Domingo Benavides can be seen on YouTube.

13. Hank Killam – killed because he knew too much.[3274] Killam was married to Wanda Joyce Killam, one of Ruby's strippers, and Hank worked with Oswald's roommate, John Carter.[3275] Killam was harassed and warned repeatedly by "government agents" that he knew too much and he moved multiple times to get away from the harassment.[3276] Finally he was killed and thrown through a window to cover up the fact that his throat was slit.[3277]

14. Bill Waters – killed because he knew too much.[3278] Waters tried to talk Hank Killam and Lee Oswald out of being involved.[3279] Waters made the mistake of calling the FBI to tell them what he knew after the Kennedy assassination.[3280]

They told him he knew too much and to keep his mouth shut, then he suddenly turned up dead.[3281]

15. Gary Underhill – killed because he knew too much.[3282] Gary was CIA and had figured out what happened.[3283] He went on the run and told some friends what he had figured out, but then changed his mind about running and went home where he was later found shot to death.[3284]

16. Maurice Gatlin – killed because he knew too much. During the Garrison investigation, Gatlin was sought for questioning.[3285] Maurice Gatlin had served as a bag man for the CIA, Clay Shaw and Guy Banister.[3286] He had brought cash to France to pay for the assassins to kill Charles de Gaulle. He suddenly became unavailable for questioning because he died suddenly from a fall from a sixth-floor balcony.[3287]

17. Lee Bowers – killed because he knew too much.[3288] Lee Bowers was the railroad yard tower man who saw the killers shoot from behind the fence at the top of the grassy knoll.[3289] He was intimidated, kidnapped, had his finger cut off and eventually murdered to keep him quiet.[3290] (See the sections on Lee Bowers.)

18. Mary Pinchot Meyer – killed because she knew too much and was willing to go public.[3291] (See the chapter on the Murder of Mary Pinchot Meyer.)

19. William Pitzer – killed because he knew too much and was willing to go public.[3292] (See the section on the murder of William Pitzer.)

20. Manuel Rodriguez Quesada – anti-Castro Cuban exile killed because he was involved in the JFK assassination, knew too much and was wanted for questioning in the Garrison investigation.[3293]

21. Gilberto Hernandez – anti-Castro Cuban exile killed because he was involved in the JFK assassination, knew too much and was wanted for questioning in the Garrison investigation.[3294]

22. Eladio del Valle – anti-Castro Cuban exile killed because he was involved in the JFK assassination, knew too much and was wanted for questioning in the Garrison investigation.[3295]

23. David Ferrie – killed because he was involved in the JFK assassination, knew too much and was wanted for questioning in the Garrison investigation.[3296] Ferrie was the original target of the Garrison investigation.[3297] After Ferrie was killed Garrison focused his investigation on Clay Shaw.[3298] Ferrie had worked with Oswald and Banister and Shaw and others in New Orleans on various projects related to the Kennedy assassination.[3299] (See the section on David Ferrie.)

24. Guy Banister – killed because he was involved in the Kennedy assassination and knew too much.[3300] Banister ran the office in New Orleans where Lee Harvey Oswald, David Ferrie, Sergio Arcacha Smith and others worked on various CIA and Kennedy assassination projects in the summer of 1963.[3301] His files disappeared when he died.[3302] (See the section on Guy Banister.)

25. Rolando Masferrer – anti-Castro Cuban exile killed by car bomb because he was involved in the Kennedy assassination and knew too much.[3303]

26. Dr. Mary Sherman – killed because she knew too much.[3304] The murder was staged to look like a robbery.[3305] Mary Sherman had been working with Lee Harvey Oswald, David Ferrie, Clay Shaw, Judyth Vary Baker and Dr. Alton Ochsner on a fast-acting cancer originally meant for Fidel Castro, but eventually used on Jack Ruby.[3306]

27. William Sullivan, FBI – killed because he knew too much.[3307] Sullivan worked directly for J. Edgar Hoover and was killed only days before he was to testify before the HSCA.[3308] He was shot in a faked hunting accident, and the authorities said he was shot by fellow hunter Robert Daniels.[3309] Robert Novak reported that Sullivan had been fired by Hoover and Sullivan himself warned that someday he would die in an accident and not to believe it, he will have been murdered.[3310]

28. Louis Nichols, FBI – another of Hoover's Assistant FBI Directors and Hoover's conduit to the Warren Commission.[3311] Nichols was killed because he had been involved in the cover-up and knew too much.[3312] He was scheduled to testify before the HSCA.[3313]

29. Alan Belmont, FBI – special assistant to Hoover.[3314] Killed because he knew too much.[3315] As an FBI liaison to the Warren Commission, Belmont ran the cover up after the Kennedy hit and was scheduled to testify before the House Select Committee on Assassinations.[3316]

30. James Cadigan, FBI – killed because he knew too much.[3317] James Cadigan, an FBI document expert who worked on the cover-up of the Kennedy assassination.[3318] Was scheduled to testify before the House Select Committee on Assassinations.[3319]

31. Donald Kaylor, FBI – killed because he knew too much.[3320] As the FBI fingerprint expert who worked on the cover-up of the Kennedy case and the Oswald palm print.[3321] Kaylor was scheduled to testify before the House Select Committee on Assassinations.[3322]

32. J.M. English, FBI – killed because he knew too much.[3323] Head of FBI forensics and was involved in the cover-up because he worked on the Mannlicher-Carcano rifle and Tippit pistol, and was scheduled to testify before the House Select Committee on Assassinations.[3324]

33. John Paisley – killed because he knew too much.[3325] Paisley was a CIA officer who knew too much and was about to blow the whistle during the HSCA investigation.[3326] Paisley was shot in the head with diving weights fixed to his body and tossed in the ocean.[3327] The kill shot was behind left ear and Paisley was right handed.[3328] There was no gun found on the boat, and he was eating a meal when he was killed.[3329]

34. Roger Craig – killed because he knew too much and was going to be called by the HSCA.[3330] Craig was a deputy sheriff who had seen too much and refused to lie.[3331] (See the section on Roger Craig and the Other Oswald.)

35. David Sanchez Morales – killed because he knew too much. Morales was a hitman for the CIA and was involved in the Kennedy assassination.[3332] (See the Section on David Sanchez Morales.)

36. George de Mohrenschildt – killed because he knew too much and was going to talk to the House Select Committee on Assassinations.[3333] He had been one of Oswald's CIA

babysitters in Dallas.[3334]   Later, when he was giving interviews and scheduled to talk to the HSCA, his murder was made to look like a suicide.[3335] (See the section on George de Mohrenschildt.)

37. Sam Giancana – mafia boss killed because he was involved in the Kennedy assassination, knew too much and was scheduled to talk to the Church Committee.[3336] (See the section on Sam Giancana.)

38. Johnny Roselli – killed because he knew too much and was talking.[3337] Johnny was in the mafia and had been heavily involved in the planning of the Kennedy assassination.[3338] He was there in Dallas that day.[3339] He was part of the mafia link to the CIA.[3340]

39. Chuck Nicoletti – killed because he knew too much and was scheduled to talk to the House Select Committee on Assassinations.[3341] Chuck was a hitman for mafia boss Sam Giancana and was on one of the shooting teams in Dallas that day.[3342]

40. Carlos Prio Socarras – anti-Castro Cuban exile killed because he was involved in the Kennedy assassination, knew too much and was murdered before he could testify to the House Select Committee on Assassinations.[3343]

41. Richard Case Nagell – killed because he knew too much. He was a spy who had been told to go pretend to work for the Russians.[3344] The Russians told him to stop the assassination of JFK by either warning Oswald off or killing him.[3345] He had evidence that he kept as proof in addition to just what he knew. He was murdered and his evidence was stolen.[3346] (See the section on Richard Case Nagell.)

42. Ralph Leon Yates – driven to an early grave because he had seen too much and refused to lie.[3347] He would not change his story so he was put in an insane asylum and tortured for eleven years until he died at age 39.[3348] (See the section on The Ralph Yates Incident.)

43. Robert Kennedy – killed because he was going to become president and run a real investigation. (See the chapter on The Murder of Robert Kennedy).

44. Mac Wallace – Mac Wallace was Johnson's hitman who left his fingerprint at the Texas School Book Depository.[3349] He was killed because he was involved and knew too much and was a liability.[3350] In 1971 Mac Wallace was murdered as he was pressuring Johnson's partner Ed Clark for more money.[3351]

45. Harold Russell, witness to escape of Tippit shooter, shot because he knew too much.[3352]

46. William Whaley, Oswald's cab driver – killed in motor vehicle.[3353] Whaley knew too much. He could testify that there was more than one Oswald, because he gave Oswald a ride the day of the assassination.

47. James Worrell, Jr., saw man escape from book depository, killed in motor vehicle.[3354] Worrell knew too much. He was a witness who could identify one of the real shooters.

48. Hale Boggs, former member of the Warren Commission, died under mysterious circumstances and his records mysteriously disappeared – he had announced that he had some startling revelations about the Kennedy assassination.[3355]

49. Cliff Carter, aide to Johnson, also died in 1971 when he got pneumonia and no penicillin could be located anywhere in Washington D.C.[3356] As an aide to Johnson, he was involved and knew too much.

50. Clint Peoples was killed as he was about to publish his research into the JFK assassination.[3357] He had looked into the death of Henry Marshall and had done fresh research into the Kennedy assassination.[3358] He knew too much and had to be killed to keep him quiet.[3359] He was run off the road.[3360] (See the section on the Murder of Henry Marshall.)

And that's not counting the half dozen murders Johnson committed before the JFK assassination, or the death of Lisa Howard, which likely should have been included. There were a considerable number of "suspicious" deaths like Lisa Howard's which didn't quite make the cut. These were deaths and disappearances which came close, but did not make The List because there just wasn't enough proof. William Harvey, who was involved in the JFK assassination, just happened to die when he was talking to the Church Committee. Janet Cuffari was one of Jack Ruby's strippers, and her stage name was Jada. Beverly Oliver worked in Ruby's club and was there in Dealey Plaza the day Kennedy was killed. She wrote a book, and she said that Ruby brought Oswald into his club and introduced him as being CIA. She also said that a dancer named Jada disappeared leaving some of her clothes after telling reporters that Ruby had introduced her to Oswald.[3361] There is every chance that Janet Cuffari was murdered to keep her quiet. Witness Earlene Roberts was harassed to death because she could prove that Oswald was not guilty of shooting Police Officer J.D. Tippit. Her death is not on The List because she was in poor health before the harassment started and her death is difficult to link to her testimony. Singer Jim Reeves had ties to the Kennedy assassination and he died under suspicious circumstances, as did people who knew too much about his death. William Pawley was involved in the anti-Castro Cubans and very likely knew too much. He died under suspicious circumstances just before he could be questioned by the HSCA. The list goes on and on, but there was not enough concrete information for these folks to make "The List" above. I have no doubt we would be appalled to know how many people really lost their lives to keep a lid on the Kennedy assassination conspiracy.

The Warren Commission – The First Whitewash

The Warren Commission's many critics claim that it failed in its mission. I disagree. I think the Warren Commission succeeded at its intended purpose. The difference is easily explained. The public was told that the Warren Commission was created to investigate the assassination of President Kennedy and report its findings. This was a lie. The real purpose of the Warren Commission was to do a whitewash and produce a report that Oswald was a lone nut killer so that fiction could be sold to the public with the help of the mainstream media. In this the Warren Commission fulfilled its purpose. It allowed the conspirators to convict Oswald in the court of public opinion, which was the whole point. Johnson was forced to create the Warren Commission and he picked people he could control and who would produce the result he wanted. This strategy worked and Johnson and the conspirators got what they needed. The Warren Report conclusion that Oswald acted alone could then be sold to the public because the commissioners were prominent and distinguished public figures who were willing to lend their credibility to the whitewash.

This chapter is organized into eleven sections. Sections two through eight deal with the commissioners:

1. Prelude – the reason Johnson reluctantly created the Warren Commission – describes how Johnson was content to have the Texas authorities do the whitewash until Congress threatened to create an inquiry and Johnson was forced to create a commission he could control

2. Earl Warren – describes Earl Warren's background as the reluctant chairman who was eventually convinced to participate because Johnson said there were rumors of a conspiracy that could lead to World War Three and tens of millions of American lives lost

3. Allen Dulles – describes how Allen Dulles actually ran the commission because he was the only one without a full-time job – Dulles was Johnson's first choice for chairman until he realized that Warren would be better as a figurehead while Dulles ran the commission in the background

4. Gerald Ford – describes how Gerald Ford changed the location of the wounds to facilitate the cover up – also describes how Ford was controlled by Hoover and the other conspirators

5. John McCloy – describes how Dulles and McCloy go way back as fellow Cold Warriors and how McCloy, Ford and Dulles controlled the Warren Commission and the Warren Report

6. Richard Russell – describes how Russell was a friend and mentor to Johnson which was why Johnson appointed him – he could be controlled – and Johnson was able to control Russell

7. John Sherman Cooper – describes how Cooper, Russell and Boggs were in the minority "southern wing" of the commission and were sidelined by the majority on the commission

8. Hale Boggs – describes how Boggs was one of the first representatives calling for a Congressional inquiry and how Johnson included Boggs because he thought he could control him

9. The Magic Bullet Fiction – describes why the commission had to create the concept of the magic bullet to minimize the number of shots so as to pretend that there was only one shooter

10. Dissention – describes how several of the commissioners didn't buy the Magic Bullet fiction and how Johnson handled the dissention and bullied and tricked the dissenters into going along

11. The Commission – describes the day-to-day workings of how the commission either intimidated witnesses or ignored evidence that didn't fit the fairy tale that Oswald was the lone shooter

Prelude – Why Johnson Reluctantly Created the Warren Commission

The original plan was for Oswald to be killed in a "shootout" with police while being arrested. The original plan also did not include the Warren Commission. Against all odds, Oswald was taken alive and mafia functionary Ruby then had to be sent in to silence him. The public watched on national television as Ruby walked into the Dallas Police Department with a loaded pistol and gunned Oswald down while he was surrounded by police. That was a tipping point where the whole "Oswald as lone gunman" thing really started to wear thin with the American public. Anyone with half a brain could see that there was something fishy going on. It looked like Oswald was killed to keep him from talking. The reason it *looked* like Oswald was killed to keep him from talking was because Oswald was, in fact, killed to keep him from talking. Then people started to look closer at the other, rather strange, aspects of the official version of the Kennedy case. The foreign press, not under the sway of the Deep State, was blatant in their accusations that the Kennedy assassination was a coup d'état. All of the pressure of this public opinion caused Congress to get involved, and several Senate and House efforts were underway to investigate the Kennedy assassination. This then forced Johnson to create the Warren Commission. Had Johnson done nothing, Congress would have created investigations that were not under his control. The last thing he could afford was an actual investigation into the Kennedy assassination, so he reluctantly created what became the Warren Commission.

The task he gave the Warren Commission was simple – create a report that says Oswald did it alone so the mainstream media can then sell it to the public. The whole point of the Warren Commission was to have a bunch of distinguished "public servants" put their stamp of approval on the foregone conclusion that Oswald did it alone. The commissioners were recruited by Johnson with that criteria in mind. He needed people who would be seen as distinguished and who he could control. And he wanted a unanimous decision, so Earl Warren was chosen as the perfect person to lend his name to the process.

The foreign press was highly critical of the Oswald-as-lone-gunman theory, especially among people familiar with the Mannlicher-Carcano, a rifle with a well-deserved reputation as a piece of junk.[3362] When Dallas Police Chief Curry said that Oswald's death meant they could close the case, the London *Daily Telegraph* accurately referred to this statement as a "monumental absurdity."[3363] Charles de Gaulle expressed his contempt for the lone gunman theory. He predicted the cover up.[3364]

A close associate of Gandhi in India expressed his skepticism. He claimed:[3365]

> "he said he was fearful that the enemies of peace might have used Oswald as a tool, and then silenced him"[3366]

A paper called *The Patriot* published an editorial called Murder Politics which said:[3367]

> "It looks now as though Oswald, who was silenced so quickly, was only an agent. ... The ease with which a nightclub keeper with a criminal record could get access to a prisoner in police custody and shoot him suggests collusion. ... Obviously, the effort of the Dallas authorities ... was to insinuate Oswald was connected with communism and the Soviet Union. ... This taken together with the Dallas police chief's haste in declaring that the 'case had been closed' with the killing of Oswald, points to the existence of influences bent on changing Mr. Kennedy's policies at whatever cost. ... We cannot but be conscious of the fact that the man who was assassinated a few days ago was able to show men and women everywhere how to proceed along the path that will lead us to peace."[3368]

In Germany the *Homburger Echo* said:[3369]

> "Dallas police had an understandable interest in producing any suspect as quickly as possible while the rest of the country doubts that Oswald was the only or even the real assassin." It said "Oswald's murder raised suspicions that would make Kennedy's assassination a gang plot."[3370]

On November 24, 1963 Hoover created a memo. He also called Johnson aide Walter Jenkins to relay the sentiment in the memo, which included the following passage:[3371]

> "The thing I am most concerned about, and so is Mr. Katzenbach, is having something issued so we can convince the public that Oswald is the real assassin. Mr. Katzenbach

thinks that the president might appoint a presidential commission of three outstanding citizens, to make a determination. I countered with a suggestion that we make an investigative report to the Attorney General with pictures, laboratory work, etc., then the Attorney General can make the report to the president and the president can decide whether to make it public. We have no information on Ruby that is firm, although there are some rumors of underworld activity in Chicago."[3372]

On November 25, 1963 Hale Boggs of Louisiana called for a Congressional investigation into the Kennedy assassination.[3373] On November 26, 1963 the Senate and the House announced that they would make full investigations of the Kennedy assassination. Representative Hale Boggs of Louisiana was the first to suggest it and Senator Dirksen of Illinois made the announcement that both parties had approved the move after getting great numbers of telegrams from constituents requesting an investigation.[3374] That same day Deputy Attorney General Nicholas Katzenbach sent a message to presidential assistant Bill Moyers as follows:[3375]

"It is important that all the facts surrounding President Kennedy's assassination be made public in such a way which will satisfy people in the United States and abroad that all the facts have been told."

1. "The public must be satisfied that Oswald was the assassin, that he did not have confederates who are still at large and that the evidence was such that he would have been convicted at trial."

2. "Speculation about Oswald's motivation ought to be cut off and we should have some basis for rebutting thought that this was a right-wing conspiracy."

The FBI had been given jurisdiction over the investigation and had already prepared a report naming Oswald as the lone nut gunman.[3376]

Hoover had helped draft Katzenbach's warning message.[3377] FBI liaison to the White House Courtney Evans sends an internal FBI memo to Alan Belmont to say:[3378]

"Katzenbach noted. ... There have also been allegations that Oswald and Ruby were known to each other and were part of a conspiracy. It has been further alleged that Oswald was killed to silence him. ... It is [Katzenbach's] belief there might have to be some so-called editorial interpretation. He noted that the report will be subjected to the closest scrutiny by the worldwide press and foreign government representatives, as well as the American people. He knew that we were keeping this in mind in preparation of the report. ... The problem is to show motive, and this ... is a condition of Oswald's mind ... Oswald has admitted he was an avowed Marxist. ... While neither the White House nor the Department should be able to contend that our report does not meet the required purpose, we must be factual and recognize that a matter of this magnitude cannot be fully investigated in a week's time."[3379]

Congressional investigations would have their own investigative staff and therefore be dangerous. This is a key point. If Johnson creates a commission, he can limit it to having to rely on the FBI, the CIA, the Secret Service and the Dallas police for information. The threat of Congressional investigations forces Johnson to create a presidential commission. The last thing Johnson or Hoover want is an investigation that is not under Johnson's control, so LBJ agrees to create what becomes the Warren Commission.[3380]

Phillip Nelson, in his book *LBJ: THE MASTERMIND OF THE JFK ASSASSINATION*, said that:[3381]

> "It was J. Edgar Hoover's original statement that became the "mission statement" for the Warren Commission: "The thing I am concerned about, and so is Katzenbach, is having something issued so we can convince the public that Oswald is the real assassin.""[3382]

Johnson was originally going to let the corrupt Dallas authorities, who he could control, run the 'investigation' into the Kennedy assassination. The original plan did not call for Ruby to shoot Oswald on national television, and Johnson had not anticipated the public groundswell and call for a congressional investigation into the assassination. Once it became apparent that there was going to be an official federal investigation he realized he needed to get out in front of it. His solution to this was to create a presidential commission that he could control and which would come to the foregone conclusion that Oswald was the assassin and that he had acted alone. To do this Johnson created the Warren Commission and tasked it with finding Oswald guilty.

Johnson knew how to do this. He had done it before. He himself had chaired a committee where he, for his own purposes, needed to find Leland Olds 'guilty' of being a communist so he could be fired. Olds had done nothing wrong except to do his job, and that was the point.

Olds had been the head of the Federal Power Commission and he was forcing the utilities to provide competitive rates for utilities to consumers. Johnson's financial backers wanted Olds fired so they could make higher profits. Johnson had chaired the committee which held hearings on the issue and he stacked the committee with anticommunists and then painted Olds out to be a communist. The committee voted Olds out and Johnson's financial backers got what they wanted. In his book series *THE YEARS OF LYNDON JOHNSON*, Johnson biographer Robert Caro describes in detail how Johnson used his committee to smear and destroy Olds. Johnson understood, from his own experience, that a committee could be created and controlled to come to a foregone conclusion. He put this experience to good use with the creation of the Warren Commission. He created a commission stocked with people he could control who would come to the conclusion he wanted, and it worked. They came to the conclusion that Oswald was a lone nut who killed Kennedy all by himself.

As I mentioned before, I was shocked when I first found out that Allen Dulles was on the Warren Commission. Allen Dulles was, in my opinion, the prime suspect in the assassination of Kennedy and should have been the one being investigated, not the one running the investigation. As I dug into it I saw Johnson's genius once again at work. A careful look at the list of commissioners will show that all of them have full-time jobs except Dulles. Having recently been fired by Kennedy, Dulles had the time to devote to the commission that the others did not. That meant that it was Dulles and not Warren who was the commissioner in day-to-day charge of the commission. Dulles could be there onsite to make sure things didn't stray from the pre-ordained script. It was called the Warren Commission because Warren was the figurehead. This was on purpose. The fairy tale it produced would have the stamp of approval of the Chief Justice of the Supreme Court of the United States of America. Chief Justice Earl Warren after all was the Chief Justice who had produced the unanimous decision in the landmark Brown v. Board of Education case which forced the desegregation of schools in America.

Warren at first turned Johnson down. He was then persuaded by Johnson to put his stamp on the foregone conclusion that Oswald acted alone. Johnson did this by claiming that there were too many wild rumors circulating that the Cubans and/or the Russians were behind Oswald and this could spiral out of control and start World War Three and kill forty million Americans in a nuclear war. President Johnson told Warren that his country needed him to help avert this disaster, and Warren reluctantly agreed.

Johnson also asked his longtime mentor and friend Senator Richard Russell to be on the commission. Johnson no doubt assumed he could control Russell. The same was true of John McCloy, who was a former president of the World Bank and member of the Council on Foreign Relations and was friends with the wealthy oil barons. The oil barons would have vouched for McCloy if Johnson had needed them to. More importantly, McCloy had been very good friends with Allen Dulles for decades. They thought alike. He could be counted on to help keep things on track.

Congressman Gerald Ford was seen by Johnson and Hoover as someone who could be controlled. He had been caught in a honey trap set by Hoover and had been doing Hoover's bidding ever since. Hoover had evidence of his infidelity and no doubt used this as subtle pressure to make sure Ford was a reliable tool.

Hale Boggs was one of the Congressional representatives who had originally called for a Congressional investigation, so it would look good to have him involved. As a representative from Louisiana, Johnson probably thought that, since mafia boss Carlos Marcello was also from Louisiana, he could use Marcello's influence to keep Boggs in line.

Johnson rounded out the group with Senator John Sherman Cooper. Johnson's bureaucratic instincts were, as always, right on the money. The Warren Commission produced exactly what he wanted – a report saying Oswald was the lone nut shooter who did not have any accomplices.

Warren Commissioners:

- Earl Warren – Chief Justice of the U.S. Supreme Court
- Allen Dulles – former Director of Central Intelligence Agency
- Gerald Ford – Republican Congressional Representative from Michigan
- John McCloy – former president of the World Bank and Chairman of the Council on Foreign Relations
- Richard Russell – Democratic Senator from Georgia
- John Sherman Cooper – Republican Senator from Kentucky
- Hale Boggs – Democratic Congressional Representative from Louisiana

The CIA had set up Oswald as a patsy with a bonus. The bonus was that he had been to Russia and had even been to New Orleans for the express purpose of hanging a pro-Castro sign around his neck. He had been manipulated into doing things that would implicate both Cuba and Russia in the Kennedy assassination. This was because the CIA and the Pentagon still wanted an excuse to start World War Three. Johnson, once he was president, decided against this option. The Russians, as Kennedy had pointed out to his generals, were likely to shoot back. So, Johnson jettisoned the whole idea of using the Kennedy assassination as a pretext to invade Cuba or attack the Soviet Union. However, the concept could still be useful to him before he abandoned it entirely. The threat of World War Three was just the leverage he needed to get a reluctant Chief Justice Earl Warren and an equally reluctant Senator Richard Russell to join his new commission.[3383] Johnson told them that the job of the commission was to squash the rumors circulating that there was a conspiracy. Johnon told them this had to be done so that Khrushchev didn't think that we were going to attack the Soviet Union in retaliation for killing Kennedy and then one thing leads to another and we end up in a nuclear war that could cost the lives of forty million Americans.[3384] For the good of the country these nasty conspiracy rumors had to be squashed. The cost of a nuclear war was just so high that we couldn't afford to risk these rumors getting traction. Oswald had to be painted out to be a lone nut, no matter what. This was Johnson at his manipulative best. He convinced Warren and Russell, neither of whom wanted anything to do with the commission, to go along. Warren at first said he was too busy, and Russell hated Warren for his civil rights rulings and did not want to be in the same room with him, but Johnson overcame all their objections with the 'nuclear option' sales pitch and it worked.[3385] Johnson was a genius. He was an evil genius, but he was a genius. The rest of the commissioners were relatively easy to recruit once Warren and Russell were in.

Author Phillip Nelson, in his book *LBJ: THE MASTERMIND OF THE JFK ASSASSINATION*, expressed the opinion that Johnson chose Gerald Ford, John McCloy and Allen Dulles because he could control them.[3386] I agree with Nelson's assessment, but I would also add that Russell and Johnson were extremely close. Russell was a mentor to Johnson going back to the 1940's. Johnson assumed, correctly as it turned out, that he could also control Russell. Warren had his marching orders – squash all rumors of a conspiracy for the good of the country. Russell had been recruited with the same angle. Ford, McCloy and Dulles were picked for their dependable loyalty. Hale Boggs was added because he had been the first to call for an investigation, but he was vastly outnumbered. Johnson had his hand-picked team with

Dulles, not Warren, in charge. Warren lent his name to the enterprise, but Dulles was the only one of the seven with the time available to attend the meetings and run things on a day-to-day basis.

On November 29, 1963 the Warren Commission was announced to the public. One of the first things Warren did was to make sure that the Warren Commission would conduct business in secret.[3387] The last thing he was going to do was have an open, transparent investigation.

Years later, Senator Schweiker had this to say regarding the results of the Warren Commission:[3388]

> "The Warren Commission has collapsed like a house of cards. I believe that the Warren Commission was set up at the time to feed pabulum to the American people for reasons not yet known, and that one of the biggest cover-ups in the history of our country occurred at that time."[3389]

The reason for the collapse of the reputation of the Warren Commission, as well as for the collapse of the public's opinion of the results published in the Warren Report, are easy to understand. It was a house of cards from the beginning, only meant to hold up long enough to give the commissioner's collective blessing to the theory that Oswald was a lone nut who shot Kennedy. The Warren Commission was never created to do an investigation. As such, it had no investigators. The commission was completely dependent on J. Edgar Hoover, the FBI, the CIA, the Secret Service, the Dallas police and other government agencies for information.[3390] The last thing Hoover and the other conspirators were going to do was hand over any relevant or incriminating evidence on themselves. Dulles' loyal troops at the CIA certainly weren't going to incriminate themselves. The Warren Commission never stood a chance to run a real investigation of the Kennedy assassination, as Johnson had promised the American people when he created it. And, once the commissioners had been carefully chosen to make sure the Warren Commission came up with the foregone conclusion, the staff they hired and managed for the actual tasks of holding hearings and writing a report didn't stand a chance. At one point, Lee Rankin caught Hoover lying about Oswald and lying also about the involvement of the mafia. Oswald had been an FBI informant and the mafia had been involved in the Kennedy assassination, but the commissioners closed ranks and let Hoover get away with saying that none of this was true. The staff hired by the commission, almost all capable lawyers, were mostly competent and patriotic people who did the best they could but they were caught in a hopeless charade where they had no chance of coming up with the truth. Johnson was able, just barely, to keep control of the commissioners long enough to get the appearance of a unanimous decision. That was what he needed to then get the mainstream media to kick in and sell the result to the public.

Author Mark North, in his book ACT OF TREASON, said:[3391]

> "Because of the basic issues raised by the crisis, the controlling faction within the commission made the decision to withhold the truth from the public. John Kennedy was dead. In their minds, the integrity of the presidency and FBI could not be allowed to follow him. Tragically this decision had the disastrous effect of ensuring both Hoover and Johnson's positions in power, not to mention the general chilling effect on the efforts of others to prosecute the mafia."[3392]

Walter Cronkite told us "we must have faith" in the commission.[3393]

Earl Warren

Allen Dulles was Johnson's first choice to be the chairman of what became the Warren Commission but then he went for Warren as a better choice.[3394] Dulles was not someone who should spend a lot of time in the spotlight. Warren had arranged for the famously unanimous U.S. Supreme Court decision in Brown vs. Board of Education in 1954 that declared "separate but equal" to be unconstitutional.[3395] This ability to get a unanimous decision from a divided group likely played a part in Johnson's decision to pick Warren for the job of chairman of his commission. By stacking the commission, Johnson knew he could get a majority of the commission to go along. After all, Johnson got to choose the members of the commission. But he would need someone with Warren's skills to get the rest of the group to make it unanimous.[3396] And Warren himself desperately wanted the decision of the commission to be unanimous.[3397]

On December 27, 1963 there were press reports that Chief Justice Earl Warren was hanged in effigy from the Santa Barbara, California county courthouse flagpole with a sign describing him as the "head of the Oswald whitewash committee."[3398]

Warren went along with the idea that the commission was not going to do any investigating, and simply relied on the results of investigations of other government agencies. He also did not want public hearings, and there were almost none.[3399] Thus, almost all the work of the commission was carried out in secret, and the press was banned from the hearings.[3400]   The Warren Commission took statements from witnesses and then sealed them so the American people could not see them.[3401] This was the whole point. The last thing Johnson and the other conspirators wanted the public to see was actual evidence.

On February 4, 1964 a reporter asked Warren if the full report was to be made public. Warren replied: "Yes. There will come a time, but it might not be in your lifetime. ... There may be some things that would involve security."[3402]   This, of course, is Warren saying "NO" without using the word "no." The real answer to the question was no, the full report, for what it's worth, will never be made public. Warren, a career politician, had learned how to say "no" in a politically correct manner, making it sound like "yes." Notice the first word in his answer is "yes."

Allen Dulles

As mentioned above, Allen Dulles was Johnson's first choice to be the chairman of what became the Warren Commission but then went for Warren as a better choice.[3403]   While Warren had his name on the commission for public relations purposes (which was the whole point of the commission in the first place), Dulles was clearly Johnson's choice to run the commission.[3404] To begin with, he was the only one of the seven commissioners who had the time. Having been fired by Kennedy, he was available to do the day-to-day work necessary to keep the commission from jumping the tracks laid out for it.[3405] "I don't think Allen Dulles ever missed a meeting." Said Warren.[3406]   Dulles micro-managed the committee and its General Counsel Lee Rankin. There was no detail too small.[3407]

Allen Dulles should have been a prime suspect in the Kennedy assassination, not running the investigation. As David Talbot points out in his book *THE DEVIL'S CHESSBOARD: ALLEN DULLES, THE CIA, AND THE RISE OF AMERICA'S SECRET GOVERNMENT*:[3408]

> "In the weeks leading up to the assassination of President Kennedy on November 22, 1963, the flurry of meetings at Dulles' house intensified. Among the CIA men coming in and out of Q Street were several who later came under investigation by the House Select Committee on Assassinations and other probes for their possible connection to the president's murder. And on the weekend of the assassination, Dulles hunkered down for unexplained reasons

at a secret CIA facility in northern Virginia known as "The Farm" despite the fact that he had been removed from the Agency two years earlier."[3409]

Dulles had the means, the motive and the opportunity to be part of the conspiracy to assassinate Kennedy. The assassination and cover-up would be difficult to imagine without his direct involvement.

Through his entire time on the commission, Dulles never told the others on the commission that the CIA had been trying to kill Castro continuously since he first came to power in Cuba. Earl Warren only read about it in the newspapers in January of 1967.[3410]

At the first meeting of the Warren Commission Allen Dulles handed out a book that claimed that the assassinations of American presidents were all done by lone nuts.[3411] At that meeting he also said that an atmosphere of rumor and suspicion interferes with the functioning of the government, especially abroad, and one of the main tasks of the commission was to dispel rumors.[3412]

Author Mark Lane, in his book *LAST WORD: MY INDICTMENT OF THE CIA IN THE MURDER OF JFK*, points out that:[3413]

> "Dulles even told the other members that they needn't worry about anyone doubting their false conclusions because maybe, at worst, it would be some professor off in the distant future who would study the evidence and by that time it wouldn't matter."[3414]

Dulles used his press connections, like the *New York Times*, to issue leaks and control the spin.[3415]

Author Mark North, in his book *ACT OF TREASON: THE ROLE OF J. EDGAR HOOVER IN THE ASSASSINATION OF PRESIDENT KENNEDY*, pointed out that:[3416]

> "Shortly after his appointment to the commission, Dulles told *New York Post* columnist Murray Kempton that he was certain no evidence of a conspiracy would be found..."[3417]

North goes on to say that "This belief is logical. Dulles, schooled in intelligence work, has been placed on the commission for the very purposes of containment." North also points out that Dulles knew that Hoover was hiding evidence from the commission.[3418]

Author David Talbot, in his book *THE DEVIL'S CHESSBOARD: ALLEN DULLES, THE CIA, AND THE RISE OF AMERICA'S SECRET GOVERNMENT*, recounts the confrontation at UCLA between David Lifton and Allen Dulles. In December of 1965 Dulles went to UCLA as a well-paid guest lecturer where he got questioned by some folks who had hard questions for him.[3419] David Lifton was a graduate student at UCLA who was an engineering and physics major.[3420] He had attended a Mark Lane lecture and had decided to focus on the Kennedy assassination.[3421] Lifton brought some documents with him.[3422] There was ample evidence of a conspiracy because someone had to have fired from the front.[3423] Lifton confronted Dulles with hard evidence that there were plenty of witnesses who saw smoke, giving names of people that author and assassination researcher Harold Feldman had dug up.[3424] Dulles laughed at the mention of *The Nation* writer, but he laughed alone.[3425] Then Dulles tried to move on and failed.[3426] Lifton passed the photos around and the students could see for themselves.[3427] When Dulles finally left Lifton gave a two-hour presentation to the gathered students on the evidence of a conspiracy.[3428] Talbot said this was as close as Dulles came to actually having to answer questions about the Kennedy assassination.[3429]

Gerald Ford

J. Edgar Hoover at the FBI very much wanted Gerald Ford to be elected to Congress and helped Ford get elected.[3430] Ford immediately reciprocated in his first speech to Congress by asking for an increase in Hoover's salary.[3431]

Congressman Gerald Ford got caught in a honey trap. Bobby Baker and Fred Black had a suite at the Sheraton Carlton Hotel where they arranged for call girls to entertain guests like congressmen and senators.[3432] Ford was a frequent visitor according to Baker, and the FBI filmed the action.[3433] Hoover had decided to monitor the hotel suite that Baker and Black used for their 'friends' to meet women.[3434] Since Hoover had information on what was going on in the suite and he shared everything with Johnson, Johnson had that same information. The suite was originally bugged to spy on Baker, but Ford was caught in the same honey trap when he borrowed the key to the suite to use for the same purpose.[3435] This may help explain why Ford was so willing to go to such great lengths to assist in the cover-up of the Kennedy assassination, including moving the entry wound bullet hole in Kennedy's back so that it lined up with the Magic Bullet fiction.[3436]

At the first meeting of the Warren Commission Ford said that dispelling damaging rumors was a major concern of the commission.[3437]

Author Mark North, in his book *ACT OF TREASON: THE ROLE OF J.
EDGAR HOOVER IN THE ASSASSINATION OF PRESIDENT
KENNEDY*, documents that Assistant FBI Director Sullivan will later
state:

> "Hoover was delighted when Ford was named to the Warren
> Commission. The Director wrote in one of his internal memos
> that the Bureau could expect Ford to 'look after FBI interests'
> and he did, keeping us fully advised of what was going on
> behind closed doors. He was our ... informant on the Warren
> Commission"[3438]

North goes on to point out that, in an internal FBI memo from Deke
DeLoach to Hoover regarding a meeting with Ford:

> "He asked that I come up to see him. Upon arriving he told
> me he wanted to talk in the strictest of confidence. This was
> agreed to. Ford indicated he would keep me thoroughly
> advised as to the activities of the commission."[3439]

And that:

> "Ford apparently discusses the fact that he, Dulles and Boggs
> had successfully opposed Warren's choice for general counsel
> (Warren Olney). He states he is "disturbed about the manner
> in which Chief Justice Warren is carrying on his chairmanship
> of the Presidential Commission." Warren's defeat on this
> issue, in conjunction with other data he possesses, may well
> have convinced him that he should do nothing more than go
> along with Hoover and Johnson. Ford's data is very good
> news to Hoover, as he had, of course, also opposed Olney.
> Ford is fundamentally at odds with Warren from the outset,
> presumably believing he is trying to deflect attention from the
> fact that Oswald was a "kill-crazy communist." He feels that
> Warren is dangerously liberal, a belief that is undoubtedly
> reinforced by the FBI. Hoover loathes Warren. Ford also tells
> DeLoach that CIA Director McCone has informed him of an
> Oswald/Cuban contact in Mexico City during which Oswald
> had accepted money. DeLoach informs Ford that the report is
> baseless, no doubt being fully aware of the CIA's ongoing
> effort to implicate Cuba in any way it can. By this point Ford
> is unknowingly eating out of Hoover's hand, providing
> considerable aid to a traitor."[3440]

In order for the conspiracy to be covered up, evidence of a shot from
the front had to be covered up. In order for a shot from the front to be
covered up, the Magic Bullet had to have gone through Kennedy and

Connally, not only doing the work of several actual shots, but coming from behind and not in front. In order for this fiction to be sold to the public, the entry wound in Kennedy's right shoulder had to be lined up with the entry wound in his throat and the throat wound had to become an exit wound. To make this happen, Ford changed the text of a key sentence about the entrance wound on Kennedy's back.[3441] The draft originally said that "a bullet had entered his back at a point slightly above the shoulder and to the right of the spine" and Ford crossed out those words and changed them to "a bullet had entered the base of the back his neck slightly to the right of the spine" and the change was made.[3442]

Ford later insisted later that his "small change" was meant to clarify things, but the effect of the "small change" was crucial to support the magic bullet theory and make the whole lone nut theory work.[3443]

The American public only learned of Ford's evidence tampering in 1993, over three decades after the assassination, and this information was only released because of the Assassination Records Review Board (ARRB).[3444]

Gerald Ford wrote afterwards:

"There is no evidence of a second man, of other shots or other guns."[3445]

That was not true, not even back in 1964.[3446]

Ford clarified later to the History Channel that:

"We said we found no evidence of a conspiracy, we didn't say there was no conspiracy."[3447]

And finally, this quote from Gerald Ford:

"The monumental record of the President's Commission will stand like a Gibraltar of factual literature through the ages to come."[3448]

John McCloy

Harold Ickes said of John McCloy:

"He is more or less inclined to be a fascist."[3449]

McCloy became friends with Dulles thirty years before they teamed up on the Warren Commission.[3450] They met in 1930 while working together as lawyers.[3451] McCloy made a fortune as a Wall Street lawyer representing rich people getting richer running stock scams.[3452] This was where he met Allen Dulles.[3453] McCloy went to work for Secretary of War Henry Stimson and was instrumental in supporting the decision to intern Japanese Americans during World War II.[3454] McCloy was willing to consider the Constitution a "scrap of paper" where the safety of the country was concerned.[3455] McCloy also manipulated evidence in Japanese internment cases to make sure the courts ruled against the Japanese-Americans.[3456] After the war, McCloy helped Nazi Klaus Barbie, the Butcher of Lyon, to escape because McCloy thought Barbie could help in the fight against communism in the Cold War.[3457] Later, McCloy helped convince President Carter to let the Shah of Iran into the U.S., sparking the Iranian Hostage Crisis.[3458]

John McCloy presided over loans to the Nazis in Germany in the 1930's, then he was made high commissioner after the war and shipped a bunch of unrepentant Nazis over to the U.S.[3459] His protégé was Allen Dulles and McCloy, while on the Warren Commission, said "it is of paramount importance to show the world that the United States is not a banana republic were a government can be changed by conspiracy."[3460] While John McCloy was high commissioner to Germany in 1950 he appointed Nazi spy chief Reinhard Gehlen to become the chief of intelligence for what became West Germany.[3461] McCloy was a hard-line Cold Warrior who left the Kennedy administration over differences in their approach to the Soviet Union.[3462] After he left the administration, McCloy went to work for a law firm where he represented anti-Kennedy oilmen Clint Murchison and Sid Richardson, who he had known since his days at Chase Manhattan.[3463]

In addition to being a longtime associate of the oil barons, McCloy was also a certified member of the Deep State. McCloy also served as President of the World Bank and as Chairman of International House.[3464] McCloy was also Chairman of the Council on Foreign Relations.[3465] These organizations believe in elites running the world. Kennedy was against the United States becoming a colonial power and was a proponent of third-world nationalism. He wanted developing countries to elect their own leaders. The Dulles brothers and McCloy saw the world fundamentally differently, which was why neither of them lasted long in the Kennedy administration.

In choosing McCloy to help with the Warren Commission whitewash, Johnson was picking an insider who was already "on the team."

Dulles, McCloy and Ford took control of the committee right away. The first thing they did was block Warren from appointing Warren Olney as chief counsel.[3466]

John McCloy was at the meeting of the other conspirators the night before JFK was killed.

Richard Russell

Senator Russell also turned Johnson down at first. He hated Warren for his civil rights rulings and did not want to be in the same room with him. He was also persuaded by Johnson to put his stamp on the foregone conclusion that Oswald acted alone. Johnson did this by claiming that there were too many wild rumors circulating that the Cubans and/or the Russians were behind Oswald and this could spiral out of control and start World War Three and kill forty million Americans in a nuclear war. His country needed him to help avert this potential disaster. Russell's last-ditch effort to avoid serving on the commission was to claim that he did not have the time. In response Johnson told Russell that:[3467]

> "There's not going to be any time to begin with. All you got to do is evaluate a Hoover report he's already written."[3468]

When Johnson also told Russell that his name had already been announced as being on the commission, Russell reluctantly agreed.

Johnson and Russell talk almost daily, sometimes twice a day, during the time of the Warren Commission, although Russell, for his part, attended few of the commission meetings.[3469] By February of 1964 Russell was tired of the Warren Commission while doing his best in the Senate to block the civil rights legislation that Johnson was now backing.[3470] Russell had decided to quit the commission and wrote a letter of resignation to Johnson, then didn't send it.[3471] Russell was the only member of the commission who did not show up regularly.[3472] Rankin went to see Russell and told him that Warren had offered to hire a lawyer to help Russell keep up with the commission and Russell agreed to stay on the commission.[3473]

In the end, Johnson was right. He was able to use his deep relationship with Russell to keep Russell from publicly voicing his doubts about the conclusions of the Warren Report, which hung on the slender thread of the Magic Bullet fiction.[3474]

Russell voiced his concern about this to Johnson, who replied:

"Well, what difference does it make which bullet hit Connally?"[3475]

And Russell said:

"Well, it doesn't make much difference. But they said that ... the Commission believes that the same bullet that hit Kennedy hit Connally. Well, I don't believe it."[3476]

Russell was close to Johnson, but he wasn't buying the Magic Bullet fiction, and that meant he wasn't buying the lone gunman theory. The whole point of the Magic Bullet was to be able to claim that one bullet struck both Kennedy and Connally, so there only had to be one shooter, Oswald. Russell got his assistant, Colonel Phillip Corso, to conduct his own investigation.[3477] Corso was told not to keep any written records, and he came to the conclusion that there was a conspiracy.[3478] Russell then teamed up with commissioners Boggs and Cooper to demand a private executive session to discuss their concerns.[3479] At this "no-holds barred shouting match" Russell forced their agreement that his written dissent would be published with the final Warren Report.[3480] Even with this agreement, Russell still needed the famous "Johnson treatment" to be arm-twisted into signing the Warren Report, only to be shocked later to discover that he had been swindled.[3481] After all that, his dissent was not published with the Warren Report or even buried in the twenty-six volumes of exhibits.[3482] It was only found many years later among his papers.[3483]

Author Philip Shenon, in his book *A CRUEL AND SHOCKING ACT*, pointed out that:[3484]

"Senator Richard Russell had one last way in 1964 to show how much he disapproved of the commission's report. It might bear Russell's name, but that did not mean the report had to bear his actual signature, in fresh ink."[3485]

"As a memento of the investigation, Warren had wanted to give each of the commissioners – and every member of the staff – a copy of the final report that was hand-signed by all seven of them. (The report's cover page bore a printed version of their signatures.) He also wanted to give everyone an autographed copy of the official joint portrait of the commissioners. So more than one hundred copies of the report and the photo were set aside for that purpose, and the commissioners were invited to stop by the office at their convenience to do the signings."[3486]

"On December 7, after all the other commissioners had turned up to sign copies of the report and the photograph, Julia Eide, Rankin's secretary, said she was giving up on Russell. The senator had refused to sign, insisting for weeks that he was too busy with Senate business to cross the street to the commission's offices. She called Russell's office that day and spoke to one of his secretaries, who said that the senator had just left for Georgia and did not intend to return until the new year."[3487]

"I guess they will have to be sent out without his signature," Eide wrote to Rankin, hinting that she knew just how close the commission had come to a divided report because of Russell. "And what's the difference?" she wrote. "It didn't seem to me that he did anything except cause us some trouble, so perhaps the books don't deserve his 'John Henry.'"[3488]

"We have not been told the truth about Oswald." Senator Richard Russell, former Warren Commission member, 1970.[3489]

In the 1970's Richard Russell declared to the press that he believed someone else had worked with Oswald.[3490]

John Sherman Cooper

Senator John Cooper and John McCloy appear to have known each other from their time in Germany during and after World War Two. Perhaps McCloy suggested Cooper to Johnson as someone who could be trusted to go along with the program. McCloy was a mentor to Dulles and perhaps he did a few favors for Cooper in Germany and was in a position to call in his markers during the Warren Commission. Perhaps Cooper was considered trustworthy because Cooper was part of the Georgetown set. All of this is pure speculation on my part, as I could not find any reason why Johnson thought he could control Cooper. Cooper appears to have been an honest man who eventually joined the dissenters on the commission.

Author Mark North, in his book *BETRAYAL IN DALLAS*, said that:[3491]

"Following the HSCA's overturning of the Warren Report's conclusions, an anguished former Warren Commission member Senator John Cooper went public with his belief in conspiracy, telling the press, "I heard Governor Connally testify very strongly that he was not struck by the same bullet, and I could not convince myself that the same bullet struck both of them." Cooper knew, as did the other commissioners, that separate bullets meant two shooters and conspiracy."[3492]

Hale Boggs

On November 25, 1963 Hale Boggs of Louisiana is the first to call for a congressional investigation into the Kennedy assassination.[3493] This is likely how he came to be on the Warren Commission.

Hale Boggs later said that "Hoover lied his eyes out to the Commission, on Oswald, on Ruby, on their friends, the bullets, the gun, you name it …"[3494]

Author Phillip Nelson, in his book *LBJ: THE MASTERMIND OF THE JFK ASSASSINATION*, says that, during the Garrison investigation in 1976:[3495]

> "Hale Boggs, a former member of the Warren Commission, had commented to several people that the assassination might be linked directly back to Lyndon Johnson."[3496]

Nelson goes on to say that before Boggs died under mysterious circumstances and his Warren Commission records disappeared from Tulane he had announced that he had some startling revelations about the Kennedy assassination.[3497]

The Magic Bullet Fiction

The Warren Commission had too many shots to deal with. Their charter was to come up with the conclusion that Oswald was a lone shooter from the Texas School Book Depository, which was behind the president as he was being shot. The problem was that there were multiple shooters from multiple directions and they were having a hard time dealing with all of them. They had come up with three shots, which was the maximum anyone could have physically gotten off with a bolt action rifle in the six seconds during which there was shooting. Never mind aiming, just pumping the bolt and squeezing the trigger took a few seconds for each shot, so the most anyone could physically accomplish was three shots.[3498]

So, the first thing the authorities did was bury the evidence of as many shots as possible. All the photographs of the puff of smoke from the fence at the top of the knoll had been confiscated. The bullet found in the grass had been sent down a black hole. The shot to the chrome strip at the top of the limousine had been ignored. The limousine itself had been sent to be rebuilt so the crime scene would be destroyed. The bullet fragments in the limousine had been cleaned out. The scar on the sidewalk had been ignored. Even the chunk of curb where they tried to hide the Tague shot had been removed and sent to Washington. This still left too many shots to account for. The conspirators had planned on a minimum of at least three shooting teams (each team with a shooter and a spotter) from different directions. They could not take any chances of Kennedy getting out of Dealey Plaza alive. They understood the seriousness of what they were doing. They were going to the electric chair if Kennedy was just wounded. As long as he died, the evidence of the number of shots could be covered up later. After all, they had already made pre-assassination plans to:

- Confiscate all the photographs and film from bystanders and witnesses in Dealey Plaza
- Intimidate any witnesses who got stubborn and didn't want to change their story
- Kill any really brave and reluctant witnesses who refused to go along with the party line
- Grab the body from Parkland to make sure that the Dallas doctors didn't do a real autopsy
- Switch the body to a shipping casket and work on it for a while before the official autopsy

- Have the official autopsy at either Walter Reed or Bethesda where they could control the military doctors and keep them from tracking the wounds in a proper autopsy procedure
- Kill Oswald before he could talk or (God forbid) go to trial and defend himself in a court of law

Kennedy had been hit in the back, the throat and the head, and Connally had been hit at least once, not to mention bullets hitting the pavement, the turf, the chrome strip at the top of the windshield, etc. and all this had to be squeezed somehow into three shots. Then came the news that Tague was hit, and it blew up their chances of getting anyone to believe that all this happened by three shots from one shooter. This was why they tried to ignore Tague, and only acknowledged his wound when they were forced by Martha Jo Stroud. During the shooting, James Tague was struck by a fragment of a bullet that first hit the curb. He reported the incident to Dallas Deputy Sheriff Walters and Dallas Police Officer Haygood.[3499] Two journalists, Tom Dillard and James Underwood also took photographs of the mark on the curb.[3500] Tague as interviewed by FBI Agent Kreutzer.[3501] The authorities did their best to bury the incident. They did this because the last thing they needed was to have to account for more shots. Not until July of 1964 when Martha Jo Stroud, Assistant U.S. Attorney for Dallas, sent an official letter to the Warren Commission with a photograph did the Commission ask the FBI to look into it, which they reluctantly did.[3502] The authorities eventually had to admit it existed. There was just too much evidence for them to bury it.

There were obviously more than three shots, and with the missed shot that struck the curb and then Tague, they had to come up with *something* to explain them all. The Tague fragment may have been the tipping point that forced the Warren Commission to create the Magic Bullet fiction. About that time was when Arlen Specter, who at that time was the assistant counsel to the Warren Commission, came up with the idea of combining several shots into one, and why we now we have the Magic Bullet fiction. By claiming it had gone into Kennedy's back and come out his throat and then went on to cause all of Connally's wounds, Specter could combine at least three shots into one. A bullet passed completely through Connally's chest, fracturing ribs, collapsing his right lung and causing massive bleeding.[3503] The bullet fractured his right forearm and penetrated his thigh.[3504] He was on the brink of death.[3505] Assuming Connally's multiple wounds came from one bullet, which was at least possible, the other two shots that the Magic Bullet theory covered were the entrance wound (shot from the front) in Kennedy's throat and the shoulder wound (from behind) in Kennedy's back. By literally moving the wound in Kennedy's back from his shoulder to his neck, and by changing the entrance wound in his throat (from the front) to an exit wound of a bullet that then went on to almost kill Connally with multiple wounds, Specter was able to combine at least three shots into one. At first this didn't even pass the laugh test at the Warren Commission. Then they slowly came to realize that they were stuck with it, like it or not, because they had to make the facts fit the 'lone gunman' theory. They slowly stopped laughing and eventually went along. They had to. There was no other way to fit all the damage into three shots.

According to author Mark Lane, in his book LAST WORD: *MY INDICTMENT OF THE CIA IN THE MURDER OF JFK*:[3506]

> "Another problem was that Connally was able to locate the frame at which he was first struck. It took place 1.8 seconds after JFK was hit. The commission got around this by saying that Connally had not noticed when he was hit a "glancing blow." But Connally was absolutely sure he had noticed when his ribs were smashed."[3507]

The Magic Bullet is fiction, but just to be clear, there is plenty of hard evidence to that effect. The bullet holes in the shirt and coat that Kennedy was wearing that day are hard proof that the Magic Bullet theory is not possible.[3508] Gerald Ford could use his position on the commission to "move" the wounds on paper and in the Warren Report, but the shirt and coat show that Kennedy was shot from behind in the right shoulder, not in the back of the neck.

Arlen Specter also bullied Darryl Tomlinson, who found the magic bullet, into saying he found it on a stretcher that connected it to Connally.[3509]

The Magic Bullet, officially known as CE 399, for Commission Exhibit #399, was magically found at Parkland Hospital on a stretcher. The stretcher was never tied to Connally, who it supposedly came out of. One of two people is likely to have planted the bullet. The first person was an FBI agent who tried to barge into the emergency room at Parkland Hospital and failed. The second person is Jack Ruby. Either one of them could have planted the bullet that was later found. Someone who claimed to be FBI named either Doyle Williams (or perhaps a different FBI agent named Robert Barrett, who was at the Texas theatre when Oswald was arrested) tried to barge his way past the Secret Service agents into the emergency room and was knocked to the floor by a Secret Service agent named Andrew Berger.[3510] Jack Ruby was also seen at Parkland Hospital at around 1:00 PM on the day of the assassination.[3511] Either the FBI agent or Ruby could have been there to plant a bullet that later became known as the Magic Bullet.

CE 399 has to be seen to be believed. I urge anyone to Google a picture of the Magic Bullet. It has been described by many people as in "pristine" condition. It is a copper-coated military bullet and it appears to be in remarkably excellent shape for having done all the damage attributed to it by the Warren Commission.

Nurse Audrey Bell, the supervisor who handled the fragments that came out of Connally, said that:[3512]

> "The smallest was the size of a striking end of a match, and the largest at least twice that big. I've seen the picture of the magic bullet, and I can't see how it could be the bullet from which the fragments I saw came."[3513]

This is one of the reasons I urge anyone to look up a picture of CE 399. You can see there are no fragments missing from it. The reason it is not smashed or flattened by having crashed through two human bodies and multiple ribs is that CE 399 didn't do any of those things. It was likely recovered from having been shot into a barrel of water and then planted as evidence. However, it wasn't originally planted at Parkland. CE 399 is, as mentioned earlier, a copper-coated military round. The original bullet that was planted at Parkland was a lead-colored hunting round. In 1996 author Josiah Thompson showed O.P. Wright, the Parkland Hospital security chief who turned the bullet over to the Secret Service, a picture of CE 399. Wright said he had turned over a lead-colored, sharp-pointed hunting round. Having worked for the sheriff's department he knew the difference.[3514]

Josiah Thompson wrote a book, *SIX SECONDS IN DALLAS*, that proves multiple shooters and demolishes the 'Magic Bullet' fiction.[3515]

Dissention

Author Philip Shenon, in his book *A CRUEL AND SHOCKING ACT*, documents the dissent:[3516]

> "Warren was more determined than ever to produce a unanimous report; anything less might lead the public to conclude that the facts about the president's murder were still uncertain or that they were being hidden."[3517]

> "Russell told aides after the meeting that Warren had, at first, stubbornly refused to alter the report to raise any questions about the single-bullet theory. "Warren just wouldn't give in," he told his longtime Senate secretary. "He was adamant that this was the way it was gonna be." According to Russell's account, Warren explained the necessity for a unanimous report and then urged the commission to adopt the findings as they had been laid out by the staff: Russell recalled that Warren looked around the room at the other commissioners and declared, before inviting any discussion, "We're all agreed and we're going to sign the report."[3518]

> "That was when Russell spoke up to correct – and to challenge – the chief justice. They were *not* in agreement. There would be a dissent, he warned, especially about the single-bullet theory. "I'll never sign the report if this commission says categorically that the second shot passed through both" Kennedy and Connally, he declared. He was offended, he said, by the idea that the commission would challenge Connally's certainty that he had been hit by a separate bullet. Senator Cooper spoke up to support Russell, saying he also believed Connally and would sign the dissent. Russell remembered Boggs suggested that he, too, was not fully convinced by the single-bullet theory."[3519]

The result was a change in the language that allowed for the possibility of separate bullets hitting Kennedy and Connally, but that all bullets had come from the sixth floor of the Texas School Book Depository.[3520]

> "Although it is not necessary to any essential findings of the commission to determine just which shot hit Governor Connally, there is very persuasive evidence from the experts to indicate that the same bullet which pierced the President's throat also caused Governor Connally's wounds. However, Connally's testimony and certain other factors have given rise

to some difference of opinion as to this probability, but there is no question in the mind of any member of the Commission that all the shots which caused the President's and Governor Connally's wounds were fired from the sixth-floor window of the Texas School Book Depository."[3521]

The Warren Commission was not unanimous.[3522] Richard Russell led a group of three that included himself, Senator John Sherman Cooper and Congressman Hale Boggs, who only accepted the final report after some changes and only after Warren insisted that the final report had to be unanimous.[3523]

Later they found that, of the 13 executive sessions of the commission, the only one not transcribed was the session where the three had objected.[3524] All that was published were brief minutes that left out any mention of dissent.[3525] In a 1966 article Senator Russell said he had doubts that Oswald acted alone.[3526]

Ford, Dulles and McCloy were dominant and Russell, Boggs and Cooper were marginalized and tricked into signing the report.[3527]

Hale Boggs later said that "Hoover lied his eyes out to the Commission, on Oswald, on Ruby, on their friends, the bullets, the gun, you name it …"[3528]

The Commission

Given the secrecy in which the Warren Commission worked, some time elapsed until we got a clear picture of what went on behind the scenes. What has emerged over the years is a picture of the Warren Commission as having a brief and dysfunctional childhood followed by a premature death. Hoover and Johnson only reluctantly created the commission, and then tried their best to strangle it. Johnson, having created the commission, continually hounded Warren to wrap things up and finish as quickly as possible.[3529] Hoover, having pushed Johnson to create the commission, immediately resented its existence and refused to participate. He sent them a summary report and demanded that they rubber stamp it. When they asked for information, he went to Johnson and tried to figure out how to avoid giving them any. Failing that, he inundated them with a mountain of trivial paperwork in the hope they could not find what they were looking for. When they asked Hoover about mafia involvement or if Oswald was an FBI informant and Hoover lied, they questioned his answer. Upon being questioned,

Hoover attacked each of them personally, using the resources of the FBI to open files on all of them and "investigate" them, looking for dirt to destroy them with. They were stunned by the attack and a truce was called where Hoover was let off the hook and he backed down.

The whole time this fight between the FBI and the commission was going on, the CIA was simply stonewalling the Warren Commission, giving them little or no information at all while pretending to be as open and accommodating as possible.

Then came the Warren Report, a deliberate lie which can best be described as propaganda. And the way the volumes of exhibits were released later was an additional subterfuge.

Author Phillip Nelson, in his book *LBJ: THE MASTERMIND OF THE JFK ASSASSINATION*, does an excellent job of summarizing the report itself:[3530]

> "Its decision to publish a 912-page book just before the 1964 presidential election, followed by twenty-six volumes and fifty-thousand more pages of documents, was designed to show the public that the investigation was thorough and complete; in truth, this was done to obfuscate the fact that they had explored only one very narrow lead, effectively excluding all others. In order to "paper the files," the staff was, evidently, instructed to include thousands of pages of extraneous material having nothing to do with the pertinent issues. This effort apparently led to someone gathering miscellaneous debris collected during the course of the "investigation." Some of the examples of this are legendary:"[3531]

>> "Three pages devoted to David Belin's efforts to elicit from Mrs. Barbara Rowland that she got As and Bs in high school and that her husband had fudged his high school grades to her when they were courting since she later saw one of his report cards and noted that it had some Cs on it; also included was a review in minute detail of his entire work history."[3532]

>> "Jack Ruby's mother's dental records from 1938, including a comment from the dentist that "patient states she has teeth but was not wearing them." Evidently, at least someone on the staff had a rather perverse sense of humor to have gratuitously included such a document obviously intended to disparage Jack Ruby's mother, Fannie Rubenstein. But this was not the only instance of the

> commission's staff attacking the integrity of completely innocent American citizens."[3533]

> "Finally, among many other such irrelevant files, there is yet another enigmatic item buried in the thousands of pages, which relates to a nail file purportedly owned by Lee Oswald's mother."[3534]

A 912-page report plus an additional twenty-six volumes constitute a huge amount of data, and the sheer size did several things for the conspirators. First, it gave the *appearance* of the Warren Commission having done an exhaustive investigation. This is both the opposite of what actually happened and exactly the impression the conspirators wanted to give the American people. Second, by having a mountain of mostly irrelevant data to bury the relevant data in, the conspirators made it that much harder for anyone to determine what was actually going on. The task of anyone who was interested in the truth was made even harder by the lack of an index to the twenty-six volumes, which was probably why it was skipped.

And the Warren Commission cleverly withheld the twenty-six volumes of evidence until more than two months after the release of its report.[3535] In the meantime, the mainstream media praised the Warren Report without benefit of seeing the evidence exhibits.[3536] *The New York Times* called the report "comprehensive, careful, compendious and competent."[3537]

And, once it had produced the report, the Warren Commission was quickly disbanded so as to avoid having to answer questions from the many critics who sprung up.

Thus, my contention that the Warren Report succeeded in its purpose. The commission was created to do a whitewash so the conspirators would not get caught. It worked. They escaped punishment.

Hoover's Long Shadow

The Warren Commission was at the mercy of Hoover for information, and J. Edgar Hoover was feeding it only what he wanted it to know. Hoover wanted to be the choke point for all information, and the Warren Commission was no exception. Having gotten Johnson to create the Warren Commission as a means of avoiding congressional investigations which might involve people doing actual investigating, Hoover had no intention of allowing the commission access to any meaningful information. On the day after Kennedy's assassination Hoover had produced a 5-page report which said Oswald was guilty and he acted alone.[3538] As far as Hoover was concerned, the purpose of the Warren Commission was just to read his report and turn around and tell the American people that yes, Hoover was right and Oswald was guilty. Move along folks, nothing to see here.

On December 2, 1962 Hoover sent his report to Johnson saying that Oswald and Ruby each acted alone. He also leaked the results of the report to the press.[3539] Hoover used press leaks to force the public and the Warren Commission to come to his conclusions about the assassination.[3540] On December 3, 1963 the *New York Journal American* ran the headline "Oswald Lone Killer – FBI Report to Prove It" the story quoted 'anonymous government sources' but the FBI was the obvious source.[3541]

The Warren commission was stonewalled by Hoover who had already concluded that Oswald and Ruby were lone nuts who acted independently and demanded that the Warren Commission publicly agree with him.[3542] On December 5, 1963 the Warren Commission held its first meeting. Hoover sent them a summary report.[3543] When they confronted Hoover and demanded the details backing up his conclusions, he delayed for a month while trying to find a way around sending them the details.[3544] Lee Rankin had to suck up to Hoover to get information and therefore never challenged or questioned the FBI findings.[3545]

At the first meeting of the commission Warren said there was no need for the commission to issue subpoenas. He was overruled by the other commissioners. He also said they have no need for their own investigators and the other commissioners agreed.[3546] This left the commission at the mercy of Hoover, and the first thing the Warren Commission did was hit a brick wall. Hoover would not even send a representative to the first meeting of the commission. They had a decision to make. Did they want to charge the new president as having been behind a coup d'état? The controlling faction on the commission did not want to do that, and the others were simply too timid to open a can of worms labeled "constitutional crisis," so the Warren Commission stayed on track and did not stray outside its charter of rubber-stamping the 'Oswald did it alone' theory. Thus, Hoover was allowed, for the most part, to get away with stonewalling the Warren Commission.

On December 9, 1963 the FBI report was given to the Warren Commission which asked that nothing be made public until the report had been reviewed by the commission. The next morning the *New York Times* had a substantial story on the report headlined "Oswald Assassin Beyond a Doubt, FBI Concludes – He Acted Alone and Did Not Know Ruby Says Report to Warren Inquiry Panel"[3547]

By March 10, 1964 Johnson is openly saying that he intends to waive Hoover's retirement.[3548] This is a clear message to the Warren Commission that Hoover is not going anywhere and they will have to deal with him remaining in power.[3549] Hoover personally reviewed every document sent to the commission, often several a day, sent directly to Warren Commission General Counsel Lee Rankin.[3550]

For the commission, getting information was like pulling teeth. Hoover only told the Warren Commission what he wanted them to know, and the last thing he wanted the commission to hear about was any hint of conspiracy. For example, there was an incident in Clinton, Louisiana where Oswald, Ferrie and Shaw were seen together in the late summer of 1963. Reeves Morgan, a member of the Louisiana State Legislature, informed the FBI of the Clinton sighting almost immediately after the assassination.[3551] The FBI did not investigate, and the Warren Commission never learned of it.[3552]

Another example of Hoover and the FBI filtering what the Warren Commission saw was the office in New Orleans where ex-FBI agent Guy Banister had Oswald working with Clay Shaw, David Ferrie, Sergio Arcacha Smith and others on several projects, including the Kennedy assassination. The office is on the corner of Camp and Lafayette in New Orleans and has two entrances.[3553] The official address was 544 Camp Street, which was stamped on several of Oswald's leaflets which he handed out.[3554] The FBI in New Orleans went to interview Banister and claimed that he was at 532 Lafayette Street.[3555] No mention of the 544 Camp Street address was made, even though it was the same place.[3556] 532 Lafayette Street was just a side entrance to the same office at 544 Camp Street. The Warren Commission was never told this.[3557]

On December 10, 1963 Hoover clamps down and disciplines half a dozen FBI officials. They have done nothing wrong, but Hoover wants to send a warning message to make sure that he has control of any information about the Kennedy assassination. Anyone who values their career was warned to follow orders.[3558]

On December 16, 1963 the Warren Commission formally requested from Hoover that they be allowed to see the details that led up to the summary report.[3559]

"RESOLVED, that the commission request promptly from all government agencies and departments of the government the raw materials upon which any reports given to the commission are based."[3560]

Once Chief Justice Warren publicly called on Hoover to send over the details, Hoover had no choice but to comply.[3561] He stalled for a month, then decided to try to bury the Warren Commission in paper.[3562] He began sending hundreds of FBI reports to the commission, including huge piles of crank allegations.[3563]

On December 18, 1963 Hoover leaked selective information on Kennedy's wounds to make it appear that there were only shots from behind.[3564] This pattern of leaking information to the press before giving it to the Warren Commission was meant to force the commission to come to his conclusion.[3565] He only feeds them what he wants them to know and, by the time they get it, the press has already published the conclusion Hoover wants.[3566] In the meantime, Hoover is using Gerald Ford and Richard Russell as his eyes and ears on the commission.[3567]

Author Mark North, in his book *ACT OF TREASON: THE ROLE OF J. EDGAR HOOVER IN THE ASSASSINATION OF PRESIDENT KENNEDY*, says that by January 27, 1964:[3568]

"The overall situation regarding Hoover has now become a topic of grave concern."[3569]

McCloy "The time is almost overdue for us to have a better perspective of the FBI investigation than we now have. We are so dependent on them for our facts."[3570]

Rankin: "Part of our difficulty in regard to it is that they have no problem. They have decided that no one else is involved."[3571]

Russell: "They have tried the case and reached a verdict on every aspect."[3572]

Boggs: "You have just put your finger on it."[3573]

At some point Lee Rankin realized that Hoover was lying about Oswald not being an informant for the FBI. There are also much more serious questions about whether or not Hoover knows about any mafia connections. On March 26, 1964 Rankin requests that the FBI answer several questions in writing. This is in preparation for questioning Hoover in person when he appears before the commission on May 14.

Hoover fights back by his usual tactics, opening files and collecting information that can be used against his perceived "enemies." He claimed that staff attorney Norman Redich was a communist. He also lined up a few key allies in Congress to go to bat for him. Senator Karl Mundt of South Dakota demanded that the Warren Commission stop work until they all passed security investigations by the FBI.[3574] This attack by Hoover has the desired effect.[3575] The commissioners rein in Rankin and Hoover is let off the hook.

When Ranking moves in on Hoover at the meeting on May 14, the committee closes ranks. Rankin is cut off several times and eventually drops the matter. Hoover is allowed to get away with lying to the committee.[3576] After this, there are no more attempts to challenge Hoover. Years later Rankin will say:[3577]

> "Who could protest against what Mr. Hoover did, back in those days?"[3578]

When the Warren Report came out and was critical of the FBI, Hoover initiated a search for dirt on the commission personnel – all 84 of them – including secretaries and clerks, and the search turned up dirt on sixteen people and their relatives.[3579]

The CIA Stonewalls the Commission

CIA Director John McCone and Deputy Director of Plans Richard Helms testified before the Warren Commission. McCone was an outsider and was able to have plausible deniability and Helms just flat lied. Helms knew that Oswald was a CIA creation and lied about it.[3580] He also made sure that the files that were handed over were scrubbed prior to being delivered.[3581]

Author Anthony Summers, in his book *NOT IN YOUR LIFETIME, THE ASSASSINATION OF JFK*, says:[3582]

> "Former Warren Commission counsel Burt Griffin, a judge in later life, blamed the federal intelligence agencies for the failings of both the official investigations:"[3583]

> "I feel betrayed." he said "I feel that the CIA lied to us, that we had an agency of government here which we were depending upon, that we expected to be truthful with us and to cooperate with us and they didn't do it. The CIA concealed from us the fact that they were involved in efforts to

assassinate Castro, which could have been of extreme importance to us, especially the fact that they were involved in working with the mafia."[3584]

"Griffin felt the same about the FBI because it had not pursued the leads that pointed to possible conspiracy "What is most disturbing to me" he said "is that these two agencies of government that were supposed to be loyal and faithful to us deliberately misled us."[3585]

"Consider the possible reality" he had suggested to the House Assassinations Committee "that under the American system of civil liberties and the requirement of proof beyond a reasonable doubt it is virtually impossible to prosecute or uncover a well-conceived and well-executed conspiracy."[3586]

Summers also said, in reference to the Warren Commission and the later HSCA investigation:[3587]

"The Warren Commission, scholars now know, did not see a multitude of documents that are today deemed assassination related. Senior Assassinations Committee staff, empowered to investigate the president's murder with the authority of the House of Representatives, ended their probe still stymied by CIA procrastination and evasiveness."[3588]

The Warren Commission Ignores Evidence

In addition to having the FBI and the CIA stonewall and lie to the Warren Commission, the members and staff of the commission themselves did their best to avoid seeing things that they did not want to see. Below are a few examples.

Jack Ruby, who murdered Oswald two days after Kennedy was shot, was seen at Parkland Hospital at 1:30 PM on November 22, 1963 by journalist Seth Kantor, who knew Ruby.[3589] But Jack Ruby said he wasn't there, so the Warren Commission took the murderer's word for it and ignored what Seth Kantor said.[3590]

The Warren Commission carefully avoided asking any questions about Oswald's involvement with the CIA or Office of Naval Intelligence (ONI) or Oswald's time in Japan working on the U-2 program.[3591] Oswald's commanding officer, Marine Corps Lieutenant John E. Donovan, was prepared to answer questions about Oswald's time working on the U-2 program.[3592] The Warren Commission did not ask him about it.[3593] When Donovan asked a commission lawyer about this he was told:[3594]

> "We asked you exactly what we wanted to know from you and we asked you everything we wanted for now and that's all. And if there is anything else we want to ask you, we will."[3595]

Dallas Police Officer Joe Marshall Smith encountered a fake Secret Service agent who produced real Secret Service credentials, but during his testimony before the Warren Commission he was not asked about this.[3596] Wesley Liebler was the attorney questioning Smith and he did not dig into this. Smith had also smelled gunpowder, but Liebler did not want to know about this either.[3597]

The Warren Commission ignored anyone who said they saw more than one person on the sixth floor. Carolyn Walters said she saw two men in an upper floor of the book depository, one with blonde hair and a white shirt and a rifle and the other with a brown suit jacket, so she was not called to testify.[3598] Instead the Warren Commission asked to hear from 16-year-old African American Amos Lee Euins who said he saw a man with a rifle shooting out of the sixth floor window of the book depository.[3599] Forrest Sorrels of the Secret Service discounted Amos Lee's testimony because he did not see the shooter well enough to tell if he was white or black, but because he saw a lone shooter he was good enough for the Warren Commission.[3600]

Victoria Adams was watching the motorcade with her friend Sandra Styles from the fourth floor of the Texas School Book Depository.[3601] Adams said there was no one else on the stairs when she and Sandra ran down to see what was going on.[3602] She said she was harassed, questioned multiple times and changes were made in her testimony.[3603] She decided to disappear for her own safety.[3604] It took author Barry Earnest thirty-five years to find Victoria Adams.[3605] The Warren Commission disregarded Victoria's testimony because it didn't fit their theory.[3606]

Twenty-five witnesses gave sworn affidavits within forty-eight hours of the assassination, and twenty-two of them pointed to the grassy knoll as the source of the shots.[3607] The Warren Commission ignored them, as it ignored the opinion of fifty-one of the 121 total witnesses who gave evidence to the commission who said the shots came from the grassy knoll.[3608] Even though only thirty-two of those 121 thought the shots came from the Texas School Book Depository, the Warren Report would state their conclusion that:[3609]

"No credible evidence suggests that the shots were fired from the railroad bridge over the Triple Underpass, the nearby railroad yards, or any place other than the Texas School Book Depository."[3610]

Commission critic Harold Feldman wrote:[3611]

"In what other murder case would the testimony of fifty-one sworn and many other unheard witnesses be dismissed so cavalierly as 'no credible evidence.'"[3612]

Reports from three Dallas cops, Seymour Weitzman, D.V. Harkness and Joe Marshall Smith, were also dismissed by the commission.[3613] Smith pointed out that he had run into someone with Secret Service credentials, as did Jean Hill and other witnesses.[3614] The commission not only ignored their evidence of shots from the grassy knoll and of fake Secret Service agents, they went out of their way to bully witnesses into agreeing with the official story. Jean Hill later recounted her experience to assassination researcher Jim Marrs:[3615]

"He kept trying to get me to change my story, particularly regarding the number of shots. He said that I had been told how many shots there were, and I figured he was talking about what the Secret Service told me right after the assassination. His inflection and attitude were that I knew what I was supposed to be saying, why wouldn't I just say it. I asked him, "Look, do you want the truth or just what you want me to say?" He said he wanted the truth, so I said "The truth is that I heard between four and six shots." I told him, "I'm not going to lie for you." So, he starts talking off the record. He told me about my life, my family, and even mentioned that my marriage was in trouble. I said "What's the point of interviewing me if you already know everything about me?" He got angrier and angrier and finally told me, "Look, we can make you look as crazy as [Marina] Oswald and everybody knows how crazy she is. We could have you put in a mental institution if you don't cooperate with us.""[3616]

Having Jean Hill put in a mental institution was not an idle threat. Eugene Dinkin, Ralph Yates and others had been hustled into insane asylums to be tortured into changing their stories. She added that:

"He was so mean I could hardly believe it."[3617]

Specter's bullying was not limited to Jean Hill. He also used this tactic on Darryl Tomlinson, who found the magic bullet, into saying he found it on a stretcher that connected it to Connally.[3618] The Magic Bullet fiction was Specter's creation, and he also bullied one of the Parkland Doctors into changing his story to go along with the lie. Dr. Ronald Jones later testified in front of the Assassination Records Review Board (ARRB) that Specter had followed him out into the hallway and pressured him into changing the entry wound in the throat to be an exit wound to fit Specter's Magic Bullet theory.[3619]

Mark Lane submitted a 10,000-word brief to the Warren Commission pointing out the many holes in the prevailing 'Oswald as lone gunman' theory.[3620] Lane was one of the critics who couldn't be ignored because he had gathered hard evidence and was making it known in the media and in personal appearances. He also refused to be intimidated into silence. The commission reluctantly agreed to meet with him, and Lane requested that the meeting be open and not a secret session like all the others. The commission let him have his say and then ignored him and his input. This was just done for the sake of appearances, so they could say they met with him.

The *Dallas Morning News* had four people in Dealey Plaza when Kennedy was murdered; Mary Woodward, Maggie Brown, Aurelio Lorenzo and Ann Donaldson.[3621] They were all on the grassy knoll and said the shots came from behind them, which was printed in the newspaper the next day.[3622] They were all ignored by the Warren Commission.[3623]

John Chisolm and his wife were on the grassy knoll and said the shots came from behind them.[3624] They were ignored by the Warren Commission.[3625] A.J. Milliken was on the grassy knoll where he heard a total of five shots originate.[3626] He was ignored by the Warren Commission.[3627] Jean Newman was on the knoll and she said the shots had come from there.[3628] She was ignored by the Warren Commission.[3629] Abraham Zapruder, filming the assassination from the grassy knoll, said that at least one of the shots came from the grassy knoll because it was so much louder than the others.[3630] His testimony was ignored.

Sam Holland was a railway supervisor who was on the railroad bridge over the Triple Underpass directly in front of Kennedy's car when he was assassinated. Holland said:

> "I looked over to where the shots came from and I saw a puff of smoke still lingering underneath the trees in front of the wooden fence."[3631]

Asked where the shots came from, he said:

> "Behind that picket fence, close to the little plaza. There's no doubt whatsoever in my mind."[3632]

The Warren Commission listened to what Holland had to say and then ignored him.[3633]

Lee Bowers was a railroad man in a tower in the railroad yard behind the fence at the top of the grassy knoll. He had an excellent view of the parking area behind the fence. He testified before the Warren Commission that "something out of the ordinary" happened over by the fence that caught his attention as the shooting started, but was cut off in mid-sentence as he started to describe what that something was.[3634]

The Zapruder film was seen by commissioners and staff, yet nowhere does the Warren Report mention the sudden, obvious backward movement of Kennedy's head upon being shot from the front.[3635]

Warren made the autopsy photos off-limits to the commission staffers.[3636]

Several witnesses spotted two men on the sixth floor of the Texas School Book Depository.[3637] Arnold Rowland pointed out to his wife that a man there was holding a high-powered rifle with a scope.[3638] This man was in the window on the west end of the sixth floor, while there was another man in the window on the east end, the 'sniper's nest' window.[3639] This second man had a darker complexion and Rowland thought he was black.[3640] Rowland mentioned that the FBI had no interest in his testimony:[3641]

> "They told me it didn't have any bearing or such on the case right then. In fact, they just the same as told me to forget it now. They didn't seem interested at all. They didn't pursue this point. They didn't take it down in the notation as such."[3642]

Witnesses Ruby Henderson and Carolyn Walther also saw two men on the sixth floor of the Texas School Book Depository, one with a dark complexion, but they saw the two men both in the right-hand or eastern window.[3643] They were ignored by the Warren Commission.[3644]

John Powell was on the sixth floor of the Dallas County building, directly across from the sixth floor of the Texas School Book Depository, when he saw a man with a rifle that had a scope.[3645] He also remembered two men, one with dark skin.[3646] He was never interviewed by either the FBI or the Warren Commission.[3647]

All testimony of two shooters was ignored by the Warren Commission.[3648]

Charles Drehm was within ten feet of the president when Kennedy was shot from the front, according to Drehm.[3649] He was not called by the Warren Commission.[3650] The grassy knoll was in front of the limousine, so shots from the knoll were shots from the front. O.V. Campbell was a Vice President of the Texas School Book Depository and was standing in front of the building when Kennedy was shot.[3651] He ran toward the grassy knoll where he thought the shots had come from.[3652] He was not called by the Warren Commission.[3653]

B.W. Hargis was a motorcycle cop riding just to the left and rear of the limousine.[3654] When the shots were fired he ditched the motorcycle and charged up the grassy knoll where the shots were coming from.[3655] He appears to have been called by the Warren Commission but his testimony also appears to have been omitted.[3656] Hargis was not the only police officer to have sworn testimony buried by the commission. Clyde Haywood also left his motorcycle and charged up the grassy knoll, and Seymour Weitzman swore in an affidavit that he ran to the fence at the top of the knoll:[3657]

> "I ran in a northwest direction and scaled a fence towards where we (he and his police partner) thought the shots came from."[3658]

The Warren Commission ignored their testimony.[3659]

Between the FBI filtering out testimony or witnesses who did not fit the 'Oswald did it alone' theory and the Warren Commission willfully ignoring testimony or bullying witnesses, the truth never stood a chance. The public interest was never high on the list of concerns of the Deep State.

The Warren Commission also used the fact that Jack Ruby was on trial for murdering Oswald as an excuse to avoid digging too deeply into that aspect of the conspiracy.[3660]

In early December of 1963 Ruby employee William Abade was interviewed by the FBI.[3661] In that interview he discussed his bookmaking activities for Ruby's establishment and how he observed that Ruby had police officers there on a regular basis.[3662] The FBI report in the National Archives is five pages, but the Warren Commission only published four of those pages.[3663] The missing page covers Abade's employment by Ruby as a bookmaker, thus either the Warren Commission or the FBI was attempting to hide this aspect of Ruby's background.[3664]

The front page of the *Dallas Morning News* for December 22, 1962 depicted the route of the motorcade, in a graphic covering five-sixths of the page, as staying on Main Street through the center of Dealey Plaza and not making the detour to go past the Texas School Book Depository.[3665] Anyone seeing this would assume that the actual route the motorcade took through Dealey Plaza was a last-minute change, and perhaps suspect that the president had been set up to be murdered.[3666]

The Warren Commission printed, as an official exhibit, the front page of the *Dallas Morning News* for December 22, 1962, but replaced the map covering most of the page with a solid gray blank where the motorcade route was.[3667] In this way they helped hide the evidence of the coup d'état.[3668]

Authors Roger Stone and Mike Colapietro, in their book *THE MAN WHO KILLED KENNEDY: THE CASE AGAINST LBJ*, said:[3669]

> "The witnesses to the assassination who were to testify were presupposed to follow the established conclusions set for the Commission. If the witnesses testified contrarily, they were led or coerced to present their case otherwise. If they did not, their account was altered or discarded."[3670]

They go on to say that even George de Mohrenschildt complained that his testimony was changed.[3671]

Author Jim Marrs, in his book *CROSSFIRE*, documents that there was a memo where the Warren Commission admitted that they were changing evidence:[3672]

> "On April 10, 1964, in a memo to Commission assistant counsel Albert Jenner regarding a chronology of Oswald's background by staffer John Hart Ely, Rankin wrote, "Our depositions and examinations of records and other data disclose that there are details in Mr. Ely's memoranda which will require material alterations and, in some instances, omission.""[3673]

Joachim Joesten, in his book *OSWALD, ASSASSIN OR FALL GUY?*, describes how Lee Rankin of the Warren Commission reached out to him for a pre-publication copy of his manuscript while he was getting his book published.[3674] He also describes how the FBI kept an eye on him while claiming they could not find him even after the Warren Commission sent someone to talk to him.[3675] Joesten said of the 'interview':[3676]

> "Our interview became rather animated, and from his questioning it was apparent (though Mr. Morris never said so outright) that he, or rather his agency, was particularly concerned with the fact that I believed Oswald had been connected with both the Central Intelligence Agency and with the Federal Bureau of Investigation. I had a definite impression, from his questions, that he was trying to ascertain whether or not I had any inside information, or any documents, from within the CIA or FBI. I put his mind at rest:

all my information on these points had come from published sources but I couldn't help feeling from his concern that my speculations had cut close to the bone. That same concern of his leads inevitably to a fundamental question: If the CIA or the FBI had no relations with Oswald, why would they worry where I got my information from? If they had no relations, if they have no documents in their files relating to Oswald before the assassination, if, to put it bluntly, they have nothing to hide, why are they worrying?"[3677]

To me this clearly shows that the Warren Commission understood that its job was damage control. This is the Deep State mentality at work. The Warren Commission was there so the establishment could claim to the voters that they looked into the Kennedy assassination, but the real work of the Warren Commission was to do the exact opposite. The real work was to make sure the truth stayed hidden.

Mark Lane wrote to Chief Justice Warren pointing out that he had been retained by Oswald's mother to represent Oswald's interests, which was confirmed by Mrs. Marguerite Oswald.[3678] Warren Commission General Counsel Lee Rankin said they were not going to have a lawyer for Oswald, claiming:[3679]

"The commission is not engaged in determining the guilt of anybody."[3680]

Dr. Crenshaw at Parkland Hospital was one of many doctors who saw the entry wound at the front of Kennedy's neck, and more than forty witnesses saw the large exit wound at the back of the head.[3681] This did not matter to the Warren Commission, who asserted they were all mistaken and said the wound in Kennedy's head was caused by a bullet that:[3682]

"entered through the right rear of the president's head and exited from the right side of the head, causing a large wound."[3683]

The Warren Commission version of the wounds was contradicted in 1988 in a Nova television interview where the doctors confirmed their original findings.[3684]

Author Mark North, in his book *ACT OF TREASON*, summed up the work of the Warren Commission:[3685]

"The Warren Commission, the reluctant invention of both Johnson and Hoover, failed in its primary purpose. Suspicious of the Director from the beginning and mystified by LBJ's brazen promotion of the man, the immensity of their task soon became all too apparent. Perhaps as a consequence of this, the commission split along ideological lines with some only wanting to prove the guilt of a deceased "kill-crazy communist," others to obtain the truth. In effectuating the first line of thought, the controlling faction within the group (Warren, Dulles, Ford and McCloy) was ultimately forced to prevent its general counsel, Rankin, from exposing the Director. To the same end members Russell and Cooper were forced to sign a report they did not agree with. Boggs, with his special perspective (i.e. being a U.S. representative from Louisiana) acquiesced in signing the report but in the coming years became bitter and openly challenged the Director, calling for his removal."[3686]

"With the Commission members' knowledge of Hoover's complicity and Johnson's unquestioning support of him because of his own associations, the question of institutional integrity became paramount. Their problem was three-fold: they knew that if they scrutinized and revealed the mafia's role, that in itself would alarm the general population. Exposure of Oswald's and Ruby's relationship to Marcello and the Bureau would then greatly exacerbate the crisis by focusing attention on Hoover. While the commission did not know of the September 1962 Jose Aleman/Trafficante surveillance data revealing the existence of the Marcello contract, other information that was available to them, taken as a whole, clearly raised the disturbing issue of foreknowledge on the part of the Director. His initial refusal to supply data had only strengthened those concerns. From this arose the third and most unsettling issue: that of Johnson's own relationship to the mafia. To expose the mob and the Director to prosecution might ultimately lead to the downfall of the President himself."[3687]

The origin of, and motivations behind, the Warren Commission help to explain what happened once the Warren Reoprt was published. Anyone who was paying attention, and there were quite a few, could see that there were obvious holes in it. American citizens, having been failed by their government, started looking into the Kennedy assassination on their own. They believed that they had a right to know what really happened in Dealey Plaza that day. The Deep State, as usual, put the pubic interest dead last.

The Murder of Mary Meyer

The murder of Mary Pinchot Meyer, one of many people who lost their lives as a result of the Kennedy assassination, is highlighted here because the direct connection between her murder and the CIA is so well documented. Mary was killed in October of 1964 because she knew too much and was going to go public. Many years later author Leo Damore started to look into the murder of Mary Meyer. He spent years researching the murder but died before he could write a book about it. Author Peter Janney took up the project and, combining his own research and first-hand knowledge of the situation as a family friend, published a book in 2012 called *MARY'S MOSAIC: THE CIA CONSPIRACY TO MURDER JOHN F. KENNEDY, MARY PINCHOT MEYER, AND THEIR VISION FOR WORLD PEACE.* I highly recommend it.

All the research done first by Leo Damore and then by Peter Janney has given us considerable detail on the murder of Mary Meyer and the circumstances surrounding it. It shows the lengths the CIA would go to keep a lid on the assassination of Kennedy. Having murdered Kennedy, the conspirators could not afford to leave any loose ends. They murdered dozens of people who knew too much, Mary is just one of the most well-documented of those murders.

This chapter is organized into seven sections:

1. Mary and JFK cross paths – describes how Mary Pinchot and John Kennedy knew each other since their college days and how Kennedy tried several times to date Mary

2. Cord Meyer joins the CIA – describes how Mary eventually meets and marries Cord Meyer and how Cord goes from working with Mary for world peace to joining the CIA as a Cold Warrior

3. Mary Meyer and John Kennedy – describes how, after Mary's divorce, she and Kennedy become lovers and Mary influences Kennedy to try marijuana and LSD and work for world peace

4. The Cuban Missile Crisis Effect – describes how the Cuban Missile Crisis scares JFK and convinces him that he needs to work with Khrushchev toward a peaceful resolution of their differences

5. Mary plans to expose the conspiracy – after Kennedy is murdered and the Warren Report is issued, Mary is infuriated and plans to expose the conspiracy with her insider knowledge

6. Another Covert Operation is Necessary – once the conspirators can't convince Mary to keep quiet they decide to kill her and stage another covert operation, including a cover up

7. Leo Damore and Peter Janney – describes how authors Leo Damore and Peter Janney looked into the murder of Mary Meyer and how this resulted in the book *MARY'S MOSAIC*

Author Peter Janney was friends with Mary Meyer's son Michael. Wistar Janney (Peter's father) worked with Cord Meyer at the CIA and the two families were close. Their children grew up together and played together. Peter Janney and Michael Meyer were childhood friends until Michael's death in December of 1956 when they were both about ten years old.[3688]

Mary's murder affected Peter Janney deeply and he decided to tell her story. He took the time to research and document a very compelling case that the CIA had Mary murdered to silence her. Most of the people who have been murdered because they knew too much about Kennedy's assassination died without having someone like Peter Janney to do such a thorough job of digging up all the incriminating evidence and writing a book about it. They just died in such large numbers that it's mathematically impossible to believe they were *all* just a coincidence. Mary is different. Peter Janney cared enough to see to it that we can all know what happened.

Mary was murdered for a combination of reasons. She knew too much, she wouldn't shut up and she couldn't be ignored. She had put it together. She had figured out that Oswald wasn't a lone nut killer like the Warren Commission said he was. And she was so outraged that Kennedy was murdered that she ignored the obvious danger to herself and went ahead with her plans to go public with what she knew. And she could not be ignored. As the (now ex) wife of a high-level CIA chief she was part of the inner circle. The public would take her seriously. She would appear to the public to have inside knowledge and therefore have credibility. The conspirators were working overtime in the shadows to keep a lid on their conspiracy and the last thing they needed was Mary Meyer shining a spotlight on them. So, they ran a covert operation to murder her and make it look like an ordinary murder by pinning it on some poor guy who just happened to be in the wrong place at the wrong time.

Mary and JFK Cross Paths

Mary Pinchot and John F. Kennedy crossed paths several times when they were both single and in school or college. He tried several times to take her to bed and she always turned him down, but they continued to bump into each other because they ran in the same social circles.

During the 1930's a young John Kennedy met Mary at a dance at Choate and he was interested in her but she was not as interested in him.[3689] The same happened when they again crossed paths in the early 1940's when Mary was at Vassar – she seemed unimpressed by yet another rich college boy just looking to get laid.[3690]

John Kennedy and Mary (now Mary Meyer) continued to cross paths, including in 1959 when he was preparing to run for president.[3691] Kennedy had married Jackie on the orders of his father, who wanted JFK in the White House and he would need the proper wife. Kennedy continued to fool around and Jackie went into the marriage knowing who he was.[3692] John and Jackie Kennedy had a dysfunctional relationship from the beginning.[3693]

By 1956 John F. Kennedy and his wife Jackie had moved in next door to Cord and Mary Meyer, at Hickory Hill.[3694] Later Jack and Jackie would move to Georgetown.[3695]

Kennedy was always attracted to Mary, partly because she had never given in and gone to bed with him, and partly because she understood him.[3696] As he got closer to running for the White House she asked him why he couldn't get his womanizing under control because it was a huge risk and a liability for a man attempting to get to the White House.[3697]

Cord Meyer Joins the CIA

Cord Meyer was a war hero who was against war.[3698] He had a vision of a world without war. He wanted to see "a genuine federation of the nations so they would not be free to make war, but would be subordinate to a higher law."[3699]

In 1945, around the same time as the United Nations conference on International Organization was taking place in San Francisco, he married Mary Pinchot and they went to the conference together.[3700]

Cord Meyer was a young political hopeful at the conference.[3701] Also attending the conference, as a journalist, was John Kennedy.[3702] They ran in the same social circles and knew each other and spent time together at the conference.[3703] Kennedy and Cord had a confrontation at the conference.[3704]

John Kennedy was still attracted to Mary. Cord realized this and when Kennedy asked to interview Cord, Cord snubbed Kennedy, who never forgot it.[3705] Years later when Cord wanted out of the CIA and asked President Kennedy to make him the U.S. Ambassador to Guatemala, Kennedy turned him down.[3706]

Cord Meyer was idealistic and became a prominent writer and scholar, advocating world government through global federalism.[3707] The world federalist movement ran out of steam in the face of the budding Cold War.[3708] Cord became disillusioned by his apparently futile efforts to promote world federalism.[3709] This affected his personal life and marriage and by 1951 their marriage was strained and the Cold War was in full swing.[3710] Allen Dulles recruited Cord Meyer into the CIA.[3711] By joining the CIA Cord Meyer was admitting that he was turning his back on the ideal of world federalism and world peace and joining in the fight to win the Cold War against communism.[3712] Cord became a rising star in the CIA running operations like Mockingbird and Radio Free Europe. He was awarded the Distinguished Intelligence Medal three times, one of only two people to be so honored.[3713]

Cord Meyer had always despised John Kennedy and other newly rich folks he considered inferior.[3714] Cord Meyer came from old money.[3715] Mary Meyer divorced Cord and eventually started having an affair with Kennedy while he was in the White House.[3716] Cord had started out disliking Kennedy, then came the incident at the United Nations conference in 1945, at which point Cord started to hate Kennedy. By the time Mary was having an affair with President Kennedy, his hatred for Kennedy had metastasized.

Mary and Cord moved to Washington for Cord's job but they could no longer be partners[3717] CIA employees were not allowed to discuss their work with their spouses.[3718] While Mary had started out as a partner with Cord, editing his work and supporting his efforts at world peace, now she was shut out and increasingly opposed to, and critical of, the CIA and its mission, strategies and tactics.[3719] Mary also detested Allen Dulles and compared him to Machiavelli, only worse.[3720] Mary had gone from being Cord's partner and biggest supporter to being shut out and opposed to what he was doing – Mary was uncomfortable as a "CIA wife" and was increasingly alienated from Cord.[3721] During the mid-1950's Cord considered leaving the CIA but ended up getting a promotion and staying with the CIA.[3722] Mary and her sister Tony went on a 'husband dumping' trip to Europe and both had affairs with other men and decided to divorce their husbands.[3723] Tony got a divorce and Married Ben Bradlee and Mary had an affair with a man she eventually decided she wanted to marry.[3724]

Cord Meyer had gone completely over to the dark side from once being the foremost proponent of world peace.[3725] In December of 1956 Michael Meyer was hit by a car and killed.[3726] He had been a young boy of only 9 years old.[3727] This was a shock to his best friend Peter Janney, the author of the book *MARY'S MOSAIC*.[3728] In 1956 Mary told Cord she wanted a divorce.[3729] Not long after this, in 1957, Mary and Cord were divorced.[3730] They had grown apart. Mary was free and uninhibited and Cord was cold and dismissive.[3731] She thought he betrayed the ideals which they shared and was increasingly unhappy about the direction the CIA was taking, considering it immoral.[3732] Mary cited "extreme mental cruelty" as her reason for the divorce.[3733] In the meantime, Mary had become increasingly outspoken with her criticism of the CIA.[3734] Mary was a pacifist opposed to war and armed conflict.[3735] During that same time Cord Meyer and James Jesus Angleton had become friends and coworkers at the CIA.[3736]

Mary Meyer and John Kennedy

After the divorce, Mary Pinchot Meyer and President John F. Kennedy started having an affair that became serious. Mary introduced Kennedy to marijuana and LSD and encouraged him to work toward world peace. How much influence Mary had on Kennedy's outlook is hard to tell, but he did turn away from the Cold War and toward peace, and he tried to take the country and the world with him. Jackie knew about Kennedy's affair with Mary and knew that this affair was more serious than the usual flings Kennedy had.[3737] In the end Kennedy had a much deeper attraction to and relationship with Mary than the many other women he had affairs with.[3738]

She had been telling Kennedy about LSD and he wanted to experiment so she went to see LSD proponent Timothy Leary to learn how to guide others in LSD sessions.[3739] Leary showed Mary how to help her 'important friend' turn on and expand his thinking.[3740] When she first visited with Leary she did not tell him the identity of her 'important friend' and at first she only identified herself to him as Mary Pinchot.[3741] She wanted to recruit a bunch of women in Washington D.C. to get the important men in their lives to 'turn on' and hoped this would help to influence events toward world peace.[3742] She would start by getting the women to turn on and then get their husbands and boyfriends to turn on.[3743]

Leary later confirmed that Mary was on a mission to recruit a group of half a dozen women in Washington with powerful husbands and boyfriends to get their men to 'turn on' in an effort to influence events toward world peace.[3744] CIA officer James Jesus Angleton had Mary's real diary (not just her sketch book) and was reported to have said that Mary and Kennedy took LSD trips together.[3745] This is something that, if this is true, he could have learned and would have known from reading her diary.[3746] Leary also believed that Mary Meyer and John Kennedy took LSD trips together during their affair.[3747] The accounts of their affair and marijuana use are well documented by friends of Mary.[3748] Mary and Kennedy saw each other often at the White House where she was a frequent visitor.[3749] They also met at Joseph Alsop's house when he was away and at Mary's house in Georgetown.[3750] Kenny O'Donnell said that Mary was outspoken and confrontational with Kennedy.[3751] Kennedy is reported to have told Kenny O'Donnell that he was in love with Mary and was looking forward to a life with her after leaving the White House.[3752] Mary was a regular visitor at the White House because she and Kennedy were lovers.[3753] Mary was not asked to leave the room when Kennedy discussed business.[3754] By all accounts Mary was treated very differently from other women in Kennedy's life.[3755]

The Cuban Missile Crisis Effect

After the Cuban Missile Crisis Kennedy accelerated the shift in his thinking away from the logic of the Cold War and the domino theory. He decided to try to work with Khrushchev to achieve world peace. Kennedy gave the Peace Speech at American University, negotiated the test ban treaty with Khrushchev and reached out to Castro to normalize relations. Castro was reaching back and they were making progress when Kennedy was assassinated.

Leo Damore claimed that Mary and Kennedy had taken a mild LSD trip several weeks before his Peace Speech on June 10, 1963 at American University.[3756]   During the Peace Speech Kennedy articulated the vision that Cord Meyer had once championed. Kennedy went around his own national security apparatus and crafted a nuclear test ban treaty to propose to the Soviet Union. Mary told Timothy Leary that she and her circle had been 'turning on' some very important people in Washington.[3757]

During the Cuban Missile Crisis the CIA and the Pentagon tried to undermine Kennedy.[3758] Robert Kennedy told Anatoly Dobrynin that President Kennedy was worried that the military would overthrow him if the crisis went on much longer.[3759] In the early days of the crisis Air Force Chief of Staff General LeMay wanted to immediately initiate a bombing campaign against the Soviet missile sites in Cuba, and this was followed a few days later by Pentagon recommendations of a full-scale U.S. invasion of Cuba to follow LeMay's air strikes.[3760] Unknown to the CIA and the Pentagon at the time was that the Russians had over forty thousand troops in Cuba to resist just such an invasion.[3761] They were armed not just with strategic missiles, the medium and intermediate range ICBMs discovered by the American U-2 photography, but, completely unknown to the military and CIA at the time, also with 98 tactical or low-yield nuclear warheads along with the appropriate short-range missiles and bombers to deliver them.[3762] These had been placed in Cuba with the specific intent of being actively used to oppose any U.S. invasion of the island.[3763] Former Defense Secretary Robert McNamara said in an interview in 1998:[3764]

> "We didn't learn until nearly thirty years later that the Soviets had roughly 162 nuclear warheads on this isle of Cuba at a time when our CIA said they believed there were none. And included in the 162 were some 90 tactical warheads to be used against a U.S. invasion force. Had we ... attacked Cuba and invaded Cuba at the time we almost surely would have been involved in nuclear war. And when I say "we," I mean you – it would not have been the U.S. alone. It would have endangered the security of the West, without any question."[3765]

During the Cuban Missile Crisis, the CIA and the Pentagon were doing everything possible, behind Kennedy's back, to push the situation over the brink into all-out nuclear war.[3766] On October 28, 1962 the Air Force launched an unarmed ICBM from Vandenberg AFB in California destined for the Marshall Islands in the Pacific.[3767] The Russians had no way to know the missile was unarmed and the whole point was to push them over the edge of an already tense situation.[3768] The relationship between Kennedy and his own military got worse.[3769]

The U.S. had, at that time, a program where Strategic Air Command (SAC) bombers flew in shifts so they were always in the air. They had established "turn around points" where they normally turned back. During the Cuban Missile Crisis, they went past their established "turn around points." Given the heightened tensions of the crisis, this also could have easily been interpreted by the Russians as a sign of a preemptive strike.[3770]

Air Force Generals Thomas Power and Curtis LeMay came up with the concept of Mutually Assured Destruction (M.A.D.). During the Cuban Missile Crisis General Power made the decision on his own to raise the security level of the Strategic Air Command to DEFCON 2, only one step away from active nuclear war, without telling President Kennedy before he did so.[3771]

With each provocation, the gulf between Kennedy and his military leaders became more and more obvious. The same thing was happening with the CIA, who were also off on their own trying to throw gasoline on the fire and turn the Cuban Missile Crisis into an all-out war. On October 21, 1962 during the Cuban Missile Crisis, after Robert Kennedy told CIA Director McCone to immediately halt all operations against Cuba, CIA Task Force W chief William Harvey sendt two raiding parties into Cuba.[3772]

Kennedy and Khrushchev were able to work out an agreement that avoided nuclear war. The Pentagon and CIA were furious with the negotiated compromise while Kennedy's opinion of the U.S. military leadership hit an all-time low.[3773] The day after the crisis ended Kennedy told Arthur Schlesinger "The military are mad. They wanted to do this."[3774] Two weeks later Kennedy told Schlesinger:

> "The first advice I'm going to give my successor is going to be to watch the generals and to avoid feeling that just because they were military men that their opinions were worth a damn."[3775]

The Joint Chiefs were enraged that Cuba had not been attacked.[3776] They were also indignant that Kennedy had made concessions to Khrushchev.[3777] The Bay of Pigs fiasco in 1961 had already humiliated the military-intelligence establishment and the Cuban Missile Crisis in 1962 had made things worse.[3778]

Mary Plans to Expose the Conspiracy

Mary was suspicious of the 'lone nut gunman' theory and started to look into the Kennedy assassination. Leo Damore said Mary read the Warren Report carefully and became enraged at the cover up.[3779] After Mary had read the Warren report, she confronted Cord who told Angleton.[3780] By that time, she had compiled a journal of information on the assassination that she planned to go public with. Around that same time Mary Meyer was sure someone was breaking into her house and searching it.[3781] She had found a heavy door in her basement ajar.[3782] This door was so heavy neither she nor her sons could move it without help.[3783] The incidents continued and got worse throughout 1964.[3784] Mary even saw someone leaving as she was entering.[3785] John Bross was a CIA chief and CIA officer James Jesus Angleton bragged to John's wife Joan Bross that he had bugged Mary's phone and bedroom.[3786] Joe Shimon was also CIA and was the principal CIA liaison to mafia member Johnny Roselli.[3787] Shimon said that Angleton was spying on Mary and this escalated into full-blown surveillance of Mary at the time of the release of the Warren Report in late September 1964.[3788]

Mary blamed CIA officer James Angleton for the surveillance she knew she was under.[3789] This did not stop her plans to go public with her findings. She rebuffed several attempts to get her to keep quiet.

Jimmy Smith was a lawyer and part of Bobby Kennedy's inner circle.[3790] He was a pall bearer at Bobby Kennedy's funeral.[3791] Author Leo Damore had called Smith to discuss how he had solved the murder of Mary Meyer, and Smith took notes that he later shared with author Peter Janney.[3792] Smith's notes indicated that it had to have been Cord Meyer who conveyed to Jim Angleton how infuriated Mary had become.[3793] Whether Mary subsequently had a separate confrontation with Jim Angleton alone or with Cord present wasn't clear, but it was almost certain both men realized, knowing Mary as well as they did, that she wasn't the kind of person who was going to keep quiet.[3794]

Another Covert Operation is Necessary

The CIA mounted a covert operation to murder Mary and blame it on a guy named Ray Crump who happened to be in the wrong place at the wrong time.

Author Leo Damore called Jimmy Smith and said he had solved the case. Smith took six pages of notes, which he saved and later recounted for author Peter Janney.[3795] Damore said that an ex-FBI man using the alias "William L. Mitchell" had murdered Mary Meyer.[3796] Damore also said he had Mary's real diary in his possession, and that the murder had been a CIA operation.[3797] 'Mitchell' had been assigned to be part of a surveillance team keeping watch on Mary Meyer starting in September of 1964 when the release of the Warren Report made her so angry that she confronted the CIA chiefs.[3798] Damore said that 'Mitchell' was a trained hitman for the CIA's "K contracts" office in Washington, D.C..[3799] The plan to murder Mary Meyer was a scaled-down version of the plan to kill Kennedy.[3800] It took place in an open setting, away from home and appeared to be the work of a deranged loser who had been set up to be the patsy.[3801]

The surveillance team got to know Mary's routine and her regular noon walk on the tow path by the C&O Canal was the place they chose when they got the order to go ahead with the murder.[3802] Her regular four-mile walk gave them the flexibility to pick the place where they would have just enough witnesses to get the patsy convicted of the crime.[3803] They picked where Canal Road and Fox Hall Road crossed.[3804] The team had to be ready to go when the right conditions, like the availability of a patsy, all came together.[3805] Only the CIA had the resources to disguise someone on short notice to look and dress like the patsy.[3806]

Ray Crump, Jr. and his girlfriend Vivian had decided to use the park that day since they did not have money for a hotel room.[3807] Once the patsy, Ray Crump, was spotted, the team had to assemble clothing close enough to Crumps that he would be convicted in court.[3808] The only problem the CIA's Technical Services Division (TSD) encountered that day was that Crump was a small man, and the man they had picked to pretend to be Crump was larger than Crump.[3809] In the end, this discrepancy and a good lawyer would allow Crump to escape being convicted of the crime.[3810] On October 12, 1964 everything came together for the surveillance team and they got the green light to go ahead with the hit.[3811] At that time several things were put in place, including a stalled car where a witness was going to be needed.[3812] The purpose of the stalled car was to use as an excuse to call a tow truck driver to be there as a witness.[3813] The team had about two hours to get everything in place and pull off the murder of Mary Meyer.[3814] In the meantime Vivian had left and Ray Crump had either fallen asleep or passed out from drinking, and then he had fallen in the river and struggled to get back to the bank.[3815] The tow truck driver, Henry Wiggins, and his assistant, Bill Branch, had shown up, which was the final necessary condition and the team was told to go ahead with the murder of Mary Meyer.[3816] Wiggins would later say that Mary's screams lasted about twenty seconds before the first gunshot.[3817] Her killer held her from behind and allowed her to scream to draw the attention of the witnesses before shooting her.[3818] Mary was wounded by the first shot but broke away, and then 'Mitchell' forced her to the edge of the canal where he executed her with the second shot and slipped away into the woods.[3819] The Ray Crump imposter then stood over the body so he could be seen by Wiggins who came to the wall of the canal where he could see the crime scene.[3820] Ray Crump was arrested between 1:15 and 1:30 PM.[3821] Crump got lucky and got an excellent lawyer, and he was eventually found not guilty.[3822]

James Jesus Angleton located, stole and got away with Mary's real diary on the night of her murder.[3823]

Leo Damore and Peter Janney

The day after the murder of Mary Meyer her killer, "U.S. Army Lieutenant William Mitchell" showed up at the local police station and volunteered to be a witness, saying he had passed Mary Meyer on the tow path and described seeing Ray Crump just before she was murdered.[3824] 'Mitchell' said he was stationed at the Pentagon and, in fact, a listing for him was eventually found.[3825] He also gave an address in Arlington, Virginia which turned out to be a CIA safe house.[3826] His stated job at Georgetown University turned out to be a cover, like the Pentagon job.[3827] Leo Damore and later Peter Janney were eventually able to partly follow the trail of "William Mitchell."[3828] Damore had a phone conversation with Mary's killer in late March of 1993.[3829] Immediately after that call, Damore called Jimmy Smith and related the conversation.[3830]

Very late in his life Cord Meyer was asked who killed his wife and he responded "The same sons of bitches that killed John F. Kennedy."[3831]

In his book *MARY'S MOSAIC*, author Peter Janney goes into great detail to document all the ways in which he managed to corroborate the CIA involvement in Mary Meyer's murder. I highly recommend reading the book for those who want to know more about how the Deep State spends their tax dollars.

Jack Ruby

Clearly the plan went wrong. No one who is trying to plan an operation like this says "Gee, let's have Lee Harvey Oswald murdered in front of millions of live television viewers. And for good measure, let's do it while he's in police custody, right in Dallas police headquarters." The plan was for Lee Harvey Oswald to die in a shootout while being arrested. Oswald somehow managed, against all odds, to be arrested alive. Even pulling a gun and trying to shoot the arresting officers in the Texas Theatre didn't get Oswald killed. So, Ruby was sent in to silence him.

Jack Ruby was a mafia functionary who was involved in the Kennedy assassination. Once Oswald was taken alive Ruby was sent in to kill Oswald to keep him quiet. He was told he would spend a few years in jail and then be set free and paid off. Once he was on trial for murder however, his mafia lawyer went for the insanity defense to paint Ruby out as a nut. This was good for the mafia and the conspirators but bad for Ruby, who was convicted and later decided to talk. Things predictably went downhill from there and Ruby himself then had to be eliminated to keep him quiet.

This chapter is organized into five sections:

1. Who was Jack Ruby – describes Ruby's background as a mafia functionary in the Dallas wing of Carlos Marcello's organization – Ruby reported to Joseph Civello who reported to Marcello

2. Ruby's involvement in the JFK assassination – describes the part Ruby played in the Kennedy hit until things went wrong and he was sent in to murder Oswald to keep Oswald from talking

3. Ruby is sent in to silence Oswald – describes how, when the plan goes wrong and Oswald was taken alive, Ruby is sent in to kill him on the expectation he will get a short prison term

4. The Mafia sends Ruby a lawyer – describes how the mafia supplies Ruby with a lawyer who only looks out for the mafia's interests and Ruby ended up convicted of murder and on death row

5. Now Ruby needs to be silenced – describes how Ruby, sitting
   on death row, now wants to start talking and how Ruby now
   has to be murdered to keep him quiet, and how this was done

Who Was Jack Ruby?

Jack Ruby used to work for Sam Giancana, the mafia boss in Chicago.[3832]
Ruby then came to Dallas in the late 1940's.[3833] He was sent to Dallas
by the mafia in Chicago.[3834] In Dallas, he got involved in all kinds of
illegal activity, including running guns to Cuba in the 1950's.[3835] By
the late 1950's Ruby was smuggling guns from Galveston, Texas to a
young revolutionary leader named Fidel Castro in Cuba.[3836] With his
connections in Cuba, Ruby was able to move freely between the U.S.
and Cuba. This was handy when mafia boss Santo Trafficante, who
had been imprisoned by Castro for running Cuban casinos, was in the
Triscornia detention camp near Havana.[3837] Ruby would come by to
bring food and allow Trafficante to keep in touch with his empire.[3838]
Robert McKeown, an arms dealer, was asked by Jack Ruby for a letter
of introduction to Fidel Castro.[3839] Ruby claimed McKeown wanted to
sell Castro some jeeps and Ruby also wanted to get some folks released
who Castro was holding in prison.[3840]

Edward Brower was a gun smuggler for the CIA.[3841] He said Ruby
became involved with the CIA in the late 1950's smuggling guns to
Castro.[3842] Once Castro was in power, Ruby started selling guns to the
anti-Castro forces in Cuba.[3843] He was just doing it for the money, not
ideology.[3844] Once Castro was in power, the CIA wanted to help the
anti-Castro forces. As New Orleans District Attorney Jim Garrison
said:[3845]

> "When you understand that that part of the mafia which was
> the ally in the late '50's, early '60's, of the CIA is working
> with the Agency like it used to before, as Ruby was doing,
> actually the evidence is overwhelming that he was working for
> the intelligence community, not as Agent #352 with a gold
> badge, but as a member of the mafia, part of which had
> become subservient to the CIA."[3846]

After Castro took over and kicked the mafia out of the casinos in Cuba,
the mob bosses switched their allegiance and started backing the anti-
Castro CIA plans to oust Castro.[3847]

In Dallas, Ruby worked as a mafia functionary in the Marcello/Civello organization. Joe Civello was the guy who ran the Dallas operations for Carlos Marcello, who was based in New Orleans. In an FBI interview on January 14, 1964 Civello acknowledged having known Ruby for about ten years.[3848] Ruby also ran a couple of strip clubs in Dallas. He was involved in the corruption in Dallas and was likely to be rolled up in the indictments coming down from the Kennedy crackdown on mafia in general and Marcello's organization in particular in the early 1960's during the Kennedy administration.

In early December of 1963 Ruby employee William Abade was interviewed by the FBI.[3849] In that interview he discussed his bookmaking activities for Ruby's establishment and how he observed that Ruby had police officers there on a regular basis.[3850] The FBI report in the National Archives is five pages, but the Warren Commission only published four of the pages.[3851] The missing page covers Abade's employment by Ruby as a bookmaker, thus either the Warren Commission or the FBI was attempting to hide this aspect of Ruby's background.[3852]

Hoover did not want Ruby to be seen as a part of the mafia. An FBI report of Ruby visiting mafia boss Santo Trafficante while Trafficante was in one of Castro's prisons was created but not shared. The FBI also knew that John Wilson, a British journalist who was also in prison with Trafficante, knew of Ruby's connections.[3853] Hoover tried to discredit Wilson because he said he saw Ruby visit Santo Trafficante while Trafficante was in a Cuban prison. The day after Wilson reported this, an FBI report says:[3854]

> "John Wilson likely be psychopath – we gather he gave this impression when testifying before Eastland committee in '59"[3855]

Hoover does this because he is trying to keep Ruby's ties to the mafia from becoming known.[3856] If Hoover can discredit Wilson, his account of Ruby's mafia connections can be dismissed as coming from a nut.

Robert Moore, a piano player who worked for Ruby, also worked for Joseph Civello.[3857] He is interviewed by the FBI and said:

> "Ruby was a frequent visitor at Civello's store and an associate of Civello"[3858]

Hoover had no intention of pursuing this lead. He ordered a superficial 'investigation' and then buried the results and ignored Ruby's mafia connections, hoping no one will notice.[3859] The last thing Hoover wanted was for the connection between Ruby and Marcello to come to light. In early December Hoover again attacked the Dallas and New

Orleans FBI agents investigating the Marcello organization and the investigation slowed to a crawl.[3860]

On November 12, 1963 two ex-convicts then currently employed by the Chicago mafia, Paul Jones and Alex Kruger, showed up in Dallas and met with Jack Ruby.[3861]

Ruby's Involvement in the JFK Assassination

When Ruby's drug mule Rose Cherami was taken to the hospital in Louisiana after being found in the road, she not only correctly predicted the Kennedy assassination, which happened two days later, she also said she worked for Jack Ruby.[3862] She also testified that Ruby and Oswald knew each other.[3863]

Julia Ann Mercer was stalled in traffic at 11:00 AM on the day of the assassination next to a green pickup truck parked on the north side of Elm just west of Dealey Plaza.[3864] She watched as a man pulled out a rifle case wrapped in paper and carried it up the slope.[3865] She then pulled up next to the driver, who she did not know, and they made eye contact.[3866] The driver was Jack Ruby, which she would later realize when she saw his picture in the news media after he shot Oswald.[3867] When Kennedy was assassinated she gave the FBI her statement.[3868] She later recognized Jack Ruby from his pictures in the media.[3869]

Ruby's involvement in the Kennedy assassination went much deeper than just giving snipers a ride to Dealey Plaza. Ruby had developed relationships with much of the Dallas police force. Peace Justice David L. Johnson reported to Dallas FBI agents Harden and Wilkison that Ruby had cosigned Dallas bank loans for some police officers.[3870] In Ruby's clubs the cops were treated like kings. The bartender in Ruby's club had a standing order that he could serve cops hard liquor and that cops never had to pay for drinks at Ruby's club.[3871] He fixed them up with women from his strip joints. Jack Hardee knew Jack Ruby and he said that J.D. Tippit was a frequent visitor to Ruby's club.[3872] Ruby's relationships with the Dallas police were put to use by the conspirators. Ruby was paid to use his relationships with the cops to make sure Oswald was killed while being arrested for the assassination of Kennedy.[3873]

On June 08, 1963 Ruby visited New Orleans.[3874] While he was there, Ruby, whose nickname was "Sparky," pointed out that he had known Oswald since he a young boy.[3875] On July 6, 1963 Ruby called the Old

French Opera House in New Orleans, which was owned by Frank Caracci, a capo in the Marcello organization.[3876] Ruby makes many calls there during the planning of the Kennedy assassination.[3877] On October 1, 1963 Ruby was spotted in the French Quarter with Frank Caracci by New Orleans Detective O'Sullivan.[3878] On October 9, 1963 Ruby flew to New Orleans and is seen with Frank Caracci.[3879] On November 21, 1963 by Thursday afternoon Ruby was in Houston where President Kennedy was visiting prior to his visit to Dallas the next day.[3880]

Jack Ruby was broke in early 1963.[3881] He was struggling to pay his bills, and the IRS was after him for tens of thousands of dollars in back taxes.[3882] On November 15, 1963 he suddenly was expecting a windfall and started looking to have a safe put in concrete in his office.[3883] And Ruby had recently moved into a newer, much nicer apartment building.[3884] On November 19, 1963 Ruby gave his lawyer power of attorney to deal with his IRS issues.[3885] He told the lawyer that he now had a "connection" where he can get the money he needs to settle his debt with the IRS.[3886] The afternoon of the assassination he went into his bank with $7,000 in cash.[3887]

Mark North, in his book *ACT OF TREASON*, points out that, in early November, 1963:[3888]

> "This evening at Ruby's Carousel Club in Dallas an individual named Wilbur Waldon Litchfield waits to speak with the mobster. "The next to see Ruby, Litchfield reported, was a man in a V-neck sweater who had been sitting four tables front of Litchfield. [He] had paid particular attention to that man, he explained, 'because of his sloppy dress'; the man's 'hair was not combed,' and he stood out from the other men in suits or sport jackets. . . . Fifteen or twenty minutes after entering Ruby's office, the man . . . came out with Ruby. . . . As the man left, he passed within two feet of Litchfield underneath a bright light. [He] observed that that man was 'in his middle 20's, 5'7" – 5'9"; and very slender. . . . After President Kennedy was assassinated' . . . . Litchfield positively identified the man as Oswald. . . . The Dallas Police immediately took the highly unusual step of giving Litchfield a polygraph exam. The police's curt conclusion was that Litchfield 'ha[d] been untruthful.' . . . Officials attempted to shake his testimony through a questionable means of pressure, again highly irregular. . . . '. . . When the federal agents talked to me, they said, "You know, if you say you are positive and it wasn't him," it's a Federal charge. . . .'"[3889]

Oswald was also seen in Ruby's club by stripper Karen Harlen.[3890] Lots of witnesses, including musicians, strippers and comedians, also saw Oswald at Ruby's club.[3891]

Ruby and Oswald were seen together by, for example, by Bill DeMar.[3892] Under the stage name of Bill Crowe, DeMar was master of ceremonies at Ruby's Carousel club.[3893] DeMar was ignored by the FBI because Hoover was trying to bury the link between Ruby and Oswald. A reporter tracked DeMar down and he also said:[3894]

> "I gave the FBI a statement about seeing Oswald in the club and that was it. I told them the same thing I'm telling you. I signed it and have heard nothing more about the incident to this day."[3895]

One of the strippers in Ruby's club was called Jada. She was with Ruby at an all-night party on November 20, 1963, two days before the Kennedy assassination, at the apartment of Frank Tortoriello[3896] Beverly Oliver also worked in Jack Ruby's club, and she later wrote a book. She reported that Ruby brought Oswald into the club and introduced him as being CIA. She also said that a dancer named Jada simply disappeared, leaving some of her clothes, after telling reporters that Ruby had introduced her to Oswald.[3897] Jada is not listed among the fifty murdered JFK assassination witnesses (see the section called The List) for the simple reason that there is no proof linking her disappearance to the murder. However, Jada's 'disappearance' does fit the pattern of people who knew too much, talked, and died.

Author Jerome Corsi, in his book *WHO REALLY KILLED KENNEDY?*, said:[3898]

> "Sam Giancana claimed that the original plan to eliminate Oswald involved having Officer Tippit and Roscoe White kill Oswald in what would have been portrayed as an attempt to apprehend the escaping assassin."[3899]

> "According to Giancana the plan went awry when Tippit lost his nerve."[3900]

> Giancana also said "When the plan to kill Oswald failed, the assignment went to Jack Ruby."[3901]

The original plan was for Oswald to be shot while being arrested.[3902] That plan failed and the conspirators had to improvise. It was Jack Ruby's job to arrange with the Dallas cops to kill Oswald during his arrest. The mafia paid Ruby to set up the death of Oswald because he had the relationships with the Dallas cops.[3903] It was his responsibility.

When it failed and Oswald was in custody, it then fell to Ruby to go to Dallas Police Headquarters and kill Oswald while he was in custody. Johnny Roselli said Ruby was ordered by the mafia to kill Oswald to shut him up.[3904]

The second attempt to kill Oswald while being arrested was at the Texas Theatre. Ruby was even at the Texas Theatre to watch. He was hoping Oswald would be killed. George Applin was attending the movie when Oswald was arrested, and he got up and moved to the back when the lights came on and the police moved in on Oswald.[3905] While in the back, he warned Jack Ruby, who he did not know, that he would be safer if he moved.[3906] Ruby ignored him as Oswald tried to use his gun on the police at the last minute.[3907] Two days later Applin recognized Ruby from the television news.[3908] This second attempt to have Oswald killed while being arrested also failed and Oswald was taken alive, but Oswald's luck was about to run out.

Ruby had agreed to make sure Oswald was dead, but then he had failed. Oswald was alive, and starting to talk. At one point, Oswald, while being transferred, blurted out to reporters "I'm just a patsy!"[3909] This was very bad news for Ruby's boss, Carlos Marcello. Once Oswald was taken alive, Ruby was between a rock and hard place. He had failed, and the price for failure in the mafia wasn't just getting fired. He would die a slow and painful death if he did not kill Oswald himself. The Chicago mafia had recently put a loan shark named William "Action" Jackson on a meat hook and brutally tortured him to death for a few days for the sin of talking to the FBI.[3910] This was what was in store for Ruby if he failed again.[3911] At this point, Ruby was desperate. While at his sister's place, he threw up.[3912] His next move was to place calls to the FBI and Dallas police to warn them that Oswald would be killed while being transferred. These gambits failed, and Ruby had no choice but to kill Oswald. He was in much greater fear of the mafia than of the Dallas authorities. As a long-time Dallas local Ruby thought that he would be safe in the hands of the local authorities.[3913] There was a way that he could have gotten a maximum sentence of five years for killing Oswald, and while he would rather not have had to do it, that was preferable to facing the meat hook. It was his responsibility to have Oswald killed. When the original plan failed and Oswald was in custody, it fell to Ruby to go to Dallas Police Headquarters and kill Oswald while he was in police custody. He was seen as the only one who had the relationships with the cops that would allow him to get to Oswald while Oswald was in police custody.

Eugene Brading (a.k.a. Jim Braidon) arrived in Dallas on November 21, the day before the assassination, and checked into suite 301 of the

Cabana hotel with Morgan Brown.[3914] On November 22, 1963 at 1:30 AM Ruby went to the Lucas B&B restaurant where he had arranged to meet a man.[3915] Ruby was known to the staff as a regular, but they did not know the man he met there.[3916] Ruby paid for the bill for both of them and they left together, and an hour later Ruby called his club from the Cabana hotel.[3917]

On November 22, 1963 John F. Kennedy was assassinated in Dealey Plaza.

Morgan Brown checked out of the Cabana hotel at 2:00 PM on November 22, 1963.[3918]

Immediately after the assassination Ruby went to Parkland Hospital.[3919] He may have planted what became known as the Magic Bullet. Then he went to the Texas Theatre to see Oswald's arrest.

Ruby is Sent in to Silence Oswald

Once Oswald was taken alive, Ruby was stuck. He had twice failed to fulfill his assigned task, to have Oswald killed while being arrested, for which he had already accepted at least partial payment. Worse, the people who assigned him that task were brutal mafia thugs who would put him on a meat hook and torture him to death if he failed again. Ruby actually had two chances that weekend to kill Oswald. He lost his nerve the first time.

After Oswald's arrest on November 22, 1963, Ruby showed up on the third floor of the Dallas Police Headquarters.[3920] Oswald was in Captain Will Fritz's office, and Ruby tried to open the door and go in when he was pulled back by police officers.[3921] Then at 11:30 PM Ruby was again at police headquarters and was seen by UPI photographer Pete Fisher, who said:[3922]

> "The Dallas police brought Oswald through this entrance, and Oswald passed not more than three feet from Ruby as he was led up on the stage." Fisher pointed out that "If Ruby had wanted to shoot Oswald at that time he could easily have done it because of the fact that he was so close to Oswald."[3923]

Ruby later confirmed that he had a loaded snub-nosed revolver with him at the time, but he passed up that chance to shoot Oswald.[3924] Clearly, he did not want to shoot Oswald, and he lost his nerve at that first chance.

In the middle of the night of November 23-24 Jack Ruby called both the Dallas County sheriff's office and the Dallas FBI office to warn them that Oswald would be killed if he was transferred.[3925] Then Ruby called the Dallas police and Officer Billy Grammer thought the voice sounded familiar.[3926] He knew Jack Ruby, but couldn't quite put a name with the voice until later.[3927] The caller knew details of the transfer that were not public.[3928] Ruby said:

> "You're going to have to make some other plans or we're going to kill Oswald right there in the basement."[3929]

Reports were filed, but no changes were made.[3930] This was clearly an attempt by Ruby to get out of killing Oswald. He then gathered his courage and succeeded in murdering Oswald the second time he had the chance. The event was covered on national television with millions of people watching. Ruby looked, acted and dressed like the gangster he was. The murder looked like a scene out of a gangster movie. Watching all this, the public became skeptical of the official story, and letters poured in to Congress requesting an investigation. The result was the Warren Commission.

On November 24, 1963 Oswald was shot by Jack Ruby in the basement of Dallas Police Headquarters while surrounded by police during his transfer. He was rushed to Parkland Memorial Hospital, but died on the operating table.

Author Dr. Charles Crenshaw, in his book *JFK HAS BEEN SHOT*, documents how Jack Ruby reacted to Oswald's death:[3931]

> "Standing nearby, Detective Don Archer witnesses the shooting and assists in apprehending Ruby. He and other officers place Ruby in a fifth-floor cell. Archer, staying behind to guard the prisoner, observes Ruby's strange behavior. Ruby was "very hyper" and "sweating profusely." He had been stripped down for security purposes and his rapid heartbeat could be readily seen. Ruby requested and was given a cigarette. Later, word came that Oswald had died as a result of the shooting. Archer conveys this information to Ruby, telling him that, "It looks like it's going to be the electric chair for you." Instead of becoming more agitated, Ruby became calm, ceased perspiring, and his rapid heartbeat slowed to normal. Archer then asks Ruby if he would like another cigarette. Ruby replied "I don't smoke." Ruby's behavior, Archer noted, was a "complete turnaround." It was apparent that his life depended on getting Oswald."[3932]

Ruby was considerably more worried about the meat hook. He was more afraid of mob justice than the Dallas legal system. He and his mafia bosses had the Dallas justice system wired and he thought it would treat him well.

Mark North, in his book *ACT OF TREASON*, said that on December 23, 1963:

> "Ruby employee Karen Bennett and his roommate George Senator testify at a hearing in Dallas. Bennet, who within months will be found shot to death in a Houston hotel, is carrying a gun in her purse, wearing sunglasses and appears frightened. She testifies that the morning Ruby murdered Oswald he had wired money to her for rent prior to entering the police station basement."[3933]

On November 25, 1963 Ruby was transferred to the Dallas County Jail where he stayed until he died a few years later.[3934] That same day, the *Los Angeles Times* reported that "Ruby spoke to his sister, apparently on Sunday. Ruby: "Take care of yourself and don't worry, the FBI and the officers are treating me well. I've got friends."[3935] As a long-time Dallas local Ruby thought he would be safe in the hands of the local authorities.[3936]

New Orleans mafia boss Carlos Marcello sent Sam Campisi to meet with Jack Ruby in jail on November 30.[3937] Clearly the reason for the visit was to tell Ruby to keep his mouth shut and everything would work out well.[3938]

The involvement of the mafia in the Kennedy assassination was becoming rather obvious.[3939] When Attorney General Robert Kennedy had his investigators look into the phone records of Jack Ruby in the time leading up to the assassination he said:[3940]

> "The list [of names] was almost a duplicate of the people I called before the Rackets Committee."[3941]

Once he shot Oswald, Ruby worried that his background running guns to Cuba with Thomas Ely Davis might be brought up.[3942] Davis was connected with the CIA and was, at that time, in prison in Algeria in connection with the plot against Charles de Gaulle.[3943] Ruby's attorneys and the authorities were working overtime to keep Ruby's CIA and mafia connections from becoming known.

The Mafia Sends Ruby a Lawyer

The judge in Ruby's case, Joe Brown, was wired into the local corruption and did his best to help Ruby and prevent disclosures about Ruby's ties to the mafia.[3944]

Just as the conspirators tried to portray Oswald as a lone nut gunman, the same authorities tried to portray Ruby as just a strip-joint owner who decided, on his own, to murder Oswald. Nothing to see here folks, move along. And once Ruby had accomplished his task for them he had become a liability. Had Oswald died as per the original plan Ruby would have been much better off. Having to murder Oswald on national television had made Ruby disposable.

At first Ruby was relieved that Oswald died and he was saved from the meat hook. Then things slowly started to change for Ruby. The wrong legal strategy for Ruby's defense was to try for temporary insanity. This meant the jury had almost no choice but to send him away. The right strategy would have been to try for Murder Without Malice. The penalty would have likely been five years or less. The lawyer the mafia sent in to defend Ruby went for Temporary Insanity instead of Murder Without Malice. This was good for the mafia but bad for Ruby. It meant that, once Ruby was labeled as 'crazy,' anything he might say could be discounted. It also, unfortunately for Ruby, meant that he would spend what little was left of his life in jail.

As far as Ruby's fate was concerned, the mafia was calling the shots. They sent in mafia lawyer Melvin Belli to take charge of Ruby's growing defense team. Above all, their interest was to keep Ruby quiet. This meant permanently, but in the short run he would not be allowed to take the stand in his own defense. The last thing the mafia wanted was Ruby talking. It also meant that Ruby would not be pursuing the legal strategy that was in his best interest.

At first, Ruby's attorney was Tom Howard.[3945] Before mafia lawyer Melvin Belli arrived, Tom Howard was pursuing a legal strategy of Murder Without Malice for Ruby.[3946] This was the right legal strategy for Ruby. The idea was that everybody hated Oswald for killing Kennedy and Ruby was almost a hero for killing Oswald. Give the jury the option of letting Ruby off with five years (at most) in jail and everybody goes home happy.

In his book *THE POISON PATRIARCH*, author Mark Shaw documents that Ruby prosecutor Bill Alexander disputed lawyer Melvin Belli's statement that no plea bargain was possible. He quotes Alexander:[3947]

"Belli never approached us about settling the case prior to trial. He never made an offer, no effort there. It was the opinion, and I was not alone on this, that the case needed to be tried so the public would know what the facts were. But if Ruby had wanted to plead guilty, there could have been the possibility of probation or short-term imprisonment because we did not want to see him convicted."[3948]

This would have been the kind of treatment Ruby, a longtime local who knew the Dallas system, was expecting. He would have been expecting to spend little, if any, time behind bars and then be free. Ruby's first defense attorney, Tom Howard, had a similar strategy to appeal to the jury who, in his words, wanted "to pin a medal on Jack" for killing Oswald, and this would have resulted in a light punishment – a few years in prison at worst.[3949]

Belli decided to go with an insanity defense instead, painting Ruby out as crazy. This helped the mafia but not Ruby, who ended up sentenced to die in the electric chair. Judge Brown was critical of the way Belli handled the defense.[3950] He talked to the jury and they said Belli offered them no alternatives except acquittal or extreme penalty, and acquittal was impossible since Ruby had murdered Oswald on national television.[3951] Melvin Belli's defense strategy only make sense if you understand who was pulling the strings and why.

The expense of paying for Ruby's legal defense also only make sense if you know who was pulling the strings. In addition to the other half a dozen lawyers already on Ruby's legal team, Belli brought a staff of fourteen people with him to Dallas and they camped out in a dozen rooms of a hotel.[3952] The airfare, meals and other travel expenses must have created an enormous travel bill in addition to the normal trial expenses like paying for multiple prominent psychiatrists.[3953] And that's not counting the money Belli charged for his time and the time his staff spent on the Ruby trial. Jack Ruby did not have the money for this kind of defense team, but he wasn't the one paying the bill or calling the shots.

Belli told Milton Hunt, his driver and friend who accompanied him to Dallas, that:[3954]

"The Ruby case is fixed. I'm just going through the motions. It's simply being staged for the sake of publicity. There's an inside thing, and that there was no way to win. It's a whitewash."[3955]

Author Mark Shaw, in his book *THE POISON PARTIARCH*, documents how two independent sources both claimed that Belli was offered a million dollars by the mafia to take the Ruby case.[3956] He was also told not to talk about the trial.

Melvin Belli loved to hear himself talk, especially about himself and his accomplishments.[3957] However, he never talked about the Ruby case.[3958] Mafia boss Santo Trafficante kept telling mafia lawyer Frank Ragano not to ask Belli about the Ruby case "whatever you do, don't ask him about Jack Ruby. Don't get involved. It's none of your business."[3959]

Now Ruby Needs to be Silenced

Once he realized that he too had been thrown under the bus, Ruby decided to talk. He eventually got a few members of the Warren Commission to come to Dallas to talk to him. Unfortunately for Ruby they were just there for show. They had no interest in what he had to say. Like everyone else who tried to talk, he then had to be murdered. He was eventually murdered a few years later with the fast-acting cancer that had been developed in New Orleans by the CIA for use on Castro.

By mid-1964 Ruby no longer felt safe in the hands of the authorities in Dallas. He would like to talk, but thought he would be murdered if he did. He knew David Ferrie and Lee Oswald and had been to New Orleans to visit them while they were working on the fast-acting cancer program for the CIA.[3960] On June 7, 1964 Jack Ruby begged Earl Warren to take him to Washington so he could reveal the truth about the assassination and Warren refused.[3961]

When Warren refused to take him back to Washington, Ruby then insisted on being given a lie-detector test. Warren reluctantly agreed. This created a problem for the conspirators. If Ruby got a legitimate test then the truth might come out, so Hoover arranged for an FBI polygraph expert to make sure the test indicated that Ruby did not know Oswald prior to the assassination. The test was faked, but this did not come to light until 1978 during the House Select Committee on Assassinations (HSCA) investigation.

Author Donald Byron Thomas, in his book *HEAR NO EVIL*, documents how the panel of experts hired by the House Select Committee on Assassinations (HSCA) in 1978 described in detail how Ruby's polygraph had been faked by the FBI's polygraph expert, Bell

P. Hearndon, in 1964.[3962] Hearndon violated all the normal principles of how to give a legitimate polygraph test.[3963]

> "The evidence shows that the FBI's polygraph expert, Bell Hearndon, deliberately sabotaged Ruby's polygraph exam and then gave false testimony to the Warren Commission."[3964]

Ruby also had a letter smuggled out of prison where he pointed the finger at President Johnson as being behind the Kennedy assassination.[3965]

Dorothy Kilgallen wrote a column saying that the Federal government was keeping Oswald in the shadows by not releasing what it knew about him and this column impressed Ruby who agreed to an interview which turned into two interviews.[3966] Kilgallen told several friends that "this (the Kennedy assassination) has to be a conspiracy" she was planning a trip to New Orleans to get more information for her research when she died under suspicious circumstances.[3967]

Authors Roger Stone and Mike Colapietro, in their book *THE MAN WHO KILLED KENNEDY: THE CASE AGAINST LBJ*, said:[3968]

> "Kilgallen had more pieces of the assassination puzzle, including that Texas oil barons – Lyndon Johnson moneyman H.L. Hunt in particular and Carlos Marcello – were involved in the plot. Following her interview with Jack Ruby, Kilgallen announced to friends that the information she was privy to in the Ruby interview was game-changing, and that she was "about to blow the JFK case sky high." The new information was to be released in a book Kilgallen was writing titled *Murder One*, which she hoped would finally reveal elements of the conspiracy and cover-up integral to the assassination."[3969]

Dorothy Kilgallen was murdered on November 8, 1965 and her notes were stolen.[3970] She had given a backup copy of her notes to her neighbor and friend Florence Pritchett Smith, who was murdered the next day and the backup copy of Kilgallen's notes were also stolen.[3971] At this point the conspirators knew that Ruby was trying to get word out, so he had to be murdered.

Author Phillip Nelson, in his book *LBJ: THE MASTEMIND OF THE JFK ASSASSINATION*, documented that:[3972]

> "One of the doctors assigned to Ruby was Dr. Louis Joy Ion West, a psychiatrist who had worked with the CIA's MK-ULTRA program, which involved the use of LSD and other experimental psychological procedures. Dr. West was brought

in mysteriously, by persons unknown, as he had no previous connections to Ruby or Dallas."[3973]

Author Phillip Nelson, in his book *LBJ: THE MASTEMIND OF THE JFK ASSASSINATION*, documented that:[3974]

> "According to Jim Maars, Deputy Sheriff Al Madox said "We had a phony doctor come in to [the Dallas County Jail] from Chicago, just as phony and queer as a three-dollar bill. And he worked his way in through – I don't know, whoever supplied the county at that time with doctors ... you could tell he was Ruby's doctor. He spent half his time up there talking with Ruby." Ruby told me, "Well they injected me for a cold. It was cancer cells." DPD Officer Tom Tilson said that "it was the opinion of a number of other police officers that Ruby had received injections of cancer." Bruce McCarthy, operated an electron microscope at Southwest Medical School near Parkland Hospital, was asked to analyze Ruby's cancer cells and explained there are two types of cancer cells: cilia (which affect the respiratory system) and microvilli (affecting the digestive system). McCarthy identified Ruby's cells as microvilli, indicating they originated in the digestive system. He was shocked when it was announced that Ruby died from lung cancer."[3975]

Author Phillip Nelson, in his book *LBJ: THE MASTEMIND OF THE JFK ASSASSINATION*, documented that:[3976]

> "Dr. Earl Rose ... discovered that the heaviest concentration of cancer cells was in the right lung, with traces of white cancerous tumors throughout the body. According to the doctors who had treated Ruby, his cancer had originated in the pancreas, but Rose saw a normal pancreas."[3977]

Had the cancer grown organically in Ruby, his pancreas would have shown signs of it, because that was where it would have started. Ruby was injected with the fast-acting cancer developed by the CIA in the summer of 1963 at the direction of Dr. Alton Ochsner. This is how he ended up dying from a cancer that did not originate in his own body.

On January 3, 1967, Jack Ruby died of cancer as a prisoner in Dallas.[3978]

The CIA and the Mainstream Media

History is full of examples where good propaganda helped to sell a big lie. The conspirators needed the mainstream media to help them sell the American people on the lie that Oswald was a lone shooter. Our mainstream media, those vigilant guardians of our democracy, were more than happy to oblige.

The CIA used the American mainstream media to put the CIA's spin on the news. The idea was to make sure the media was saying what the CIA wanted said, not the truth of what was actually happening. An example of this was the Bay of Pigs fiasco. The CIA had the media blame it on Kennedy when really it was the CIA's fault. Another example is the Kennedy assassination. The mainstream media praised the Warren Report and basically said we should all believe it. Just move along folks, nothing to see here.

Anyone who views the Zapruder film can plainly see Kennedy's head go backward due to a shot from the front. Help to the conspirators from the mainstream media came in two forms. The first kind of help was what was said, like having the mainstream media praise the Warren Commission for doing a thorough job or having Dan Rather claim that he had seen the Zapruder film and it showed the president's head go forward (as if shot from behind) when in fact the exact opposite happened. The second kind of help was what was not said, like when Mark Lane distributed 100 copies of the Zapruder film to prominent journalists in the late 1960's, including Walter Cronkite, and none of them used it or even commented on it. They sat on the information contained in the film.

It gets worse. The mainstream media allowed itself to be used as a weapon by the CIA against those who the CIA saw as enemies. An example of this is Jim Garrison, who tried to prosecute CIA operative Clay Shaw for conspiracy to murder President Kennedy. The CIA used the mainstream media as part of their all-out attack on Garrison in an attempt to destroy him as an example to others who might try to expose the conspiracy.

The name for the CIA program that controlled the mainstream media was Operation Mockingbird. It started out innocently enough as patriotic journalists and publishers who wanted to help their country. It eventually grew into a systematic undermining of one of the basic pillars of democracy. We the people, in order to make well-informed decisions about the future of our country, need to have the facts. The CIA was making sure that didn't happen.

Operation Mockingbird

Operation Mockingbird started out innocently enough. It was a program by the CIA to get newspapers and other media outlets to put the CIA's spin on the news. Eventually it turned into something worse.

Phil Graham was a high-ranking Army Intelligence officer in World War II.[3979] He was close to MacArthur in the Pacific and he was also close to high-ranking CIA officers like Allen Dulles, Frank Wisner, Richard Helms, Cord Meyer and Desmond Fitzgerald, and they were all in the same social class and saw each other regularly on a social basis.[3980] Phil Graham was put in charge by his father in law of the *Washington Post*.[3981] In the late 1940's Frank Wisner of the CIA began recruiting American news organizations and journalists to become spies and disseminators of propaganda on the CIA payroll.[3982]

In the early 1950's the CIA formalized its direct ties with the mainstream media and this was the beginning of Operation Mockingbird to influence American public opinion.[3983] In 1951 Frank Wisner recruited Philip Graham, publisher of the *Washington Post* and from there went on to recruit prominent journalists at CBS, *New York Times*, *Newsweek* and others with Graham's help.[3984] Joseph Alsop once said that it was his patriotic duty to carry water for the CIA.[3985] This was no doubt part of the recruiting pitch. Wisner also recruited *Time* and *Life* magazine publisher Henry Luce and CBS head William Paley.[3986] Also recruited were Joseph Alsop (300 different newspapers), Stewart Alsop (*New York Herald Tribune*), Ben Bradlee (*Newsweek*), James Reston (*New York Times*), Walter Pincus (*Washington Post*), Herb Gold (*Miami News*) and Charles Bartlett (*Chattanooga Times*).[3987] By 1953 the CIA had influence over 25 major media outlets.[3988]

Author Peter Janney, in his book *MARY'S MOSAIC*, pointed out that:[3989]

> "During the 1950's, the CIA initiated Operation Mockingbird, a project designed, the reader will recall, to influence the American media to slant news stories favoring the CIA's

agenda or point of view, particularly those having to do with international events and foreign policy. The program had been started by Allen Dulles's top lieutenant Frank Wisner, a friend of Phil Graham's and at one time Cord Meyer's boss. Wisner successfully "recruited" a number of prominent journalists to the CIA, including his friend Phil Graham, who soon helped run Mockingbird within mainstream media outlets. Using newspapers, magazines, radio and television, even Hollywood, the CIA's disinformation spin machine went to work shaping public opinion and perceptions, undermining the integrity and independence of an indispensable pillar of the democratic process."[3990]

Author Peter Janney, in his book *MARY'S MOSAIC*, points out that:[3991]

"Under Cord Meyer's tutelage, Mockingbird became a stunning success. Whenever the CIA wanted a news story slanted in a particular way, it got it. This amounted to a subversion of democracy's most precious cornerstone, the free press."[3992]

In a 25,000-word cover story published in Rolling Stone on October 20, 1977 entitled *The CIA and the Media: How American's Most Powerful News Media Worked Hand in Glove with the Central Intelligence Agency and Why the Church Committee Covered It Up*, Carl Bernstein documents Operation Mockingbird. By the CIA's own admission, at least 25 organizations and 400 journalists will become CIA 'assets.' Here is a quote from the article:

"Among the executives who lent their cooperation to the Agency were William Paley of CBS, Henry Luce of Time, Inc., Arthur Hays Sulzberger of the *New York Times*, Barry Bingham, Sr. of the *Louisville Courier-Journal* and James Copley of the Copley News Service. Other organizations which cooperated with the CIA include the American Broadcasting Company, The National Broadcasting Company, the Associated Press, United Press International, Reuters, Hearst Newspapers, Scripps-Howard, *Newsweek* Magazine, the Mutual Broadcasting System, the *Miami Herald* and the old *Saturday Evening Post* and *New York Herald-Tribune*.

By far the most valuable of these associations, according to CIA officials, have been with the *New York Times*, CBS and Time, Inc."

An example of how this works was given by Mark Lane in his book *LAST WORD: MY INDICTMENT OF THE CIA IN THE MURDER OF*

JFK. Lane and the ACLU brought a lawsuit against the CIA under the Freedom of Information Act (FOIA) and obtained internal CIA documents describing how the process works:[3993]

> "This is the method now employed. An independent publication is chosen to mask the source. A CIA puppet is placed there and given an impressive title. The CIA then provides the propaganda. It appears as an independent concept when published. The CIA, employing its official website, cia.gov, then cites the "independent" writer and the "independent" publication as the source as it spreads its false allegations throughout the world."[3994]

Lane also points out that the CIA singled him out for an attack:[3995]

> "The CIA instructed its "assets" in the national news media in detail to criticize me and my work because, it said, the agency had been involved in the assassination. One CIA memorandum specifically stated the journalists who were their "assets" should employ in that effort, even suggesting the language that should be used to destroy me. Remarkably, New York Times journalist Anthony Lewis, referred to as "a prominent liberal intellectual," used in his stories the numerous and specific arguments suggested by the CIA; echoes of that campaign to falsify the record still persist."[3996]

In addition to putting the CIA spin on news, the CIA used its control of the media to avoid publication of anything that didn't fit their narrative. Truman's critique of the CIA was pulled from the *Washington Post*. Mark Lane had to go to London to get his first book *RUSH TO JUDGEMENT*, published, but not before the CIA tried to have it edited to its liking.[3997]

By 1962 Phil and Katharine Graham's marriage had come apart.[3998] Phil got drunk and told off the mid-winter dinner meeting of the Associated Press directors at the Arizona Biltmore Hotel.[3999] He referred to them as "having no balls."[4000] He also complained about the CIA manipulation of journalists, and was clearly no longer recruiting them to join Operation Mockingbird.[4001] This meant he was a danger to the CIA, who wanted someone reliable in charge of the *Washington Post*. Phil was committed to the Chestnut Lodge sanitarium and was home on a weekend pass when he was found dead of a shotgun blast.[4002] He was recovering and was going to be once again in control of the *Post*. Having Phil's death ruled a suicide nullified the revisions he made to his will in 1963, cutting Katherine out.[4003] Katherine Graham said that Phil had gone downstairs and shot himself in the bathroom.[4004]

That's not what happened. Barbara Smith was the granddaughter of William Wadsworth Smith, the caretaker of the Graham's Glen Welby estate when Phil died.[4005] When Phil died he had been asked to go upstairs and bring the body downstairs.[4006] After Phil's death, Katherine Graham had complete control of the *Washington Post*.[4007] Katherine was loyal to the Deep State and Phil was not, and they needed to have someone dependable in charge of the *Post* when they took Kennedy out. However Phil died, now they had someone they could control in charge of the *Post*.

How the Mainstream Media Helped the Conspiracy

The foreign press was not under the control of the CIA and they were much more critical of the official story that Oswald was a lone nut and Ruby was a lone nut. They were openly skeptical of the authorities and printed accusations that the assassination was a coup d'état. This was in direct contrast to the American mainstream media which had been effectively turned into a propaganda arm by the CIA.

Having Oswald convicted in the court of public opinion was of paramount importance. The public had to be sold the lie that Oswald, and only Oswald, was guilty. That meant a disinformation campaign and it would eventually involve several levels:

- Having Hoover come up with the FBI's official report that Oswald, and only Oswald, was guilty and leaking it to the press.
- Having Oswald on the cover of *Life* magazine with a pistol on his hip, the sniper rifle in one hand and some communist literature in the other.
- Having the Warren Commission lend its credibility to the notion that Oswald was a lone gunman.
- Having the mainstream media then trumpet the conclusions of the Warren Commission to the public.
- Having *Life* magazine publish only carefully selected frames from the Zapruder film, which was otherwise buried away from public view. The frames were selected to support the 'lone gunman' lie.
- Having the Warren Report omit evidence of shots coming from the front. Having the Warren report omit, for example, any reference to the dozens of witnesses who saw gun smoke and heard shots from the front.

- Having the Warren Commission publish its huge report two months before publishing the twenty-six volumes of backup material. This allowed the mainstream media to praise the report without even seeing the twenty-six volumes of supporting material, some of which contradicted the Warren Report.
- Having the twenty-six volumes published without an index, which makes it almost unusable except by someone with too much time on their hands.
- Having twenty-six volumes of backup material to give the public the impression that the Warren Commission did an exhaustive job.
- Having the mainstream media tell the public that, because there were twenty-six volumes, the Warren Commission did an exhaustive job.
- Having the mainstream media either ignore or smear anyone who criticized the Warren Report, marginalizing anyone who disagreed with it as a 'conspiracy kook' to blunt the criticism.

In fact, the Warren Commission studiously ignored any evidence that did not fit their preconceived notion that Oswald alone was guilty. The Warren Commission had no investigative staff and relied on other agencies like the FBI, the CIA and the Secret Service for their information. The twenty-six volumes are filled depositions of over 500 witnesses and over three thousand exhibits. Unloading all this data onto the printed page gives bulk to the Warren Report while obscuring the fact that much of the publicly available data is irrelevant.

The hefty Warren Report of almost 1,000 pages and the twenty-six volumes of exhibits also masked the fact that the Warren Commission only looked at one possible scenario and no actual investigating was done. The size of the report and the exhibits make it appear to be the result of an enormous amount of work, and this theme was then picked up and trumpeted by the media. The Warren Report was described as exhaustive and thorough.

The government had its agents harass and intimidate witnesses who saw evidence of a conspiracy, like Lee Bowers. Those same agents also destroyed or buried evidence that didn't fit, like the Mauser rifle. They also manufactured evidence, like the Magic Bullet, to make their story appear more plausible.

After all of this they handed the "evidence" to the Warren Commission to place their stamp of approval on it and publish a whitewash. Then the mainstream media told us all that the Warren Commission had done a thorough and exhaustive job and come to the conclusion that Oswald did it alone. They point to the Warren Report and the massive twenty-six volumes of backup material as evidence of how hard the Warren Commission worked to bring their conclusion to the American public.

But the job was not done. Anyone who had doubts or questions about the Warren Report and its conclusions had to be painted out to be a 'conspiracy kook' and marginalized by the mainstream media. Anyone with a dissenting opinion had to be either ignored or laughed at. And our mainstream media was up to the task. This went on for decades, with the mainstream media propping up the Warren Commission conclusions and suppressing dissent for two generations.

In mid-November of 1963 President Kennedy had already confided to his secretary that Johnson was about to be dumped from the ticket for the 1964 election.[4008] Johnson's scandals had come home to roost and he had become a liability. His political future was hanging by a thread and Bobby Kennedy was vigorously chopping away at that thread. Bobby leaked information to *Life* magazine on Johnson's scandals so they could help Johnson over the cliff. The idea was to have the media expose Johnson's baggage to the public as a prelude to dumping Johnson off the ticket. *Life* magazine was preparing a major feature story about Johnson and the Baker scandal. Phil Wooton of *Life* had an assistant named James Wagenvoord, who recalled:[4009]

> "It was all coming from Bobby. It was going to blow Johnson right out of the water. We had him. He was done. Bobby Baker had taken the fall for Johnson. Johnson would have been finished and off the 1964 ticket, and would have probably been facing prison time."[4010]

Hearings were underway in the Senate where insurance agent Don Reynolds was testifying that he had seen Bobby Baker with a suitcase full of $100,000 in cash as a payoff to Johnson for his influence in swinging the TFX contract to General Dynamics.[4011] Reynolds also said he had refused several attempts by Johnson to buy his silence. Then word arrived about the Kennedy assassination and everything changed.[4012] The testimony ended, the hearings stalled, and the *Life* magazine story was killed.[4013] *Life* magazine was under the control of the CIA's Operation Mockingbird.[4014] Edward K Thompson, senior editor at *Life* at that time was, according to Wagenvoord, a close friend of Allen Dulles.[4015] The story about Johnson was in final editing, and everything went in the shredder.[4016] The issue of *Life* magazine that was going to expose Johnson instead had an article featuring still shots from the Zapruder film of the Kennedy assassination.[4017] Not long after that, an FBI agent dropped off a lumpy package to Wagenvoord of

"Oswald material" which turned out to be a film of Oswald handing out communist flyers in New Orleans.[4018]

The Zapruder film was set to be auctioned off the day after the assassination.[4019] The large news organizations, including CBS, were admitted to a one-time screening of the film before the auction.[4020] *Life* magazine bought the film for $150,000 before the auction could begin.[4021] Richard Stalling, who handled the purchase for *Life* magazine, said that orders to buy the film and keep it from public view came directly from *Life* publisher C.D. Jackson.[4022]

Author Donald Byron Thomas, in his book *HEAR NO EVIL*, points out that:[4023]

> "Researcher Peter Dale Scott notes that *Life* publisher C.D. Jackson had unusually close ties to the CIA, including active participation in the intelligence operations during this era. Reporter Carl Bernstein described Jackson in an article for *Rolling Stone* as "Henry Luce's personal emissary to the CIA"."[4024]

> "In October 1964, when *Life* published its special issue on the Warren Commission, it was C.D. Jackson who stepped in to stop the presses and order major revisions to the issue. The original version contained a print of Z frame 323. That frame showed the president slumped against the back of the rear seat, revealing that he had fallen backwards not forwards as the Warren Report stated. The still of Z 323 was replaced by Z frame 313 and a caption reading "The assassin's shot struck the right rear portion of the President's skull causing a massive wound and snapping his head to one side."[4025]

The Deep State was trying to keep from the public that there were shots from the front. One of the reasons the Zapruder film was not shown to the public was because it shows the violent backward movement of Kennedy's head as he is shot from the front. CBS, where Dan Rather worked, was participating in the CIA's Operation Mockingbird.[4026] On November 25, 1963 Dan Rather said on national television that he had seen the Zapruder film and that Kennedy's head went forward when he was hit.[4027] This is the opposite of what the Zapruder film actually shows, as the public will see in 1975 when the film is finally shown on national television.[4028] Dan Rather won't admit to this until 1993, almost two decades after everyone already knows what the film actually shows.[4029]

Once the Zapruder film was purchased by *Life* magazine, it was immediately turned over to the CIA so it can be altered (see the section on the Zapruder film).[4030] Then the film was buried and only still shots were released. The few still shots which were released were either irrelevant or appear to support the Deep State's version of events.[4031]

Author Mark North, in his book *ACT OF TREASON*, points out that:[4032]

> "CIA begins a disinformation campaign designed to create the public perception that Oswald is a pro-Castroite contract killer with direct links to Cuba. The goal is to implicate Castro formally and trigger another invasion of Cuba."[4033]

In the early evening of the day of the Kennedy assassination, the CIA, through one of its media "assets" named Hal Hendricks at the Scripps Howard chain, was feeding Dallas journalist Seth Kantor background information on Lee Harvey Oswald.[4034] Hendricks supplied Kantor with details of Oswald's past, his defection to Russia and his recent pro-Castro activities.[4035] In 1976 Hendricks would plead guilty to having withheld information from a Senate Committee probe into multinational corporations and the CIA.[4036] Hendricks had lied to the committee with the collusion of the CIA and had concealed his access to CIA information.[4037]

Life magazine continued to help by denying access to the Zapruder film as a moving picture or video. This was because anyone who viewed the film could see that Kennedy was shot from the front. *Life* only published still shots. In its regular weekly issue on November 29, 1963 *Life* published only 31 out of over 400 frames of the Zapruder film.[4038] They are careful not to include any sequence of frames which would depict Kennedy's head moving backward as a result of a shot from the front.[4039]

J. Edgar Hoover fed stories to the press that counter eyewitness statements of a gunman on the grassy knoll.[4040] Oswald was portrayed in the media as a lone nut gunman.[4041] The statements of the doctors at Parkland Hospital about wounds from the front were contradicted.[4042] The net result of all of this effort at propaganda and disinformation was that the public was told that Oswald was guilty and he acted alone.[4043]

On Tuesday, November 26, 1963 an article in the *Washington Daily News* states:[4044]

> "Two amateur photographers from Dallas … have gotten close-up films of the assassination of President Kennedy. One film, bought by *Life* magazine for $40,000, is in color. Of the three copies made by … Zapruder … one went to *Life*, one to the FBI and one to the Secret Service … The FBI and Secret Service declined comment on the films, since they contain

'evidentiary' matter ... Persons who saw the color film ... say it shows the following sequence: ... the first of three ... shots appear to strike ... Kennedy in the shoulder or back. ...Governor Connally turns toward the right ... [and is struck] ... then a third shot strikes Mr. Kennedy in the head and he lurches forward."[4045]

Of the various lies in this article, the worst is the assertion that Kennedy's head lurched forward when he was shot.[4046] This was the opposite of what happened, but the lie fit the official story and the film would not be shown to the public for over a decade.[4047]

Hoover at the FBI used press leaks to force the public and the Warren Commission to come to his conclusions about the assassination.[4048]

On December 3, 1963 the *New York Journal American* ran the headline "Oswald Lone Killer – FBI Report to Prove It" the story quoted 'anonymous government sources' but the FBI was the obvious source.[4049]

On December 9, 1963 the FBI report was given to the Warren Commission which asked that nothing be made public until the report had been reviewed by the commission. The next morning the *New York Times* had a substantial story on the report headlined "Oswald Assassin Beyond a Doubt, FBI Concludes – He Acted Alone and Did Not Know Ruby Says Report to Warren Inquiry Panel."[4050]

Author Mark North, in his book *ACT OF TREASON: THE ROLE OF J. EDGAR HOOVER IN THE ASSASSINATION OF PRESIDENT KENNEDY*, has an excellent summary of the kind of deception used by *Life* magazine to support the official version of events:[4051]

> "On December 6, 1963 ... *Life* magazine releases its memorial edition on the Kennedy assassination. The cover is captioned "All of *LIFE'S* Pictures on the Most Shocking Event of Our Time." In reality, only an additional nine frames are released: Z-183, 226, 232, 258, 277, 309, 347, 371, and one other between 371 and the end of the film. Once again, key frames are withheld. Three of the nine are again of Jackie trying to escape the limousine. Captions create a near completely false description of the killing. " ... the first bullet struck [Kennedy] in the neck ... The president slumped forward in his seat and down toward his wife. ... The second shot struck governor Connally. ... Oswald's last bullet ... struck the President in the rear right part of his head." With a federally appointed investigative body already in place, *Life*, with this fabrication, very probably violates obstruction-of-justice statutes. Further, as ultimately discussed in *Reasonable Doubt*, citing the

Zapruder film, which *Life* owned and which the public was not allowed to see until 1975, the article reported that the film showed JFK turned completely around so that he was facing the sniper's nest, thus explaining the entry wound in the throat. As any viewer of the Zapruder film can instantly discern, no such turn was made by the president. Not coincidentally, around the time (1975) Life returns the film to the Zapruder family for the sum of $1.00, congress begins to closely scrutinize the activities of the FBI during the 1960's."[4052]

Back in 1963 the vast majority of the American people still trusted their institutions like the government and the media, and the Deep State took advantage of this, violated that trust, and used it to give credibility to the lies being sold to the public. This was the era before Watergate and the massive escalation of the Vietnam War that caused the American public to learn not to trust their institutions.

Author Mark North, in his book *ACT OF TREASON*, shows how Hoover manages the spin on the news to make sure that any actual facts that escape aren't allowed to live long in the open:[4053]

"On December 16, 1962 there are reports that some of the shots came from the front."[4054]

"On December 17, 1963 Hoover attempts to counter the revelations of the prior day with regard to the nature of Kennedy's wounds by leaking the following distortion to the press: "The first shot fired by President Kennedy's assassin struck Mr. Kennedy in the back and did not hit any vital organ, a reliable source familiar with the autopsy findings reported tonight. The second bullet to hit Mr. Kennedy – after another had struck ... Connally ... hit the president in the back of the skull and proved fatal." – in reality, of course, one of the two fatal head shots hit Kennedy in the right temple and *exited* the "back of the skull.""[4055]

"On December 18, 1963 Hoover again leaks selective information regarding the nature of Kennedy's wounds to make it appear as if the FBI report is correct. This is accomplished by asserting that the autopsy report will show only shots from behind. The second head wound, inflicted from the right front, is omitted from the discussion. "Officials declined all comment today on reports of what pathologists found in an autopsy on President Kennedy's body. The reports gave detailed support to the Federal Bureau of Investigation's finding that two bullets had hit Mr. Kennedy from the rear. The FBI came to this conclusion in its report on the assassination. The pathologists were said to have found that a first bullet hit the president in the back. The bullet lodged in the body. It assertedly not hit any vital organs. The second shot, it said, hit the right rear of Mr. Kennedy's head and caused fatal injury. A fragment of this bullet, according to the reports, passed out the front of the throat. This presumably would account for various reports suggesting – on the basis of the hurried observations of doctors in Dallas after the shooting … that there was an 'entry wound' in the front of the throat … The talk of a front 'entry wound' had caused wide speculation about a second assassin's firing at Mr. Kennedy from in front of his car. The man who was accused of the killing … Oswald, was said to have shot from a window above and behind the car. The FBI, in its report to the special commission … stated flatly that both bullets had come from the window where Oswald assertedly was but the report did not mention the autopsy." – Note that this story is not based on any "official" statement and that both the FBI and autopsy reports have not been released to the public. The FBI, of course, attended the autopsy. Through articles such as this, Hoover is scrambling to fix his conclusions in the public's mind, to preempt the commission."[4056]

This was Hoover using a willing media to get out in front of the spin and make sure that the official story of Oswald as the lone nut who shot Kennedy became the commonly accepted version of events in Dallas.

Author Joachim Joesten, in his book *OSWALD: ASSASSIN OR FALL GUY?*, said that:[4057]

"*Time* magazine, which with its fellow traveler *Life*, has led the pack in foisting a version of the Oswald case on the American public which is demonstrably false, is satisfied with pious generalizations."[4058]

One month after the assassination of Kennedy, former President Harry Truman published an editorial that said the CIA should be returned to being the intelligence arm of the president (see the section on Truman's warning in the chapter on the CIA). This editorial was suppressed by the mainstream media. In *MARY'S MOSAIC*, author Peter Janney points out that:[4059]

"According to veteran researcher and author Ray Marcus, the editorial appeared only in the first edition of the *Post* that morning. It was omitted from all subsequent editions that day.

Who would have the decision to limit its publication? Moreover, the editorial was never picked up by any other media outlet, nor discussed by any other journalist, columnist, or broadcast communicator. It simply evaporated from the public landscape."[4060]

On February 21, 1964 *Life* magazine used the cover of the magazine to publish a photograph of Oswald holding a rifle in one hand and communist literature on the other while wearing a pistol on his hip. The problem was that the photograph was fake. Oswald's face was added to someone else's body who had posed for the photograph. Like everything else about the Kennedy assassination, the first impression upon seeing the photograph was that it appeared plausible. Oswald must have been guilty. Then upon closer examination there are many, many discrepancies and eventually the whole thing collapses. But what was important here is not that the photograph turned out to be a fake, it was the impression it left on the public in early 1964. It achieved its intended purpose. Everyone who casually looked at the photographs took it for its intended purpose – as proof of Oswald's guilt. There he was, proudly holding up the murder weapon and the communist literature. Case closed.

Upon closer examination, the photograph turned out to be a fake. In his book, *CIA ROGUES AND THE KILLING OF THE KENNEDYS*, author Patrick Nolan documents that:[4061]

> "Photo experts have since analyzed the pictures and found clear evidence that the shots were faked. One of the experts was Major John Pickard of the Canadian Department of Defense and another was past president of the Evidence Photographers International Council, detective Malcom Thompson, who was recommended by Kodak and Scotland Yard.[4062]

> "Their analysis found, first, that the shadows on the face do not correspond to the shadows on the ground – the face shot was taken when the sun was high in the sky and the body shot was taken when the sun was low in the sky. Secondly, the chin on the face does not resemble Lee's. It is square, while Lee's is more pointed. And third, the experts discovered a faint line that reveals the demarcation between the body shot and the pasted-on head.[4063]

> "Another discrepancy in the photo was found in the comparison of the size of the Mannlicher-Carcano to the height of Oswald. Measuring the two, experts found a

significant difference between the photo and the true measurements of Lee and the rifle: either the man is five inches shorter than Lee or the rifle 2.4 inches longer than the Mannlicher-Carcano.[4064]

"Finally, the photos were obviously taken on a sunny day. Marina Oswald told the Warren Commission that she had taken the incriminating pictures on March 31, 1963. Yet according to the US Weather Bureau reports for that day in Dallas, it was a cloudy, rainy day.[4065]

Nolan goes on to document that there were similar discrepancies in the story about the camera that was supposedly used and how the pictures were "found" by the authorities.[4066]

Author Jim Marrs, in his book *CROSSFIRE*, also points out a number of issues with the backyard photos.[4067] For example, there are multiple photographs of Oswald in that pose, but the background is the exact same in all of them.[4068] This is impossible with a handheld camera, as we're told by the authorities the picture was taken.[4069] He also points out that Oswald's face is exactly the same in all of the shots.[4070] This is the result of using the same face shot on all the different poses of the rest of the body.[4071] And Oswald had a pointed chin while the picture is of someone with a flat, square chin.[4072]

The net result of all this is that the picture on the cover of *Life* magazine was fake, but, like all the other information on the Kennedy assassination, the real story would not be told until much later. The real impact of the picture of Oswald on the cover of *Life* magazine in early 1964 was to further convict Oswald in the court of public opinion, which was the whole point.

The CIA's hold on the mainstream media allowed it to clamp down on what was and was not published. When the assassination first happened, Mark Lane wrote an article which questioned the official version of events and he had a very difficult time getting it published.[4073] The same happened with his first book on the assassination. He had to go to London to get it published.[4074] However, there was a considerable interest among the American people in real information on the Kennedy assassination. Lane went through the case against Oswald and refuted it point by point.[4075] When Mark Lane offered his article "Oswald Innocent? A Lawyer's Brief" for free to whoever would publish it, he tried a list of periodicals, including the *New Republic*, *Look*, *Life*, the *Saturday Evening Post* and the *Progressive*.[4076] They all turned him down, so he published it in the leftist *National Guardian*.[4077]

There was so much interest in the article that they had to print additional press runs and eventually just published it as a pamphlet.[4078]

Mark Lane was not the only critic of the official version of events who had a hard time getting his point across in the mainstream media. When Jim Garrison tried to prosecute Clay Shaw for the murder of John Kennedy, he was attacked by the mainstream media.[4079] He had to use non-traditional media outlets like giving an interview to *Playboy* magazine to be published at all.[4080]

During the Garrison prosecution of Shaw, Garrison issued a subpoena to get his hands on the Zapruder film.[4081] Mark Lane made 100 copies of the film and handed them out to mainstream media personalities like Walter Cronkite.[4082] Not one of them used the film or told the American people about the obvious evidence of the shot from the front.[4083]

Author Anthony Summers, in his book *NOT IN YOUR LIFETIME*, points out that:[4084]

> "In 1977, when the FBI went through the motions of releasing 100,000 pages from its Kennedy assassination files, the U.S. media uttered an uncritical cheer. At the press conference to mark the event, reporters seemed uninterested or ill-equipped to ask probing questions. The author found himself virtually alone in pressing the FBI spokesman into an admission that up to 10% of the Kennedy file will not be released. One reason for retaining the records, the spokesman said, was to protect individual's privacy. The other was the familiar one – national security – even after the passage of the JFK Records Act in 1992, which mandated the release of all Kennedy assassination material unless a real case could be made for retention, the FBI continued to resist full disclosure."[4085]

In 1985 the *Washington Post* and the rest of the mainstream media avoided coverage of the verdict in the trial where E. Howard Hunt lost in court and it was obvious that the CIA was involved in the Kennedy assassination.[4086]

James DiEugenio, in his book *RECLAIMING PARKLAND*, documents the bias in the mainstream media (which he refers to below as the 'MSM'):[4087]

> "The *New York Times* had irresponsibly accepted the Warren verdict in September 1964 without even reading the twenty-six volumes of evidence which were not released until the following month. Once the newspaper had done that, they then had to taper and censor all of their subsequent coverage

in order to not admit they had made a huge error which had resulted in misleading their reading public about who had killed their president. In fact, this censorship extended as far as editing book reviews that were too favorable to critics in their original form and consciously bypassing the regular book review editor by assigning reviews of Kennedy assassination books to certain writers in advance."[4088]

"This is just one example of how controlled the press is in regard to President Kennedy's assassination and books like *Reclaiming History*. The review of *Reclaiming History* in the *Wall Street Journal* which appeared on May 20, 2007, is another example. This review was written by Max Holland. For twenty years, perhaps no other single person has more vociferously attempted to revive the moribund Warren Commission through a variety of media – books, newspaper editorials, TV specials, academic journals and magazine articles – than Max Holland. In 2001 he became the first author working outside the government to be given a Studies in Intelligence Award from the Central Intelligence Agency. This might have been because in the fall of 2001 an article of his on the JFK case appeared on the CIA's own website. Today he supports the commission and demeans its critics through his own website, www.washingtondecoded.com. As with the *New York Times* practice of prescreening writers, giving Holland the assignment to review Bugliosi's book was guaranteeing the result in advance."[4089]

"Another example of this would be the review of *Reclaiming History* in the *Atlantic,* which echoed the *New York Times* practice. That review was written by novelist Thomas Mallon, who in 2002, five years before the publication of *Reclaiming History*, had written a nonfiction book entitled *Mrs. Paine's Garage.* Previously the work of Carol Hewitt, Steve Jones and Barbara LaMonica had brought serious suspicion about the enigmatic figures of Ruth and Michael Paine; Mallon's book was an apologia for them. It ignored or discounted all the evidence those three writers, and many others, had recently brought to bear on the pair. The *Atlantic*, which is one of the worst periodicals on this subject, allowed Mallon to begin his review with the following: "Several years ago I spent a portion of one November afternoon in Irving, Texas, inside the home garage where Lee Harvey Oswald had hidden his rifle in the months before he killed John F. Kennedy." Mallon then described Ruth Paine as "an admirable Quaker who, as a young housewife, became innocently enmeshed in the assassination. . . ." He added that Ruth was a person "of idealistic nature and fine character." As we will see, it is highly doubtful that Oswald ever had a rifle in the Paine garage and even more doubtful that it was the rifle the Warren Commission accused him of having. We will also see that the character of Ruth Paine is, to say the least, not as saintly as Mallon implies. Therefore, this review of *Reclaiming History* was typical MSM: "hear no evil, see no evil, say no evil" on the JFK case. The editors made sure of that in advance."[4090]

"The reaction from the *Los Angeles Times* was also rather predictable. As Warren Commission critic Pat Spear has noted, it looks like this particular review of *Reclaiming History* was written with the help of Bugliosi's publicist. In a taped interview conducted before the release of the book, Bugliosi said he wanted his work to be considered "a book for the ages." Well, on cue, Jim Newton's review ended with the following two sentences: "With this work, Bugliosi has definitively explained the murder that recalibrated modern America. *It is a book for the ages*." (emphasis added.)"[4091]

Selling the Warren Report to the Public

A 912-page report plus an additional twenty-six volumes constitute a huge amount of data, and the sheer size did several things for the conspirators. First, it gave the appearance of the Warren Commission having done an exhaustive investigation. This is both the opposite of what actually happened and exactly the impression the conspirators wanted to give the American people. Second, by having a mountain of mostly irrelevant data to bury the relevant data in, the conspirators made it that much harder for anyone to determine what was actually going on. The task of anyone who was interested in the truth was made even harder by the lack of an index to the twenty-six volumes, which was probably why it was skipped.

The Warren Commission cleverly withheld the twenty-six volumes of evidence until more than two months after the release of its report.[4092] The mainstream media praised the Warren Report without benefit of seeing the evidence.[4093] *The New York Times* called the report "comprehensive, careful, compendious and competent."[4094] The *New York Times* praised the Warren Report in September of 1964 before the twenty-six volumes of exhibits were published the following month.[4095]

Author Mark Lane, in his book *LAST WORD: MY INDICTMENT OF THE CIA IN THE MURDER OF JFK*, points out that *New York Times* journalist Anthony Lewis, who was one of the CIA's "media assets," praised the Warren Report the day that the twenty-six volumes of exhibits were released. As Lane says:

> "Later, when the commission released twenty-six volumes of thousands of pages of testimony and exhibits, Lewis, that very day, wrote that all the evidence demonstrated that the Warren Commission conclusions were accurate. I studied the material for the better part of a year, working almost eighteen hours each day. It was only after I completed that enormous task that I wrote to Lewis and asked him how he had been able to get through the material in just a few hours."[4096]

Author Vincent Salandria claimed that the basic facts in the Warren Report did not square with the evidence in the twenty-six volumes of the Warren Commission Hearings and Exhibits issued two months after the Warren Report.[4097] Unlike most people, Salandria had actually studied the twenty-six volumes and compared the evidence to the conclusions.[4098]

Within three days of the release of the Warren Report, the *New York Times* and Bantam Books issued a one-dollar paperback edition of the Warren Report that sold millions of copies.[4099] Within a month of the release of the twenty-six volumes of exhibits, the *New York Times* and Bantam Books issued a paperback book, *The Witnesses*, which also sold for one dollar.[4100] *The Witnesses* was claimed to consist of "the highlights of Hearings before the Warren Commission ... selected and edited by *The New York Times*."[4101]

Author Sylvia Meagher, in her book *ACCESSORIES AFTER THE FACT*, points out, in regard to *The Witnesses*, that:[4102]

> "...indeed, the testimony was very carefully selected and edited to present only those passages which supported the Commission's assertions and conclusions while excluding all inconsistent or inimical parts of the transcripts. Thus, for example, the excerpts from Abraham Zapruder's testimony do not include his remarks that he had believed the shot to come from behind him (the grassy knoll)..."[4103]

Walter Cronkite told us "we must have faith" in the commission.[4104]

The Attack on Dr. Crenshaw

Dr. Charles Crenshaw was one of the doctors who attended Kennedy at Parkland Hospital right after he had been shot. He was one of the doctors who saw an entry wound in the throat from a shot that had come from the front and thus was evidence of more than one shooter and therefore evidence of the conspiracy. Dr. Crenshaw said later that he had kept quiet out of fear for his life. He said that these folks had killed the president of the United States and would not hesitate to kill a doctor.[4105]

Dr. Charles Crenshaw and the other Parkland doctors kept quiet for 30 years, but they agreed on a few things. The wound in Kennedy's throat was an entry wound, as was the entry wound at the right front by the hairline that blew out the back of his head. Crenshaw broke his silence 30 years later. He and the other doctors had kept quiet out of fear.[4106] After thirty years of keeping his mouth shut, Dr. Crenshaw wrote a book where he said that the shots had come from the front.[4107]

The Journal of the American Medical Association (JAMA) viciously attacked Dr. Crenshaw when he told the truth about Kennedy being shot from the front.[4108] George Lundberg, editor of the JAMA, assigned Dennis Breo to write for the JAMA.[4109] Breo claimed in the JAMA that Dr. Crenshaw had not even been one of the doctors working on Kennedy that day.[4110] This was later proven to be false as Dr. Crenshaw was in fact there.[4111]

In April of 1992 Dr. Crenshaw came out with his book, *JFK: CONSPIRACY OF SILENCE*, which contradicted the Warren Report by saying that Kennedy had wounds from the front, and it became number one on the *New York Times* bestseller list.[4112] In the May 27, 1992 issue of *JAMA* were two articles claiming Dr. Crenshaw was not even in the trauma room that day and, when Dr. Crenshaw tried to set the record straight, ignored him.[4113] Dr. Crenshaw then sued the *JAMA* which ended up having to pay money to Dr. Crenshaw and his co-author Gary Shaw.[4114]

The mainstream media continues today to both protect the Deep State and undermine our democracy. This can be seen in the contrast between how the mainstream media treated Obama and Trump. In their book *THE WORST PRESIDENT IN HISTORY*, authors Matt Margolis and Mark Noonan detail the many failures and scandals which went unreported during the Obama administration. The mainstream media ignored anything bad about Obama while relentlessly attacking Trump at every opportunity, even when they had to create opportunities to attack.

The last chapter, Why This Matters Today, goes into detail on how the mainstream media continues to help the Deep State to undermine our representative republic.

The Truth Seeps Out Over the Years

One of the advantages of hindsight is more complete information. The conspiracy had a lid on it, but the truth seeped out around the edges over the years. In this way many of the questions asked about the Kennedy assassination were slowly answered over the years. In some cases, this took decades. For example, some of the witnesses who were intimidated into either silence or changing their stories finally felt that it was safe to talk honestly thirty years later. Sometimes it was a deathbed confession that brought information to light.

Here are a few examples:

- Witness Ed Hoffman saw one of the shooters behind the fence on the grassy knoll. His family convinced him to sit on what he knew for his own safety. His story didn't come out for years.

- Witness Gordon Arnold's story of having shots go past him on the grassy knoll was not published until 1978. He kept quiet out of fear.

- During the Garrison prosecution and trial of Clay Shaw we learned from the testimony of Dr. Pierre Finck, who very reluctantly, and only because he was under oath and forced by the judge to answer the question, testified that he was ordered to botch the autopsy (this was so there would be no evidence on record of shots coming from the front and therefore a conspiracy)

- George Whitaker at the Ford plant in Detroit, who saw the bullet hole in the windshield of Kennedy's limousine, only spoke out many years later – he had kept quiet out of fear

- Victoria Adams, the "girl on the stairs" was found thirty-five years later and now her story is known – because of this we now can prove that Oswald was not on the sixth floor when Kennedy was shot

- Doctor Crenshaw, who could clearly see that Kennedy had been shot from the front, finally felt safe to tell his story thirty years after he had been intimidated into silence.

- Robert Vinson was on the secret CIA flight with the Oswald double who was spirited away from Dallas the evening of the assassination. His story only came out decades after the fact.

- In 1992 the JFK Records Act was enacted by Congress to create the Assassination Records Review Board and mandate the release of government documents relating to the Kennedy assassination

- In 1993 Dan Marvin realized while watching a documentary on television about William Pitzer being murdered that he had been recruited by the CIA to kill Pitzer in 1966 but turned the job down. The realization that the CIA had gone through with the hit caused him to come forward

- In 2005 a CIA memo was declassified and it showed conclusively that the CIA knew that the Bay of Pigs operation would not succeed unless Kennedy agreed to U.S. military involvement

- In 2009 we learned how the Zapruder film was altered so as to minimize the evidence of a shot from the front and therefore proves that there was a conspiracy to assassinate John F. Kennedy

- Judyth Vary Baker, Lee Harvey Oswald's girlfriend in New Orleans was warned to keep her mouth shut if she wanted to live and only told her story forty years later

These were puzzle pieces which were not available to researchers who were skeptical of the Warren Report when it first came out. Now they are available to us and we can add them to what is already known. Another advantage is YouTube, which allows anyone with a browser to view interviews taped with witnesses while they were still alive. Some of this is from old black-and-white footage shot in the sixties. The cumulative effect of all of the evidence now publicly available provides a much more complete picture than was available to the public at the time of Kennedy's assassination. There are still holes in the picture, but we can see the broad outlines of what happened. As the puzzle pieces have fallen into place the picture has slowly emerged over the decades.

Since the professionals working for the authorities failed to investigate, the amateurs were the only option for those interested in the truth about who killed their president. And they've found out considerably more than the professionals. This is not because they were more skilled or had the resources of the government at their disposal. They found out more because the authorities were doing their best to hide the truth while the amateurs were doing their best to find the truth.

Witness Victoria Adams was watching the motorcade with her friend Sandra Styles from the fourth floor of the Texas School Book Depository.[4115] Adams said there was no one else on the stairs when she and Sandra ran down to see what was going on.[4116] It took author Barry Earnest thirty-five years to find Victoria Adams.[4117] She said she was harassed, questioned multiple times and changes were made in her testimony.[4118] She decided to disappear for her own safety.[4119]

Robert Vinson was on the CIA flight out of Dallas the evening of the Kennedy assassination with the Oswald double (see the section on the Oswald double).[4120] He had been drafted into the CIA as a means of keeping him quiet.[4121] Once the JFK Records Act in 1992 released him from his nondisclosure agreements with the government he was able to tell his story thirty years after the assassination.[4122]

James Wilcott was a CIA finance officer. Fifteen years after the Kennedy assassination, Wilcott testified before the House Select Committee on Assassinations (HSCA) that Oswald was a double agent for the CIA.[4123] He also testified that the CIA was involved in the Kennedy assassination.[4124]

The kill shot clearly came from the right front, entered at the hairline in Kennedy's temple and took off part of the back of his head. The two motorcycle cops riding to the left and rear of the limousine were both splattered with blood and brains. Bobby Hargis was one of the cops who got splattered. He was the closest of the two to the left and rear. To his left and rear was B.J. Martin. He was also splattered. Officer Martin saw Johnson duck 30 to 40 seconds before the shooting began. His statements were suppressed for 30 years.[4125]

Author David Talbot, in his book *THE DEVIL'S CHESSBOARD*, documents that:[4126]

> "Perhaps the most devastating revelation about the CIA operations emerged years later, in 2005, when the agency was compelled to release the minutes of a meeting held by its Cuba task force on November 15, 1960, one week after the Kennedy election. The group, which was deliberating on how to brief the president-elect on the pending invasion, came to an eye-

opening conclusion. In the face of strong security measures that Castro had implemented, the CIA task force admitted, their invasion plan was "now seen to be unachievable, except as a joint [CIA/Department of Defense] action." In other words, the CIA realized that its Bay of Pigs expedition was doomed to fail unless its exile brigade was reinforced by the power of the U.S military. But the CIA never shared this sobering assessment with the president."[4127]

Proof that the Zapruder film was altered came to light in 2009 when author Peter Janney interviewed National Photographic Interpretation Center (NPIC) photo expert Dino Brugioni about the briefing boards he prepared for the CIA the weekend of the assassination.[4128] This is when the discrepancies between the original Zapruder film and the altered version became known.[4129] (See the section on the Zapruder film)

To a large extent this book was made possible by those ordinary citizens who, over the years, tried to get at the truth and get it out to the public. Without the mountain of output from independent researchers and authors who have, for a few generations now, dug into the Kennedy assassination and published what they found, this book would not have been possible. Only now that we can finally put enough of the pieces in place can we start to see enough of the picture to know what went on. There are details that we will never know, but over time enough has leaked out or been found that we can know enough to realize that what we now call the Deep State was behind the Kennedy assassination.

The Murder of Robert Kennedy

Robert Kennedy came to the realization that his brother had been murdered as the result of a conspiracy. His strategy for dealing with it was to keep that conclusion to himself and to attempt to run for president. Once in the White House he would be in a position to order a real investigation into what happened to JFK. The conspirators could not allow that to happen, so they killed him just after he had won the California Democratic primary and was poised to win the presidential election and the White House.

His murder and the subsequent 'lone nut gunman' conclusion by law enforcement authorities had as many unanswered questions as President Kennedy's assassination. The government claimed that Sirhan acted alone, but there were between ten and fourteen shots fired at the scene while Sirhan's gun only held eight shots. In addition, Sirhan and his gun were a few feet in front of Senator Kennedy who was shot from behind at point blank range. There are many other unanswered questions about the murder of Robert Kennedy, and the story told by the authorities is clearly not the whole story. This is another example where the Deep State decided to keep the American people from being able to choose the occupant of the White House. In this case it was done to protect the conspirators from the exposure that would come from a real investigation into the murder of President Kennedy and also to make sure that a Kennedy in the White House didn't reverse U.S. policy in Vietnam.

This chapter is organized into five sections:

1. The Wayne January incident – describes how the hits on both JFK and RFK were predicted by an anti-Castro Cuban exile who warned Wayne January that they would both be assassinated

2. Why RFK had to be Murdered – describes why Senator Robert F. Kennedy had to be assassinated by the same conspirators who assassinated his brother, President John F. Kennedy

3. The official story is an obvious lie – describes the differences between reality and the story put out by the authorities – another 'lone nut gunman' (sound familiar?)

4. Sirhan goes missing – describes how Sirhan was hypnotized and programmed using techniques developed by the CIA in the MK-ULTRA program

5. The cover up – describes the witness intimidation and evidence tampering that went on to make sure that the evidence of a conspiracy was covered up, just like when JFK was assassinated

When Attorney General Robert Kennedy tried to have two of his investigators participate in the investigation into John Kennedy's death, Hoover blocked them.[4130] Hoover also blocked and filtered what little information Robert Kennedy got about the death of his brother.[4131] Hoover's relationship with Johnson trumped Robert Kennedy's position above Hoover in the Federal organization chart.[4132]

Not long after the assassination of John Kennedy, Robert Kennedy said to his press secretary, Edwin O. Guthman:

> "I thought they might get one of us, but Jack, after all he'd been through, never worried about it. I thought it would be me."[4133]

In 1963 the Elkins mafia family warned the Kennedys about a planned mafia hit on President Kennedy – from a high building with a high-powered rifle with a scope shooting at the motorcade.[4134]

In 1968 the top mafia lawyer for the Elkins clan flew to Portland, Oregon and warned Robert Kennedy that there would be a hit on him during his trip to Los Angeles and that a small caliber handgun would be used to kill him from behind.[4135] Robert Kennedy was warned that the assassin would be one of his bodyguards and was urged to change his plans and fire his protection detail.[4136] Then on October 17, 1968 J.B. Elkins died when the car he was driving was pushed off the road and he hit a telephone pole.[4137]

The Wayne January Incident

The day before the JFK assassination Wayne January was at Redbird Airfield in Dallas preparing a DC-3 for a flight the next day.[4138] He had been working with another man for a few days on the job of preparing the plane for the flight.[4139] The other man was Cuban, and the two had become friends while working on the plane.[4140] The Cuban kept to himself except to talk with January, and the man who bought the plane had only made the one visit to Redbird for the purchase.[4141] The plane was bought by the Houston Air Center, which January would find out later was a front for the CIA.[4142] While eating lunch that day, the Cuban said "Wayne, they're going to kill your president."[4143] Wayne asked him to repeat this and then said "You mean President Kennedy?"[4144] Then the Cuban explained that he was a pilot for the CIA and that he had been involved in the Bay of Pigs invasion.[4145] He also said that a lot of the survivors of that operation bitterly blamed the Kennedys for not providing the air cover that the CIA said they had promised.[4146] Wayne January asked if that was why they were going to kill Kennedy and the Cuban said "They are not only going to kill the president, they are going to kill Robert Kennedy, and any other Kennedy that gets into that position."[4147] Wayne January thought the guy was nuts, and the Cuban said "You will see." and later added "They want Robert Kennedy real bad."[4148] When Wayne asked "But, what for?" the man replied "Never mind, you don't need to know."[4149] The next day the plane was ready by lunchtime and suddenly they got the news that the president had been shot.[4150] Wayne January kept the discussion to himself out of fear until 1992 when author Matthew Smith was interviewing him about the Oswald incident at Redbird (see the section on the Redbird Incident).[4151] In 2003 Smith got permission from January's widow to publish the incident using Wayne January's real name.[4152]

In their book *THE MAN WHO KILLED KENNEDY*, authors Roger Stone and Mike Colapietro documented that:[4153]

> "Morales's lawyer Robert Walton had said multiple times that El Indio confessed his guilt in the JFK assassination. Morales told Walton, "I was in Dallas when we got that mother fucker, and I was in Los Angeles [where Robert Kennedy was murdered] when we got the little bastard."[4154]

Why Robert Kennedy Had to be Murdered

Robert Kennedy had to be murdered because he was going to become president and then not only run a real investigation into his brother's murder, but also pull the United States out of Vietnam. The conspirators could not afford to be exposed for their part in the murder of President John Kennedy and did not want to have the country pull out of Vietnam, so they arranged another hit on Robert Kennedy.

When John Kennedy was murdered, Robert Kennedy at first suspected that the guys the CIA had lined up to kill Castro had turned and used the plan against President Kennedy.[4155]   His suspicions were well founded. That was pretty much what happened. The CIA plan to kill Castro had been turned on President Kennedy. Then RFK became depressed and isolated as Hoover cut him off and went around him directly to Johnson.[4156] So he kept quiet for a while because he did not have enough political power to follow through on any criticism of the conspirators or even of the Warren Commission.[4157] By 1967 he was starting to see a path to the White House and, with it, a chance to open a real investigation of JFK's assassination.[4158] When he declared his candidacy for president he became a threat to the conspirators, and the closer he got to winning first the Democratic nomination and then the White House, the bigger threat he became.   When he won the California primary, and looked like he was going on to the White House, he had to be stopped or they would all end up in the electric chair.

Robert Kennedy told New Orleans District Attorney Jim Garrison that he was going to look into the JFK assassination when he got to the White House.[4159]   He also told Garrison that, once he won the California primary, he would go public with his doubts about the Warren Report.[4160]

Bill Walton, a friend of Robert Kennedy, said that RFK suspected the worst of foul play but kept a low profile because it was too dangerous.[4161] His plan was to position himself to get to the White House himself and then he could open a real investigation.[4162] Bill Walton was sent by Robert Kennedy to let Khrushchev know that he and Jackie thought President Kennedy was killed by domestic enemies and not by the Russians.[4163]

If the threat of the electric chair wasn't enough incentive for the conspirators to kill Robert Kennedy, there was the added threat that, like JFK, RFK wanted to get the United States out of Vietnam. Johnson pulled out of the race and Robert Kennedy looked sure to win the White House.[4164] In the meantime, the Pentagon and the CIA knew that, without Johnson, they would need Nixon in the White House to continue the war.[4165] The CIA and the Pentagon still thought they could win the Vietnam War, but not if Bobby Kennedy won the White House.[4166] To the Pentagon and the CIA Robert Kennedy's opposition to the Vietnam War and his chances of winning the White House made him a marked man.[4167]

In Nebraska for the 1968 primary, Robert Kennedy told the farmers that he was taking on the Deep State.[4168] He said:

"I came to Nebraska in my campaign because I need your help. We're taking on the Establishment. And we are taking on the political figures of this country."[4169]

In February of 1968 Robert Kennedy said, in a speech in Chicago, that his brother's decision to go to Vietnam in the first place had been wrong and that now was the time to change course.[4170]

The Official Story Is an Obvious Lie

Just like the assassination of President John Kennedy, the murder of Senator Robert Kennedy had the authorities attempting to convince the public of an obvious lie. The murder of Robert Kennedy simply could not have happened the way they said it did. So, this led, once again, to the obvious question – if it didn't happen the way the authorities said it happened, what did happen?

In their book *DEAD WRONG*, authors Richard Belzer and David Wayne said that the Official Verdict on Robert Kennedy's death was that:[4171]

> "Senator Kennedy was assassinated by a lone gunman, Sirhan Bishara Sirhan, who fired from a distance, not at point-blank range, in the kitchen of the Ambassador Hotel. Sirhan was found guilty "alone and not in concert with anyone else" of Murder in the First Degree."[4172]

Belzer and Wayne go on to say that the actual circumstances were that Kennedy was:[4173]

> "Shot three times from behind, bullets traversing body at an upward angle, back-to-front. Coroner determined that the kill shot came from directly behind the right ear and at point-blank range. Defendant was never anywhere near enough to the victim to have fired the kill shot and, furthermore, shots from the Defendant could not have left a back-to-front bullet path, because Defendant was in front of the victim. Therefore, bullet trajectory would necessarily have been front-to-back."[4174]

Belzer and Wayne also point out that Sirhan's gun only held eight bullets but fourteen bullets were fired, necessitating two shooters.[4175] So who was the other shooter?

Author David Talbot, in his book *THE DEVIL'S CHESSBOARD*, said:[4176]

"As in Dallas, official reports immediately pinned sole responsibility for the shooting on a troubled loner, a twenty-four-year-old Palestinian immigrant named Sirhan Sirhan. The accused assassin was undeniably involved in the assault on Kennedy as the senator and his entourage made their way through the crowded, dimly lit hotel pantry on the way to a press briefing room. But numerous eyewitnesses – including one of the men who subdued Sirhan – insisted that the alleged assassin could not have fired the shot that killed Kennedy. Sirhan was several feet in front of Kennedy when he began firing with his revolver. But the fatal shot – which struck RFK at point-blank range behind the right ear, penetrating his brain – was fired from behind. Furthermore, evidence indicated that thirteen shots were fired in the pantry that night – five more than the number of bullets that Sirhan's gun could hold."[4177]

Talbot went on to say:

"A security guard named Thane Eugene Cesar who guided Kennedy into the pantry later fell under suspicion. He was seen pulling his gun as the chaos erupted that night in the cramped passageway. But investigators quickly cleared Cesar, and his gun was never tested. Over the years, Cesar's possible role in the assassination of Robert Kennedy has been debated by researchers and lawyers associated with the case. Some – like Sirhan's current legal team – declare that Cesar, if not the actual assassin, played a role in the plot, perhaps helping set up Kennedy as a target."[4178]

According to Los Angeles coroner Dr. Thomas Noguchi, it was not possible for Sirhan to have fired the fatal shots.[4179] Bullets test-fired from Sirhan's gun did not match the bullets pulled out of Robert Kennedy's body, according to a panel led by Judge Robert A. Wenke in 1975.[4180]

Sirhan Goes Missing

The CIA's MK-ULTRA program had progressed to the point where a hypnotized subject would, on cue, pull out a weapon and fire and later not remember what had happened.[4181] However, it was unreliable so you would have to have two shooters – one patsy and one to do the kill shot.[4182] The CIA had a file on Sirhan since well before the Robert Kennedy assassination.[4183]

Sirhan disappeared from his home in Pasadena and returned three months later with amnesia about the time gap.[4184] He was gone from December of 1967 through February of 1968.[4185] Memory and mind control conditioning takes up to three months, and Sirhan was missing for three months.[4186] And Sirhan was in the top five to ten percent in terms of susceptibility to being hypnotized.[4187]

When Sirhan returned from his absence his personality had changed and now he was irritable and withdrawn.[4188] This is a symptom of people who have been programmed with mind control techniques. He also was now very much into the Arab cause and had significant political views.[4189]

Dr. William Bryan in Los Angeles later admitted to having been the one who hypnotized Sirhan.[4190] He had done extensive work for the CIA beginning in Korea during the Korean War in the 1950's with the MK-ULTRA program.[4191] His specialty was in hypnotizing people with amnesia memory blocks so they would not remember later what they had done while under hypnosis.[4192] Sirhan was tested after the Robert Kennedy assassination and found to have been brainwashed and programmed with hypnosis.[4193] Dr. William Bryant was scheduled to testify before the House Select Committee on Assassinations in the spring of 1977, but he was found dead before he could testify before the HSCA.[4194]

The attractive woman in the polka dot dress may have been controlling Sirhan.[4195] She was with him in the pantry before the shooting and then she ran away after the shooting.[4196] This same woman was seen repeatedly by multiple witnesses in multiple places as being with Sirhan.[4197] She was consistently described as being in her early twenties and having an hourglass figure and a prominent nose.[4198] She is also frequently described as having, in addition to Sirhan, a tall man standing nearby.[4199] Author Patrick Nolan, in his book *CIA ROGUES AND THE KILLING OF THE KENNEDYS*, said that the tall man was likely there to keep an eye on both the woman and Sirhan while the woman was controlling Sirhan.[4200]

Sirhan's programmers had him write forty-eight pages of incriminating handwriting and then left it where it could be easily found and used against him at his trial.[4201]

There is a moral imperative exception to the rule that someone would not do under hypnosis what they would not otherwise do.[4202] For example, if a hypnotized person thinks their family is in danger they will act to protect them even if that means attacking someone.[4203] This is how a hypnotized person can be made to do something they would not otherwise do.[4204] Resistance to hypnosis can be bypassed through the use of drugs and brainwashing techniques like sensory deprivation, and no one knows where Sirhan was when he disappeared.[4205]

Sirhan was one of the easiest to program through hypnosis as Dr. Seymour Pollack and Dr. Bernard Diamond were able to demonstrate this in his cell.[4206]

The Cover Up

The CIA had cops on the payroll in major cities in the U.S. like Los Angeles, including LAPD cops Manny Pena and Hank Hernandez who helped with the cover up of the Robert Kennedy hit.[4207]

Authors Roger Stone and Mike Colapietro, in their book *THE MAN WHO KILLED KENNEDY*, commented on a similarity between the murders of John and Robert Kennedy:[4208]

> "The official truth in Robert Kennedy's death, much like his brother's, would be reached by distorting facts, destroying evidence, devaluing contrary testimony, and harassing naysayers."[4209]

> "When County Coroner Dr. Thomas T. Noguchi performed Bobby's autopsy, he found that the three bullets that had hit Kennedy had entered from the rear. Sirhan fired his .22-caliber, eight-shot revolver a few feet in front of Kennedy, yet the fatal shot was fired from "less than one inch from Kennedy's head, behind his right ear." Noguchi also found that the bullets had entered Senator Kennedy at an upward angle."[4210]

> "Noguchi's autopsy confirmed that it would have been impossible for Sirhan, who was standing to the front of Kennedy and whom not a single witness would testify was shooting any closer than one-and-a-half to two feet away from Kennedy, to have fired any shot, never mind the fatal shot with the gun barrel nearly pressed to the back of the senator's head. One of the closest witnesses to the shooting, busboy Juan Romero, saw the gun of Sirhan "approximately one yard from Senator Kennedy's head."[4211]

> "Investigators responded to Noguchi's autopsy evidence by slandering the doctor. Law enforcement officers investigating

the assassination accused the doctor of intentionally cooking up the autopsy report for self-promotion."[4212]

""I hope he dies because if he dies, then my international reputation will be established," Noguchi was reported to have exclaimed with Kennedy on his deathbed. He was also alleged to have been a drug user, who displayed "erratic behavior" and danced around Kennedy's corpse with apparent delight. His reputation was damaged, and he was temporarily fired due to the allegations."[4213]

""Some people believe that the problems I had resulted from my work on the Kennedy case," Noguchi later said. "One of the charges was that the Kennedy autopsy was 'botched up.' The first thing they did was withdraw that particular charge. There were sixty-four charges in all. They were prepared to show a shock value. They didn't expect me to fight back. And I was fully vindicated in the end.""[4214]

Authors Roger Stone and Mike Colapietro, in their book *THE MAN WHO KILLED KENNEDY*, documented that there was another possible gunman there right behind Kennedy, Thane Eugene Cesar:[4215]

"...Thane Eugene Cesar, a security guard who was escorting Kennedy through the kitchen. Cesar was in the right position to have caused the wounds to Kennedy and had been carrying a gun, which was not examined by police. Witnesses said that Cesar had fired shots, but their testimonies were neglected. Years later, Cesar intimated to investigators that he was not carrying the type of gun that killed Kennedy. He did say that he had owned the type, a .22 caliber, but had sold it four months before the assassination. It was later discovered that Cesar sold the gun three months *after* the killing of Kennedy. It mattered not. Law enforcement had their man."[4216]

Author Patrick Nolan, in his book *CIA ROGUES AND THE KILLING OF THE KENNEDYS*, said:

"A thorough examination and analysis of those who had ample motive, means, and opportunity concludes that only a small group stands alone: the CIA's Richard Helms and James Angleton and their rogue band of conspirators and mob allies."[4217]

"Only Richard Helms and James Angleton, the CIA's chief of counterintelligence, possessed the means of planning and executing this type of operation without drawing suspicion, albeit in part by relying on their closest officers: David Atlee Phillips, the head of CIA Latin American Affairs; E. Howard Hunt, sabotage expert; and other confidants."[4218]

The LAPD ignored any witnesses who said that they saw Sirhan with the attractive woman.[4219]   Two examples of this were two RFK campaign workers, Laverne Botting and Ethel Creehan.[4220]   They both remembered Sirhan visiting the campaign office with the woman and both their accounts were dismissed even though they gave accurate descriptions of both Sirhan and the woman.[4221]   And there were attempts to intimidate Mrs. Botting into silence.[4222]

Police Officer William Schneid saw Sirhan with the woman on May 20, 1968 at Robbie's Restaurant in Pomona, California when Senator Kennedy was scheduled to speak there.[4223]   He told this to the FBI, but was never interviewed by the LAPD.[4224]   Philip Melanson uncovered multiple witnesses who saw Sirhan with the woman, all of whom were ignored by the LAPD.[4225]

Albert LeBeau was collecting tickets at the Kennedy event at Robbie's Restaurant and when he asked Sirhan and the woman for tickets they turned back.[4226]   Later, he saw they made it in somehow and confronted them about tickets again.[4227]   He later identified Sirhan, but the LAPD said that he "admitted he lied" about this, which was just the LAPD, once again, trying to discredit a credible witness.[4228]

Sirhan's controllers had to be sure he would fire on command, so, on the same day Sirhan was witnessed buying ammunition, he was also seen practicing shooting in the Santa Ana mountains by a man hiking with his son.[4229]   The woman and another man were seen with him.[4230]   The LAPD dismissed this sighting as mistaken even though they did not even show the witness, Dean Pack, a photo of Sirhan because the discussion took place over the phone.[4231]

On the day of the assassination, fifteen witnesses saw Sirhan with the woman and the other man at the San Gabriel Gun Club shooting range in Duarte, California.[4232]   The witnesses were all dismissed by the authorities for one reason or another.[4233]   Richard and Roberta Grijalva reported seeing Sirhan, by all accounts the only person there who looked like him, but their account was dismissed by the LAPD who claimed they mistook Sirhan for someone else who resembled him.[4234] When too many witnesses came forward for the LAPD to credibly dismiss, they made arrangements for a woman who worked at a local bar frequented by cops to say she was at the gun range with Sirhan.[4235] This would keep them from having to investigate the mystery woman or acknowledge the existence of a conspiracy.[4236]

At 11:30 PM Sandra Serrano went outside to cool off for a minute and was on the steps of an emergency exit when three people brushed past her.[4237] One was the woman in the polka dot dress, one was Sirhan and the other was the tall man that always seemed to accompany Sirhan and the woman.[4238] Other witnesses at the Ambassador Hotel also accurately described the trio, including Darnell Johnson, Robin Casden, Thomas Vincent, George Green, Evan Freed and Booker Griffin.[4239] Sirhan and the woman were seen in the pantry between the Embassy Room and the Colonial Room.[4240] Sirhan then poured himself and the woman a cup of coffee just before the shooting.[4241] According to witnesses Darnell Johnson and Robin Casden, Sirhan and the woman were then joined in the pantry by the taller man who they came in with and two men in suits, one suit was darker and the other was lighter.[4242]

Author Patrick Nolan, in his book *CIA ROGUES AND THE KILLING OF THE KENNEDYS*, documents that:[4243]

> "Based on the accounts of five witnesses, there were two gunmen besides Sirhan. One was on the side of Robert Kennedy and one directly behind him. Sirhan was in front of Kennedy. One gunman wore a dark suit, and the other a lighter color. The five witnesses were Evan Freed, Dr. Marcus McBroom, Lisa Urso, Don Schulman, and Martha Raines (a pseudonym supplied by author Philip Melanson)."[4244]

Nelson also said:[4245]

> "According to witness Evan Freed, who was standing four feet from Kennedy, the first shot came from the man in the dark suit who had stepped behind Kennedy, opposite Sirhan. He fired upwards at point-blank range. The angle and muzzle distance – less than one inch away – corresponds with Dr. Thomas Noguchi's autopsy findings. Another witness, interviewed by author Philip Melanson, Martha Raines (pseudonym) also saw the dark-haired man in a suit firing a weapon. Kennedy's head jerked forward, from the impact of the being shot from behind. He then fell backwards and collapsed onto the floor, stated witness Lisa Urso. At the same time, Urso saw the blond man in the light suit, who was standing "by Kennedy," placing a handgun back into a holster."[4246]

Author Patrick Nolan, in his book *CIA ROGUES AND THE KILLING OF THE KENNEDYS*, said that Cesar had CIA connections:[4247]

> "As authors Turner and Christian have pointed out, his day job was with Lockheed working in a restricted area related to the

CIA's U-2 spy plane facility. As author Philip Melanson has shown that Cesar was hired by Ace Guard Service for part-time work only a few days before the assassination, according to company records."[4248]

Author Patrick Nolan, in his book *CIA ROGUES AND THE KILLING OF THE KENNEDYS*, also pointed out that Cesar correctly identified Kennedy's wounds twenty minutes before the doctors did and expressed the opinion that Cesar may have been the real assassin or, alternatively, may have been there to kill Sirhan after the assassination.[4249] Nolan also said that LAPD Sergeant Paul Schraga happened to be in the area and set up a command post in the parking lot of the hotel just after the assassination:[4250]

> "As soon as he arrived, a couple in their fifties named Bernstein rushed up to him. They reported that they had seen a young woman in a polka-dot dress and a man run by them. The woman had shouted "We shot him!" The Berensteins asked, "Who?" "Senator Kennedy," was the reply. Sergeant Schraga called in the report. Minutes after the assassination, LAPD issued an all-point bulletin that read: "Prior to shooting, suspect observed with a female cau. Twenty-three to twenty-seven [years old], five feet six inches, wearing a white viole dress, three-fourth inch sleeves, with small black polka dots..." At 1:41 a.m., a senior LAPD officer canceled the bulletin. Later on, according to Sergeant Schraga, his reports of the incident ended up "missing." When he eventually refused to go along with the official version of the assassination, Schraga said, his service ratings began to fall. As a result, a year later he chose to leave the department."[4251]

> "In addition to those mentioned above, others who came forward to report seeing the woman in the polka dot dress in the Embassy Room, most of the time with Sirhan, were Lonny Worthy, Margaret Hahn, Judith Groves, John Ludlow, Eve Hansen, Nina Ballantyne, Susan Locke, and Jeanette Prudhomme. The woman in the polka dot dress may have been involved in the assassination. The LAPD tried to stem the publicity by producing a Santa Barbara college student who had been at the Ambassador Hotel that night and had worn polka dots. Her name was Valerie Schulte. She had been some fifteen feet behind Senator Kennedy – not next to Sirhan as the polka dot dress woman had been. Also, her dress was green with yellow dots, and she had, in fact, been on

crutches that night with a cast on one leg, barely able to walk, let alone run."[4252]

The LAPD set up a separate and special unit to investigate the Robert Kennedy shooting.[4253] It was called Special Unit Senator (SUS).[4254] LAPD Detective Lieutenant Manuel Pena and LAPD Detective Sargent Hank Hernandez were the key investigators.[4255] They were both CIA, but that fact did not come to light until much later.[4256] They kept the investigation focused on Sirhan as a lone gunman.[4257]

Witnesses who didn't follow the "lone nut gunman" theory were harassed and made to change their story.[4258] Sandra Serrano was a good example. Author Patrick Nolan, in his book, *CIA ROGUES AND THE KILLING OF THE KENNEDYS*, documents the following:[4259]

> "The SUS team was particularly adept at handling reports of accomplices and other conspiracy theories by preventing corroborating accounts from surfacing. For example, witnesses who saw the young woman in the polka dot dress in the pantry were either ignored or pressured into revising their stories. One key witness who strayed from the lone assassin theory was Sandra Serrano. As noted earlier, she had seen the young woman and her male companion rushing down the Ambassador Hotel's outside staircase, the same route they had used earlier with Sirhan when entering the kitchen. Serrano was still sitting on the steps sipping a vodka and orange juice, when, as she has stated, the fleeing woman shouted "We shot him!" "We shot him!" Serrano asked who, and she replied, "We've shot Senator Kennedy." Another witness, Albert Ellis, later told the FBI that he, too, had heard the same cry."[4260]

> "Soon after the assassination, NBC's Sander Vanocur interviewed Serrano for nationwide television. She gave the same account she later gave the police. In fact, her description of the young woman and her male companion and Sirhan match those of other witnesses who also saw them in the pantry, either just prior to the shooting, or while running out afterwards. The LAPD tried numerous times to persuade Serrano to changer her story with regard to the woman announcing, "We shot him." She steadfastly refused. Two weeks after the assassination, on June 20, 1968, at 9 p.m., Serrano submitted to a polygraph test administered by Sgt. Hank Hernandez."[4261]

> "Professor Philip Melanson has chronicled the methods employed against Serrano based on a surviving audiotape of

the test. Hernandez insisted to Serrano that she did not hear the young woman say "We shot him." And rather than asking "yes" or "no" questions, Hernandez's approach involved using harassment and intimidation to persuade her to change her story. His stream of rhetoric resulted in continual arguing with the witness. Excerpts of his statements demonstrated the lengths to which SUS would go to suppress evidence of a plot. The following is a quote of Hernandez's voice on tape: "You owe it to Senator Kennedy. . . . Be a woman about this. . . . Don't shame his death by keeping this up. . . . What you saw is not true. Tell me why you made up this story. . . . If you loved the man, the least you owe him is letting him rest in peace, and he can't. . . . This is going to make an old woman out of you before your time. . . . There's people out there waiting for you if you don't tell the truth." On the verge of tears, the twenty-year-old caved in. She agreed to recant her statements. Twenty years later, in 1988, when the California State Archives released the LAPD's files on the case, Serrano was asked to speak on a local radio program. She summed up her Hank Hernandez polygraph test by saying, "I became unglued. . . . I said what he wanted me to say."[4262]

Any evidence of a conspiracy was buried.[4263] Sirhan went to a gun shop called the Lock, Stock and Barrel on June 1, 1968.[4264] He was seen by two reliable witnesses, the clerk and the owner, when he went there to buy ammo with two men, but the subject of the two men with Sirhan was avoided at trial, even by Sirhan's own defense attorney.[4265] And after one of the witnesses, store clerk Larry Arnot, had been given a 'polygraph exam' by LAPD Detective Hank Hernandez he suddenly didn't remember Sirhan at all.[4266]

Author Patrick Nolan, in his book, *CIA ROGUES AND THE KILLING OF THE KENNEDYS*, points out that the authorities worked to hide evidence of more shots:[4267]

> "The facts regarding the physical evidence found in the kitchen pantry were the key to proving whether there was more than one gunman. If more than eight shots were fired, then there had to be a second gunman. LAPD's lead criminalist, DeWayne Wolfer, reported to SUS team leaders Manny Pena and Hank Hernandez that seven bullets were recovered and one was lost in the ceiling space. According to LAPD's official ballistics report, two bullets were recovered from Senator Kennedy's body, five bullets were taken from the five surviving victims, and one bullet was lost in the

"ceiling interspace," for a total of eight bullets. But FBI documents, released under the Freedom of Information Act, reveal evidence of five additional bullets. In its examination of the murder scene, the FBI reported finding two bullet holes in the doorjamb of the pantry's swinging doors, two in the center dividing post, and one in the stage door jamb. These five added to the LAPD list produce total of thirteen bullets fired."[4268]

"FBI agent William Bailey, who inspected the crime scene shortly after the assassination, discovered the evidence of two unaccounted for bullets lodged in the center divider between the swinging doors in the kitchen pantry. Two additional bullets that SUS neglected to report became public information when FBI photos of the hotel kitchen pantry evidence were released in 1975. Since both the LAPD and the FBI knew of these in 1968, it is clear that both were working together to ensure that evidence of a conspiracy remained secret, at least initially. Another hole with a bullet in it was discovered by two LAPD officers, Robert Rozzi and Charles Wright. The two policemen were photographed by the AP at the crime scene pointing to the bullet hole, which was located in a doorjamb a foot above the floor in a hallway leading into the pantry. The door frames were quickly removed by the police and destroyed by them a year later."[4269]

"In the decade following the assassination, a battle raged over the exact bullet count due to the serious consequences of having more than eight, the alleged murder weapon having been an 8-shot Iver-Johnson. One witness, Nina Rhodes, whose account mentioned hearing more than eight shots, found out in 1992 that her statement to the FBI, given in 1968, had been rewritten. The summary released in 1992 indicated that while at the hotel kitchen entrance on the night of the murder she had heard "eight distinct shots." Upon reading the report, she was amazed. She immediately wrote back to inform the Los Angeles grand jury, "I would like to stress . . . I heard twelve to fourteen shots, some originating in the vicinity of the senator not from where I saw Sirhan . . ."[4270]

"LAPD has maintained its position that no additional bullets were found at the scene of the assassination. In addition, when asked to produce a spectrographic report, which would determine if all the recovered bullets had the same metallic makeup and hence were likely from the same "batch," the department responded that the scientific evidence was "either lost or destroyed."[4271]

"An acoustic analysis of ABC's broadcast tape from the Embassy Room was conducted in 1982 at the Stanford Research Institute in Menlo Park, California, according to writers Klaber and Melanson. The results ascertained that no fewer than ten gunshots were fired."[4272]

The one photographer, Scott Enyart, who was in the pantry taking photographs at the time of the assassination had his film confiscated by the authorities.[4273]

Jim Garrison Tries Clay Shaw in 1969

Jim Garrison was the District Attorney in New Orleans in the 1960's. He attempted to investigate the death of President Kennedy and bring one of the conspirators to justice. He instigated the only prosecution in the assassination of John F. Kennedy. The conspirators could not allow this to happen and they first tried to bribe Garrison into dropping the case. When he couldn't be bribed they effectively destroyed the case he was trying to build against Clay Shaw, the CIA operative who Garrison chose to prosecute. They also attempted to destroy Garrison himself. They succeeded in using the mainstream media to have Garrison removed from office. They were unsuccessful in their attempts to have him put behind bars, and Garrison did the public a great service by hammering more cracks into the Deep State's cover-up of the Kennedy assassination. Because of this we have more information on the assassination.

The Garrison investigation is interesting for several reasons. First, it was good to see that there was at least one honest public servant willing to look into the Kennedy assassination. Second, Garrison uncovered some useful information. One good example of useful information uncovered by the Garrison prosecution is the Finck testimony in the Clay Shaw trial. Putting Finck on the stand proved that the orders to hamstring the autopsy came from high up in the Pentagon. Dr. Finck did not want to answer the question. The answer had to be dragged out of him. We would never have known the answer unless a judge had ordered him to answer the question, under oath. The Garrison investigation also forced the Zapruder film out into the open, which showed that some of the shots came from the front. The Garrison investigation was also notable for the lengths the CIA went to in order to derail it. They ran a multi-level covert operation to destroy both Garrison's case and Garrison personally. Garrison wrote a book called ON THE TRAIL OF THE ASSASSINS where he described the experience of being attacked. Many years later, after the revelations that came to light from the JFK Records Act of 1992 and the subsequent Assassination Records Review Board, James DiEugenio was able to document many of the details of how the CIA worked behind the scenes to launch all these attacks. He wrote a book called DESTINY BETRAYED. It makes for eye-opening reading.

Numerous witnesses from Dallas testified at the trial of Clay Shaw that there were shots from the front. This was to establish that there was a conspiracy to murder President Kennedy. As Jim Garrison said, in his book ON THE TRAIL OF THE ASSASSINS:[4274]

"To establish that the president had to have been shot by more than one gunman and that there had to have been a conspiracy, we called a number of witnesses from Dallas who saw and heard shooting from in front of the motorcade. William E. Newman, a young design engineer from Dallas, described how he had been only 10 or 15 feet away from the limousine when he saw the first shot hit the President in front of the head. Kennedy fell backwards violently. The shots, Newman recalled, were coming from the grassy knoll right behind where he was standing. His testimony was corroborated by Frances Newman, his wife. And by James Simmons, an employee of the Union Terminal Railway. And by Mrs. Mary Moorman, a housewife from Dallas, and Mrs. Philip Willis."[4275]

The Zapruder film was also shown for the first time at the trial of Clay Shaw. The film showed Kennedy and the violent backward movement of his head upon being shot from the front.[4276]

When I first heard that New Orleans was involved in the Kennedy assassination, I wondered why the prosecution was not in Dallas. Once I dug into it I discovered that New Orleans was involved because that's where a lot of the setup for the murder happened. As discussed earlier in the sections on the additional setups in Tampa and Chicago, there were multiple cities which were considered as alternate sites for the actual murder of President Kennedy. The idea was to have a flexible plan that was not dependent on a presidential trip to any one city and therefore did not have a single potential point of failure. New Orleans was where many of the conspirators (mafia boss Carlos Marcello and CIA assets Guy Banister, Sergio Arcacha Smith, David Ferrie and Clay Shaw among others) lived and where Marcello had his power base. It was also near where many of the anti-Castro Cuban exiles were being trained.

This chapter is organized into five sections:

1. Who was Jim Garrison? – gives some background on Garrison, who he was and why he chose to risk everything to expose the conspiracy to assassinate John F. Kennedy

2. Garrison's Investigation Was Infiltrated – describes how the CIA and the mainstream media infiltrated and tried to sabotage the Garrison investigation and trial of Clay Shaw

3. The Trial of Clay Shaw – describes the Garrison prosecution of CIA operative Clay Shaw for participation in the conspiracy to assassinate President Kennedy

4.   The Attempt to Destroy Garrison – describes how the CIA decided to teach Garrison a lesson so that no one else would ever again attempt to investigate the Kennedy assassination

5.   The Media Attack on Garrison – describes how the attempt to destroy Garrison personally is coordinated with a media attack on Garrison to destroy him in the mind of the public

There was just no way the CIA wing of the Deep State was going to allow Jim Garrison, the District Attorney of New Orleans, to successfully prosecute Clay Shaw for participation in a conspiracy to murder President Kennedy. Had he been allowed to succeed it would have opened a huge can of worms. If someone was guilty of conspiracy to murder Kennedy, who else was involved? If Clay Shaw was CIA and he was involved in the Kennedy assassination, what was the CIA doing taking out a hit on the President of the United States? If Clay Shaw was found guilty, the list of questions that would bring up would be endless. Garrison had to not only be stopped from getting a guilty verdict, he had to be personally discredited and destroyed. He had to end up behind bars as an object lesson to anyone else who might consider doing something similar. He had to be made an example.

In order to make sure that Garrison not only failed to get a guilty verdict but also ended up disgraced and behind bars, the Deep State conspirators, including Lyndon Johnson, J. Edgar Hoover, the CIA and the mainstream media, orchestrated a campaign against Garrison which was impressive in its scope. Here is a list of the levels on which the they attacked Garrison:

- Kill David Ferrie before he could be a material witness
- Kill any other witnesses who might be useful
- Cut his budget by claiming in the newspaper he was squandering money on the JFK investigation
- Set him up for prosecution in the men's room of the Los Angeles airport
- Harass his witnesses
- Get his witnesses out of the state of Louisiana
- Quash any extradition requests to get those witnesses back
- Quash any subpoenas he tried to use
- Spy on him and his investigation
- Infiltrate his office with plants to spy on him and hurt the prosecution
- Send him on wild goose chases to waste his time and money
- Send him fake witnesses planted to hurt his case

- Get the mainstream media to smear him
- Get him tossed out of office by a coordinated media campaign
- Have him prosecuted on trumped-up charges of bribery of pinball operators
- Have him arrested in front of his wife and children
- Have his home searched

Who was Jim Garrison?

Jim Garrison was the duly elected District Attorney of New Orleans who tried to investigate the murder of President Kennedy and prosecute some of those who conspired to assassinate him. He was an honest public servant who was doing the job he was elected to do. As a result, the Deep State turned on him and attacked him with everything they had. Once they prevented him from getting a guilty verdict in the Shaw trial they then went after him personally. This was to make an example out of him so no one else in an official capacity tried to look too closely at the Kennedy assassination.

At first David Ferrie was Garrison's star witness. He was the primary focus of Garrison's investigation, and then he was murdered.[4277] Clay Shaw worked with David Ferrie, Dr. Alton Ochsner and Lee Oswald on several CIA and Kennedy assassination projects in New Orleans during the summer of 1963. After Ferrie's murder Shaw became the primary focus of Garrison's investigation and prosecution.[4278] Clay Shaw did work for the CIA, but Garrison couldn't prove that until after the trial when it was too late to do any good.[4279] Richard Helms had a long career with the CIA, topped off by being Director of the CIA from 1966 to 1973. In 1979 Helms testified under oath that Clay Shaw was connected to the CIA. Had this been known at the time of the Garrison prosecution, Clay Shaw would have been convicted of conspiracy to murder President Kennedy and Garrison would have been proven to be right. Since this was not known at the time, Garrison was almost destroyed for trying to prosecute Clay Shaw.

Oswald was sent to New Orleans to make him look like a Castro supporter. He was given a fake cover job with the Reily Coffee Company in the same neighborhood with all the intelligence offices. The Reily Coffee Company was owned by William B. Reily who was linked to the CIA front Cuban Revolutionary Council. Within sight of each other in that part of New Orleans were the offices of the CIA, FBI,

ONI (Office of Naval Intelligence), the Secret Service and Guy Banister's office.[4280]

Author James DiEugenio, in his book *DESTINY BETRAYED*, says of Garrison:[4281]

> "One of the many criticisms brought against Jim Garrison when his inquiry into President Kennedy's death was made public was this: He was doing it to advance his political career. In fact, one newspaper even wrote that Garrison hoped to become Vice-President because of the fame to be garnered from his inquiry. This is one of the worst things one can say about a District Attorney. Since it implies that he is willing to indict and prosecute someone only to advance his political ambition. This was only the beginning of a two-year war of character assassination that would turn Garrison into a caricature and Clay Shaw into a martyr. As we will later see, in reality, it was this campaign of calumny that was politically motivated. And it was performed by some journalists of rather questionable ethics. The truth is actually the opposite. In pursuing his Kennedy investigation, Garrison threw away a political career of great promise. And along with it, the two offices he most aspired to: District Attorney and the U.S. Senate. This part of the story was not told to the public. We should relate it here."[4282]

DiEugenio then goes into seven pages of details to document what he asserts here.[4283] I would urge anyone interested in the real Jim Garrison to read it.

On February 17, 1967 the *New Orleans States-Item* published a story about Garrison's investigation that complained about the $8,000 spent by Garrison's office on travel and expenses in the investigation.[4284] This alerted the world, including the Deep State, that Garrison was on the case and suggested a reason to criticize his efforts. Once they knew Garrison was looking into the Kennedy assassination, the Deep State sprang into action and went after Garrison with everything they had.

Jim Garrison, in his book *ON THE TRAIL OF THE ASSASSINS*, describes David Ferrie's bitter reaction to the story being published:[4285]

> "You know what this news story does to me, don't you?" said Ferrie. "I'm a dead man. From here on. Believe me, I'm a dead man."[4286]

And within a week Ferrie was found dead under suspicious circumstances.[4287]

Garrison's Investigation Was Infiltrated

Dean Andrews was a lawyer in New Orleans who had been called by Clay Shaw to represent Oswald and when Garrison asked him about it he got scared and did not want to answer Garrison's questions.[4288] Andrews had a right to be frightened. By that time Garrison's witnesses were dying left and right (see the chapter on the Murder of Anyone Who Would Talk). David Ferrie, Guy Bannister, Rose Cherami, Dr. Mary Sherman, Maurice Gatlin, Manuel Rodriguez Quesada, Gilberto Hernandez and Eladio del Valle all died violent or suspicious deaths, and that was just in New Orleans. Clearly Andrews did not want his name added to this list.

Author Phillip Nelson, in his book *LBJ: THE MASTERMIND OF THE JFK ASSASSINATION*, says, in regard to the Garrison investigation:[4289]

> "It is abundantly clear now that a lot of high-level officials in the CIA, the FBI, the Justice Department, and the White House were very worried about what might be revealed in that trial and nothing was spared in getting it shut down before it got out of control."[4290]

> "... the plain fact was that D.A. Garrison was getting much too close to people and evidence that had not been sufficiently buried."[4291]

> "On February 16, 1967, Hoover had been shown an article from the *New Orleans States-Item* about the reinvestigation being launched by Garrison into the Kennedy assassination, and that one of his chief suspects was David Ferrie, who had known Lee Harvey Oswald for at least eight years and was then working for Carlos Marcello. Author John H. Davis described what happened next. "FBI cable traffic during the last two weeks of February reveals that news of the Garrison investigation convulsed Hoover. Immediately he began marshalling his allies in the government and the media in a discreet, behind-the-scenes effort to discredit Garrison and undermine his investigation." His "allies in the government" would have certainly included President Johnson and James Angleton, and clearly many others on down the hierarchy. Immediately after that, Garrison arranged to put Ferrie up at the Fontainebleau Hotel but for some inexplicable reason, he

left the hotel on February 21 and returned to his apartment. In the early hours of the next morning, he was found dead..."[4292]

President Johnson tried to get his Attorney General, Ramsey Clark, to shut down the Garrison investigation.[4293] Clark announced publicly that they had already looked into Clay Shaw and exonerated him in the Kennedy assassination.[4294] By this time Johnson had promoted Richard Helms from Deputy Director to Director of the CIA and now the CIA joined the coordinated attack on Garrison.[4295]

Author Gaeton Fonzi, in his book *THE LAST INVESTIGATION*, put it this way:[4296]

> "Agency Director Richard Helms, according to his former staff assistant Victor Marchetti, was very concerned that Garrison, despite his wild scatter-gun approach, might blow open some doors the Agency preferred to be kept closed. The House Assassinations Committee would later learn that the Agency, in order to keep close track of where Garrison was going, planted several undercover operatives on his staff."[4297]

In February of 1967 a man calling himself "John Miller," and who described himself as an oil man from Denver came to visit Garrison, ostensibly to offer help paying for the investigation.[4298] Garrison and Andrew Sciambra were in Garrison's office when "Miller" claimed he could guarantee Garrison a federal district court judgeship if Garrison shut down the investigation.[4299] Garrison refused to be bribed.[4300]

Garrison was running the investigation on a shoestring budget, so when volunteers showed up, he welcomed the free help.[4301] One of these was a former CIA case officer named William Wood. He was called Bill Boxley as an alias so as not to alert the establishment that there was a former CIA employee on the team.[4302] "Boxley" then recommended another former CIA employee named Jim Rose.[4303] As it turned out in the end, by Garrison's estimate, half of the volunteers were planted there to spy on Garrison's investigation.[4304] According to Garrison, in his book *ON THE TRAIL OF THE ASSASSINS*, what the CIA had done to his investigation was obstruction of justice.[4305] At every level of his investigation Garrison was obstructed by the Deep State. Gordon Novel of the CIA had been involved with Guy Banister and Garrison wanted to talk to him but he left for Ohio before Garrison could get to him. Garrison tried to extradite Novel to Louisiana in April of 1967.[4306] Novel had notified the CIA that Garrison was looking for him and suggested that the CIA activate Garrison, who was in the reserves. Under pressure from the Deep State, Ohio refused to extradite Gordon Novel.[4307] Garrison was also stopped from extraditing other witnesses.[4308]

Garrison then tried to subpoena Allen Dulles only to have the U.S. Attorney in Washington, D.C. decline to serve the subpoena.[4309] The Deep State was moving decisively to keep Garrison from success in his investigation and prosecution. Garrison's book makes interesting reading.

Richard Case Nagell had tried to warn Oswald and the federal government about the plan to assassinate Kennedy, and he reached out through relatives to assist Garrison now that he was out of prison (see the section on Richard Case Nagell).[4310] Nagell and Garrison agreed on a place to meet in the open in New York and Garrison flew up for the meeting.[4311] Nagell described to Garrison how he had tried to warn first Oswald and then the government about the plan to kill President Kennedy.[4312] Nagell named Shaw, Ferrie and Bannister as having worked with Oswald and described how the FBI had ignored his warning.[4313]

Garrison ended up paying the expenses of the investigation out of his own pocket and he was taking trips to speak at universities as a means of both helping to pay for the investigation and countering the media assault on him and his investigation.[4314] On one such trip Garrison was set up to be arrested in the men's room at the Los Angeles airport and he only narrowly escaped.[4315] The conspirators sent a homosexual who knew Garrison into the next stall and the police were gathered outside the men's room.[4316] Garrison luckily realized what was going on and managed to avoid the trap.[4317] Had Garrison been convicted on a trumped-up sex misdemeanor charge in California it would have made headlines and cost him his job.[4318] Having Garrison removed from office would have stopped the investigation.[4319] "Boxley" had helped to set him up.[4320] Garrison describes this episode in detail in his book ON THE TRAIL OF THE ASSASSINS.[4321] As a parting shot, "Boxley" tried to smear Garrison as a drug addict.[4322]

William Wood ("Boxley") was finally gone, but he had led Garrison down numerous false paths during his tenure with the investigation.[4323] This had wasted precious time, money and credibility that Garrison and the investigation could not afford to spare.[4324] In the meantime he had also been spying on Garrison and his investigation for the CIA and keeping them up to date on Garrison's progress.[4325]

Another disastrous plant was Charles Spiesel, who was sent in to discredit the Clay Shaw prosecution in the eyes of the jury.[4326] He claimed to Garrison that he had been drinking with David Ferrie and Ferrie had said he wanted to kill Kennedy.[4327] He also said that the two of them had visited Clay Shaw's home and Shaw had said that Ferrie would have to fly the assassins out of Dallas on the evening of the hit.[4328]

Spiesel fell apart on the stand and appeared to be a flake, at one point admitting that he had fingerprinted his daughter before and after her going to college to make sure it was really her.[4329] This had the desired effect of destroying the credibility of the prosecution in the eyes of the jury.[4330]

James DiEugenio does a good job, in his book *DESTINY BETRAYED*, of documenting how the CIA infiltrated Garrison's office. Garrison was trying to investigate and build a case in the massive Kennedy conspiracy with the very limited budget of a local district attorney's office. People came from all over to volunteer to help and Garrison was in no position to turn them down. This allowed the CIA to plant double agents in Garrison's office to both keep tabs on Garrison and try to discredit Garrison and the case he was building. And this was just the beginning. Once the case was over the Deep State continued the multi-level attack on Garrison. There's no other explanation for why the Deep State continued to pursue the attacks. This was clearly done to make an example out of him so that no one else would ever dare to try to find the truth of who was behind the Kennedy assassination. In the interest of not trying to repeat what DiEugenio wrote in his book I would suggest that anyone who doubts the depth and breadth of the attacks on Garrison should read his excellent book. I would start by reading Garrison's book *ON THE TRAIL OF THE ASSASSINS*, then read *DESTINY BETRAYED*. DiEugenio expands and builds on what Garrison wrote by adding new information that goes into considerably more detail on what happened. Garrison was aware of the multiple attacks on him at the time, and he described this in his book. DiEugenio adds to this by documenting who was involved behind the scenes to make these attacks happen. He describes in detail how the mechanism worked between the CIA and the "assets" that they employed to attempt to destroy Garrison for daring to challenge them. It's eye-opening reading for those of us with naïve ideas about living in a free society. For example, DiEugenio goes into detail on how the CIA had Garrison's subpoenas quashed.[4331]

Author Phillip Nelson, in his book *LBJ: THE MASTERMIND OF THE JFK ASSASSINATION*, points out that, during the Garrison prosecution of Clay Shaw, CIA Director Richard Helms was putting the resources of the CIA at the disposal of those trying to derail Garrison:[4332]

> "As Jim Garrison prosecuted the Clay Shaw trial in New Orleans, Helms was also said to have routinely started his daily 9:00 AM meetings at CIA headquarters with questions like "How is the Shaw trial going? Are we giving them all the help they need? Is everything going all right down there?"

This information was revealed by a former CIA agency staff employee, Victor Marchetti, who said that comments like "We'll pick this up later in my office," or "talk to me about it after the meeting" were used to tightly control who was privy to certain information."[4333]

The FBI also sent infiltrators into Garrison's office.[4334] The Gurvich brothers, William and Louis, offered their private investigation services for free and Garrison accepted, and they also turned out to be spies.[4335]

The Trial of Clay Shaw

On March 1, 1967 Garrison arrested prominent New Orleans businessman and CIA asset Clay Shaw for conspiring to murder President Kennedy.[4336]

During the trial, Clay Shaw took the stand and denied knowing David Ferrie or Lee Harvey Oswald.[4337] This was a lie and opened him up to prosecution for perjury.[4338]

As mentioned earlier, the trial of Clay Shaw accomplished several good things, including:

- The testimony of witnesses that there were shots from the front, which proved a conspiracy
- The testimony of Dr. Finck, which proved that the Pentagon brass ordered him not to complete a proper autopsy which would have resulted in proof of shots from the front
- The first public viewing of the Zapruder film, which proved that shots came from the front

However, the predictable result, given that the Deep State had the resources of the Federal Government and the mass media to use against Garrison, was that he was ultimately unsuccessful in proving at that time that Clay Shaw was part of the conspiracy to assassinate President Kennedy. On March 1, 1969 Clay Shaw was found not guilty.[4339]

Garrison charged Shaw with perjury after his acquittal, but the United States District Court and the appellate courts backed Shaw and stopped his prosecution for perjury.[4340]

Federal courts are not legally allowed to overrule state courts and stop a prosecution, but the judge ignored the law and stopped Garrison from prosecuting Shaw for perjury in this case.[4341] Many years later a letter was found in the National Archives among Clay Shaw's personal papers.[4342] It was from the wife of Herbert Christenberry, the judge who ruled to stop the prosecution of Shaw for perjury, and it was sent after his acquittal.[4343] It reads in part:

> "Our most sincere congratulations! We shared your anxieties over the past two outrageous years. Should your case have eventually found its way to Federal Court and been allotted to my husband you most certainly would have had a fair trial. He felt we should not risk the possibility of being considered "prejudiced" in advance. This is our reason for not openly expressing these sentiments earlier."[4344]

After Clay Shaw was acquitted the newspapers called for Garrison's resignation.[4345] Author James DiEugenio, in his book *DESTINY BETRAYED*, describes how the FBI and *Look* magazine pitched in to help smear Garrison between the time of Shaw's acquittal and his trial for perjury:[4346]

> "While this was ongoing, the other side continued their covert defense of Shaw. In August of 1969, the mass circulation magazine *Look*, ran a long article entitled "The Persecution of Clay Shaw." This piece appears to be a joint operation between Hoover and Cartha DeLoach in Washington, and locally, Aaron Kohn and Bill Gurvich. The information in the article is essentially all the phony Mafia smears that David Chandler and Aaron Kohn had manufactured and utilized to tar Garrison. The photographs accompanying the article were taken by Bill Gurvich. The man who officially received the byline for the article, but who really served as a fig leaf for Kohn and Gurvich, was Warren Rogers. This could not be known at the time of the publication. But Rogers, like Phelan and Sandy Smith, was a reliable asset for the FBI. That is, he could be counted on to do favors for them when called upon. The public did not know this until the 1979 posthumous publication of William Sullivan's book about the FBI called *The Bureau*. Sullivan had been a top echelon officer in the FBI for many years. In his book there is a chapter entitled "Flacking for the Bureau." Listed as one of the reporters who would often write articles with information fed to them by the FBI was Warren Rogers. In addition to the FBI, the CIA was also on the ready. Headquarters in Langley wanted to remove the teletype machine from the local station after the trial was over and Shaw had been acquitted. But Hunter Leake requested that the communications keystone stay in New

Orleans until after the Shaw perjury trial was complete. Leake got his request fulfilled."[4347]

The Attempt to Destroy Garrison

Author David Talbot, in his book *THE DEVIL'S CHESSBOARD*, points out that Garrison was harassed by the entire Deep State establishment and the national media:[4348]

> "The Garrison investigation set off alarm bells in CIA headquarters. It soon became clear, however, that the authority of a crusading district attorney was no match for the U.S. intelligence establishment. Days after Garrison sent off the Dulles subpoena to the nation's capital, he received a letter from the United States attorney in Washington, D.C., who tersely informed the DA that he "declined" to serve the subpoena on Dulles. Meanwhile, the CIA – which by then, was led by Helms – mounted an aggressive counterattack on the district attorney. Subpoenas like the one sent to Dulles were simply ignored, government records were destroyed, Garrison's office was infiltrated by spies, and agency assets in the media worked to turn the DA into a crackpot in the public eye. Even the private investigator Garrison hired to sweep his office for electronic bugs turned out to be a CIA operative. After Dulles was subpoenaed by Garrison, the security specialist – Gordon Novel – phoned the spymaster to slip him inside information about the DA's strategy."[4349]

> "In the end, Garrison's powerful enemies managed to turn the tables on him, and the New Orleans prosecutor himself became the target of an investigation, on trumped-up federal corruption charges. "This is what happens to you," he observed years later, "when you do not go along with the new government's ratification of the coup.""[4350]

The attempt to destroy Garrison continued.[4351] A phony case was manufactured against him and Garrison was acquitted.[4352] The media pilloried Garrison and he narrowly lost the next election.[4353]

The trial of Clay Shaw was over, but the Deep State wasn't done with Garrison. He had dared to challenge them and this would not go unpunished. He had to be destroyed – personally. On June 30, 1971 Garrison was arrested at his home by the IRS.[4354] Garrison was charged in a pinball bribery racket, which was the opposite of the truth as Garrison had vigorously enforced the laws against pinball payoffs.[4355] Garrison hired F. Lee Bailey to defend him and Bailey agreed to take the case on the condition that Garrison allow Bailey to defend him for free.[4356] The federal government dragged on the legal proceedings for years and put together a team of lawyers who had been after Garrison for several years.[4357]

At one point in the past Garrison had personally loaned Pershing Gervais $5,000 after Garrison had to ask for his resignation from the New Orleans DA's office.[4358] Gervais paid back the money in five payments of $1,000 and the feds had used these payments as the basis for their case against Garrison.[4359] They had even edited the tapes to put incriminating words in Garrison's mouth.[4360] The trial of Garrison started on August 20, 1973 and was expected to last 4 to 6 weeks and end just before Garrison's next election as District Attorney.[4361] The reason for the timing was because this was a setup in an attempt to get Garrison removed from office.[4362] The judge, Herbert Christenberry, was the same judge who had overridden the clearly explicit federal law that allowed Garrison to prosecute Shaw for perjury.[4363] Garrison decided to represent himself in the courtroom because the government's case was a fabrication and it was Garrison vs. the Federal Government and Garrison thought the jury would get this better from him than from an out of town lawyer.[4364] Garrison brought a book to read during the trial because none of the pinball operators had any relationship to Garrison and when it was his time to question each pinball operator Garrison would put his book down briefly and ask if they knew each other.[4365] They would say they did not and Garrison would go back to reading.[4366] The cop who collected the protection money, Sargent Soule, then testified and he also had no relationship with Garrison[4367] Then Pershing Gervais was called to testify and then the doctored tape recordings were played and Garrison appeared to be guilty of taking payoffs.[4368] Gervais claimed that $150,000 was paid to Garrison and the prosecution played the doctored tapes that made Garrison sound guilty.[4369] On cross examination Garrison got Gervais to admit he had lied, and then got an audio expert to demonstrate how the tapes had been doctored.[4370] Garrison was acquitted but lost the next election by a narrow margin, so the attack on Garrison had accomplished at least one of its objectives for the Deep State.[4371] Garrison had finally been removed from office. They had been hoping to land Garrison in prison, but had to settle for getting him out of office.

Once Garrison was out of office the next step was to destroy the files he had gathered during his investigation and prosecution of Clay Shaw so Garrison's successor tried to burn the files Garrison left behind.[4372] He seems to have burned most of them.[4373]

The Media Attack on Garrison

The CIA used Operation Mockingbird to control the media (see the section on Operation Mockingbird). This meant more than just spinning stories to support the CIA's point of view. It even meant more than just squashing stories that the CIA wanted squashed. In addition to spinning and squashing, it meant that the media could be used as a weapon to destroy someone, especially an elected official who depended on getting votes to keep their job. The CIA used all three against Jim Garrison.

Author Mark Lane, in his book *LAST WORD: MY INDICTMENT OF THE CIA IN THE MURDER OF JFK*, describes how the CIA attacked Garrison:[4374]

> "From the moment his investigation of the JFK assassination became public, Garrison was pilloried in the press. This treatment was part of an orchestrated effort by the CIA to discredit critics of the Warren Commission. A CIA memo dated April 1, 1967 ... outlines the strategy and calls for the Agency's "assets" in the media (writers and editors) to publish stories saying the critics were politically motivated, financially motivated, egomaniacal, sloppy in their research, supported by the Soviet Union, etc. This is exactly the inaccurate portrait of Garrison that emerged in the press."[4375]

With the CIA controlling the mainstream media, Garrison had to resort to alternative media to get his side of the story out. At one point, Garrison agreed to an interview with *Playboy* magazine in order to respond to the smears and other media attacks on himself and his investigation and get the facts out.[4376]

Henry Luce, the publisher of *Time*, *Life* and *Fortune* magazines, was a charter member of the CIA's Operation Mockingbird.[4377] He was close to Allen Dulles and they shared the same Cold War view of the world and America's place in it. Luce was also an enemy of President Kennedy. [4378] And his *Life* magazine had gone out of its way to peddle the 'Oswald did it' lie to the public.[4379] In early 1967 Dick Billings from *Life* magazine showed up in New Orleans to claim that *Life* magazine and Jim Garrison should combine their efforts and share their results in order to help each other uncover the conspiracy to assassinate Kennedy.[4380] In Billing's defense, he may have actually believed this. In any case, Garrison believed him and gratefully accepted the 'help' from *Life* magazine.[4381] In hindsight this appears to have been an effort by *Life* magazine to spy on Garrison and see what he knew by "sharing their results." This is because later, as Garrison put it in his book *ON THE TRAIL OF THE ASSASSINS*:[4382]

> "Without any warning, Dick Billings, the friendly editor of *Life* magazine, suddenly flew in from New York. He seemed amiable enough, but he appeared to have lost a great deal of weight. He had deep circles under his eyes. His ivy league clothes hung loosely on his thin frame. He informed me that *Life* would no longer be able to support me and work with me in the investigation. The magazine, he said, had come to the conclusion that I was not the vigorous opponent of organized crime that it had first thought I was."[4383]

> ""What on earth are you talking about?" I asked. He then mentioned a name, asking me if I knew the man. I shook my head and answered that I had never heard of him. The editor held out his hands. "There you are," he said. "You should have a dossier on him by now.""[4384]

> "I pulled over a phone directory and located the name he had mentioned in the small town of Covington, a listing which indicated that he lived immediately north of the lake. "Is this who you mean?" I asked."[4385]

> ""That's the man," he said. "He's one of the top racketeers down here.""[4386]

> ""And you're the starting quarterback for the Green Bay Packers," I responded. If that fellow had been engaged in any extended criminality in and around New Orleans, I would have known his name well. As it turned out, I could find no one in the office who ever had heard his name. Nor did the name ever come up again."[4387]

> "I studied my visitor. It was obvious that he was an unhappy man executing a bad assignment which he had been ordered to carry out. I was angry, but not at him."[4388]

Life magazine then proceeded to smear Garrison as a free-wheeling visitor to Las Vegas casinos, even though Garrison did not gamble at all.[4389] Garrison was described as having a special Las Vegas connection who was a lieutenant of a New Orleans mobster.[4390] Garrison was reported by *Life* as being granted a five-thousand-dollar credit at the cashier's cage, the implication was that Garrison used the credit during his alleged gambling.[4391]

Time magazine also pitched in to help, as Garrison put it in his book *ON THE TRAIL OF THE ASSASSINS*:[4392]

> "Around the time the *Life* article about my fictional gaming proclivities in Las Vegas, *Time* magazine – a sister publication of *Life*'s and a part of the Luce empire – ran a series of articles on our investigation. It was pictured as an indefensible sham, and I was a demented buffoon, hungry for headlines."[4393]

When Clay Shaw was indicted Garrison was attacked by the mainstream media, including *Newsweek*, *Time*, The *New York Times*, *The New York Post*, *The Saturday Evening Post*, etc.[4394] In *Newsweek*'s May 15, 1967 issue under the heading The JFK Conspiracy, Hugh Aynesworth wrote:[4395]

> "Jim Garrison is right, there has been a conspiracy in New Orleans, but it is a plot of Garrison's own making. It is a scheme to concoct a fantastic "solution" to the death of John F. Kennedy and to make it stick. In this case the district attorney and his staff have been indirect parties to the death of one man and have humiliated, harassed and financially gutted several others."[4396]

> "Indeed, Garrison's tactics have been even more questionable than his case. I have evidence that one of the strapping D.A.'s investigators offered an unwilling "witness" $3,000 and a job with an airline – if only he would "fill in the facts" of an alleged meeting to plot the death of the president. I also know that when the D.A.'s office learned that this entire bribery attempt had been tape recorded two of Garrison's men returned to the "witness" and, he says, threatened him with physical harm."[4397]

Garrison, in his book *ON THE TRAIL OF THE ASSASSINS*, said that:[4398]

> "Ainsworth, who seemed a gentle and fair enough man when he interviewed me for several hours in my home, never did get around to revealing whose life our office had shortened. As for the $3,000 bribe, by the time I came across Aynesworth's

revelation, the witness our office had supposedly offered it to, Alvin Babeouf, had admitted to us that it had never happened. Aynesworth, of course, never explained what he did with the "evidence" allegedly in his possession, and the so-called bribery tape recording had not, in fact, ever existed."[4399]

"If this article was a typical Aynesworth product one could hardly help but wonder how a newsman with so rampant an imagination could continue to find a market for his stories. Yet, in fairness to Aynesworth, I must say that this "news" story was all too typical of what my office staff found itself reading in newspaper and magazine articles by writers from distant cities who had not the remotest awareness of what my office had been attempting to accomplish."[4400]

"James Phelan, who had written a highly supportive lead article for the *Saturday Evening Post* about my office's success in fighting crime in New Orleans, ("The Vice Man Commeth"), returned to do an article about the JFK investigation. In a piece entitled "Rush to Judgement in New Orleans", Phelan claimed that Perry Russo never told Assistant D.A. Andrew Sciambra about any conspiracy until he was "drugged." The clear implication was that our office had drugged Russo and then planted the conspiracy story in his brain while he was in a highly suggestible state. The truth, of course, was quite different. In fact, Phelan himself was aware of what Russo had told us about the conspiracy well before it occurred to me that we might be able to verify Russo's testimony with medically supervised hypnosis and Sodium Pentathol. I knew this because I was the one who first told Phelan about Russo's story. Phelan's colorful fiction later fell apart at Clay Shaw's trial when it was made clear that Russo had provided Sciambra with the full description of all significant events prior to any medical treatments. Moreover, as was obvious to the reporters in Baton Rouge, Russo gave interviews to the press in which he discussed a conspiracy – although he did not know at the time that Shaw and Bertrand were one and the same – before he ever met with Sciambra."[4401]

"The simple truth is that public officials really do not go unobserved so long by the people who elect them. I have never heard of a district attorney who was able to build a career on drugging witnesses so they would say whatever he ordered them to say."[4402]

In the spring of 1967 Walter Sheridan came to New Orleans to create an investigative special for NBC with Garrison and his office as the target of the investigation.[4403] They had been threatening Gordon Novel's ex-wife to try to get her to tell lies about Garrison, and she warned Garrison.[4404] The NBC special aired in June of 1967.[4405] Garrison got the FCC to force NBC to give him time for rebuttal.[4406] CBS then did a hit piece where they supported the Warren Commission and cut Garrison from 30 minutes to 30 seconds.[4407]

Comedian Mort Sahl had arranged with Johnny Carson for Garrison to appear on Carson's show.[4408] He did this by putting Carson on the spot in front of Carson's live audience.[4409] When Carson reluctantly agreed, Sahl told Garrison and he agreed.[4410] When Garrison went to the studios a day early, as requested, they grilled him for hours and recorded his answers.[4411] They then prepared "gotcha" questions for Carson to hit Garrison with while on the air.[4412] Garrison's appearance on the Carson show made it apparent that NBC was doing its best to suppress Garrison's point of view.[4413]

Garrison survived the attack on his personal life, although the ordeal cost him the job he wanted and was so well suited for. He continued to try to get the truth out about the Kennedy assassination.

Garrison was an elected official who challenged the Deep State and they threw everything they had at him. Being an elected official made Garrison particularly vulnerable to the multi-level attack where they find *something* to charge him with and then try him both in court and in the court of public opinion. Even if only *some* of the mud sticks, it may be enough to get the voters to remove him from office. This tactic will later be used against President Trump.

The House Assassinations Committee – The Second Whitewash

The House Select Committee on Assassinations (HSCA) started as an honest attempt to investigate the murders of John F. Kennedy and Martin Luther King, Jr. Unfortunately for the American people, it too was compromised by the Deep State and ultimately became a second whitewash. The HSCA only grudgingly admitted that, yes there was overwhelming evidence of another shooter, but not to worry about it. Since evidence of another shooter meant that therefore President Kennedy was murdered as a result of a conspiracy, they threw the mafia under the bus as the likely additional conspirators. That way no one had to admit that it was the government itself, the Deep State, which needed to be investigated. Move along folks, nothing to see here.

This chapter is organized into four sections:

1. What prompted the HSCA? – describes how author Mark Lane tapped into a groundswell of interest among the American people to take another look at the Kennedy assassination

2. How did the HSCA get off track? – describes how it started off with the intention to do the right thing but was captured by the Deep State and was kept from doing much real investigating

3. How did the HSCA function? – describes the dysfunctional way the HSCA operated while hamstrung by the strictures imposed on it by the Deep State and how the HSCA staff struggled to accomplish something meaningful in spite of the limitations they worked under

4. What were the HSCA's conclusions? – describes how the HSCA ended up doing some useful work and bringing some information to light – including that there were shots from the front

What Prompted the HSCA?

In 1975 Mark Lane started his campaign for what eventually became the House Select Committee on Assassinations (HSCA) legislation.[4414] Along the way he got an FOIA court order for the government to start releasing documents.[4415] The argument he used on the judge was that, if Oswald was a lone nut gunman, then there was no 'national security' argument to keeping all the documents secret.[4416] Among the documents released was an internal CIA review of his book *RUSH TO JUDGEMENT*.[4417] Also included were instructions from the CIA to media "assets" on how to discredit any critics of the CIA, the FBI or the Warren Commission.[4418] There were even specific instructions on how to smear Mark Lane.[4419] Then Senator Richard Schweiker got in touch with Lane and he was able to have input into what became the Church Committee.[4420] Senator Schweiker thought the Warren Report had "collapsed like a house of cards."[4421] In 1976 there were over 100 congressional sponsors of the HSCA legislation.[4422] Lane kept up his campaign and was ultimately successful in getting enough support to get the legislation passed.[4423] In 1991 81% of Americans believed that there was a conspiracy to kill Kennedy, and this had been true for years, going back as far as 1976.[4424]

On August 7, 1976 the body of mobster Johnny Roselli, one of the links between the CIA and organized crime leaders involved in Castro's assassination plots, was found mutilated, stuffed into a drum floating in Biscayne Bay.[4425] The next month the House of Representatives established the House Select Committee on Assassinations (HSCA).[4426]

How Did the HSCA Get Off Track?

The HSCA started out as a legitimate attempt to investigate the murders of John F. Kennedy and Martin Luther King, Jr. The critics of the Warren Report had raised enough doubts among the voters that there was a groundswell of interest in an official investigation. The closest thing to a real investigation was Jim Garrison's prosecution of Clay Shaw, and Shaw was a peripheral figure in the plot. The last thing the Deep State wanted was a real investigation. The first investigation, the Warren Commission, had been a whitewash, so there had yet to be a real official federal investigation of the Kennedy assassination. The public had requested another investigation and Johnson wasn't there to appoint a commission that he could control. Now the Deep State had a problem. They had to figure out how to get control of the HSCA so that it did not run a real investigation. The Kennedy assassination was less fifteen years before the HSCA, so some of the principal players were still alive and liable for prosecution. Some of the witnesses were still alive. Some evidence still existed. The Deep State was not going to just allow the HSCA to do its job. They were going to attack the HSCA on multiple levels while killing off the most important witnesses.

On October 10, 1976 HSCA Chairman Thomas Downing of Virginia appointed Philadelphia First Assistant District Attorney Richard Sprague as Chief Counsel and Staff Director and Sprague announced he would conduct the Kennedy probe as a murder investigation.[4427] The CIA and FBI immediately tried to gag the HSCA.[4428]

The first thing the CIA did was refuse to give the HSCA any information unless Richard Sprague agreed to sign a non-disclosure agreement that forced him to keep quiet on anything he learned, forever.[4429] Sprague refused to sign, asking how he could "possibly sign an agreement with an agency I'm supposed to be investigating."[4430]

Robert Tannenbaum was a lawyer with the District Attorney's office in New York who later became chief of homicide and bureau chief of the criminal courts before Sprague hired him to run the HSCA investigation.[4431] Author Mark Lane, in his book *LAST WORD: MY INDICTMENT OF THE CIA IN THE MURDER OF JFK*, described the backgrounds of Sprague and Tannenbaum and said that:[4432]

> "Both Sprague and Tannenbaum were honest, intelligent and skillful lawyers committed to learning and publishing the truth. When both the CIA and the FBI, aided by powerful media allies, began the campaign to have Sprague fired, Rep. Harold Ford, a member of the HSCA, stated that "the FBI has hired former agents to lobby with Congress against the continuation of the Select Committee."[4433]

The HSCA started out well, with Sprague and Tanenbaum and Representative Thomas Downing from Virginia as the chairman.[4434] Downing was supportive of doing it right.[4435] They were not going to make the same mistake the Warren Commission made and rely on the FBI and CIA for their information.[4436] They were going to have their own investigation staff, for which they would need a budget of $6.5 million.[4437] They were going to do a professional job and get to the truth.[4438] At first, they were going to give Sprague the $6.5M budget he requested.[4439] Then Downing announced he was going to retire at the end of his term.[4440] His retirement gave the Deep State the opening they needed.

On November 27, 1976 David Atlee Phillips was questioned by the HSCA about the CIA giving the Warren Commission photographs, tape recordings and transcripts from Mexico City, where a man misidentified as Oswald visited the Soviet embassy.[4441] Phillips lied and said that the tape recordings were routinely destroyed before the Kennedy assassination and were therefore unavailable.[4442] Mark Lane then delivered to Tannenbaum a copy of an FBI memo which proved that the tapes had not been destroyed because the FBI had listened to the tapes after the assassination and therefore the tapes had still existed.[4443] Phillips was called back and asked to repeat his testimony and then handed the memo which proved he had just perjured himself.[4444] Phillips took the document without a word, got up and left the building.[4445]

The reaction of the Deep State was predictable. They were outraged. They were not going to let the HSCA get away with a real investigation, especially with the convenient resignation of Downing. Once he left, the Deep State had an opening to capture the HSCA.[4446] Sprague did not realize at first that, once Downing left, his support had collapsed.[4447] Things went downhill from there.

The Deep State, including the mainstream media, had mobilized to cripple the HSCA. Author James DiEugenio, in his book *DESTINY BETRAYED*, documents that the same media attack that happened to Jim Garrison happened to Richard Sprague, even though Sprague had a distinguished career before and after his time at the HSCA:[4448]

> "The first attacks on Sprague began with the *Los Angeles Times*. These were then picked up and amplified by the *New York Times*. And then the *Washington Post* jumped into it. Their reporter was Walter Pincus, who called the HSCA in February of 1977, "perhaps the worst example of Congressional inquiry run amok." The man who led the charge at the *LA Times* was, predictably, Jack Nelson. The reporter who previously went after Jim Garrison. At the *New York Times*, something very revealing occurred. The first reporter that the *Times* had on the beat was Ben Franklin. Franklin had covered the prosecution of Tony Boyle by Sprague. And he had given Sprague some fair press so far. But at about the time of Sprague's budget submission, they replaced Franklin with David Burnham. Burnham went to the newspaper morgue in Philadelphia and wrote a long series about Sprague's career in the Philadelphia DA's office. He picked five small points of controversy in Sprague's illustrious

eighteen-year career. When the series was over, the *Times* ran an editorial asking Sprague to resign. Once this happened, Burnham was rotated out of the assignment."[4449]

Sprague decided to subpoena the CIA's records.[4450] Shortly afterwards, the attempt to get the committee reconstituted was blocked, and one of the critics of the approach that Sprague was taking with the HSCA was Robert Michel of Illinois who accused Sprague of wanting to investigate the CIA.[4451] Sprague agreed that was his intention, and also later agreed that was the beginning of the end of his tenure with the HSCA.[4452]

On January 7, 1977 William Pawley died under suspicious circumstances before he could be questioned by an investigator for the House Select Committee on Assassinations (HSCA).[4453] On March 29, 1977 Chicago mafia boss Sam Giancana's hitman, Chuck Nicoletti, was murdered before he could testify. His boss, Sam Giancana, had already been killed two years earlier to keep him from talking to the Church Committee.[4454] On April 5, 1977 Anti-Castro Cuban exile Carlos Prio Socarras was murdered before he could testify before the HSCA.[4455]

Author Gaeton Fonzi was an investigator for the HSCA, and he thought Sprague was forced out.[4456] He was of the opinion that the Washington establishment was not going to fund the HSCA going forward if Sprague stayed on because Sprague wanted a real investigation and the establishment did not.[4457] In his book *THE LAST INVESTIGATION*, Fonzi documents the following series of events:[4458]

> "On February 1, 1977 – The House Rules Committee, deviating from its normal procedure of automatically reconstituting standing committees from the previous congressional session, gives the Assassinations Committee funding for only two months and an order to justify its existence during that two-month period. The Committee and Chief Counsel Sprague had been under heavy attack by the major media, notably the *New York Times* and politicians claiming Sprague is planning to employ hidden tape recorders and lie detectors in the probe. Attacks have increased since Sprague, refusing to use other federal agencies in the investigation as the Warren Commission did, said he needed $6.5 Million for the first year of investigation. With Downing's retirement, Texas Democrat Henry Gonzalez assumes chairmanship of the committee."[4459]

"On February 11, 1977, angered by Sprague's refusal to relinquish the power of staff appointments to him, Gonzalez begins a feud with Sprague that culminates in Gonzalez firing Sprague and ordering the Capitol police to evict the chief counsel from his office – within hours, Gonzalez's dismissal of Sprague is rescinded by the other members of the committee."[4460]

"On March 1, 1977, frustrated by the lack of support from his fellow committee members, Gonzalez resigns as chairman, calls Sprague an "unconscionable scoundrel." Ohio Congressman Louis Stokes is appointed the new committee chairman."[4461]

"On March 16, 1977, with general congressional support for continuing the Assassinations Committee fading as a result of its internal feuding, Sprague offers to resign if committee members feel he is a millstone that would prevent the committee's reconstitution. The members refuse his offer."[4462]

"On March 29, 1977, in Florida, George de Mohrenschildt dies of a shotgun wound to the head hours after receiving a notice from HSCA investigator Fonzi that he is being sought to testify. That evening in Washington, with the committee on the verge of losing a House vote for reconstitution and funding, Chief Counsel Sprague resigns. The next morning, the news of de Mohrenschildt's death and Sprague's resignation produce a victory for the Committee's continuation, although at $2.5 Million per year, with much less funding than Sprague had requested."[4463]

"On May 6, 1977 Carlos Prio, former president of Cuba linked to the mob's control of Havana casinos and involved with Frank Sturgis in anti-Castro activities, kills himself outside his Miami beach home before he can be questioned by Committee investigator Fonzi."[4464]

"On May 13, 1977, in an interview with *New York Times* reporter Robert Sam Anson, former Committee Chief Counsel Sprague says he believes his problems with Gonzalez and certain members of Congress about funding was a smoke screen, that his conflict with the CIA was the underlying source of his troubles. If he had to do it all over again, he said, he would begin by probing "Oswald's ties to the Central Intelligence Agency.""[4465]

While looking for a replacement for Sprague, Stansfield Turner, then the Director of the CIA, was clear that he would not cooperate so Supreme Court Justice Arthur Goldberg turned down the job of heading up the HSCA.[4466] Then they hired G. Robert Blakey, who thought the mafia was involved in the Kennedy hit and was friendly with the CIA and trusted them.[4467] So, Richard Sprague resigned and was replaced by G. Robert Blakey, and after Sprague was forced out Tannenbaum was replaced by Gary Cornwell.[4468] Blakey agreed to allow the CIA to filter what the HSCA could see.[4469] Cornwell then announced that the time for "foraging" was over and now the HSCA must limit itself to issues which could be covered in the limited time remaining before writing a final report.[4470]

Author James DiEugenio, in his book *DESTINY BETRAYED*, points out that:[4471]

> "When Robert Blakey took charge of the House Select Committee on Assassinations he agreed to do something that Richard Sprague would not. In return for access to classified materials, members and employees of the committee signed agreements pledging not to disclose any information they gathered while doing their work. Then, when Blakey, Gary Cornwell and Dick Billings edited the report and volumes, the agencies they made agreements with were allowed to veto what information was included in the published volumes."[4472]

Blakey relied on the CIA and FBI for his input and agreed to have George Joannides as the CIA-assigned liaison to make sure he and the HSCA never got to see any actual evidence unless the CIA wanted them to.[4473] George Joannides was involved in the CIA operations in 1963 and was the CIA officer in charge of one of the anti-Castro Cuban exile groups and was therefore the worst possible choice if you wanted the truth.[4474] He would have been called as a material witness if the HSCA was run the way it should have been run.[4475]

On October 31, 1977 Richard Helms, Director of the CIA pleaded guilty to lying to the Church Senate Intelligence Committee about the CIA's involvement in overthrowing Salvador Allende in Chile.[4476]

On November 18, 1977 Cuban exile leader Manuel Artime, a close associate of E. Howard Hunt, died at the age of 45 within weeks of being told he has cancer and before he can be questioned by the HSCA.[4477]

The HSCA wasn't born into captivity like the Warren Commission, so The Deep State had found it necessary to capture the HSCA and crippled it. This way the HSCA was guaranteed not to produce anything of real danger to the Deep State.

How Did the HSCA Function?

Gaeton Fonzi, in his book *THE LAST INVESTIGATION*, documents what happened on June 12, 1978:[4478]

> "Blakey announces that, because of an unforeseen budget crunch, there will have to be a drastic reduction in committee staff personnel, when the specific cuts are later announced, two-thirds of the committee's investigative staff are dismissed."[4479]

> "Of the 25 staffers given their walking papers, the majority were investigators. In June, just before the cut, the Committee employed 118 persons; in the end, only 83 staffers remained. Of those, only four were Kennedy assassination investigators."[4480]

Author Gaeton Fonzi, in his book *THE LAST INVESTIGATION*, describes the work of Robert Groden, who was hired by the HSCA as their photographic expert:[4481]

> ""One of the first things I did," Groden recalls, "was to ask to see the autopsy photographs in the National Archives. I wanted to find out how it was the Warren Commission concluded the shots came from the rear when all the doctors at Parkland Hospital, every one of them, wrote in their reports that Kennedy's head was blasted out. When I saw the autopsy photographs I was shocked. After years in photo optic work I knew what I saw, and what I saw was a matte line in the photograph of the back of the president's head. That's when two photographic elements come together visually and there's an overlap. I saw a soft edged matte insertion forgery of very high quality which made it appear as if there was a small wound of entry in the rear of the president's head.""[4482]

> "Groden did some photo-optical tests on copies of the photographs to confirm what he saw. "Then," he says, "I wrote a report about it to Blakey saying that based on my professional opinion the autopsy photographs of the President's head had been retouched.""[4483]

> "Says Groden: "Blakey suppressed my results. He refused to let me present my evidence to the Committee. I was a consultant who wasn't permitted to consult.""[4484]

Fonzi also said that Blakey never wanted to follow up on the report by Groden, and then Blakey said they had to finish up and produce a report even if it meant they would not really investigate what they were supposed to investigate.[4485] After that the motto of the group became "Reality is Irrelevant" and they had shirts printed with that tag line on the front. In Fonzi's book, *THE LAST INVESTIGATION*, there is a picture of one of the staff modeling one of the shirts.[4486]

A week after Groden submitted that report a very strange incident occurred at HSCA Committee headquarters.[4487] The CIA had agreed to allow some evidence to be kept in a secure area at Committee headquarters.[4488] The CIA security representative, Regis Blahut, turned out to be the one who had gone into the secure area to look at the evidence, then he blurted to a reporter "there are other things involved that are detrimental to other things" and the CIA then fired Blahut.[4489]

The HSCA's Conclusions

Author Gaeton Fonzi, in his book *THE LAST INVESTIGATION*, documents that the HSCA concluded that there was a 95% chance that a fourth shot came from the grassy knoll and therefore concluded that Kennedy was assassinated as the result of a conspiracy:[4490]

> "On December 29, 1978, after further acoustical tests at Dealey Plaza, and a reevaluation of Dr. Barger's earlier analysis, two other acoustical consultants, Mark Weiss and Ernest Aschkenasy, testify there is more than a 95 percent probability of a shot having been fired from the grassy knoll."[4491]

> "On March 29, 1979 the House Assassinations Committee issues its report, concluding that President Kennedy was probably assassinated by Lee Harvey Oswald in a conspiracy with other unknown individuals. Chief Counsel Robert Blakey announces his conclusion that "the mob did it.""[4492]

Fonzi also said that the HSCA did not fulfill its mandate to investigate the death of President Kennedy.[4493]

Why This Matters Today

The U.S. Government continues to suppress documents relating to the Kennedy assassination to this day.[4494] The assassinations of the Kennedys are relevant today because the Deep State is still at it, and we need to start by recognizing that fact so we can deal with it. The Deep State is, as I write this, trying once again to overturn the will of the voters. The only difference between 1963 and 2018 is that they're no longer using bullets.

In 1963 the Deep State – the crooked politicians, the intelligence community, the mafia, the FBI and the mainstream media (among others) got together and decided to get rid of President Kennedy. In August of 1963 the polls showed John Kennedy running well ahead of any potential Republican presidential candidates.[4495] On October 13, 1963 President Kennedy had an approval rating of 57 percent.[4496] He was therefore very likely to be reelected the next year.[4497] If the Deep State wanted Kennedy out, they were going to have to take him out themselves because the voters liked him and wanted to keep him for another term. The Deep State decided to kill Kennedy and thereby replace him with Lyndon Johnson.

They also very likely did the same to Robert Kennedy as he was just about to win the 1968 presidential election.

The same cast of characters is trying once more to overturn the will of the voters. Recently the crooked politicians, the intelligence community, the Department of Justice, the FBI and the mainstream media have been trying to get rid of President Trump. That's why what happened in 1963 is still relevant today. The Deep State rides again.

In 1963 the Deep State got what it wanted and America and the world paid the price. One of the consequences of the Kennedy assassination was the Vietnam War. Kennedy would have pulled out of Vietnam before we sent combat troops. This would have been painful, but not nearly as painful for America and Vietnam as what happened. Another consequence was that Hoover was able to ramp up programs like COINTELPRO where the FBI was used against African Americans. The surveillance state created by J. Edgar Hoover is well documented by author Betty Medsger in her book *THE BURGLARY* about a group of American citizens who decided to break into an FBI office in Media, Pennsylvania in 1971 to steal documents and publish them in the media to expose what was going on at the FBI. These are just two examples of the larger price we paid for letting the Deep State take over.

The American people are in a fight with the Deep State for control of our country, and we need to acknowledge that fact. By my count, the effort to dump Trump is the third attempt by the Deep State to overturn the will of the voters. The first two, President John F. Kennedy and Senator Robert F. Kennedy, succeeded. John F. Kennedy was already president and he was murdered so that the Deep State could have Johnson, who would follow the policies the Deep State wanted. Johnson was in alignment with the CIA and the Pentagon on making war instead of peace. Robert F. Kennedy was on the verge of becoming president, and he was killed to keep those policies from being reversed and to keep his brother's murder from being investigated. Robert Kennedy was very likely to have been elected president in 1968, and taking him out as he was about to enter the White House amounts to the same thing. The Deep State wanted Nixon instead of Bobby Kennedy because Nixon was a Cold Warrior and he was not a Kennedy, so they killed Bobby and got Nixon in the White House.

Starting during the 2016 presidential campaign, the Deep State spied on candidate Trump, tapping his phones. The mainstream media wing of the Deep State has done its best from the beginning to stall or stop Trump's candidacy and presidency. Once he was elected, the Deep State tried to have the Electoral College overturn the will of the voters by trying to convince the electors not to confirm Trump in office once he had won the election. When that effort failed, the Deep State tried to use the 25th amendment to the Constitution to have Trump removed from office. This amendment provides for the removal of the president if the vice president and a majority of the cabinet agree that the president is unable to perform the duties of president. Here the mainstream media pitched in again with "news" stories of Trump being mentally unfit for office. That effort failed, and then there was talk of impeachment. While all this was going on, the Deep State tried to destroy Trump's campaign and then his presidency with a completely fake dossier. This collection of made-up documents was used as the basis for false accusations that Trump had done some disgusting and potentially illegal things involving Russia and working with the Russians to rig the U.S. presidential election. The fake dossier claimed that Trump was in collusion with the Russians to help him win the White House, and it became the basis for the investigation headed by Special Counsel Robert Mueller. This investigation is just another attempt by the Deep State to remove Trump from office by any means necessary. Using 'collusion with the Russians to subvert the U.S. electoral process,' this investigation in search of a crime is the Deep State's attempt to find *something* to use or charge Trump with in order to get rid of him.

Hillary Clinton was supposed to become president, at least that was what the Deep State was expecting to have happen. It appears not to have occurred to them that Trump might actually win and that some of their actions would subsequently come to light under a Trump administration.

While Secretary of State, Hillary Clinton appears to have had a pay-to-play scheme going to sell influence. Author Gregg Jarrett, in his book *THE RUSSIA HOAX: THE ILLICIT SCHEME TO CLEAR HILLARY CLINTON AND FRAME DONALD TRUMP*, documents how FBI Director James Comey, in 2016, launched an effort to both exonerate Hillary Clinton for her multiple crimes and find some way to use the legal system to get rid of Donald Trump. Hillary Clinton had sold influence as Secretary of State and had used a private email system to hide these dealings from public scrutiny. One of the reasons that government officials are not allowed to use private email systems for official business is so that they cannot hide what they are doing. One of the reasons for the Freedom of Information Act (FOIA) is to make sure that the public can force public officials to be transparent about the things they do with the authority and power entrusted to them by the public. Hillary Clinton circumvented all those controls by using her own private email server for official government business. Lyndon Johnson made tens of millions of dollars selling influence in the time he was an elected official. Hillary and Bill Clinton made hundreds of millions of dollars selling influence while Hillary was Secretary of State and as a presidential candidate.[4498] This was made possible by the perception that she would soon be back in the White House, and the Clintons mined a rich vein of people willing to pay for access to American power. While Hillary Clinton was Secretary of State, the Russians were able, with Hillary's help, to buy a controlling stake in Uranium One, a company that owned uranium mines in the United States.[4499] Frank Giustra was involved in the deal, and he gave the Clintons over $145 million.[4500] Bill Clinton got a $500,000 speaking fee from a Russian bank just before the Uranium One deal closed.[4501] That vein became considerably less lucrative once Hillary Clinton lost the 2016 presidential election and was no longer seen as having influence to peddle.

In an article titled "Donations to Clinton Foundation plunged along with Hillary's election defeat," the *NEW YORK POST*, on November 18, 2017 said that:

> "Contributions to the Bill, Hillary & Chelsea Clinton Foundation fell by 42%, from $108 million to $63 million in 2016 – the year that Hillary Clinton lost her bid for president..."

Author Gregg Jarrett, in his book *THE RUSSIA HOAX*, points out that:[4502]

> "Once Hillary Clinton lost the presidential election, contributions to the Clinton Foundation and the Clinton Global Initiative began to dwindle. What foreign business or government wanted to shell out big bucks for nothing in return? Hillary was no longer in office, with little prospects for returning to power. She was in no position to confer benefits in exchange for money. No chance for a quid pro quo of favors for cash."[4503]

Jarrett also refers to two excellent quotes from author Peter Schweizer's well-researched book *CLINTON CASH* to make his point:[4504]

> "Who else in American politics would be so audacious as to have one spouse accept money from foreign governments and businesses while the other charted American foreign policy? Or would permit one spouse to conduct sensitive negotiations with foreign entities while in some instances the other collected large speaking fees from some of those same entities?"[4505]

> "Meanwhile, bureaucratic or legislative obstacles were mysteriously cleared or approvals granted within the purview of his wife, the powerful secretary of state. Huge donations then flowed into the Clinton Foundation while Bill received enormous speaking fees underwritten by the very businessmen who benefitted from these apparent interventions."[4506]

To exonerate Clinton for the email abuses, Comey simply took over the function of the U.S. Attorney General and said that, in his opinion, Hillary should not be prosecuted for her illegal use of a private email system to hide her actions.[4507] Comey used the lame excuse that Clinton did not intend to break the law as his reason for not recommending prosecution.[4508] Comey had written this statement long before the 'investigation' was over, demonstrating that the 'investigation' was just for show.[4509] Since the Deep State did not want Clinton prosecuted, there was no one with both the power and the will to object, and Clinton was not prosecuted, either for the email abuses or the influence peddling.

Author Gregg Jarrett, in his book *THE RUSSIA HOAX*, goes into detail on how the 'investigation' into Clinton's email activities was compromised. In his chapter on "The Fix" he details how the various players were used to make sure the end result was predictable. It makes interesting reading, and confirms how the internal workings of the Deep State function to get the outcome they want.

The other objective was to destroy Trump, and to do this Comey had to use a dossier that was created out of thin air by the Clinton presidential campaign. The Clinton camp paid millions for this made-up collection of documents with which to instigate legal proceedings against Donald Trump. And, once this process was started, the corrupt political wing of the Deep State leaked the dossier to the mainstream media wing, who took the ball and ran with it, making as much as possible out of the allegations of 'collusion' with the Russians.[4510] There were a few problems with all of this. First, the whole thing was based on a fictional dossier that turned out to have been made up by the Clinton campaign. Second, Trump was not guilty of collusion with the Russians. Third, collusion in politics is not a crime.[4511] This was all an attempt to frame Trump for crimes he did not commit. This is an attempt by the Deep State to, once again, overturn the will of the voters.

While the 2016 presidential campaign was going on, the Clinton campaign and the Democratic National Committee (DNC) paid to have dirt on Trump created. Author Theodore Roosevelt Malloch, in his book *THE PLOT TO DESTROY TRUMP: HOW THE DEEP STATE FABRICATED THE RUSSIAN DOSSIER TO SUBVERT THE PRESIDENT*, documents that:[4512]

> "We know that the Democratic National Committee and the Clinton campaign – using Fusion GPS and the law firm Perkins Coie to funnel the money – financed the dossier."[4513]

Fusion GPS paid retired British spy Christopher Steele $168,000 to create a fictional dossier on Trump's alleged ties to Russia.[4514] Fusion GPS was founded by Glenn Simpson, a longtime Democrat.[4515] The Clinton campaign and the Democratic National Committee (DNC) then had the law firm, Perkins Coie, pay for the dossier.[4516]

Author Theodore Malloch, in his book, *THE PLOT TO DESTROY TRUMP*, refers to Professor Stephen F. Cohen of Princeton and points out that John Brennan, CIA Director from 2013 to 2017, shared the dossier with James Clapper, Director of National Intelligence from from 2010 to 2017, and FBI Director James Comey to get the anti-Trump ball rolling:[4517]

"It was John Brennan at the CIA who started the whole thing. Brennan played a crucial role in promoting Russia gate from the get-go. He briefed members of Congress and President Obama as early as July or August of 2016, using Steele's dossier. He shared information with James Clapper and FBI Director, James Comey."[4518]

Malloch also claims:[4519]

"It was Brennan who provided information to Christopher Steele – he spoon-fed it to him. Steele did not have deep contacts in Russia since he had not been there for about twenty years. He was badly out of touch. Steele's sources are incredible. He doesn't and won't name them."[4520]

Author Gregg Jarrett, in his book *THE RUSSIA HOAX*, points out that:[4521]

"What exactly did Brennan do? When He learned of the "dossier," he allegedly gave the information contained therein to the FBI and Democrats on Capitol Hill, and certain members of the media were alerted. According to his testimony before the House Intelligence Committee, Brennan seemed to acknowledge that he was among the first individuals to have access to the "dossier" and soon alerted the FBI which then opened its Trump-Russia investigation."[4522]

In June 2016 Bruce Ohr was an Associate Deputy General in the Department of Justice, and he met with Christopher Steele and with Glenn Simpson.[4523] Simpson of Fusion GPS was trying to convince Ohr to use the dossier to start an investigation of Trump. At the same time, Fusion GPS was paying Ohr's wife Nellie to provide opposition research on Trump.[4524] Maybe they learned this tactic (paying the spouse) from the Clintons.

Author Gregg Jarrett, in his book *THE RUSSIA HOAX*, points out that:[4525]

"Distilled to its essence, the scam worked like this: Clinton's campaign paid Simpson who paid Steele who allegedly got information from Moscow intended to damage Trump and help Clinton. Then the FBI and the Justice Department exploited the dubious information as a pretense to open an investigation of Trump, while the media ran with their stories intended to bring down the new president. The government abused its powers and the press was shamefully complicit."[4526]

"...the FBI is specifically prohibited from searching for evidence of a crime that does not exist under law. There must be "an articulable factual basis for the investigation" that indicates that a crime has or will take place."[4527]

"Former federal prosecutor Andrew McCarthy in writing about the Trump-Russia probe warned, "The government is not supposed to use its foreign-intelligence collection authority as a pretext for building criminal cases." Yet, this appears to be what the FBI did. Under the guise of a baseless counterintelligence probe, it began investigating the Republican candidate for president."[4528]

Using the fake dossier, the government eventually got an FISA (Foreign Intelligence Surveillance Act) warrant to tap the phone of a Trump aide named Carter Page.

Author Gregg Jarrett, in his book *THE RUSSIA HOAX*, points out that the House Intelligence Committee looked into the corrupt process by which the government claimed "probable cause" to get a FISA warrant and:[4529]

"The results of the committee's investigation were stunning. The FBI and DOJ *knew* that the "dossier" was unverified conjecture. They *knew* it was paid for by Clinton and Democrats and was politically motivated. They *knew* the person who compiled it despised Trump and harbored a clear bias. And they *knew* they could not spy on a Trump associate without the "dossier." Despite all this, the FBI and DOJ used it anyway, deceiving the court by actively withholding or obscuring every bit of vital information."[4530]

The dossier was first published in *Mother Jones* and, once it was published, the mainstream media wing of the Deep State takes the ball and runs with it.[4531] Then, in May of 2017, former FBI Director Robert Mueller is appointed as a special counsel to head up an investigation in search of a crime. And he hires a staff dominated by Deep State partisans who all have the same goal – get Trump.

Author Sidney Powell, in her book *LICENSED TO LIE: EXPOSING CORRUPTION IN THE DEPARTMENT OF JUSTICE*, details how the Justice Department has taken to using illegal tactics to convict innocent people of crimes they haven't committed. She gives several examples including the trial of Alaska Senator Ted Stevens. Stevens was wrongfully convicted of fraud just in time for him to lose his senate seat. This seat was key to changing the balance of power in the Senate. The conviction was later overturned, but it was too late for Ted Stevens or the Republican party to get back the senate seat. Powell describes in detail how the Justice Department used illegal tactics to both make up "evidence" of guilt and hide evidence favorable to the defense. This toxic combination allowed them to get a conviction. One of the tactics Powell describes is illegal witness intimidation – the prosecution threatens the witnesses with an indictment if they don't testify the way they're told. This tactic is used to both silences witnesses for the defense and creates false witnesses for the prosecution. Powell describes this from the perspective of having been an attorney defending innocent people. In his book *SILENT NO MORE: HOW I BECAME A POLITICAL PRISONER OF MUELLER'S "WITCH HUNT"* author Jerome Corsi describes these tactics from the perspective of having been a witness threatened with prison time if he does not say what the prosecution wants him to say. He was called by the Mueller team who were trying to frame President Trump for crimes he did not commit so they can have him thrown out of office. They wanted Corsi to claim to be a key link in a chain that led from Trump to the Russians so they could charge Trump with collusion with the Russians. They threatened Corsi with indictment and prosecution if he did not go along and help them get Trump. The Deep State is clearly out of control and needs to be reined in. The government is not supposed to be spending our tax money overthrowing the will of the voters. They are not supposed to be using the authority we delegate to them to get rid of the duly elected leaders we put in office. And they're not supposed to be bullying and threatening innocent people into lying under oath to help them "get" whoever they're targeting. They're also not supposed to be hiding exculpatory evidence from the defense. They believe themselves to be above the law. The law is something they use on other people, but they protect each other from subpoenas, indictment and prosecution.

In the early 1960's Allen Dulles himself admitted to the other Warren Commission members that a CIA agent or officer would lie under oath.[4532] Things have gone downhill since then. Now we have government employees from almost every agency who are willing to lie to Congressional oversight committees. And sometimes they don't even bother to lie, they simply refuse to answer questions. The Deep State not only rides again, it rides out of control.

Jason Chaffetz served as a U.S. Congressional Representative from Utah. While in the House, he served as the Chairman of the House Committee on Oversight and Government Reform. In his book *THE DEEP STATE*, he goes into detail on the abuses of power by the Deep State. In the last chapter he suggests some practical steps that could be taken to curb the Deep State, sorting them into three main categories:[4533]

> "We must start by empowering Congress to use, and perhaps modernize, existing constitutional checks against the executive branch that have fallen into disuse. We have to restore the penalties, rewards, and incentives that govern the federal workforce. And finally, we must expose corruption by bringing hidden things into the light."[4534]

Chaffetz also points out that, as it stands now, inheirent contempt power relies on the District Attorney for the District of Columbia, and that this concept must be abandoned because the D.A. does not always comply.[4535]

Chaffetz, in his book *THE DEEP STATE*, points out that:[4536]

> "A range of options exists for restoring to Congress the ability to enforce contempt citations. Legislation could be passed denying the district attorney the ability to substitute his own discretion for that of Congress. Congress could unilaterally impose fines, even going so far as to withhold the fines from federal paychecks. As a last resort, Congress could even return to the days of remanding into custody those unwilling to cooperate. Having failed to assert enforcement powers in the past, Congress must take some of the blame for the emergence of today's powerful Deep State, which now routinely refuses to cooperate with Congress."[4537]

Judicial Watch, for example, is more successful at getting information than Congressional oversight committees because they have a direct route to the courts.[4538] And the courts, unlike Congress, are willing to impose penalties like fines and imprisonment for noncompliance.[4539] Congress needs an expedited pathway to the courts for immediate consideration.[4540] The current system takes a few years to get to the merits of the case and this gives the agencies an incentive to stonewall.[4541] By the time the case gets to court the people pushing the case may no longer be in power or the situation could change in some other way to cause the issue to be dropped.[4542] On most matters that are not generating big headlines, the agencies know they can just withhold information and run out the clock, and this works in most cases.[4543]

Chaffetz also suggests other remedies. He suggests that prosecution be mandated for lying to Congress.[4544] He points out that the impeachment power of Congress should be used more often, and that Congress should use the power of the purse.[4545] He also acknowledges that Congress would first have to fix the broken budget process in order to use the power of the purse.[4546] Another suggestion is rescinding the ability of agencies to make de-facto laws.[4547] Finally, he points out that Federal workforce incentives need to be overhauled to restore accountability.[4548] He goes into each of these in detail in his book, *THE DEEP STATE*, and I highly recommend it to anyone wanting to know more.

Each generation is supposed to be good stewards of the things they are given and pass them on to the next generation in good shape. But that's not what's happening. Our generation has failed the next generation. The country I was born into just before Kennedy was murdered had considerably more freedom than the one we will be passing on to the next generation. The Deep State chips away at our Constitution a little every day while the rest of us are distracted. They do this while the rest of us are going about our business and working to support ourselves and our families. And the end result is that every generation gets a country that is a little less free than the last. Like the proverbial frog that gets boiled by raising the water temperature just a little at a time, we don't seem to notice the trend. But the result is the same. If we don't reverse the trend, then one day we will wake up and it will be too late. Jason Chaffetz has outlined the steps we need to demand from our elected representatives. We should take those steps while we still have the vote, and therefore the power, to take them.

Lincoln was concerned that government "of the people, by the people, for the people" should not be allowed to "perish from the earth." We owe it to the next generation to not let democracy slip through our fingers. We need to get control of the Deep State while we still have the power to do so.

Acknowledgements

Many people helped me create this book. My wife Joyce Browne tolerated my making time to write the book, and Randy Roth, Char Peck, Roger Brown, John Fortunato, Ray McGury, Mike Eynon, Lori Browne and Marv Lind all helped me by proofreading the rough draft and providing feedback to show me what I had missed.

Bibliography

1. Baker, Judyth, *ME & LEE*
2. Belzer, Richard and David Wayne, *DEAD WRONG*
3. Belzer, Richard and David Wayne, *HIT LIST*
4. Caro, Robert, *THE YEARS OF LYNDON JOHNSON – THE PATH TO POWER*
5. Caro, Robert, *THE YEARS OF LYNDON JOHNSON – MEANS OF ASCENT*
6. Caro, Robert, *THE YEARS OF LYNDON JOHNSON – MASTER OF THE SENATE*
7. Caro, Robert, *THE YEARS OF LYNDON JOHNSON – THE PASSAGE OF POWER*
8. Chaffetz, Jason, *THE DEEP STATE*
9. Childs, Allen, *WE WERE THERE*
10. Corsi, Jerome, *KILLING THE DEEP STATE*
11. Corsi, *SILENT NO MORE*
12. Corsi, Jerome, *WHO REALLY KILLED KENNEDY?*
13. Crenshaw, Charles, Jens Hansen and Gary Shaw, *JFK HAS BEEN SHOT*
14. DiEugenio, James, *DESTINY BETRAYED*
15. DiEugenio, James, *RECLAIMING PARKLAND*
16. Douglass, James, *JFK AND THE UNSPEAKABLE*
17. English, T.J., *HAVANA NOCTURNE*
18. Ernest, Barry, *THE GIRL ON THE STAIRS*
19. Fleming, Tim, *JFK AND THE END OF AMERICA*
20. Fonzi, Gaeton, *THE LAST INVESTIGATION*
21. Garrison, Jim, *ON THE TRAIL OF THE ASSASSINS*
22. Hack, Richard, *PUPPETMASTER: THE SECRET LIFE OF J. EDGAR HOOVER*
23. Hornberger, Jacob, *THE KENNEDY AUTOPSY*
24. Janney, Peter, *MARY'S MOSAIC*
25. Jarrett, Gregg, *THE RUSSIA HOAX*
26. Joesten, Joachim, *OSWALD: ASSASSIN OR FALL GUY?*
27. Kessler, Ronald, *The SECRETS OF THE FBI*
28. Kinzer, Stephen, *THE BROTHERS*
29. Lane, Mark, *LAST WORD*
30. Malloch, Theodore, *THE PLOT TO DESTROY TRUMP*
31. Margolis, Matt and Mark Noonan, *THE WORST PRESIDENT IN HISTORY*
32. Marrs, Jim, *CROSSFIRE*
33. McClellan, Barr, *BLOOD, MONEY & POWER*
34. Meagher, Sylvia, *ACCESSORIES AFTER THE FACT*

35. Medsger, *THE BURGLARY*
36. Minutaglio, Bill and Steven Davis, *DALLAS 1963*
37. Morley, Jefferson, *THE GHOST*
38. Nelson, Phillip, *LBJ: THE MASTERMIND OF THE JFK ASSASSINATION*
39. Newman, John, *OSWALD AND THE CIA*
40. Nolan, Patrick, *CIA ROGUES AND THE KILLING OF THE KENNEDYS*
41. North, Mark, *ACT OF TREASON*
42. North, Mark, *BETRAYAL IN DALLAS*
43. O'Reilly, Bill and Martin Dugard, *KILLING KENNEDY*
44. Pirro, Jeanine, *LIARS, LEAKERS, AND LIBERALS*
45. Powell, Sidney, *LICENSED TO LIE*
46. Russell, Dick, *THE MAN WHO KNEW TOO MUCH*
47. Schweizer, Peter, *CLINTON CASH*
48. Scott, Peter, *DEEP POLITICS ON OSWALD, MEXICO AND CUBA*
49. Shaw, Mark, *THE POISON PATRIARCH*
50. Shenon, Philip, *A CRUEL AND SHOCKING ACT*
51. Stone, Roger and Mike Colapietro, *THE MAN WHO KILLED KENNEDY*
52. Summers, Anthony, *NOT IN YOUR LIFETIME*
53. Talbot, David, *THE DEVIL'S CHESSBOARD*
54. Thomas, Donald, *HEAR NO EVIL*
55. Thompson, Josiah, *SIX SECONDS IN DALLAS*
56. VanDeMark, *ROAD TO DISASTER*
57. Ventura, Jesse and Dick Russell, *THEY KILLED OUR PRESIDENT*
58. Weberman, Alan and Michael Canfield, *COUP D'ETAT IN AMERICA*
59. Weiner, Tim, *ENEMIES: A HISTORY OF THE FBI*
60. Weiner, Tim, *LEGACY OF ASHES: A HISTORY OF THE CIA*

Index

End Notes (References)

1 Ernest, *THE GIRL ON THE STAIRS,* p. 287
2 Ernest, *THE GIRL ON THE STAIRS,* pp. 248-249
3 Ernest, *THE GIRL ON THE STAIRS,* pp. 248-249
4 Joesten, *OSWALD: ASSASSIN OR FALL GUY?,* p. 120
5 Joesten, *OSWALD: ASSASSIN OR FALL GUY?,* p. 120
6 Marrs, *CROSSFIRE,* p. 420
7 Summers, *NOT IN YOUR LIFETIME,* p. 85
8 Lane, *LAST WORD,* p. 16
9 Marrs, *CROSSFIRE,* pp. 421-422
10 Belzer & Wayne, *DEAD WRONG,* p. 88
11 Summers, *NOT IN YOUR LIFETIME,* p. 117
12 Summers, *NOT IN YOUR LIFETIME,* p. 117
13 Nelson, *LBJ: THE MASTERMIND OF THE JFK ASSASSINATION,* p. 396
14 Douglass, *JFK AND THE UNSPEAKABLE,* p. 113
15 Nelson, *LBJ: THE MASTERMIND OF THE JFK ASSASSINATION,* p. 608
16 Nelson, *LBJ: THE MASTERMIND OF THE JFK ASSASSINATION,* p. 376
17 Nelson, *LBJ: THE MASTERMIND OF THE JFK ASSASSINATION,* p. 376
18 Nelson, *LBJ: THE MASTERMIND OF THE JFK ASSASSINATION,* p. 603
19 Stone & Colapietro, *THE MAN WHO KILLED KENNEDY,* p. 350
20 Stone & Colapietro, *THE MAN WHO KILLED KENNEDY,* p. 353
21 Stone & Colapietro, *THE MAN WHO KILLED KENNEDY,* p. 377
22 Stone & Colapietro, *THE MAN WHO KILLED KENNEDY,* pp. 214-215
23 Nelson, *LBJ: THE MASTERMIND OF THE JFK ASSASSINATION,* pp. 37, 198
24 Nelson, *LBJ: THE MASTERMIND OF THE JFK ASSASSINATION,* pp. 39-40
25 Caro, *THE YEARS OF LYNDON JOHNSON – MEANS OF ASCENT,* p. 8
26 Caro, *THE YEARS OF LYNDON JOHNSON – MEANS OF ASCENT,* p. 8
27 McClellan, *BLOOD, MONEY & POWER,* p. 121
28 McClellan, *BLOOD, MONEY & POWER,* p. 132
29 McClellan, *BLOOD, MONEY & POWER,* p. 133
30 McClellan, *BLOOD, MONEY & POWER,* p. 133
31 Nelson, *LBJ: THE MASTERMIND OF THE JFK ASSASSINATION,* p. 616
32 McClellan, *BLOOD, MONEY & POWER,* p. 47
33 Nelson, *LBJ: THE MASTERMIND OF THE JFK ASSASSINATION,* p. 610

[34] McClellan, *BLOOD, MONEY & POWER*, p. 13

[35] Nelson, *LBJ: THE MASTERMIND OF THE JFK ASSASSINATION*, p. 616

[36] Nelson, *LBJ: THE MASTERMIND OF THE JFK ASSASSINATION*, p. 30

[37] McClellan, *BLOOD, MONEY & POWER*, pp. 91-92

[38] McClellan, *BLOOD, MONEY & POWER*, p. 92

[39] McClellan, *BLOOD, MONEY & POWER*, p. 93

[40] McClellan, *BLOOD, MONEY & POWER*, p. 95

[41] North, *BETRAYAL IN DALLAS*, p. 7

[42] Nelson, *LBJ: THE MASTERMIND OF THE JFK ASSASSINATION*, p. 36

[43] North, *ACT OF TREASON*, p. 354

[44] North, *ACT OF TREASON*, p. 354

[45] North, *ACT OF TREASON*, p. 230

[46] North, *ACT OF TREASON*, p. 477

[47] North, *ACT OF TREASON*, pp. 335-336

[48] Nelson, *LBJ: THE MASTERMIND OF THE JFK ASSASSINATION*, p. 307

[49] Nelson, *LBJ: THE MASTERMIND OF THE JFK ASSASSINATION*, p. 146-147

[50] North, *ACT OF TREASON*, p. 371

[51] Nelson, *LBJ: THE MASTERMIND OF THE JFK ASSASSINATION*, p. 147

[52] Stone & Colapietro, *THE MAN WHO KILLED KENNEDY*, p. 172

[53] Nelson, *LBJ: THE MASTERMIND OF THE JFK ASSASSINATION*, p. 147

[54] North, *ACT OF TREASON*, p. 395

[55] North, *ACT OF TREASON*, p. 77

[56] Stone & Colapietro, *THE MAN WHO KILLED KENNEDY*, p. 352-353

[57] North, *ACT OF TREASON*, p. 495

[58] North, *ACT OF TREASON*, p. 495

[59] North, *ACT OF TREASON*, p. 495

[60] Stone & Colapietro, *THE MAN WHO KILLED KENNEDY*, p. 201

[61] Stone & Colapietro, *THE MAN WHO KILLED KENNEDY*, p. 201

[62] McClellan, *BLOOD, MONEY AND POWER*, p. 126

[63] McClellan, *BLOOD, MONEY AND POWER*, p. 126

[64] McClellan, *BLOOD, MONEY AND POWER*, p. 126

[65] Stone & Colapietro, *THE MAN WHO KILLED KENNEDY*, p. 202

[66] Stone & Colapietro, *THE MAN WHO KILLED KENNEDY*, p. 202

[67] Stone & Colapietro, *THE MAN WHO KILLED KENNEDY*, p. 202

[68] McClellan, *BLOOD, MONEY AND POWER*, p. 168

[69] McClellan, *BLOOD, MONEY AND POWER*, p. 156

[70] McClellan, *BLOOD, MONEY AND POWER*, p. 126

[71] Nelson, *LBJ: THE MASTERMIND OF THE JFK ASSASSINATION*, p.232

[72] Nelson, *LBJ: THE MASTERMIND OF THE JFK ASSASSINATION*, p.233

[73] Nelson, *LBJ: THE MASTERMIND OF THE JFK ASSASSINATION*, pp. 232-234

[74] North, *BETRAYAL IN DALLAS*, pp. 31-32

[75] Nelson, *LBJ: THE MASTERMIND OF THE JFK ASSASSINATION*, p. 202

[76] North, *ACT OF TREASON*, p. 139

[77] North, *ACT OF TREASON*, p. 140

[78] Stone & Colapietro, *THE MAN WHO KILLED KENNEDY*, p. 206

[79] North, *ACT OF TREASON*, p. 142

[80] North, *ACT OF TREASON*, p. 142

[81] North, *ACT OF TREASON*, pp. 142-143

[82] North, *ACT OF TREASON*, pp. 142-143

[83] North, *ACT OF TREASON*, pp. 142-143

[84] North, *ACT OF TREASON*, pp. 157-158

[85] North, *ACT OF TREASON*, pp. 157-158

[86] North, *ACT OF TREASON*, pp. 157-158

[87] North, *ACT OF TREASON*, p. 158

[88] McClellan, *BLOOD, MONEY AND POWER*, p. 157

[89] McClellan, *BLOOD, MONEY AND POWER*, p. 157

[90] McClellan, *BLOOD, MONEY AND POWER*, p. 157

[91] Stone & Colapietro, *THE MAN WHO KILLED KENNEDY*, p. 211

[92] Nelson, *LBJ: THE MASTERMIND OF THE JFK ASSASSINATION*, p. 243

[93] Nelson, *LBJ: THE MASTERMIND OF THE JFK ASSASSINATION*, p. 243

[94] Nelson, *LBJ: THE MASTERMIND OF THE JFK ASSASSINATION*, p. 228

[95] McClellan, *BLOOD, MONEY AND POWER*, p. 158

[96] McClellan, *BLOOD, MONEY AND POWER*, pp. 158-159

[97] McClellan, *BLOOD, MONEY AND POWER*, pp. 158-159

[98] McClellan, *BLOOD, MONEY AND POWER*, p. 159

[99] Nelson, *LBJ: THE MASTERMIND OF THE JFK ASSASSINATION*, p. 226

[100] Nelson, *LBJ: THE MASTERMIND OF THE JFK ASSASSINATION*, p. 228

[101] Stone & Colapietro, *THE MAN WHO KILLED KENNEDY*, p.p 203-205

[102] McClellan, *BLOOD, MONEY AND POWER*, pp. 172-173

[103] North, *ACT OF TREASON*, p. 148

[104] Nelson, *LBJ: THE MASTERMIND OF THE JFK ASSASSINATION*, p. 228

[105] Nelson, *LBJ: THE MASTERMIND OF THE JFK ASSASSINATION*, p. 228

[106] Nelson, *LBJ: THE MASTERMIND OF THE JFK ASSASSINATION*, p. 228

[107] Stone & Colapietro, *THE MAN WHO KILLED KENNEDY*, p. 204

[108] Stone & Colapietro, *THE MAN WHO KILLED KENNEDY*, p. 204

[109] North, *ACT OF TREASON*, p. 148

[110] North, *ACT OF TREASON*, p. 149

[111] North, *ACT OF TREASON*, p. 149

[112] North, *ACT OF TREASON*, p. 149

[113] North, *ACT OF TREASON*, p. 149

[114] North, *ACT OF TREASON*, p. 149

[115] North, *ACT OF TREASON*, p. 150

[116] North, *ACT OF TREASON*, p. 152

[117] North, *ACT OF TREASON*, p. 152

[118] North, *ACT OF TREASON*, p. 156

[119] North, *ACT OF TREASON*, pp. 150-151

[120] North, *ACT OF TREASON*, p. 110

[121] North, *ACT OF TREASON*, p. 110

[122] North, *ACT OF TREASON*, p. 149

[123] North, *ACT OF TREASON*, p. 111

[124] North, *ACT OF TREASON*, p. 117

[125] McClellan, *BLOOD, MONEY AND POWER*, p. 168

[126] McClellan, *BLOOD, MONEY AND POWER*, p. 168

[127] McClellan, *BLOOD, MONEY AND POWER*, p. 160

[128] McClellan, *BLOOD, MONEY AND POWER*, p. 159

[129] Nelson, *LBJ: THE MASTERMIND OF THE JFK ASSASSINATION*, pp. 46-247

[130] North, *ACT OF TREASON*, p. 173

[131] Nelson, *LBJ: THE MASTERMIND OF THE JFK ASSASSINATION*, p. 204

[132] Nelson, *LBJ: THE MASTERMIND OF THE JFK ASSASSINATION*, p. 204

[133] Nelson, *LBJ: THE MASTERMIND OF THE JFK ASSASSINATION*, p. 204

[134] Nelson, *LBJ: THE MASTERMIND OF THE JFK ASSASSINATION*, pp. 204-205

[135] North, *ACT OF TREASON*, p. 215

[136] North, *ACT OF TREASON*, p. 217

[137] North, *ACT OF TREASON*, p. 218

[138] North, *ACT OF TREASON*, p. 219

[139] North, *ACT OF TREASON*, p. 222

[140] McClellan, *BLOOD, MONEY AND POWER*, p. 174

[141] North, *ACT OF TREASON*, p. 247

[142] North, *ACT OF TREASON*, p. 247

[143] North, *ACT OF TREASON*, p. 259

[144] North, *ACT OF TREASON*, p. 352

[145] North, *ACT OF TREASON*, p. 357

[146] North, *ACT OF TREASON*, p. 357

[147] McClellan, *BLOOD, MONEY AND POWER*, p. 172

[148] Stone & Colapietro, *THE MAN WHO KILLED KENNEDY*, p. 206

[149] North, *ACT OF TREASON*, p. 503

[150] North, *ACT OF TREASON*, p. 503

[151] North, *ACT OF TREASON*, p. 503

[152] North, *ACT OF TREASON*, p. 503

[153] McClellan, *BLOOD, MONEY AND POWER*, p. 123

[154] Stone & Colapietro, *THE MAN WHO KILLED KENNEDY*, p. 46

[155] Stone & Colapietro, *THE MAN WHO KILLED KENNEDY*, p. 188

[156] Stone & Colapietro, *THE MAN WHO KILLED KENNEDY*, p. 188

[157] Nelson, *LBJ: THE MASTERMIND OF THE JFK ASSASSINATION*, p. 38

[158] Nelson, *LBJ: THE MASTERMIND OF THE JFK ASSASSINATION*, p. 38

[159] Nelson, *LBJ: THE MASTERMIND OF THE JFK ASSASSINATION*, p. 38

[160] Stone & Colapietro, *THE MAN WHO KILLED KENNEDY*, p. 188

[161] Stone & Colapietro, *THE MAN WHO KILLED KENNEDY*, p. 189

[162] Stone & Colapietro, *THE MAN WHO KILLED KENNEDY*, p. 189

[163] Stone & Colapietro, *THE MAN WHO KILLED KENNEDY*, pp. 189-190

[164] Stone & Colapietro, *THE MAN WHO KILLED KENNEDY*, p. 191

[165] Stone & Colapietro, *THE MAN WHO KILLED KENNEDY*, p. 191

[166] Stone & Colapietro, *THE MAN WHO KILLED KENNEDY*, p. 192

[167] Stone & Colapietro, *THE MAN WHO KILLED KENNEDY*, p. 193

[168] Nelson, *LBJ: THE MASTERMIND OF THE JFK ASSASSINATION*, p. 117

[169] Nelson, *LBJ: THE MASTERMIND OF THE JFK ASSASSINATION*, p. 117

[170] North, *ACT OF TREASON*, p. 104

[171] North, *ACT OF TREASON*, p. 104

[172] North, *ACT OF TREASON*, p. 121

[173] Nelson, *LBJ: THE MASTERMIND OF THE JFK ASSASSINATION*, p. 183

[174] Nelson, *LBJ: THE MASTERMIND OF THE JFK ASSASSINATION*, p. 183

[175] Nelson, *LBJ: THE MASTERMIND OF THE JFK ASSASSINATION*, pp. 183, 250

[176] Nelson, *LBJ: THE MASTERMIND OF THE JFK ASSASSINATION*, p. 183

[177] Stone & Colapietro, *THE MAN WHO KILLED KENNEDY*, p. 198

[178] Stone & Colapietro, *THE MAN WHO KILLED KENNEDY*, p. 198

[179] Stone & Colapietro, *THE MAN WHO KILLED KENNEDY*, p. 198

[180] Stone & Colapietro, *THE MAN WHO KILLED KENNEDY*, pp. 198-199

[181] Stone & Colapietro, *THE MAN WHO KILLED KENNEDY*, p. 199

[182] Stone & Colapietro, *THE MAN WHO KILLED KENNEDY*, p. 199

[183] Stone & Colapietro, *THE MAN WHO KILLED KENNEDY*, p. 200

[184] North, *ACT OF TREASON*, p. 509-510

[185] North, *ACT OF TREASON*, p. 509-510
[186] North, *ACT OF TREASON*, p. 509-510
[187] North, *ACT OF TREASON*, p. 509-510
[188] North, *ACT OF TREASON*, p. 309
[189] North, *ACT OF TREASON*, p. 193
[190] North, *ACT OF TREASON*, p. 322
[191] North, *ACT OF TREASON*, p. 322
[192] North, *ACT OF TREASON*, p. 332
[193] North, *ACT OF TREASON*, p. 337
[194] North, *ACT OF TREASON*, p. 337
[195] North, *ACT OF TREASON*, p. 345
[196] North, *ACT OF TREASON*, p. 347
[197] North, *ACT OF TREASON*, p. 347
[198] North, *ACT OF TREASON*, p. 348
[199] North, *ACT OF TREASON*, p. 368
[200] North, *ACT OF TREASON*, p. 368
[201] North, *ACT OF TREASON*, p. 368
[202] North, *ACT OF TREASON*, p. 368
[203] North, *ACT OF TREASON*, p. 368
[204] North, *ACT OF TREASON*, p. 370
[205] North, *ACT OF TREASON*, p. 370
[206] North, *ACT OF TREASON*, p. 400
[207] North, *ACT OF TREASON*, p. 400
[208] North, *ACT OF TREASON*, p. 415
[209] North, *ACT OF TREASON*, p. 417
[210] North, *ACT OF TREASON*, p. 417
[211] North, *ACT OF TREASON*, p. 415
[212] North, *ACT OF TREASON*, p. 482
[213] North, *ACT OF TREASON*, p. 482
[214] North, *ACT OF TREASON*, p. 485
[215] North, *ACT OF TREASON*, p. 485
[216] North, *ACT OF TREASON*, p. 485
[217] North, *ACT OF TREASON*, p. 485
[218] North, *ACT OF TREASON*, pp. 501-502
[219] North, *ACT OF TREASON*, pp. 501-502
[220] North, *ACT OF TREASON*, p. 502
[221] North, *ACT OF TREASON*, p. 502
[222] Nelson, *LBJ: THE MASTERMIND OF THE JFK ASSASSINATION*, pp. 572-574
[223] North, *ACT OF TREASON*, p. 516
[224] North, *ACT OF TREASON*, p. 516
[225] North, *ACT OF TREASON*, p. 518
[226] North, *ACT OF TREASON*, p. 518
[227] North, *ACT OF TREASON*, p. 518
[228] North, *ACT OF TREASON*, p. 519
[229] North, *ACT OF TREASON*, p. 519
[230] North, *ACT OF TREASON*, p. 526

[231] Nelson, *LBJ: THE MASTERMIND OF THE JFK ASSASSINATION*, p. 190

[232] McClellan, *BLOOD, MONEY AND POWER*, p. 189

[233] Nelson, *LBJ: THE MASTERMIND OF THE JFK ASSASSINATION*, p. 191

[234] North, *ACT OF TREASON*, p.193

[235] North, *ACT OF TREASON*, p.367

[236] Nelson, *LBJ: THE MASTERMIND OF THE JFK ASSASSINATION*, p. 564

[237] Nelson, *LBJ: THE MASTERMIND OF THE JFK ASSASSINATION*, p. 194

[238] Nelson, *LBJ: THE MASTERMIND OF THE JFK ASSASSINATION*, p. 194

[239] Nelson, *LBJ: THE MASTERMIND OF THE JFK ASSASSINATION*, pp. 210-211, 217-218

[240] McClellan, *BLOOD, MONEY AND POWER: HOW LBJ KILLED JFK*, pp. 106-107

[241] McClellan, *BLOOD, MONEY AND POWER: HOW LBJ KILLED JFK*, pp. 108-109

[242] McClellan, *BLOOD, MONEY AND POWER: HOW LBJ KILLED JFK*, pp. 108-109

[243] Stone & Colapietro, *THE MAN WHO KILLED KENNEDY*, p. 210

[244] Stone & Colapietro, *THE MAN WHO KILLED KENNEDY*, p. 210

[245] Stone & Colapietro, *THE MAN WHO KILLED KENNEDY*, p. 210

[246] Talbot, *THE DEVIL'S CHESSBOARD*, p. 539

[247] Stone & Colapietro, *THE MAN WHO KILLED KENNEDY*, p. 212

[248] Nelson, *LBJ: THE MASTERMIND OF THE JFK ASSASSINATION*, p. 225

[249] Nelson, *LBJ: THE MASTERMIND OF THE JFK ASSASSINATION*, p. 225

[250] Nelson, *LBJ: THE MASTERMIND OF THE JFK ASSASSINATION*, p. 225

[251] Nelson, *LBJ: THE MASTERMIND OF THE JFK ASSASSINATION*, p. 225

[252] Nelson, *LBJ: THE MASTERMIND OF THE JFK ASSASSINATION*, p. 225

[253] Nelson, *LBJ: THE MASTERMIND OF THE JFK ASSASSINATION*, p. 225

[254] Nelson, *LBJ: THE MASTERMIND OF THE JFK ASSASSINATION*, p. 210

[255] Nelson, *LBJ: THE MASTERMIND OF THE JFK ASSASSINATION*, p. 210

[256] Nelson, *LBJ: THE MASTERMIND OF THE JFK ASSASSINATION*, p. 210

[257] Nelson, *LBJ: THE MASTERMIND OF THE JFK ASSASSINATION*, p. 210

[258] Nelson, *LBJ: THE MASTERMIND OF THE JFK ASSASSINATION*,

p. 220
[259] Nelson, *LBJ: THE MASTERMIND OF THE JFK ASSASSINATION*, p. 220
[260] Nelson, *LBJ: THE MASTERMIND OF THE JFK ASSASSINATION*, p. 220
[261] Nelson, *LBJ: THE MASTERMIND OF THE JFK ASSASSINATION*, p. 220
[262] Nelson, *LBJ: THE MASTERMIND OF THE JFK ASSASSINATION*, pp. 220-221
[263] Nelson, *LBJ: THE MASTERMIND OF THE JFK ASSASSINATION*, p. 220
[264] Nelson, *LBJ: THE MASTERMIND OF THE JFK ASSASSINATION*, p. 230
[265] Nelson, *LBJ: THE MASTERMIND OF THE JFK ASSASSINATION*, p. 230
[266] Nelson, *LBJ: THE MASTERMIND OF THE JFK ASSASSINATION*, p. 230
[267] Nelson, *LBJ: THE MASTERMIND OF THE JFK ASSASSINATION*, p. 230
[268] McClellan, *BLOOD, MONEY AND POWER*, p. 171
[269] McClellan, *BLOOD, MONEY AND POWER*, p. 171
[270] Nelson, *LBJ: THE MASTERMIND OF THE JFK ASSASSINATION*, p. 231
[271] Nelson, *LBJ: THE MASTERMIND OF THE JFK ASSASSINATION*, p. 231
[272] Stone & Colapietro, *THE MAN WHO KILLED KENNEDY*, p. 209
[273] Stone & Colapietro, *THE MAN WHO KILLED KENNEDY*, p. 209
[274] Nelson, *LBJ: THE MASTERMIND OF THE JFK ASSASSINATION*, p. 231
[275] McClellan, *BLOOD, MONEY AND POWER*, p. 171
[276] Nelson, *LBJ: THE MASTERMIND OF THE JFK ASSASSINATION*, p. 231
[277] Stone & Colapietro, *THE MAN WHO KILLED KENNEDY*, p. 212
[278] Nelson, *LBJ: THE MASTERMIND OF THE JFK ASSASSINATION*, p. 249
[279] Nelson, *LBJ: THE MASTERMIND OF THE JFK ASSASSINATION*, p. 249
[280] Nelson, *LBJ: THE MASTERMIND OF THE JFK ASSASSINATION*, p. 223
[281] Nelson, *LBJ: THE MASTERMIND OF THE JFK ASSASSINATION*, p. 223
[282] Nelson, *LBJ: THE MASTERMIND OF THE JFK ASSASSINATION*, p. 223
[283] Nelson, *LBJ: THE MASTERMIND OF THE JFK ASSASSINATION*, p. 224
[284] Nelson, *LBJ: THE MASTERMIND OF THE JFK ASSASSINATION*, p. 224

[285] Nelson, *LBJ: THE MASTERMIND OF THE JFK ASSASSINATION*, p. 224

[286] Nelson, *LBJ: THE MASTERMIND OF THE JFK ASSASSINATION*, p. 224

[287] Stone & Colapietro, *THE MAN WHO KILLED KENNEDY*, p. 134

[288] Nelson, *LBJ: THE MASTERMIND OF THE JFK ASSASSINATION*, pp. 272-273

[289] Summers, *NOT IN YOUR LIFETIME*, pp. 202-203

[290] Summers, *NOT IN YOUR LIFETIME*, pp. 202-203

[291] Corsi, *WHO REALLY KILLED KENNEDY*, pp. 226-229

[292] Corsi, *WHO REALLY KILLED KENNEDY*, pp. 226-229

[293] Corsi, *WHO REALLY KILLED KENNEDY*, pp. 226-229

[294] Corsi, *WHO REALLY KILLED KENNEDY*, pp. 226-229

[295] Corsi, *WHO REALLY KILLED KENNEDY*, pp. 226-229

[296] Corsi, *WHO REALLY KILLED KENNEDY*, pp. 226-229

[297] Corsi, *WHO REALLY KILLED KENNEDY*, pp. 226-229

[298] Corsi, *WHO REALLY KILLED KENNEDY*, pp. 226-229

[299] Corsi, *WHO REALLY KILLED KENNEDY*, pp. 229-230

[300] Caro, *THE YEARS OF LYNDON JOHNSON – MASTER OF THE SENATE*, p. 111

[301] Nelson, *LBJ: THE MASTERMIND OF THE JFK ASSASSINATION*, p. 267

[302] Nelson, *LBJ: THE MASTERMIND OF THE JFK ASSASSINATION*, p. 59

[303] Nelson, *LBJ: THE MASTERMIND OF THE JFK ASSASSINATION*, p. 269

[304] Nelson, *LBJ: THE MASTERMIND OF THE JFK ASSASSINATION*, p. 268

[305] Nelson, *LBJ: THE MASTERMIND OF THE JFK ASSASSINATION*, p. 268

[306] Nelson, *LBJ: THE MASTERMIND OF THE JFK ASSASSINATION*, p. 279

[307] Nelson, *LBJ: THE MASTERMIND OF THE JFK ASSASSINATION*, p. 272

[308] Nelson, *LBJ: THE MASTERMIND OF THE JFK ASSASSINATION*, p. 272

[309] Nelson, *LBJ: THE MASTERMIND OF THE JFK ASSASSINATION*, p. 280

[310] Nelson, *LBJ: THE MASTERMIND OF THE JFK ASSASSINATION*, p. 280

[311] Nelson, *LBJ: THE MASTERMIND OF THE JFK ASSASSINATION*, p. 281

[312] Nelson, *LBJ: THE MASTERMIND OF THE JFK ASSASSINATION*, p. 282

[313] Nelson, *LBJ: THE MASTERMIND OF THE JFK ASSASSINATION*, p. 284

[314] Nelson, *LBJ: THE MASTERMIND OF THE JFK ASSASSINATION*,

pp. 298-299

[315] Caro, *THE YEARS OF LYNDON JOHNSON – MASTER OF THE SENATE*, p. 1035

[316] Caro, *THE YEARS OF LYNDON JOHNSON – MASTER OF THE SENATE*, p. 1038

[317] Talbot, *THE DEVIL'S CHESSBOARD*, p. 493

[318] Nelson, *LBJ: THE MASTERMIND OF THE JFK ASSASSINATION*, p. 298-299

[319] Nelson, *LBJ: THE MASTERMIND OF THE JFK ASSASSINATION*, p. 298-299

[320] Joesten, *OSWALD: ASSASSIN OR FALL GUY?*, p. 236

[321] Nelson, *LBJ: THE MASTERMIND OF THE JFK ASSASSINATION*, pp. 298-299

[322] Nelson, *LBJ: THE MASTERMIND OF THE JFK ASSASSINATION*, pp. 298-299

[323] Nelson, *LBJ: THE MASTERMIND OF THE JFK ASSASSINATION*, p. 59

[324] Nelson, *LBJ: THE MASTERMIND OF THE JFK ASSASSINATION*, p. 59

[325] Nelson, *LBJ: THE MASTERMIND OF THE JFK ASSASSINATION*, p. 59

[326] Nelson, *LBJ: THE MASTERMIND OF THE JFK ASSASSINATION*, p. 300

[327] Nelson, *LBJ: THE MASTERMIND OF THE JFK ASSASSINATION*, p. 301

[328] Nelson, *LBJ: THE MASTERMIND OF THE JFK ASSASSINATION*, p. 301

[329] Nelson, *LBJ: THE MASTERMIND OF THE JFK ASSASSINATION*, p. 114

[330] North, *ACT OF TREASON*, p 246

[331] North, *ACT OF TREASON*, p 246

[332] Nelson, *LBJ: THE MASTERMIND OF THE JFK ASSASSINATION*, p. 195

[333] Nelson, *LBJ: THE MASTERMIND OF THE JFK ASSASSINATION*, p. 230

[334] Nelson, *LBJ: THE MASTERMIND OF THE JFK ASSASSINATION*, p. 237

[335] Nelson, *LBJ: THE MASTERMIND OF THE JFK ASSASSINATION*, p. 237

[336] Nelson, *LBJ: THE MASTERMIND OF THE JFK ASSASSINATION*, p. 238

[337] Nelson, *LBJ: THE MASTERMIND OF THE JFK ASSASSINATION*, p. 238

[338] McClellan, *BLOOD, MONEY AND POWER*, p. 188

[339] North, *ACT OF TREASON*, p 281

[340] North, *ACT OF TREASON*, p 281

[341] North, *ACT OF TREASON*, p 275

[342] Nelson, *LBJ: THE MASTERMIND OF THE JFK ASSASSINATION*, p. 307

[343] Nelson, *LBJ: THE MASTERMIND OF THE JFK ASSASSINATION*, pp. 307-309

[344] Nelson, *LBJ: THE MASTERMIND OF THE JFK ASSASSINATION*, p. 114

[345] Nelson, *LBJ: THE MASTERMIND OF THE JFK ASSASSINATION*, p. 301

[346] Nelson, *LBJ: THE MASTERMIND OF THE JFK ASSASSINATION*, p. 307

[347] Nelson, *LBJ: THE MASTERMIND OF THE JFK ASSASSINATION*, pp. 307-309

[348] Corsi, *WHO REALLY KILLED KENNEDY*, p. 285

[349] Corsi, *WHO REALLY KILLED KENNEDY*, p. 285

[350] Corsi, *WHO REALLY KILLED KENNEDY*, p. 286

[351] Corsi, *WHO REALLY KILLED KENNEDY*, pp. 285-286

[352] Corsi, *WHO REALLY KILLED KENNEDY*, p. 286

[353] Corsi, *WHO REALLY KILLED KENNEDY*, p. 286

[354] Corsi, *WHO REALLY KILLED KENNEDY*, p. 286

[355] Corsi, *WHO REALLY KILLED KENNEDY*, p. 289

[356] Corsi, *WHO REALLY KILLED KENNEDY*, p. 290

[357] Corsi, *WHO REALLY KILLED KENNEDY*, pp. 290-291

[358] Corsi, *WHO REALLY KILLED KENNEDY*, p. 291

[359] Nelson, *LBJ: THE MASTERMIND OF THE JFK ASSASSINATION*, p. 310

[360] Nelson, *LBJ: THE MASTERMIND OF THE JFK ASSASSINATION*, p. 310

[361] Nelson, *LBJ: THE MASTERMIND OF THE JFK ASSASSINATION*, p. 310

[362] Nelson, *LBJ: THE MASTERMIND OF THE JFK ASSASSINATION*, p. 261

[363] Nelson, *LBJ: THE MASTERMIND OF THE JFK ASSASSINATION*, p. 261

[364] Nelson, *LBJ: THE MASTERMIND OF THE JFK ASSASSINATION*, p. 261

[365] Nelson, *LBJ: THE MASTERMIND OF THE JFK ASSASSINATION*, p. 261

[366] Nelson, *LBJ: THE MASTERMIND OF THE JFK ASSASSINATION*, p. 261

[367] Nelson, *LBJ: THE MASTERMIND OF THE JFK ASSASSINATION*, p. 261

[368] Nelson, *LBJ: THE MASTERMIND OF THE JFK ASSASSINATION*, pp. 261-262

[369] Nelson, *LBJ: THE MASTERMIND OF THE JFK ASSASSINATION*, pp. 261-262

[370] Nelson, *LBJ: THE MASTERMIND OF THE JFK ASSASSINATION*, pp. 261-262

[371] Nelson, *LBJ: THE MASTERMIND OF THE JFK ASSASSINATION*, pp. 261-262

[372] Nelson, *LBJ: THE MASTERMIND OF THE JFK ASSASSINATION*, pp. 261-262

[373] Nelson, *LBJ: THE MASTERMIND OF THE JFK ASSASSINATION*, p. 597

[374] Douglass, *JFK AND THE UNSPEAKABLE*, p. 189

[375] Marrs, *CROSSFIRE*, p. 286

[376] Talbot, *THE DEVIL'S CHESSBOARD*, p. 504

[377] Stone & Colapietro, *THE MAN WHO KILLED KENNEDY*, p. 374

[378] Stone & Colapietro, *THE MAN WHO KILLED KENNEDY*, p. 226

[379] Stone & Colapietro, *THE MAN WHO KILLED KENNEDY*, p. 226

[380] Stone & Colapietro, *THE MAN WHO KILLED KENNEDY*, p. 227

[381] Stone & Colapietro, *THE MAN WHO KILLED KENNEDY*, p. 229

[382] Nelson, *LBJ: THE MASTERMIND OF THE JFK ASSASSINATION*, p. 194

[383] Nelson, *LBJ: THE MASTERMIND OF THE JFK ASSASSINATION*, p. 194

[384] Nelson, *LBJ: THE MASTERMIND OF THE JFK ASSASSINATION*, p. 576

[385] Nelson, *LBJ: THE MASTERMIND OF THE JFK ASSASSINATION*, p. 567

[386] Nelson, *LBJ: THE MASTERMIND OF THE JFK ASSASSINATION*, pp. 567-568

[387] Nelson, *LBJ: THE MASTERMIND OF THE JFK ASSASSINATION*, pp. 567-568

[388] Nelson, *LBJ: THE MASTERMIND OF THE JFK ASSASSINATION*, p. 568

[389] Nelson, *LBJ: THE MASTERMIND OF THE JFK ASSASSINATION*, p. 568

[390] Nelson, *LBJ: THE MASTERMIND OF THE JFK ASSASSINATION*, pp. 568-569

[391] Nelson, *LBJ: THE MASTERMIND OF THE JFK ASSASSINATION*, pp. 568-569

[392] North, *ACT OF TREASON,* p. 509-510

[393] North, *ACT OF TREASON,* p. 509-510

[394] Nelson, *LBJ: THE MASTERMIND OF THE JFK ASSASSINATION*, pp. 568-569

[395] Nelson, *LBJ: THE MASTERMIND OF THE JFK ASSASSINATION*, pp. 568-569

[396] Nelson, *LBJ: THE MASTERMIND OF THE JFK ASSASSINATION*, p. 565

[397] Nelson, *LBJ: THE MASTERMIND OF THE JFK ASSASSINATION*, p. 566

[398] Nelson, *LBJ: THE MASTERMIND OF THE JFK ASSASSINATION*, p. 566

[399] Nelson, *LBJ: THE MASTERMIND OF THE JFK ASSASSINATION*,

p. 565

[400] Nelson, *LBJ: THE MASTERMIND OF THE JFK ASSASSINATION*, p. 565

[401] Nelson, *LBJ: THE MASTERMIND OF THE JFK ASSASSINATION*, p. 573

[402] Nelson, *LBJ: THE MASTERMIND OF THE JFK ASSASSINATION*, p. 575

[403] Nelson, *LBJ: THE MASTERMIND OF THE JFK ASSASSINATION*, p. 194

[404] North, *ACT OF TREASON*, p. 402

[405] North, *ACT OF TREASON*, p. 488

[406] North, *ACT OF TREASON*, p. 488

[407] North, *ACT OF TREASON*, p. 498

[408] North, *ACT OF TREASON*, p. 498

[409] North, *ACT OF TREASON*, p. 503

[410] North, *ACT OF TREASON*, p. 503

[411] North, *ACT OF TREASON*, p. 504

[412] North, *ACT OF TREASON*, p. 504

[413] Nolan, *CIA ROGUES AND THE KILLING OF THE KENNEDYS*, pp. 26-27

[414] Nolan, *CIA ROGUES AND THE KILLING OF THE KENNEDYS*, pp. 26-27

[415] Nolan, *CIA ROGUES AND THE KILLING OF THE KENNEDYS*, pp. 26-27

[416] North, *ACT OF TREASON*, p. 300

[417] North, *ACT OF TREASON*, p. 300

[418] Morley, *THE GHOST*, pp. 62-63

[419] Nelson, *LBJ: THE MASTERMIND OF THE JFK ASSASSINATION*, p. 143

[420] Nelson, *LBJ: THE MASTERMIND OF THE JFK ASSASSINATION*, p. 143

[421] Talbot, *THE DEVIL'S CHESSBOARD*, p. 539

[422] Garrison, *ON THE TRAIL OF THE ASSASSINS*, p. 104

[423] North, *BETRAYAL IN DALLAS*, p. 80

[424] Nelson, *LBJ: THE MASTERMIND OF THE JFK ASSASSINATION*, p. 321

[425] Nelson, *LBJ: THE MASTERMIND OF THE JFK ASSASSINATION*, p. 322

[426] Nelson, *LBJ: THE MASTERMIND OF THE JFK ASSASSINATION*, p. 323

[427] Nelson, *LBJ: THE MASTERMIND OF THE JFK ASSASSINATION*, pp. 322-324

[428] Nelson, *LBJ: THE MASTERMIND OF THE JFK ASSASSINATION*, p. 321

[429] Nelson, *LBJ: THE MASTERMIND OF THE JFK ASSASSINATION*, p. 322

[430] North, ACT OF TREASON, pp. 183-184

[431] Corsi, *WHO REALLY KILLED KENNEDY*, pp. 291-294

[432] Corsi, *WHO REALLY KILLED KENNEDY*, p. 301

[433] Corsi, *WHO REALLY KILLED KENNEDY*, p. 302

[434] Summers, *NOT IN YOUR LIFETIME*, p. 293

[435] Summers, *NOT IN YOUR LIFETIME*, p. 293

[436] Nelson, *LBJ: THE MASTERMIND OF THE JFK ASSASSINATION*, pp. 324-325

[437] Nelson, *LBJ: THE MASTERMIND OF THE JFK ASSASSINATION*, p. 325

[438] Nelson, *LBJ: THE MASTERMIND OF THE JFK ASSASSINATION*, p. 325

[439] Nelson, *LBJ: THE MASTERMIND OF THE JFK ASSASSINATION*, p. 325

[440] Marrs, *CROSSFIRE*, p. 554

[441] Stone & Colapietro, *THE MAN WHO KILLED KENNEDY*, p. 134

[442] Corsi, *WHO REALLY KILLED KENNEDY*, p. 217

[443] Corsi, *WHO REALLY KILLED KENNEDY*, p. 217

[444] Corsi, *WHO REALLY KILLED KENNEDY*, pp. 217-218

[445] Corsi, *WHO REALLY KILLED KENNEDY*, p. 218

[446] Corsi, *WHO REALLY KILLED KENNEDY*, p. 218

[447] Corsi, *WHO REALLY KILLED KENNEDY*, p. 218

[448] Corsi, *WHO REALLY KILLED KENNEDY*, p. 218

[449] Corsi, *WHO REALLY KILLED KENNEDY*, p. 216

[450] Corsi, *WHO REALLY KILLED KENNEDY*, p. 216

[451] Corsi, *WHO REALLY KILLED KENNEDY*, p. 216

[452] Corsi, *WHO REALLY KILLED KENNEDY*, p. 216

[453] Corsi, *WHO REALLY KILLED KENNEDY*, p. 217

[454] Corsi, *WHO REALLY KILLED KENNEDY*, p. 217

[455] Corsi, *WHO REALLY KILLED KENNEDY*, pp. 216-217

[456] Summers, *NOT IN YOUR LIFETIME*, p. 221

[457] Summers, *NOT IN YOUR LIFETIME*, pp. 221-222

[458] Summers, *NOT IN YOUR LIFETIME*, pp. 221-222

[459] Corsi, *WHO REALLY KILLED KENNEDY*, p. 216

[460] Corsi, *WHO REALLY KILLED KENNEDY*, p. 218

[461] Corsi, *WHO REALLY KILLED KENNEDY*, p. 218

[462] Corsi, *WHO REALLY KILLED KENNEDY*, pp. 218-219

[463] Corsi, *WHO REALLY KILLED KENNEDY*, pp. 219-220

[464] Corsi, *WHO REALLY KILLED KENNEDY*, p. 220

[465] Corsi, *WHO REALLY KILLED KENNEDY*, p. 220

[466] Corsi, *WHO REALLY KILLED KENNEDY*, p. 220

[467] Stone & Colapietro, *THE MAN WHO KILLED KENNEDY*, p. 134

[468] Corsi, *WHO REALLY KILLED KENNEDY*, pp. 220-221

[469] Shaw, *THE POISON PATRIARCH*, p. 226

[470] Shaw, *THE POISON PATRIARCH*, p. 227

[471] Shaw, *THE POISON PATRIARCH*, p. 230

[472] Shaw, *THE POISON PATRIARCH*, p. 230

[473] Shaw, *THE POISON PATRIARCH*, p. 233

[474] Shaw, *THE POISON PATRIARCH*, pp. 235-236
[475] Shaw, *THE POISON PATRIARCH*, p. 236
[476] Shaw, *THE POISON PATRIARCH*, pp. 236-237
[477] Shaw, *THE POISON PATRIARCH*, pp. 236-237
[478] Shaw, *THE POISON PATRIARCH*, p. 237
[479] North, *ACT OF TREASON*, pp. 117-118
[480] Shaw, *THE POISON PATRIARCH*, p. 238
[481] Shaw, *THE POISON PATRIARCH*, p. 238
[482] Shaw, *THE POISON PATRIARCH*, p. 239
[483] Shaw, *THE POISON PATRIARCH*, p. 238
[484] Shaw, *THE POISON PATRIARCH*, pp. 239-240
[485] Shaw, *THE POISON PATRIARCH*, p. 241
[486] Shaw, *THE POISON PATRIARCH*, p. 226
[487] Summers, *NOT IN YOUR LIFETIME*, p. 224
[488] Summers, *NOT IN YOUR LIFETIME*, p. 224
[489] Summers, *NOT IN YOUR LIFETIME*, p. 224
[490] Summers, *NOT IN YOUR LIFETIME*, p. 226
[491] Summers, *NOT IN YOUR LIFETIME*, p. 226
[492] Summers, *NOT IN YOUR LIFETIME*, p. 226
[493] Summers, *NOT IN YOUR LIFETIME*, p. 226
[494] North, *ACT OF TREASON*, p. 106
[495] North, *ACT OF TREASON*, p. 230
[496] Corsi, *WHO REALLY KILLED KENNEDY*, p. 221
[497] Corsi, *WHO REALLY KILLED KENNEDY*, p. 209
[498] Corsi, *WHO REALLY KILLED KENNEDY*, pp. 209-210
[499] Fonzi, *THE LAST INVESTIGATION*, p. 437
[500] Fonzi, *THE LAST INVESTIGATION*, p. 373
[501] Fonzi, *THE LAST INVESTIGATION*, p. 373
[502] Fonzi, *THE LAST INVESTIGATION*, p. 373
[503] Newman, *OSWALD AND THE CIA*, pp. 202-203
[504] Summers, *NOT IN YOUR LIFETIME*, p. 215
[505] Janney, *MARY'S MOSAIC*, p. 389
[506] Douglass, *JFK AND THE UNSPEAKABLE*, p. 34
[507] Douglass, *JFK AND THE UNSPEAKABLE*, p. 34
[508] Douglass, *JFK AND THE UNSPEAKABLE*, p. 34
[509] Summers, *NOT IN YOUR LIFETIME*, pp. 217-218
[510] Summers, *NOT IN YOUR LIFETIME*, p. 217
[511] Summers, *NOT IN YOUR LIFETIME*, pp. 217-218
[512] North, *ACT OF TREASON*, p. 114
[513] North, *ACT OF TREASON*, p. 114
[514] North, *ACT OF TREASON*, p. 116
[515] North, *ACT OF TREASON*, p. 116
[516] Summers, *NOT IN YOUR LIFETIME*, p. 220
[517] North, *ACT OF TREASON*, pp. 116-117
[518] North, *ACT OF TREASON*, pp. 117-118
[519] Nelson, *LBJ: THE MASTERMIND OF THE JFK ASSASSINATION*, p. 146

[520] Nelson, *LBJ: THE MASTERMIND OF THE JFK ASSASSINATION*, p. 146

[521] Belzer & Wayne, *DEAD WRONG*, p. 152

[522] Belzer & Wayne, *DEAD WRONG*, p. 152

[523] North, *ACT OF TREASON,* pp. 457-458

[524] North, *ACT OF TREASON,* pp. 457-458

[525] Fonzi, *THE LAST INVESTIGATION*, p. 437

[526] Summers, *NOT IN YOUR LIFETIME*, pp. 422-423

[527] Summers, *NOT IN YOUR LIFETIME*, pp. 422-423

[528] Fonzi, *THE LAST INVESTIGATION*, p. 438

[529] Shaw, *THE POISON PATRIARCH*, pp. 186-187

[530] Stone & Colapietro, *THE MAN WHO KILLED KENNEDY*, p. 171

[531] Nelson, *LBJ: THE MASTERMIND OF THE JFK ASSASSINATION*, p. 144

[532] Nelson, *LBJ: THE MASTERMIND OF THE JFK ASSASSINATION*, p. 144

[533] Stone & Colapietro, *THE MAN WHO KILLED KENNEDY*, pp. 173-174

[534] Stone & Colapietro, *THE MAN WHO KILLED KENNEDY*, pp. 173-174

[535] Stone & Colapietro, *THE MAN WHO KILLED KENNEDY*, pp. 173-174

[536] Stone & Colapietro, *THE MAN WHO KILLED KENNEDY*, pp. 173-174

[537] Stone & Colapietro, *THE MAN WHO KILLED KENNEDY*, pp. 173-174

[538] Stone & Colapietro, *THE MAN WHO KILLED KENNEDY*, pp. 173-174

[539] North, *ACT OF TREASON*, p. 274

[540] North, *ACT OF TREASON*, p. 274

[541] Summers, *NOT IN YOUR LIFETIME*, p. 288

[542] Summers, *NOT IN YOUR LIFETIME*, p. 288

[543] North, ACT OF TREASON, p. 183

[544] North, *ACT OF TREASON,* p. 538

[545] North, *ACT OF TREASON,* p. 538

[546] North, *ACT OF TREASON*, p. 15

[547] North, *ACT OF TREASON*, p. 15

[548] Summers, *NOT IN YOUR LIFETIME*, pp. 234-235

[549] Summers, *NOT IN YOUR LIFETIME*, pp. 234-235

[550] Summers, *NOT IN YOUR LIFETIME*, pp. 234-235

[551] Summers, *NOT IN YOUR LIFETIME*, pp. 234-235

[552] Summers, *NOT IN YOUR LIFETIME*, pp. 234-235

[553] North, *ACT OF TREASON*, p. 184

[554] North, *ACT OF TREASON*, p. 184

[555] North, *ACT OF TREASON*, p. 13

[556] North, *ACT OF TREASON*, p. 189

[557] North, *ACT OF TREASON*, p. 189

[558] North, *ACT OF TREASON*, p. 189

[559] North, *ACT OF TREASON*, p. 189

[560] North, *ACT OF TREASON*, p. 189

[561] North, *ACT OF TREASON*, p. 198

[562] North, *ACT OF TREASON,* p. 216

[563] North, *ACT OF TREASON*, p. 222

[564] North, *ACT OF TREASON*, p. 224

[565] North, *ACT OF TREASON*, p. 224

[566] North, *ACT OF TREASON*, p. 363

[567] Nelson, *LBJ: THE MASTERMIND OF THE JFK ASSASSINATION*, p. 146

[568] Nelson, *LBJ: THE MASTERMIND OF THE JFK ASSASSINATION*, p. 146

[569] Nelson, *LBJ: THE MASTERMIND OF THE JFK ASSASSINATION*, p. 146

[570] Nelson, *LBJ: THE MASTERMIND OF THE JFK ASSASSINATION*, p. 146

[571] North, *ACT OF TREASON*, p. 408

[572] Corsi, *WHO REALLY KILLED KENNEDY*, pp. 206-208

[573] Corsi, *WHO REALLY KILLED KENNEDY*, pp. 206-208

[574] Corsi, *WHO REALLY KILLED KENNEDY*, pp. 206-208

[575] Corsi, *WHO REALLY KILLED KENNEDY*, pp. 206-208

[576] Corsi, *WHO REALLY KILLED KENNEDY*, pp. 206-208

[577] Stone & Colapietro, *THE MAN WHO KILLED KENNEDY*, pp. 178-179

[578] Stone & Colapietro, *THE MAN WHO KILLED KENNEDY*, pp. 178-179

[579] Corsi, *WHO REALLY KILLED KENNEDY?*, p. 210

[580] Belzer & Wayne, *HIT LIST*, p. 40

[581] Summers, *NOT IN YOUR LIFETIME*, p. 419-420

[582] North, *ACT OF TREASON,* p. 420

[583] North, *ACT OF TREASON,* p. 420

[584] North, *ACT OF TREASON,* p. 420

[585] North, *ACT OF TREASON,* p. 395

[586] North, *ACT OF TREASON,* p. 395

[587] North, *ACT OF TREASON*, p. 432

[588] North, *ACT OF TREASON*, p. 432

[589] North, *ACT OF TREASON,* p. 441

[590] North, *ACT OF TREASON,* p. 441

[591] North, *ACT OF TREASON,* p. 439

[592] North, *ACT OF TREASON,* p. 439

[593] Shaw, *THE POISON PATRIARCH*, p. 194

[594] North, *ACT OF TREASON,* p. 405

[595] North, *ACT OF TREASON,* p. 395

[596] North, *ACT OF TREASON,* p. 395

[597] North, *ACT OF TREASON,* p. 487

[598] Summers, *NOT IN YOUR LIFETIME*, p. 216

[599] Summers, *NOT IN YOUR LIFETIME*, p. 216

[600] Summers, *NOT IN YOUR LIFETIME*, p. 216

[601] Summers, *NOT IN YOUR LIFETIME*, p. 216

[602] Nelson, *LBJ: THE MASTERMIND OF THE JFK ASSASSINATION*, pp. 144-145

[603] Shaw, *THE POISON PATRIARCH*, p. 66

[604] Summers, *NOT IN YOUR LIFETIME*, p. 405

[605] Summers, *NOT IN YOUR LIFETIME*, p. 405

[606] Summers, *NOT IN YOUR LIFETIME*, p. 405

[607] Summers, *NOT IN YOUR LIFETIME*, p. 405

[608] North, *ACT OF TREASON,* pp. 443-444

[609] Douglass, *JFK AND THE UNSPEAKABLE*, p. 34

[610] Douglass, *JFK AND THE UNSPEAKABLE*, p. 34

[611] Douglass, *JFK AND THE UNSPEAKABLE*, p. 34

[612] Janney, *MARY'S MOSAIC*, p. 253

[613] Janney, *MARY'S MOSAIC*, p. 312

[614] Janney, *MARY'S MOSAIC*, p. 389

[615] Janney, *MARY'S MOSAIC*, pp. 386-387

[616] Janney, *MARY'S MOSAIC*, p. 387

[617] Janney, *MARY'S MOSAIC*, p. 387

[618] Janney, *MARY'S MOSAIC*, p. 387

[619] Janney, *MARY'S MOSAIC*, p. 387

[620] Janney, *MARY'S MOSAIC*, p. 387

[621] Summers, *NOT IN YOUR LIFETIME*, pp. 229-230

[622] Summers, *NOT IN YOUR LIFETIME*, p. 230

[623] Summers, *NOT IN YOUR LIFETIME*, p. 230

[624] Summers, *NOT IN YOUR LIFETIME*, p. 230

[625] North, *ACT OF TREASON,* pp. 196-197

[626] North, *ACT OF TREASON,* pp. 196-197

[627] North, *ACT OF TREASON,* pp. 196-197

[628] North, *ACT OF TREASON,* pp. 196-197

[629] Summers, *NOT IN YOUR LIFETIME*, p. 231

[630] Nelson, *LBJ: THE MASTERMIND OF THE JFK ASSASSINATION*, p. 146

[631] Nelson, *LBJ: THE MASTERMIND OF THE JFK ASSASSINATION*, p. 146

[632] Summers, *NOT IN YOUR LIFETIME*, p. 429

[633] Summers, *NOT IN YOUR LIFETIME*, p. 429

[634] North, *ACT OF TREASON*, p. 410

[635] Corsi, *WHO REALLY KILLED KENNEDY*, p. 214

[636] Corsi, *WHO REALLY KILLED KENNEDY*, p. 214

[637] Summers, *NOT IN YOUR LIFETIME*, pp. 422-423

[638] Summers, *NOT IN YOUR LIFETIME*, pp. 422-423

[639] DiEugenio, *RECLAIMING PARKLAND*, p. 361

[640] Fonzi, *THE LAST INVESTIGATION*, p. 132

[641] Lane, *LAST WORD*, pp. 19-20

[642] Lane, *LAST WORD*, pp. 19-20

[643] Lane, *LAST WORD*, pp. 19-20

[644] Lane, *LAST WORD*, p. 21

[645] Lane, *LAST WORD*, p. 21

[646] Lane, *LAST WORD*, p. 21

[647] Lane, *LAST WORD*, p. 22

[648] Talbot, *THE DEVIL'S CHESSBOARD*, p. 25

[649] Talbot, *THE DEVIL'S CHESSBOARD*, p. 28

[650] Corsi, *WHO REALLY KILLED KENNEDY*, p. 304

[651] Talbot, *THE DEVIL'S CHESSBOARD*, p. 29

[652] Talbot, *THE DEVIL'S CHESSBOARD*, p. 29

[653] Talbot, *THE DEVIL'S CHESSBOARD*, p. 29

[654] Talbot, *THE DEVIL'S CHESSBOARD*, p. 29

[655] Talbot, *THE DEVIL'S CHESSBOARD*, p. 29

[656] Talbot, *THE DEVIL'S CHESSBOARD*, p. 29

[657] Talbot, *THE DEVIL'S CHESSBOARD*, p. 47

[658] DiEugenio, *RECLAIMING PARKLAND*, pp. 329-330

[659] DiEugenio, *RECLAIMING PARKLAND*, p. 332

[660] Weiner, *LEGACY OF ASHES*, pp. 47-48

[661] Weiner, *LEGACY OF ASHES*, pp. 47-48

[662] Talbot, *THE DEVIL'S CHESSBOARD*, p. 122

[663] Talbot, *THE DEVIL'S CHESSBOARD*, p. 96

[664] Talbot, *THE DEVIL'S CHESSBOARD*, p. 97

[665] Talbot, *THE DEVIL'S CHESSBOARD*, p. 147

[666] Talbot, *THE DEVIL'S CHESSBOARD*, p. 203

[667] Talbot, *THE DEVIL'S CHESSBOARD*, p. 203

[668] Talbot, *THE DEVIL'S CHESSBOARD*, p. 204

[669] Talbot, *THE DEVIL'S CHESSBOARD*, p. 204

[670] Talbot, *THE DEVIL'S CHESSBOARD*, p. 204

[671] Weiner, *LEGACY OF ASHES*, p. 87

[672] Weiner, *LEGACY OF ASHES*, pp. 94-105

[673] Weiner, *LEGACY OF ASHES*, pp. 110-117

[674] Talbot, *THE DEVIL'S CHESSBOARD*, p. 231

[675] Talbot, *THE DEVIL'S CHESSBOARD*, p. 232

[676] Talbot, *THE DEVIL'S CHESSBOARD*, p. 231

[677] Talbot, *THE DEVIL'S CHESSBOARD*, p. 232

[678] Talbot, *THE DEVIL'S CHESSBOARD*, p. 232

[679] Garrison, *ON THE TRAIL OF THE ASSASSINS*, p. 291

[680] Garrison, *ON THE TRAIL OF THE ASSASSINS*, p. 291

[681] Janney, *MARY'S MOSAIC*, p. 234

[682] Janney, *MARY'S MOSAIC*, p. 234

[683] Janney, *MARY'S MOSAIC*, p. 234

[684] Janney, *MARY'S MOSAIC*, p. 234

[685] Garrison, *ON THE TRAIL OF THE ASSASSINS*, p. 291

[686] Janney, *MARY'S MOSAIC*, p. 234

[687] Garrison, *ON THE TRAIL OF THE ASSASSINS*, p. 291

[688] Talbot, *THE DEVIL'S CHESSBOARD*, pp. 287-290

[689] Talbot, *THE DEVIL'S CHESSBOARD*, pp. 287-290

[690] Talbot, *THE DEVIL'S CHESSBOARD*, pp. 287-290

[691] Talbot, *THE DEVIL'S CHESSBOARD*, pp. 287-290

[692] Talbot, *THE DEVIL'S CHESSBOARD*, p. 288

[693] Talbot, *THE DEVIL'S CHESSBOARD*, p. 290

[694] Talbot, *THE DEVIL'S CHESSBOARD*, pp. 287-290

[695] Talbot, *THE DEVIL'S CHESSBOARD*, pp. 290-297

[696] Talbot, *THE DEVIL'S CHESSBOARD*, p. 309

[697] Talbot, *THE DEVIL'S CHESSBOARD*, p. 309

[698] Talbot, *THE DEVIL'S CHESSBOARD*, p. 322

[699] Talbot, *THE DEVIL'S CHESSBOARD*, p. 322

[700] Talbot, *THE DEVIL'S CHESSBOARD*, pp. 322-324

[701] Talbot, *THE DEVIL'S CHESSBOARD*, pp. 322-323

[702] Talbot, *THE DEVIL'S CHESSBOARD*, pp. 322-323

[703] Newman, *OSWALD AND THE CIA*, p. 40

[704] Weiner, *LEGACY OF ASHES*, p. 184

[705] Weiner, *LEGACY OF ASHES*, p. 184

[706] Weiner, *LEGACY OF ASHES*, p. 184

[707] Weiner, *LEGACY OF ASHES*, p. 184

[708] Janney, *MARY'S MOSAIC*, p. 232

[709] Janney, *MARY'S MOSAIC*, p. 232

[710] Talbot, *THE DEVIL'S CHESSBOARD*, p. 366

[711] Talbot, *THE DEVIL'S CHESSBOARD*, p. 366

[712] Talbot, *THE DEVIL'S CHESSBOARD*, p. 367

[713] Belzer & Wayne, *DEAD WRONG*, p. 120

[714] Garrison, *ON THE TRAIL OF THE ASSASSINS*, p. 292

[715] Talbot, *THE DEVIL'S CHESSBOARD*, p. 371

[716] Talbot, *THE DEVIL'S CHESSBOARD*, p. 374

[717] Talbot, *THE DEVIL'S CHESSBOARD*, p. 374

[718] Talbot, *THE DEVIL'S CHESSBOARD*, pp. 374-375

[719] DiEugenio, *RECLAIMING PARKLAND*, p. 361

[720] DiEugenio, *RECLAIMING PARKLAND*, p. 361

[721] Talbot, *THE DEVIL'S CHESSBOARD*, p. 375

[722] Talbot, *THE DEVIL'S CHESSBOARD*, p. 375

[723] Talbot, *THE DEVIL'S CHESSBOARD*, p. 375

[724] Talbot, *THE DEVIL'S CHESSBOARD*, p. 375

[725] Talbot, *THE DEVIL'S CHESSBOARD*, p. 375-376

[726] Talbot, *THE DEVIL'S CHESSBOARD*, p. 375-376

[727] Talbot, *THE DEVIL'S CHESSBOARD*, p. 377

[728] Talbot, *THE DEVIL'S CHESSBOARD*, p. 377

[729] Talbot, *THE DEVIL'S CHESSBOARD*, p. 379

[730] Talbot, *THE DEVIL'S CHESSBOARD*, pp. 381-382

[731] Talbot, *THE DEVIL'S CHESSBOARD*, p. 383

[732] Talbot, *THE DEVIL'S CHESSBOARD*, p. 386

[733] Talbot, *THE DEVIL'S CHESSBOARD*, p. 386

[734] Talbot, *THE DEVIL'S CHESSBOARD*, p. 387

[735] Talbot, *THE DEVIL'S CHESSBOARD*, p. 387

[736] Weiner, *LEGACY OF ASHES*, p. 190

[737] Weiner, *LEGACY OF ASHES*, p. 191

[738] Weiner, *LEGACY OF ASHES*, p. 190

[739] Weiner, *LEGACY OF ASHES*, p. 192

[740] Weiner, *LEGACY OF ASHES*, p. 192

[741] Weiner, *LEGACY OF ASHES*, p. 193

[742] Weiner, *LEGACY OF ASHES*, p. 193

[743] Weiner, *LEGACY OF ASHES*, p. 193

[744] Weiner, *LEGACY OF ASHES*, p. 193

[745] Weiner, *LEGACY OF ASHES*, pp. 193-194

[746] Weiner, *LEGACY OF ASHES*, p. 194

[747] Weiner, *LEGACY OF ASHES*, p. 194

[748] Corsi, *WHO REALLY KILLED KENNEDY*, p. 224

[749] Corsi, *WHO REALLY KILLED KENNEDY*, pp. 225-226

[750] Corsi, *WHO REALLY KILLED KENNEDY*, pp. 226-229

[751] Corsi, *WHO REALLY KILLED KENNEDY*, pp. 226-229

[752] Corsi, *WHO REALLY KILLED KENNEDY*, pp. 226-229

[753] Corsi, *WHO REALLY KILLED KENNEDY*, pp. 226-229

[754] Corsi, *WHO REALLY KILLED KENNEDY*, pp. 226-229

[755] Corsi, *WHO REALLY KILLED KENNEDY*, pp. 226-229

[756] Corsi, *WHO REALLY KILLED KENNEDY*, pp. 226-229

[757] Corsi, *WHO REALLY KILLED KENNEDY*, pp. 226-229

[758] Corsi, *WHO REALLY KILLED KENNEDY*, pp. 229-230

[759] Corsi, *WHO REALLY KILLED KENNEDY*, pp. 226-229

[760] Corsi, *WHO REALLY KILLED KENNEDY*, pp. 229-230

[761] DiEugenio, *DESTINY BETRAYED*, p. 34

[762] DiEugenio, *DESTINY BETRAYED*, p. 34

[763] DiEugenio, *DESTINY BETRAYED*, p. 34

[764] DiEugenio, *DESTINY BETRAYED*, p. 34

[765] DiEugenio, *DESTINY BETRAYED*, p. 34

[766] DiEugenio, *DESTINY BETRAYED*, p. 34

[767] DiEugenio, *DESTINY BETRAYED*, pp. 34-35

[768] DiEugenio, *DESTINY BETRAYED*, p. 35

[769] DiEugenio, *DESTINY BETRAYED*, p. 35

[770] DiEugenio, *DESTINY BETRAYED*, p. 35

[771] Weiner, *LEGACY OF ASHES*, p. 204

[772] Weiner, *LEGACY OF ASHES*, p. 204

[773] Weiner, *LEGACY OF ASHES*, p. 204

[774] Halberstam, *THE FIFTIES*, p. 376

[775] Halberstam, *THE FIFTIES*, p. 376

[776] Halberstam, *THE FIFTIES*, p. 385

[777] DiEugenio, *DESTINY BETRAYED*, p. 47

[778] Janney, *MARY'S MOSAIC*, p. 235

[779] Janney, *MARY'S MOSAIC*, p. 236

[780] Janney, *MARY'S MOSAIC*, pp. 236-237

[781] Janney, *MARY'S MOSAIC*, pp. 236-237

[782] Janney, *MARY'S MOSAIC*, p. 235

[783] Talbot, *THE DEVIL'S CHESSBOARD*, p. 398

588

784 Talbot, *THE DEVIL'S CHESSBOARD*, p. 398
785 Talbot, *THE DEVIL'S CHESSBOARD*, p. 398
786 Talbot, *THE DEVIL'S CHESSBOARD*, p. 399
787 Summers, *NOT IN YOUR LIFETIME*, p. 204
788 Summers, *NOT IN YOUR LIFETIME*, p. 204
789 Weiner, *LEGACY OF ASHES*, p. 204
790 Weiner, *LEGACY OF ASHES*, p. 204
791 Weiner, *LEGACY OF ASHES*, p. 204
792 Corsi, *WHO REALLY KILLED KENNEDY*, p. 312
793 DiEugenio, *DESTINY BETRAYED*, p. 46
794 Talbot, *THE DEVIL'S CHESSBOARD*, p. 410
795 Talbot, *THE DEVIL'S CHESSBOARD*, pp. 410-411
796 Weiner, *LEGACY OF ASHES*, p. 206
797 DiEugenio, *DESTINY BETRAYED*, p. 45
798 DiEugenio, *DESTINY BETRAYED*, p. 45
799 DiEugenio, *DESTINY BETRAYED*, p. 45
800 Weiner, *LEGACY OF ASHES*, p. 206
801 Talbot, *THE DEVIL'S CHESSBOARD*, p. 411
802 Talbot, *THE DEVIL'S CHESSBOARD*, p. 411
803 Talbot, *THE DEVIL'S CHESSBOARD*, p. 411
804 Talbot, *THE DEVIL'S CHESSBOARD*, p. 411
805 Talbot, *THE DEVIL'S CHESSBOARD*, p. 412
806 DiEugenio, *DESTINY BETRAYED*, p. 48
807 DiEugenio, *DESTINY BETRAYED*, p. 48
808 DiEugenio, *DESTINY BETRAYED*, p. 48
809 Talbot, *THE DEVIL'S CHESSBOARD*, p. 406
810 Talbot, *THE DEVIL'S CHESSBOARD*, p. 406
811 Talbot, *THE DEVIL'S CHESSBOARD*, p. 407
812 Talbot, *THE DEVIL'S CHESSBOARD*, p. 407
813 Talbot, *THE DEVIL'S CHESSBOARD*, p. 407
814 Summers, *NOT IN YOUR LIFETIME*, p. 204
815 Summers, *NOT IN YOUR LIFETIME*, p. 204
816 Summers, *NOT IN YOUR LIFETIME*, p. 204
817 Summers, *NOT IN YOUR LIFETIME*, p. 204
818 Summers, *NOT IN YOUR LIFETIME*, p. 205
819 DiEugenio, *DESTINY BETRAYED*, p. 47
820 DiEugenio, *DESTINY BETRAYED*, p. 47
821 DiEugenio, *DESTINY BETRAYED*, p. 47
822 DiEugenio, *DESTINY BETRAYED*, p. 47
823 Douglass, *JFK AND THE UNSPEAKABLE*, p. 381
824 Douglass, *JFK AND THE UNSPEAKABLE*, pp. 381-382
825 Weiner, *LEGACY OF ASHES*, p. 206
826 Weiner, *LEGACY OF ASHES*, p. 207
827 Weiner, *LEGACY OF ASHES*, p. 207
828 Weiner, *LEGACY OF ASHES*, p. 207
829 Weiner, *LEGACY OF ASHES*, p. 208
830 Douglass, *JFK AND THE UNSPEAKABLE*, p. 116

[831] Douglass, *JFK AND THE UNSPEAKABLE*, p. 116

[832] Douglass, *JFK AND THE UNSPEAKABLE*, p. 116

[833] Douglass, *JFK AND THE UNSPEAKABLE*, p. 152

[834] Douglass, *JFK AND THE UNSPEAKABLE*, p. 116

[835] Douglass, *JFK AND THE UNSPEAKABLE*, pp. 15-16

[836] Douglass, *JFK AND THE UNSPEAKABLE*, pp. 15-16

[837] Douglass, *JFK AND THE UNSPEAKABLE*, pp. 15-16

[838] Douglass, *JFK AND THE UNSPEAKABLE*, pp. 15-16

[839] Talbot, *THE DEVIL'S CHESSBOARD*, p. 428

[840] Talbot, *THE DEVIL'S CHESSBOARD*, p. 428

[841] Talbot, *THE DEVIL'S CHESSBOARD*, p. 449

[842] Talbot, *THE DEVIL'S CHESSBOARD*, p. 453

[843] Talbot, *THE DEVIL'S CHESSBOARD*, p. 473

[844] Janney, *MARY'S MOSAIC*, pp. 236-237

[845] Janney, *MARY'S MOSAIC*, pp. 236-237

[846] Nolan, *CIA ROGUES AND THE KILLING OF THE KENNEDYS*, p. 60

[847] Nolan, *CIA ROGUES AND THE KILLING OF THE KENNEDYS*, p. 60

[848] Nelson, *LBJ: THE MASTERMIND OF THE JFK ASSASSINATION*, p. 372

[849] Douglass, *JFK AND THE UNSPEAKABLE*, p. 341

[850] Douglass, *JFK AND THE UNSPEAKABLE*, p. 342

[851] Douglass, *JFK AND THE UNSPEAKABLE*, p. 342

[852] Douglass, *JFK AND THE UNSPEAKABLE*, p. 345

[853] Fonzi, *THE LAST INVESTIGATION*, p. 132

[854] Stone & Colapietro, *THE MAN WHO KILLED KENNEDY*, pp. 116-117

[855] Lane, *LAST WORD*, p. 283

[856] Janney, *MARY'S MOSAIC*, pp. 262-263

[857] Talbot, *THE DEVIL'S CHESSBOARD*, p. 146

[858] Talbot, *THE DEVIL'S CHESSBOARD*, pp. 565-566

[859] Lane, *LAST WORD*, p. 238

[860] Lane, *LAST WORD*, p. 281

[861] Douglass, JFK AND THE UNSPEAKABLE, p. 331

[862] Douglass, JFK AND THE UNSPEAKABLE, p. 331

[863] Douglass, JFK AND THE UNSPEAKABLE, p. 331

[864] Talbot, *THE DEVIL'S CHESSBOARD*, pp. 569-572

[865] Talbot, *THE DEVIL'S CHESSBOARD*, pp. 569-572

[866] Weiner, *LEGACY OF ASHES*, p. 244

[867] Weiner, *LEGACY OF ASHES*, pp. 244-245

[868] Douglass, *JFK AND THE UNSPEAKABLE*, pp. 116-117

[869] Douglass, *JFK AND THE UNSPEAKABLE*, pp. 116-117

[870] Douglass, *JFK AND THE UNSPEAKABLE*, pp. 116-117

[871] Douglass, *JFK AND THE UNSPEAKABLE*, pp. 116-117

[872] Douglass, *JFK AND THE UNSPEAKABLE*, pp. 116-117

[873] Douglass, *JFK AND THE UNSPEAKABLE*, pp. 116-117

[874] Douglass, *JFK AND THE UNSPEAKABLE*, pp. 116-117
[875] Douglass, *JFK AND THE UNSPEAKABLE*, p. 118
[876] Douglass, *JFK AND THE UNSPEAKABLE*, p. 118
[877] Douglass, *JFK AND THE UNSPEAKABLE*, p. 118
[878] Nelson, *LBJ: THE MASTERMIND OF THE JFK ASSASSINATION*, p. 125
[879] Nelson, *LBJ: THE MASTERMIND OF THE JFK ASSASSINATION*, p. 104
[880] Nelson, *LBJ: THE MASTERMIND OF THE JFK ASSASSINATION*, p. 104
[881] Nelson, *LBJ: THE MASTERMIND OF THE JFK ASSASSINATION*, p. 104
[882] Nelson, *LBJ: THE MASTERMIND OF THE JFK ASSASSINATION*, p. 104
[883] Nelson, *LBJ: THE MASTERMIND OF THE JFK ASSASSINATION*, pp. 120-121
[884] Nelson, *LBJ: THE MASTERMIND OF THE JFK ASSASSINATION*, pp. 120-121
[885] Nelson, *LBJ: THE MASTERMIND OF THE JFK ASSASSINATION*, pp. 120-121
[886] Nelson, *LBJ: THE MASTERMIND OF THE JFK ASSASSINATION*, pp. 120-121
[887] Nelson, *LBJ: THE MASTERMIND OF THE JFK ASSASSINATION*, pp. 122-123
[888] Nelson, *LBJ: THE MASTERMIND OF THE JFK ASSASSINATION*, pp. 122-123
[889] Nelson, *LBJ: THE MASTERMIND OF THE JFK ASSASSINATION*, pp. 122-123
[890] Nelson, *LBJ: THE MASTERMIND OF THE JFK ASSASSINATION*, pp. 124-125
[891] Douglass, *JFK AND THE UNSPEAKABLE*, p. 148
[892] Douglass, *JFK AND THE UNSPEAKABLE*, p. 148
[893] Douglass, *JFK AND THE UNSPEAKABLE*, p. 192
[894] Douglass, *JFK AND THE UNSPEAKABLE*, p. 192
[895] Douglass, *JFK AND THE UNSPEAKABLE*, p. 192
[896] Joesten, *OSWALD: ASSASSIN OR FALL GUY?*, pp. 234-235
[897] Joesten, *OSWALD: ASSASSIN OR FALL GUY?*, pp. 234-235
[898] Joesten, *OSWALD: ASSASSIN OR FALL GUY?*, pp. 234-235
[899] Joesten, *OSWALD: ASSASSIN OR FALL GUY?*, pp. 234-235
[900] Douglass, *JFK AND THE UNSPEAKABLE*, p. 152
[901] Douglass, *JFK AND THE UNSPEAKABLE*, p. 152
[902] Douglass, *JFK AND THE UNSPEAKABLE*, p. 152
[903] Lane, *LAST WORD*, p. 274
[904] Lane, *LAST WORD*, p. 274
[905] Lane, *LAST WORD*, p. 274
[906] Lane, *LAST WORD*, p. 279
[907] Lane, *LAST WORD*, p. 279

[908] Douglass, *JFK AND THE UNSPEAKABLE*, pp. 165-166
[909] Douglass, *JFK AND THE UNSPEAKABLE*, pp. 165-166
[910] Douglass, *JFK AND THE UNSPEAKABLE*, pp. 165-166
[911] Douglass, *JFK AND THE UNSPEAKABLE*, pp. 165-166
[912] Douglass, *JFK AND THE UNSPEAKABLE*, pp. 165-166
[913] Douglass, *JFK AND THE UNSPEAKABLE*, pp. 166-167
[914] Douglass, *JFK AND THE UNSPEAKABLE*, pp. 166-167
[915] Douglass, *JFK AND THE UNSPEAKABLE*, p. 168
[916] Douglass, *JFK AND THE UNSPEAKABLE*, p. 183
[917] Douglass, *JFK AND THE UNSPEAKABLE*, p. 191
[918] Douglass, *JFK AND THE UNSPEAKABLE*, p. 189
[919] North, *ACT OF TREASON,* p. 325
[920] Douglass, *JFK AND THE UNSPEAKABLE*, p. 219
[921] Douglass, *JFK AND THE UNSPEAKABLE*, p. 197
[922] Douglass, *JFK AND THE UNSPEAKABLE*, p. 202
[923] Douglass, *JFK AND THE UNSPEAKABLE*, p. 209
[924] Lane, *LAST WORD*, p. 138
[925] Lane, *LAST WORD*, p. 138
[926] Lane, *LAST WORD*, p. 138
[927] Lane, *LAST WORD*, p. 138
[928] Lane, *LAST WORD*, p. 138
[929] Lane, *LAST WORD*, p. 138
[930] Lane, *LAST WORD*, p. 138
[931] Nelson, *LBJ: THE MASTERMIND OF THE JFK ASSASSINATION,* p. 128
[932] Douglass, *JFK AND THE UNSPEAKABLE*, p. 146
[933] Douglass, *JFK AND THE UNSPEAKABLE*, p. 146
[934] Douglass, *JFK AND THE UNSPEAKABLE*, p. 146
[935] Douglass, *JFK AND THE UNSPEAKABLE*, p. 146
[936] Douglass, *JFK AND THE UNSPEAKABLE*, p. 146
[937] Douglass, *JFK AND THE UNSPEAKABLE*, p. 146
[938] Douglass, *JFK AND THE UNSPEAKABLE*, p. 146
[939] Douglass, *JFK AND THE UNSPEAKABLE*, p. 147
[940] Douglass, *JFK AND THE UNSPEAKABLE*, p. 147
[941] Douglass, *JFK AND THE UNSPEAKABLE*, p. 147
[942] Douglass, *JFK AND THE UNSPEAKABLE*, p. 148
[943] Douglass, *JFK AND THE UNSPEAKABLE*, p. 148
[944] Douglass, *JFK AND THE UNSPEAKABLE*, p. 148
[945] Douglass, *JFK AND THE UNSPEAKABLE*, p. 148
[946] Belzer & Wayne, *DEAD WRONG*, pp. 120-125
[947] Belzer & Wayne, *DEAD WRONG*, pp. 120-125
[948] Belzer & Wayne, *DEAD WRONG*, pp. 120-125
[949] Belzer & Wayne, *DEAD WRONG*, pp. 120-125
[950] Belzer & Wayne, *DEAD WRONG*, pp. 120-125
[951] Belzer & Wayne, *DEAD WRONG*, pp. 120-125
[952] Belzer & Wayne, *DEAD WRONG*, pp. 120-125
[953] Belzer & Wayne, *DEAD WRONG*, pp. 120-125

[954] Belzer & Wayne, *DEAD WRONG*, pp. 120-125

[955] Belzer & Wayne, *DEAD WRONG*, pp. 120-125

[956] DiEugenio, *DESTINY BETRAYED*, p. 164

[957] DiEugenio, *DESTINY BETRAYED*, p. 164

[958] DiEugenio, *DESTINY BETRAYED*, p. 164-165

[959] DiEugenio, *DESTINY BETRAYED*, p. 164-165

[960] Joesten, *OSWALD: ASSASSIN OR FALL GUY?*, p. 202

[961] Joesten, *OSWALD: ASSASSIN OR FALL GUY?*, p. 203

[962] Joesten, *OSWALD: ASSASSIN OR FALL GUY?*, p. 207

[963] Fonzi, *THE LAST INVESTIGATION*, p. 10

[964] Janney, *MARY'S MOSAIC*, p. 21

[965] Janney, *MARY'S MOSAIC*, p. 21

[966] Janney, *MARY'S MOSAIC*, p. 21

[967] Talbot, *THE DEVIL'S CHESSBOARD*, p. 511

[968] Talbot, *THE DEVIL'S CHESSBOARD*, p. 511

[969] Talbot, *THE DEVIL'S CHESSBOARD*, p. 511

[970] Talbot, *THE DEVIL'S CHESSBOARD*, p. 510

[971] Talbot, *THE DEVIL'S CHESSBOARD*, pp. 511-512

[972] North, *ACT OF TREASON*, p. 460

[973] Talbot, *THE DEVIL'S CHESSBOARD*, p. 512

[974] DiEugenio, *DESTINY BETRAYED*, p. 84

[975] DiEugenio, *DESTINY BETRAYED*, pp. 84-85

[976] DiEugenio, *RECLAIMING PARKLAND*, pp. 176-177

[977] DiEugenio, *DESTINY BETRAYED*, p. 84

[978] Summers, *NOT IN YOUR LIFETIME*, p. 286

[979] Summers, *NOT IN YOUR LIFETIME*, p. 128

[980] Summers, *NOT IN YOUR LIFETIME*, p. 128

[981] Summers, *NOT IN YOUR LIFETIME*, p. 128

[982] Summers, *NOT IN YOUR LIFETIME*, p. 142

[983] Summers, *NOT IN YOUR LIFETIME*, p. 143

[984] Summers, *NOT IN YOUR LIFETIME*, p. 143

[985] Summers, *NOT IN YOUR LIFETIME*, p. 144

[986] DiEugenio, *DESTINY BETRAYED*, p. 143

[987] DiEugenio, *DESTINY BETRAYED*, p. 143

[988] DiEugenio, *DESTINY BETRAYED*, p. 143

[989] Nolan, *CIA ROGUES AND THE KILLING OF THE KENNEDYS*, p. 96

[990] Nolan, *CIA ROGUES AND THE KILLING OF THE KENNEDYS*, p. 96

[991] Nolan, *CIA ROGUES AND THE KILLING OF THE KENNEDYS*, p. 96

[992] Nolan, *CIA ROGUES AND THE KILLING OF THE KENNEDYS*, p. 96

[993] Nolan, *CIA ROGUES AND THE KILLING OF THE KENNEDYS*, p. 96

[994] Nelson, *LBJ: THE MASTERMIND OF THE JFK ASSASSINATION*, p. 336

[995] Nelson, *LBJ: THE MASTERMIND OF THE JFK ASSASSINATION*, p. 336

[996] Summers, *NOT IN YOUR LIFETIME*, p. 140

[997] Summers, *NOT IN YOUR LIFETIME*, p. 140

[998] Summers, *NOT IN YOUR LIFETIME*, pp. 140-141

[999] Nolan, *CIA ROGUES AND THE KILLING OF THE KENNEDYS*, p. 95

[1000] Summers, *NOT IN YOUR LIFETIME*, p. 133

[1001] Summers, *NOT IN YOUR LIFETIME*, p. 133

[1002] Summers, *NOT IN YOUR LIFETIME*, p. 138

[1003] Summers, *NOT IN YOUR LIFETIME*, p. 138

[1004] Summers, *NOT IN YOUR LIFETIME*, p. 138

[1005] Summers, *NOT IN YOUR LIFETIME*, p. 138

[1006] Douglass, *JFK AND THE UNSPEAKABLE*, p. 40

[1007] Douglass, *JFK AND THE UNSPEAKABLE*, p. 40

[1008] Douglass, *JFK AND THE UNSPEAKABLE*, p. 40

[1009] Douglass, *JFK AND THE UNSPEAKABLE*, p. 40

[1010] DiEugenio, *DESTINY BETRAYED*, p. 132

[1011] Summers, *NOT IN YOUR LIFETIME*, p. 135

[1012] DiEugenio, *DESTINY BETRAYED*, p. 136

[1013] DiEugenio, *DESTINY BETRAYED*, p. 136

[1014] DiEugenio, *DESTINY BETRAYED*, p. 136

[1015] DiEugenio, *DESTINY BETRAYED*, p. 136

[1016] DiEugenio, *DESTINY BETRAYED*, p. 136

[1017] DiEugenio, *DESTINY BETRAYED*, p. 136

[1018] DiEugenio, *DESTINY BETRAYED*, p. 138

[1019] DiEugenio, *DESTINY BETRAYED*, p. 139

[1020] Nelson, *LBJ: THE MASTERMIND OF THE JFK ASSASSINATION*, pp. 334

[1021] Douglass, *JFK AND THE UNSPEAKABLE*, p. 365

[1022] Summers, *NOT IN YOUR LIFETIME*, p. 144

[1023] Nolan, *CIA ROGUES AND THE KILLING OF THE KENNEDYS*, p. 99

[1024] Nolan, *CIA ROGUES AND THE KILLING OF THE KENNEDYS*, p. 99

[1025] Summers, *NOT IN YOUR LIFETIME*, p. 151

[1026] Summers, *NOT IN YOUR LIFETIME*, p. 151

[1027] Summers, *NOT IN YOUR LIFETIME*, p. 154

[1028] Summers, *NOT IN YOUR LIFETIME*, p. 154

[1029] (Summers, *NOT IN YOUR LIFETIME*, pp. 155-156

[1030] Newman, *OSWALD AND THE CIA*, pp. 205-206

[1031] Newman, *OSWALD AND THE CIA*, p. 209

[1032] Newman, *OSWALD AND THE CIA*, p. 209

[1033] Newman, *OSWALD AND THE CIA*, p. 209

[1034] Douglass, *JFK AND THE UNSPEAKABLE*, p. 38

[1035] Fonzi, *THE LAST INVESTIGATION*, p. 425

[1036] Fonzi, *THE LAST INVESTIGATION*, p. 425

[1037] Summers, *NOT IN YOUR LIFETIME*, p. 174

[1038] Douglass, *JFK AND THE UNSPEAKABLE*, pp. 46-47

[1039] Fonzi, *THE LAST INVESTIGATION*, p. 425

[1040] Fonzi, *THE LAST INVESTIGATION*, p. 426

[1041] Newman, *OSWALD AND THE CIA*, p. 248

[1042] Joesten, *OSWALD: ASSASSIN OR FALL GUY?*, p. 207

[1043] Newman, *OSWALD AND THE CIA*, p. 212

[1044] Fonzi, *THE LAST INVESTIGATION*, p. 427

[1045] Garrison, *ON THE TRAIL OF THE ASSASSINS*, pp. 57-59

[1046] Garrison, *ON THE TRAIL OF THE ASSASSINS*, pp. 57-59

[1047] Garrison, *ON THE TRAIL OF THE ASSASSINS*, pp. 57-59

[1048] Garrison, *ON THE TRAIL OF THE ASSASSINS*, pp. 57-59

[1049] Garrison, *ON THE TRAIL OF THE ASSASSINS*, pp. 57-59

[1050] Garrison, *ON THE TRAIL OF THE ASSASSINS*, pp. 57-59

[1051] Garrison, *ON THE TRAIL OF THE ASSASSINS*, pp. 57-59

[1052] Garrison, *ON THE TRAIL OF THE ASSASSINS*, pp. 57-59

[1053] Garrison, *ON THE TRAIL OF THE ASSASSINS*, pp. 57-59

[1054] Garrison, *ON THE TRAIL OF THE ASSASSINS*, pp. 57-59

[1055] Nelson, *LBJ: THE MASTERMIND OF THE JFK ASSASSINATION*, pp. 343

[1056] Nelson, *LBJ: THE MASTERMIND OF THE JFK ASSASSINATION*, pp. 343

[1057] Fonzi, *THE LAST INVESTIGATION*, pp. 427-428

[1058] Fonzi, *THE LAST INVESTIGATION*, pp. 427-428

[1059] Fonzi, *THE LAST INVESTIGATION*, pp. 427-428

[1060] Fonzi, *THE LAST INVESTIGATION*, pp. 427-428

[1061] Garrison, *ON THE TRAIL OF THE ASSASSINS*, pp. 58-59

[1062] Douglass, *JFK AND THE UNSPEAKABLE*, pp. 61-62

[1063] Douglass, *JFK AND THE UNSPEAKABLE*, pp. 61-62

[1064] Douglass, *JFK AND THE UNSPEAKABLE*, pp. 61-62

[1065] Douglass, *JFK AND THE UNSPEAKABLE*, pp. 61-62

[1066] Douglass, *JFK AND THE UNSPEAKABLE*, pp. 61-62

[1067] Douglass, *JFK AND THE UNSPEAKABLE*, p. 62

[1068] Garrison, *ON THE TRAIL OF THE ASSASSINS*, p. 116

[1069] Nelson, *LBJ: THE MASTERMIND OF THE JFK ASSASSINATION*, p. 346

[1070] Douglass, *JFK AND THE UNSPEAKABLE*, p. 62

[1071] Summers, *NOT IN YOUR LIFETIME*, p. 278

[1072] Fonzi, *THE LAST INVESTIGATION*, p. 428

[1073] Fonzi, *THE LAST INVESTIGATION*, p. 428

[1074] Fonzi, *THE LAST INVESTIGATION*, p. 428

[1075] North, *ACT OF TREASON*, p. 280

[1076] North, *ACT OF TREASON*, p. 300

[1077] DiEugenio, *DESTINY BETRAYED*, p. 159

[1078] DiEugenio, *DESTINY BETRAYED*, p. 159

[1079] Newman, *OSWALD AND THE CIA*, p. 323

[1080] North, *ACT OF TREASON*, p. 296

[1081] Douglass, *JFK AND THE UNSPEAKABLE*, p. 65
[1082] Fonzi, *THE LAST INVESTIGATION*, p. 429
[1083] Baker, *ME & LEE*, p. 21
[1084] Baker, *ME & LEE*, p. 53
[1085] Baker, *ME & LEE*, p. 95
[1086] Baker, *ME & LEE*, p. 96
[1087] Baker, *ME & LEE*, p. 96
[1088] Baker, *ME & LEE*, p. 208
[1089] Baker, *ME & LEE*, p. 208
[1090] Baker, *ME & LEE*, p. 261
[1091] Baker, *ME & LEE*, p. 262
[1092] Baker, *ME & LEE*, pp. 262-264
[1093] Baker, *ME & LEE*, p. 173
[1094] Baker, *ME & LEE*, p. 174
[1095] Baker, *ME & LEE*, p. 251
[1096] Baker, *ME & LEE*, p. 158
[1097] Baker, *ME & LEE*, p. 191
[1098] Baker, *ME & LEE*, p. 251
[1099] Baker, *ME & LEE*, p. 235
[1100] Baker, *ME & LEE*, p. 287
[1101] Baker, *ME & LEE*, p. 380
[1102] Baker, *ME & LEE*, p. 126
[1103] Baker, *ME & LEE*, p. 211
[1104] Baker, *ME & LEE*, p. 320
[1105] Baker, *ME & LEE*, p. 183
[1106] Baker, *ME & LEE*, p. 183
[1107] Baker, *ME & LEE*, p. 179
[1108] Baker, *ME & LEE*, pp. 423-440
[1109] Baker, *ME & LEE*, p. 444
[1110] Baker, *ME & LEE*, pp. 423-440
[1111] Baker, *ME & LEE*, p. 466
[1112] Baker, *ME & LEE*, p. 466
[1113] Baker, *ME & LEE*, p. 467
[1114] Baker, *ME & LEE*, p. 470
[1115] Baker, *ME & LEE*, p. 470
[1116] Baker, *ME & LEE*, p. 470
[1117] Baker, *ME & LEE*, p. 471
[1118] Baker, *ME & LEE*, p. 471
[1119] Baker, *ME & LEE*, p. 522
[1120] Baker, *ME & LEE*, p. 521
[1121] Baker, *ME & LEE*, p. 533
[1122] Baker, *ME & LEE*, p. 540
[1123] Lane, *LAST WORD*, p. 286
[1124] Douglass, *JFK AND THE UNSPEAKABLE*, p. 81
[1125] Douglass, *JFK AND THE UNSPEAKABLE*, p. 81
[1126] Douglass, *JFK AND THE UNSPEAKABLE*, p. 81
[1127] Summers, *NOT IN YOUR LIFETIME*, p. 315

[1128] Summers, *NOT IN YOUR LIFETIME*, p. 323

[1129] Summers, *NOT IN YOUR LIFETIME*, p. 323

[1130] Summers, *NOT IN YOUR LIFETIME*, p. 323

[1131] Summers, *NOT IN YOUR LIFETIME*, p. 321

[1132] Summers, *NOT IN YOUR LIFETIME*, pp. 321-322

[1133] Summers, *NOT IN YOUR LIFETIME*, p. 322

[1134] Summers, *NOT IN YOUR LIFETIME*, p. 322

[1135] Summers, *NOT IN YOUR LIFETIME*, p. 322

[1136] North, *ACT OF TREASON,* p. 319

[1137] Summers, *NOT IN YOUR LIFETIME*, p. 322

[1138] Summers, *NOT IN YOUR LIFETIME*, pp. 322-323

[1139] Fonzi, *THE LAST INVESTIGATION*, pp. 288-289

[1140] Fonzi, *THE LAST INVESTIGATION*, pp. 288-289

[1141] Fonzi, *THE LAST INVESTIGATION*, pp. 288-289

[1142] Fonzi, *THE LAST INVESTIGATION*, pp. 288-289

[1143] Fonzi, *THE LAST INVESTIGATION*, pp. 288-289

[1144] Shenon, *A CRUEL AND SHOCKING ACT*, p. 384

[1145] Lane, *LAST WORD*, pp. 196-197

[1146] Lane, *LAST WORD*, pp. 196-197

[1147] Nelson, *LBJ: THE MASTERMIND OF THE JFK ASSASSINATION*, pp. 531-532

[1148] Lane, *LAST WORD*, p. 197

[1149] Lane, *LAST WORD*, p. 197

[1150] Lane, *LAST WORD*, p. 199

[1151] Fonzi, *THE LAST INVESTIGATION*, p. 430

[1152] Fonzi, *THE LAST INVESTIGATION*, p. 430

[1153] Fonzi, *THE LAST INVESTIGATION*, p. 430

[1154] Douglass, *JFK AND THE UNSPEAKABLE*, p. 82

[1155] Douglass, *JFK AND THE UNSPEAKABLE*, p. 82

[1156] Douglass, *JFK AND THE UNSPEAKABLE*, p. 82

[1157] Fonzi, *THE LAST INVESTIGATION*, p. 430

[1158] Fonzi, *THE LAST INVESTIGATION*, p. 430

[1159] Fonzi, *THE LAST INVESTIGATION*, p. 439

[1160] Fonzi, *THE LAST INVESTIGATION*, p. 294

[1161] Fonzi, *THE LAST INVESTIGATION*, p. 294

[1162] Fonzi, *THE LAST INVESTIGATION*, p. 294

[1163] Summers, *NOT IN YOUR LIFETIME*, pp. 329-334

[1164] Nelson, *LBJ: THE MASTERMIND OF THE JFK ASSASSINATION*, p. 351

[1165] Nelson, *LBJ: THE MASTERMIND OF THE JFK ASSASSINATION*, p. 351

[1166] Nelson, *LBJ: THE MASTERMIND OF THE JFK ASSASSINATION*, p. 351

[1167] Nelson, *LBJ: THE MASTERMIND OF THE JFK ASSASSINATION*, pp. 351-352

[1168] Morley, *THE GHOST*, p. 215

[1169] Summers, *NOT IN YOUR LIFETIME*, p. 342

[1170] Summers, *NOT IN YOUR LIFETIME*, p. 342

[1171] Douglass, *JFK AND THE UNSPEAKABLE*, p. 81

[1172] Nelson, *LBJ: THE MASTERMIND OF THE JFK ASSASSINATION*, p. 540

[1173] Nelson, *LBJ: THE MASTERMIND OF THE JFK ASSASSINATION*, p. 540

[1174] North, *ACT OF TREASON*, pp. 355-356

[1175] Douglass, *JFK AND THE UNSPEAKABLE*, p. xxix

[1176] North, *ACT OF TREASON*, p. 417

[1177] Fonzi, *THE LAST INVESTIGATION*, p. 432

[1178] Fonzi, *THE LAST INVESTIGATION*, p. 432

[1179] Douglass, *JFK AND THE UNSPEAKABLE*, p. 196

[1180] Douglass, *JFK AND THE UNSPEAKABLE*, p. 196

[1181] Douglass, *JFK AND THE UNSPEAKABLE*, p. 196

[1182] Douglass, *JFK AND THE UNSPEAKABLE*, p. 197

[1183] Douglass, *JFK AND THE UNSPEAKABLE*, p. 197

[1184] Douglass, *JFK AND THE UNSPEAKABLE*, p. 197

[1185] Douglass, *JFK AND THE UNSPEAKABLE*, p. 197

[1186] Douglass, *JFK AND THE UNSPEAKABLE*, p. 197

[1187] Douglass, *JFK AND THE UNSPEAKABLE*, p. 196

[1188] Douglass, *JFK AND THE UNSPEAKABLE*, p. 177

[1189] Douglass, *JFK AND THE UNSPEAKABLE*, p. 177

[1190] Douglass, *JFK AND THE UNSPEAKABLE*, pp. 177-178

[1191] Douglass, *JFK AND THE UNSPEAKABLE*, pp. 177-178

[1192] Douglass, *JFK AND THE UNSPEAKABLE*, pp. 177-178

[1193] Douglass, *JFK AND THE UNSPEAKABLE*, p. 178

[1194] Nelson, *LBJ: THE MASTERMIND OF THE JFK ASSASSINATION*, p. 327

[1195] Nelson, *LBJ: THE MASTERMIND OF THE JFK ASSASSINATION*, p. 327

[1196] Corsi, *WHO REALLY KILLED KENNEDY*, p. 304

[1197] Corsi, *WHO REALLY KILLED KENNEDY*, p. 304

[1198] Talbot, *THE DEVIL'S CHESSBOARD*, p. 28

[1199] Talbot, *THE DEVIL'S CHESSBOARD*, p. 29

[1200] Talbot, *THE DEVIL'S CHESSBOARD*, p. 29

[1201] Talbot, *THE DEVIL'S CHESSBOARD*, p. 77

[1202] Talbot, *THE DEVIL'S CHESSBOARD*, p. 77

[1203] Corsi, *WHO REALLY KILLED KENNEDY*, pp. 304-305

[1204] Corsi, *WHO REALLY KILLED KENNEDY*, p. 305

[1205] Corsi, *WHO REALLY KILLED KENNEDY*, p. 306

[1206] Talbot, *THE DEVIL'S CHESSBOARD*, p. 122

[1207] Talbot, *THE DEVIL'S CHESSBOARD*, p. 148

[1208] Talbot, *THE DEVIL'S CHESSBOARD*, p. 146

[1209] Talbot, *THE DEVIL'S CHESSBOARD*, p. 148

[1210] Talbot, *THE DEVIL'S CHESSBOARD*, pp. 148-149

[1211] Talbot, *THE DEVIL'S CHESSBOARD*, p. 146

[1212] Talbot, *THE DEVIL'S CHESSBOARD*, p. 149

1213 Talbot, *THE DEVIL'S CHESSBOARD*, p. 149
1214 Talbot, *THE DEVIL'S CHESSBOARD*, p. 77
1215 Talbot, *THE DEVIL'S CHESSBOARD*, p. 149
1216 Talbot, *THE DEVIL'S CHESSBOARD*, p. 147
1217 Talbot, *THE DEVIL'S CHESSBOARD*, p. 366
1218 Talbot, *THE DEVIL'S CHESSBOARD*, p. 149
1219 Talbot, *THE DEVIL'S CHESSBOARD*, p. 160
1220 Talbot, *THE DEVIL'S CHESSBOARD*, p. 219
1221 Talbot, *THE DEVIL'S CHESSBOARD*, p. 219
1222 Talbot, *THE DEVIL'S CHESSBOARD*, p. 219
1223 Talbot, *THE DEVIL'S CHESSBOARD*, p. 221
1224 Talbot, *THE DEVIL'S CHESSBOARD*, p. 223
1225 Talbot, *THE DEVIL'S CHESSBOARD*, pp. 287-290
1226 Talbot, *THE DEVIL'S CHESSBOARD*, p. 290
1227 Talbot, *THE DEVIL'S CHESSBOARD*, p. 290
1228 Talbot, *THE DEVIL'S CHESSBOARD*, p. 290
1229 Talbot, *THE DEVIL'S CHESSBOARD*, pp. 290-297
1230 Talbot, *THE DEVIL'S CHESSBOARD*, p. 309
1231 Talbot, *THE DEVIL'S CHESSBOARD*, p. 309
1232 Talbot, *THE DEVIL'S CHESSBOARD*, p. 309
1233 Janney, *MARY'S MOSAIC*, p. 184
1234 Talbot, *THE DEVIL'S CHESSBOARD*, p. 366
1235 Talbot, *THE DEVIL'S CHESSBOARD*, p. 413
1236 Talbot, *THE DEVIL'S CHESSBOARD*, p. 414
1237 Talbot, *THE DEVIL'S CHESSBOARD*, pp. 414-415
1238 Talbot, *THE DEVIL'S CHESSBOARD*, p. 416
1239 Talbot, *THE DEVIL'S CHESSBOARD*, p. 416
1240 Talbot, *THE DEVIL'S CHESSBOARD*, p. 416
1241 Talbot, *THE DEVIL'S CHESSBOARD*, p. 417
1242 Talbot, *THE DEVIL'S CHESSBOARD*, p. 418
1243 Talbot, *THE DEVIL'S CHESSBOARD*, p. 420
1244 Talbot, *THE DEVIL'S CHESSBOARD*, p. 424
1245 Talbot, *THE DEVIL'S CHESSBOARD*, pp. 7, 428
1246 Talbot, *THE DEVIL'S CHESSBOARD*, p. 449
1247 Talbot, *THE DEVIL'S CHESSBOARD*, p. 449
1248 Nolan, *CIA ROGUES AND THE KILLING OF THE KENNEDYS*, p. 60
1249 Corsi, *WHO REALLY KILLED KENNEDY*, p. 308
1250 Corsi, *WHO REALLY KILLED KENNEDY*, p. 308
1251 Corsi, *WHO REALLY KILLED KENNEDY*, p. 308
1252 Nelson, *LBJ: THE MASTERMIND OF THE JFK ASSASSINATION*, p. 123
1253 Talbot, *THE DEVIL'S CHESSBOARD*, p. 493
1254 Talbot, THE DEVIL'S CHESSBOARD, p. 488
1255 Talbot, *THE DEVIL'S CHESSBOARD*, pp. 487-488
1256 Talbot, *THE DEVIL'S CHESSBOARD*, p. 539
1257 Talbot, *THE DEVIL'S CHESSBOARD*, p. 8

[1258] Talbot, *THE DEVIL'S CHESSBOARD*, p. 8

[1259] Janney, *MARY'S MOSAIC*, p. 286

[1260] Janney, *MARY'S MOSAIC*, p. 286

[1261] Janney, *MARY'S MOSAIC*, p. 286

[1262] Talbot, *THE DEVIL'S CHESSBOARD*, p. 575

[1263] Corsi, *WHO REALLY KILLED KENNEDY*, p. 301

[1264] Corsi, *WHO REALLY KILLED KENNEDY*, p. 301

[1265] Corsi, *WHO REALLY KILLED KENNEDY*, p. 301

[1266] North, *ACT OF TREASON,* p. 465

[1267] North, *ACT OF TREASON,* p. 465

[1268] North, *ACT OF TREASON,* p. 465

[1269] Douglass, *JFK AND THE UNSPEAKABLE*, p. 16

[1270] Lane, *LAST WORD*, pp. 257-258

[1271] Nolan, *CIA ROGUES AND THE KILLING OF THE KENNEDYS*, p. 16

[1272] Nolan, *CIA ROGUES AND THE KILLING OF THE KENNEDYS*, p. 17

[1273] Nolan, *CIA ROGUES AND THE KILLING OF THE KENNEDYS*, p. 23

[1274] Nolan, *CIA ROGUES AND THE KILLING OF THE KENNEDYS*, p. 19

[1275] Nolan, *CIA ROGUES AND THE KILLING OF THE KENNEDYS*, p. 23

[1276] Nolan, *CIA ROGUES AND THE KILLING OF THE KENNEDYS*, p. 27

[1277] Lane, *LAST WORD*, pp. 256-257

[1278] Nolan, *CIA ROGUES AND THE KILLING OF THE KENNEDYS*, pp. 17-18

[1279] Weiner, *LEGACY OF ASHES*, pp. 73-74

[1280] Weiner, *LEGACY OF ASHES*, pp. 73-74

[1281] Weiner, *LEGACY OF ASHES*, p. 74

[1282] Nolan, *CIA ROGUES AND THE KILLING OF THE KENNEDYS*, p. 18

[1283] Lane, *LAST WORD*, p. 256

[1284] Lane, *LAST WORD*, pp. 257-258

[1285] Weiner, *LEGACY OF ASHES*, p. 74

[1286] Lane, *LAST WORD*, p. 256

[1287] Weiner, *LEGACY OF ASHES*, p. 73

[1288] Weiner, *LEGACY OF ASHES*, p. 74

[1289] Nolan, *CIA ROGUES AND THE KILLING OF THE KENNEDYS*, p. 17

[1290] Nolan, *CIA ROGUES AND THE KILLING OF THE KENNEDYS*, p. 63

[1291] Nolan, *CIA ROGUES AND THE KILLING OF THE KENNEDYS*, p. 59

[1292] Janney, *MARY'S MOSAIC*, pp. 203-204

[1293] Janney, *MARY'S MOSAIC*, pp. 203-204

[1294] Janney, *MARY'S MOSAIC*, pp. 203-204

[1295] Nolan, *CIA ROGUES AND THE KILLING OF THE KENNEDYS*, p. 20

[1296] Nolan, *CIA ROGUES AND THE KILLING OF THE KENNEDYS*, p. 27

[1297] Nolan, *CIA ROGUES AND THE KILLING OF THE KENNEDYS*, p. 28

[1298] Nolan, *CIA ROGUES AND THE KILLING OF THE KENNEDYS*, p. 28

[1299] Lane, *LAST WORD*, pp. 265-266

[1300] Lane, *LAST WORD*, pp. 265-266

[1301] Lane, *LAST WORD*, pp. 265-266

[1302] Lane, *LAST WORD*, pp. 265-266

[1303] Nolan, *CIA ROGUES AND THE KILLING OF THE KENNEDYS*, p. 27

[1304] Nolan, *CIA ROGUES AND THE KILLING OF THE KENNEDYS*, p. 27

[1305] Nolan, *CIA ROGUES AND THE KILLING OF THE KENNEDYS*, p. 27

[1306] Nolan, *CIA ROGUES AND THE KILLING OF THE KENNEDYS*, p. 28

[1307] Nolan, *CIA ROGUES AND THE KILLING OF THE KENNEDYS*, p. 28

[1308] Nolan, *CIA ROGUES AND THE KILLING OF THE KENNEDYS*, p. 28

[1309] Lane, *LAST WORD*, pp. 255-256

[1310] Lane, *LAST WORD*, pp. 255-256

[1311] Lane, *LAST WORD*, pp. 255-256

[1312] Lane, *LAST WORD*, pp. 255-256

[1313] Lane, *LAST WORD*, p. 257

[1314] Lane, *LAST WORD*, p. 267

[1315] Lane, *LAST WORD*, p. 267

[1316] Lane, *LAST WORD*, pp. 267-268

[1317] Lane, *LAST WORD*, p. 269

[1318] Lane, *LAST WORD*, p. 269

[1319] Lane, *LAST WORD*, p. 269

[1320] Lane, *LAST WORD*, p. 269

[1321] Lane, *LAST WORD*, pp. 269-270

[1322] Lane, *LAST WORD*, p. 270

[1323] Lane, *LAST WORD*, p. 270

[1324] Lane, *LAST WORD*, p. 270

[1325] Lane, *LAST WORD*, p. 270

[1326] Lane, *LAST WORD*, p. 270

[1327] Lane, *LAST WORD*, p. 270

[1328] Talbot, *THE DEVIL'S CHESSBOARD*, pp. 579-580

[1329] Talbot, *THE DEVIL'S CHESSBOARD*, pp. 579-580

[1330] Talbot, *THE DEVIL'S CHESSBOARD*, pp. 579-580

[1331] Douglass, *JFK AND THE UNSPEAKABLE*, p. 34

[1332] Douglass, *JFK AND THE UNSPEAKABLE*, p. 34

[1333] Morley, *THE GHOST*, p. 220

[1334] Summers, *NOT IN YOUR LIFETIME*, p. 146

[1335] Nolan, *CIA ROGUES AND THE KILLING OF THE KENNEDYS*, pp. 26-27

[1336] Nolan, *CIA ROGUES AND THE KILLING OF THE KENNEDYS*, pp. 26-27

[1337] Nelson, *LBJ: THE MASTERMIND OF THE JFK ASSASSINATION*, p. 100

[1338] Douglass, *JFK AND THE UNSPEAKABLE*, p. 252

[1339] Douglass, *JFK AND THE UNSPEAKABLE*, p. 252

[1340] Lane, *LAST WORD*, p. 282

[1341] Nelson, *LBJ: THE MASTERMIND OF THE JFK ASSASSINATION*, p. 175

[1342] Nolan, *CIA ROGUES AND THE KILLING OF THE KENNEDYS*, pp. 46-51

[1343] Nolan, *CIA ROGUES AND THE KILLING OF THE KENNEDYS*, pp. 46-51

[1344] Fonzi, *THE LAST INVESTIGATION*, p. 441

[1345] Summers, *NOT IN YOUR LIFETIME*, p. 147

[1346] Fonzi, *THE LAST INVESTIGATION*, p. 144

[1347] Fonzi, *THE LAST INVESTIGATION*, p. 144

[1348] Weiner, *LEGACY OF ASHES*, p. 329

[1349] Weiner, *LEGACY OF ASHES*, p. 329

[1350] Weiner, *LEGACY OF ASHES*, p. 329

[1351] Weiner, *LEGACY OF ASHES*, pp. 329-330

[1352] Weiner, *LEGACY OF ASHES*, p. 330

[1353] Weiner, *LEGACY OF ASHES*, p. 330

[1354] Fonzi, *THE LAST INVESTIGATION*, p. 433

[1355] Garrison, *ON THE TRAIL OF THE ASSASSINS*, pp. 129-130

[1356] Nelson, *LBJ: THE MASTERMIND OF THE JFK ASSASSINATION*, p. 557

[1357] Nelson, *LBJ: THE MASTERMIND OF THE JFK ASSASSINATION*, p. 557

[1358] Nelson, *LBJ: THE MASTERMIND OF THE JFK ASSASSINATION*, p. 557

[1359] Nelson, *LBJ: THE MASTERMIND OF THE JFK ASSASSINATION*, p. 605

[1360] Nelson, *LBJ: THE MASTERMIND OF THE JFK ASSASSINATION*, p. 605

[1361] DiEugenio, *DESTINY BETRAYED*, pp. 75-76

[1362] Talbot, *THE DEVIL'S CHESSBOARD*, p. 97

[1363] Talbot, *THE DEVIL'S CHESSBOARD*, p. 97

[1364] Talbot, *THE DEVIL'S CHESSBOARD*, pp. 465-466

[1365] Talbot, *THE DEVIL'S CHESSBOARD*, pp. 465-466

[1366] Morley, *THE GHOST*, p. 255

[1367] Summers, *NOT IN YOUR LIFETIME*, pp. 197-198

[1368] Summers, *NOT IN YOUR LIFETIME*, pp. 197-198

[1369] Nelson, *LBJ: THE MASTERMIND OF THE JFK ASSASSINATION*, pp. 327-328

[1370] Nelson, *LBJ: THE MASTERMIND OF THE JFK ASSASSINATION*, p. 468

[1371] Nelson, *LBJ: THE MASTERMIND OF THE JFK ASSASSINATION*, p. 468

[1372] Nelson, *LBJ: THE MASTERMIND OF THE JFK ASSASSINATION*, p. 468

[1373] Janney, *MARY'S MOSAIC*, p. 286

[1374] DiEugenio, *DESTINY BETRAYED*, p. 164

[1375] Nelson, *LBJ: THE MASTERMIND OF THE JFK ASSASSINATION*, p. 605

[1376] Nelson, *LBJ: THE MASTERMIND OF THE JFK ASSASSINATION*, p. 605

[1377] Morley, *THE GHOST*, p. 151

[1378] Morley, *THE GHOST*, p. 153

[1379] Morley, *THE GHOST*, p. 153

[1380] Morley, *THE GHOST*, p. 153

[1381] Janney, *MARY'S MOSAIC*, p. 356

[1382] Nolan, *CIA ROGUES AND THE KILLING OF THE KENNEDYS*, p. 58

[1383] Nolan, *CIA ROGUES AND THE KILLING OF THE KENNEDYS*, p. 58

[1384] Nelson, *LBJ: THE MASTERMIND OF THE JFK ASSASSINATION*, p. 182

[1385] Nolan, *CIA ROGUES AND THE KILLING OF THE KENNEDYS*, p. 59

[1386] Nolan, *CIA ROGUES AND THE KILLING OF THE KENNEDYS*, p. 59

[1387] Weiner, *LEGACY OF ASHES*, pp. 208-209

[1388] Weiner, *LEGACY OF ASHES*, pp. 208-209

[1389] Weiner, *LEGACY OF ASHES*, pp. 208-209

[1390] Nelson, *LBJ: THE MASTERMIND OF THE JFK ASSASSINATION*, pp. 351-352

[1391] Fonzi, *THE LAST INVESTIGATION*, p. 436

[1392] Fonzi, *THE LAST INVESTIGATION*, p. 436

[1393] Janney, *MARY'S MOSAIC*, p. 325

[1394] Janney, *MARY'S MOSAIC*, p. 326

[1395] Janney, *MARY'S MOSAIC*, p. 326

[1396] Janney, *MARY'S MOSAIC*, p. 326

[1397] Morley, *THE GHOST*, p. 248

[1398] Morley, *THE GHOST*, pp. 248-249

[1399] Morley, *THE GHOST*, p. 249

[1400] Shenon, *A CRUEL AND SHOCKING ACT*, p. 538

[1401] Shenon, *A CRUEL AND SHOCKING ACT*, p. 538

[1402] Shenon, *A CRUEL AND SHOCKING ACT*, p. 538
[1403] Shenon, *A CRUEL AND SHOCKING ACT*, p. 538
[1404] Shenon, *A CRUEL AND SHOCKING ACT*, pp. 537-538
[1405] Shenon, *A CRUEL AND SHOCKING ACT*, pp. 537-538
[1406] Talbot, *THE DEVIL'S CHESSBOARD*, p. 620
[1407] Douglass, *JFK AND THE UNSPEAKABLE*, p. 75
[1408] Baker, *ME & LEE*, p. 521
[1409] Fonzi, *THE LAST INVESTIGATION*, p. 422
[1410] Fonzi, *THE LAST INVESTIGATION*, p. 423
[1411] Fonzi, *THE LAST INVESTIGATION*, pp. 141-142
[1412] Fonzi, *THE LAST INVESTIGATION*, pp. 141-142
[1413] Fonzi, *THE LAST INVESTIGATION*, pp. 141-142
[1414] Talbot, *THE DEVIL'S CHESSBOARD*, p. 504
[1415] Baker, *ME & LEE*, p. 521
[1416] Nelson, *LBJ: THE MASTERMIND OF THE JFK ASSASSINATION*, p. 327
[1417] Baker, *ME & LEE*, p. 521
[1418] Baker, *Me & Lee*, p. 521
[1419] Nelson, *LBJ: THE MASTERMIND OF THE JFK ASSASSINATION*, p. 468
[1420] Nelson, *LBJ: THE MASTERMIND OF THE JFK ASSASSINATION*, p. 468
[1421] Lane, *LAST WORD*, pp. xi-xii
[1422] Lane, *LAST WORD*, pp. xi-xii
[1423] Lane, *LAST WORD*, pp. xi-xii
[1424] Lane, *LAST WORD*, p. xii
[1425] Lane, *LAST WORD*, p. xii
[1426] Lane, *LAST WORD*, p. xii
[1427] Lane, *LAST WORD*, p. xii
[1428] Lane, *LAST WORD*, p. xii
[1429] Lane, *LAST WORD*, pp. 136-137
[1430] Douglass, *JFK AND THE UNSPEAKABLE*, p. 75
[1431] Fonzi, *THE LAST INVESTIGATION*, p. 426
[1432] Fonzi, *THE LAST INVESTIGATION*, p. 426
[1433] Fonzi, *THE LAST INVESTIGATION*, p. 132
[1434] Douglass, *JFK AND THE UNSPEAKABLE*, p. 57
[1435] Douglass, *JFK AND THE UNSPEAKABLE*, p. 57
[1436] Fonzi, *THE LAST INVESTIGATION*, p. 425
[1437] Nelson, *LBJ: THE MASTERMIND OF THE JFK ASSASSINATION*, p. 81
[1438] Fonzi, *THE LAST INVESTIGATION*, p. 425
[1439] Fonzi, *THE LAST INVESTIGATION*, p. 425
[1440] Fonzi, *THE LAST INVESTIGATION*, p. 425
[1441] Fonzi, *THE LAST INVESTIGATION*, p. 425
[1442] Nolan, *CIA ROGUES AND THE KILLING OF THE KENNEDYS*, p. 14
[1443] Fonzi, *THE LAST INVESTIGATION*, p. 425

[1444] Fonzi, *THE LAST INVESTIGATION*, p. 425

[1445] Fonzi, *THE LAST INVESTIGATION*, p. 425

[1446] Fonzi, *THE LAST INVESTIGATION*, p. 46

[1447] Nelson, *LBJ: THE MASTERMIND OF THE JFK ASSASSINATION*, p. 83

[1448] Nelson, *LBJ: THE MASTERMIND OF THE JFK ASSASSINATION*, p. 84

[1449] Nelson, *LBJ: THE MASTERMIND OF THE JFK ASSASSINATION*, p. 88

[1450] Summers, *NOT IN YOUR LIFETIME*, p. 205

[1451] Summers, *NOT IN YOUR LIFETIME*, p. 205

[1452] Morley, *THE GHOST*, p. 116

[1453] Morley, *THE GHOST*, p. 116

[1454] Nelson, *LBJ: THE MASTERMIND OF THE JFK ASSASSINATION*, p. 363

[1455] Nelson, *LBJ: THE MASTERMIND OF THE JFK ASSASSINATION*, p. 363

[1456] Nelson, *LBJ: THE MASTERMIND OF THE JFK ASSASSINATION*, p. 363

[1457] Nelson, *LBJ: THE MASTERMIND OF THE JFK ASSASSINATION*, p. 363

[1458] Nelson, *LBJ: THE MASTERMIND OF THE JFK ASSASSINATION*, p. 363

[1459] Nolan, *CIA ROGUES AND THE KILLING OF THE KENNEDYS*, p. 60

[1460] Nolan, *CIA ROGUES AND THE KILLING OF THE KENNEDYS*, p. 60

[1461] Nelson, *LBJ: THE MASTERMIND OF THE JFK ASSASSINATION*, p. 468

[1462] Nelson, *LBJ: THE MASTERMIND OF THE JFK ASSASSINATION*, p. 468

[1463] Fonzi, *THE LAST INVESTIGATION*, p. 122

[1464] Nolan, *CIA ROGUES AND THE KILLING OF THE KENNEDYS*, p. 37

[1465] Talbot, *THE DEVIL'S CHESSBOARD*, pp. 500-501

[1466] Nelson, *LBJ: THE MASTERMIND OF THE JFK ASSASSINATION*, p. 102

[1467] Talbot, *THE DEVIL'S CHESSBOARD*, p. 471

[1468] Belzer & Wayne, *DEAD WRONG*, p. 151

[1469] Nelson, *LBJ: THE MASTERMIND OF THE JFK ASSASSINATION*, p. 543

[1470] Belzer & Wayne, *DEAD WRONG*, p. 152

[1471] Nelson, *LBJ: THE MASTERMIND OF THE JFK ASSASSINATION*, p. 543

[1472] Nelson, *LBJ: THE MASTERMIND OF THE JFK ASSASSINATION*, p. 175

[1473] Nelson, *LBJ: THE MASTERMIND OF THE JFK ASSASSINATION*,

p. 175

[1474] Nelson, *LBJ: THE MASTERMIND OF THE JFK ASSASSINATION*, p. 175

[1475] Nelson, *LBJ: THE MASTERMIND OF THE JFK ASSASSINATION*, p. 175

[1476] Nelson, *LBJ: THE MASTERMIND OF THE JFK ASSASSINATION*, p. 468

[1477] Nelson, *LBJ: THE MASTERMIND OF THE JFK ASSASSINATION*, p. 468

[1478] Nelson, *LBJ: THE MASTERMIND OF THE JFK ASSASSINATION*, p. 321

[1479] Nelson, *LBJ: THE MASTERMIND OF THE JFK ASSASSINATION*, p. 323

[1480] Nelson, *LBJ: THE MASTERMIND OF THE JFK ASSASSINATION*, p. 343

[1481] Nelson, *LBJ: THE MASTERMIND OF THE JFK ASSASSINATION*, p. 338

[1482] Nelson, *LBJ: THE MASTERMIND OF THE JFK ASSASSINATION*, p. 342

[1483] Nelson, *LBJ: THE MASTERMIND OF THE JFK ASSASSINATION*, p. 342

[1484] Nelson, *LBJ: THE MASTERMIND OF THE JFK ASSASSINATION*, p. 342

[1485] Weiner, *LEGACY OF ASHES*, p. 316

[1486] Weiner, *LEGACY OF ASHES*, p. 316

[1487] Weiner, *LEGACY OF ASHES*, p. 316

[1488] Stone & Colapietro, *THE MAN WHO KILLED KENNEDY*, p. 156

[1489] Fonzi, *THE LAST INVESTIGATION*, p. 77

[1490] Weiner, *ENEMIES*, p. 220

[1491] Weiner, *ENEMIES*, p. 220

[1492] Fonzi, *THE LAST INVESTIGATION*, p. 86

[1493] Fonzi, *THE LAST INVESTIGATION*, p. 86

[1494] Fonzi, *THE LAST INVESTIGATION*, p. 78

[1495] Fonzi, *THE LAST INVESTIGATION*, p. 79

[1496] Fonzi, *THE LAST INVESTIGATION*, p. 79

[1497] Talbot, *THE DEVIL'S CHESSBOARD*, p. 501

[1498] Talbot, *THE DEVIL'S CHESSBOARD*, p. 501

[1499] Talbot, *THE DEVIL'S CHESSBOARD*, p. 501

[1500] Talbot, *THE DEVIL'S CHESSBOARD*, p. 501

[1501] Talbot, *THE DEVIL'S CHESSBOARD*, p. 502

[1502] Nelson, *LBJ: THE MASTERMIND OF THE JFK ASSASSINATION*, p. 327

[1503] Fonzi, *THE LAST INVESTIGATION*, p. 49

[1504] Fonzi, *THE LAST INVESTIGATION*, p. 49

[1505] Fonzi, *THE LAST INVESTIGATION*, p. 49

[1506] Corsi, *WHO REALLY KILLED KENNEDY*, p. 317

[1507] Corsi, *WHO REALLY KILLED KENNEDY*, p. 317

[1508] Corsi, *WHO REALLY KILLED KENNEDY*, p. 236
[1509] Corsi, *WHO REALLY KILLED KENNEDY*, p. 236
[1510] Corsi, *WHO REALLY KILLED KENNEDY*, pp. 236-237
[1511] Corsi, *WHO REALLY KILLED KENNEDY*, pp. 236-237
[1512] Corsi, *WHO REALLY KILLED KENNEDY*, pp. 236-237
[1513] Lane, *LAST WORD*, p. 65
[1514] Corsi, *WHO REALLY KILLED KENNEDY*, p. 237
[1515] Corsi, *WHO REALLY KILLED KENNEDY*, p. 237
[1516] Lane, *LAST WORD*, p. 58
[1517] Lane, *LAST WORD*, p. 58
[1518] Corsi, *WHO REALLY KILLED KENNEDY*, p. 237
[1519] Corsi, *WHO REALLY KILLED KENNEDY*, p. 237
[1520] Lane, *LAST WORD*, p. 62
[1521] Lane, *LAST WORD*, p. 62
[1522] Fonzi, *THE LAST INVESTIGATION*, p. 435
[1523] Corsi, *WHO REALLY KILLED KENNEDY*, pp. 312-313
[1524] Fonzi, *THE LAST INVESTIGATION*, p. 422
[1525] Newman, *OSWALD AND THE CIA*, pp. 126-127
[1526] Fonzi, *THE LAST INVESTIGATION*, p. 423
[1527] Fonzi, *THE LAST INVESTIGATION*, p. 423
[1528] Weiner, *ENEMIES*, p. 220
[1529] Weiner, *ENEMIES*, p. 220
[1530] Fonzi, *THE LAST INVESTIGATION*, p. 41
[1531] Fonzi, *THE LAST INVESTIGATION*, p. 41
[1532] Fonzi, *THE LAST INVESTIGATION*, p. 41
[1533] Fonzi, *THE LAST INVESTIGATION*, p. 41
[1534] Fonzi, *THE LAST INVESTIGATION*, p. 41
[1535] DiEugenio, *DESTINY BETRAYED*, p. 46
[1536] DiEugenio, *DESTINY BETRAYED*, pp. 54-56
[1537] DiEugenio, *DESTINY BETRAYED*, pp. 55-56
[1538] DiEugenio, *DESTINY BETRAYED*, pp. 55-56
[1539] Summers, *NOT IN YOUR LIFETIME*, p. 204
[1540] Summers, *NOT IN YOUR LIFETIME*, p. 204
[1541] Summers, *NOT IN YOUR LIFETIME*, p. 205
[1542] Corsi, *WHO REALLY KILLED KENNEDY*, p. 312
[1543] Corsi, *WHO REALLY KILLED KENNEDY*, p. 312
[1544] Corsi, *WHO REALLY KILLED KENNEDY*, p. 312
[1545] Fonzi, *THE LAST INVESTIGATION*, p. 40
[1546] Fonzi, *THE LAST INVESTIGATION*, p. 40
[1547] Summers, *NOT IN YOUR LIFETIME*, p. 202
[1548] Summers, *NOT IN YOUR LIFETIME*, p. 202
[1549] Summers, *NOT IN YOUR LIFETIME*, p. 202
[1550] Fonzi, *THE LAST INVESTIGATION*, p. 308
[1551] Fonzi, *THE LAST INVESTIGATION*, p. 308
[1552] Fonzi, *THE LAST INVESTIGATION*, p. 308
[1553] Fonzi, *THE LAST INVESTIGATION*, p. 308
[1554] Fonzi, *THE LAST INVESTIGATION*, p. 308

[1555] Fonzi, *THE LAST INVESTIGATION*, pp. 426-427
[1556] Talbot, *THE DEVIL'S CHESSBOARD*, p. 501
[1557] Talbot, *THE DEVIL'S CHESSBOARD*, p. 501
[1558] Talbot, *THE DEVIL'S CHESSBOARD*, p. 501
[1559] Talbot, *THE DEVIL'S CHESSBOARD*, p. 501
[1560] Talbot, *THE DEVIL'S CHESSBOARD*, p. 502
[1561] Nelson, *LBJ: THE MASTERMIND OF THE JFK ASSASSINATION*, p. 468
[1562] Nelson, *LBJ: THE MASTERMIND OF THE JFK ASSASSINATION*, p. 468
[1563] DiEugenio, *DESTINY BETRAYED*, p. 190
[1564] DiEugenio, *DESTINY BETRAYED*, p. 191
[1565] Fonzi, *THE LAST INVESTIGATION*, p. 435
[1566] Lane, *LAST WORD*, pp. 45-46
[1567] Lane, *LAST WORD*, pp. 45-46
[1568] Lane, *LAST WORD*, pp. 45-46
[1569] Lane, *LAST WORD*, pp. 45-46
[1570] Lane, *LAST WORD*, p. 47
[1571] Lane, *LAST WORD*, p. 48
[1572] Lane, *LAST WORD*, p. 48
[1573] Lane, *LAST WORD*, p. 49
[1574] Lane, *LAST WORD*, p. 51
[1575] Lane, *LAST WORD*, p. 52
[1576] Lane, *LAST WORD*, pp. 55-62
[1577] Lane, *LAST WORD*, p. 62
[1578] Lane, *LAST WORD*, p. 63
[1579] Lane, *LAST WORD*, p. 63
[1580] Lane, *LAST WORD*, p. 65
[1581] Fonzi, *THE LAST INVESTIGATION*, pp. 338-339
[1582] Stone & Colapietro, *THE MAN WHO KILLED KENNEDY*, p. 152
[1583] Janney, *MARY'S MOSAIC*, p. 299
[1584] Belzer & Wayne, *HIT LIST*, p. 149
[1585] Talbot, *THE DEVIL'S CHESSBOARD*, p. 504
[1586] Corsi, *WHO REALLY KILLED KENNEDY*, pp. 243-244
[1587] Corsi, *WHO REALLY KILLED KENNEDY*, p. 314
[1588] Corsi, *WHO REALLY KILLED KENNEDY*, p. 312
[1589] Corsi, *WHO REALLY KILLED KENNEDY*, p. 312
[1590] Corsi, *WHO REALLY KILLED KENNEDY*, p. 313
[1591] Corsi, *WHO REALLY KILLED KENNEDY*, p. 313
[1592] Corsi, *WHO REALLY KILLED KENNEDY*, p. 313
[1593] Belzer & Wayne, *HIT LIST*, pp. 125-126
[1594] Belzer & Wayne, *HIT LIST*, pp. 125-126
[1595] Lane, *LAST WORD*, p. 132
[1596] Lane, *LAST WORD*, p. 132
[1597] Nelson, *LBJ: THE MASTERMIND OF THE JFK ASSASSINATION*, p. 468
[1598] Nelson, *LBJ: THE MASTERMIND OF THE JFK ASSASSINATION*,

p. 468

[1599] DiEugenio, *DESTINY BETRAYED*, pp. 55-56

[1600] Nelson, *LBJ: THE MASTERMIND OF THE JFK ASSASSINATION*, p. 468

[1601] Nelson, *LBJ: THE MASTERMIND OF THE JFK ASSASSINATION*, pp. 344-346

[1602] Baker, *ME & LEE*, p. 466

[1603] Baker, *ME & LEE*, p. 466

[1604] Baker, *ME & LEE*, p. 466

[1605] Baker, *ME & LEE*, p. 467

[1606] Nelson, *LBJ: THE MASTERMIND OF THE JFK ASSASSINATION*, pp. 344-346

[1607] Nelson, *LBJ: THE MASTERMIND OF THE JFK ASSASSINATION*, pp. 344-346

[1608] Lane, *LAST WORD*, p. 132

[1609] Lane, *LAST WORD*, p. 132

[1610] Nelson, *LBJ: THE MASTERMIND OF THE JFK ASSASSINATION*, p. 146

[1611] Talbot, *THE DEVIL'S CHESSBOARD*, p. 512

[1612] Summers, *NOT IN YOUR LIFETIME*, p. 286

[1613] Summers, *NOT IN YOUR LIFETIME*, pp. 282-283

[1614] Summers, *NOT IN YOUR LIFETIME*, p. 282

[1615] Summers, *NOT IN YOUR LIFETIME*, p. 286

[1616] Nelson, *LBJ: THE MASTERMIND OF THE JFK ASSASSINATION*, p. 468

[1617] DiEugenio, *DESTINY BETRAYED*, pp. 55-56

[1618] Summers, *NOT IN YOUR LIFETIME*, pp. 283-284

[1619] Fonzi, *THE LAST INVESTIGATION*, p. 428

[1620] Fonzi, *THE LAST INVESTIGATION*, p. 428

[1621] Fonzi, *THE LAST INVESTIGATION*, p. 428

[1622] Douglass, *JFK AND THE UNSPEAKABLE*, p. 248

[1623] Douglass, *JFK AND THE UNSPEAKABLE*, p. 248

[1624] Douglass, *JFK AND THE UNSPEAKABLE*, p. 248

[1625] Douglass, *JFK AND THE UNSPEAKABLE*, p. 248

[1626] Douglass, *JFK AND THE UNSPEAKABLE*, p. 248

[1627] Corsi, *WHO REALLY KILLED KENNEDY*, p. 139

[1628] Fonzi, *THE LAST INVESTIGATION*, p. 428

[1629] Summers, *NOT IN YOUR LIFETIME*, p. 288

[1630] Summers, *NOT IN YOUR LIFETIME*, p. 289

[1631] Summers, *NOT IN YOUR LIFETIME*, p. 289

[1632] North, *ACT OF TREASON*, p. 353

[1633] Nelson, *LBJ: THE MASTERMIND OF THE JFK ASSASSINATION*, p. 325

[1634] North, *ACT OF TREASON*, p. 412

[1635] North, *ACT OF TREASON*, p. 412

[1636] Nelson, *LBJ: THE MASTERMIND OF THE JFK ASSASSINATION*, p. 325

[1637] North, *ACT OF TREASON,* p. 420

[1638] North, *ACT OF TREASON,* p. 395

[1639] North, *ACT OF TREASON,* p. 430

[1640] North, *ACT OF TREASON,* p. 440

[1641] North, *ACT OF TREASON,* p. 440

[1642] DiEugenio, *DESTINY BETRAYED,* p. 84

[1643] DiEugenio, *DESTINY BETRAYED,* p. 84

[1644] DiEugenio, *DESTINY BETRAYED,* pp. 84-85

[1645] DiEugenio, *DESTINY BETRAYED,* pp. 84-85

[1646] DiEugenio, *DESTINY BETRAYED,* pp. 84-85

[1647] Corsi, *WHO REALLY KILLED KENNEDY,* pp. 206-208

[1648] Corsi, *WHO REALLY KILLED KENNEDY,* pp. 206-208

[1649] Corsi, *WHO REALLY KILLED KENNEDY,* pp. 206-208

[1650] Corsi, *WHO REALLY KILLED KENNEDY,* pp. 206-208

[1651] Corsi, *WHO REALLY KILLED KENNEDY,* pp. 206-208

[1652] Corsi, *WHO REALLY KILLED KENNEDY,* pp. 206-208

[1653] North, *ACT OF TREASON,* p. 487

[1654] Garrison, *ON THE TRAIL OF THE ASSASSINS,* p. 178

[1655] DiEugenio, *DESTINY BETRAYED,* p. 260

[1656] Belzer & Wayne, *HIT LIST,* pp. 171-179

[1657] Belzer & Wayne, *HIT LIST,* pp. 171-179

[1658] Belzer & Wayne, *HIT LIST,* pp. 171-179

[1659] Belzer & Wayne, *HIT LIST,* pp. 171-179

[1660] Fonzi, *THE LAST INVESTIGATION,* p. 433

[1661] Belzer & Wayne, *HIT LIST,* pp. 115-119

[1662] Summers, *NOT IN YOUR LIFETIME,* p. 274

[1663] Summers, *NOT IN YOUR LIFETIME,* p. 283

[1664] Summers, *NOT IN YOUR LIFETIME,* p. 274

[1665] Summers, *NOT IN YOUR LIFETIME,* p. 280

[1666] Summers, *NOT IN YOUR LIFETIME,* p. 280

[1667] Summers, *NOT IN YOUR LIFETIME,* p. 280

[1668] Summers, *NOT IN YOUR LIFETIME,* p. 283

[1669] Douglass, *JFK AND THE UNSPEAKABLE,* p. 62

[1670] Douglass, *JFK AND THE UNSPEAKABLE,* pp. 62-63

[1671] Douglass, *JFK AND THE UNSPEAKABLE,* pp. 62-63

[1672] Summers, *NOT IN YOUR LIFETIME,* pp. 278-279

[1673] Summers, *NOT IN YOUR LIFETIME,* p. 278

[1674] Nelson, *LBJ: THE MASTERMIND OF THE JFK ASSASSINATION,* pp. 182-183

[1675] Fonzi, *THE LAST INVESTIGATION,* p. 428

[1676] Fonzi, *THE LAST INVESTIGATION,* p. 428

[1677] Fonzi, *THE LAST INVESTIGATION,* p. 428

[1678] Douglass, *JFK AND THE UNSPEAKABLE,* pp. 248-249

[1679] Douglass, *JFK AND THE UNSPEAKABLE,* pp. 248-249

[1680] Douglass, *JFK AND THE UNSPEAKABLE,* p. 249

[1681] Nelson, *LBJ: THE MASTERMIND OF THE JFK ASSASSINATION,* p. 343

[1682] Nelson, *LBJ: THE MASTERMIND OF THE JFK ASSASSINATION*, pp. 343-344

[1683] Nelson, *LBJ: THE MASTERMIND OF THE JFK ASSASSINATION*, p. 468

[1684] DiEugenio, *DESTINY BETRAYED*, pp. 55-56

[1685] Summers, *NOT IN YOUR LIFETIME*, pp. 289-290

[1686] Summers, *NOT IN YOUR LIFETIME*, pp. 289-290

[1687] Summers, *NOT IN YOUR LIFETIME*, pp. 289-290

[1688] Summers, *NOT IN YOUR LIFETIME*, pp. 289-290

[1689] North, *ACT OF TREASON*, p. 412

[1690] North, *ACT OF TREASON*, p. 412

[1691] North, *ACT OF TREASON*, p. 412

[1692] North, *ACT OF TREASON*, p. 412

[1693] Summers, *NOT IN YOUR LIFETIME*, p. 274

[1694] Summers, *NOT IN YOUR LIFETIME*, p. 274

[1695] Summers, *NOT IN YOUR LIFETIME*, p. 280

[1696] Fonzi, *THE LAST INVESTIGATION*, p. 432

[1697] Belzer & Wayne, *HIT LIST*, pp. 115-119

[1698] Janney, *MARY'S MOSAIC*, p. 171

[1699] Janney, *MARY'S MOSAIC*, p. 170

[1700] Janney, *MARY'S MOSAIC*, p. 171

[1701] Janney, *MARY'S MOSAIC*, p. 172

[1702] Janney, *MARY'S MOSAIC*, p. 172

[1703] Janney, *MARY'S MOSAIC*, p. 175

[1704] Janney, *MARY'S MOSAIC*, p. 178

[1705] Janney, *MARY'S MOSAIC*, p. 180

[1706] Janney, *MARY'S MOSAIC*, p. 181

[1707] Janney, *MARY'S MOSAIC*, p. 182

[1708] Janney, *MARY'S MOSAIC*, p. 184

[1709] Janney, *MARY'S MOSAIC*, p. 184

[1710] Janney, *MARY'S MOSAIC*, p. 186

[1711] Janney, *MARY'S MOSAIC*, p. 14

[1712] Janney, *MARY'S MOSAIC*, p. 189

[1713] Belzer & Wayne, *HIT LIST*, pp. 143-152

[1714] Janney, *MARY'S MOSAIC*, p. 357

[1715] Janney, *MARY'S MOSAIC*, p. 357

[1716] Nelson, *LBJ: THE MASTERMIND OF THE JFK ASSASSINATION*, p. 174

[1717] Nelson, *LBJ: THE MASTERMIND OF THE JFK ASSASSINATION*, p. 174

[1718] Talbot, *THE DEVIL'S CHESSBOARD*, p. 504

[1719] Janney, *MARY'S MOSAIC*, pp. 191-192, 248

[1720] Janney, *MARY'S MOSAIC*, pp. 191-192

[1721] Janney, *MARY'S MOSAIC*, p. 248

[1722] Janney, *MARY'S MOSAIC*, pp. 263-265

[1723] Janney, *MARY'S MOSAIC*, p. 275

[1724] Nelson, *LBJ: THE MASTERMIND OF THE JFK ASSASSINATION*,

p. 468

[1725] Belzer & Wayne, *HIT LIST*, p. 149

[1726] Talbot, *THE DEVIL'S CHESSBOARD*, p. 504

[1727] Nelson, *LBJ: THE MASTERMIND OF THE JFK ASSASSINATION*, p. 468

[1728] Nelson, *LBJ: THE MASTERMIND OF THE JFK ASSASSINATION*, p. 468

[1729] Janney, *MARY'S MOSAIC*, p. 286

[1730] Janney, *MARY'S MOSAIC*, p. 286

[1731] Janney, *MARY'S MOSAIC*, p. 286

[1732] Janney, *MARY'S MOSAIC*, p. 32

[1733] Janney, *MARY'S MOSAIC*, p. 391

[1734] Janney, *MARY'S MOSAIC*, p. 391

[1735] Janney, *MARY'S MOSAIC*, p. 391

[1736] Janney, *MARY'S MOSAIC*, p. 391

[1737] Janney, *MARY'S MOSAIC*, pp. 370-371

[1738] Janney, *MARY'S MOSAIC*, p. 340

[1739] Janney, *MARY'S MOSAIC*, p. 346

[1740] Stone & Colapietro, *THE MAN WHO KILLED KENNEDY*, p. 156

[1741] Stone & Colapietro, *THE MAN WHO KILLED KENNEDY*, p. 156

[1742] Talbot, *THE DEVIL'S CHESSBOARD*, p. 500

[1743] Talbot, *THE DEVIL'S CHESSBOARD*, p. 500

[1744] Nelson, *LBJ: THE MASTERMIND OF THE JFK ASSASSINATION*, p. 165

[1745] DiEugenio, *DESTINY BETRAYED*, pp. 55-56

[1746] Nelson, *LBJ: THE MASTERMIND OF THE JFK ASSASSINATION*, p. 510

[1747] Stone & Colapietro, *THE MAN WHO KILLED KENNEDY*, pp. 155-156

[1748] Stone & Colapietro, *THE MAN WHO KILLED KENNEDY*, pp. 155-156

[1749] Nelson, *LBJ: THE MASTERMIND OF THE JFK ASSASSINATION*, pp. 168-169

[1750] Nelson, *LBJ: THE MASTERMIND OF THE JFK ASSASSINATION*, p. 468

[1751] Nelson, *LBJ: THE MASTERMIND OF THE JFK ASSASSINATION*, p. 468

[1752] Talbot, *THE DEVIL'S CHESSBOARD*, p. 504

[1753] Talbot, *THE DEVIL'S CHESSBOARD*, p. 501

[1754] Talbot, *THE DEVIL'S CHESSBOARD*, p. 501

[1755] Talbot, *THE DEVIL'S CHESSBOARD*, p. 501

[1756] Talbot, *THE DEVIL'S CHESSBOARD*, p. 501

[1757] Talbot, *THE DEVIL'S CHESSBOARD*, p. 502

[1758] Nelson, *LBJ: THE MASTERMIND OF THE JFK ASSASSINATION*, p. 327

[1759] Fonzi, *THE LAST INVESTIGATION*, p. 433

[1760] Fonzi, *THE LAST INVESTIGATION*, p. 433

[1761] Fonzi, *THE LAST INVESTIGATION*, p. 433
[1762] Fonzi, *THE LAST INVESTIGATION*, p. 375
[1763] Fonzi, *THE LAST INVESTIGATION*, p. 376
[1764] Fonzi, *THE LAST INVESTIGATION*, p. 376
[1765] Fonzi, *THE LAST INVESTIGATION*, pp. 377-379
[1766] Fonzi, *THE LAST INVESTIGATION*, p. 389
[1767] Fonzi, *THE LAST INVESTIGATION*, pp. 388-389
[1768] Fonzi, *THE LAST INVESTIGATION*, p. 441
[1769] Fonzi, *THE LAST INVESTIGATION*, p. 441
[1770] Malloch, *THE PLOT TO DESTROY TRUMP*, p. 95
[1771] North, *ACT OF TREASON,* pp. 352-353
[1772] North, *ACT OF TREASON,* pp. 352-353
[1773] North, *ACT OF TREASON,* pp. 352-353
[1774] North, *ACT OF TREASON,* p. 375
[1775] North, *ACT OF TREASON,* pp. 378-379
[1776] North, *ACT OF TREASON,* p. 366
[1777] North, *ACT OF TREASON,* p. 366
[1778] Douglass, *JFK AND THE UNSPEAKABLE*, pp. 370-371
[1779] Summers, *NOT IN YOUR LIFETIME*, p. 205
[1780] Summers, *NOT IN YOUR LIFETIME*, pp. 205-206
[1781] Summers, *NOT IN YOUR LIFETIME*, pp. 205-206
[1782] Summers, *NOT IN YOUR LIFETIME*, p. 206
[1783] Summers, *NOT IN YOUR LIFETIME*, p. 204
[1784] Summers, *NOT IN YOUR LIFETIME*, p. 204
[1785] Talbot, *THE DEVIL'S CHESSBOARD*, p. 406
[1786] Talbot, *THE DEVIL'S CHESSBOARD*, p. 406
[1787] Talbot, *THE DEVIL'S CHESSBOARD*, p. 406
[1788] Talbot, *THE DEVIL'S CHESSBOARD*, p. 406
[1789] DiEugenio, *DESTINY BETRAYED*, p. 54
[1790] DiEugenio, *DESTINY BETRAYED*, p. 54
[1791] DiEugenio, *DESTINY BETRAYED*, p. 54
[1792] DiEugenio, *DESTINY BETRAYED*, p. 54
[1793] DiEugenio, *DESTINY BETRAYED*, p. 54
[1794] DiEugenio, *DESTINY BETRAYED*, p. 55
[1795] DiEugenio, *DESTINY BETRAYED*, p. 55
[1796] DiEugenio, *DESTINY BETRAYED*, p. 55
[1797] DiEugenio, *DESTINY BETRAYED*, p. 55
[1798] DiEugenio, *DESTINY BETRAYED*, p. 55
[1799] DiEugenio, *DESTINY BETRAYED*, p. 55
[1800] DiEugenio, *DESTINY BETRAYED*, p. 56
[1801] DiEugenio, *DESTINY BETRAYED*, pp. 55-56
[1802] Fonzi, *THE LAST INVESTIGATION*, p. 45
[1803] Fonzi, *THE LAST INVESTIGATION*, p. 425
[1804] Nolan, *CIA ROGUES AND THE KILLING OF THE KENNEDYS*, p. 14
[1805] Fonzi, *THE LAST INVESTIGATION*, p. 425
[1806] Fonzi, *THE LAST INVESTIGATION*, p. 425

[1807] Fonzi, *THE LAST INVESTIGATION*, p. 425

[1808] Fonzi, *THE LAST INVESTIGATION*, p. 46

[1809] Fonzi, *THE LAST INVESTIGATION*, p. 40

[1810] Fonzi, *THE LAST INVESTIGATION*, p. 424

[1811] Fonzi, *THE LAST INVESTIGATION*, p. 132

[1812] Fonzi, *THE LAST INVESTIGATION*, p. 426

[1813] Weiner, *LEGACY OF ASHES*, p. 236

[1814] Weiner, *LEGACY OF ASHES*, pp. 230-234

[1815] Weiner, *LEGACY OF ASHES*, pp. 232-234

[1816] Nolan, *CIA ROGUES AND THE KILLING OF THE KENNEDYS*, p. 60

[1817] Nolan, *CIA ROGUES AND THE KILLING OF THE KENNEDYS*, p. 60

[1818] Fonzi, *THE LAST INVESTIGATION*, p. 48

[1819] Fonzi, *THE LAST INVESTIGATION*, p. 48

[1820] Fonzi, *THE LAST INVESTIGATION*, pp. 48-49

[1821] Summers, *NOT IN YOUR LIFETIME*, p. 208

[1822] Fonzi, *THE LAST INVESTIGATION*, p. 49

[1823] Fonzi, *THE LAST INVESTIGATION*, p. 79

[1824] Summers, *NOT IN YOUR LIFETIME*, p. 210

[1825] Summers, *NOT IN YOUR LIFETIME*, p. 210

[1826] Summers, *NOT IN YOUR LIFETIME*, p. 210

[1827] Talbot, *THE DEVIL'S CHESSBOARD*, p. 456

[1828] Talbot, *THE DEVIL'S CHESSBOARD*, p. 456

[1829] Summers, *NOT IN YOUR LIFETIME*, p. 210

[1830] Summers, *NOT IN YOUR LIFETIME*, pp. 436-437

[1831] Summers, *NOT IN YOUR LIFETIME*, pp. 436-437

[1832] Douglass, *JFK AND THE UNSPEAKABLE*, p. 75

[1833] Fonzi, *THE LAST INVESTIGATION*, p. 427

[1834] Douglass, *JFK AND THE UNSPEAKABLE*, p. 57

[1835] Fonzi, *THE LAST INVESTIGATION*, p. 49

[1836] Fonzi, *THE LAST INVESTIGATION*, p. 49

[1837] Fonzi, *THE LAST INVESTIGATION*, p. 50

[1838] Fonzi, *THE LAST INVESTIGATION*, p. 50

[1839] Fonzi, *THE LAST INVESTIGATION*, p. 50

[1840] Fonzi, *THE LAST INVESTIGATION*, p. 427

[1841] Summers, *NOT IN YOUR LIFETIME*, p. 304

[1842] Talbot, *THE DEVIL'S CHESSBOARD*, p. 454

[1843] Summers, *NOT IN YOUR LIFETIME*, p. 210

[1844] Summers, *NOT IN YOUR LIFETIME*, p. 210

[1845] Summers, *NOT IN YOUR LIFETIME*, p. 210

[1846] Douglass, *JFK AND THE UNSPEAKABLE*, p. 177

[1847] Summers, *NOT IN YOUR LIFETIME*, p. 364

[1848] Summers, *NOT IN YOUR LIFETIME*, p. 365

[1849] Douglass, *JFK AND THE UNSPEAKABLE*, p. 61

[1850] Douglass, *JFK AND THE UNSPEAKABLE*, p. 61

[1851] Douglass, *JFK AND THE UNSPEAKABLE*, p. 61

[1852] Douglass, *JFK AND THE UNSPEAKABLE*, p. 61

[1853] Summers, *NOT IN YOUR LIFETIME*, p. 365

[1854] DiEugenio, *DESTINY BETRAYED*, p. 70

[1855] Lane, *LAST WORD*, p. 282

[1856] Douglass, *JFK AND THE UNSPEAKABLE*, p. 35

[1857] Summers, *NOT IN YOUR LIFETIME*, p. 367

[1858] Douglass, *JFK AND THE UNSPEAKABLE*, p. 252

[1859] Douglass, *JFK AND THE UNSPEAKABLE*, p. 252

[1860] Douglass, *JFK AND THE UNSPEAKABLE*, p. 252

[1861] Douglass, *JFK AND THE UNSPEAKABLE*, p. 249

[1862] Douglass, *JFK AND THE UNSPEAKABLE*, p. 249

[1863] Douglass, *JFK AND THE UNSPEAKABLE*, p. 250

[1864] DiEugenio, *DESTINY BETRAYED*, p. 74

[1865] DiEugenio, *DESTINY BETRAYED*, p. 74

[1866] Douglass, *JFK AND THE UNSPEAKABLE*, p. 251

[1867] Douglass, *JFK AND THE UNSPEAKABLE*, p. 251

[1868] Douglass, *JFK AND THE UNSPEAKABLE*, p. 253

[1869] Lane, *LAST WORD*, p. 37

[1870] Lane, *LAST WORD*, p. 37

[1871] Lane, *LAST WORD*, pp. 39-40

[1872] Lane, *LAST WORD*, p. 40

[1873] Lane, *LAST WORD*, pp. 40-41

[1874] Lane, *LAST WORD*, pp. 40-41

[1875] Lane, *LAST WORD*, pp. 40-41

[1876] Summers, *NOT IN YOUR LIFETIME*, pp. 369-370

[1877] Fonzi, *THE LAST INVESTIGATION*, p. 431

[1878] Fonzi, *THE LAST INVESTIGATION*, p. 431

[1879] Fonzi, *THE LAST INVESTIGATION*, p. 431

[1880] Douglass, *JFK AND THE UNSPEAKABLE*, p. 247

[1881] Douglass, *JFK AND THE UNSPEAKABLE*, p. 247

[1882] Douglass, *JFK AND THE UNSPEAKABLE*, p. 249

[1883] Douglass, *JFK AND THE UNSPEAKABLE*, p. 245

[1884] Belzer & Wayne, *HIT LIST*, p. 48

[1885] Belzer & Wayne, *HIT LIST*, pp. 51-52

[1886] Corsi, *WHO REALLY KILLED KENNEDY*, pp. 138-139

[1887] Corsi, *WHO REALLY KILLED KENNEDY*, p. 139

[1888] Douglass, *JFK AND THE UNSPEAKABLE*, p. 247

[1889] Corsi, *WHO REALLY KILLED KENNEDY*, p. 138

[1890] Corsi, *WHO REALLY KILLED KENNEDY*, p. 138

[1891] Corsi, *WHO REALLY KILLED KENNEDY*, p. 138

[1892] Douglass, *JFK AND THE UNSPEAKABLE*, p. 245

[1893] Corsi, *WHO REALLY KILLED KENNEDY*, pp. 138-139

[1894] Corsi, *WHO REALLY KILLED KENNEDY*, p. 139

[1895] Corsi, *WHO REALLY KILLED KENNEDY*, pp. 140-141

[1896] Corsi, *WHO REALLY KILLED KENNEDY*, pp. 140-141

[1897] Corsi, *WHO REALLY KILLED KENNEDY*, pp. 140-141

[1898] Corsi, *WHO REALLY KILLED KENNEDY*, pp. 140-141

[1899] Corsi, *WHO REALLY KILLED KENNEDY*, pp. 140-141
[1900] Douglass, *JFK AND THE UNSPEAKABLE*, p. 246
[1901] Douglass, *JFK AND THE UNSPEAKABLE*, p. 246
[1902] Douglass, *JFK AND THE UNSPEAKABLE*, pp. 245-246
[1903] Douglass, *JFK AND THE UNSPEAKABLE*, p. 246
[1904] Douglass, *JFK AND THE UNSPEAKABLE*, p. 246
[1905] Douglass, *JFK AND THE UNSPEAKABLE*, p. 247
[1906] Belzer & Wayne, *HIT LIST*, pp. 51-52
[1907] Belzer & Wayne, *HIT LIST*, pp. 51-52
[1908] DiEugenio, *DESTINY BETRAYED*, p. 329
[1909] Joesten, *OSWALD: ASSASSIN OR FALL GUY?*, p. 287
[1910] Nelson, *LBJ: THE MASTERMIND OF THE JFK ASSASSINATION*, p. 143
[1911] North, *ACT OF TREASON*, p. 261
[1912] DiEugenio, *RECLAIMING PARKLAND*, p. 237
[1913] DiEugenio, *RECLAIMING PARKLAND*, pp. 237-238
[1914] DiEugenio, *RECLAIMING PARKLAND*, pp. 237-238
[1915] DiEugenio, *RECLAIMING PARKLAND*, pp. 237-238
[1916] Weiner, *ENEMIES*, p. 36
[1917] Weiner, *ENEMIES*, p. 36
[1918] Weiner, *ENEMIES*, p. 38
[1919] Weiner, *ENEMIES*, p. 38
[1920] Weiner, *ENEMIES*, p. 40
[1921] Weiner, *ENEMIES*, pp. 40-41
[1922] Weiner, *ENEMIES*, p. 41
[1923] Weiner, *ENEMIES*, pp. 40-41
[1924] Weiner, *ENEMIES*, p. 41
[1925] Weiner, *ENEMIES*, pp. 42-43
[1926] Weiner, *ENEMIES*, pp. 42-43
[1927] Weiner, *ENEMIES*, p. 42
[1928] Weiner, *ENEMIES*, pp. 42-44
[1929] Weiner, *ENEMIES*, pp. 43-44
[1930] Weiner, *ENEMIES*, pp. 44-45
[1931] Weiner, *ENEMIES*, p. 48
[1932] Weiner, *ENEMIES*, p. 48
[1933] Weiner, *ENEMIES*, p. 83
[1934] Weiner, *ENEMIES*, p. 83
[1935] Weiner, *ENEMIES*, p. 83
[1936] Weiner, *ENEMIES*, pp. 83-84
[1937] DiEugenio, *RECLAIMING PARKLAND*, pp. 237-238
[1938] DiEugenio, *RECLAIMING PARKLAND*, p. 238
[1939] DiEugenio, *RECLAIMING PARKLAND*, p. 238
[1940] DiEugenio, *RECLAIMING PARKLAND*, pp. 237-238
[1941] DiEugenio, *RECLAIMING PARKLAND*, p. 238
[1942] DiEugenio, *RECLAIMING PARKLAND*, p. 240
[1943] DiEugenio, *RECLAIMING PARKLAND*, p. 238
[1944] DiEugenio, *RECLAIMING PARKLAND*, p. 238

[1945] DiEugenio, *RECLAIMING PARKLAND*, p. 239
[1946] DiEugenio, *RECLAIMING PARKLAND*, p. 240
[1947] DiEugenio, *RECLAIMING PARKLAND*, p. 240
[1948] DiEugenio, *RECLAIMING PARKLAND*, pp. 238-239
[1949] DiEugenio, *RECLAIMING PARKLAND*, pp. 238-239
[1950] DiEugenio, *RECLAIMING PARKLAND*, pp. 238-239
[1951] Hack, *PUPPETMASTER*, pp. 165-166, 301
[1952] Hack, *PUPPETMASTER*, p. 126
[1953] Hack, *PUPPETMASTER*, p. 132
[1954] Hack, *PUPPETMASTER*, p. 136
[1955] Hack, *PUPPETMASTER*, pp. 155-158
[1956] Hack, *PUPPETMASTER*, pp. 164-165
[1957] Hack, *PUPPETMASTER*, p. 171
[1958] Hack, *PUPPETMASTER*, pp. 174-176
[1959] Hack, *PUPPETMASTER*, pp. 228-232
[1960] Hack, *PUPPETMASTER*, pp. 228-232
[1961] Hack, *PUPPETMASTER*, pp. 182-183
[1962] Hack, *PUPPETMASTER*, pp. 182-183
[1963] Hack, *PUPPETMASTER*, p. 176
[1964] Hack, *PUPPETMASTER*, p. 176
[1965] Hack, *PUPPETMASTER*, pp. 306-307
[1966] Hack, *PUPPETMASTER*, p. 178
[1967] Hack, *PUPPETMASTER*, p. 181
[1968] North, *ACT OF TREASON*, p. 210
[1969] Hack, *PUPPETMASTER*, pp. 188-193
[1970] Hack, *PUPPETMASTER*, p. 100
[1971] Hack, *PUPPETMASTER*, p. 213
[1972] Hack, *PUPPETMASTER*, p. 284
[1973] Hack, *PUPPETMASTER*, p. 284
[1974] Nelson, *LBJ: THE MASTERMIND OF THE JFK ASSASSINATION*, p. 144
[1975] Nelson, *LBJ: THE MASTERMIND OF THE JFK ASSASSINATION*, p. 144
[1976] Nelson, *LBJ: THE MASTERMIND OF THE JFK ASSASSINATION*, p. 144
[1977] Hack, *PUPPETMASTER*, p. 284
[1978] Hack, *PUPPETMASTER*, p. 284
[1979] Hack, *PUPPETMASTER*, p. 285
[1980] Hack, *PUPPETMASTER*, p. 285
[1981] Hack, *PUPPETMASTER*, p. 285
[1982] Nelson, *LBJ: THE MASTERMIND OF THE JFK ASSASSINATION*, p. 141
[1983] Nelson, *LBJ: THE MASTERMIND OF THE JFK ASSASSINATION*, p. 141
[1984] Nelson, *LBJ: THE MASTERMIND OF THE JFK ASSASSINATION*, p. 141
[1985] Nelson, *LBJ: THE MASTERMIND OF THE JFK ASSASSINATION*,

pp. 141-142
[1986] North, *ACT OF TREASON*, p. 91
[1987] North, *ACT OF TREASON*, p. 37
[1988] North, *ACT OF TREASON*, p. 37
[1989] North, *ACT OF TREASON*, p. 41
[1990] North, *ACT OF TREASON*, p. 43
[1991] North, *ACT OF TREASON*, p. 43
[1992] North, *ACT OF TREASON*, p. 43
[1993] North, *ACT OF TREASON*, p. 44
[1994] North, *ACT OF TREASON*, pp. 43-45
[1995] North, *ACT OF TREASON*, p. 119
[1996] Nelson, *LBJ: THE MASTERMIND OF THE JFK ASSASSINATION*, p. 142
[1997] Nelson, *LBJ: THE MASTERMIND OF THE JFK ASSASSINATION*, p. 142
[1998] Hack, *PUPPETMASTER*, p. 209
[1999] Hack, *PUPPETMASTER*, p. 209
[2000] Hack, *PUPPETMASTER*, pp. 316-317
[2001] Hack, *PUPPETMASTER*, p. 255
[2002] Hack, *PUPPETMASTER*, p. 248
[2003] Hack, *PUPPETMASTER*, p. 249
[2004] Hack, *PUPPETMASTER*, p. 249
[2005] Hack, *PUPPETMASTER*, p. 249
[2006] Hack, *PUPPETMASTER*, p. 261
[2007] Hack, *PUPPETMASTER*, pp. 316-317
[2008] Nelson, *LBJ: THE MASTERMIND OF THE JFK ASSASSINATION*, p. 150
[2009] Nelson, *LBJ: THE MASTERMIND OF THE JFK ASSASSINATION*, pp. 150-151
[2010] DiEugenio, *RECLAIMING PARKLAND*, p. 235
[2011] North, *ACT OF TREASON*, p. 376
[2012] Hack, *PUPPETMASTER*, p. 313
[2013] Hack, *PUPPETMASTER*, pp. 313-314
[2014] Hack, *PUPPETMASTER*, pp. 314-315
[2015] North, *ACT OF TREASON*, p. 282
[2016] North, *ACT OF TREASON*, p. 282
[2017] North, *ACT OF TREASON*, p. 289
[2018] North, *ACT OF TREASON*, p. 289
[2019] Hack, *PUPPETMASTER*, p. 290
[2020] Hack, *PUPPETMASTER*, p. 291
[2021] Hack, *PUPPETMASTER*, p. 291
[2022] Hack, *PUPPETMASTER*, p. 300
[2023] Hack, *PUPPETMASTER*, p. 300
[2024] Hack, *PUPPETMASTER*, p. 300
[2025] Hack, *PUPPETMASTER*, p. 300
[2026] Hack, *PUPPETMASTER*, p. 301
[2027] Douglass, *JFK AND THE UNSPEAKABLE*, p. 204

[2028] Douglass, *JFK AND THE UNSPEAKABLE*, p. 204

[2029] Douglass, *JFK AND THE UNSPEAKABLE*, p. 204

[2030] Douglass, *JFK AND THE UNSPEAKABLE*, p. 204

[2031] Hack, *PUPPETMASTER*, pp. 380-383

[2032] North, *ACT OF TREASON,* p. 364

[2033] Hack, *PUPPETMASTER*, p. 246

[2034] Hack, *PUPPETMASTER*, pp. 246-247

[2035] Hack, *PUPPETMASTER*, pp. 246-247

[2036] Hack, *PUPPETMASTER*, p. 247

[2037] Hack, *PUPPETMASTER*, p. 247

[2038] Hack, *PUPPETMASTER*, pp. 247-248

[2039] Hack, *PUPPETMASTER*, pp. 247-248

[2040] Hack, *PUPPETMASTER*, pp. 255-256

[2041] Hack, *PUPPETMASTER*, pp. 255-256

[2042] Hack, *PUPPETMASTER*, pp. 261-263

[2043] Hack, *PUPPETMASTER*, pp. 261-263

[2044] Hack, *PUPPETMASTER*, pp. 261-263

[2045] Hack, *PUPPETMASTER*, p. 263

[2046] Nelson, *LBJ: THE MASTERMIND OF THE JFK ASSASSINATION*, p. 140

[2047] Nelson, *LBJ: THE MASTERMIND OF THE JFK ASSASSINATION*, p. 140

[2048] Nelson, *LBJ: THE MASTERMIND OF THE JFK ASSASSINATION*, p. 140

[2049] North, *ACT OF TREASON*, p. 27

[2050] North, *ACT OF TREASON*, p. 68

[2051] North, *ACT OF TREASON*, p. 68

[2052] North, *ACT OF TREASON*, pp. 68-69

[2053] North, *ACT OF TREASON*, p. 69

[2054] North, *ACT OF TREASON*, p. 69

[2055] North, *ACT OF TREASON*, p. 70

[2056] North, *ACT OF TREASON*, p. 71

[2057] Newman, *OSWALD AND THE CIA*, p. 144

[2058] Newman, *OSWALD AND THE CIA*, p. 144

[2059] Newman, *OSWALD AND THE CIA*, p. 144

[2060] North, *ACT OF TREASON*, p. 74

[2061] North, *ACT OF TREASON*, p. 130

[2062] North, *ACT OF TREASON*, p. 133

[2063] North, *BETRAYAL IN DALLAS*, pp. 31-32

[2064] North, *ACT OF TREASON*, p. 131

[2065] North, *ACT OF TREASON*, p. 131

[2066] North, *ACT OF TREASON,* p. 152

[2067] Nelson, *LBJ: THE MASTERMIND OF THE JFK ASSASSINATION*, pp. 320-321

[2068] North, *ACT OF TREASON*, p. 13

[2069] North, *ACT OF TREASON*, p. 13

[2070] North, *ACT OF TREASON*, p. 13

[2071] North, *ACT OF TREASON*, p. 15

[2072] North, *ACT OF TREASON*, p. 15

[2073] North, *ACT OF TREASON*, p. 189

[2074] North, *ACT OF TREASON*, p. 224

[2075] North, *BETRAYAL IN DALLAS*, p. 53

[2076] North, *ACT OF TREASON,* p. 279

[2077] North, *ACT OF TREASON,* p. 279

[2078] North, *ACT OF TREASON,* p. 280

[2079] North, *ACT OF TREASON,* p. 160

[2080] North, *ACT OF TREASON,* p. 163

[2081] North, *ACT OF TREASON,* p. 185

[2082] North, *ACT OF TREASON,* p. 185

[2083] North, *ACT OF TREASON,* p. 198

[2084] North, *ACT OF TREASON,* pp. 231-233

[2085] North, *ACT OF TREASON,* pp. 243-244

[2086] North, *ACT OF TREASON,* pp. 243-244

[2087] North, *ACT OF TREASON,* pp. 243-244

[2088] North, *ACT OF TREASON,* p. 74

[2089] Douglass, *JFK AND THE UNSPEAKABLE*, p. 154

[2090] Douglass, *JFK AND THE UNSPEAKABLE*, p. 154

[2091] Douglass, *JFK AND THE UNSPEAKABLE*, p. 154

[2092] Douglass, *JFK AND THE UNSPEAKABLE*, p. 154

[2093] Douglass, *JFK AND THE UNSPEAKABLE*, p. 154

[2094] Douglass, *JFK AND THE UNSPEAKABLE*, p. 154

[2095] North, *ACT OF TREASON,* pp. 444-445

[2096] North, *ACT OF TREASON,* pp. 444-445

[2097] North, *ACT OF TREASON,* pp. 351-352

[2098] North, *ACT OF TREASON,* pp. 352-353

[2099] North, *ACT OF TREASON,* pp. 352-353

[2100] North, *ACT OF TREASON,* pp. 352-353

[2101] Baker, *ME & LEE*, p. 516

[2102] Baker, *ME & LEE*, p. 516

[2103] Garrison, *ON THE TRAIL OF THE ASSASSINS*, pp. 219-221

[2104] Garrison, *ON THE TRAIL OF THE ASSASSINS*, pp. 219-221

[2105] Garrison, *ON THE TRAIL OF THE ASSASSINS*, pp. 219-221

[2106] Garrison, *ON THE TRAIL OF THE ASSASSINS*, pp. 219-221

[2107] Garrison, *ON THE TRAIL OF THE ASSASSINS*, pp. 219-221

[2108] Garrison, *ON THE TRAIL OF THE ASSASSINS*, pp. 219-221

[2109] North, *ACT OF TREASON,* p. 392

[2110] North, *ACT OF TREASON,* p. 392

[2111] North, *ACT OF TREASON,* p. 392

[2112] Stone & Colapietro, *THE MAN WHO KILLED KENNEDY*, p. 264

[2113] Stone & Colapietro, *THE MAN WHO KILLED KENNEDY*, p. 264

[2114] Stone & Colapietro, *THE MAN WHO KILLED KENNEDY*, p. 264

[2115] North, *ACT OF TREASON,* p. 395

[2116] North, *ACT OF TREASON,* p. 396

[2117] North, *ACT OF TREASON,* p. 396

[2118] North, *BETRAYAL IN DALLAS*, p. 53
[2119] North, *ACT OF TREASON*, p. 395
[2120] North, *ACT OF TREASON*, p. 395
[2121] North, *ACT OF TREASON*, p. 394
[2122] North, *ACT OF TREASON*, pp. 394-395
[2123] North, *ACT OF TREASON*, p. 395
[2124] North, *ACT OF TREASON*, p. 425
[2125] North, *ACT OF TREASON*, p. 395
[2126] North, *ACT OF TREASON*, p. 395
[2127] North, *ACT OF TREASON*, p. 394
[2128] North, *ACT OF TREASON*, p. 394
[2129] North, *ACT OF TREASON*, p. 392
[2130] North, *ACT OF TREASON*, p. 393
[2131] North, *ACT OF TREASON*, p. 393
[2132] North, *ACT OF TREASON*, p. 392
[2133] North, *ACT OF TREASON*, p. 392
[2134] North, *ACT OF TREASON*, p. 392
[2135] North, *ACT OF TREASON*, p. 395
[2136] Nelson, *LBJ: THE MASTERMIND OF THE JFK ASSASSINATION*, p. 149
[2137] North, *ACT OF TREASON*, p. 427
[2138] North, *ACT OF TREASON*, p. 427
[2139] North, *ACT OF TREASON*, p. 397
[2140] North, *ACT OF TREASON*, p. 396
[2141] North, *ACT OF TREASON*, p. 401
[2142] North, *ACT OF TREASON*, p. 401
[2143] North, *ACT OF TREASON*, p. 451
[2144] North, *ACT OF TREASON*, p. 499
[2145] Summers, *NOT IN YOUR LIFETIME*, pp. 116-117
[2146] Summers, *NOT IN YOUR LIFETIME*, pp. 116-117
[2147] Nelson, *LBJ: THE MASTERMIND OF THE JFK ASSASSINATION*, p. 505
[2148] Douglass, *JFK AND THE UNSPEAKABLE*, p. 113
[2149] Nelson, *LBJ: THE MASTERMIND OF THE JFK ASSASSINATION*, pp. 176-177
[2150] Nelson, *LBJ: THE MASTERMIND OF THE JFK ASSASSINATION*, pp. 176-177
[2151] Nelson, *LBJ: THE MASTERMIND OF THE JFK ASSASSINATION*, p. 178
[2152] Nelson, *LBJ: THE MASTERMIND OF THE JFK ASSASSINATION*, p. 178
[2153] Nelson, *LBJ: THE MASTERMIND OF THE JFK ASSASSINATION*, p. 526
[2154] Talbot, *THE DEVIL'S CHESSBOARD*, p. 459
[2155] Talbot, *THE DEVIL'S CHESSBOARD*, p. 459
[2156] Janney, *MARY'S MOSAIC*, p. 245
[2157] Janney, *MARY'S MOSAIC*, p. 245

[2158] Janney, *MARY'S MOSAIC*, p. 245

[2159] Janney, *MARY'S MOSAIC*, pp. 245-246

[2160] Janney, *MARY'S MOSAIC*, pp. 245-246

[2161] Janney, *MARY'S MOSAIC*, pp. 245-246

[2162] Morley, *THE GHOST*, p. 114

[2163] Morley, *THE GHOST*, p. 114

[2164] Hornberger, THE *KENNEDY AUTOPSY*, p. 81

[2165] Summers, *NOT IN YOUR LIFETIME*, p. 197

[2166] Morley, *THE GHOST*, p. 114

[2167] Morley, *THE GHOST*, p. 115

[2168] Morley, *THE GHOST*, p. 115

[2169] Morley, *THE GHOST*, pp. 117-118

[2170] Morley, *THE GHOST*, pp. 117-118

[2171] Morley, *THE GHOST*, p. 118

[2172] Morley, *THE GHOST*, p. 118

[2173] Janney, *MARY'S MOSAIC*, p. 247

[2174] Janney, *MARY'S MOSAIC*, p. 246

[2175] Janney, *MARY'S MOSAIC*, p. 246

[2176] Janney, *MARY'S MOSAIC*, p. 247

[2177] Douglass, *JFK AND THE UNSPEAKABLE*, p. 30

[2178] Morley, *THE GHOST*, p. 118

[2179] Morley, *THE GHOST*, p. 118

[2180] Morley, *THE GHOST*, pp. 118-119

[2181] Morley, *THE GHOST*, pp. 118-119

[2182] Morley, *THE GHOST*, p. 119

[2183] Nelson, *LBJ: THE MASTERMIND OF THE JFK ASSASSINATION*, pp. 79-80

[2184] Talbot, *THE DEVIL'S CHESSBOARD*, p. 453

[2185] Talbot, *THE DEVIL'S CHESSBOARD*, p. 453

[2186] Kohn, *STRATEGIC AIR WARFARE: AN INTERVIEW WITH THE GENERALS*, pp. 113-114

[2187] Kohn, *STRATEGIC AIR WARFARE: AN INTERVIEW WITH THE GENERALS*, pp. 113-114

[2188] Kohn, *STRATEGIC AIR WARFARE: AN INTERVIEW WITH THE GENERALS*, pp. 113-114

[2189] Nolan, *CIA ROGUES AND THE KILLING OF THE KENNEDYS*, pp. 26-27

[2190] Nelson, *LBJ: THE MASTERMIND OF THE JFK ASSASSINATION*, p. 100

[2191] Nelson, *LBJ: THE MASTERMIND OF THE JFK ASSASSINATION*, p. 100

[2192] Janney, *MARY'S MOSAIC*, p. 262

[2193] Nelson, *LBJ: THE MASTERMIND OF THE JFK ASSASSINATION*, p. 121

[2194] Nelson, *LBJ: THE MASTERMIND OF THE JFK ASSASSINATION*, pp. 122-123

[2195] Nelson, *LBJ: THE MASTERMIND OF THE JFK ASSASSINATION*,

pp. 122-123

[2196] Douglass, *JFK AND THE UNSPEAKABLE*, p. 54

[2197] Marrs, *CROSSFIRE*, p. 288

[2198] Marrs, *CROSSFIRE*, p. 288

[2199] Marrs, *CROSSFIRE*, p. 288

[2200] Marrs, *CROSSFIRE*, p. 288

[2201] Marrs, *CROSSFIRE*, p. 288

[2202] Marrs, *CROSSFIRE*, p. 288

[2203] Marrs, *CROSSFIRE*, p. 288

[2204] Marrs, *CROSSFIRE*, p. 288

[2205] Marrs, *CROSSFIRE*, p. 288

[2206] Marrs, *CROSSFIRE*, p. 289

[2207] Douglass, *JFK AND THE UNSPEAKABLE*, p. 236

[2208] Janney, *MARY'S MOSAIC*, p. 238

[2209] Janney, *MARY'S MOSAIC*, p. 238

[2210] Janney, *MARY'S MOSAIC*, p. 238

[2211] Janney, *MARY'S MOSAIC*, p. 238

[2212] Douglass, *JFK AND THE UNSPEAKABLE*, p. 236

[2213] Douglass, *JFK AND THE UNSPEAKABLE*, p. 113

[2214] Douglass, *JFK AND THE UNSPEAKABLE*, p. 113

[2215] Douglass, *JFK AND THE UNSPEAKABLE*, p. 113

[2216] Douglass, *JFK AND THE UNSPEAKABLE*, p. 113

[2217] Douglass, *JFK AND THE UNSPEAKABLE*, p. 96

[2218] Douglass, *JFK AND THE UNSPEAKABLE*, p. 98

[2219] Douglass, *JFK AND THE UNSPEAKABLE*, p. 98

[2220] Douglass, *JFK AND THE UNSPEAKABLE*, p. 98

[2221] Nelson, *LBJ: THE MASTERMIND OF THE JFK ASSASSINATION*, p. 372

[2222] Janney, *MARY'S MOSAIC*, p. 246

[2223] Janney, *MARY'S MOSAIC*, p. 246

[2224] Janney, *MARY'S MOSAIC*, p. 246

[2225] Nelson, *LBJ: THE MASTERMIND OF THE JFK ASSASSINATION*, p. 181

[2226] Nelson, *LBJ: THE MASTERMIND OF THE JFK ASSASSINATION*, p. 181

[2227] Halberstam, *THE FIFTIES*, p. 56

[2228] Halberstam, *THE FIFTIES*, p. 56

[2229] Douglass, *JFK AND THE UNSPEAKABLE*, pp. 98-99

[2230] Douglass, *JFK AND THE UNSPEAKABLE*, pp. 98-99

[2231] Douglass, *JFK AND THE UNSPEAKABLE*, pp. 101-102

[2232] Douglass, *JFK AND THE UNSPEAKABLE*, p. 101

[2233] Douglass, *JFK AND THE UNSPEAKABLE*, p. 101

[2234] Douglass, *JFK AND THE UNSPEAKABLE*, p. 101

[2235] Douglass, *JFK AND THE UNSPEAKABLE*, p. 109

[2236] Douglass, *JFK AND THE UNSPEAKABLE*, p. 109

[2237] Douglass, *JFK AND THE UNSPEAKABLE*, p. 109

[2238] Douglass, *JFK AND THE UNSPEAKABLE*, p. 109

[2239] Douglass, *JFK AND THE UNSPEAKABLE*, p. 121

[2240] Douglass, *JFK AND THE UNSPEAKABLE*, p. 121

[2241] Douglass, *JFK AND THE UNSPEAKABLE*, p. 121

[2242] Nelson, *LBJ: THE MASTERMIND OF THE JFK ASSASSINATION*, p. 120

[2243] Nelson, *LBJ: THE MASTERMIND OF THE JFK ASSASSINATION*, p. 120

[2244] Douglass, *JFK AND THE UNSPEAKABLE*, p. 197

[2245] Douglass, *JFK AND THE UNSPEAKABLE*, pp. 210-211

[2246] Douglass, *JFK AND THE UNSPEAKABLE*, p. 211

[2247] Douglass, *JFK AND THE UNSPEAKABLE*, p. 189

[2248] Marrs, *CROSSFIRE*, p. 286

[2249] Marrs, *CROSSFIRE*, p. 286

[2250] Nelson, *LBJ: THE MASTERMIND OF THE JFK ASSASSINATION*, p. 125

[2251] Nelson, *LBJ: THE MASTERMIND OF THE JFK ASSASSINATION*, p. 104

[2252] Nelson, *LBJ: THE MASTERMIND OF THE JFK ASSASSINATION*, p. 104

[2253] Nelson, *LBJ: THE MASTERMIND OF THE JFK ASSASSINATION*, p. 104

[2254] Janney, *MARY'S MOSAIC*, p. 277

[2255] Janney, *MARY'S MOSAIC*, p. 277

[2256] Nelson, *LBJ: THE MASTERMIND OF THE JFK ASSASSINATION*, pp. 360-361

[2257] Nelson, *LBJ: THE MASTERMIND OF THE JFK ASSASSINATION*, pp. 360-361

[2258] Nelson, *LBJ: THE MASTERMIND OF THE JFK ASSASSINATION*, pp. 360-361

[2259] Nelson, *LBJ: THE MASTERMIND OF THE JFK ASSASSINATION*, pp. 360-361

[2260] Nelson, *LBJ: THE MASTERMIND OF THE JFK ASSASSINATION*, pp. 360-361

[2261] Nelson, *LBJ: THE MASTERMIND OF THE JFK ASSASSINATION*, pp. 360-361

[2262] Nelson, *LBJ: THE MASTERMIND OF THE JFK ASSASSINATION*, pp. 360-361

[2263] Nelson, *LBJ: THE MASTERMIND OF THE JFK ASSASSINATION*, pp. 360-361

[2264] Stone & Colapietro, *THE MAN WHO KILLED KENNEDY*, p. 253

[2265] Joesten, *OSWALD: ASSASSIN OR FALL GUY?*, p. 144

[2266] Joesten, *OSWALD: ASSASSIN OR FALL GUY?*, p. 144

[2267] Joesten, *OSWALD: ASSASSIN OR FALL GUY?*, p. 144

[2268] Douglass, *JFK AND THE UNSPEAKABLE*, p. 306

[2269] Douglass, *JFK AND THE UNSPEAKABLE*, p. 306

[2270] Douglass, *JFK AND THE UNSPEAKABLE*, p. 306

[2271] Douglass, *JFK AND THE UNSPEAKABLE*, p. 306

[2272] Summers, *NOT IN YOUR LIFETIME*, p. 53

[2273] Summers, *NOT IN YOUR LIFETIME*, p. 53

[2274] Summers, *NOT IN YOUR LIFETIME*, p. 53

[2275] Douglass, *JFK AND THE UNSPEAKABLE*, pp. 306-307

[2276] Douglass, *JFK AND THE UNSPEAKABLE*, pp. 306-307

[2277] Douglass, *JFK AND THE UNSPEAKABLE*, p. 307

[2278] Douglass, *JFK AND THE UNSPEAKABLE*, p. 307

[2279] Nelson, *LBJ: THE MASTERMIND OF THE JFK ASSASSINATION*, pp. 404-405

[2280] Nelson, *LBJ: THE MASTERMIND OF THE JFK ASSASSINATION*, p. 404

[2281] North, *ACT OF TREASON,* pp. 403-404

[2282] Corsi, *WHO REALLY KILLED KENNEDY*, pp. 20-21

[2283] Belzer & Wayne, *DEAD WRONG*, pp. 97-98

[2284] Stone & Colapietro, *THE MAN WHO KILLED KENNEDY*, p. 253

[2285] Nelson, *LBJ: THE MASTERMIND OF THE JFK ASSASSINATION*, p. 406

[2286] Summers, *NOT IN YOUR LIFETIME*, pp. 14-15

[2287] Nelson, *LBJ: THE MASTERMIND OF THE JFK ASSASSINATION*, pp. 514-515

[2288] Nelson, *LBJ: THE MASTERMIND OF THE JFK ASSASSINATION*, pp. 514-515

[2289] Nelson, *LBJ: THE MASTERMIND OF THE JFK ASSASSINATION*, pp. 514-515

[2290] Nelson, *LBJ: THE MASTERMIND OF THE JFK ASSASSINATION*, pp. 514-515

[2291] Hornberger, *THE KENNEDY AUTOPSY*, p. 88

[2292] Hornberger, *THE KENNEDY AUTOPSY*, p. 88

[2293] Hornberger, *THE KENNEDY AUTOPSY*, p. 88

[2294] Hornberger, *THE KENNEDY AUTOPSY*, pp. 88-89

[2295] Hornberger, *THE KENNEDY AUTOPSY*, p. 89

[2296] Hornberger, *THE KENNEDY AUTOPSY*, p. 89

[2297] Hornberger, *THE KENNEDY AUTOPSY*, pp. 89-90

[2298] Hornberger, *THE KENNEDY AUTOPSY*, pp. 89-90

[2299] Hornberger, *THE KENNEDY AUTOPSY*, p. 90

[2300] Hornberger, *THE KENNEDY AUTOPSY*, p. 90

[2301] Hornberger, *THE KENNEDY AUTOPSY*, p. 91

[2302] Hornberger, *THE KENNEDY AUTOPSY*, p. 91

[2303] Hornberger, *THE KENNEDY AUTOPSY*, pp. 91-92

[2304] Hornberger, *THE KENNEDY AUTOPSY*, p. 99

[2305] Nelson, *LBJ: THE MASTERMIND OF THE JFK ASSASSINATION*, pp. 520-521

[2306] Nelson, *LBJ: THE MASTERMIND OF THE JFK ASSASSINATION*, pp. 520-521

[2307] Nelson, *LBJ: THE MASTERMIND OF THE JFK ASSASSINATION*, pp. 520-521

[2308] Hornberger, *THE KENNEDY AUTOPSY*, p. 92

[2309] Hornberger, *THE KENNEDY AUTOPSY*, p. 101
[2310] Janney, *MARY'S MOSAIC*, p. 294
[2311] Janney, *MARY'S MOSAIC*, p. 294
[2312] Wayne, *HIT LIST*, p. 156
[2313] Wayne, *HIT LIST*, p. 156
[2314] Wayne, *HIT LIST*, p. 156
[2315] Janney, *MARY'S MOSAIC*, p. 295
[2316] Nelson, *LBJ: THE MASTERMIND OF THE JFK ASSASSINATION*, p. 525
[2317] Nelson, *LBJ: THE MASTERMIND OF THE JFK ASSASSINATION*, p. 526
[2318] Nelson, *LBJ: THE MASTERMIND OF THE JFK ASSASSINATION*, pp. 527-529
[2319] Douglass, *JFK AND THE UNSPEAKABLE*, p. 313
[2320] Douglass, *JFK AND THE UNSPEAKABLE*, p. 313
[2321] Nelson, *LBJ: THE MASTERMIND OF THE JFK ASSASSINATION*, pp. 527-529
[2322] Fonzi, *THE LAST INVESTIGATION*, p. 22
[2323] Fonzi, *THE LAST INVESTIGATION*, p. 23
[2324] Fonzi, *THE LAST INVESTIGATION*, p. 23
[2325] Fonzi, *THE LAST INVESTIGATION*, p. 23
[2326] Fonzi, *THE LAST INVESTIGATION*, p. 408
[2327] Marrs, *CROSSFIRE*, p. 302
[2328] Marrs, *CROSSFIRE*, p. 302
[2329] Marrs, *CROSSFIRE*, p. 302
[2330] Marrs, *CROSSFIRE*, p. 302
[2331] Marrs, *CROSSFIRE*, p. 302
[2332] Marrs, *CROSSFIRE*, p. 302
[2333] Fonzi, *THE LAST INVESTIGATION*, p. 404
[2334] Marrs, *CROSSFIRE*, pp. 364-365
[2335] North, *ACT OF TREASON*, p. 487
[2336] North, *ACT OF TREASON*, p. 487
[2337] Corsi, *WHO REALLY KILLED KENNEDY*, pp. 22-23
[2338] Corsi, *WHO REALLY KILLED KENNEDY*, p. 23
[2339] North, *ACT OF TREASON*, p. 487
[2340] North, *ACT OF TREASON*, p. 487
[2341] Summers, *NOT IN YOUR LIFETIME*, p. 52
[2342] Summers, *NOT IN YOUR LIFETIME*, p. 52
[2343] Summers, *NOT IN YOUR LIFETIME*, p. 52
[2344] Fonzi, *THE LAST INVESTIGATION*, p. 217
[2345] Fonzi, *THE LAST INVESTIGATION*, p. 218
[2346] Fonzi, *THE LAST INVESTIGATION*, p. 218
[2347] Fonzi, *THE LAST INVESTIGATION*, p. 218
[2348] Fonzi, *THE LAST INVESTIGATION*, p. 218
[2349] Joesten, *OSWALD: ASSASSIN OR FALL GUY?*, p. 288
[2350] Joesten, *OSWALD: ASSASSIN OR FALL GUY?*, p. 288
[2351] Joesten, *OSWALD: ASSASSIN OR FALL GUY?*, p. 288

[2352] Marrs, *CROSSFIRE*, pp. 364-365

[2353] Nelson, *LBJ: THE MASTERMIND OF THE JFK ASSASSINATION*, p. 530

[2354] Summers, *NOT IN YOUR LIFETIME*, p. 54

[2355] DiEugenio, *RECLAIMING PARKLAND*, p. xxiii

[2356] DiEugenio, *RECLAIMING PARKLAND*, p. xxiii

[2357] Garrison, *ON THE TRAIL OF THE ASSASSINS*, p. 244

[2358] Garrison, *ON THE TRAIL OF THE ASSASSINS*, p. 244

[2359] Thomas, *HEAR NO EVIL*, p. 284

[2360] Thomas, *HEAR NO EVIL*, p. 284

[2361] Thomas, *HEAR NO EVIL*, p. 284

[2362] Douglass, *JFK AND THE UNSPEAKABLE*, pp. xxx, xxxi

[2363] Douglass, *JFK AND THE UNSPEAKABLE*, p. 282

[2364] Douglass, *JFK AND THE UNSPEAKABLE*, p. 283

[2365] Douglass, *JFK AND THE UNSPEAKABLE*, p. 283

[2366] Douglass, *JFK AND THE UNSPEAKABLE*, p. 283

[2367] Douglass, *JFK AND THE UNSPEAKABLE*, p. 283

[2368] Douglass, *JFK AND THE UNSPEAKABLE*, p. 284

[2369] Douglass, *JFK AND THE UNSPEAKABLE*, p. 284

[2370] Douglass, *JFK AND THE UNSPEAKABLE*, p. 310

[2371] Douglass, *JFK AND THE UNSPEAKABLE*, p. 310

[2372] Douglass, *JFK AND THE UNSPEAKABLE*, p. 310

[2373] Douglass, *JFK AND THE UNSPEAKABLE*, p. 310

[2374] Belzer & Wayne, *HIT LIST*, p. 158

[2375] North, *ACT OF TREASON,* p. 425

[2376] Stone & Colapietro, *THE MAN WHO KILLED KENNEDY*, pp. 258-260

[2377] Stone & Colapietro, *THE MAN WHO KILLED KENNEDY*, pp. 258-260

[2378] DiEugenio, *RECLAIMING PARKLAND*, pp. 143-144

[2379] DiEugenio, *RECLAIMING PARKLAND*, pp. 143-144

[2380] DiEugenio, *RECLAIMING PARKLAND*, pp. 143-144

[2381] DiEugenio, *RECLAIMING PARKLAND*, pp. 143-144

[2382] DiEugenio, *RECLAIMING PARKLAND*, pp. 143-144

[2383] DiEugenio, *RECLAIMING PARKLAND*, pp. 143-144

[2384] DiEugenio, *RECLAIMING PARKLAND*, pp. 143-144

[2385] Janney, *MARY'S MOSAIC*, p. 296

[2386] Janney, *MARY'S MOSAIC*, p. 296

[2387] DiEugenio, *RECLAIMING PARKLAND*, pp. 166-167

[2388] DiEugenio, *RECLAIMING PARKLAND*, p. 167

[2389] DiEugenio, *RECLAIMING PARKLAND*, p. 167

[2390] DiEugenio, *RECLAIMING PARKLAND*, p. 168

[2391] Douglass, *JFK AND THE UNSPEAKABLE*, p. 308

[2392] Douglass, *JFK AND THE UNSPEAKABLE*, p. 308

[2393] Douglass, *JFK AND THE UNSPEAKABLE*, p. 308

[2394] Douglass, *JFK AND THE UNSPEAKABLE*, p. 308

[2395] Douglass, *JFK AND THE UNSPEAKABLE*, p. 308

[2396] Douglass, *JFK AND THE UNSPEAKABLE*, p. 308

[2397] Douglass, *JFK AND THE UNSPEAKABLE*, p. 314

[2398] Douglass, *JFK AND THE UNSPEAKABLE*, p. 314

[2399] Nelson, *LBJ: THE MASTERMIND OF THE JFK ASSASSINATION*, p. 560

[2400] Nelson, *LBJ: THE MASTERMIND OF THE JFK ASSASSINATION*, p. 560

[2401] Nelson, *LBJ: THE MASTERMIND OF THE JFK ASSASSINATION*, p. 560

[2402] Nelson, *LBJ: THE MASTERMIND OF THE JFK ASSASSINATION*, p. 560

[2403] Crenshaw, *JFK HAS BEEN SHOT*, p. 257

[2404] Douglass, *JFK AND THE UNSPEAKABLE*, p. 314

[2405] Douglass, *JFK AND THE UNSPEAKABLE*, p. 315

[2406] Douglass, *JFK AND THE UNSPEAKABLE*, p. 315

[2407] Douglass, *JFK AND THE UNSPEAKABLE*, p. 315

[2408] Douglass, *JFK AND THE UNSPEAKABLE*, p. 316

[2409] Douglass, *JFK AND THE UNSPEAKABLE*, p. 317

[2410] Douglass, *JFK AND THE UNSPEAKABLE*, p. 317

[2411] Douglass, *JFK AND THE UNSPEAKABLE*, p. 319

[2412] Joesten, *OSWALD: ASSASSIN OR FALL GUY?*, p. 239

[2413] Joesten, *OSWALD: ASSASSIN OR FALL GUY?*, p. 239

[2414] Joesten, *OSWALD: ASSASSIN OR FALL GUY?*, p. 241

[2415] Nelson, *LBJ: THE MASTERMIND OF THE JFK ASSASSINATION*, p. 144

[2416] Nelson, *LBJ: THE MASTERMIND OF THE JFK ASSASSINATION*, p. 144

[2417] Nelson, *LBJ: THE MASTERMIND OF THE JFK ASSASSINATION*, p. 144

[2418] Corsi, *WHO REALLY KILLED KENNEDY*, pp. 209-210

[2419] Corsi, *WHO REALLY KILLED KENNEDY*, pp. 209-210

[2420] Nelson, *LBJ: THE MASTERMIND OF THE JFK ASSASSINATION*, p. 321

[2421] Nelson, *LBJ: THE MASTERMIND OF THE JFK ASSASSINATION*, p. 322

[2422] Nelson, *LBJ: THE MASTERMIND OF THE JFK ASSASSINATION*, p. 323

[2423] Nelson, *LBJ: THE MASTERMIND OF THE JFK ASSASSINATION*, pp. 322-324

[2424] Nelson, *LBJ: THE MASTERMIND OF THE JFK ASSASSINATION*, p. 321

[2425] Nelson, *LBJ: THE MASTERMIND OF THE JFK ASSASSINATION*, p. 322

[2426] Baker, *ME & LEE*, p. 504

[2427] Nelson, *LBJ: THE MASTERMIND OF THE JFK ASSASSINATION*, p. 221

[2428] Stone & Colapietro, *THE MAN WHO KILLED KENNEDY*, p. 210

[2429] Talbot, *THE DEVIL'S CHESSBOARD*, p. 539

[2430] Nelson, *LBJ: THE MASTERMIND OF THE JFK ASSASSINATION*, p. 221

[2431] Talbot, *THE DEVIL'S CHESSBOARD*, p. 539

[2432] Talbot, *THE DEVIL'S CHESSBOARD*, p. 540

[2433] Stone & Colapietro, *THE MAN WHO KILLED KENNEDY*, p. 374

[2434] Stone & Colapietro, *THE MAN WHO KILLED KENNEDY*, p. 226

[2435] Stone & Colapietro, *THE MAN WHO KILLED KENNEDY*, pp. 226-227

[2436] Stone & Colapietro, *THE MAN WHO KILLED KENNEDY*, pp. 226-227

[2437] Stone & Colapietro, *THE MAN WHO KILLED KENNEDY*, p. 227

[2438] Stone & Colapietro, *THE MAN WHO KILLED KENNEDY*, p. 229

[2439] Corsi, *WHO REALLY KILLED KENNEDY*, p. 283

[2440] Corsi, *WHO REALLY KILLED KENNEDY*, p. 283

[2441] Talbot, *THE DEVIL'S CHESSBOARD*, p. 573

[2442] Nelson, *LBJ: THE MASTERMIND OF THE JFK ASSASSINATION*, p. 183

[2443] Douglass, *JFK AND THE UNSPEAKABLE*, p. 246

[2444] Douglass, *JFK AND THE UNSPEAKABLE*, p. 247

[2445] Belzer & Wayne, *HIT LIST*, pp. 51-52

[2446] Ventura, *THEY KILLED OUR PRESIDENT*, p. 320

[2447] Ventura, *THEY KILLED OUR PRESIDENT*, p. 320

[2448] Ventura, *THEY KILLED OUR PRESIDENT*, p. 320

[2449] Summers, *NOT IN YOUR LIFETIME*, p. 5

[2450] Joesten, *OSWALD: ASSASSIN OR FALL GUY?*, p. 239

[2451] Talbot, THE DEVIL'S CHESSBOARD, p. 488

[2452] Nelson, *LBJ: THE MASTERMIND OF THE JFK ASSASSINATION*, p. 77

[2453] Nelson, *LBJ: THE MASTERMIND OF THE JFK ASSASSINATION*, p. 362

[2454] Nelson, *LBJ: THE MASTERMIND OF THE JFK ASSASSINATION*, p. 362

[2455] Nelson, *LBJ: THE MASTERMIND OF THE JFK ASSASSINATION*, p. 362

[2456] Nelson, *LBJ: THE MASTERMIND OF THE JFK ASSASSINATION*, p. 363

[2457] Nelson, *LBJ: THE MASTERMIND OF THE JFK ASSASSINATION*, p. 363

[2458] Nelson, *LBJ: THE MASTERMIND OF THE JFK ASSASSINATION*, p. 363

[2459] North, *BETRAYAL IN DALLAS*, p. 7

[2460] North, *BETRAYAL IN DALLAS*, pp. 19-20

[2461] North, *BETRAYAL IN DALLAS*, p. xi

[2462] North, *BETRAYAL IN DALLAS*, p. 5

[2463] North, *BETRAYAL IN DALLAS*, p. 6

[2464] North, *BETRAYAL IN DALLAS*, p. 45

[2465] North, *BETRAYAL IN DALLAS*, p. 94

[2466] North, *BETRAYAL IN DALLAS*, p. 27

[2467] North, *BETRAYAL IN DALLAS*, pp. 19-20

[2468] North, *BETRAYAL IN DALLAS*, p. xi

[2469] North, *BETRAYAL IN DALLAS*, p. xi

[2470] North, *BETRAYAL IN DALLAS*, p. xi

[2471] North, *BETRAYAL IN DALLAS*, p. xi

[2472] North, *BETRAYAL IN DALLAS*, p. xi

[2473] DiEugenio, *RECLAIMING PARKLAND*, p. 196

[2474] DiEugenio, *RECLAIMING PARKLAND*, p. 196

[2475] DiEugenio, *RECLAIMING PARKLAND*, p. 196

[2476] DiEugenio, *RECLAIMING PARKLAND*, pp. 196-197

[2477] DiEugenio, *RECLAIMING PARKLAND*, p. 197

[2478] Stone & Colapietro, *THE MAN WHO KILLED KENNEDY*, p. 219

[2479] North, *BETRAYAL IN DALLAS*, p. 80

[2480] Stone & Colapietro, *THE MAN WHO KILLED KENNEDY*, p. 219

[2481] Joesten, *OSWALD: ASSASSIN OR FALL GUY?*, p. 146

[2482] Joesten, *OSWALD: ASSASSIN OR FALL GUY?*, p. 146

[2483] Joesten, *OSWALD: ASSASSIN OR FALL GUY?*, p. 146

[2484] Garrison, *ON THE TRAIL OF THE ASSASSINS*, p. 202

[2485] Garrison, *ON THE TRAIL OF THE ASSASSINS*, p. 202

[2486] Garrison, *ON THE TRAIL OF THE ASSASSINS*, p. 202

[2487] Garrison, *ON THE TRAIL OF THE ASSASSINS*, p. 202

[2488] Garrison, *ON THE TRAIL OF THE ASSASSINS*, p. 202

[2489] Garrison, *ON THE TRAIL OF THE ASSASSINS*, p. 202

[2490] North, *ACT OF TREASON,* p. 428

[2491] Garrison, *ON THE TRAIL OF THE ASSASSINS*, p. 205

[2492] Garrison, *ON THE TRAIL OF THE ASSASSINS*, p. 205

[2493] Garrison, *ON THE TRAIL OF THE ASSASSINS*, pp. 205-206

[2494] Garrison, *ON THE TRAIL OF THE ASSASSINS*, pp. 205-206

[2495] Garrison, *ON THE TRAIL OF THE ASSASSINS*, pp. 205-206

[2496] Garrison, *ON THE TRAIL OF THE ASSASSINS*, pp. 205-206

[2497] Garrison, *ON THE TRAIL OF THE ASSASSINS*, pp. 205-206

[2498] Garrison, *ON THE TRAIL OF THE ASSASSINS*, pp. 205-206

[2499] Garrison, *ON THE TRAIL OF THE ASSASSINS*, pp. 205-206

[2500] Corsi, *WHO REALLY KILLED KENNEDY*, pp. 140-141

[2501] Douglass, *JFK AND THE UNSPEAKABLE*, p. 246

[2502] Garrison, *ON THE TRAIL OF THE ASSASSINS*, p. 202

[2503] Garrison, *ON THE TRAIL OF THE ASSASSINS*, p. 202

[2504] North, *BETRAYAL IN DALLAS*, p. 9

[2505] North, *BETRAYAL IN DALLAS*, p. 9

[2506] North, *BETRAYAL IN DALLAS*, p. 10

[2507] North, *BETRAYAL IN DALLAS*, p. 31

[2508] North, *BETRAYAL IN DALLAS*, p. 10

[2509] North, *BETRAYAL IN DALLAS*, p. 10

[2510] North, *BETRAYAL IN DALLAS*, p. 13

[2511] North, *BETRAYAL IN DALLAS*, p. 13

[2512] North, *BETRAYAL IN DALLAS*, p. 27

[2513] North, *BETRAYAL IN DALLAS*, p. 66

[2514] North, *BETRAYAL IN DALLAS*, pp. 53-55

[2515] North, *BETRAYAL IN DALLAS*, p. 61

[2516] North, *BETRAYAL IN DALLAS*, p. 62

[2517] North, *BETRAYAL IN DALLAS*, p. 48

[2518] North, *BETRAYAL IN DALLAS*, p. 35

[2519] North, *BETRAYAL IN DALLAS*, pp. 24-25

[2520] North, *BETRAYAL IN DALLAS*, p. 38

[2521] North, *BETRAYAL IN DALLAS*, p. 35

[2522] North, *BETRAYAL IN DALLAS*, p. 50

[2523] North, *BETRAYAL IN DALLAS*, p. 50

[2524] North, *BETRAYAL IN DALLAS*, p. 50

[2525] North, *BETRAYAL IN DALLAS*, p. 50

[2526] North, *BETRAYAL IN DALLAS*, p. 58

[2527] North, *BETRAYAL IN DALLAS*, pp. 53-55

[2528] North, *BETRAYAL IN DALLAS*, p. 61

[2529] North, *BETRAYAL IN DALLAS*, p. 62

[2530] North, *BETRAYAL IN DALLAS*, p. 48

[2531] North, *BETRAYAL IN DALLAS*, p. 63

[2532] North, *BETRAYAL IN DALLAS*, p. 63

[2533] North, *BETRAYAL IN DALLAS*, p. 65

[2534] North, *BETRAYAL IN DALLAS*, pp. 48-49

[2535] North, *BETRAYAL IN DALLAS*, pp. 69-70

[2536] North, *BETRAYAL IN DALLAS*, p. 92

[2537] North, *BETRAYAL IN DALLAS*, p. 93

[2538] North, *BETRAYAL IN DALLAS*, p. 93

[2539] North, *BETRAYAL IN DALLAS*, p. 93

[2540] North, *BETRAYAL IN DALLAS*, p. 102

[2541] North, *BETRAYAL IN DALLAS*, pp. 104-105

[2542] North, *BETRAYAL IN DALLAS*, p. 105

[2543] North, *BETRAYAL IN DALLAS*, p. 107

[2544] North, *BETRAYAL IN DALLAS*, p. 117

[2545] North, *BETRAYAL IN DALLAS*, p. 117

[2546] North, *BETRAYAL IN DALLAS*, p. 117

[2547] North, *BETRAYAL IN DALLAS*, p. 118

[2548] North, *ACT OF TREASON*, p. 335

[2549] Corsi, *WHO REALLY KILLED KENNEDY*, pp. 176-177

[2550] Corsi, *WHO REALLY KILLED KENNEDY*, pp. 176-177

[2551] Douglass, *JFK AND THE UNSPEAKABLE*, p. 200

[2552] Douglass, *JFK AND THE UNSPEAKABLE*, p. 201

[2553] Corsi, *WHO REALLY KILLED KENNEDY*, p. 177

[2554] Corsi, *WHO REALLY KILLED KENNEDY*, p. 177

[2555] Corsi, *WHO REALLY KILLED KENNEDY*, p. 177

[2556] Janney, *MARY'S MOSAIC*, p. 282

[2557] Corsi, *WHO REALLY KILLED KENNEDY*, p. 178

[2558] Corsi, *WHO REALLY KILLED KENNEDY*, pp. 178-179

[2559] Nelson, *LBJ: THE MASTERMIND OF THE JFK ASSASSINATION*, p. 362

[2560] Douglass, *JFK AND THE UNSPEAKABLE*, p. 200

[2561] Douglass, *JFK AND THE UNSPEAKABLE*, p. 214

[2562] Douglass, *JFK AND THE UNSPEAKABLE*, p. 214

[2563] Douglass, *JFK AND THE UNSPEAKABLE*, p. 214

[2564] Douglass, *JFK AND THE UNSPEAKABLE*, p. 214

[2565] Douglass, *JFK AND THE UNSPEAKABLE*, pp. 214-215

[2566] Douglass, *JFK AND THE UNSPEAKABLE*, p. 215

[2567] Douglass, *JFK AND THE UNSPEAKABLE*, p. 215

[2568] Douglass, *JFK AND THE UNSPEAKABLE*, p. 215

[2569] Douglass, *JFK AND THE UNSPEAKABLE*, p. 216

[2570] Douglass, *JFK AND THE UNSPEAKABLE*, p. 216

[2571] Douglass, *JFK AND THE UNSPEAKABLE*, p. 216

[2572] Douglass, *JFK AND THE UNSPEAKABLE*, p. 216

[2573] Douglass, *JFK AND THE UNSPEAKABLE*, p. 216

[2574] Nelson, *LBJ: THE MASTERMIND OF THE JFK ASSASSINATION*, p. 368

[2575] North, *ACT OF TREASON,* pp. 352-353

[2576] Corsi, *WHO REALLY KILLED KENNEDY*, p. 179

[2577] Corsi, *WHO REALLY KILLED KENNEDY*, p. 180

[2578] Corsi, *WHO REALLY KILLED KENNEDY*, p. 180

[2579] Corsi, *WHO REALLY KILLED KENNEDY*, pp. 180-182

[2580] Corsi, *WHO REALLY KILLED KENNEDY*, pp. 180-182

[2581] Corsi, *WHO REALLY KILLED KENNEDY*, pp. 180-182

[2582] Douglass, *JFK AND THE UNSPEAKABLE*, p. 153

[2583] Douglass, *JFK AND THE UNSPEAKABLE*, pp. 153-154

[2584] Douglass, *JFK AND THE UNSPEAKABLE*, p. 154

[2585] Douglass, *JFK AND THE UNSPEAKABLE*, p. 154

[2586] Douglass, *JFK AND THE UNSPEAKABLE*, p. 154

[2587] Douglass, *JFK AND THE UNSPEAKABLE*, p. 154

[2588] Douglass, *JFK AND THE UNSPEAKABLE*, p. 154

[2589] Garrison, *ON THE TRAIL OF THE ASSASSINS*, pp. 182-186

[2590] Douglass, *JFK AND THE UNSPEAKABLE*, p. 156

[2591] Douglass, *JFK AND THE UNSPEAKABLE*, p. 157

[2592] Douglass, *JFK AND THE UNSPEAKABLE*, p. 157

[2593] Douglass, *JFK AND THE UNSPEAKABLE*, p. 350

[2594] Janney, *MARY'S MOSAIC*, p. 21

[2595] Janney, *MARY'S MOSAIC*, p. 21

[2596] Corsi, *WHO REALLY KILLED KENNEDY?*, p. 162

[2597] Douglass, *JFK AND THE UNSPEAKABLE*, p. 47

[2598] Douglass, *JFK AND THE UNSPEAKABLE*, p. 47

[2599] Douglass, *JFK AND THE UNSPEAKABLE*, p. 47

[2600] Fonzi, *THE LAST INVESTIGATION*, p. 424

[2601] North, *ACT OF TREASON,* p. 212

[2602] Douglass, *JFK AND THE UNSPEAKABLE*, p. 48

[2603] Nelson, *LBJ: THE MASTERMIND OF THE JFK ASSASSINATION*,

p. 468

[2604] Nelson, *LBJ: THE MASTERMIND OF THE JFK ASSASSINATION*, p. 468

[2605] Fonzi, *THE LAST INVESTIGATION*, p. 427

[2606] Douglass, *JFK AND THE UNSPEAKABLE*, p. 48

[2607] Douglass, *JFK AND THE UNSPEAKABLE*, p. 48

[2608] Corsi, *WHO REALLY KILLED KENNEDY*, p. 168

[2609] Douglass, *JFK AND THE UNSPEAKABLE*, p. 48

[2610] Talbot, *THE DEVIL'S CHESSBOARD*, p. 531

[2611] Talbot, *THE DEVIL'S CHESSBOARD*, pp. 532-533

[2612] Talbot, *THE DEVIL'S CHESSBOARD*, pp. 532-533

[2613] Corsi, *WHO REALLY KILLED KENNEDY*, p. 171

[2614] Talbot, *THE DEVIL'S CHESSBOARD*, p. 533

[2615] Belzer & Wayne, HIT LIST, p. 236

[2616] Belzer & Wayne, HIT LIST, p. 236

[2617] Belzer & Wayne, HIT LIST, p. 237

[2618] Belzer & Wayne, HIT LIST, p. 236

[2619] Baker, Me & Lee, p. 292

[2620] DiEugenio, *DESTINY BETRAYED*, p. 199

[2621] DiEugenio, *DESTINY BETRAYED*, pp. 199-200

[2622] Douglass, *JFK AND THE UNSPEAKABLE*, p. 170

[2623] Douglass, *JFK AND THE UNSPEAKABLE*, p. 170

[2624] Douglass, *JFK AND THE UNSPEAKABLE*, pp. 170-171

[2625] Douglass, *JFK AND THE UNSPEAKABLE*, pp. 170-171

[2626] Douglass, *JFK AND THE UNSPEAKABLE*, pp. 169-170

[2627] Douglass, *JFK AND THE UNSPEAKABLE*, p. 169

[2628] Fonzi, *THE LAST INVESTIGATION*, pp. 50-51

[2629] Douglass, *JFK AND THE UNSPEAKABLE*, pp. 168-169

[2630] Douglass, *JFK AND THE UNSPEAKABLE*, p. 168

[2631] North, *ACT OF TREASON,* p. 270

[2632] North, *ACT OF TREASON,* p. 279

[2633] North, *ACT OF TREASON,* p. 288

[2634] Nolan, *CIA ROGUES AND THE KILLING OF THE KENNEDYS*, p. 136

[2635] Summers, *NOT IN YOUR LIFETIME*, p. 352

[2636] Joesten, *OSWALD: ASSASSIN OR FALL GUY?*, pp. 45-46

[2637] Douglass, *JFK AND THE UNSPEAKABLE*, p. 171

[2638] DiEugenio, *DESTINY BETRAYED*, p. 199

[2639] Douglass, *JFK AND THE UNSPEAKABLE*, pp. 158-162

[2640] Douglass, *JFK AND THE UNSPEAKABLE*, pp. 158-162

[2641] Douglass, *JFK AND THE UNSPEAKABLE*, pp. 158-162

[2642] Douglass, *JFK AND THE UNSPEAKABLE*, pp. 158-162

[2643] Fonzi, *THE LAST INVESTIGATION*, p. 114

[2644] DiEugenio, *DESTINY BETRAYED*, p. 352

[2645] Douglass, *JFK AND THE UNSPEAKABLE*, pp. 158-162

[2646] Fonzi, *THE LAST INVESTIGATION*, p. 433

[2647] Fonzi, *THE LAST INVESTIGATION*, p. 433

[2648] Douglass, *JFK AND THE UNSPEAKABLE*, p. 222

[2649] North, *ACT OF TREASON*, pp. 342-343

[2650] Douglass, *JFK AND THE UNSPEAKABLE*, p. 222

[2651] Douglass, *JFK AND THE UNSPEAKABLE*, p. 222

[2652] North, *ACT OF TREASON*, p. 338

[2653] North, *ACT OF TREASON*, pp. 341-342

[2654] North, *ACT OF TREASON*, pp. 348-349

[2655] North, *ACT OF TREASON*, pp. 425-426

[2656] Douglass, *JFK AND THE UNSPEAKABLE*, p. xxx

[2657] Douglass, *JFK AND THE UNSPEAKABLE*, p. xxx

[2658] Douglass, *JFK AND THE UNSPEAKABLE*, p. xxx

[2659] Douglass, *JFK AND THE UNSPEAKABLE*, p. xxx

[2660] Douglass, *JFK AND THE UNSPEAKABLE*, p. 244

[2661] Douglass, *JFK AND THE UNSPEAKABLE*, p. 244

[2662] Douglass, *JFK AND THE UNSPEAKABLE*, p. 244

[2663] Douglass, *JFK AND THE UNSPEAKABLE*, p. 350

[2664] Douglass, *JFK AND THE UNSPEAKABLE*, p. 350

[2665] Douglass, *JFK AND THE UNSPEAKABLE*, p. 351

[2666] Douglass, *JFK AND THE UNSPEAKABLE*, pp. 351-352

[2667] Douglass, *JFK AND THE UNSPEAKABLE*, p. 352

[2668] Douglass, *JFK AND THE UNSPEAKABLE*, p. 352

[2669] Douglass, *JFK AND THE UNSPEAKABLE*, p. 352

[2670] Douglass, *JFK AND THE UNSPEAKABLE*, p. 353

[2671] Douglass, *JFK AND THE UNSPEAKABLE*, p. 354

[2672] Douglass, *JFK AND THE UNSPEAKABLE*, p. 227

[2673] Douglass, *JFK AND THE UNSPEAKABLE*, p. 227

[2674] Joesten, *OSWALD: ASSASSIN OR FALL GUY?*, p. 127

[2675] Douglass, *JFK AND THE UNSPEAKABLE*, p. 226

[2676] Douglass, *JFK AND THE UNSPEAKABLE*, pp. 226-227

[2677] Douglass, *JFK AND THE UNSPEAKABLE*, p. 227

[2678] Joesten, *OSWALD: ASSASSIN OR FALL GUY?*, pp. 128-129

[2679] North, *ACT OF TREASON*, p. 369

[2680] North, *ACT OF TREASON*, p. 474

[2681] North, *ACT OF TREASON*, p. 362

[2682] North, *ACT OF TREASON*, p. 362

[2683] North, *ACT OF TREASON*, p. 354

[2684] North, *ACT OF TREASON*, p. 354

[2685] Meagher, *ACCESSORIES AFTER THE FACT*, pp. 353

[2686] Garrison, *ON THE TRAIL OF THE ASSASSINS*, p. 57

[2687] Douglass, *JFK AND THE UNSPEAKABLE*, p. 223

[2688] Douglass, *JFK AND THE UNSPEAKABLE*, p. 223

[2689] Belzer & Wayne, *HIT LIST*, p. 133

[2690] Belzer & Wayne, *HIT LIST*, p. 132

[2691] Belzer & Wayne, *HIT LIST*, p. 133

[2692] Belzer & Wayne, *HIT LIST*, p. 131

[2693] Belzer & Wayne, *HIT LIST*, p. 131

[2694] Joesten, *OSWALD: ASSASSIN OR FALL GUY?*, p. 193

[2695] North, *ACT OF TREASON,* p. 427

[2696] North, *ACT OF TREASON,* p. 445

[2697] North, *ACT OF TREASON,* p. 344

[2698] Joesten, *OSWALD: ASSASSIN OR FALL GUY?*, pp. 114-115

[2699] Joesten, *OSWALD: ASSASSIN OR FALL GUY?*, pp. 114-115

[2700] Joesten, *OSWALD: ASSASSIN OR FALL GUY?*, p. 115

[2701] Summers, *NOT IN YOUR LIFETIME*, pp. 354-355

[2702] Summers, *NOT IN YOUR LIFETIME*, pp. 354-355

[2703] North, *ACT OF TREASON,* p. 366

[2704] North, *ACT OF TREASON,* p. 366

[2705] Belzer & Wayne, *DEAD WRONG*, p. 123

[2706] Summers, *NOT IN YOUR LIFETIME*, p. 156

[2707] Belzer & Wayne, *DEAD WRONG*, p. 123

[2708] Lane, *LAST WORD*, p. 197

[2709] Lane, *LAST WORD*, p. 197

[2710] Lane, *LAST WORD*, p. 197

[2711] North, *ACT OF TREASON,* p. 393

[2712] North, *ACT OF TREASON,* p. 354

[2713] North, *ACT OF TREASON,* p. 354

[2714] North, *ACT OF TREASON,* p. 354

[2715] North, *ACT OF TREASON,* p. 354

[2716] North, *ACT OF TREASON,* p. 354

[2717] North, *ACT OF TREASON,* p. 354

[2718] DiEugenio, *RECLAIMING PARKLAND*, p. 82

[2719] DiEugenio, *RECLAIMING PARKLAND*, p. 81

[2720] DiEugenio, *RECLAIMING PARKLAND*, p. 81

[2721] DiEugenio, *RECLAIMING PARKLAND*, p. 81

[2722] DiEugenio, *RECLAIMING PARKLAND*, p. 83

[2723] DiEugenio, *RECLAIMING PARKLAND*, p. 83

[2724] Joesten, *OSWALD: ASSASSIN OR FALL GUY?*, p. 120

[2725] Joesten, *OSWALD: ASSASSIN OR FALL GUY?*, p. 120

[2726] Summers, *NOT IN YOUR LIFETIME*, p. 190

[2727] Nelson, *LBJ: THE MASTERMIND OF THE JFK ASSASSINATION,* p. 374

[2728] Nelson, *LBJ: THE MASTERMIND OF THE JFK ASSASSINATION,* p. 375

[2729] Stone & Colapietro, *THE MAN WHO KILLED KENNEDY*, p. 222

[2730] Nelson, *LBJ: THE MASTERMIND OF THE JFK ASSASSINATION,* p. 376

[2731] North, *ACT OF TREASON,* p. 367

[2732] Nolan, *CIA ROGUES AND THE KILLING OF THE KENNEDYS,* p. 145

[2733] Joesten, *OSWALD: ASSASSIN OR FALL GUY?*, pp. 14-16

[2734] Joesten, *OSWALD: ASSASSIN OR FALL GUY?*, pp. 14-16

[2735] Nolan, *CIA ROGUES AND THE KILLING OF THE KENNEDYS,* pp. 143-144

[2736] Nolan, *CIA ROGUES AND THE KILLING OF THE KENNEDYS,*

pp. 143-144

[2737] Nolan, *CIA ROGUES AND THE KILLING OF THE KENNEDYS*, pp. 143-144

[2738] Nolan, *CIA ROGUES AND THE KILLING OF THE KENNEDYS*, pp. 143-144

[2739] Talbot, *THE DEVIL'S CHESSBOARD*, p. 563

[2740] Douglass, *JFK AND THE UNSPEAKABLE*, p. 352

[2741] Joesten, *OSWALD: ASSASSIN OR FALL GUY?*, p. 7

[2742] Joesten, *OSWALD: ASSASSIN OR FALL GUY?*, p. 7

[2743] Douglass, *JFK AND THE UNSPEAKABLE*, p. 365

[2744] Douglass, *JFK AND THE UNSPEAKABLE*, p. 365

[2745] Stone & Colapietro, *THE MAN WHO KILLED KENNEDY*, p. 220

[2746] Stone & Colapietro, *THE MAN WHO KILLED KENNEDY*, p. 220

[2747] Nelson, *LBJ: MASTERMIND OF THE JFK ASSASSINATION*, p. 321

[2748] Nelson, *LBJ: MASTERMIND OF THE JFK ASSASSINATION*, p. 321

[2749] North, *ACT OF TREASON*, p. 102

[2750] Nelson, *LBJ: THE MASTERMIND OF THE JFK ASSASSINATION*, pp. 387-388

[2751] Nelson, *LBJ: THE MASTERMIND OF THE JFK ASSASSINATION*, pp. 387-388

[2752] Stone & Colapietro, *THE MAN WHO KILLED KENNEDY*, p. 234

[2753] Douglass, *JFK AND THE UNSPEAKABLE*, p. 271

[2754] Douglass, *JFK AND THE UNSPEAKABLE*, p. 271

[2755] Joesten, *OSWALD: ASSASSIN OR FALL GUY?*, p. 279

[2756] Nelson, *LBJ: THE MASTERMIND OF THE JFK ASSASSINATION*, pp. 379-380

[2757] Stone & Colapietro, *THE MAN WHO KILLED KENNEDY*, p. 219

[2758] Stone & Colapietro, *THE MAN WHO KILLED KENNEDY*, p. 219

[2759] Nelson, *LBJ: THE MASTERMIND OF THE JFK ASSASSINATION*, p. 379

[2760] DiEugenio, *RECLAIMING PARKLAND*, p. 367

[2761] DiEugenio, *RECLAIMING PARKLAND*, p. 367

[2762] Lane, *LAST WORD*, p. 164

[2763] Nelson, *LBJ: THE MASTERMIND OF THE JFK ASSASSINATION*, p. 403

[2764] Nelson, *LBJ: THE MASTERMIND OF THE JFK ASSASSINATION*, p. 471

[2765] Nelson, *LBJ: THE MASTERMIND OF THE JFK ASSASSINATION*, p. 471

[2766] Nelson, *LBJ: THE MASTERMIND OF THE JFK ASSASSINATION*, p. 498

[2767] Nelson, *LBJ: THE MASTERMIND OF THE JFK ASSASSINATION*, pp. 473-478

[2768] Nelson, *LBJ: THE MASTERMIND OF THE JFK ASSASSINATION*, pp. 473-478

[2769] Stone & Colapietro, *THE MAN WHO KILLED KENNEDY*, p. 237

[2770] Nelson, *LBJ: THE MASTERMIND OF THE JFK ASSASSINATION*, pp. 498-499

[2771] Janney, *MARY'S MOSAIC*, pp. 253-254

[2772] Nelson, *LBJ: THE MASTERMIND OF THE JFK ASSASSINATION*, pp. 494-497

[2773] Lane, *LAST WORD*, p. 12

[2774] Lane, *LAST WORD*, p. 12

[2775] Summers, *NOT IN YOUR LIFETIME*, pp. 59-60

[2776] Summers, *NOT IN YOUR LIFETIME*, p. 60

[2777] Nelson, *LBJ: THE MASTERMIND OF THE JFK ASSASSINATION*, p. 493

[2778] Nelson, *LBJ: THE MASTERMIND OF THE JFK ASSASSINATION*, p. 493

[2779] Summers, *NOT IN YOUR LIFETIME*, pp. 60-61

[2780] Nelson, *LBJ: THE MASTERMIND OF THE JFK ASSASSINATION*, p. 491

[2781] Nelson, *LBJ: THE MASTERMIND OF THE JFK ASSASSINATION*, p. 491

[2782] Nelson, *LBJ: THE MASTERMIND OF THE JFK ASSASSINATION*, p. 491

[2783] Stone & Colapietro, *THE MAN WHO KILLED KENNEDY*, p. 212

[2784] McClellan, *BLOOD, MONEY AND POWER*, pp. 326-327

[2785] Talbot, *THE DEVIL'S CHESSBOARD*, p. 501

[2786] Fonzi, *THE LAST INVESTIGATION*, p. 346

[2787] McClellan, *BLOOD, MONEY AND POWER*, p. 195

[2788] McClellan, *BLOOD, MONEY AND POWER*, p. 195

[2789] Corsi, *WHO REALLY KILLED KENNEDY*, pp. 71-72

[2790] Corsi, *WHO REALLY KILLED KENNEDY*, pp. 71-72

[2791] Corsi, *WHO REALLY KILLED KENNEDY*, pp. 71-72

[2792] Corsi, *WHO REALLY KILLED KENNEDY*, pp. 71-72

[2793] Corsi, *WHO REALLY KILLED KENNEDY*, pp. 71-72

[2794] North, *BETRAYAL IN DALLAS*, pp. 71-72

[2795] Summers, *NOT IN YOUR LIFETIME*, pp. 37-38

[2796] Crenshaw, *JFK HAS BEEN SHOT*, p. 66

[2797] Crenshaw, *JFK HAS BEEN SHOT*, p. 66

[2798] Nolan, *CIA ROGUES AND THE KILLING OF THE KENNEDYS*, p. 8

[2799] Joesten, *OSWALD: ASSASSIN OR FALL GUY?*, p. 286

[2800] Joesten, *OSWALD: ASSASSIN OR FALL GUY?*, p. 286

[2801] Summers, *NOT IN YOUR LIFETIME*, p. 40

[2802] Summers, *NOT IN YOUR LIFETIME*, p. 40

[2803] Summers, *NOT IN YOUR LIFETIME*, p. 41

[2804] Summers, *NOT IN YOUR LIFETIME*, p. 41

[2805] Summers, *NOT IN YOUR LIFETIME*, p. 41

[2806] Summers, *NOT IN YOUR LIFETIME*, pp. 42-43

[2807] Summers, *NOT IN YOUR LIFETIME*, p. 43

[2808] Summers, *NOT IN YOUR LIFETIME*, pp. 56-57

[2809] Summers, *NOT IN YOUR LIFETIME*, pp. 58-59

[2810] Summers, *NOT IN YOUR LIFETIME*, pp. 58-59

[2811] Summers, *NOT IN YOUR LIFETIME*, pp. 58-59

[2812] Joesten, *OSWALD: ASSASSIN OR FALL GUY?*, p. 284

[2813] Joesten, *OSWALD: ASSASSIN OR FALL GUY?*, p. 284

[2814] Crenshaw, *JFK HAS BEEN SHOT*, p. 66

[2815] Crenshaw, *JFK HAS BEEN SHOT*, p. 66

[2816] Crenshaw, *JFK HAS BEEN SHOT*, p. 66

[2817] Douglass, *JFK AND THE UNSPEAKABLE*, pp. 263-264

[2818] Douglass, *JFK AND THE UNSPEAKABLE*, p. 264

[2819] Douglass, *JFK AND THE UNSPEAKABLE*, p. 264

[2820] Douglass, *JFK AND THE UNSPEAKABLE*, pp. 264-265

[2821] Douglass, *JFK AND THE UNSPEAKABLE*, p. 264

[2822] Marrs, *CROSSFIRE*, p. 73

[2823] Stone & Colapietro, *THE MAN WHO KILLED KENNEDY*, p. 239

[2824] Joesten, *OSWALD: ASSASSIN OR FALL GUY?*, p. 282

[2825] Stone & Colapietro, *THE MAN WHO KILLED KENNEDY*, p. 238-239

[2826] Douglass, *JFK AND THE UNSPEAKABLE*, pp. 264-265

[2827] Belzer & Wayne, *DEAD WRONG*, p. 134

[2828] Belzer & Wayne, *DEAD WRONG*, p. 134

[2829] Belzer & Wayne, *DEAD WRONG*, p. 134

[2830] Belzer & Wayne, *DEAD WRONG*, p. 134

[2831] Summers, *NOT IN YOUR LIFETIME*, p. 42

[2832] Nelson, *LBJ: THE MASTERMIND OF THE JFK ASSASSINATION*, p. 469

[2833] Summers, *NOT IN YOUR LIFETIME*, p. 42

[2834] Douglass, *JFK AND THE UNSPEAKABLE*, p. 262

[2835] Douglass, *JFK AND THE UNSPEAKABLE*, p. 262

[2836] Douglass, *JFK AND THE UNSPEAKABLE*, p. 262

[2837] Summers, *NOT IN YOUR LIFETIME*, p. 40

[2838] Douglass, *JFK AND THE UNSPEAKABLE*, pp. 262-263

[2839] Douglass, *JFK AND THE UNSPEAKABLE*, p. 263

[2840] Summers, *NOT IN YOUR LIFETIME*, p. 41

[2841] Summers, *NOT IN YOUR LIFETIME*, p. 40

[2842] Summers, *NOT IN YOUR LIFETIME*, p. 41

[2843] Summers, *NOT IN YOUR LIFETIME*, p. 41

[2844] Nelson, *LBJ: THE MASTERMIND OF THE JFK ASSASSINATION*, pp. 492-493

[2845] Nelson, *LBJ: THE MASTERMIND OF THE JFK ASSASSINATION*, pp. 492-493

[2846] Nelson, *LBJ: THE MASTERMIND OF THE JFK ASSASSINATION*, pp. 492-493

[2847] Douglass, *JFK AND THE UNSPEAKABLE*, p. 263

[2848] Summers, *NOT IN YOUR LIFETIME*, p. 43

[2849] Nelson, *LBJ: THE MASTERMIND OF THE JFK ASSASSINATION*,

p. 494
[2850] Nelson, *LBJ: THE MASTERMIND OF THE JFK ASSASSINATION*, p. 494
[2851] Nelson, *LBJ: THE MASTERMIND OF THE JFK ASSASSINATION*, p. 494
[2852] Nelson, *LBJ: THE MASTERMIND OF THE JFK ASSASSINATION*, p. 494
[2853] Nelson, *LBJ: THE MASTERMIND OF THE JFK ASSASSINATION*, pp. 494-497
[2854] Nelson, *LBJ: THE MASTERMIND OF THE JFK ASSASSINATION*, pp. 494-497
[2855] Nelson, *LBJ: THE MASTERMIND OF THE JFK ASSASSINATION*, pp. 494-497
[2856] Nelson, *LBJ: THE MASTERMIND OF THE JFK ASSASSINATION*, pp. 494-497
[2857] Nelson, *LBJ: THE MASTERMIND OF THE JFK ASSASSINATION*, pp. 494-497
[2858] Nelson, *LBJ: THE MASTERMIND OF THE JFK ASSASSINATION*, pp. 494-497
[2859] Nelson, *LBJ: THE MASTERMIND OF THE JFK ASSASSINATION*, pp. 494-497
[2860] Nelson, *LBJ: THE MASTERMIND OF THE JFK ASSASSINATION*, pp. 494-497
[2861] Nelson, *LBJ: THE MASTERMIND OF THE JFK ASSASSINATION*, pp. 494-497
[2862] Nelson, *LBJ: THE MASTERMIND OF THE JFK ASSASSINATION*, pp. 494-497
[2863] Nelson, *LBJ: THE MASTERMIND OF THE JFK ASSASSINATION*, pp. 494-497
[2864] Nelson, *LBJ: THE MASTERMIND OF THE JFK ASSASSINATION*, p. 498
[2865] Joesten, *OSWALD: ASSASSIN OR FALL GUY?*, p. 287
[2866] Belzer & Wayne, *DEAD WRONG*, p. 151
[2867] Belzer & Wayne, *DEAD WRONG*, p. 151
[2868] Nelson, *LBJ: THE MASTERMIND OF THE JFK ASSASSINATION*, p. 543
[2869] Belzer & Wayne, *DEAD WRONG*, p. 152
[2870] Nelson, *LBJ: THE MASTERMIND OF THE JFK ASSASSINATION*, p. 543
[2871] Corsi, *WHO REALLY KILLED KENNEDY*, pp. 291-294
[2872] Corsi, *WHO REALLY KILLED KENNEDY*, pp. 291-294
[2873] Nelson, *LBJ: THE MASTERMIND OF THE JFK ASSASSINATION*, pp. 360-361
[2874] Stone & Colapietro, *THE MAN WHO KILLED KENNEDY*, p. 171
[2875] Belzer & Wayne, *HIT LIST*, pp. 125-126
[2876] Nelson, *LBJ: THE MASTERMIND OF THE JFK ASSASSINATION*, p. 331

[2877] Nelson, *LBJ: THE MASTERMIND OF THE JFK ASSASSINATION*, p. 331

[2878] Nelson, *LBJ: THE MASTERMIND OF THE JFK ASSASSINATION*, p. 331

[2879] Nelson, *LBJ: THE MASTERMIND OF THE JFK ASSASSINATION*, p. 331

[2880] Nelson, *LBJ: THE MASTERMIND OF THE JFK ASSASSINATION*, pp. 360-361

[2881] Joesten, *OSWALD: ASSASSIN OR FALL GUY?*, p. 287

[2882] North, *ACT OF TREASON*, p. 372

[2883] Ventura, *THEY KILLED OUR PRESIDENT*, p. 320

[2884] Corsi, *WHO REALLY KILLED KENNEDY?*, p. 213

[2885] Corsi, *WHO REALLY KILLED KENNEDY?*, p. 213

[2886] Garrison, *ON THE TRAIL OF THE ASSASSINS*, p. 205

[2887] Garrison, *ON THE TRAIL OF THE ASSASSINS*, p. 205

[2888] North, *ACT OF TREASON*, p. 390

[2889] North, *ACT OF TREASON*, p. 390

[2890] Summers, *NOT IN YOUR LIFETIME*, p. 33

[2891] Summers, *NOT IN YOUR LIFETIME*, p. 33

[2892] North, *ACT OF TREASON*, p. 440

[2893] North, *ACT OF TREASON*, p. 440

[2894] Fonzi, *THE LAST INVESTIGATION*, p. 442

[2895] Fonzi, *THE LAST INVESTIGATION*, p. 404

[2896] DiEugenio, *RECLAIMING PARKLAND*, p. 212

[2897] Crenshaw, *JFK HAS BEEN SHOT*, p. 135

[2898] Thomas, *HEAR NO EVIL*, pp. 400-404

[2899] Thomas, *HEAR NO EVIL*, pp. 400-404

[2900] Thomas, *HEAR NO EVIL*, pp. 400-404

[2901] Meagher, *ACCESSORIES AFTER THE FACT*, pp. 5-8

[2902] Meagher, *ACCESSORIES AFTER THE FACT*, pp. 5-8

[2903] Meagher, *ACCESSORIES AFTER THE FACT*, pp. 5-8

[2904] Meagher, *ACCESSORIES AFTER THE FACT*, pp. 5-8

[2905] Crenshaw, *JFK HAS BEEN SHOT*, p. 136

[2906] Summers, *NOT IN YOUR LIFETIME*, pp. 44-45

[2907] Belzer & Wayne, *DEAD WRONG*, p. 94

[2908] Belzer & Wayne, *DEAD WRONG*, p. 93

[2909] Summers, *NOT IN YOUR LIFETIME*, p. 45

[2910] Nelson, *LBJ: THE MASTERMIND OF THE JFK ASSASSINATION*, pp. 397-398

[2911] Thomas, *HEAR NO EVIL*, p. 437

[2912] Thomas, *HEAR NO EVIL*, p. 322

[2913] Thomas, *HEAR NO EVIL*, p. 326

[2914] Lane, *LAST WORD*, p. 272

[2915] Lane, *LAST WORD*, p. 272

[2916] Douglass, *JFK AND THE UNSPEAKABLE*, p. 267

[2917] McClellan, *BLOOD, MONEY AND POWER*, p. 184

[2918] Belzer & Wayne, *DEAD WRONG*, p. 133

[2919] Summers, *NOT IN YOUR LIFETIME*, p. 57

[2920] Summers, *NOT IN YOUR LIFETIME*, p. 57

[2921] Corsi, *WHO REALLY KILLED KENNEDY*, p. 68

[2922] Corsi, *WHO REALLY KILLED KENNEDY*, pp. 68-69

[2923] Douglass, *JFK AND THE UNSPEAKABLE*, pp. 262-263

[2924] Douglass, *JFK AND THE UNSPEAKABLE*, p. 263

[2925] Crenshaw, *JFK HAS BEEN SHOT*, pp. 68-69

[2926] Douglass, *JFK AND THE UNSPEAKABLE*, p. 261

[2927] Douglass, *JFK AND THE UNSPEAKABLE*, p. 267

[2928] North, *ACT OF TREASON*, p. 377

[2929] North, *ACT OF TREASON*, p. 377

[2930] North, *ACT OF TREASON*, p. 377

[2931] Joesten, *OSWALD: ASSASSIN OR FALL GUY?*, p. 53

[2932] North, *ACT OF TREASON*, p. 377

[2933] North, *ACT OF TREASON*, pp. 377-378

[2934] Meagher, *ACCESSORIES AFTER THE FACT*, p. 225

[2935] Crenshaw, *JFK HAS BEEN SHOT*, pp. 70-71

[2936] Summers, *NOT IN YOUR LIFETIME*, p. 96

[2937] Douglass, *JFK AND THE UNSPEAKABLE*, p. 285

[2938] DiEugenio, *RECLAIMING PARKLAND*, p. 121

[2939] DiEugenio, *RECLAIMING PARKLAND*, p. 121

[2940] Nolan, *CIA ROGUES AND THE KILLING OF THE KENNEDYS*, p. 8

[2941] North, *ACT OF TREASON*, p. 377

[2942] North, *ACT OF TREASON*, p. 377

[2943] North, *ACT OF TREASON*, p. 378

[2944] North, *ACT OF TREASON*, pp. 377-378

[2945] North, *ACT OF TREASON*, p. 438

[2946] North, *ACT OF TREASON*, p. 438

[2947] Corsi, *WHO REALLY KILLED KENNEDY*, pp. 94-95

[2948] Corsi, *WHO REALLY KILLED KENNEDY*, pp. 94-95

[2949] Douglass, *JFK AND THE UNSPEAKABLE*, p. 274

[2950] Douglass, *JFK AND THE UNSPEAKABLE*, p. 274

[2951] Douglass, *JFK AND THE UNSPEAKABLE*, pp. 274-275

[2952] Douglass, *JFK AND THE UNSPEAKABLE*, pp. 274-275

[2953] Douglass, *JFK AND THE UNSPEAKABLE*, p. 275

[2954] Douglass, *JFK AND THE UNSPEAKABLE*, p. 275

[2955] Douglass, *JFK AND THE UNSPEAKABLE*, p. 277

[2956] Douglass, *JFK AND THE UNSPEAKABLE*, p. 277

[2957] Nelson, *LBJ: THE MASTERMIND OF THE JFK ASSASSINATION*, p. 408

[2958] Douglass, *JFK AND THE UNSPEAKABLE*, p. 275

[2959] Douglass, *JFK AND THE UNSPEAKABLE*, p. 275

[2960] Douglass, *JFK AND THE UNSPEAKABLE*, p. 275

[2961] Douglass, *JFK AND THE UNSPEAKABLE*, p. 278

[2962] Lane, *LAST WORD*, p. 34

[2963] Lane, *LAST WORD*, p. 35

[2964] Lane, *LAST WORD*, p. 35

[2965] Lane, *LAST WORD*, p. 35

[2966] Lane, *LAST WORD*, p. 35

[2967] Nelson, *LBJ: THE MASTERMIND OF THE JFK ASSASSINATION*, p. 464

[2968] Nelson, *LBJ: THE MASTERMIND OF THE JFK ASSASSINATION*, p. 464

[2969] Nelson, *LBJ: THE MASTERMIND OF THE JFK ASSASSINATION*, p. 464

[2970] Douglass, *JFK AND THE UNSPEAKABLE*, p. 261

[2971] North, *BETRAYAL IN DALLAS*, p. 53

[2972] North, *BETRAYAL IN DALLAS*, p. 92

[2973] Talbot, *THE DEVIL'S CHESSBOARD*, p. 563

[2974] Douglass, *JFK AND THE UNSPEAKABLE*, p. 352

[2975] Talbot, *THE DEVIL'S CHESSBOARD*, p. 563

[2976] Meagher, *ACCESSORIES AFTER THE FACT*, p. 323

[2977] Meagher, *ACCESSORIES AFTER THE FACT*, p. 323

[2978] North, *ACT OF TREASON,* p. 377

[2979] Meagher, *ACCESSORIES AFTER THE FACT*, pp. 225-226

[2980] Douglass, *JFK AND THE UNSPEAKABLE*, p. 244

[2981] Douglass, *JFK AND THE UNSPEAKABLE*, p. 244

[2982] Joesten, *OSWALD: ASSASSIN OR FALL GUY?*, pp. 223-224

[2983] Joesten, *OSWALD: ASSASSIN OR FALL GUY?*, p. 224

[2984] Joesten, *OSWALD: ASSASSIN OR FALL GUY?*, p. 224

[2985] Joesten, *OSWALD: ASSASSIN OR FALL GUY?*, pp. 224-225

[2986] Joesten, *OSWALD: ASSASSIN OR FALL GUY?*, pp. 225-226

[2987] North, *ACT OF TREASON,* p. 395

[2988] North, *ACT OF TREASON,* p. 440

[2989] North, *ACT OF TREASON,* p. 440

[2990] Fonzi, *THE LAST INVESTIGATION*, p. 10

[2991] Fonzi, *THE LAST INVESTIGATION*, p. 10

[2992] Fonzi, *THE LAST INVESTIGATION*, p. 10

[2993] Fonzi, *THE LAST INVESTIGATION*, p. 10

[2994] Fonzi, *THE LAST INVESTIGATION*, p. 10

[2995] Fonzi, *THE LAST INVESTIGATION*, p. 10

[2996] Fonzi, *THE LAST INVESTIGATION*, p. 10

[2997] Fonzi, *THE LAST INVESTIGATION*, p. 10

[2998] Joesten, *OSWALD: ASSASSIN OR FALL GUY?*, p. 157

[2999] Joesten, *OSWALD: ASSASSIN OR FALL GUY?*, p. 157

[3000] Belzer & Wayne, *DEAD WRONG*, p. 107

[3001] Belzer & Wayne, *DEAD WRONG*, p. 107

[3002] Stone & Colapietro, *THE MAN WHO KILLED KENNEDY*, pp. 249-250

[3003] Stone & Colapietro, *THE MAN WHO KILLED KENNEDY*, pp. 249-250

[3004] Stone & Colapietro, *THE MAN WHO KILLED KENNEDY*, pp. 249-250

[3005] Nelson, *LBJ: THE MASTERMIND OF THE JFK ASSASSINATION*, p. 538

[3006] Stone & Colapietro, *THE MAN WHO KILLED KENNEDY*, p. 249

[3007] Stone & Colapietro, *THE MAN WHO KILLED KENNEDY*, p. 249

[3008] North, *ACT OF TREASON,* p. 394

[3009] Crenshaw, *JFK HAS BEEN SHOT*, p. 198

[3010] Crenshaw, *JFK HAS BEEN SHOT*, pp. 51-52

[3011] Crenshaw, *JFK HAS BEEN SHOT*, pp. 51-52

[3012] Crenshaw, *JFK HAS BEEN SHOT*, pp. 51-52

[3013] Crenshaw, *JFK HAS BEEN SHOT*, p. 67

[3014] Crenshaw, *JFK HAS BEEN SHOT*, p. 67

[3015] Crenshaw, *JFK HAS BEEN SHOT*, p. 67

[3016] Crenshaw, *JFK HAS BEEN SHOT*, p. 67

[3017] Crenshaw, *JFK HAS BEEN SHOT*, p. 67

[3018] Crenshaw, *JFK HAS BEEN SHOT*, p. 67

[3019] Crenshaw, *JFK HAS BEEN SHOT*, p. 67

[3020] Meagher, *ACCESSORIES AFTER THE FACT*, pp. 5-8

[3021] Meagher, *ACCESSORIES AFTER THE FACT*, pp. 5-8

[3022] Meagher, *ACCESSORIES AFTER THE FACT*, p. 20

[3023] Meagher, *ACCESSORIES AFTER THE FACT*, p. 20

[3024] Meagher, *ACCESSORIES AFTER THE FACT*, p. 21

[3025] DiEugenio, *RECLAIMING PARKLAND*, p. 121

[3026] DiEugenio, *RECLAIMING PARKLAND*, p. 121

[3027] Stone & Colapietro, *THE MAN WHO KILLED KENNEDY*, p. 253

[3028] Nelson, *LBJ: THE MASTERMIND OF THE JFK ASSASSINATION*, p. 149

[3029] Nelson, *LBJ: THE MASTERMIND OF THE JFK ASSASSINATION*, p. 372

[3030] Nelson, *LBJ: THE MASTERMIND OF THE JFK ASSASSINATION*, p. 372

[3031] Nelson, *LBJ: THE MASTERMIND OF THE JFK ASSASSINATION*, p. 372

[3032] Nelson, *LBJ: THE MASTERMIND OF THE JFK ASSASSINATION*, p. 448

[3033] Nelson, *LBJ: THE MASTERMIND OF THE JFK ASSASSINATION*, p. 448

[3034] Nelson, *LBJ: THE MASTERMIND OF THE JFK ASSASSINATION*, p. 448

[3035] Nelson, *LBJ: THE MASTERMIND OF THE JFK ASSASSINATION*, p. 448

[3036] Nelson, *LBJ: THE MASTERMIND OF THE JFK ASSASSINATION*, p. 450

[3037] Nelson, *LBJ: THE MASTERMIND OF THE JFK ASSASSINATION*, p. 450

[3038] Nelson, *LBJ: THE MASTERMIND OF THE JFK ASSASSINATION*, pp. 450-451

[3039] Nelson, *LBJ: THE MASTERMIND OF THE JFK ASSASSINATION*,

pp. 450-451

[3040] Nelson, *LBJ: THE MASTERMIND OF THE JFK ASSASSINATION*, pp. 450-451

[3041] Nelson, *LBJ: THE MASTERMIND OF THE JFK ASSASSINATION*, p. 451

[3042] Nelson, *LBJ: THE MASTERMIND OF THE JFK ASSASSINATION*, p. 451

[3043] Nelson, *LBJ: THE MASTERMIND OF THE JFK ASSASSINATION*, p. 451

[3044] Nelson, *LBJ: THE MASTERMIND OF THE JFK ASSASSINATION*, p. 452

[3045] Nelson, *LBJ: THE MASTERMIND OF THE JFK ASSASSINATION*, p. 452

[3046] Nelson, *LBJ: THE MASTERMIND OF THE JFK ASSASSINATION*, pp. 454-457

[3047] Nelson, *LBJ: THE MASTERMIND OF THE JFK ASSASSINATION*, pp. 454-457

[3048] Nelson, *LBJ: THE MASTERMIND OF THE JFK ASSASSINATION*, pp. 454-457

[3049] Nelson, *LBJ: THE MASTERMIND OF THE JFK ASSASSINATION*, pp. 454-457

[3050] Nelson, *LBJ: THE MASTERMIND OF THE JFK ASSASSINATION*, pp. 454-457

[3051] Belzer & Wayne, HIT LIST, p. 137

[3052] Belzer & Wayne, HIT LIST, p. 137

[3053] Belzer & Wayne, HIT LIST, p. 138

[3054] Belzer & Wayne, HIT LIST, p. 138

[3055] Belzer & Wayne, HIT LIST, p. 138

[3056] Belzer & Wayne, HIT LIST, pp. 135-139

[3057] Douglass, *JFK AND THE UNSPEAKABLE*, p. 263

[3058] Douglass, *JFK AND THE UNSPEAKABLE*, pp. 263-264

[3059] Douglass, *JFK AND THE UNSPEAKABLE*, p. 264

[3060] Douglass, *JFK AND THE UNSPEAKABLE*, p. 264

[3061] Douglass, *JFK AND THE UNSPEAKABLE*, pp. 264-265

[3062] Douglass, *JFK AND THE UNSPEAKABLE*, p. 265

[3063] Douglass, *JFK AND THE UNSPEAKABLE*, p. 265

[3064] Douglass, *JFK AND THE UNSPEAKABLE*, p. 265

[3065] Douglass, *JFK AND THE UNSPEAKABLE*, p. 265

[3066] Douglass, *JFK AND THE UNSPEAKABLE*, p. 265

[3067] Nelson, *LBJ: THE MASTERMIND OF THE JFK ASSASSINATION*, p. 408

[3068] Lane, *LAST WORD*, p. 16

[3069] Lane, *LAST WORD*, p. 16

[3070] Joesten, *OSWALD: ASSASSIN OR FALL GUY?*, pp. 117-118

[3071] Lane, *LAST WORD*, p. 16

[3072] Nelson, *LBJ: THE MASTERMIND OF THE JFK ASSASSINATION*, p. 409

[3073] Nelson, *LBJ: THE MASTERMIND OF THE JFK ASSASSINATION*, p. 409

[3074] Lane, *LAST WORD*, p. 34

[3075] Lane, *LAST WORD*, p. 35

[3076] Lane, *LAST WORD*, p. 35

[3077] Lane, *LAST WORD*, p. 35

[3078] Lane, *LAST WORD*, p. 35

[3079] Nelson, *LBJ: THE MASTERMIND OF THE JFK ASSASSINATION*, pp. 490-491

[3080] Nelson, *LBJ: THE MASTERMIND OF THE JFK ASSASSINATION*, pp. 490-491

[3081] Nelson, *LBJ: THE MASTERMIND OF THE JFK ASSASSINATION*, pp. 490-491

[3082] Nelson, *LBJ: THE MASTERMIND OF THE JFK ASSASSINATION*, pp. 490-491

[3083] Douglass, *JFK AND THE UNSPEAKABLE*, pp. 255-256

[3084] Douglass, *JFK AND THE UNSPEAKABLE*, p. 255

[3085] Douglass, *JFK AND THE UNSPEAKABLE*, p. 256

[3086] Douglass, *JFK AND THE UNSPEAKABLE*, p. 256

[3087] Douglass, *JFK AND THE UNSPEAKABLE*, p. 256

[3088] Douglass, *JFK AND THE UNSPEAKABLE*, p. 256

[3089] Douglass, *JFK AND THE UNSPEAKABLE*, p. 256

[3090] Douglass, *JFK AND THE UNSPEAKABLE*, pp. 256-257

[3091] Douglass, *JFK AND THE UNSPEAKABLE*, pp. 256-257

[3092] Douglass, *JFK AND THE UNSPEAKABLE*, pp. 256-257

[3093] Douglass, *JFK AND THE UNSPEAKABLE*, p. 257

[3094] Douglass, *JFK AND THE UNSPEAKABLE*, p. 257

[3095] Corsi, *WHO REALLY KILLED KENNEDY*, pp. 86-87

[3096] Corsi, *WHO REALLY KILLED KENNEDY*, pp. 86-87

[3097] Corsi, *WHO REALLY KILLED KENNEDY*, pp. 86-87

[3098] North, *ACT OF TREASON,* p. 404

[3099] North, *ACT OF TREASON,* p. 395

[3100] Summers, *NOT IN YOUR LIFETIME*, p. 64

[3101] Summers, *NOT IN YOUR LIFETIME*, p. 64

[3102] Corsi, *WHO REALLY KILLED KENNEDY?*, p. 210

[3103] Corsi, *WHO REALLY KILLED KENNEDY?*, p. 210

[3104] Corsi, *WHO REALLY KILLED KENNEDY?*, p. 210

[3105] Corsi, *WHO REALLY KILLED KENNEDY?*, p. 210

[3106] Corsi, *WHO REALLY KILLED KENNEDY?*, p. 210

[3107] Belzer & Wayne, *HIT LIST*, p. 40

[3108] Summers, *NOT IN YOUR LIFETIME*, p. 419-420

[3109] Belzer & Wayne, *HIT LIST*, p. 18

[3110] Belzer & Wayne, *HIT LIST*, p. 18

[3111] Belzer & Wayne, *DEAD WRONG*, p. 134

[3112] DiEugenio, *RECLAIMING PARKLAND*, p. 125

[3113] Belzer & Wayne, *HIT LIST*, p. 99

[3114] http://spartacus-educational.com/JFKbenavides.htm

[3115] DiEugenio, *RECLAIMING PARKLAND*, p. 125

[3116] Belzer & Wayne, *HIT LIST*, pp. 127-130

[3117] Belzer & Wayne, *HIT LIST*, pp. 127-130

[3118] Belzer & Wayne, *HIT LIST*, pp. 127-130

[3119] Belzer & Wayne, *HIT LIST*, pp. 127-130

[3120] Belzer & Wayne, *HIT LIST*, pp. 127-130

[3121] Belzer & Wayne, *HIT LIST*, p. 95

[3122] Belzer & Wayne, *HIT LIST*, p. 95

[3123] Belzer & Wayne, *HIT LIST*, p. 96

[3124] Meagher, *ACCESSORIES AFTER THE FACT*, pp. 293-295

[3125] Meagher, *ACCESSORIES AFTER THE FACT*, pp. 293-295

[3126] Corsi, *WHO REALLY KILLED KENNEDY*, p. 116

[3127] Garrison, *ON THE TRAIL OF THE ASSASSINS*, p. 197

[3128] Garrison, *ON THE TRAIL OF THE ASSASSINS*, p. 197

[3129] Garrison, *ON THE TRAIL OF THE ASSASSINS*, p. 197

[3130] Lane, *LAST WORD*, pp. 25-26

[3131] Lane, *LAST WORD*, pp. 25-26

[3132] Lane, *LAST WORD*, p. 26

[3133] Lane, *LAST WORD*, p. 26

[3134] Joesten, *OSWALD: ASSASSIN OR FALL GUY?*, p. 270

[3135] Joesten, *OSWALD: ASSASSIN OR FALL GUY?*, p. 270

[3136] Summers, *NOT IN YOUR LIFETIME*, p. 105

[3137] Summers, *NOT IN YOUR LIFETIME*, p. 106

[3138] Summers, *NOT IN YOUR LIFETIME*, p. 106

[3139] Joesten, *OSWALD: ASSASSIN OR FALL GUY?*, p. 271

[3140] Joesten, *OSWALD: ASSASSIN OR FALL GUY?*, p. 271

[3141] Joesten, *OSWALD: ASSASSIN OR FALL GUY?*, p. 271

[3142] Joesten, *OSWALD: ASSASSIN OR FALL GUY?*, p. 271

[3143] Joesten, *OSWALD: ASSASSIN OR FALL GUY?*, p. 272

[3144] Joesten, *OSWALD: ASSASSIN OR FALL GUY?*, p. 273

[3145] Joesten, *OSWALD: ASSASSIN OR FALL GUY?*, p. 273

[3146] Nelson, *LBJ: THE MASTERMIND OF THE JFK ASSASSINATION*, p. 503

[3147] Nelson, *LBJ: THE MASTERMIND OF THE JFK ASSASSINATION*, pp. 504-505

[3148] Nelson, *LBJ: THE MASTERMIND OF THE JFK ASSASSINATION*, pp. 504-505

[3149] Thomas, *HEAR NO EVIL*, pp. 498-500

[3150] North, *ACT OF TREASON,* p. 407

[3151] Nolan, *CIA ROGUES AND THE KILLING OF THE KENNEDYS*, p. 160

[3152] Joesten, *OSWALD: ASSASSIN OR FALL GUY?*, p. 163

[3153] Joesten, *OSWALD: ASSASSIN OR FALL GUY?*, p. 163-164

[3154] Nolan, *CIA ROGUES AND THE KILLING OF THE KENNEDYS*, pp. 154-156

[3155] Corsi, *WHO REALLY KILLED KENNEDY*, p. 129

[3156] Corsi, *WHO REALLY KILLED KENNEDY*, p. 129

3157 Summers, *NOT IN YOUR LIFETIME*, p. 104
3158 Summers, *NOT IN YOUR LIFETIME*, p. 104
3159 Summers, *NOT IN YOUR LIFETIME*, p. 105
3160 Garrison, *ON THE TRAIL OF THE ASSASSINS*, pp. 195-107
3161 Garrison, *ON THE TRAIL OF THE ASSASSINS*, p. 196
3162 North, *ACT OF TREASON,* p. 412
3163 Douglass, *JFK AND THE UNSPEAKABLE*, p. 290
3164 Douglass, *JFK AND THE UNSPEAKABLE*, p. 290
3165 Douglass, *JFK AND THE UNSPEAKABLE*, p. 290
3166 Douglass, *JFK AND THE UNSPEAKABLE*, p. 290
3167 Douglass, *JFK AND THE UNSPEAKABLE*, p. 291
3168 Douglass, *JFK AND THE UNSPEAKABLE*, p. 291
3169 Douglass, *JFK AND THE UNSPEAKABLE*, p. 361
3170 Douglass, *JFK AND THE UNSPEAKABLE*, p. 361
3171 Douglass, *JFK AND THE UNSPEAKABLE*, p. 361
3172 Douglass, *JFK AND THE UNSPEAKABLE*, p. 361
3173 Douglass, *JFK AND THE UNSPEAKABLE*, p. 361
3174 Douglass, *JFK AND THE UNSPEAKABLE*, p. 361
3175 Douglass, *JFK AND THE UNSPEAKABLE*, p. 291
3176 Douglass, *JFK AND THE UNSPEAKABLE*, p. 291
3177 Douglass, *JFK AND THE UNSPEAKABLE*, p. 292
3178 Douglass, *JFK AND THE UNSPEAKABLE*, p. 292
3179 Douglass, *JFK AND THE UNSPEAKABLE*, p. 292
3180 Newman, *OSWALD AND THE CIA*, p. 144
3181 Newman, *OSWALD AND THE CIA*, p. 144
3182 Newman, *OSWALD AND THE CIA*, p. 144
3183 Fonzi, *THE LAST INVESTIGATION*, p. 431
3184 Douglass, *JFK AND THE UNSPEAKABLE*, p. 293
3185 Douglass, *JFK AND THE UNSPEAKABLE*, p. 293
3186 Douglass, *JFK AND THE UNSPEAKABLE*, p. 293
3187 Douglass, *JFK AND THE UNSPEAKABLE*, p. 293
3188 Douglass, *JFK AND THE UNSPEAKABLE*, p. 293
3189 Douglass, *JFK AND THE UNSPEAKABLE*, p. 294
3190 Douglass, *JFK AND THE UNSPEAKABLE*, p. 294
3191 Douglass, *JFK AND THE UNSPEAKABLE*, p. 295
3192 Douglass, *JFK AND THE UNSPEAKABLE*, p. 295
3193 Douglass, *JFK AND THE UNSPEAKABLE*, p. 295
3194 Douglass, *JFK AND THE UNSPEAKABLE*, p. xxx
3195 Douglass, *JFK AND THE UNSPEAKABLE*, p. 296
3196 Douglass, *JFK AND THE UNSPEAKABLE*, p. 297
3197 Douglass, *JFK AND THE UNSPEAKABLE*, p. 297
3198 Douglass, *JFK AND THE UNSPEAKABLE*, p. 297
3199 Douglass, *JFK AND THE UNSPEAKABLE*, p. 298
3200 Douglass, *JFK AND THE UNSPEAKABLE*, p. 298
3201 Douglass, *JFK AND THE UNSPEAKABLE*, p. 299
3202 Douglass, *JFK AND THE UNSPEAKABLE*, p. 299
3203 Douglass, *JFK AND THE UNSPEAKABLE*, p. 299

[3204] Douglass, *JFK AND THE UNSPEAKABLE*, p. 299

[3205] Douglass, *JFK AND THE UNSPEAKABLE*, p. 299

[3206] Douglass, *JFK AND THE UNSPEAKABLE*, p. 299

[3207] Douglass, *JFK AND THE UNSPEAKABLE*, p. 299

[3208] Douglass, *JFK AND THE UNSPEAKABLE*, p. 300

[3209] Douglass, *JFK AND THE UNSPEAKABLE*, p. 300

[3210] Douglass, *JFK AND THE UNSPEAKABLE*, p. 300

[3211] Douglass, *JFK AND THE UNSPEAKABLE*, p. 301

[3212] Douglass, *JFK AND THE UNSPEAKABLE*, p. 301

[3213] Douglass, *JFK AND THE UNSPEAKABLE*, p. 301

[3214] Douglass, *JFK AND THE UNSPEAKABLE*, p. 303

[3215] Talbot, *THE DEVIL'S CHESSBOARD*, p. 563

[3216] Janney, *MARY'S MOSAIC*, pp. 291-292

[3217] Nelson, *LBJ: THE MASTERMIND OF THE JFK ASSASSINATION*, p. 400

[3218] Meagher, *ACCESSORIES AFTER THE FACT*, pp. 3-4

[3219] Nelson, *LBJ: THE MASTERMIND OF THE JFK ASSASSINATION*, p. 400

[3220] Nelson, *LBJ: THE MASTERMIND OF THE JFK ASSASSINATION*, p. 400

[3221] Marrs, *CROSSFIRE*, p. 455

[3222] Nelson, *LBJ: THE MASTERMIND OF THE JFK ASSASSINATION*, pp. 400-401

[3223] Janney, *MARY'S MOSAIC*, p. 287

[3224] Janney, *MARY'S MOSAIC*, p. 287

[3225] Janney, *MARY'S MOSAIC*, pp. 287-290

[3226] Janney, *MARY'S MOSAIC*, pp. 287-290

[3227] Janney, *MARY'S MOSAIC*, pp. 291-292

[3228] Janney, *MARY'S MOSAIC*, pp. 291-292

[3229] Janney, *MARY'S MOSAIC*, pp. 291-292

[3230] Janney, *MARY'S MOSAIC*, pp. 287-290

[3231] Janney, *MARY'S MOSAIC*, p. 290

[3232] Janney, *MARY'S MOSAIC*, p. 290

[3233] Janney, *MARY'S MOSAIC*, p. 290

[3234] Janney, *MARY'S MOSAIC*, p. 293

[3235] DiEugenio, *DESTINY BETRAYED*, p. 325

[3236] Nelson, *LBJ: THE MASTERMIND OF THE JFK ASSASSINATION*, pp. 546-553

[3237] Nelson, *LBJ: THE MASTERMIND OF THE JFK ASSASSINATION*, pp. 546-553

[3238] Nelson, *LBJ: THE MASTERMIND OF THE JFK ASSASSINATION*, pp. 546-553

[3239] North, *ACT OF TREASON,* p. 449

[3240] North, *ACT OF TREASON,* p. 449

[3241] Marrs, *CROSSFIRE*, p. 302

[3242] Corsi, *WHO REALLY KILLED KENNEDY?*, p. 210

[3243] Corsi, *WHO REALLY KILLED KENNEDY?*, p. 210

[3244] Corsi, *WHO REALLY KILLED KENNEDY?*, p. 210

[3245] Belzer & Wayne, *HIT LIST*, p. 40

[3246] Belzer & Wayne, *HIT LIST*, p. 40

[3247] Belzer & Wayne, *HIT LIST*, pp. 43-45

[3248] Belzer & Wayne, *HIT LIST*, pp. 43-45

[3249] Belzer & Wayne, *HIT LIST*, pp. 43-45

[3250] Belzer & Wayne, *HIT LIST*, pp. 47-52

[3251] Belzer & Wayne, *HIT LIST*, pp. 44-52

[3252] Belzer & Wayne, *HIT LIST*, pp. 53-63

[3253] Belzer & Wayne, *HIT LIST*, pp. 53-63

[3254] Belzer & Wayne, *HIT LIST*, pp. 53-63

[3255] Belzer & Wayne, *HIT LIST*, pp. 71-74

[3256] Belzer & Wayne, *HIT LIST*, pp. 71-74

[3257] Belzer & Wayne, *HIT LIST*, pp. 75-90

[3258] Belzer & Wayne, *HIT LIST*, pp. 75-90

[3259] Belzer & Wayne, *HIT LIST*, pp. 75-90

[3260] Belzer & Wayne, *HIT LIST*, pp. 75-90

[3261] Belzer & Wayne, *HIT LIST*, pp. 75-90

[3262] Belzer & Wayne, *HIT LIST*, pp. 91-92

[3263] Belzer & Wayne, *HIT LIST*, pp. 91-92

[3264] Belzer & Wayne, *HIT LIST*, pp. 91-92

[3265] Meagher, *ACCESSORIES AFTER THE FACT*, pp. 293-295

[3266] Meagher, *ACCESSORIES AFTER THE FACT*, pp. 293-295

[3267] Meagher, *ACCESSORIES AFTER THE FACT*, pp. 293-295

[3268] Meagher, *ACCESSORIES AFTER THE FACT*, pp. 293-295

[3269] Meagher, *ACCESSORIES AFTER THE FACT*, pp. 293-295

[3270] DiEugenio, *RECLAIMING PARKLAND*, p. 125

[3271] Belzer & Wayne, *HIT LIST*, p. 99

[3272] http://spartacus-educational.com/JFKbenavides.htm

[3273] DiEugenio, *RECLAIMING PARKLAND*, p. 125

[3274] Belzer & Wayne, *HIT LIST*, pp. 103-109

[3275] Belzer & Wayne, *HIT LIST*, pp. 103-109

[3276] Belzer & Wayne, *HIT LIST*, pp. 103-109

[3277] Belzer & Wayne, *HIT LIST*, pp. 103-109

[3278] Belzer & Wayne, *HIT LIST*, pp. 103-109

[3279] Belzer & Wayne, *HIT LIST*, pp. 103-109

[3280] Belzer & Wayne, *HIT LIST*, pp. 103-109

[3281] Belzer & Wayne, *HIT LIST*, pp. 103-109

[3282] Belzer & Wayne, *HIT LIST*, pp. 111-114

[3283] Belzer & Wayne, *HIT LIST*, pp. 111-114

[3284] Belzer & Wayne, *HIT LIST*, pp. 111-114

[3285] Belzer & Wayne, *HIT LIST*, pp. 125-126

[3286] Belzer & Wayne, *HIT LIST*, pp. 125-126

[3287] Belzer & Wayne, *HIT LIST*, pp. 125-126

[3288] Belzer & Wayne, *HIT LIST*, pp. 135-139

[3289] Belzer & Wayne, *HIT LIST*, pp. 135-139

[3290] Belzer & Wayne, *HIT LIST*, pp. 135-139

[3291] Belzer & Wayne, *HIT LIST*, pp. 143-152

[3292] Belzer & Wayne, *HIT LIST*, pp. 153-164

[3293] Belzer & Wayne, *HIT LIST*, pp. 165-166

[3294] Belzer & Wayne, *HIT LIST*, pp. 165-166

[3295] Belzer & Wayne, *HIT LIST*, pp. 167-169

[3296] Belzer & Wayne, *HIT LIST*, pp. 171-179

[3297] DiEugenio, *DESTINY BETRAYED*, p. 260

[3298] DiEugenio, *DESTINY BETRAYED*, p. 260

[3299] Belzer & Wayne, *HIT LIST*, pp. 171-179

[3300] Belzer & Wayne, *HIT LIST*, pp. 115=119

[3301] Belzer & Wayne, *HIT LIST*, pp. 115=119

[3302] Belzer & Wayne, *HIT LIST*, pp. 115=119

[3303] Belzer & Wayne, *HIT LIST*, pp. 181-183

[3304] Belzer & Wayne, *HIT LIST*, pp. 185-196

[3305] Belzer & Wayne, *HIT LIST*, pp. 185-196

[3306] Belzer & Wayne, *HIT LIST*, pp. 185-196

[3307] Belzer & Wayne, *HIT LIST*, pp. 201-208

[3308] Belzer & Wayne, *HIT LIST*, pp. 201-208

[3309] Stone & Colapietro, *THE MAN WHO KILLED KENNEDY*, p. 326

[3310] Stone & Colapietro, *THE MAN WHO KILLED KENNEDY*, p. 326

[3311] Stone & Colapietro, *THE MAN WHO KILLED KENNEDY*, p. 326

[3312] Belzer & Wayne, *HIT LIST*, pp. 201-208

[3313] Belzer & Wayne, *HIT LIST*, pp. 201-208

[3314] Stone & Colapietro, *THE MAN WHO KILLED KENNEDY*, p. 326

[3315] Belzer & Wayne, *HIT LIST*, pp. 201-208

[3316] Belzer & Wayne, *HIT LIST*, pp. 201-208

[3317] Belzer & Wayne, *HIT LIST*, pp. 201-208

[3318] Belzer & Wayne, *HIT LIST*, pp. 201-208

[3319] Belzer & Wayne, *HIT LIST*, pp. 201-208

[3320] Belzer & Wayne, *HIT LIST*, pp. 201-208

[3321] Belzer & Wayne, *HIT LIST*, pp. 201-208

[3322] Belzer & Wayne, *HIT LIST*, pp. 201-208

[3323] Belzer & Wayne, *HIT LIST*, pp. 201-208

[3324] Belzer & Wayne, *HIT LIST*, pp. 201-208

[3325] Belzer & Wayne, *HIT LIST*, pp. 255-258

[3326] Belzer & Wayne, *HIT LIST*, pp. 255-258

[3327] Belzer & Wayne, *HIT LIST*, pp. 255-258

[3328] Belzer & Wayne, *HIT LIST*, pp. 255-258

[3329] Belzer & Wayne, *HIT LIST*, pp. 255-258

[3330] Lane, *LAST WORD*, p. 35

[3331] Lane, *LAST WORD*, p. 34

[3332] Stone & Colapietro, *THE MAN WHO KILLED KENNEDY*, pp. 155-156

[3333] Belzer & Wayne, *HIT LIST*, pp. 229-238

[3334] Nelson, *LBJ: THE MASTERMIND OF THE JFK ASSASSINATION*, p. 468

[3335] Belzer & Wayne, *HIT LIST*, pp. 229-238

[3336] Belzer & Wayne, *HIT LIST*, pp. 213-220

[3337] Belzer & Wayne, *HIT LIST*, pp. 221-225
[3338] Belzer & Wayne, *HIT LIST*, pp. 221-225
[3339] Belzer & Wayne, *HIT LIST*, pp. 221-225
[3340] Belzer & Wayne, *HIT LIST*, pp. 221-225
[3341] Belzer & Wayne, *HIT LIST*, pp. 227-228
[3342] Belzer & Wayne, *HIT LIST*, pp. 221-225
[3343] Fonzi, *THE LAST INVESTIGATION*, p. 440
[3344] Douglass, *JFK AND THE UNSPEAKABLE*, p. 154
[3345] Douglass, *JFK AND THE UNSPEAKABLE*, p. 154
[3346] Douglass, *JFK AND THE UNSPEAKABLE*, p. 157
[3347] Douglass, *JFK AND THE UNSPEAKABLE*, p. 354
[3348] Douglass, *JFK AND THE UNSPEAKABLE*, p. 354
[3349] Stone & Colapietro, *THE MAN WHO KILLED KENNEDY*, p. 212
[3350] Stone & Colapietro, *THE MAN WHO KILLED KENNEDY*, p. 212
[3351] Nelson, *LBJ: THE MASTERMIND OF THE JFK ASSASSINATION*, p. 249
[3352] Meagher, *ACCESSORIES AFTER THE FACT*, pp. 299-302
[3353] Meagher, *ACCESSORIES AFTER THE FACT*, pp. 299-302
[3354] Meagher, *ACCESSORIES AFTER THE FACT*, pp. 299-302
[3355] Nelson, *LBJ: THE MASTERMIND OF THE JFK ASSASSINATION*, pp. 558-559
[3356] Nelson, *LBJ: THE MASTERMIND OF THE JFK ASSASSINATION*, p. 249
[3357] Nelson, *LBJ: THE MASTERMIND OF THE JFK ASSASSINATION*, p. 249
[3358] Nelson, *LBJ: THE MASTERMIND OF THE JFK ASSASSINATION*, p. 249
[3359] Nelson, *LBJ: THE MASTERMIND OF THE JFK ASSASSINATION*, p. 249
[3360] Stone & Colapietro, *THE MAN WHO KILLED KENNEDY*, p. 214
[3361] Corsi, *WHO REALLY KILLED KENNEDY*, p. 133
[3362] Talbot, *THE DEVIL'S CHESSBOARD*, p. 566
[3363] Talbot, *THE DEVIL'S CHESSBOARD*, p. 566
[3364] Talbot, *THE DEVIL'S CHESSBOARD*, p. 567
[3365] North, *ACT OF TREASON*, pp. 440-441
[3366] North, *ACT OF TREASON*, pp. 440-441
[3367] North, *ACT OF TREASON*, pp. 440-441
[3368] North, *ACT OF TREASON*, pp. 440-441
[3369] North, *ACT OF TREASON*, p. 436
[3370] North, *ACT OF TREASON*, p. 436
[3371] North, *ACT OF TREASON*, p. 427
[3372] North, *ACT OF TREASON*, p. 427
[3373] North, *ACT OF TREASON*, p. 432
[3374] North, *ACT OF TREASON*, p. 434
[3375] North, *ACT OF TREASON*, p. 437

[3376] North, *ACT OF TREASON,* p. 392

[3377] North, *ACT OF TREASON,* p. 438

[3378] North, *ACT OF TREASON,* p. 438

[3379] North, *ACT OF TREASON,* p. 438

[3380] McClellan, *BLOOD, MONEY AND POWER*, p. 218

[3381] Nelson, *LBJ: THE MASTERMIND OF THE JFK ASSASSINATION,* p. 444

[3382] Nelson, *LBJ: THE MASTERMIND OF THE JFK ASSASSINATION,* p. 444

[3383] Douglass, *JFK AND THE UNSPEAKABLE*, p. 83

[3384] Douglass, *JFK AND THE UNSPEAKABLE*, p. 83

[3385] Douglass, *JFK AND THE UNSPEAKABLE*, p. 83

[3386] Nelson, *LBJ: THE MASTERMIND OF THE JFK ASSASSINATION,* p. 179

[3387] North, *ACT OF TREASON,* p. 452

[3388] Summers, *NOT IN YOUR LIFETIME*, p. 243

[3389] Summers, *NOT IN YOUR LIFETIME*, p. 243

[3390] Nelson, *LBJ: THE MASTERMIND OF THE JFK ASSASSINATION,* pp. 445-446

[3391] North, *ACT OF TREASON,* p. 540

[3392] North, *ACT OF TREASON,* p. 540

[3393] Lane, *LAST WORD*, p. 16

[3394] Talbot, *THE DEVIL'S CHESSBOARD*, p. 575

[3395] Lane, *LAST WORD*, pp. 8-9

[3396] Lane, *LAST WORD*, p. 9

[3397] Shenon, *A CRUEL AND SHOCKING ACT*, p. 472

[3398] North, *ACT OF TREASON,* p. 492

[3399] Nelson, *LBJ: THE MASTERMIND OF THE JFK ASSASSINATION,* pp. 445-446

[3400] Lane, *LAST WORD*, p. 7

[3401] Lane, *LAST WORD*, p. 141

[3402] North, *ACT OF TREASON,* p. 517

[3403] Talbot, *THE DEVIL'S CHESSBOARD*, p. 575

[3404] Talbot, *THE DEVIL'S CHESSBOARD*, p. 575

[3405] Lane, *LAST WORD*, p. 7

[3406] Talbot, *THE DEVIL'S CHESSBOARD*, p. 575

[3407] Talbot, *THE DEVIL'S CHESSBOARD*, p. 577

[3408] Talbot, *THE DEVIL'S CHESSBOARD*, p. 8

[3409] Talbot, *THE DEVIL'S CHESSBOARD*, p. 8

[3410] Fonzi, *THE LAST INVESTIGATION*, p. 374

[3411] Janney, *MARY'S MOSAIC*, p. 301

[3412] North, *ACT OF TREASON,* p. 465

[3413] Lane, *LAST WORD*, p. 9

[3414] Lane, *LAST WORD*, p. 9

[3415] Talbot, *THE DEVIL'S CHESSBOARD*, p. 583

[3416] North, *ACT OF TREASON,* p. 478

[3417] North, *ACT OF TREASON,* p. 478

3418 North, *ACT OF TREASON,* p. 478

3419 Talbot, *THE DEVIL'S CHESSBOARD*, p. 588

3420 Talbot, *THE DEVIL'S CHESSBOARD*, p. 588

3421 Talbot, *THE DEVIL'S CHESSBOARD*, p. 588

3422 Talbot, *THE DEVIL'S CHESSBOARD*, p. 589

3423 Talbot, *THE DEVIL'S CHESSBOARD*, p. 589

3424 Talbot, *THE DEVIL'S CHESSBOARD*, p. 590

3425 Talbot, *THE DEVIL'S CHESSBOARD*, p. 590

3426 Talbot, *THE DEVIL'S CHESSBOARD*, p. 591

3427 Talbot, *THE DEVIL'S CHESSBOARD*, p. 591

3428 Talbot, *THE DEVIL'S CHESSBOARD*, p. 591

3429 Talbot, *THE DEVIL'S CHESSBOARD*, p. 591

3430 DiEugenio, *RECLAIMING PARKLAND*, p. 335

3431 DiEugenio, *RECLAIMING PARKLAND*, p. 335

3432 Stone & Colapietro, *THE MAN WHO KILLED KENNEDY*, p. 328

3433 Stone & Colapietro, *THE MAN WHO KILLED KENNEDY*, p. 328

3434 Nelson, *LBJ: THE MASTERMIND OF THE JFK ASSASSINATION,* p. 444

3435 Nelson, *LBJ: THE MASTERMIND OF THE JFK ASSASSINATION,* p. 444

3436 Nelson, *LBJ: THE MASTERMIND OF THE JFK ASSASSINATION,* p. 444

3437 North, *ACT OF TREASON,* p. 465

3438 North, *ACT OF TREASON,* pp. 448-449

3439 North, *ACT OF TREASON,* pp. 480-481

3440 North, *ACT OF TREASON,* pp. 480-481

3441 Shenon, *A CRUEL AND SHOCKING ACT*, p. 472

3442 Shenon, *A CRUEL AND SHOCKING ACT*, p. 472

3443 Stone & Colapietro, *THE MAN WHO KILLED KENNEDY*, p. 328

3444 Stone & Colapietro, *THE MAN WHO KILLED KENNEDY*, p. 329

3445 Summers, *NOT IN YOUR LIFETIME*, p. 35

3446 Summers, *NOT IN YOUR LIFETIME*, p. 35

3447 Shaw, *THE POISON PATRIARCH*, p. 64

3448 DiEugenio, *RECLAIMING PARKLAND*, p. 335

3449 DiEugenio, *RECLAIMING PARKLAND*, p. 321

3450 DiEugenio, *RECLAIMING PARKLAND*, p. 321

3451 DiEugenio, *RECLAIMING PARKLAND*, p. 321

3452 DiEugenio, *RECLAIMING PARKLAND*, p. 321

3453 DiEugenio, *RECLAIMING PARKLAND*, p. 321

3454 DiEugenio, *RECLAIMING PARKLAND*, p. 322

3455 DiEugenio, *RECLAIMING PARKLAND*, p. 322

3456 DiEugenio, *RECLAIMING PARKLAND*, p. 322

3457 DiEugenio, *RECLAIMING PARKLAND*, p. 324

3458 DiEugenio, *RECLAIMING PARKLAND*, p. 325

3459 Marrs, *CROSSFIRE*, p. 443

3460 Marrs, *CROSSFIRE*, p. 441

3461 Corsi, *WHO REALLY KILLED KENNEDY*, p. 305

[3462] Talbot, *THE DEVIL'S CHESSBOARD*, p. 573

[3463] Talbot, *THE DEVIL'S CHESSBOARD*, p. 573

[3464] Corsi, *WHO REALLY KILLED KENNEDY*, p. 314

[3465] Talbot, *THE DEVIL'S CHESSBOARD*, p. 555

[3466] Talbot, *THE DEVIL'S CHESSBOARD*, p. 576

[3467] DiEugenio, *RECLAIMING PARKLAND*, p. 244

[3468] DiEugenio, *RECLAIMING PARKLAND*, p. 244

[3469] North, *ACT OF TREASON,* p. 501

[3470] Shenon, *A CRUEL AND SHOCKING ACT*, pp. 184-185

[3471] Shenon, *A CRUEL AND SHOCKING ACT*, pp. 184-185

[3472] Shenon, *A CRUEL AND SHOCKING ACT*, pp. 184-185

[3473] Shenon, *A CRUEL AND SHOCKING ACT*, pp. 184-185

[3474] Stone & Colapietro, *THE MAN WHO KILLED KENNEDY*, p. 329

[3475] Stone & Colapietro, *THE MAN WHO KILLED KENNEDY*, p. 329

[3476] Stone & Colapietro, *THE MAN WHO KILLED KENNEDY*, p. 330

[3477] Nelson, *LBJ: THE MASTERMIND OF THE JFK ASSASSINATION*, p. 443

[3478] Nelson, *LBJ: THE MASTERMIND OF THE JFK ASSASSINATION*, p. 443

[3479] Nelson, *LBJ: THE MASTERMIND OF THE JFK ASSASSINATION*, p. 443

[3480] Nelson, *LBJ: THE MASTERMIND OF THE JFK ASSASSINATION*, p. 443

[3481] Nelson, *LBJ: THE MASTERMIND OF THE JFK ASSASSINATION*, p. 443

[3482] Nelson, *LBJ: THE MASTERMIND OF THE JFK ASSASSINATION*, p. 443

[3483] Nelson, *LBJ: THE MASTERMIND OF THE JFK ASSASSINATION*, p. 443

[3484] Shenon, *A CRUEL AND SHOCKING ACT*, p. 488

[3485] Shenon, *A CRUEL AND SHOCKING ACT*, p. 488

[3486] Shenon, *A CRUEL AND SHOCKING ACT*, p. 488

[3487] Shenon, *A CRUEL AND SHOCKING ACT*, p. 489

[3488] Shenon, *A CRUEL AND SHOCKING ACT*, p. 488

[3489] Summers, *NOT IN YOUR LIFETIME*, p. 138

[3490] North, *BETRAYAL IN DALLAS*, p. 116

[3491] North, *BETRAYAL IN DALLAS*, p. 131

[3492] North, *BETRAYAL IN DALLAS*, p. 131

[3493] North, *ACT OF TREASON,* p. 432

[3494] Nelson, *LBJ: THE MASTERMIND OF THE JFK ASSASSINATION*, pp. 358-359

[3495] Nelson, *LBJ: THE MASTERMIND OF THE JFK ASSASSINATION*, pp. 557-558

[3496] Nelson, *LBJ: THE MASTERMIND OF THE JFK ASSASSINATION*, pp. 557-558

[3497] Nelson, *LBJ: THE MASTERMIND OF THE JFK ASSASSINATION*, pp. 558-559

[3498] Lane, *LAST WORD*, p. 17

[3499] Meagher, *ACCESSORIES AFTER THE FACT*, pp. 5-8

[3500] Meagher, *ACCESSORIES AFTER THE FACT*, pp. 5-8

[3501] Meagher, *ACCESSORIES AFTER THE FACT*, pp. 5-8

[3502] Meagher, *ACCESSORIES AFTER THE FACT*, pp. 5-8

[3503] North, *ACT OF TREASON,* p. 444

[3504] North, *ACT OF TREASON,* p. 444

[3505] North, *ACT OF TREASON,* p. 444

[3506] Lane, *LAST WORD*, p. 11

[3507] Lane, *LAST WORD*, p. 11

[3508] Fonzi, *THE LAST INVESTIGATION*, p. 405

[3509] Stone & Colapietro, *THE MAN WHO KILLED KENNEDY*, p. 336

[3510] Thomas, *HEAR NO EVIL*, p. 412

[3511] Marrs, *CROSSFIRE*, p. 356

[3512] Summers, *NOT IN YOUR LIFETIME*, p. 51

[3513] Summers, *NOT IN YOUR LIFETIME*, p. 51

[3514] DiEugenio, *RECLAIMING PARKLAND*, p. xxii

[3515] Nelson, *LBJ: THE MASTERMIND OF THE JFK ASSASSINATION*, p. 467

[3516] Shenon, *A CRUEL AND SHOCKING ACT*, p. 473

[3517] Shenon, *A CRUEL AND SHOCKING ACT*, p. 473

[3518] Shenon, *A CRUEL AND SHOCKING ACT*, p. 474

[3519] Shenon, *A CRUEL AND SHOCKING ACT*, p. 474

[3520] Shenon, *A CRUEL AND SHOCKING ACT*, p. 475

[3521] Shenon, *A CRUEL AND SHOCKING ACT*, p. 475

[3522] Corsi, *WHO REALLY KILLED KENNEDY*, p. iii

[3523] Corsi, *WHO REALLY KILLED KENNEDY*, p. iii

[3524] Corsi, *WHO REALLY KILLED KENNEDY*, p. iii

[3525] Corsi, *WHO REALLY KILLED KENNEDY*, p. iii

[3526] Corsi, *WHO REALLY KILLED KENNEDY*, pp. iii-iv

[3527] Nelson, *LBJ: THE MASTERMIND OF THE JFK ASSASSINATION*, p. 447

[3528] Nelson, *LBJ: THE MASTERMIND OF THE JFK ASSASSINATION*, pp. 358-359

[3529] Nelson, *LBJ: THE MASTERMIND OF THE JFK ASSASSINATION*, p. 445

[3530] Nelson, *LBJ: THE MASTERMIND OF THE JFK ASSASSINATION*, pp. 452-453

[3531] Nelson, *LBJ: THE MASTERMIND OF THE JFK ASSASSINATION*, pp. 452-453

[3532] Nelson, *LBJ: THE MASTERMIND OF THE JFK ASSASSINATION*, pp. 452-453

[3533] Nelson, *LBJ: THE MASTERMIND OF THE JFK ASSASSINATION*, pp. 452-453

[3534] Nelson, *LBJ: THE MASTERMIND OF THE JFK ASSASSINATION*, pp. 452-453

[3535] Fonzi, *THE LAST INVESTIGATION*, p. 4

[3536] Fonzi, *THE LAST INVESTIGATION*, p. 4

[3537] Fonzi, *THE LAST INVESTIGATION*, p. 4

[3538] North, *ACT OF TREASON,* p. 415

[3539] North, *ACT OF TREASON,* p. 457

[3540] Joesten, *OSWALD: ASSASSIN OR FALL GUY?*, p. 97

[3541] Joesten, *OSWALD: ASSASSIN OR FALL GUY?*, pp. 96-97

[3542] North, *ACT OF TREASON*, p. 14

[3543] Nelson, *LBJ: THE MASTERMIND OF THE JFK ASSASSINATION*, pp. 541-542

[3544] Nelson, *LBJ: THE MASTERMIND OF THE JFK ASSASSINATION*, pp. 541-542

[3545] Nelson, *LBJ: THE MASTERMIND OF THE JFK ASSASSINATION*, p. 459

[3546] North, *ACT OF TREASON,* p. 465

[3547] Joesten, *OSWALD: ASSASSIN OR FALL GUY?*, pp. 96-97

[3548] North, *ACT OF TREASON,* p. 401

[3549] North, *ACT OF TREASON,* p. 401

[3550] Shenon, *A CRUEL AND SHOCKING ACT*, p. 381

[3551] North, *ACT OF TREASON,* p. 411

[3552] North, *ACT OF TREASON,* p. 411

[3553] Summers, *NOT IN YOUR LIFETIME*, pp. 269-274

[3554] Summers, *NOT IN YOUR LIFETIME*, pp. 269-274

[3555] Summers, *NOT IN YOUR LIFETIME*, pp. 269-274

[3556] Summers, *NOT IN YOUR LIFETIME*, pp. 269-274

[3557] Summers, *NOT IN YOUR LIFETIME*, pp. 269-274

[3558] North, *ACT OF TREASON,* pp. 477-478

[3559] North, *ACT OF TREASON,* pp. 482-483

[3560] North, *ACT OF TREASON,* pp. 482-483

[3561] North, *ACT OF TREASON,* p. 484

[3562] North, *ACT OF TREASON,* p. 506

[3563] North, *ACT OF TREASON,* p. 506

[3564] North, *ACT OF TREASON,* p. 486

[3565] North, *ACT OF TREASON,* p. 486

[3566] North, *ACT OF TREASON,* p. 486

[3567] North, *ACT OF TREASON,* p. 489

[3568] North, *ACT OF TREASON,* pp. 515-516

[3569] North, *ACT OF TREASON,* pp. 515-516

[3570] North, *ACT OF TREASON,* pp. 515-516

[3571] North, *ACT OF TREASON,* pp. 515-516

[3572] North, *ACT OF TREASON,* pp. 515-516

[3573] North, *ACT OF TREASON,* pp. 515-516

[3574] North, *ACT OF TREASON,* p. 527-528

[3575] North, *ACT OF TREASON,* p. 399

[3576] North, *ACT OF TREASON,* pp. 528-534

[3577] North, *ACT OF TREASON,* p. 535

[3578] North, *ACT OF TREASON,* p. 535

[3579] Shenon, *A CRUEL AND SHOCKING ACT*, p. 487

[3580] Talbot, *THE DEVIL'S CHESSBOARD*, pp. 579-580

[3581] Talbot, *THE DEVIL'S CHESSBOARD*, pp. 579-580

[3582] Summers, *NOT IN YOUR LIFETIME*, pp. 443-444

[3583] Summers, *NOT IN YOUR LIFETIME*, pp. 443-444

[3584] Summers, *NOT IN YOUR LIFETIME*, pp. 443-444

[3585] Summers, *NOT IN YOUR LIFETIME*, p. 444

[3586] Summers, *NOT IN YOUR LIFETIME*, p. 444

[3587] Summers, *NOT IN YOUR LIFETIME*, p. 117

[3588] Summers, *NOT IN YOUR LIFETIME*, p. 117

[3589] Douglass, *JFK AND THE UNSPEAKABLE*, p. 359

[3590] Douglass, *JFK AND THE UNSPEAKABLE*, p. 360

[3591] Nelson, *LBJ: THE MASTERMIND OF THE JFK ASSASSINATION*, p. 359

[3592] Nelson, *LBJ: THE MASTERMIND OF THE JFK ASSASSINATION*, p. 359

[3593] Nelson, *LBJ: THE MASTERMIND OF THE JFK ASSASSINATION*, p. 359

[3594] Nelson, *LBJ: THE MASTERMIND OF THE JFK ASSASSINATION*, p. 359

[3595] Nelson, *LBJ: THE MASTERMIND OF THE JFK ASSASSINATION*, p. 359

[3596] Lane, *LAST WORD*, p. 189

[3597] Lane, *LAST WORD*, p. 191

[3598] Corsi, *WHO REALLY KILLED KENNEDY*, pp. 86-87

[3599] Corsi, *WHO REALLY KILLED KENNEDY*, pp. 86-87

[3600] Corsi, *WHO REALLY KILLED KENNEDY*, pp. 86-87

[3601] Corsi, *WHO REALLY KILLED KENNEDY*, pp. 94-95

[3602] Corsi, *WHO REALLY KILLED KENNEDY*, pp. 94-95

[3603] Corsi, *WHO REALLY KILLED KENNEDY*, pp. 94-95

[3604] Corsi, *WHO REALLY KILLED KENNEDY*, pp. 94-95

[3605] Corsi, *WHO REALLY KILLED KENNEDY*, pp. 94-95

[3606] Corsi, *WHO REALLY KILLED KENNEDY*, pp. 94-95

[3607] Stone & Colapietro, *THE MAN WHO KILLED KENNEDY*, p. 331

[3608] Stone & Colapietro, *THE MAN WHO KILLED KENNEDY*, p. 331

[3609] Stone & Colapietro, *THE MAN WHO KILLED KENNEDY*, p. 331

[3610] Stone & Colapietro, *THE MAN WHO KILLED KENNEDY*, p. 331

[3611] Stone & Colapietro, *THE MAN WHO KILLED KENNEDY*, p. 331

[3612] Stone & Colapietro, *THE MAN WHO KILLED KENNEDY*, p. 331

[3613] Stone & Colapietro, *THE MAN WHO KILLED KENNEDY*, pp. 331-332

[3614] Stone & Colapietro, *THE MAN WHO KILLED KENNEDY*, pp. 331-332

[3615] Stone & Colapietro, *THE MAN WHO KILLED KENNEDY*, pp. 336-337

[3616] Stone & Colapietro, *THE MAN WHO KILLED KENNEDY*, pp. 336-337

[3617] Lane, *LAST WORD*, pp. 14-15

[3618] Stone & Colapietro, *THE MAN WHO KILLED KENNEDY*, p. 336
[3619] Stone & Colapietro, *THE MAN WHO KILLED KENNEDY*, pp. 335-336
[3620] North, *ACT OF TREASON*, p. 488
[3621] Summers, *NOT IN YOUR LIFETIME*, p. 40
[3622] Summers, *NOT IN YOUR LIFETIME*, p. 40
[3623] Summers, *NOT IN YOUR LIFETIME*, p. 40
[3624] Summers, *NOT IN YOUR LIFETIME*, p. 40
[3625] Summers, *NOT IN YOUR LIFETIME*, p. 40
[3626] Summers, *NOT IN YOUR LIFETIME*, p. 41
[3627] Summers, *NOT IN YOUR LIFETIME*, p. 41
[3628] Summers, *NOT IN YOUR LIFETIME*, p. 41
[3629] Summers, *NOT IN YOUR LIFETIME*, p. 41
[3630] Summers, *NOT IN YOUR LIFETIME*, p. 41
[3631] Summers, *NOT IN YOUR LIFETIME*, p. 41
[3632] Summers, *NOT IN YOUR LIFETIME*, p. 41
[3633] Summers, *NOT IN YOUR LIFETIME*, p. 41
[3634] Summers, *NOT IN YOUR LIFETIME*, p. 42
[3635] Summers, *NOT IN YOUR LIFETIME*, p. 44
[3636] Shenon, *A CRUEL AND SHOCKING ACT*, p. 331
[3637] Summers, *NOT IN YOUR LIFETIME*, p. 59
[3638] Summers, *NOT IN YOUR LIFETIME*, p. 59
[3639] Summers, *NOT IN YOUR LIFETIME*, p. 59
[3640] Summers, *NOT IN YOUR LIFETIME*, pp. 59-60
[3641] Summers, *NOT IN YOUR LIFETIME*, p. 60
[3642] Summers, *NOT IN YOUR LIFETIME*, p. 60
[3643] Summers, *NOT IN YOUR LIFETIME*, pp. 60-61
[3644] Summers, *NOT IN YOUR LIFETIME*, p. 62
[3645] Summers, *NOT IN YOUR LIFETIME*, p. 61
[3646] Summers, *NOT IN YOUR LIFETIME*, p. 61
[3647] Summers, *NOT IN YOUR LIFETIME*, p. 61
[3648] Summers, *NOT IN YOUR LIFETIME*, p. 61
[3649] Joesten, *OSWALD: ASSASSIN OR FALL GUY?*, p. 283
[3650] Joesten, *OSWALD: ASSASSIN OR FALL GUY?*, p. 283
[3651] Joesten, *OSWALD: ASSASSIN OR FALL GUY?*, p. 284
[3652] Joesten, *OSWALD: ASSASSIN OR FALL GUY?*, p. 284
[3653] Joesten, *OSWALD: ASSASSIN OR FALL GUY?*, p. 284
[3654] Joesten, *OSWALD: ASSASSIN OR FALL GUY?*, pp. 284-285
[3655] Joesten, *OSWALD: ASSASSIN OR FALL GUY?*, pp. 284-285
[3656] Joesten, *OSWALD: ASSASSIN OR FALL GUY?*, pp. 284-285
[3657] Joesten, *OSWALD: ASSASSIN OR FALL GUY?*, p. 285
[3658] Joesten, *OSWALD: ASSASSIN OR FALL GUY?*, p. 285
[3659] Joesten, *OSWALD: ASSASSIN OR FALL GUY?*, p. 285
[3660] North, *ACT OF TREASON*, p. 466
[3661] North, *ACT OF TREASON*, p. 472
[3662] North, *ACT OF TREASON*, p. 472
[3663] North, *ACT OF TREASON*, p. 472

[3664] North, *ACT OF TREASON,* p. 472

[3665] Garrison, *ON THE TRAIL OF THE ASSASSINS*, pp. 101-103

[3666] Garrison, *ON THE TRAIL OF THE ASSASSINS*, pp. 101-103

[3667] Garrison, *ON THE TRAIL OF THE ASSASSINS*, pp. 101-103

[3668] Garrison, *ON THE TRAIL OF THE ASSASSINS*, pp. 101-103

[3669] Stone and Colapietro, *THE MAN WHO KILLED KENNEDY: THE CASE AGAINST LBJ*, p. 330

[3670] Stone and Colapietro, *THE MAN WHO KILLED KENNEDY: THE CASE AGAINST LBJ*, p. 330

[3671] Stone and Colapietro, *THE MAN WHO KILLED KENNEDY: THE CASE AGAINST LBJ*, p. 330

[3672] Marrs, *CROSSFIRE*, p. 458

[3673] Marrs, *CROSSFIRE*, p. 458

[3674] Joesten, *OSWALD: ASSASSIN OR FALL GUY?*, pp. 1-4

[3675] Joesten, *OSWALD: ASSASSIN OR FALL GUY?*, pp. 5-6

[3676] Joesten, *OSWALD: ASSASSIN OR FALL GUY?*, pp. 5-6

[3677] Joesten, *OSWALD: ASSASSIN OR FALL GUY?*, pp. 5-6

[3678] North, *ACT OF TREASON,* pp. 502-503

[3679] North, *ACT OF TREASON,* pp. 502-503

[3680] North, *ACT OF TREASON,* pp. 502-503

[3681] Stone & Colapietro, *THE MAN WHO KILLED KENNEDY*, p. 251

[3682] Stone & Colapietro, *THE MAN WHO KILLED KENNEDY*, p. 252

[3683] Stone & Colapietro, *THE MAN WHO KILLED KENNEDY*, p. 252

[3684] Stone & Colapietro, *THE MAN WHO KILLED KENNEDY*, p. 253

[3685] North, *ACT OF TREASON,* pp. 539-540

[3686] North, *ACT OF TREASON,* pp. 539-540

[3687] North, *ACT OF TREASON,* pp. 539-540

[3688] Janney, *MARY'S MOSAIC*, pp. 8, 14

[3689] Janney, *MARY'S MOSAIC*, p. 151

[3690] Janney, *MARY'S MOSAIC*, p. 156

[3691] Janney, *MARY'S MOSAIC*, p. 209

[3692] Janney, *MARY'S MOSAIC*, p. 209

[3693] Janney, *MARY'S MOSAIC*, p. 209

[3694] Janney, *MARY'S MOSAIC*, pp. 188-189

[3695] Janney, *MARY'S MOSAIC*, p. 199

[3696] Janney, *MARY'S MOSAIC*, p. 207

[3697] Janney, *MARY'S MOSAIC*, p. 207

[3698] Janney, *MARY'S MOSAIC*, p. 171

[3699] Janney, *MARY'S MOSAIC*, p. 171

[3700] Janney, *MARY'S MOSAIC*, p. 171

[3701] Janney, *MARY'S MOSAIC*, pp. 171-172

[3702] Janney, *MARY'S MOSAIC*, pp. 171-172

[3703] Janney, *MARY'S MOSAIC*, pp. 171-172

[3704] Janney, *MARY'S MOSAIC*, p. 172

[3705] Janney, *MARY'S MOSAIC*, p. 172

[3706] Janney, *MARY'S MOSAIC*, p. 172

[3707] Janney, *MARY'S MOSAIC*, p. 175

[3708] Janney, *MARY'S MOSAIC*, p. 177

[3709] Janney, *MARY'S MOSAIC*, p. 178

[3710] Janney, *MARY'S MOSAIC*, pp. 179-180

[3711] Janney, *MARY'S MOSAIC*, p. 180

[3712] Janney, *MARY'S MOSAIC*, p. 181

[3713] Janney, *MARY'S MOSAIC*, p. 182

[3714] Nelson, *LBJ: THE MASTERMIND OF THE JFK ASSASSINATION*, p. 174

[3715] Nelson, *LBJ: THE MASTERMIND OF THE JFK ASSASSINATION*, p. 174

[3716] Nelson, *LBJ: THE MASTERMIND OF THE JFK ASSASSINATION*, p. 174

[3717] Janney, *MARY'S MOSAIC*, p. 184

[3718] Janney, *MARY'S MOSAIC*, p. 184

[3719] Janney, *MARY'S MOSAIC*, p. 184

[3720] Janney, *MARY'S MOSAIC*, p. 184

[3721] Janney, *MARY'S MOSAIC*, p. 184

[3722] Janney, *MARY'S MOSAIC*, p. 186

[3723] Janney, *MARY'S MOSAIC*, p. 187

[3724] Janney, *MARY'S MOSAIC*, p. 187

[3725] Janney, *MARY'S MOSAIC*, pp. 194-195

[3726] Janney, *MARY'S MOSAIC*, pp. 14-15

[3727] Janney, *MARY'S MOSAIC*, p. 189

[3728] Janney, *MARY'S MOSAIC*, pp. 14-15

[3729] Janney, *MARY'S MOSAIC*, p. 189

[3730] Janney, *MARY'S MOSAIC*, pp. 14-15

[3731] Janney, *MARY'S MOSAIC*, p. 14

[3732] Janney, *MARY'S MOSAIC*, p. 66

[3733] Belzer & Wayne, *HIT LIST*, pp. 143-152

[3734] Janney, *MARY'S MOSAIC*, p. 67

[3735] Janney, *MARY'S MOSAIC*, p. 217

[3736] Janney, *MARY'S MOSAIC*, p. 14

[3737] Janney, *MARY'S MOSAIC*, p. 252

[3738] Janney, *MARY'S MOSAIC*, p. 218

[3739] Janney, *MARY'S MOSAIC*, p. 216

[3740] Janney, *MARY'S MOSAIC*, p. 217

[3741] Janney, *MARY'S MOSAIC*, p. 216

[3742] Janney, *MARY'S MOSAIC*, p. 218

[3743] Janney, *MARY'S MOSAIC*, p. 219

[3744] Janney, *MARY'S MOSAIC*, p. 223

[3745] Janney, *MARY'S MOSAIC*, p. 224

[3746] Janney, *MARY'S MOSAIC*, p. 224

[3747] Janney, *MARY'S MOSAIC*, p. 224

[3748] Janney, *MARY'S MOSAIC*, p. 224

[3749] Janney, *MARY'S MOSAIC*, p. 228

[3750] Janney, *MARY'S MOSAIC*, p. 226

[3751] Janney, *MARY'S MOSAIC*, p. 228

[3752] Janney, *MARY'S MOSAIC*, pp. 230-231

[3753] Janney, *MARY'S MOSAIC*, p. 218

[3754] Janney, *MARY'S MOSAIC*, p. 231

[3755] Janney, *MARY'S MOSAIC*, p. 231

[3756] Janney, *MARY'S MOSAIC*, p. 256

[3757] Janney, *MARY'S MOSAIC*, p. 265

[3758] Janney, *MARY'S MOSAIC*, p. 242

[3759] Janney, *MARY'S MOSAIC*, p. 245

[3760] Janney, *MARY'S MOSAIC*, pp. 245-246

[3761] Janney, *MARY'S MOSAIC*, pp. 245-246

[3762] Janney, *MARY'S MOSAIC*, pp. 245-246

[3763] Janney, *MARY'S MOSAIC*, pp. 245-246

[3764] Janney, *MARY'S MOSAIC*, pp. 245-246

[3765] Janney, *MARY'S MOSAIC*, pp. 245-246

[3766] Janney, *MARY'S MOSAIC*, p. 246

[3767] Janney, *MARY'S MOSAIC*, p. 246

[3768] Janney, *MARY'S MOSAIC*, p. 246

[3769] Janney, *MARY'S MOSAIC*, p. 246

[3770] Janney, *MARY'S MOSAIC*, p. 246

[3771] Nelson, *LBJ: THE MASTERMIND OF THE JFK ASSASSINATION*, p. 181

[3772] Fonzi, *THE LAST INVESTIGATION*, p. 122

[3773] Janney, *MARY'S MOSAIC*, p. 246

[3774] Janney, *MARY'S MOSAIC*, pp. 246-247

[3775] Janney, *MARY'S MOSAIC*, p. 247

[3776] Janney, *MARY'S MOSAIC*, p. 247

[3777] Janney, *MARY'S MOSAIC*, p. 247

[3778] Janney, *MARY'S MOSAIC*, p. 247

[3779] Janney, *MARY'S MOSAIC*, p. 312

[3780] Janney, *MARY'S MOSAIC*, p. 32

[3781] Janney, *MARY'S MOSAIC*, p. 311

[3782] Janney, *MARY'S MOSAIC*, p. 311

[3783] Janney, *MARY'S MOSAIC*, p. 311

[3784] Janney, *MARY'S MOSAIC*, p. 311

[3785] Janney, *MARY'S MOSAIC*, p. 311

[3786] Janney, *MARY'S MOSAIC*, p. 312

[3787] Janney, *MARY'S MOSAIC*, p. 312

[3788] Janney, *MARY'S MOSAIC*, p. 312

[3789] Belzer, *HIT LIST*, p. 144

[3790] Janney, *MARY'S MOSAIC*, p. 328

[3791] Janney, *MARY'S MOSAIC*, p. 328

[3792] Janney, *MARY'S MOSAIC*, pp. 328-329

[3793] Janney, *MARY'S MOSAIC*, p. 329

[3794] Janney, *MARY'S MOSAIC*, p. 329

[3795] Janney, *MARY'S MOSAIC*, p. 328

[3796] Janney, *MARY'S MOSAIC*, p. 328

[3797] Janney, *MARY'S MOSAIC*, p. 328

[3798] Janney, *MARY'S MOSAIC*, p. 329
[3799] Janney, *MARY'S MOSAIC*, p. 329
[3800] Janney, *MARY'S MOSAIC*, p. 329
[3801] Janney, *MARY'S MOSAIC*, p. 330
[3802] Janney, *MARY'S MOSAIC*, p. 331
[3803] Janney, *MARY'S MOSAIC*, p. 331
[3804] Janney, *MARY'S MOSAIC*, p. 331
[3805] Janney, *MARY'S MOSAIC*, p. 331
[3806] Janney, *MARY'S MOSAIC*, p. 332
[3807] Janney, *MARY'S MOSAIC*, p. 332
[3808] Janney, *MARY'S MOSAIC*, pp. 332-333
[3809] Janney, *MARY'S MOSAIC*, pp. 332-333
[3810] Janney, *MARY'S MOSAIC*, pp. 332-333
[3811] Janney, *MARY'S MOSAIC*, p. 333
[3812] Janney, *MARY'S MOSAIC*, p. 333
[3813] Janney, *MARY'S MOSAIC*, p. 333
[3814] Janney, *MARY'S MOSAIC*, p. 333
[3815] Janney, *MARY'S MOSAIC*, p. 334
[3816] Janney, *MARY'S MOSAIC*, p. 334
[3817] Janney, *MARY'S MOSAIC*, p. 334
[3818] Janney, *MARY'S MOSAIC*, p. 335
[3819] Janney, *MARY'S MOSAIC*, p. 335
[3820] Janney, *MARY'S MOSAIC*, p. 335
[3821] Janney, *MARY'S MOSAIC*, p. 336
[3822] Janney, *MARY'S MOSAIC*, p. 106, 136
[3823] Janney, *MARY'S MOSAIC*, p. 80
[3824] Janney, *MARY'S MOSAIC*, pp. 61-62
[3825] Janney, *MARY'S MOSAIC*, pp. 321-322
[3826] Janney, *MARY'S MOSAIC*, p. 322
[3827] Janney, *MARY'S MOSAIC*, p. 322
[3828] Janney, *MARY'S MOSAIC*, p. 324
[3829] Janney, *MARY'S MOSAIC*, p. 327
[3830] Janney, *MARY'S MOSAIC*, pp. 327-328
[3831] Nelson, *LBJ: THE MASTERMIND OF THE JFK ASSASSINATION*, p. 175
[3832] Belzer & Wayne, *DEAD WRONG*, p. 133
[3833] North, *BETRAYAL IN DALLAS*, p. 9
[3834] Summers, *NOT IN YOUR LIFETIME*, p. 403
[3835] Summers, *NOT IN YOUR LIFETIME*, p. 403
[3836] Douglass, *JFK AND THE UNSPEAKABLE*, p. 357
[3837] Summers, *NOT IN YOUR LIFETIME*, p. 405
[3838] Summers, *NOT IN YOUR LIFETIME*, p. 405
[3839] Fonzi, *THE LAST INVESTIGATION*, p. 305
[3840] Fonzi, *THE LAST INVESTIGATION*, p. 305
[3841] Douglass, *JFK AND THE UNSPEAKABLE*, p. 357
[3842] Douglass, *JFK AND THE UNSPEAKABLE*, p. 357
[3843] Douglass, *JFK AND THE UNSPEAKABLE*, p. 357

3844 Douglass, *JFK AND THE UNSPEAKABLE*, p. 357
3845 Douglass, *JFK AND THE UNSPEAKABLE*, p. 359
3846 Douglass, *JFK AND THE UNSPEAKABLE*, p. 359
3847 Summers, *NOT IN YOUR LIFETIME*, p. 406
3848 North, *ACT OF TREASON*, p. 502
3849 North, *ACT OF TREASON*, p. 472
3850 North, *ACT OF TREASON*, p. 472
3851 North, *ACT OF TREASON*, p. 472
3852 North, *ACT OF TREASON*, p. 472
3853 North, *ACT OF TREASON*, p. 438
3854 North, *ACT OF TREASON*, pp. 443-444
3855 North, *ACT OF TREASON*, pp. 443-444
3856 North, *ACT OF TREASON*, pp. 443-444
3857 North, *ACT OF TREASON*, p. 439
3858 North, *ACT OF TREASON*, p. 439
3859 North, *ACT OF TREASON*, p. 441
3860 North, *ACT OF TREASON*, p. 395
3861 North, *ACT OF TREASON*, p. 357
3862 North, *ACT OF TREASON*, p. 369
3863 Douglass, *JFK AND THE UNSPEAKABLE*, p. 249
3864 Nelson, *LBJ: THE MASTERMIND OF THE JFK ASSASSINATION*, pp. 490-491
3865 Nelson, *LBJ: THE MASTERMIND OF THE JFK ASSASSINATION*, pp. 490-491
3866 Nelson, *LBJ: THE MASTERMIND OF THE JFK ASSASSINATION*, pp. 490-491
3867 Nelson, *LBJ: THE MASTERMIND OF THE JFK ASSASSINATION*, pp. 490-491
3868 Douglass, *JFK AND THE UNSPEAKABLE*, pp. 255-256
3869 Douglass, *JFK AND THE UNSPEAKABLE*, p. 255
3870 North, *ACT OF TREASON*, p. 480
3871 North, *ACT OF TREASON*, p. 261
3872 North, *ACT OF TREASON*, p. 261
3873 Corsi, *WHO REALLY KILLED KENNEDY?*, p. 210
3874 North, *ACT OF TREASON*, p. 279
3875 Baker, *ME & LEE*, p. 235
3876 North, *ACT OF TREASON*, p. 287
3877 North, *ACT OF TREASON*, p. 287
3878 North, *ACT OF TREASON*, p. 319
3879 North, *ACT OF TREASON*, p. 323
3880 North, *ACT OF TREASON*, p. 371
3881 Summers, *NOT IN YOUR LIFETIME*, p. 408
3882 Summers, *NOT IN YOUR LIFETIME*, p. 408
3883 Summers, *NOT IN YOUR LIFETIME*, pp. 408-409
3884 North, *ACT OF TREASON*, p. 460
3885 North, *ACT OF TREASON*, p. 368
3886 North, *ACT OF TREASON*, p. 368

[3887] Summers, *NOT IN YOUR LIFETIME*, pp. 408-409

[3888] North, *ACT OF TREASON*, pp. 345-346

[3889] North, *ACT OF TREASON*, pp. 345-346

[3890] North, *ACT OF TREASON*, p. 361

[3891] Nolan, *CIA ROGUES AND THE KILLING OF THE KENNEDYS*, pp. 142-143

[3892] Joesten, *OSWALD: ASSASSIN OR FALL GUY?*, p. 197

[3893] Joesten, *OSWALD: ASSASSIN OR FALL GUY?*, p. 197

[3894] Joesten, *OSWALD: ASSASSIN OR FALL GUY?*, p. 197

[3895] Joesten, *OSWALD: ASSASSIN OR FALL GUY?*, p. 197

[3896] North, *ACT OF TREASON*, p. 369

[3897] Corsi, *WHO REALLY KILLED KENNEDY*, p. 133

[3898] Corsi, *WHO REALLY KILLED KENNEDY?*, p. 210

[3899] Corsi, *WHO REALLY KILLED KENNEDY?*, p. 210

[3900] Corsi, *WHO REALLY KILLED KENNEDY?*, p. 210

[3901] Corsi, *WHO REALLY KILLED KENNEDY?*, p. 210

[3902] Corsi, *WHO REALLY KILLED KENNEDY?*, p. 210

[3903] Belzer & Wayne, *HIT LIST*, p. 40

[3904] Summers, *NOT IN YOUR LIFETIME*, p. 419-420

[3905] Douglass, *JFK AND THE UNSPEAKABLE*, p. 361

[3906] Douglass, *JFK AND THE UNSPEAKABLE*, p. 361

[3907] Douglass, *JFK AND THE UNSPEAKABLE*, p. 361

[3908] Douglass, *JFK AND THE UNSPEAKABLE*, p. 361

[3909] North, *ACT OF TREASON*, p. 424

[3910] Belzer & Wayne, *HIT LIST*, p. 40

[3911] Belzer & Wayne, *HIT LIST*, p. 40

[3912] North, *ACT OF TREASON*, p. 412

[3913] North, *BETRAYAL IN DALLAS*, p. 85

[3914] North, *ACT OF TREASON*, p. 372

[3915] North, *ACT OF TREASON*, pp. 373-374

[3916] North, *ACT OF TREASON*, pp. 373-374

[3917] North, *ACT OF TREASON*, pp. 373-374

[3918] North, *ACT OF TREASON*, p. 408

[3919] Summers, *NOT IN YOUR LIFETIME*, p. 410

[3920] Douglass, *JFK AND THE UNSPEAKABLE*, p. 361

[3921] Douglass, *JFK AND THE UNSPEAKABLE*, p. 361

[3922] Douglass, *JFK AND THE UNSPEAKABLE*, pp. 361-362

[3923] Douglass, *JFK AND THE UNSPEAKABLE*, pp. 361-362

[3924] Douglass, *JFK AND THE UNSPEAKABLE*, p. 362

[3925] North, *ACT OF TREASON*, pp. 420-421

[3926] North, *ACT OF TREASON*, pp. 420-421

[3927] North, *ACT OF TREASON*, pp. 420-421

[3928] North, *ACT OF TREASON*, pp. 420-421

[3929] North, *ACT OF TREASON*, pp. 420-421

[3930] North, *ACT OF TREASON*, pp. 420-421

[3931] Crenshaw, *JFK HAS BEEN SHOT*, pp. 177-178

[3932] Crenshaw, *JFK HAS BEEN SHOT*, pp. 177-178

[3933] North, *ACT OF TREASON,* p. 491

[3934] North, *ACT OF TREASON,* p. 432

[3935] North, *ACT OF TREASON,* p. 429

[3936] North, *BETRAYAL IN DALLAS,* p. 85

[3937] North, *ACT OF TREASON,* p. 405

[3938] North, *ACT OF TREASON,* p. 405

[3939] Talbot, *THE DEVIL'S CHESSBOARD,* pp. 564-565

[3940] Talbot, *THE DEVIL'S CHESSBOARD,* pp. 564-565

[3941] Talbot, *THE DEVIL'S CHESSBOARD,* pp. 564-565

[3942] Douglass, *JFK AND THE UNSPEAKABLE,* p. 357

[3943] Douglass, *JFK AND THE UNSPEAKABLE,* pp. 357-358

[3944] North, *BETRAYAL IN DALLAS,* p. 87

[3945] Nolan, *CIA ROGUES AND THE KILLING OF THE KENNEDYS,* p. 168

[3946] Shaw, *THE POISON PATRIARCH,* p. 161

[3947] Shaw, *THE POISON PATRIARCH,* pp. 148-149

[3948] Shaw, *THE POISON PATRIARCH,* pp. 148-149

[3949] Shaw, *THE POISON PATRIARCH,* pp. 93-94

[3950] Shaw, *THE POISON PATRIARCH,* p. 161

[3951] Shaw, *THE POISON PATRIARCH,* p. 161

[3952] Shaw, *THE POISON PATRIARCH,* pp. 171-172

[3953] Shaw, *THE POISON PATRIARCH,* pp. 171-172

[3954] Shaw, *THE POISON PATRIARCH,* p. 153

[3955] Shaw, *THE POISON PATRIARCH,* p. 153

[3956] Shaw, *THE POISON PATRIARCH,* p. 132

[3957] Shaw, *THE POISON PATRIARCH,* p. 119

[3958] Shaw, *THE POISON PATRIARCH,* p. 169

[3959] Shaw, *THE POISON PATRIARCH,* p. 74

[3960] Baker, *Me & Lee,* p. 236

[3961] Fonzi, *THE LAST INVESTIGATION,* p. 432

[3962] Thomas, *HEAR NO EVIL,* pp. 542-550

[3963] Thomas, *HEAR NO EVIL,* pp. 542-550

[3964] Thomas, *HEAR NO EVIL,* pp. 542-550

[3965] Nelson, *LBJ: THE MASTEMIND OF THE JFK ASSASSINATION,* pp. 583-584

[3966] Shaw, *THE POISON PATRIARCH,* pp. 166-168

[3967] Shaw, *THE POISON PATRIARCH,* pp. 166-168

[3968] Stone & Colapietro, *THE MAN WHO KILLED KENNEDY,* p. 291

[3969] Stone & Colapietro, *THE MAN WHO KILLED KENNEDY,* p. 291

[3970] Belzer & Wayne, *HIT LIST,* pp. 75-90

[3971] Belzer & Wayne, *HIT LIST,* pp. 91-92

[3972] Nelson, *LBJ: THE MASTEMIND OF THE JFK ASSASSINATION,* p. 585

[3973] Nelson, *LBJ: THE MASTEMIND OF THE JFK ASSASSINATION,* p. 585

[3974] Nelson, *LBJ: THE MASTEMIND OF THE JFK ASSASSINATION,* p. 584

[3975] Nelson, *LBJ: THE MASTEMIND OF THE JFK ASSASSINATION*, p. 584

[3976] Nelson, *LBJ: THE MASTEMIND OF THE JFK ASSASSINATION*, p. 585

[3977] Nelson, *LBJ: THE MASTEMIND OF THE JFK ASSASSINATION*, p. 585

[3978] Fonzi, *THE LAST INVESTIGATION*, p. 433

[3979] Janney, *MARY'S MOSAIC*, p. 248

[3980] Janney, *MARY'S MOSAIC*, p. 248

[3981] Janney, *MARY'S MOSAIC*, p. 248

[3982] Janney, *MARY'S MOSAIC*, pp. 191-192

[3983] Nelson, *LBJ: THE MASTERMIND OF THE JFK ASSASSINATION*, p. 137

[3984] Nelson, *LBJ: THE MASTERMIND OF THE JFK ASSASSINATION*, pp. 136-137

[3985] Talbot, *THE DEVIL'S CHESSBOARD*, p. 222

[3986] Nelson, *LBJ: THE MASTERMIND OF THE JFK ASSASSINATION*, p. 137

[3987] Nelson, *LBJ: THE MASTERMIND OF THE JFK ASSASSINATION*, p. 137

[3988] Nelson, *LBJ: THE MASTERMIND OF THE JFK ASSASSINATION*, p. 137

[3989] Janney, *MARY'S MOSAIC*, p. 248

[3990] Janney, *MARY'S MOSAIC*, p. 248

[3991] Janney, *MARY'S MOSAIC*, pp. 191-192

[3992] Janney, *MARY'S MOSAIC*, pp. 191-192

[3993] Lane, *LAST WORD*, p. 105

[3994] Lane, *LAST WORD*, p. 105

[3995] Lane, *LAST WORD*, p. 98

[3996] Lane, *LAST WORD*, p. 98

[3997] Lane, *LAST WORD*, p. 76

[3998] Janney, *MARY'S MOSAIC*, p. 249

[3999] Janney, *MARY'S MOSAIC*, p. 249

[4000] Janney, *MARY'S MOSAIC*, p. 249

[4001] Janney, *MARY'S MOSAIC*, p. 268

[4002] Janney, *MARY'S MOSAIC*, p. 265

[4003] Janney, *MARY'S MOSAIC*, p. 266

[4004] Janney, *MARY'S MOSAIC*, p. 266

[4005] Janney, *MARY'S MOSAIC*, p. 267

[4006] Janney, *MARY'S MOSAIC*, p. 267

[4007] Janney, *MARY'S MOSAIC*, p. 266

[4008] Janney, *MARY'S MOSAIC*, p. 306

[4009] Janney, *MARY'S MOSAIC*, p. 307

[4010] Janney, *MARY'S MOSAIC*, p. 307

[4011] Janney, *MARY'S MOSAIC*, p. 307

[4012] Janney, *MARY'S MOSAIC*, p. 307

[4013] Janney, *MARY'S MOSAIC*, p. 307

[4014] Janney, *MARY'S MOSAIC*, p. 308

[4015] Janney, *MARY'S MOSAIC*, p. 308

[4016] Janney, *MARY'S MOSAIC*, pp. 307-308

[4017] Janney, *MARY'S MOSAIC*, pp. 307-308

[4018] Janney, *MARY'S MOSAIC*, p. 308

[4019] Thomas, *HEAR NO EVIL*, p. 335

[4020] Thomas, *HEAR NO EVIL*, p. 335

[4021] Thomas, *HEAR NO EVIL*, p. 335

[4022] Thomas, *HEAR NO EVIL*, p. 335

[4023] Thomas, *HEAR NO EVIL*, pp. 335-336

[4024] Thomas, *HEAR NO EVIL*, pp. 335-336

[4025] Thomas, *HEAR NO EVIL*, pp. 335-336

[4026] Nelson, *LBJ: THE MASTERMIND OF THE JFK ASSASSINATION*, p. 545

[4027] Nelson, *LBJ: THE MASTERMIND OF THE JFK ASSASSINATION*, p. 545

[4028] DiEugenio, *DESTINY BETRAYED*, p. 325

[4029] Stone & Colapietro, *THE MAN WHO KILLED KENNEDY*, p. 241

[4030] Nelson, *LBJ: THE MASTERMIND OF THE JFK ASSASSINATION*, pp. 546-553

[4031] North, *ACT OF TREASON*, pp. 395-396

[4032] North, *ACT OF TREASON*, p. 415

[4033] North, *ACT OF TREASON*, p. 415

[4034] Summers, *NOT IN YOUR LIFETIME*, pp. 118-119

[4035] Summers, *NOT IN YOUR LIFETIME*, pp. 118-119

[4036] Summers, *NOT IN YOUR LIFETIME*, p. 119

[4037] Summers, *NOT IN YOUR LIFETIME*, p. 119

[4038] North, *ACT OF TREASON*, p. 449

[4039] North, *ACT OF TREASON*, p. 449

[4040] North, *ACT OF TREASON*, pp. 395-396

[4041] North, *ACT OF TREASON*, pp. 395-396

[4042] North, *ACT OF TREASON*, pp. 395-396

[4043] North, *ACT OF TREASON*, pp. 395-396

[4044] North, *ACT OF TREASON*, p. 433

[4045] North, *ACT OF TREASON*, p. 433

[4046] North, *ACT OF TREASON*, p. 433

[4047] North, *ACT OF TREASON*, p. 433

[4048] Joesten, *OSWALD: ASSASSIN OR FALL GUY?*, p. 97

[4049] Joesten, *OSWALD: ASSASSIN OR FALL GUY?*, pp. 96-97

[4050] Joesten, *OSWALD: ASSASSIN OR FALL GUY?*, pp. 96-97

[4051] North, *ACT OF TREASON*, pp. 470-471

[4052] North, *ACT OF TREASON*, pp. 470-471

[4053] North, *ACT OF TREASON*, pp. 483-486

[4054] North, *ACT OF TREASON*, pp. 483-484

[4055] North, *ACT OF TREASON*, p. 485

[4056] North, *ACT OF TREASON*, p. 486

[4057] Joesten, *OSWALD: ASSASSIN OR FALL GUY?*, p. 187

[4058] Joesten, *OSWALD: ASSASSIN OR FALL GUY?*, p. 187

[4059] Janney, *MARY'S MOSAIC*, p. 300

[4060] Janney, *MARY'S MOSAIC*, p. 300

[4061] Nolan, *CIA ROGUES AND THE KILLING OF THE KENNEDYS*, pp. 112-113

[4062] Nolan, *CIA ROGUES AND THE KILLING OF THE KENNEDYS*, pp. 112-113

[4063] Nolan, *CIA ROGUES AND THE KILLING OF THE KENNEDYS*, pp. 112-113

[4064] Nolan, *CIA ROGUES AND THE KILLING OF THE KENNEDYS*, pp. 112-113

[4065] Nolan, *CIA ROGUES AND THE KILLING OF THE KENNEDYS*, pp. 112-113

[4066] Nolan, *CIA ROGUES AND THE KILLING OF THE KENNEDYS*, pp. 112-113

[4067] Marrs, CROSSFIRE, pp. 432-433

[4068] Marrs, CROSSFIRE, pp. 432-433

[4069] Marrs, CROSSFIRE, pp. 432-433

[4070] Marrs, CROSSFIRE, pp. 432-433

[4071] Marrs, CROSSFIRE, pp. 432-433

[4072] Marrs, CROSSFIRE, pp. 432-433

[4073] Janney, *MARY'S MOSAIC*, p. 297

[4074] Lane, *LAST WORD*, p. 75

[4075] Janney, *MARY'S MOSAIC*, p. 297

[4076] Janney, *MARY'S MOSAIC*, p. 297

[4077] Janney, *MARY'S MOSAIC*, p. 297

[4078] Janney, *MARY'S MOSAIC*, p. 297

[4079] DiEugenio, *DESTINY BETRAYED*, pp. 220-260

[4080] Nelson, *LBJ: THE MASTERMIND OF THE JFK ASSASSINATION*, p. 556

[4081] Lane, *LAST WORD*, p. 18

[4082] Lane, *LAST WORD*, p. 18

[4083] Lane, *LAST WORD*, p. 18

[4084] Summers, *NOT IN YOUR LIFETIME*, pp. 116-117

[4085] Summers, *NOT IN YOUR LIFETIME*, pp. 116-117

[4086] Janney, *MARY'S MOSAIC*, p. 299

[4087] DiEugenio, *RECLAIMING PARKLAND*, p. xiv

[4088] DiEugenio, *RECLAIMING PARKLAND*, p. xiv

[4089] DiEugenio, *RECLAIMING PARKLAND*, p. xiv

[4090] DiEugenio, *RECLAIMING PARKLAND*, pp. xiv-xv

[4091] DiEugenio, *RECLAIMING PARKLAND*, p. xv

[4092] Fonzi, *THE LAST INVESTIGATION*, p. 4

[4093] Fonzi, *THE LAST INVESTIGATION*, p. 4

[4094] Fonzi, *THE LAST INVESTIGATION*, p. 4

[4095] DiEugenio, *RECLAIMING PARKLAND*, p. xiv

[4096] Lane, *LAST WORD*, p. 99

[4097] Fonzi, *THE LAST INVESTIGATION*, p. 15

[4098] Fonzi, *THE LAST INVESTIGATION*, p. 15
[4099] Meagher, *ACCESSORIES AFTER THE FACT*, pp. 458-459
[4100] Meagher, *ACCESSORIES AFTER THE FACT*, pp. 458-459
[4101] Meagher, *ACCESSORIES AFTER THE FACT*, pp. 458-459
[4102] Meagher, *ACCESSORIES AFTER THE FACT*, pp. 458-459
[4103] Meagher, *ACCESSORIES AFTER THE FACT*, pp. 458-459
[4104] Lane, *LAST WORD*, p. 16
[4105] Douglass, *JFK AND THE UNSPEAKABLE*, p. 314
[4106] Nelson, *LBJ: THE MASTERMIND OF THE JFK ASSASSINATION*, p. 560
[4107] Crenshaw, *JFK HAS BEEN SHOT*, p. 257
[4108] Crenshaw, *JFK HAS BEEN SHOT*, pp. 291-292
[4109] Crenshaw, *JFK HAS BEEN SHOT*, pp. 291-292
[4110] Crenshaw, *JFK HAS BEEN SHOT*, pp. 291-292
[4111] Crenshaw, *JFK HAS BEEN SHOT*, pp. 291-292
[4112] Douglass, *JFK AND THE UNSPEAKABLE*, p. 309
[4113] Douglass, *JFK AND THE UNSPEAKABLE*, p. 309
[4114] Douglass, *JFK AND THE UNSPEAKABLE*, p. 309
[4115] Corsi, *WHO REALLY KILLED KENNEDY*, pp. 94-95
[4116] Corsi, *WHO REALLY KILLED KENNEDY*, pp. 94-95
[4117] Corsi, *WHO REALLY KILLED KENNEDY*, pp. 94-95
[4118] Corsi, *WHO REALLY KILLED KENNEDY*, pp. 94-95
[4119] Corsi, *WHO REALLY KILLED KENNEDY*, pp. 94-95
[4120] Douglass, *JFK AND THE UNSPEAKABLE*, p. 300
[4121] Douglass, *JFK AND THE UNSPEAKABLE*, p. 300
[4122] Douglass, *JFK AND THE UNSPEAKABLE*, p. 301
[4123] Nelson, *LBJ: THE MASTERMIND OF THE JFK ASSASSINATION*, p. 367
[4124] Nelson, *LBJ: THE MASTERMIND OF THE JFK ASSASSINATION*, p. 367
[4125] Nelson, *LBJ: THE MASTERMIND OF THE JFK ASSASSINATION*, p. 498
[4126] Talbot, *THE DEVIL'S CHESSBOARD*, p. 398
[4127] Talbot, *THE DEVIL'S CHESSBOARD*, p. 398
[4128] Janney, *MARY'S MOSAIC*, p. 292
[4129] Janney, *MARY'S MOSAIC*, p. 292
[4130] Nelson, *LBJ: THE MASTERMIND OF THE JFK ASSASSINATION*, p. 155
[4131] Nelson, *LBJ: THE MASTERMIND OF THE JFK ASSASSINATION*, p. 155
[4132] Nelson, *LBJ: THE MASTERMIND OF THE JFK ASSASSINATION*, p. 155
[4133] North, *ACT OF TREASON,* p. 461
[4134] Corsi, *WHO REALLY KILLED KENNEDY*, p. 221
[4135] Corsi, *WHO REALLY KILLED KENNEDY*, p. 221
[4136] Corsi, *WHO REALLY KILLED KENNEDY*, p. 221
[4137] Corsi, *WHO REALLY KILLED KENNEDY*, p. 221

[4138] Douglass, *JFK AND THE UNSPEAKABLE*, p. 370
[4139] Douglass, *JFK AND THE UNSPEAKABLE*, p. 370
[4140] Douglass, *JFK AND THE UNSPEAKABLE*, p. 370
[4141] Douglass, *JFK AND THE UNSPEAKABLE*, p. 370
[4142] Douglass, *JFK AND THE UNSPEAKABLE*, p. 370
[4143] Douglass, *JFK AND THE UNSPEAKABLE*, p. 370
[4144] Douglass, *JFK AND THE UNSPEAKABLE*, pp. 370-371
[4145] Douglass, *JFK AND THE UNSPEAKABLE*, p. 371
[4146] Douglass, *JFK AND THE UNSPEAKABLE*, p. 371
[4147] Douglass, *JFK AND THE UNSPEAKABLE*, p. 371
[4148] Douglass, *JFK AND THE UNSPEAKABLE*, p. 371
[4149] Douglass, *JFK AND THE UNSPEAKABLE*, p. 371
[4150] Douglass, *JFK AND THE UNSPEAKABLE*, p. 371
[4151] Douglass, *JFK AND THE UNSPEAKABLE*, p. 372
[4152] Douglass, *JFK AND THE UNSPEAKABLE*, p. 372
[4153] Stone & Colapietro, *THE MAN WHO KILLED KENNEDY*, p. 156
[4154] Stone & Colapietro, *THE MAN WHO KILLED KENNEDY*, p. 156
[4155] Talbot, *THE DEVIL'S CHESSBOARD*, p. 606
[4156] Talbot, *THE DEVIL'S CHESSBOARD*, p. 606
[4157] Talbot, *THE DEVIL'S CHESSBOARD*, p. 607
[4158] Talbot, *THE DEVIL'S CHESSBOARD*, p. 607
[4159] Lane, *LAST WORD*, p. 42
[4160] Lane, *LAST WORD*, p. 42
[4161] Janney, *MARY'S MOSAIC*, p. 305
[4162] Janney, *MARY'S MOSAIC*, p. 305
[4163] Janney, *MARY'S MOSAIC*, p. 305
[4164] Nolan, *CIA ROGUES AND THE KILLING OF THE KENNEDYS*, p. 216-217
[4165] Nolan, *CIA ROGUES AND THE KILLING OF THE KENNEDYS*, p. 216-217
[4166] Nolan, *CIA ROGUES AND THE KILLING OF THE KENNEDYS*, p. 216-217
[4167] Nolan, *CIA ROGUES AND THE KILLING OF THE KENNEDYS*, p. 29
[4168] Nolan, *CIA ROGUES AND THE KILLING OF THE KENNEDYS*, p. 222
[4169] Nolan, *CIA ROGUES AND THE KILLING OF THE KENNEDYS*, p. 222
[4170] Nolan, *CIA ROGUES AND THE KILLING OF THE KENNEDYS*, p. 205
[4171] Belzer & Wayne, *DEAD WRONG*, p. 189
[4172] Belzer & Wayne, *DEAD WRONG*, p. 189
[4173] Belzer & Wayne, *DEAD WRONG*, pp. 189-190
[4174] Belzer & Wayne, *DEAD WRONG*, pp. 189-190
[4175] Belzer & Wayne, *DEAD WRONG*, p. 190
[4176] Talbot, *THE DEVIL'S CHESSBOARD*, pp. 610-611
[4177] Talbot, *THE DEVIL'S CHESSBOARD*, pp. 610-611

[4178] Talbot, *THE DEVIL'S CHESSBOARD*, p. 611

[4179] Nolan, *CIA ROGUES AND THE KILLING OF THE KENNEDYS*, p. 281

[4180] Nolan, *CIA ROGUES AND THE KILLING OF THE KENNEDYS*, p. 281

[4181] Nolan, *CIA ROGUES AND THE KILLING OF THE KENNEDYS*, p. 59

[4182] Nolan, *CIA ROGUES AND THE KILLING OF THE KENNEDYS*, p. 59

[4183] Nolan, *CIA ROGUES AND THE KILLING OF THE KENNEDYS*, p. 280

[4184] Nolan, *CIA ROGUES AND THE KILLING OF THE KENNEDYS*, p. 188

[4185] Nolan, *CIA ROGUES AND THE KILLING OF THE KENNEDYS*, pp. 279-280

[4186] Nolan, *CIA ROGUES AND THE KILLING OF THE KENNEDYS*, p. 192

[4187] Nolan, *CIA ROGUES AND THE KILLING OF THE KENNEDYS*, p. 192

[4188] Nolan, *CIA ROGUES AND THE KILLING OF THE KENNEDYS*, pp. 220-221

[4189] Nolan, *CIA ROGUES AND THE KILLING OF THE KENNEDYS*, pp. 220-221

[4190] Nolan, *CIA ROGUES AND THE KILLING OF THE KENNEDYS*, p. 190

[4191] Nolan, *CIA ROGUES AND THE KILLING OF THE KENNEDYS*, p. 190

[4192] Nolan, *CIA ROGUES AND THE KILLING OF THE KENNEDYS*, p. 189

[4193] Nolan, *CIA ROGUES AND THE KILLING OF THE KENNEDYS*, p. 194

[4194] Nolan, *CIA ROGUES AND THE KILLING OF THE KENNEDYS*, pp. 276-277

[4195] Nolan, *CIA ROGUES AND THE KILLING OF THE KENNEDYS*, pp. 197-198

[4196] Nolan, *CIA ROGUES AND THE KILLING OF THE KENNEDYS*, pp. 197-198

[4197] Nolan, *CIA ROGUES AND THE KILLING OF THE KENNEDYS*, pp. 227-228

[4198] Nolan, *CIA ROGUES AND THE KILLING OF THE KENNEDYS*, p. 243

[4199] Nolan, *CIA ROGUES AND THE KILLING OF THE KENNEDYS*, p. 247

[4200] Nolan, *CIA ROGUES AND THE KILLING OF THE KENNEDYS*, p. 224

[4201] Nolan, *CIA ROGUES AND THE KILLING OF THE KENNEDYS*, pp. 198-199

[4202] Nolan, *CIA ROGUES AND THE KILLING OF THE KENNEDYS*, pp. 199-200

[4203] Nolan, *CIA ROGUES AND THE KILLING OF THE KENNEDYS*, pp. 199-200

[4204] Nolan, *CIA ROGUES AND THE KILLING OF THE KENNEDYS*, pp. 199-200

[4205] Nolan, *CIA ROGUES AND THE KILLING OF THE KENNEDYS*, p. 201

[4206] Nolan, *CIA ROGUES AND THE KILLING OF THE KENNEDYS*, p. 269

[4207] Nolan, *CIA ROGUES AND THE KILLING OF THE KENNEDYS*, p. 31

[4208] Stone & Colapietro, *THE MAN WHO KILLED KENNEDY*, pp. 364-365

[4209] Stone & Colapietro, *THE MAN WHO KILLED KENNEDY*, pp. 364-365

[4210] Stone & Colapietro, *THE MAN WHO KILLED KENNEDY*, pp. 364-365

[4211] Stone & Colapietro, *THE MAN WHO KILLED KENNEDY*, pp. 364-365

[4212] Stone & Colapietro, *THE MAN WHO KILLED KENNEDY*, pp. 364-365

[4213] Stone & Colapietro, *THE MAN WHO KILLED KENNEDY*, pp. 364-365

[4214] Stone & Colapietro, *THE MAN WHO KILLED KENNEDY*, pp. 364-365

[4215] Stone & Colapietro, *THE MAN WHO KILLED KENNEDY*, p. 367

[4216] Stone & Colapietro, *THE MAN WHO KILLED KENNEDY*, p. 367

[4217] Nolan, *CIA ROGUES AND THE KILLING OF THE KENNEDYS*, p. 6

[4218] Nolan, *CIA ROGUES AND THE KILLING OF THE KENNEDYS*, p. 10

[4219] Nolan, *CIA ROGUES AND THE KILLING OF THE KENNEDYS*, pp. 227-228

[4220] Nolan, *CIA ROGUES AND THE KILLING OF THE KENNEDYS*, pp. 227-228

[4221] Nolan, *CIA ROGUES AND THE KILLING OF THE KENNEDYS*, pp. 227-228

[4222] Nolan, *CIA ROGUES AND THE KILLING OF THE KENNEDYS*, p. 228

[4223] Nolan, *CIA ROGUES AND THE KILLING OF THE KENNEDYS*, p. 224

[4224] Nolan, *CIA ROGUES AND THE KILLING OF THE KENNEDYS*, pp. 224-225

[4225] Nolan, *CIA ROGUES AND THE KILLING OF THE KENNEDYS*, pp. 224-225

[4226] Nolan, *CIA ROGUES AND THE KILLING OF THE KENNEDYS*,

p. 225

[4227] Nolan, *CIA ROGUES AND THE KILLING OF THE KENNEDYS*, p. 225

[4228] Nolan, *CIA ROGUES AND THE KILLING OF THE KENNEDYS*, p. 225

[4229] Nolan, *CIA ROGUES AND THE KILLING OF THE KENNEDYS*, pp. 230-231

[4230] Nolan, *CIA ROGUES AND THE KILLING OF THE KENNEDYS*, pp. 230-231

[4231] Nolan, *CIA ROGUES AND THE KILLING OF THE KENNEDYS*, pp. 230-231

[4232] Nolan, *CIA ROGUES AND THE KILLING OF THE KENNEDYS*, pp. 235-236

[4233] Nolan, *CIA ROGUES AND THE KILLING OF THE KENNEDYS*, pp. 235-236

[4234] Nolan, *CIA ROGUES AND THE KILLING OF THE KENNEDYS*, pp. 235-236

[4235] Nolan, *CIA ROGUES AND THE KILLING OF THE KENNEDYS*, pp. 237-238

[4236] Nolan, *CIA ROGUES AND THE KILLING OF THE KENNEDYS*, pp. 237-238

[4237] Nolan, *CIA ROGUES AND THE KILLING OF THE KENNEDYS*, p. 247

[4238] Nolan, *CIA ROGUES AND THE KILLING OF THE KENNEDYS*, p. 247

[4239] Nolan, *CIA ROGUES AND THE KILLING OF THE KENNEDYS*, p. 247

[4240] Nolan, *CIA ROGUES AND THE KILLING OF THE KENNEDYS*, p. 247

[4241] Nolan, *CIA ROGUES AND THE KILLING OF THE KENNEDYS*, p. 247

[4242] Nolan, *CIA ROGUES AND THE KILLING OF THE KENNEDYS*, p. 248

[4243] Nolan, *CIA ROGUES AND THE KILLING OF THE KENNEDYS*, pp. 248-249

[4244] Nolan, *CIA ROGUES AND THE KILLING OF THE KENNEDYS*, pp. 248-249

[4245] Nolan, *CIA ROGUES AND THE KILLING OF THE KENNEDYS*, p. 251

[4246] Nolan, *CIA ROGUES AND THE KILLING OF THE KENNEDYS*, p. 251

[4247] Nolan, *CIA ROGUES AND THE KILLING OF THE KENNEDYS*, p. 255

[4248] Nolan, *CIA ROGUES AND THE KILLING OF THE KENNEDYS*, p. 255

[4249] Nolan, *CIA ROGUES AND THE KILLING OF THE KENNEDYS*, pp. 255-256

[4250] Nolan, *CIA ROGUES AND THE KILLING OF THE KENNEDYS,* pp. 257-258

[4251] Nolan, *CIA ROGUES AND THE KILLING OF THE KENNEDYS,* pp. 257-258

[4252] Nolan, *CIA ROGUES AND THE KILLING OF THE KENNEDYS,* pp. 257-258

[4253] Nolan, *CIA ROGUES AND THE KILLING OF THE KENNEDYS,* pp. 262-263

[4254] Nolan, *CIA ROGUES AND THE KILLING OF THE KENNEDYS,* pp. 262-263

[4255] Nolan, *CIA ROGUES AND THE KILLING OF THE KENNEDYS,* pp. 262-263

[4256] Nolan, *CIA ROGUES AND THE KILLING OF THE KENNEDYS,* pp. 262-263

[4257] Nolan, *CIA ROGUES AND THE KILLING OF THE KENNEDYS,* pp. 262-263

[4258] Nolan, *CIA ROGUES AND THE KILLING OF THE KENNEDYS,* p. 265

[4259] Nolan, *CIA ROGUES AND THE KILLING OF THE KENNEDYS,* pp. 265-266

[4260] Nolan, *CIA ROGUES AND THE KILLING OF THE KENNEDYS,* pp. 265-266

[4261] Nolan, *CIA ROGUES AND THE KILLING OF THE KENNEDYS,* pp. 265-266

[4262] Nolan, *CIA ROGUES AND THE KILLING OF THE KENNEDYS,* pp. 265-266

[4263] Nolan, *CIA ROGUES AND THE KILLING OF THE KENNEDYS,* pp. 228-229

[4264] Nolan, *CIA ROGUES AND THE KILLING OF THE KENNEDYS,* pp. 228-229

[4265] Nolan, *CIA ROGUES AND THE KILLING OF THE KENNEDYS,* pp. 228-229

[4266] Nolan, *CIA ROGUES AND THE KILLING OF THE KENNEDYS,* pp. 228-229

[4267] Nolan, *CIA ROGUES AND THE KILLING OF THE KENNEDYS,* p. 267

[4268] Nolan, *CIA ROGUES AND THE KILLING OF THE KENNEDYS,* pp. 267-268

[4269] Nolan, *CIA ROGUES AND THE KILLING OF THE KENNEDYS,* pp. 267-268

[4270] Nolan, *CIA ROGUES AND THE KILLING OF THE KENNEDYS,* p. 268

[4271] Nolan, *CIA ROGUES AND THE KILLING OF THE KENNEDYS,* p. 268

[4272] Nolan, *CIA ROGUES AND THE KILLING OF THE KENNEDYS,* p. 268

[4273] Nolan, *CIA ROGUES AND THE KILLING OF THE KENNEDYS,*

p. 275

[4274] Garrison, *ON THE TRAIL OF THE ASSASSINS*, p. 238

[4275] Garrison, *ON THE TRAIL OF THE ASSASSINS*, p. 238

[4276] Garrison, *ON THE TRAIL OF THE ASSASSINS*, pp. 239-240

[4277] DiEugenio, *DESTINY BETRAYED*, p. 260

[4278] DiEugenio, *DESTINY BETRAYED*, p. 260

[4279] Garrison, *ON THE TRAIL OF THE ASSASSINS*, p. 87

[4280] Nelson, *LBJ: THE MASTERMIND OF THE JFK ASSASSINATION*, p. 342

[4281] DiEugenio, *DESTINY BETRAYED*, p. 167

[4282] DiEugenio, *DESTINY BETRAYED*, p. 167

[4283] DiEugenio, *DESTINY BETRAYED*, pp. 167-174

[4284] Garrison, *ON THE TRAIL OF THE ASSASSINS*, pp. 129-130

[4285] Garrison, *ON THE TRAIL OF THE ASSASSINS*, p. 138

[4286] Garrison, *ON THE TRAIL OF THE ASSASSINS*, p. 138

[4287] Garrison, *ON THE TRAIL OF THE ASSASSINS*, p. 138

[4288] Garrison, *ON THE TRAIL OF THE ASSASSINS*, pp. 79-83

[4289] Nelson, *LBJ: THE MASTERMIND OF THE JFK ASSASSINATION*, p. 553

[4290] Nelson, *LBJ: THE MASTERMIND OF THE JFK ASSASSINATION*, p. 553

[4291] Nelson, *LBJ: THE MASTERMIND OF THE JFK ASSASSINATION*, p. 553

[4292] Nelson, *LBJ: THE MASTERMIND OF THE JFK ASSASSINATION*, pp. 553-554

[4293] Nelson, *LBJ: THE MASTERMIND OF THE JFK ASSASSINATION*, p. 555

[4294] Garrison, *ON THE TRAIL OF THE ASSASSINS*, p. 149

[4295] Nelson, *LBJ: THE MASTERMIND OF THE JFK ASSASSINATION*, p. 556

[4296] Fonzi, *THE LAST INVESTIGATION*, p. 375

[4297] Fonzi, *THE LAST INVESTIGATION*, p. 375

[4298] Garrison, *ON THE TRAIL OF THE ASSASSINS*, pp. 132-136

[4299] Garrison, *ON THE TRAIL OF THE ASSASSINS*, pp. 132-136

[4300] Garrison, *ON THE TRAIL OF THE ASSASSINS*, pp. 132-136

[4301] Garrison, *ON THE TRAIL OF THE ASSASSINS*, pp. 174-175

[4302] Garrison, *ON THE TRAIL OF THE ASSASSINS*, pp. 174-175

[4303] Garrison, *ON THE TRAIL OF THE ASSASSINS*, pp. 174-175

[4304] Garrison, *ON THE TRAIL OF THE ASSASSINS*, pp. 174-175

[4305] Garrison, *ON THE TRAIL OF THE ASSASSINS*, p. 179

[4306] Garrison, *ON THE TRAIL OF THE ASSASSINS*, p. 181

[4307] Garrison, *ON THE TRAIL OF THE ASSASSINS*, p. 181

[4308] Garrison, *ON THE TRAIL OF THE ASSASSINS*, p. 181

[4309] Garrison, *ON THE TRAIL OF THE ASSASSINS*, p. 182

[4310] Garrison, *ON THE TRAIL OF THE ASSASSINS*, p. 182

[4311] Garrison, *ON THE TRAIL OF THE ASSASSINS*, p. 183

[4312] Garrison, *ON THE TRAIL OF THE ASSASSINS*, pp. 182-186

[4313] Garrison, *ON THE TRAIL OF THE ASSASSINS*, pp. 182-186
[4314] Garrison, *ON THE TRAIL OF THE ASSASSINS*, pp. 186-187
[4315] Garrison, *ON THE TRAIL OF THE ASSASSINS*, pp. 186-192
[4316] Garrison, *ON THE TRAIL OF THE ASSASSINS*, pp. 186-192
[4317] Garrison, *ON THE TRAIL OF THE ASSASSINS*, pp. 186-192
[4318] Garrison, *ON THE TRAIL OF THE ASSASSINS*, pp. 186-192
[4319] Garrison, *ON THE TRAIL OF THE ASSASSINS*, pp. 186-192
[4320] Garrison, *ON THE TRAIL OF THE ASSASSINS*, p. 191
[4321] Garrison, *ON THE TRAIL OF THE ASSASSINS*, pp. 186-192
[4322] Garrison, *ON THE TRAIL OF THE ASSASSINS*, pp. 191-192
[4323] DiEugenio, *DESTINY BETRAYED*, pp. 278-285
[4324] DiEugenio, *DESTINY BETRAYED*, pp. 278-285
[4325] DiEugenio, *DESTINY BETRAYED*, pp. 278-285
[4326] DiEugenio, *DESTINY BETRAYED*, p. 295
[4327] DiEugenio, *DESTINY BETRAYED*, p. 295
[4328] DiEugenio, *DESTINY BETRAYED*, p. 295
[4329] DiEugenio, *DESTINY BETRAYED*, p. 296
[4330] DiEugenio, *DESTINY BETRAYED*, p. 296
[4331] DiEugenio, *DESTINY BETRAYED*, pp. 271-274
[4332] Nelson, *LBJ: THE MASTERMIND OF THE JFK ASSASSINATION*, p. 557
[4333] Nelson, *LBJ: THE MASTERMIND OF THE JFK ASSASSINATION*, p. 557
[4334] DiEugenio, *DESTINY BETRAYED*, pp. 220-260
[4335] DiEugenio, *DESTINY BETRAYED*, pp. 229-231
[4336] Fonzi, *THE LAST INVESTIGATION*, p. 433
[4337] DiEugenio, *DESTINY BETRAYED*, p. 312
[4338] DiEugenio, *DESTINY BETRAYED*, p. 312
[4339] Fonzi, *THE LAST INVESTIGATION*, p. 434
[4340] Garrison, *ON THE TRAIL OF THE ASSASSINS*, p. 253
[4341] Garrison, *ON THE TRAIL OF THE ASSASSINS*, p. 253
[4342] DiEugenio, *DESTINY BETRAYED*, p. 315
[4343] DiEugenio, *DESTINY BETRAYED*, p. 315
[4344] DiEugenio, *DESTINY BETRAYED*, p. 315
[4345] Garrison, *ON THE TRAIL OF THE ASSASSINS*, p. 252
[4346] DiEugenio, *DESTINY BETRAYED*, pp. 312-313
[4347] DiEugenio, *DESTINY BETRAYED*, pp. 312-313
[4348] Talbot, *THE DEVIL'S CHESSBOARD*, p. 597
[4349] Talbot, *THE DEVIL'S CHESSBOARD*, p. 597
[4350] Talbot, *THE DEVIL'S CHESSBOARD*, p. 597
[4351] DiEugenio, *DESTINY BETRAYED*, pp. 316-320
[4352] DiEugenio, *DESTINY BETRAYED*, pp. 316-320
[4353] DiEugenio, *DESTINY BETRAYED*, p. 320
[4354] Garrison, *ON THE TRAIL OF THE ASSASSINS*, p. 254
[4355] Garrison, *ON THE TRAIL OF THE ASSASSINS*, p. 255
[4356] Garrison, *ON THE TRAIL OF THE ASSASSINS*, p. 256
[4357] Garrison, *ON THE TRAIL OF THE ASSASSINS*, p. 256

[4358] Garrison, *ON THE TRAIL OF THE ASSASSINS*, p. 257

[4359] Garrison, *ON THE TRAIL OF THE ASSASSINS*, pp. 259-260

[4360] Garrison, *ON THE TRAIL OF THE ASSASSINS*, pp. 259-260

[4361] Garrison, *ON THE TRAIL OF THE ASSASSINS*, p. 260

[4362] Garrison, *ON THE TRAIL OF THE ASSASSINS*, p. 260

[4363] Garrison, *ON THE TRAIL OF THE ASSASSINS*, p. 261

[4364] Garrison, *ON THE TRAIL OF THE ASSASSINS*, p. 262

[4365] Garrison, *ON THE TRAIL OF THE ASSASSINS*, p. 263

[4366] Garrison, *ON THE TRAIL OF THE ASSASSINS*, p. 263

[4367] Garrison, *ON THE TRAIL OF THE ASSASSINS*, p. 264

[4368] Garrison, *ON THE TRAIL OF THE ASSASSINS*, p. 265

[4369] Garrison, *ON THE TRAIL OF THE ASSASSINS*, p. 265

[4370] Garrison, *ON THE TRAIL OF THE ASSASSINS*, p. 268-271

[4371] Garrison, *ON THE TRAIL OF THE ASSASSINS*, p. 271

[4372] DiEugenio, *DESTINY BETRAYED*, p. 320

[4373] DiEugenio, *DESTINY BETRAYED*, pp. 321-322

[4374] Lane, *LAST WORD*, p. 75

[4375] Lane, *LAST WORD*, p. 75

[4376] Nelson, *LBJ: THE MASTERMIND OF THE JFK ASSASSINATION*, p. 556

[4377] Nelson, *LBJ: THE MASTERMIND OF THE JFK ASSASSINATION*, p. 137

[4378] Duglass, *JFK AND THE UNSPEAKABLE*, p. 164

[4379] Joesten, *OSWALD: ASSASSIN OR FALL GUY?*, p. 134

[4380] Garrison, *ON THE TRAIL OF THE ASSASSINS*, p. 114

[4381] Garrison, *ON THE TRAIL OF THE ASSASSINS*, p. 114

[4382] Garrison, *ON THE TRAIL OF THE ASSASSINS*, p. 163

[4383] Garrison, *ON THE TRAIL OF THE ASSASSINS*, p. 163

[4384] Garrison, *ON THE TRAIL OF THE ASSASSINS*, p. 163

[4385] Garrison, *ON THE TRAIL OF THE ASSASSINS*, p. 163

[4386] Garrison, *ON THE TRAIL OF THE ASSASSINS*, p. 163

[4387] Garrison, *ON THE TRAIL OF THE ASSASSINS*, pp. 163-164

[4388] Garrison, *ON THE TRAIL OF THE ASSASSINS*, p. 164

[4389] Garrison, *ON THE TRAIL OF THE ASSASSINS*, p. 164

[4390] Garrison, *ON THE TRAIL OF THE ASSASSINS*, p. 164

[4391] Garrison, *ON THE TRAIL OF THE ASSASSINS*, p. 164

[4392] Garrison, *ON THE TRAIL OF THE ASSASSINS*, p. 164

[4393] Garrison, *ON THE TRAIL OF THE ASSASSINS*, p. 164

[4394] Garrison, *ON THE TRAIL OF THE ASSASSINS*, p. 161

[4395] Garrison, *ON THE TRAIL OF THE ASSASSINS*, p. 161

[4396] Garrison, *ON THE TRAIL OF THE ASSASSINS*, p. 161

[4397] Garrison, *ON THE TRAIL OF THE ASSASSINS*, p. 161

[4398] Garrison, *ON THE TRAIL OF THE ASSASSINS*, pp. 161-162

[4399] Garrison, *ON THE TRAIL OF THE ASSASSINS*, pp. 161-162

[4400] Garrison, *ON THE TRAIL OF THE ASSASSINS*, p. 162

[4401] Garrison, *ON THE TRAIL OF THE ASSASSINS*, p. 162

[4402] Garrison, *ON THE TRAIL OF THE ASSASSINS*, pp. 162-163

[4403] Garrison, *ON THE TRAIL OF THE ASSASSINS*, pp. 165-166

[4404] Garrison, *ON THE TRAIL OF THE ASSASSINS*, p. 166

[4405] Garrison, *ON THE TRAIL OF THE ASSASSINS*, p. 168

[4406] Garrison, *ON THE TRAIL OF THE ASSASSINS*, p. 170

[4407] Garrison, *ON THE TRAIL OF THE ASSASSINS*, p. 171

[4408] Garrison, *ON THE TRAIL OF THE ASSASSINS*, p. 208

[4409] Garrison, *ON THE TRAIL OF THE ASSASSINS*, p. 208

[4410] Garrison, *ON THE TRAIL OF THE ASSASSINS*, p. 208

[4411] Garrison, *ON THE TRAIL OF THE ASSASSINS*, p. 211

[4412] Garrison, *ON THE TRAIL OF THE ASSASSINS*, pp. 210-213

[4413] Garrison, *ON THE TRAIL OF THE ASSASSINS*, pp. 210-213

[4414] Lane, *LAST WORD*, p. 207

[4415] Lane, *LAST WORD*, p. 210

[4416] Lane, *LAST WORD*, p. 210

[4417] Lane, *LAST WORD*, p. 211

[4418] Lane, *LAST WORD*, p. 212

[4419] Lane, *LAST WORD*, p. 212

[4420] Lane, *LAST WORD*, p. 214

[4421] Lane, *LAST WORD*, p. 214

[4422] Lane, *LAST WORD*, p. 215

[4423] Lane, *LAST WORD*, p. 216

[4424] Lane, *LAST WORD*, p. 216

[4425] Fonzi, *THE LAST INVESTIGATION*, p. 438

[4426] Fonzi, *THE LAST INVESTIGATION*, p. 438

[4427] Fonzi, *THE LAST INVESTIGATION*, p. 439

[4428] Lane, *LAST WORD*, p. 217

[4429] Lane, *LAST WORD*, p. 217

[4430] Lane, *LAST WORD*, p. 217

[4431] Lane, *LAST WORD*, p. 221

[4432] Lane, *LAST WORD*, p. 221

[4433] Lane, *LAST WORD*, p. 221

[4434] DiEugenio, *DESTINY BETRAYED*, p. 326

[4435] DiEugenio, *DESTINY BETRAYED*, p. 326

[4436] DiEugenio, *DESTINY BETRAYED*, p. 326

[4437] DiEugenio, *DESTINY BETRAYED*, p. 326

[4438] DiEugenio, *DESTINY BETRAYED*, p. 326

[4439] DiEugenio, *DESTINY BETRAYED*, p. 326

[4440] DiEugenio, *DESTINY BETRAYED*, p. 326

[4441] Fonzi, *THE LAST INVESTIGATION*, p. 439

[4442] Lane, *LAST WORD*, p. 226

[4443] Lane, *LAST WORD*, p. 227

[4444] Lane, *LAST WORD*, p. 228

[4445] Lane, *LAST WORD*, p. 228

[4446] DiEugenio, *DESTINY BETRAYED*, pp. 326-327

[4447] DiEugenio, *DESTINY BETRAYED*, pp. 326-327

[4448] DiEugenio, *DESTINY BETRAYED*, p. 333

[4449] DiEugenio, *DESTINY BETRAYED*, pp. 332-333

[4450] Fonzi, *THE LAST INVESTIGATION*, p. 197
[4451] Fonzi, *THE LAST INVESTIGATION*, pp. 197-198
[4452] Fonzi, *THE LAST INVESTIGATION*, pp. 197-198
[4453] Fonzi, *THE LAST INVESTIGATION*, p. 440
[4454] Fonzi, *THE LAST INVESTIGATION*, p. 437
[4455] Fonzi, *THE LAST INVESTIGATION*, p. 440
[4456] Fonzi, *THE LAST INVESTIGATION*, p. 195
[4457] Fonzi, *THE LAST INVESTIGATION*, p. 195
[4458] Fonzi, *THE LAST INVESTIGATION*, p. 439
[4459] Fonzi, *THE LAST INVESTIGATION*, p. 439
[4460] Fonzi, *THE LAST INVESTIGATION*, p. 440
[4461] Fonzi, *THE LAST INVESTIGATION*, p. 440
[4462] Fonzi, *THE LAST INVESTIGATION*, p. 440
[4463] Fonzi, *THE LAST INVESTIGATION*, p. 440
[4464] Fonzi, *THE LAST INVESTIGATION*, p. 440
[4465] Fonzi, *THE LAST INVESTIGATION*, p. 440
[4466] DiEugenio, *DESTINY BETRAYED*, p. 339
[4467] DiEugenio, *DESTINY BETRAYED*, pp. 339-340
[4468] Fonzi, *THE LAST INVESTIGATION*, p. 209
[4469] Fonzi, *THE LAST INVESTIGATION*, p. 441
[4470] Fonzi, *THE LAST INVESTIGATION*, p. 441
[4471] DiEugenio, *DESTINY BETRAYED*, p. 350
[4472] DiEugenio, *DESTINY BETRAYED*, p. 350
[4473] Lane, *LAST WORD*, p. 233
[4474] Lane, *LAST WORD*, p. 233
[4475] Lane, *LAST WORD*, p. 234
[4476] Fonzi, *THE LAST INVESTIGATION*, p. 440
[4477] Fonzi, *THE LAST INVESTIGATION*, pp. 440-441
[4478] Fonzi, *THE LAST INVESTIGATION*, p. 441
[4479] Fonzi, *THE LAST INVESTIGATION*, p. 441
[4480] Fonzi, *THE LAST INVESTIGATION*, p. 245
[4481] Fonzi, *THE LAST INVESTIGATION*, p. 218
[4482] Fonzi, *THE LAST INVESTIGATION*, p. 218
[4483] Fonzi, *THE LAST INVESTIGATION*, p. 218
[4484] Fonzi, *THE LAST INVESTIGATION*, p. 219
[4485] Fonzi, *THE LAST INVESTIGATION*, p. 222
[4486] Fonzi, *THE LAST INVESTIGATION*, p. 222
[4487] Fonzi, *THE LAST INVESTIGATION*, pp. 218-219
[4488] Fonzi, *THE LAST INVESTIGATION*, pp. 218-219
[4489] Fonzi, *THE LAST INVESTIGATION*, pp. 218-219
[4490] Fonzi, *THE LAST INVESTIGATION*, pp. 442-443
[4491] Fonzi, *THE LAST INVESTIGATION*, pp. 442-443
[4492] Fonzi, *THE LAST INVESTIGATION*, p. 443
[4493] Fonzi, *THE LAST INVESTIGATION*, pp. 12-13
[4494] Corsi, *WHO REALLY KILLED KENNEDY*, p. iv
[4495] North, *ACT OF TREASON,* p. 300
[4496] North, *ACT OF TREASON,* p. 325

[4497] North, *ACT OF TREASON,* p. 300

[4498] Jarett, *THE RUSSIA HOAX*, p. 66

[4499] Malloch, *THE PLOT TO DESTROY TRUMP*, p. 30

[4500] Malloch, *THE PLOT TO DESTROY TRUMP*, p. 34

[4501] Malloch, *THE PLOT TO DESTROY TRUMP*, p. 34

[4502] Jarett, *THE RUSSIA HOAX*, pp. 84-85

[4503] Jarett, *THE RUSSIA HOAX*, pp. 84-85

[4504] Jarett, *THE RUSSIA HOAX*, p. 67 and Schweizer, *CLINTON CASH*, pp. 15, 17

[4505] Jarett, *THE RUSSIA HOAX*, p. 67 and Schweizer, *CLINTON CASH*, p. 15

[4506] Jarett, *THE RUSSIA HOAX*, p. 67 and Schweizer, *CLINTON CASH*, p. 17

[4507] Jarett, *THE RUSSIA HOAX*, p. xi

[4508] Jarett, *THE RUSSIA HOAX*, pp. 27-28

[4509] Jarett, *THE RUSSIA HOAX*, p. 35

[4510] Jarett, *THE RUSSIA HOAX*, p. xii

[4511] Jarett, *THE RUSSIA HOAX*, p. 99

[4512] Malloch, *THE PLOT TO DESTROY TRUMP*, p. 116

[4513] Malloch, *THE PLOT TO DESTROY TRUMP*, p. 116

[4514] Malloch, *THE PLOT TO DESTROY TRUMP*, p. 18

[4515] Malloch, *THE PLOT TO DESTROY TRUMP*, p. 18

[4516] Malloch, *THE PLOT TO DESTROY TRUMP*, p. 21

[4517] Malloch, *THE PLOT TO DESTROY TRUMP*, p. 95

[4518] Malloch, *THE PLOT TO DESTROY TRUMP*, p. 95

[4519] Malloch, *THE PLOT TO DESTROY TRUMP*, p. 95

[4520] Malloch, *THE PLOT TO DESTROY TRUMP*, p. 95

[4521] Jarett, *THE RUSSIA HOAX*, p. 120

[4522] Jarett, *THE RUSSIA HOAX*, p. 120

[4523] Malloch, *THE PLOT TO DESTROY TRUMP*, pp. 22-23

[4524] Jarett, *THE RUSSIA HOAX*, p. 145

[4525] Jarett, *THE RUSSIA HOAX*, pp. 96-97, 147

[4526] Jarett, *THE RUSSIA HOAX*, p. 147

[4527] Jarett, *THE RUSSIA HOAX*, p. 96

[4528] Jarett, *THE RUSSIA HOAX*, pp. 96-97

[4529] Jarett, *THE RUSSIA HOAX*, p. 151

[4530] Jarett, *THE RUSSIA HOAX*, p. 151

[4531] Malloch, *THE PLOT TO DESTROY TRUMP*, p. 73

[4532] Summers, *NOT IN YOUR LIFETIME*, pp. 120-121

[4533] Chaffetz, *THE DEEP STATE*, p. 185

[4534] Chaffetz, *THE DEEP STATE*, p. 185

[4535] Chaffetz, *THE DEEP STATE*, p. 186

[4536] Chaffetz, *THE DEEP STATE*, p. 186

[4537] Chaffetz, *THE DEEP STATE*, p. 186

[4538] Chaffetz, *THE DEEP STATE*, p. 187

[4539] Chaffetz, *THE DEEP STATE*, p. 187

[4540] Chaffetz, *THE DEEP STATE*, p. 187

[4541] Chaffetz, *THE DEEP STATE*, p. 187

[4542] Chaffetz, *THE DEEP STATE*, p. 187

[4543] Chaffetz, *THE DEEP STATE*, p. 187

[4544] Chaffetz, *THE DEEP STATE*, p. 188

[4545] Chaffetz, *THE DEEP STATE*, pp. 189-191

[4546] Chaffetz, *THE DEEP STATE*, p. 190

[4547] Chaffetz, *THE DEEP STATE*, p. 191

[4548] Chaffetz, *THE DEEP STATE*, pp. 192-194

Made in the USA
Middletown, DE
22 September 2019